PRINCIPLES OF FOOD, BEVERAGE, AND LABOR COST CONTROLS

for Hotels and Restaurants
Sixth Edition

Paul R. Dittmer

New Hampshire College

Gerald G. Griffin

New York City Technical College
The City University of New York

JOHN WILEY & SONS, INC.
NEW YORK • CHICHESTER • WEINHEIM • BRISBANE • SINGAPORE • TORONTO

Copyright © 1999 by Paul R. Dittmer and Gerald G. Griffin. All rights reserved.
Published simultaneously in Canada.

This publication is designed to provide accurate and authoritative information in regard to the subject matter covered. It is sold with the understanding that the publisher is not engaged in rendering professional services. If professional advice or other expert assistance is required, the services of a competent professional person should be sought.

Library of Congress Cataloging-in-Publication Data:
Dittmer, Paul.
  Principles of food, beverage, and labor cost controls / Paul R.
Dittmer, Gerald G. Griffin.—6th ed.
    p. cm.
  Rev. ed. of: Principles of food, beverage, and labor cost controls
for hotels and restaurants. 5th ed. c1994.
  Includes index.
  ISBN 0-471-29325-3 (alk. paper)
  1. Food service—Cost control. I. Griffin, Gerald G., 1936– .
II. Dittmer, Paul. Principles of food, beverage, and labor cost
controls for hotels and restaurants. III. Title.
TX911.3.C65D58 1999
647.95′068′1—dc21
                                                                98-31455
                                                                    CIP

Printed in the United States of America.
10 9 8 7 6 5 4 3 2 1

PRINCIPLES OF FOOD, BEVERAGE, AND
LABOR COST CONTROLS
for Hotels and Restaurants

The 6th edition is dedicated to the memory of Gerald Griffin, co-author of this text. He unexpectedly died shortly after completion of this edition.

Paul R. Dittmer

CONTENTS

Preface

This text has been developed for use in courses introducing food, beverage, and labor cost controls to students preparing for careers in food and beverage management. The present edition consists of twenty-one chapters, divided into four parts, as follows.

Part I offers an introduction to food, beverage, and labor cost controls, defining a number of key terms and concepts and providing a foundation for the balance of the work as well as some sense of its scope. It identifies working definitions for the terms cost and sales, discusses the control process in some detail, and introduces the basics of cost-volume-profit analysis.

Part II addresses the application of the four-step control process to the primary phases of foodservice operations: purchasing, receiving, storing, issuing, and production. Specific techniques and procedures for each phase are explained and discussed in detail. Three chapters are devoted to determining costs and using them as monitoring devices in foodservice operations. One chapter deals specifically with food sales control, offering a broad definition of the term and providing detailed discussion of several approaches to sales control.

Part III discusses the application of the four-step control process to the various phases of beverage operations: purchasing, receiving, storing, issuing, and production. Here, too, specific techniques and procedures for each phase are explained and discussed in detail. One chapter is devoted to the principal methods used to monitor beverage operations. The final chapter in Part III specifically addresses beverage sales control, offering a broad definition of the term and providing detailed discussion of several approaches to controlling beverage sales.

Part IV is a four-chapter exposition of labor cost control. The first of the four explores the factors affecting labor cost and labor cost percent. Admittedly, some of these are beyond the control of management, but it is important for managers to know about them. The second chapter discusses the need for performance standards. This leads naturally to a chapter on training, a topic many believe to be central to labor cost control. The concluding chapter in Part IV deals with monitoring performance and taking corrective action.

In developing and revising the text, flexibility has always been a key concern. For example, each of the four parts can generally stand alone. Eliminating any one will not make it difficult to use others. Thus, in programs that include extensive accounting courses, some instructors may choose to disregard Part I. In courses without beverage components, instructors may prefer to skip Part III. And instructors in courses that do not include labor cost control can choose to ignore Part IV.

The book has a greater number of chapters than most instructors use in a one-term course. In our view, this is a virtue because it provides instructors with opportunities to select chapters dealing with the specific subjects identified in their course outlines. We believe this is the best way to meet the varying needs of instructors in the broad range of courses and programs in this field.

Because a great many chapters include more questions and problems than most will be inclined to assign, instructors will find it easy to make selective use of the end-of-chapter materials for written assignment or for in-class discussion.

ACKNOWLEDGMENTS

In revising this work, we had advice, assistance, cooperation, and support from many people. Without their interest and clear willingness to help, the final product would have been far less than it is. Therefore, we are glad to have this opportunity to acknowledge the considerable aid we have received and to list below the names and affiliations of those who have given it so readily:

Patricia S. Bartholomew, Frank C. Constantino, Stephen K. Holzinger, and Fedele J. Panzarino, New York City Technical College of the City University of New York; Julie Rain, New Hampshire College; Michael M. Coltman, MC Media Corporation; Warren Sackler, Rochester Institute of Technology; Robert A. Heath and Edward F. McIntyre, Birmingham (U.K.) College of Food, Tourism and Creative Studies; Kevin Bedard, of Canopy's Training Restaurant, a program of the Educational Opportunity Center, State University of New York College at Brockport; Andrew R. Schwarz, Sullivan County Community College; Marianne Gajewski and Lisa Parker Gates, the Educational Foundation of the National Restaurant Association; Allan Sherwin, Lundeberg School of Seamanship; James A. Bardi, the Berks Campus of Pennsylvania State University; Mary Ann Carroll, Keystone Junior College; George G. Fenich, University of New Orleans; John Drysdale, Johnson County Community College; Frederick Laughlin, Jr., Northwestern Michigan College; Earl Arrowwood, Jr., Bucks County Community College; Rodney Rudolph, State University of New York College of Technology at Delhi; John Stefanelli, Harrah College of Hotel Adminisration, University of Nevada, Las Vegas; Wallace Rande, Northern Arizona University; Paul McVety, Johnson and Wales University; David Tucker, Widener University; Charles Latour, Northern Virginia Community College; Larry Ross, Georgia State University; Michael Evans, Appalachian State University; Chris Letchinger, Kendall College; Anthony Bruno, Nassau Community College; Don St. Hilaire, California State Polytechnic University-Pomona.

Through the many months required to produce this work, the staff of John Wiley has been extraordinarily professional, patient, helpful, and supportive in every way. In particular, Pam Chirls, Andrea Johnson, and Stacey Guttman have all earned this public acknowledgement of their special efforts on our behalf.

If this edition of the text is successful, proving to be a useful addition to the growing number of professional texts available for those planning careers in food and beverage management, a healthy measure of the credit will be due to the many individuals whose help we have acknowledged above. If not—if the work is somehow off the mark—the authors accept full responsibility for the shortcomings.

Finally, many instructors are likely to be interested in the various additional text-based materials available from the publisher. For example, answers for all end-of chapter questions and problems can be found in the Instructor's Guide, along with various other materials designed to assist classroom teachers. The Instructor's Guide is available without charge from the publisher (ISBN 0 471293245).

Paul R. Dittmer
Gerald G. Griffin
May 1999

Part I

Introduction to Food, Beverage, and Labor Cost Control

For a business to survive, it is necessary for a profit to be achieved. Normally, profit does not automatically come; it must be planned, and procedures must be in place to keep costs sufficiently low to allow for profit. One has only to look at the large percentage of new businesses that fail (in excess of 50%) to understand how important it is to manage a business in such a way that costs are kept under control and profit is possible.

This text establishes and illustrates those principles and procedures for food and beverage operations. Part I lays a foundation for that discussion. Parts II, III, and IV outline the specific principles and procedures that keep costs of the most important elements of a food service establishment—food costs, beverage costs, and labor cost—within predetermined bounds.

1

Cost and Sales Concepts

LEARNING OBJECTIVES

After reading and studying this chapter, you should be able to:
1. Define the terms cost and sales.
2. Define and distinguish between various types of costs.
3. Distinguish between monetary and nonmonetary sales concepts.
4. Describe the significance of cost-to-sales relationships and identify several cost-to-sales ratios important in food and beverage management.
5. Perform various calculations using cost percent formulas.
6. List and discuss factors that cause industry-wide variations in cost percents.
7. Explain the value of comparing current cost-to-sales ratios with those for previous periods.
8. Define each of the Key Terms at the end of the chapter.

INTRODUCTION

The Rush Hour Inn

Until she decided to purchase a restaurant two years ago, Kim Rusher had been a successful advertising executive. Her annual income was substantial, and she augmented it by investing in some profitable real estate ventures with her brother. However, her position in advertising required that she travel several days a week, and her feeling that she was not able to spend enough time with her children made her decide to give up the advertising business in favor of operating her own business.

On the advice of her brother, she decided to go into the restaurant business, even though she lacked previous experience in the field. After all her years of travel, she felt she knew more about restaurants from the customer's point of view than most restaurateurs. So she began to look around for an appropriate property. Fortunately, she soon found a place just 12 miles from her home, located on a main road on the outskirts of a city of 75,000 people. The building and equipment were only 6 years old and apparently in fine condition, and the retiring owner was anxious to sell at a very fair price. The owner's books revealed a successful operation, with a restaurant profit of approximately $165,000 per year. Kim Rusher decided to buy. The restaurant had 100 seats. It was open seven days a week, from 6:00 A.M. to 10:00 P.M., serving a varied menu of standard American fare. Kim felt she would be able to run it successfully with a small and dedicated staff.

In the first year, Kim's profits were less than those of the previous owner. After two years, profits were continuing to decline. The restaurant was simply not showing an adequate profit, even though she had increased the volume of business over that of the previous owner. The place was reasonably busy, her customers often complimented her on the food, and her staff appeared to be loyal and helpful in every way. The truth was that Kim Rusher was operating a popular, but not very profitable, food and beverage business. At the end of the second full year of operation, the statement of income prepared by her accountant revealed a restaurant profit of $76,670 (Fig. 1.1).

It quickly became apparent to Kim, her family, and her accountant that, unless something could be done to increase the profit, continued operation would not be worth the effort required.

The Graduate Restaurant

Just a few miles down the road from the Rush Hour Inn, Bill Young owns and operates the Graduate Restaurant. After four years in the Air Force, Bill had worked for an insurance company for a few years before enrolling in a

For the Year Ended December 31, XXXX	
SALES	
Food	$1,533,400
Beverage	$ 270,600
Total Sales	$1,804,000
COST OF SALES	
Food	$ 644,028
Beverage	$ 86,592
Total Cost of Sales	$ 730,620
GROSS PROFIT	$1,073,380
CONTROLLABLE EXPENSES	
Salaries and Wages	$ 487,080
Employee Benefits	$ 121,770
Other Controllable Expenses	$ 270,600
Total Controllable Expenses	$ 879,450
INCOME BEFORE OCCUPANCY COSTS, INTEREST, DEPRECIATION, AND INCOME TAXES	$ 193,930
OCCUPANCY COSTS	$ 153,340
INTEREST EXPENSE	$ 27,060
DEPRECIATION	$ 90,200
RESTAURANT PROFIT	$ 76,670

FIGURE 1.1 *The Rush Hour Inn Income Statement*

nearby college to study hospitality management. His interest in the food and beverage sector of the hospitality industry began in his high school days when he worked part time in the local unit of a national fast-food chain. While his interest had grown steadily over the years, it took considerable courage for him to give up a fairly promising insurance career to go back to school. He earned a degree in hospitality management, and then went to work as the assistant manager in a local restaurant. Over the next several years, he worked in three food and beverage operations in the area, including the Rush Hour Inn, before deciding that he was ready to own and operate his own restaurant.

With the help of his family and a local bank, he was able to purchase the Graduate Restaurant, a fairly popular establishment with the same type of menu as the Rush Hour Inn, as well as comparable prices and hours of operation. In fact, the only differences to the casual observer were size and location: The Graduate Restaurant had only 50 seats and was in a somewhat less favorable location.

Under the previous owner, the restaurant had shown a profit of $65,000 per year. But Bill felt sure he could increase the restaurant profit by applying the principles he had learned in the college's hospitality management program. The employees he inherited with the restaurant were both loyal and coopera-

For the Year Ended December 31, XXXX	
SALES	
Food	$786,250
Beverage	$138,750
Total Sales	$925,000
COST OF SALES	
Food	$275,187
Beverage	$ 34,688
Total Cost of Sales	$309,875
GROSS PROFIT	$615,125
CONTROLLABLE EXPENSES	
Salaries and Wages	$185,000
Employee Benefits	$ 46,250
Other Controllable Expenses	$138,750
Total Controllable Expenses	$370,000
INCOME BEFORE OCCUPANCY COSTS, INTEREST, DEPRECIATION, AND INCOME TAXES	$245,125
OCCUPANCY COSTS	$ 78,625
INTEREST EXPENSE	$ 13,875
DEPRECIATION	$ 46,250
RESTAURANT PROFIT	$106,375

FIGURE 1.2 *The Graduate Restaurant Income Statement*

tive, and he found them receptive to the changes that he made gradually over the first year of operation. None of the changes were dramatically apparent to the customers; in fact, at the end of the first year, most had not noticed any changes at all. In general, they were as pleased with the establishment as they had been when Jim first took it over, and they continued to return. In addition, newcomers tried the restaurant, liked it, and became regular customers. At the end of the first full year of operation, Bill's accountant presented him with a statement of income showing a restaurant profit of $106,375 (Fig 1.2).

The statement confirmed Bill's expectations. It proved to him that his management of the operation was effective in the ways he had anticipated. At the end of his first year, he looked to the future with confidence.

A comparison of the statements of income for these two restaurants reveals some very important facts. As one might expect, the Rush Hour Inn, with twice as many seats as the Graduate Restaurant, as well as a comparable menu and comparable prices, shows approximately twice the dollar volume of sales. However, in spite of the apparently favorable sales comparison, the restaurant profit for the Rush Hour Inn is considerably less than that for the Graduate Restaurant. Since the difference between sales and restaurant profit on each statement of income is represented by costs of various kinds, we can infer that part of the difficulty with the Rush Hour Inn is somehow related to cost. The costs of operation are somehow in more favorable proportion to sales in the Graduate Restaurant. Initially, we must look to the nature of these costs and their relations to sales to find the differences between the two establishments. It is possible that the costs of operation are not well regulated, or controlled, in the Rush Hour Inn. It is also possible that sales are not well controlled and that, if Kim Rusher is going to increase her profit to a desirable level, she must begin by exercising greater control over the several kinds of operating costs, as well as over sales.

The statement of income from the Graduate Restaurant suggests that Bill Young has kept both costs and sales under control, and, as we shall see, this is critically important to the success of his business. Comparative investigation of the two restaurants would reveal that Bill Young had instituted various control procedures in the Graduate Restaurant that would be noticeably absent in Kim Rusher's business. These control procedures are important features of a computer program that plays a significant part in the operation of the Graduate Restaurant. These have enabled Jim to manage his business more effectively. It will be important, therefore, to look closely at the nature and effect of these control procedures in succeeding chapters. However, before proceeding, it will first be useful to establish clear definitions of the terms **cost, sales,** and **control.** Cost and sales will be defined and discussed in this chapter; control will be covered in Chapter 2.

COST CONCEPTS

Definition of Cost

Accountants define a **cost** as a reduction in the value of an asset for the purpose of securing benefit or gain. That definition, while technically correct, is not very useful in a basic discussion of controls, so we will modify it somewhat.

As we use the term in our discussion of cost control in the food and beverage business, cost is defined *as the expense to a hotel or restaurant for goods or services when the goods are consumed or the services rendered.* Foods and beverages are considered "consumed" when they have been used, wastefully or otherwise, and are no longer available for the purposes for which they were acquired. Thus, the cost of a piece of meat is incurred when the piece is no longer available for the purpose for which it was purchased because it has been cooked, served, or thrown away because it has spoiled, or even because it has been stolen. The cost of labor is incurred when people are on duty, whether or not they are working and whether they are paid at the end of a shift or at some later date.

The cost of any item may be expressed in a variety of units: weight, volume, or total value. The cost of meat, for example, can be expressed as a value per piece, per pound, or per individual portion. The cost of liquor can be expressed as a value per bottle, per drink, or per ounce. Labor costs can be expressed as value per hour (an hourly wage, for example) or value per week (a weekly salary).

Costs can be viewed in a number of different ways, and it will be useful to identify some of them before proceeding.

Fixed and Variable Costs

The terms **fixed** and **variable** are used to distinguish between those costs that have no direct relationship to business volume and those that do.

FIXED COSTS. **Fixed costs** are those that are normally unaffected by changes in sales volume. They are said to have little direct relationship to the business volume because they do not change significantly when the number of sales increases or decreases. Insurance premiums, real estate taxes, and depreciation on equipment are all examples of fixed costs. Real estate taxes, after all, are set by governmental authorities and are based on government's need for a determined amount of total revenue. The taxes for an individual establishment are based on the appraised value of the assessed property as real estate. Real estate taxes do not change when the sales volume in an establishment changes.

All fixed costs change over time, of course, sometimes increasing, sometimes decreasing. However, changes in fixed costs are not normally related to short-term changes in business volume. They are sometimes tied indirectly to long-term volume changes. For example, an increase in the cost of insurance premiums may be attributable to an insurance company's perception of increased risk associated with higher volume. Even though the increase in insurance cost is somehow related to an increase in volume, the cost of insurance is still considered a fixed cost. Advertising expense is another example: Larger establishments tend to spend more on advertising because their larger sales volume makes larger amounts of money available for the purpose, but advertising expense is still considered a fixed cost.

The term "fixed" should never be taken to mean static or unchanging, but merely to indicate that any changes that may occur in such costs are related only indirectly or distantly to changes in volume. Sometimes, in fact, changes in fixed costs are wholly unrelated to changes in volume, as with real estate taxes. Other examples of costs that are generally considered fixed include repairs and maintenance, rent or occupancy costs, most utility costs, and the cost of professional services, such as accounting.

VARIABLE COSTS. **Variable costs** are those that are clearly related to business volume. As business volume increases, variable costs will increase; as volume decreases, variable costs should decrease, too. The obvious examples of variable costs are food, beverages, and labor. However, there are significant differences between the behavior of food and beverage costs on the one hand and labor costs on the other.

Food and beverage costs are considered directly variable costs. **Directly variable costs** are those that are directly linked to volume of business, such that every increase or decrease in volume brings a corresponding increase or decrease in cost. Every time a restaurant sells an order of steak, it incurs a cost for the meat. Similarly, each sale of a bottle of beer at the bar brings about a cost for the beer. Total directly variable costs, then, increase or decrease—or at least should increase or decrease—in direct proportion to sales volume.

Payroll costs (including salaries and wages and employee benefits, and often referred to as **labor costs**) present an interesting contrast. Foodservice employees may be divided into two categories—those whose numbers will remain constant despite normal fluctuations in business volume, and those whose numbers and consequent total costs should logically (and often will) vary with normal changes in business volume. The first category includes such personnel as the manager, bookkeeper, chef, and cashier. In terms of the above definition, they are fixed cost personnel. Their numbers and costs may change, but not because of short-term changes in business volume. The second category would include the servers, or the waitstaff. As business volume changes, their numbers and total costs can be expected to increase or decrease accordingly.

Both fixed cost and variable cost employees are included in one category on the statement of income: "Salaries and Wages." Because payroll cost has both the fixed element and the variable element, it is known as a **semivariable cost,** meaning that a portion of it should change with short-term changes in business volume, and another portion should not.

It must be noted that each individual establishment must make its own determination of which employees should be fixed cost personnel and which should be variable-cost. In some specialized cases, it is possible for payroll to consist entirely of either fixed-cost or variable-cost personnel. For example, there are some restaurants in which the entire staff works for hourly wages. In these cases, numbers of hours worked and consequent costs are almost wholly related to business volume. Conversely, in some smaller restaurants employees may all be on regular salaries, in which case labor cost would be considered fixed.

Controllable and Noncontrollable Costs

Costs may also be labeled **controllable** and **noncontrollable. Controllable costs** are those that can be changed in the short term. Variable costs are normally controllable. The cost of food or beverages, for example, can be changed in several ways—by changing portion sizes, by changing ingredients, or by changing both of these. The cost of labor can be increased or decreased in the short term by hiring additional employees or by laying some off, by increasing or decreasing the hours of work, or, in some instances, by increasing or decreasing wages.

In addition, certain fixed costs are controllable, including advertising and promotion, utilities, repairs and maintenance, and administrative and general expenses, a category that includes office supplies, postage, and telephone expenses, among others. It is possible for owners or managers to make decisions that will change any of these in the short term.

By contrast, **noncontrollable costs** are those that cannot normally be changed in the short term. These are usually fixed costs, and a list of the more common ones would include rent, interest on a mortgage, real estate taxes, license fees, and depreciation. Managers do not normally have the ability to change any of these in the near term.

Unit and Total Costs

It is also important to distinguish between **unit costs** and **total costs.** The units may be food or beverage portions, as in the cost of one steak or one martini, or units of work, as in the hourly rate for an employee. It is also useful to discuss costs in terms of totals, as in the total cost of all food served in one period, such as a week or a month, or the total cost of labor for one period. The costs on the statement of income are all total costs, rather than unit costs.

These concepts are best illustrated by example. In Sherwin's Steak House, a restaurant where steaks are cut from strip loins, one strip loin was purchased for $52.50. If one entire strip were consumed in one day, the total cost would be $52.50. However, the cost per unit (the steak) depends on the number of steaks cut from the strip. If there are 15, the unit cost is an average of $3.50. No 2 of the 15 are likely to have identical costs because it is not normally possible for a butcher to cut all steaks exactly the same weight. In the food and beverage business we commonly deal with **average** unit costs, rather than **actual** unit costs. It is important to know unit costs for purposes of establishing menu prices and determining unit profitability. Total costs, including those that appear in statements of income, are normally used for broader purposes, including the determination of the relationship between total costs and total

	Unit Cost	Total Cost
Fixed Cost	Changes	Does not change
Variable Cost	Does not change	Changes

*It must be noted that not all will agree with this. The point must be made that actual variable costs per unit tend to decrease as volume increases. Labor becomes more productive with greater time utilization, and food purchasing at greater volume can reduce cost.

FIGURE 1.3   *Cost Behavior as Business Volume Changes**

sales—as will be discussed later in this chapter—and for determining overall profitability of operations.

It is significant to note that, as business volume changes, total and unit costs are affected in different ways. Let us assume that a restaurant has a fixed cost for rent of $2,000 per month. If 2,000 customers were served during a period of one month, the fixed cost of rent per customer would be $1. If, in the succeeding month, the number of customers increased to 4,000, the total fixed cost for rent would not change, but the fixed cost per unit (customer) would be reduced from $1.00 to $.50.

A similar analysis may be done with variable costs. The variable cost for the steak described above was $3.50 per unit. If 2,000 customers in a given month order steak, the total variable cost would be $7,000 at $3.50 average unit cost per steak. If, in the following month, 4,000 customers order steak, the variable cost per unit (the steak) should remain $3.50, while the total variable cost for 4,000 steaks increases to $14,000.

While the preceding paragraphs illustrate cost behavior only as business volume increases, it is important to recognize that costs behave similarly as business volume decreases. The relationships hold true. Figure 1.3 illustrates the behavior of fixed and variable costs per unit and in total, as discussed above.

It is important to understand these relationships when dealing with cost volume profit analysis and the calculation of break-even points, which are discussed in Chapter 3.

Prime Cost

Prime cost is a term our industry uses to refer to the costs of materials and labor: food, beverages, and payroll. Unfortunately, while everyone agrees that total food costs and total beverage costs should be included in prime cost, there is no general agreement on the payroll cost component. Some would include all payroll costs, while others would include only the cost of kitchen staff. In this text, prime cost is defined as the sum of food costs, beverage costs, and labor costs (salaries and wages, plus employee benefits). These, taken together, represent the largest portion of total costs for virtually all foodservice operations. Consequently, prime cost is of the greatest interest to most owners and managers. The level and control of prime cost play a large part in determining whether or not an establishment meets its financial goals. In this text, we will, therefore, concentrate on those controllable costs that are most important in determining profit: food cost, beverage cost, and labor cost.

Historical and Planned Costs

Two additional cost concepts are important for those seeking to comprehend cost control: **historical cost** and **planned cost.** The definition of cost at the beginning of this chapter carries with it an implication that all costs are historical—that is, that they can be found in business records, books of account, financial statements, invoices, employees' time cards, and other similar records. Historic costs are used for various important purposes, such as establishing unit costs, determining menu prices, and comparing present with past labor costs. However, the value of historic costs is not limited to these few purposes. Historic records of costs are of particular value for planning—for determining in the present what is likely to happen in the future. Planning is among the most important functions of management, and, in order to plan effectively, managers use historical costs to develop **planned costs**—projections of what costs will be or should be for a future period. Thus, historical costs are necessary for effective planning. This kind of planning is often called **budgeting,** a topic to be discussed in Chapter 2.

SALES CONCEPTS

Having provided a brief introduction to costs in food and beverage operations, we will turn our attention to sales—a word that we have taken for granted thus far. It will be useful to establish a working definition of the term and to examine some of the principal sales concepts required for an understanding of control in foodservice.

The term **sales** is used in a number of ways among professionals in the foodservice industry. In order for the term to be meaningful, one must be specific about the context in which it is used. It will, therefore, be useful to define the term and to explore some of the many ways it is used in the industry.

Sales Defined

In general, the term **sales** is defined as revenue resulting from the exchange of products and services for value. In our industry, food and beverage sales are exchanges of the products and services of a restaurant, bar, or related enterprise for value. We normally express sales in monetary terms, although there are other possibilities. Actually, there are two basic groups of terms normally used in food and beverage operations to express sales concepts: **monetary** and **nonmonetary.**

Monetary Terms

TOTAL SALES.   **Total sales** is a term that refers to the total volume of sales expressed in dollar terms. This may be for any given time period, such as a week, a month, or a year. For example, total dollar sales for the Rush Hour Inn was expressed as $1,804,000 for the year ending December 31, XXXX.

TOTAL SALES BY CATEGORY.   Examples of **total dollar sales by category** are total food sales or total beverage sales, referring to the total dollar volume of sales for all items in one category. By extension, we might see such terms as total steak sales or total seafood sales, referring to the total dollar volume of sales for all items in those particular categories.

TOTAL SALES BY SERVER.   **Total sales per server** is total dollar volume of sales for which a given server has been responsible in a given time period, such as a meal period, a day, or a week. These figures are sometimes used by management to make judgments about the comparative performance of two or more employees. It might be helpful, for example, to identify those servers responsible for the greatest and for the least dollar sales in a given period.

TOTAL SALES BY SEAT.   **Total sales per seat** is the total dollar sales for a given time period divided by the number of seats in the restaurant. The normal time period used is one year. This figure is most frequently used by chain operations as a means for comparing sales results from one unit with those of another. In addition, the National Restaurant Association determines this average nationally so that individual operators may compare their results with those of other similar restaurants.

SALES PRICE.   **Sales price** refers to the amount charged each customer purchasing one unit of a particular item. The unit may be a single item (an appetizer or an entree) or an entire meal, depending on the manner in which a restaurant prices its products. The sum of all sales prices charged for all items sold in a given time period will be total dollar sales for that time period.

AVERAGE SALE.   An **average sale** in business is determined by adding individual sales to determine a total and then dividing that total by the number of individual sales. There are two such averages commonly calculated in food and beverage operations: **average sale per customer** and **average sale per server.**

AVERAGE SALE PER CUSTOMER.   **Average sale per customer** is the result of dividing total dollar sales by the number of sales or customers. For example, if total dollar sales for a given day in a restaurant were $1,258.00 and the restaurant had served 183 customers, then the average dollar sale would be $6.87.

This average is determined as follows:

$$\text{Average sale} = \text{Total dollar sales}/\text{Total number of covers}$$

The average dollar sale concept is also expressed as the average check or the average cover, which are synonymous terms in our industry. The average dollar sale is used by foodservice operators to compare the sales performance of one employee with another, to identify sales trends, and to compare the effectiveness of various menus, menu listings, or sales promotions.

This figure is of considerable interest to managers, who are likely to be interested in following business trends. If the average sale decreases over time, management will probably investigate the reasons for the changes in customer spending habits. Some possibilities might include a deterioration in service standards, customer dissatisfaction with food quality, inadequate sales promotion, and changes in portion sizes.

AVERAGE SALE PER SERVER.   **Average sale per server** is total dollar sales for an individual server divided by the number of customers served by that individual. This, too, is a figure used for comparative purposes, and it is usually considered a better indicator of the sales ability of a particular individual because, unlike total sales per server, it eliminates differences caused by variations in the numbers of persons served.

All of these monetary sales concepts are common in the industry and are likely to be encountered quickly by those seeking careers in food and beverage management. At the same time, there are a number of nonmonetary sales concepts and terms that also should be understood.

Nonmonetary Terms

TOTAL NUMBER SOLD. **Total number sold** refers to the total number of steaks, shrimp cocktails, or any other menu item sold in a given time period. This figure is useful in a number of ways. For example, foodservice managers use total number sold to identify unpopular menu items, in order to eliminate such items from the menu. Additionally, historical records of total numbers of specific items sold are useful for forecasting sales. Such forecasts are useful for making decisions about purchasing and production. Total number of a specific item sold is a figure used to make judgments about quantities in inventory and about sales records, as we will see in later chapters.

COVERS. **Cover** is a term used in our industry to describe one diner, regardless of the quantity of food he or she consumes. An individual consuming a continental breakfast in a hotel coffee shop is counted as one cover. So is another individual in the same coffee shop who orders a full breakfast consisting of juice, eggs, bacon, toast, and coffee. These two are counted as two covers.

TOTAL COVERS. **Total covers** refers to the total number of customers served in a given period—an hour, a meal period, a day, a week, or some other. Foodservice managers are usually particularly interested in these figures, which are compared with figures for similar periods in the past so that judgments can be made about business trends.

AVERAGE COVERS. An **average number of covers** is determined by dividing the total number of covers for a given time period by some other number. That number may be a number of hours in a meal period, the number of days the establishment is open per week, or the number of servers on duty during the time period, among many other possibilities. The following are some of the more common:

Covers per hour = Total covers/Number of hours of operation

Covers per day = Total covers/Number of days of operation

Covers per server = Total covers/Number of servers

The averages so derived can be of considerable help to a manager at-

August XXXX		
Menu Item	*Portion Sales*	*Sales Mix*
A	1,000	12.5%
B	1,200	15.0%
C	1,800	22.5%
D	2,400	30.0%
E	1,600	20.0%
Totals	8,000	100.0%

FIGURE 1.4 *Sales Mix for the Sherwood Island Lodge*

tempting to make judgments about such common questions as the efficiency of service in the dining room, the effectiveness of some promotional campaign, or the effectiveness of a particular server.

SEAT TURNOVER. **Seat turnover,** most often called simply **turnover** or **turns,** refers to the number of seats occupied during a given period (or the number of customers served during that period) divided by the number of seats available. For example, if 150 persons were served luncheon in a dining room with 50 seats, seat turnover would be calculated as 3, obviously meaning that, on average, each seat had been used three times during the period. Seat turnover may be calculated for any period, but is most often calculated for a given meal period.

SALES MIX. **Sales mix** is a term used to describe the relative quantity sold of any menu item compared to other items in the same category. The relative quantities are normally percentages of total unit sales and always total 100 percent. For example, assume that the Sherwood Island Lodge offers a menu with five entree items represented by the letters A, B, C, D, and E. Total portion sales for each of these for the month of August are provided in Figure 1.4.

During August, a total of 8,000 entrees were sold, 1,000 of which were portions of A. Thus, sales of A represent 12.5% of total unit sales, calculated as follows:

$$1,000/8,000 = .125 = 12.5\%$$

Similar calculations would be performed for Items B, C, D, and E, the results of which appear in Figure 1.4. That is the sales mix for the Sherwood Island Lodge, based on historical records.

THE COST-TO-SALES RATIO: COST PERCENT

Raw dollar figures for directly variable and semivariable costs are seldom, if ever, of any particular significance for control purposes. Because these costs vary to some extent with business volume, they become significant only when expressed in relation to that volume with which they vary. Foodservice managers calculate costs in dollars and compare those costs to sales in dollars. This enables managers to discuss the relationship between costs and sales, sometimes described as the cost per dollar of sale, the ratio of costs to sales, or simply as the cost-to-sales ratio. The industry uses the following basic formula for calculating cost-to-sales ratio:

$$Cost/Sales = Cost\ per\ dollar\ of\ sale$$

The formula normally results in a decimal answer, and any decimal can be converted to a percentage if one multiplies it by 100 and adds a percent sign (%). This is the same as simply moving the decimal point two places to the right and adding a percent sign.

Because it is usually used to calculate cost percents, the formula is commonly written as:

$$Cost/Sales = Cost\ \%$$

This formula can then be extended to show the following relationships:

$$Food\ cost/Food\ sales = Food\ cost\ \%$$

$$Beverage\ cost/Beverage\ sales = Beverage\ cost\ \%$$

$$Labor\ cost/Total\ sales = Labor\ cost\ \%$$

Let us go back to the statements of income for the two establishments described earlier—the Rush Hour Inn and the Graduate Restaurant. In the case of the Graduate Restaurant, we saw that food costing $275,188 ultimately resulted in sales of $786,250. In order to determine the percentage of sales represented by cost, we divide cost by sales, as in the preceding formula, and multiply the resulting decimal answer by 100 in order to convert it to a percentage:

$$\$275,188/\$786,250 = 35.0\%$$

Thus, we learn that the food cost percent, or the food cost-to-sales ratio, in the Graduate Restaurant over the past year has been 35 percent. This tells

	Graduate Restaurant	*Rush Hour Inn*
Food Sales	$786,250	$1,533,400
Cost of Food Sold	$275,188	$ 644,028
Cost per Dollar of Sale	$.35	$.42
Food Cost %	35%	42%

FIGURE 1.5   *Comparison of Cost and Sales Graduate Restaurant and Rush Hour Inn*

us that 35 percent of the income from food sales over the year has gone to cover the cost of the food. Because the cost of food represents $.35 out of each $1.00 in sales, we can also say that food cost per dollar sale is $.35. Following the same formula, we may now take the figures for food costs and food sales from the statement of income for the Rush Hour Inn and calculate both the food cost percent and the cost per dollar of sale for purposes of comparison.

$$\$644,028/\$1,533,400 = 42\%$$

So, in the case of the Rush Hour Inn, the food cost per dollar of sale is $.42, and the food cost percent is 42 percent.

Cost percents are useful to managers in at least two ways. They provide a means of comparing costs relative to sales for two or more periods of time, and they provide a means of comparing two or more operations. When one compares cost percents for two or more operations, it is important to note that the comparisons are valid only if the operations are similar. Thus, one could compare two fast-food restaurants offering similar products, but one could not compare a French restaurant with a local diner and expect the comparison to be meaningful.

Useful information about the two restaurants is compared in Figure 1.5.

It is only at this point that the figures can begin to take on some real meaning and that one can begin to compare them intelligently. Significantly, one learns that a principal difference between the two restaurants lies in the fact that the food cost per dollar of sale is $.07 higher in one. Expressed another way, one can say that the cost-to-sales ratio for food is 7 percent higher in the Rush Hour Inn. It is not until raw dollar figures have been converted to this form that one has any useful way of comparing them.

Because food cost is variable, it increases and decreases with sales volume. It would not be possible to make useful comparisons between operating periods for one restaurant or between similar restaurants (as in a chain, for example) unless one were to work with cost percents, or with costs per dollar of sale. Since cost-control figures in the hospitality industry are most commonly

	Graduate Restaurant	Rush Hour Inn
Food Cost as a % of Food Sales	35.0%	42.0%
Beverage Cost as a % of Beverage Sales	25.0%	32.0%
Combined Food Cost and Beverage Cost as a % of Total Sales	33.5%	40.5%
Payroll Cost as a % of Total Sales	25.0%	33.8%
Overhead as a % of Total Sales	30.0%	30.0%

FIGURE 1.6   *Comparison of Cost Percentages Graduate Restaurant and Rush Hour Inn*

expressed in terms of cost percents, we will deal with those figures in this text. In addition, because real dollar figures in real restaurant operations seldom result in round numbers, our percents will be expressed in tenths of 1 percent—35.9 percent or 36.2 percent, for example. This, too, is common to the hospitality industry and permits a greater degree of accuracy. After all, in the case of the Rush Hour Inn, one-tenth of 1 percent of sales is $786.25, which is a considerable number of real dollars.

Using the formula above, it is now possible to develop a chart (Fig. 1.6) comparing cost percents in the two restaurants.

It is both interesting and significant that the cost percents for the components of prime cost—food, beverages, and labor—are all higher at the Rush Hour Inn than they are at the Graduate Restaurant. The remaining costs are the same in both establishments when expressed as percents of sales. In food-service these remaining costs are often referred to as overhead costs. In this text, we will use the term **overhead cost** to mean all costs other than prime cost. Overhead normally consists of all the fixed costs associated with operating the business.

Sometimes the formula:

$$\text{Cost}/\text{Sales} = \text{Cost \%}$$

is rearranged algebraically to facilitate other calculations. For instance, suppose that a banquet manager has been directed by her boss to ensure that all banquet functions operate at a given food cost percent, and she wants to quote a sales price for a particular menu item, the cost of which is known. The calculation of sales price is simplified if the formula is rearranged in the following form:

$$\text{Cost}/\text{Cost \%} = \text{Sales (or Sales price)}$$

If the given cost percent were 30.0 percent and the food cost for the item were $3.60, the appropriate sales price would be $12.00, as illustrated here:

$$\$3.60/0.3 = \$12.00$$

Suppose that this banquet manager is dealing with a group willing to spend $15.00 per person for a banquet, and the same given 30.0 percent cost percent is to apply. Calculation of the maximum permissible cost per person is facilitated by rearranging the formula once again:

$$\text{Sales} \times \text{Cost \%} = \text{Cost}$$

So the cost per person can be calculated as $4.50:

$$\$15.00 \times 0.3 = \$4.50$$

In summary, the cost percent formula can be written and used in any one of three possible forms:

$$\text{Cost}/\text{Sales} = \text{Cost \%}$$

$$\text{Cost}/\text{Cost \%} = \text{Sales}$$

$$\text{Sales} \times \text{Cost \%} = \text{Cost}$$

The foregoing discussion has assumed that food and beverage costs are relatively stable over time and that one can readily predict future costs accurately. Unfortunately, that is not normally the case. However, in spite of that fact, it is often necessary to quote prices for functions to be held some months in the future. To do so with some reasonable degree of accuracy, one should consider both seasonal fluctuations in costs and inflation rates. For example, the price of most shellfish is highest in New England during the winter months when the catch is smallest, and this fact should be taken into account when quoting prices in July for a function to be held in January. Moreover, in times of inflation, various food costs increase at various rates. These can frequently be anticipated by management from published information and should be taken into account when quoting future sales prices. One possible example would be the case of an establishment quoting a banquet price for a date six months in the future when the current rate of inflation is 10 percent on an annual basis. If the current food cost for the function is calculated to be $4.00, the manager could be reasonably sure that the cost would be somewhat higher in six months. While it is not possible to predict the future cost with perfect accuracy, it is possible to approximate it. One simple way would be to assume that one-half of the annual rate would apply to the first six months of the upcoming year, and thus to use 5 percent (one-half of 10 percent) as the approximate future cost—$4.20, in this case. Assuming a pre-established food cost percent of 30 percent, sales price would be increased from $13.33 to $14.00, as illustrated here:

$$\$4.00/.3 = \$13.33 \text{ versus } \$4.20/.3 = \$14.00$$

Mathematicians would immediately recognize that this is not wholly accurate. However, it does offer a simple system for attempting to take inflation into account, and is clearly better than ignoring inflation completely.

INDUSTRY-WIDE VARIATIONS IN COST PERCENTS

Cost percents vary considerably from one foodservice operation to another. There are many possible reasons for these variations, several of which are discussed below. Some of the factors contributing to these variations would be type of service, location, price structure, and type of menu.

In very broad terms, there are two basic types of foodservice operations:

- Those that operate at a low margin of profit per item served and depend on relatively high business volume.
- Those that operate at a relatively high margin of profit per item and therefore do not require such high business volume.

It is apparent that, if the two were to have any menu items in common, the menu price would tend to be lower in operations of the first type.

The following examples of the cost structures of establishments in these two categories are intended to serve only as illustrations of relative costs. The examples should not be taken to imply either that these are standards for the industry or that any particular restaurant should have or should strive to achieve the illustrated cost structure. The cost structure for each individual restaurant must be determined for that restaurant alone, the obvious point being that, as percentages of sales, costs must always total less than 100.0 percent if the operation is to be profitable.

Restaurants that depend principally on convenience foods—the so-called fast-food or quick-service operations—are generally included in the first (low margin) category above. Because of relatively lower menu prices, the food cost percents in these restaurants tend to be higher. However, they hire unskilled personnel, pay lower wages, and keep the number of employees at a minimum. This makes it possible for them to offset high food cost percent with low labor cost and low labor cost percent. A typical cost analysis for such a restaurant might be as seen in Figure 1.7.

Restaurants in the second (high margin) category tend to depend less on convenience foods, catering to customers who prefer fresh foods (often prepared gourmet style) and more personal service. This type of food preparation and service usually requires a greater number of personnel who are more highly skilled and often better paid. This tends to keep the cost of labor higher than in establishments of the first type cited. However, the food cost percent

Cost of Food and Beverages	40%
Labor Cost	20%
Other Controllable and Noncontrollable Costs	30%
Profit Before Income Taxes	10%
Total	100%

FIGURE 1.7 *Cost Analysis for Typical Low-Margin Restaurant*

in such establishments tends to be lower, partly because of higher menu prices. An analysis of costs for a typical restaurant of this type would resemble those in Figure 1.8.

It is important to note that operations in the first category require greater numbers of customers to achieve a given dollar volume of sales. In the second example, partly because of higher menu prices, fewer customers are required to reach a given dollar volume. In general, it is possible to achieve a profit with fewer customers if menu prices are high.

In the two examples cited above, profit as a percentage of sales is shown to be 10.0 percent. It must be emphasized that these figures are not to be taken as industry standards or even as necessarily desirable standards. Some experts feel that 5.0 percent profit is desirable. Others feel that a lower percentage of profit will help ensure customer satisfaction and will induce customers to return regularly. If true, this would be likely to lengthen the business life of a restaurant.

The appropriate percentage of profit for a given restaurant must be based on other factors, such as desired return on investment, the real and perceived risks of being in the foodservice business compared to other forms of investment, the return one might expect to earn in some other business, and a whole range of considerations involving the competition in a specific market. In the last analysis, evaluations and judgments about costs, sales, and profits must be made on an individual, case-by-case basis. Each restaurant tends to be unique.

Cost of Food and Beverages	25%
Labor Cost	35%
Other Controllable and Noncontrollable Costs	30%
Profit Before Income Taxes	10%
Total	100%

FIGURE 1.8 *Cost Analysis for Typical High-Margin Restaurant*

MONITORING COSTS AND SALES

It is obvious that total sales must exceed total costs if a foodservice enterprise is to be profitable. If costs exceed sales for an extended period of time, the enterprise may eventually face bankruptcy. At the very least, the owner will have to put additional funds into the business to keep it going. It is the job of the manager—and the cost controller, if there is one—to be continually aware of the costs of operating the business and to keep these costs below the level of sales. Cost information is gathered daily in many operations and compared with sales information for the day, to determine the ratios of the various costs to sales. These ratios are compared to the same ratios from previous periods, and judgments are made about whether or not the ratios are satisfactory. If not, remedial steps must be taken to bring these ratios into line with ratios from previous periods. It is important that the cost and sales data used to calculate these ratios be from like periods. Customarily, comparisons are made for specific days of the week—Monday of last week with Monday of this week, for example. Comparisons sometimes are made of like weeks in two different months—the first week in June compared with the first week in July, for example. Sometimes trends can be identified by those who track these ratios from week to week.

In many establishments, cost and sales data are seldom examined, and ratios are rarely calculated. If this is the case, it should be obvious that management is taking a high degree of risk. Establishments that gather cost and sales information only monthly, quarterly, or annually may not be able to take effective remedial action because the information is not sufficiently timely to shed light on current problems.

CHAPTER ESSENTIALS

In this chapter, we defined cost as the term is used in the foodservice industry and showed that all industry-related costs can be viewed from several perspectives, including fixed versus variable (with some variable costs being directly variable and others being semivariable), controllable versus noncontrollable, total versus unit, and historical versus planned or budgeted. We defined the term prime cost and showed how the components of the prime cost relate to one another as well as to total sales. We defined sales and illustrated a number of special terms commonly used in the industry to discuss and compare various ways of identifying and expressing sales. Monetary expressions of sales include total sales; total sales by category, by server, and by seat; sales prices; and average sale per customer and per server. We defined the term cover, and identified such nonmonetary expressions of sales as total number sold, total covers, average covers, seat turnover, and sales mix. We defined the cost-to-sales ratio and provided the formulas used in industry for various common calculations. We also showed how cost-to-sales ratios may vary from one establishment to another throughout the industry. Finally, we discussed the importance of monitoring cost and sales data and of calculating significant ratios regularly. An understanding of these concepts will provide the necessary foundation for those seeking to understand and apply the control process in foodservice.

KEY TERMS IN THIS CHAPTER

Average sale per customer
Average sale per server
Beverage cost
Budgeted cost
Controllable cost
Cost
Cost per dollar sale
Cost percent
Cover
Directly variable cost
Fixed cost
Food cost
Historical cost
Labor cost
Noncontrollable cost
Overhead
Planned cost
Prime cost
Sale
Sales mix
Sales price
Seat turnover
Semivariable cost
Total cost
Total sales
Total sales per seat
Unit cost
Variable cost

QUESTIONS AND PROBLEMS

1. Given the following information, calculate cost percentages. Round your answers to the nearest tenth of a percent.

    a. Cost $200.00; Sales $500.00.
    b. Cost $150.00; Sales $500.00.
    c. Cost $178.50; Sales $700.00.
    d. Cost $216.80; Sales $800.00.
    e. Cost $127.80; Sales $450.00.
    f. Cost $610.00; Sales $2,000.00.

2. Calculate cost, given the following figures for cost percent and sales:
    a. Cost % 28.0%; Sales $500.00.
    b. Cost % 34.5%; Sales $2,400.00.
    c. Cost % 24.8%; Sales $225.00.
    d. Cost % 31.6%; Sales $1,065.00.
    e. Cost % 29.7%; Sales $790.00.
    f. Cost % 21.2%; Sales $4,100.00.

3. Calculate sales, given the following figures for cost percent and cost:
    a. Cost % 30.0%; Cost $90.00.
    b. Cost % 25.0%; Cost $500.00.
    c. Cost % 33.3%; Cost $1,000.00.
    d. Cost % 27.3%; Cost $1,300.40.
    e. Cost % 24.5%; Cost $88.20.
    f. Cost % 34.8%; Cost $1,113.60.

4. List three examples of foodservice costs that are fixed. Are they controllable? Explain your answers.

5. List three examples of foodservice costs that are variable. Are they controllable? Explain your answers.

6. Write a short paragraph illustrating why a comparison of raw dollar costs in two restaurants would not be meaningful, but a comparison of the cost percents for food, beverages, labor, and overhead might be.

7. The present cost to Lil's Restaurant for one à la carte steak is $3.20. This is 40.0% of the menu sales price.
    a. What is the present sales price?
    b. At an annual inflation rate of 11%, what is this steak likely to cost one year from today?
    c. Using the cost calculated in (b) above, what should the menu sales price be for this item in one year if the cost percent at that time is to be 38%?
    d. If you were a banquet manager planning a function six months from now and planning to use this item, what unit cost would you plan for?

    e. The banquet manager in (d) above has already calculated that the other items included in this banquet menu will have increased in cost in six months from $2.00 to $2.11. What should the sales price per person be for this banquet if the desired cost percentage is 40%?

8. In the Loner Inn, total fixed costs for October were $28,422.80. In that month, 14,228 covers were served.
    a. What was fixed cost per cover for October?
    b. Assume that fixed costs will increase by 2% in November. Determine fixed cost per cover if the number of covers decreases by 10% in November.

9. Joe's Downtown Restaurant purchases domestic red wine at $9.20 per bottle. Each bottle contains three liters, the equivalent of 101 ounces. The wine is served in five-ounce glasses, and management allows for one ounce of spillage per three-liter bottle.
    a. What is the average unit cost per drink?
    b. What is the total cost of 60 glasses of wine?
    c. The banquet manager is planning a function for 120 persons for next Friday evening. Each guest will be given one glass of wine. How many bottles should be ordered for the party?
    d. What will be the unit cost of the wine? The total cost?

10. Sales records for luncheon in the Newmarket Restaurant for a recent week were:

Item A	196
Item B	72
Item C	142
Item D	24
Item E	112
Item F	224
Item G	162

Given this information, calculate sales mix.

11. Calculate the average dollar sale per customer from the following data:
    a. Sales: $1,000.00; Number of customers: 125.
    b. Sales: $1,300.00; Number of customers: 158.
    c. Sales: $8,720.53; Number of customers: 976.

12. The table below indicates the number of covers served and the gross sales per server for one three-hour period in Sally's Restaurant. De-

termine: (a) the average number of covers served per hour per server, and (b) the average sale per server for the three-hour period.

Server	Covers served	Gross sales per server
A	71	$237.40
B	66	$263.95
C	58	$188.25

13. Use the information about Sally's Restaurant identified in 12 above to complete the following:
    a. Calculate the average dollar sale.
    b. Calculate the turnover for the three-hour period if there are 65 seats in the restaurant.

14. Given the information about Sally's Restaurant identified in 12 and 13 above, assume the restaurant had 85,629 customers per year and gross sales were $352,783.40.
    a. Calculate average dollar sale per customer.
    b. Calculate sales per seat for the year.

15. The financial records of the Colonial Restaurant reveal the following figures for the year ending December 31, XXXX.

Depreciation	$ 25,000
Food sales	$375,000
Cost of beverages sold	$ 30,000
Other controllable expenses	$ 60,000
Salaries and wages	$130,000
Beverage sales	$125,000
Employee benefits	$ 20,000
Cost of food sold	$127,500
Occupancy costs	$ 55,000

   a. Following the form illustrated in Figure 1.1, prepare a statement of income for the business.
   b. Determine the following percentages.
      1. Food cost percent
      2. Labor cost percent (payroll, plus payroll taxes and employee benefits)
      3. Beverage cost percent
      4. Combined food and beverage cost percent
      5. Percentage of profit before income taxes
   c. Assuming the restaurant has 75 seats, determine food sales per seat for the year.

16. Define each of the following terms:

Average sale per customer
Average sale per server
Beverage cost
Budgeted cost
Controllable cost
Cost
Cost per dollar sale
Cost percent
Cover
Directly variable cost
Fixed cost
Food cost
Historical cost
Labor cost
Noncontrollable cost
Overhead
Planned cost
Prime cost
Sale
Sales mix
Sales price
Seat turnover
Semivariable cost
Total cost
Total sales
Total sales per seat
Unit cost
Variable cost

2 *The Control Process*

LEARNING OBJECTIVES

L E A R N I N G   O B J E C T I V E S

After reading and studying this chapter, you should be able to:
1. Define **control** and discuss its significance in food and beverage management.
2. Pinpoint responsibility for control in a food and beverage operation.
3. Cite examples of control techniques used in food and beverage operations.
4. Prepare an operating budget.
5. List the steps in the control process.
6. Describe the significance of the cost-benefit ratio in making control decisions.
7. Define each of the Key Terms at the end of the chapter.

INTRODUCTION

A considerable part of the previous chapter on costs and sales was devoted to explaining the meaning of those terms as they relate to the food and beverage industry. This chapter will define control, discuss the relationship of control to costs and sales, and outline how a manager institutes control in an enterprise. While later chapters will go into specific procedures used to institute control in various phases of food and beverage operations, this chapter will address control and the control process in general terms.

Before we begin the discussion, it is important to point out that in the food and beverage industry control really means controlling people rather than things. Consider the following: Food does not disappear by itself, without help. Excess quantities of liquor do not get into drinks unless put there by bartenders. Employees' wage calculations are not based on the wrong numbers of hours unless someone gives the wrong information to the paymaster. Food is not consumed by rodents unless human beings make that food accessible. Customers seldom leave without paying unless staff members make that possible.

In every one of these instances, the problem is the result of human action or lack of it. If a business is to operate profitably and reach its financial goals, people's actions must be managed.

The people involved may not be simply the personnel of the food and beverage operation; "people" may include customers of the establishment and, in some cases, intruders who may seek to steal the resources of the establishment—obviously without the knowledge and consent of the management. Thus, installing locks on both the front and back doors is one of the most basic control devices that one can use to prevent intruders from entering and stealing food, beverages, equipment, and cash when the operation is closed. Another simple control procedure is to locate the cashier near the front door in an effort to prevent customers from leaving without paying their bills. The time clock for employees is an example of a simple control device. This serves many purposes, one of which is to develop an accurate set of records of the numbers of hours worked by each of the hourly wage employees. Yet another good example is the bartender's use of a measuring device to ensure that each drink will contain the correct amount of a particular alcoholic ingredient. The need for control is not restricted to human beings, however. Instituting various sanitation procedures serves effectively to control infestation by various insects and rodents. Loss of food to non-human invaders surely constitutes unwarranted additional cost to any restaurant.

CONTROL

Control is a process used by managers to direct, regulate, and restrain the actions of people so that the established goals of an enterprise may be achieved.

If one intends to institute control in an enterprise, an obvious first step is to establish appropriate goals for the enterprise. Probably the most common goal for all private enterprises is financial success, although this is by no means the only long-range goal of business. Other goals might include operating the best restaurant in the city, providing adequate health insurance for employees, preserving the environment, promoting better health by providing nutritional information in the menu, or aiding in the integration of minority groups into national economic life.

To achieve these goals, management must set up any number of subgoals compatible with its long-range plans. These tend to be more specific and usually more immediate in nature. For example, to achieve the goal of operating the best restaurant in the city, it would be necessary to make plans to hire an excellent chef and to purchase the finest ingredients.

Discussion of general business goals and the planning required for achieving them is not within the scope of a text on cost control. On the assumption that appropriate goals have been established, we will restrict our discussion to the control procedures employed by foodservice managers to achieve one basic goal of business: operating profitably. Therefore, the focus will be on establishing control over costs and sales in food and beverage operations. Attention will center on the particular methods and procedures used by foodservice managers to direct, regulate, and restrain the actions of people, both directly and indirectly, to keep costs within acceptable bounds, to account for revenues, and to earn a profit in the process.

COST CONTROL

Cost control is defined as the process used by managers to regulate costs and guard against excessive costs. It is an ongoing process and involves every step in the chain of purchasing, receiving, storing, issuing, and preparing food and beverages for sale, as well as training and scheduling the personnel involved. The particular methods used to control costs vary from one establishment to another, depending in part on the nature and scope of operations, but the principles behind these methods are constant. The obvious goal is to eliminate excessive costs for food, beverages, and labor—to exert some governing power over costs in all areas to ensure that the enterprise will operate at a profit.

Two of the principal causes of excessive costs are inefficiency and waste. For example, storing food in refrigerators that are not cold enough or bottled beer in a warm, sunny room will cause spoilage and excessive cost. So will the preparation of an inedible beef stew or an unpalatable drink. When the stew is thrown into the garbage can or the drink poured down the drain, costs of operation are increased, but sales are not. Since profit is essentially the difference between sales and costs, it is apparent that any increases in cost that do not lead to corresponding increases in sales can have only one effect: reducing profits. Clearly, management must take steps to guard against these excessive costs.

SALES CONTROL

While cost control is critically important to the profitable operation of any business, cost control alone will not ensure profitability. Additional steps must be taken to ensure that all sales result in appropriate income to the business. For example, profits will be adversely affected if a steak listed in the menu for $18.95 is sold to a customer for $15.95 or if the drink priced to sell for $4.50 is sold for $2.50. Therefore, it is important to require that each employee record each sale accurately.

In addition, it is useful to compare sales records to production records to ensure that all quantities produced are accounted for. Although it is unfortunate that some employees are not completely honest, it is a fact of life that must be taken into account in food and beverage operations. Therefore, guest checks are usually numbered to ensure accountability. Sometimes duplicate copies of the checks, clearly identified as duplicates so they are not confused with the originals, are used to reconcile kitchen production with recorded sales. When the checks and duplicates are numbered sequentially, missing numbers can be noted and investigated at once.

These are but a few of the various approaches intended to ensure that every portion leaving a kitchen or bar has been recorded as a sale at the appropriate sales price. A number of such techniques will be discussed in Chapter 12, which includes a more thorough treatment of this complex topic.

RESPONSIBILITY FOR CONTROL

Responsibility for every aspect of any food and beverage enterprise rests with management. Control, therefore, is clearly a responsibility of management. In some food and beverage enterprises—probably the majority—managers take personal charge of directing and supervising the control procedures in every phase of operations. In others, managers delegate some or all of the work to subordinates. The nature, size, and scope of operations help determine the extent to which managers can exercise direct control rather than delegate responsibility. In general, the larger and more complex the operation, the more likely it is that control procedures will be supervised by subordinates. Job titles for these subordinates include food controller, beverage controller, assistant manager, supervisor, and a number of others.

Throughout this text, we will use several job titles for those having responsibility for supervising food, beverage, or labor control procedures. In the majority of food and beverage enterprises, one is likely to find control procedures supervised directly by managers, so that title is used most often. In larger operations, one may still find food controllers and beverage controllers. Today, there are comparatively few of these, but the job titles are still useful in discussions of control principles and will appear in various chapters.

Because food and beverage operations are so varied, it would be impossible to identify with any precision the job titles of those responsible for specific controls in a particular type of food and beverage operation. The use in this text of one job title rather than another is not intended to suggest that any particular task should be assigned to any particular job title. In that sense, the specific job titles used are of very little importance. The significant point is that management is ultimately responsible for seeing that appropriate control procedures are established either by attending to the work personally or by assigning it to others.

INSTITUTING CONTROL

The food and beverage business can be characterized as one that involves raw materials purchased, received, stored, and issued for the purpose of manufacturing products for sale. In these respects, many similarities exist between the food and beverage business and other manufacturing businesses. As an example, let us look at the steps involved in the production of wood furniture.

The furniture manufacturer must determine the kinds of woods that are best suited to the kind of furniture to be manufactured, and must purchase appropriate quantities of lumber at favorable prices. When the wood is delivered, the shipment must be checked to ensure that the material delivered is exactly as ordered. Then it must be moved into appropriate storage facilities, partly to prevent theft and partly to ensure that the characteristics of the wood will not be adversely affected by climate. The wood must then be issued in appropriate amounts for the production of various kinds of tables and chairs. During the manufacturing process, some effort must be made to maintain balanced quantities of parts so that, for example, one tabletop is made for each four legs. After tables have been manufactured and sold to customers, care must be taken to ensure that each sale is properly recorded, that the correct price is charged for each table sold, and that the total dollar value of each sale is collected.

There are a great number of similarities between the manufacturing industry just described and the typical food and beverage business. The motel coffee shop, the school cafeteria, the hotel dining room, the resort cocktail lounge—all these share with the manufacturing businesses described above the need for purchasing, receiving, storing, and issuing raw materials for the production of finished products for sale. In food and beverage operations, we deal with fruits, vegetables, meat, poultry, and a large number of other foods—fresh, frozen, and canned—as well as alcoholic beverages in many establishments, but these really serve the same purposes in our business that wood serves in the furniture manufacturing business.

In both businesses, raw materials must be carefully selected, always with the desired final products in mind, and appropriate quantities of each must be ordered to meet expected production needs. In each case, any order for raw materials should be placed with the vendor who will sell the materials at the most favorable price. As materials are received, they must be checked to see that the business is getting what it pays for. Then the materials must be stored appropriately until needed. When the person in charge of production requests materials from storage, the materials needed must be made available for the production of finished items for sale.

At each stage of operation, it is necessary to institute control in order to prevent the kinds of problems mentioned earlier. Control may be accomplished in a variety of ways, and anyone who attempts to manage a food and beverage operation should be aware of the range of techniques available.

The particular techniques selected for use in a given situation depend on the nature of the material or service requiring control and on the degree of difficulty inherent in instituting the control. Thus, deciding which control technique to adopt in a given situation is not always simple. The following are some of the more common techniques.

CONTROL TECHNIQUES

The list of control techniques available to a manager includes the following:

1. Establishing standards.
2. Establishing procedures.
3. Training.
4. Setting examples.

5. Observing and correcting employee actions.
6. Requiring records and reports.
7. Disciplining employees.
8. Preparing and following budgets.

Establishing Standards

Standards are defined as rules or measures established for making comparisons and judgments. In business, these standards are set by management and are used for judging the extent to which results meet expectations. Several types of standards are useful in establishing control over food and beverage operations. It is important to develop a working understanding of these several types of standards before proceeding.

Quality standards are used to define the degree of excellence of raw materials, finished products, and, by extension, work. In one sense, establishing quality standards is a grading process. Most food items are graded according to degree of excellence (many of them by government: the Department of Agriculture in the United States and similar agencies in other nations), and management should establish a quality standard for each food item that is to be purchased. Beef, for example, is generally available in a number of different grades for restaurant and institutional use, and it is important to determine which grade will be used for the preparation of a particular menu item.

Beverage items also require quality standards. For example, some spirits improve with age, and a 12-year-old scotch whiskey is generally considered to be of a higher quality than one that is only 8 years old. Management in beverage operations must determine which beverage items are of appropriate quality to ensure customer satisfaction. Quality standards must also be determined for the work force. In some hotels and fine restaurants, higher degrees of skill are required for the production and service of elaborate menu items. Lower levels of skill would probably be acceptable in the average roadside diner.

Quantity standards are defined as measures of weight, count, or volume used to make comparisons and judgments. Management must establish a number of quantity standards. Standard portion sizes for food and beverage products and standards for work output are simple examples. The portion size for every food item served must be clearly established. Each shrimp cocktail should contain a predetermined number of shrimp of specified size, a certain measure of sauce, and clearly identified quantities of garnishes. A portion of soup should be identified as to size of bowl or cup to be used, or the size of the ladle used to portion it, and the quantity of any garnish to be added. Similarly, entree items must be identified as to the number of ounces or pieces. Surrounding items, such as vegetables, should be portioned with a spoon of particular size, as with peas, or be identified by count, as with asparagus spears.

In bar operations, management must establish a standard quantity for each measure of liquor used. In many instances, bars operate with standard drink recipes, indicating the specific quantities of ingredients to be used in preparing particular drinks.

Quantity standards are often important in the control of labor costs as well. It is useful when planning staff schedules to know, for example, the number of tables or seats a server can cover during a given period or the number of sandwiches a pantry worker can make per hour.

In addition to quality and quantity standards, it is ultimately necessary to determine and set cost standards for operation. Cost standards are more commonly referred to as standard costs.

The term **standard cost** is defined as the cost of goods or services identified, approved, and accepted by management. Standard costs are used for various purposes. They may be compared with actual costs in order for one to make judgments about the actual costs, and they may be used as a basis for establishing sales prices. Paradoxically, a standard cost is both realistic and an ideal simultaneously. For example, if one bottle of liquor containing 33.8 ounces costs $11.83 to purchase, each ounce has a value of $.35. That is to say that the standard cost of one ounce is $.35. If the entire bottle is used to prepare drinks, each of which contains one ounce of the liquor, the standard cost of the liquor in each drink is $.35. Based on the actual purchase price of the bottle, that is the real cost of one ounce. However, this is an ideal: it does not take into account the possibility of either spillage or evaporation, both of which are likely to occur in bar operations.

Standard costs are useful in measuring the effectiveness of operations in food and beverage establishments. As we shall see, comparing standard costs with actual costs can help determine how effectively food and beverage materials and labor resources are being used in day-to-day operations. Standard costs are particularly useful in cost control because they provide a means for management to compare what is actually happening in an enterprise with what should be happening, given the standards established for operations.

Standard costs must be calculated. There are various methods for doing this, each of which will be discussed in detail in later chapters. In the case of foods and beverages, various kinds of calculations are necessary, the simplest form of which has been previously illustrated in the discussion of the standard cost of one ounce of liquor. In the case of labor, determination of standard costs is rather more complex.

Establishing Procedures

In addition to establishing standards for quality, quantity, and cost, food and beverage managers must establish standard procedures. **Procedures** are the methods employed to prepare products or perform jobs. **Standard procedures** are those that have been established as the correct methods, routines, and techniques for day-to-day operations. As we shall see in later chapters, maintaining effective control over food, beverage, and labor costs requires establishing standard procedures for every phase of operations.

Ordering and purchasing procedures must be standardized to ensure that ingredients used to make food and beverage products are purchased at appropriate times in needed quantities, at the most favorable prices, and are of appropriate quality for intended use. Receiving procedures must be standardized so that all goods received conform in quality, quantity, and cost to those ordered. Standard storing procedures must be put into effect to guard against both spoilage and theft, either of which will lead to excessive costs.

Issuing must be standardized so that food and beverage items will be used in the order they are received, thus preventing spoilage and the resulting excessive costs. To further guard against spoilage and theft, the quantities of foods and beverages issued must be linked to carefully determined production needs. Moreover, records of issues can be used to calculate cost per item produced; such costs can then be compared to standard costs to determine the efficiency of production and the effectiveness of operations.

Production procedures must be standardized for a number of reasons. One of the most important of these is customer satisfaction. Any given item should be produced by the same method and with the same ingredients every time it is served. It should also be served in the same quantity each time, partly so that regular customers will be given the same quantity each time they order the item, and partly to maintain cost standards.

Training

While establishing standards and standard procedures is necessary for control, doing so is really just the first step in a process. None of the standards are of any significance unless employees are aware of them, and employees will not become aware of the standards unless management is willing to undertake staff training. **Training** is a process by which managers teach employees how work is to be done, given the standards and standard procedures established. For example, if management has established a standard four-ounce portion size for hamburgers, then all employees responsible for producing portions of hamburgers must be made aware of the fact that four ounces is the correct portion size. Moreover, each of these employees must be trained to produce portions of the standard size at his workstation, using the correct equipment and supplies provided for doing so. If all employees are not aware of the relevant standards and standard procedures established for their work and are not trained to follow these standards, the standards are completely useless.

Any foodservice manager who trains employees would doubtless agree that training is difficult, frustrating, time-consuming, and, in the short run, costly. Perhaps that is why a substantial number of poor managers ignore it and simply put new employees to work without devoting any time to demonstrating and explaining what they are to do. Sometimes the new employee is merely introduced to a co-worker who is then expected to train him. Occasionally this works reasonably well; more often it does not, frequently because the co-worker is either unwilling or unable to train the new employee. After all, the typical foodservice employee is not hired for his ability to train others.

If employees are not suitably trained to follow established standards and standard procedures, the control aspects of the manager's job become difficult, at best; sometimes control becomes impossible. Further discussion of this topic will be deferred to suitable sections of the text and the chapters on labor control.

Setting Examples

Sometimes the process of establishing standards and standard procedures is not quite as formal as the foregoing sections might suggest. In many instances, standards are established in a very informal way: employees in an operation begin to follow the examples set by the manager—the manager's behavior, manner, responses to questions, and even a failure to speak or take action in some situations. In general, the behavior of individuals in a group tends to be influenced by the actions, statements, and attitudes of their leaders.

The attitudes and work habits of a manager are evident as she performs various tasks in the course of a work day. Her behavior will influence the manner in which employees perform their work. If the manager who has occasion to help employees plate food for the dining room serves incorrect portion sizes, employees will be more likely to do the same when the manager is not there. Similarly, if a manager is inclined to wrap parcels of food to take home for personal use, employees will be more likely to do so. And if the manager observes them doing so and fails to end the practice, the amount of food leaving the premises will usually increase.

It must be noted that any manager must be consistent in setting examples as well as in directing, regulating, and restraining employees and their actions. In far too many cases, managers appear not to have long-range and short-range goals clearly in mind as they go about the business of managing. Consequently, their examples, actions, directions, and responses to employee questions do not present a clear and consistent view to subordinates. Such inconsistency confuses employees and has the effect of working against the control processes and procedures in effect.

Observing and Correcting Employee Actions

If a manager were to see a bartender mixing drinks without measuring the ingredients and did not take time to remind the individual to measure quantities carefully, then the bartender could reasonably assume that his work met the manager's standards. The manager would have missed an excellent opportunity to improve the bartender's work habits, and to maintain control. Similarly, if a manager were to observe a receiving clerk failing to verify that quantities of meat delivered conformed to the quantity on the invoice and did not correct the individual, the employee might never know that his performance was unacceptable.

One of a manager's important tasks is to observe the actions of all employees continually as they go about their daily jobs, judging those actions in the light of the standards and standard procedures established for their work. If any are failing to follow the standards, it is a manager's responsibility to correct their performance to the extent necessary at the appropriate time.

Requiring Records and Reports

Obviously, no manager can be in all places at all times to observe employees' actions. The owner/manager of a small operation can observe employee actions to a far greater extent than can the manager of a larger operation—one consisting, for example, of several bars and dining rooms, seating hundreds of guests and employing hundreds of personnel. The larger the establishment, the more likely it is that management's observations must be indirect rather than direct. Their "observations" must be abstracted and inferred from a variety of records and reports.

One example of such a report is the statement of income illustrated in the introductory chapter. The statement of income summarizes cost and sales information for a particular period. Figures in the statement of income can be used to calculate cost-to-sales ratios of various kinds. These are normally compared to ratios for previous periods, and judgments are made about operations on the basis of these comparisons. If the comparisons are considered satisfactory to management, this implies in general terms that the performance of employees has been acceptable during the period covered by the statement. If the comparisons are unsatisfactory, the implication is that some or all of the standards and standard procedures have not been followed. The manager cannot normally pinpoint specific problems from such a general report as the statement of income; other more specific and more timely reports and records are usually required. Some of these may be developed daily, others weekly and monthly, as will be seen in later chapters. At this point, it is important to recognize that managers need timely information to determine whether or not long-range and short-range goals and subgoals are being met. If timely records and reports are not available, opportunities for taking corrective action may be lost. The variety and extent of the records and reports developed and used for control purposes will be discussed in great detail in later chapters.

Disciplining Employees

Discipline is defined as action taken to admonish, chastise, or reprimand an employee for work performance or personal behavior incompatible with established standards. It is a term with negative connotations, suggesting the threats and punishments used on children by some parents. Discipline, therefore, is a difficult topic to address.

Foodservice managers generally prefer to avoid the need for discipline by improving the hiring practices in their organizations. By selecting the right people for jobs—those with the experience, skill, and personal characteristics that match the job requirements—the number of individuals requiring some level of discipline can be reduced to a bare minimum. However, from time to time, every manager must face the fact that some individual staff member must be disciplined.

Discipline is used as a control technique in many food and beverage operations, and may take any of a number of forms, as discussed below. It is a valuable technique if used properly and judiciously.

Discipline is not the same as observing and correcting employee actions; it is the next step beyond. Before resorting to discipline, managers are likely to have made reasonable, though unsuccessful, efforts to correct the actions of some employee. Discipline would be called for only if corrective action failed. If so, managers commonly resort to some words or actions that employees normally regard as punishing, in the broadest sense of that term. One assumes that the standards for work performance and personal behavior are known and understood by all employees, either because they have been given appropriate training and instruction by management or because they should be aware of the norms for acceptable behavior in the workplace. For example, suppose an employee has been trained to follow specific performance standards and does not do so. A supervisor, given his responsibility to observe and correct employees actions, notices the employee's failure to follow the performance standards and makes some reasonable attempts to induce the employee to improve his performance. If repeated efforts aimed at obtaining improved performance from the employee were entirely unsuccessful, some discipline would be required. His poor performance would be called to his attention again by his supervisor, probably in a more direct and forceful way. On this second occasion, the supervisor's approach would likely be more severe. Most responsible managers would hope that the second such occasion would be the last and that the admonition would bring about the necessary improvement. However, if it did not, then it would be necessary to take progressively more stern, forceful, and finally punishing actions, the last of which would be firing. If an employee was worth hiring, he should be worth keeping, and all suitable efforts should be made to bring his job performance into line. Therefore, this final step—firing—is normally reserved for use only if it is simply impossible to modify the employee's job performance or personal behavior. On some rare occasions—in the case of theft, for example—it is used immediately.

On another level, the manager responsible for poor financial performance in one unit of a chain organization may have this fact pointed out to him by top management in any number of ways. The possibilities may range from quiet discussion to heated admonition, or from demotion or transfer to firing. Finally, no employee at any level of an organization is completely immune from the possibility of disciplinary action.

It is important to recognize the desirability of keeping the number of individuals terminated to a minimum. A high rate of employee turnover because of excessive firings can be very costly, leading to such additional expenses as newspaper advertising for new help, higher rates for unemployment insurance contributions in some states, lower rates of productivity, higher training costs, and a number of others.

On the one hand, it must be understood that the object of discipline is to change or modify employees' job performance or personal behavior—to improve performance so that the work is done in a manner that conforms to the standards and procedures that management has identified as the ones most likely to achieve the organization's goals and objectives. On the other hand, it should be apparent that disciplinary action generally has negative connotations in the minds of employees, most of whom would normally prefer to avoid any such unpleasantness. If certain behavior patterns (those that follow the standards and procedures established by management) lead to positive and pleasant rewards, while others (those that ignore management's standards and procedures) bring the negative and unpleasant rewards associated with disciplinary action, then most employees will generally work towards the former and avoid the latter. The very fact that employees know that continual failure to follow established standards can lead to unpleasantness tends to have the desirable effect of making job performance and personal behavior conform to appropriate standards.

Preparing and Following Budgets

Preparing and following budgets may be the most common technique for controlling business operations. A **budget** is defined as a financial plan and may be described as a realistic expression of management's goals and objectives expressed in financial terms. Many businesses establish budgets for specific aspects of operation. Thus, there are sales budgets, cash flow budgets, capital equipment budgets, and advertising budgets, among many other possibilities.

Food and beverage operations also use budgets—many of the same types of budgets as are used in other businesses. Many restaurants prepare capital equipment budgets, for example, because of the ongoing need to replace equipment that wears out and to purchase new types of equipment that becomes available in the market. Capital equipment is typically very costly, and a financial plan must be established before making the purchase. Advertising budgets are established so that appropriate levels of funds can be made available to generate a particular level of sales.

The most important type of budget that a food and beverage manager can prepare is an **operating budget.** Stated in dollar terms, it is a forecast of sales activity and an estimate of costs that will be incurred in the process of generating those sales. By extension, the budget indicates the profit that should result after the costs of producing those sales have been met. An operating budget is clearly a financial plan for the period it covers. In this text, we will restrict our discussion of budgets to operating budgets because the operating budget is most closely aligned with food, beverage, and labor cost control.

For established restaurants, preparation of an operating budget normally begins with historical information—the financial records of the business. Additionally, one needs estimates of anticipated changes in costs and sales and in the business environment. Thus, if federal or state laws will affect wage rates paid to employees in the period covered by the budget being prepared, this information must be factored into the planning. Similarly, if the establishment's real estate tax rates have been increased or decreased, that information should be reflected in the budget. More difficult to deal with, but equally important, are the effects of poor weather conditions on future crops, anticipated shortages of beef due to cattlemen's reductions in herds, and other such general conditions, including those in the economy that may affect future sales.

In new establishments that lack financial statements for previous years, information from a market analysis and from a manager's previous experience in the industry provide the best alternative sources of data for budget preparation. When no market analysis is available, or when the manager is not widely experienced in the food and beverage business, or when both of these are true, one may find that no effort is made to prepare a budget. When this is the case, management has missed an opportunity to use one of the most useful of all control techniques.

PREPARING AN OPERATING BUDGET

As previously stated, an operating budget is normally prepared using historical information from previous budgets and other financial records. This information, together with anticipated changes in sales and costs, provides the basic data needed to prepare an operating budget for an upcoming period. Operating budgets can be prepared for any period of time—a day, a week, a month, a quarter, six months, or a full year. Typically, an operating budget for one full year is prepared first and then broken down into smaller units for shorter time periods. Budgets for these shorter periods may not reflect equal sales and costs in every instance.

This is the case in seasonal restaurants. Thus, for example, if the budget for a restaurant forecasts $1,600,000 in sales for the year, each quarter would not necessarily forecast sales of $400,000. The first and fourth quarters may be busy periods for the restaurant, while the second and third quarters may be slow. The managers may forecast $500,000 in sales for the first and fourth quarters and only $300,000 in sales for each of the second and third quarters. In addition, the manager might forecast substantial profits for the busy quarters and very little for the slow quarters.

To illustrate the preparation of a budget, let us use as the example the Graduate Restaurant described in the introduction to Chapter 1. The statement of income and relevant percentages derived from it are reproduced in Figure 2.1. The illustration of budget preparation is for a static budget. A **static budget** is one that is prepared assuming only one level of business activity for the period (i.e., $1,600,000 in sales).

In the previous chapter, distinctions were drawn between controllable and noncontrollable costs, and between fixed and variable costs. To prepare an operating budget, one must determine which costs are fixed and which are variable. That can be more complex than it may sound, and the determinations made by management in one restaurant may be incorrect or inappropriate in another. Figure 2.2 lists the assumptions about fixed and variable costs that were used in the preparation of the operating budget illustrated below.

Using those assumptions, we will now begin the process of preparing an operating budget for the Graduate Restaurant for the coming fiscal year. The initial step in this process is to examine sales figures from the recent past to note evident trends, if any. In some establishments, the examination of sales records might reveal regular increases in sales from year to year; in others, decreases might be seen; in still others, changes from year to year might show no discernible pattern. In any case, it is the responsibility of the owner or

For the Year Ended December XXXX		
		Percent of Sales
SALES		
Food	$786,250	85.00%
Beverage	$138,750	15.00%
Total Sales	$925,000	100.00%
COST OF SALES		
Food	$275,187	35.00%
Beverage	$ 34,688	25.00%
Total Cost of Sales	$309,875	33.50%
GROSS PROFIT	$615,125	66.50%
CONTROLLABLE EXPENSES		
Salaries and Wages	$185,000	20.00%
Employee Benefits	$ 46,250	5.00%
Other Controllable Expenses	$138,750	15.00%
Total Controllable Expenses	$370,000	40.00%
INCOME BEFORE OCCUPANCY COSTS, INTEREST, DEPRECIATION, AND INCOME TAXES	$245,125	26.50%
OCCUPANCY COSTS	$ 78,625	8.50%
INTEREST EXPENSE	$ 13,875	1.50%
DEPRECIATION	$ 46,250	5.00%
RESTAURANT PROFIT	$106,375	11.50%

FIGURE 2.1   *The Graduate Restaurant Statement of Income*

manager to analyze past sales for this purpose. Information from such an analysis can be of great value in projecting sales levels for the period to be covered by the budget.

The next step in the budgeting process is to examine the external environment and assess any conditions or factors that could affect sales volume in the coming year. These would include general economic conditions in the nation and in the immediate geographical area; population changes; changes that could affect transportation to the establishment, including new highways and bus routes; and any number of other external variables.

Another important step is to review any planned changes in the operation that would affect sales volume. For example, any plans to increase or decrease menu prices will clearly affect sales volume, and the impact of such changes must be clearly assessed. The impact of such varied possibilities as anticipated changes in the number of seats in the restaurant, in the number of items listed in the menu, in the particular menu items offered, and in levels of advertising must also be considered.

After one conducts the assessments discussed above, the next logical pro-

For the Year Ending December 31, XXXX	
FIXED COSTS	
Occupancy costs	$ 78,625
Other controllable costs	138,750
Fixed salaries and wages	111,000 (60% of $65,000 salaries and wages)*
Employee benefits	27,750 (25% of $39,000)
Interest	13,875
Depreciation	46,250
VARIABLE COSTS	
Cost of food	35.0% of food sales
Cost of beverages	25.0% of beverage sales
Salaries and wages	9.4% of food sales**
Employee benefits	25.0% of variable salaries and wages

*Salaries and wages are a semivariable cost, so they must be divided into their fixed and variable components. In the illustration, we have assumed that 60.0% of total salaries and wages is fixed, while the remaining 40.0% is variable.
**Variable salaries and wages are assumed to be associated only with food sales. Therefore, other salaries and wages will not increase or decrease with changes in the business volume. Variable salaries and wages—40.0% of $185,000, or $74,000—are 9.4% of food sales?

FIGURE 2.2 *Fixed and Variable Costs in the Graduate Restaurant*

cedure is to determine the nature and extent of changes in cost levels, some of which will be dictated by anticipated changes in sales volume and others of which will occur independent of volume changes. Some variable costs are certain to be affected by changes in volume, but may also be affected by other factors. Increased sales volume may necessitate hiring additional servers, but a union labor contract may include a new hourly wage for all employees. There are many other possibilities for cost increases: a clause in a lease dictating a rent increase effective on a particular date, higher utility rates, anticipated increases in the costs of particular foods, and any number of others. Any anticipated changes in cost and sales levels must be considered and factored into the new operating budget.

Let us assume that the management of the Graduate Restaurant has carefully examined past cost and sales figures and has assessed the impact of various anticipated changes in both internal and external conditions on costs and sales.

The following changes are anticipated:

1. Both food and beverage sales are expected to increase by 5 percent.
2. Fixed salaries and wages will increase by 4 percent.

For the Year Ended December XXXX			
	Current Year	*Change*	*Upcoming Year*
SALES			
Food	$786,250	+$39,313	$825,563
Beverage	$138,750	+6,938	$145,688
Total Sales	$925,000	+$46,251	$971,251
COST OF SALES			
Food	$275,187	+$13,760	$288,947
Beverage	$ 34,688	+ 1,735	$ 36,423
Total Cost of Sales	$309,875	+$15,495	$325,370
GROSS PROFIT	$615,125		$645,880
CONTROLLABLE EXPENSES			
Fixed Sal. and Wages	$111,000	+$4,400	$115,400
Variable Sal. and Wages	$ 74,000	+3,603	$ 77,603
Employee Benefits	$ 46,250	+2,001	48,251
Other Controllable Expenses	$138,750	+6,500	145,250
Total Controllable Expenses	$370,000	+$16,504	$386,504
INCOME BEFORE OCCUPANCY COSTS, INTEREST, DEPRECIATION, AND INCOME TAXES	$245,125		$259,376
OCCUPANCY COSTS	$ 78,625	+$2,000	$ 80,625
INTEREST EXPENSE	$ 13,875		$ 13,875
DEPRECIATION	$ 46,250		$ 46,250
RESTAURANT PROFIT	$106,375		$118,606

FIGURE 2.3   *The Graduate Restaurant Statement of Income*

3. Variable salaries and wages will continue to be the same percentage of sales.
4. The cost of employee benefits will increase, but will continue to be the same percentage of salaries and wages.
5. Other controllable costs will increase by $6,500.
6. Occupancy costs will increase by $2,000.
7. Food and beverage cost percentages will remain the same.

Based on these anticipated changes, the budget for the Graduate Restaurant for the coming fiscal year would be as illustrated in Figure 2.3.

Assuming that the projections in the operating budget for sales, costs, and profits were acceptable to management, it would be adopted as the plan of action for the covered period. If the projections were unacceptable, management would reexamine both the assumptions on which the budget was based and the budget figures themselves. A reexamination of this nature might suggest the desirability of additional changes affecting sales or costs that might lead to more acceptable results. Before the adoption of the budget, the effects of such potential changes could be tested by means of the techniques of cost/ volume/profit analysis, the principal subject of the following chapter.

Once an operating budget is accepted and adopted for an upcoming period, it becomes a standard against which operating performance is measured as the fiscal year progresses. To use it effectively for this purpose, the operating budget may be broken down into smaller units for shorter time periods, as discussed above. This may result in monthly or quarterly budgets, with sales and cost projections with which actual figures can be compared. The budget projections become the standards or targets for the covered periods. If cost and sales figures for a given period do not meet expectations as identified in the budget, efforts will be made to identify the causes. Once the causes have been identified, it is possible and desirable to take remedial actions to ensure better performance in the next operating period. If, for example, sales do not meet budget projections and costs are too high for the level of sales recorded, some remedial action will clearly be required. If payroll or any other controllable cost is greater than the amount budgeted, then management should attempt to determine the causes of the excessive costs and take appropriate measures to keep future costs at more suitable levels.

One must recognize that budget projections are merely targets and are often incorrect. Sales levels are often higher or lower than projections because the people who prepare budgets—owners, managers, and accountants—are often unable to project the future accurately. Sometimes this is caused by their failure to take all of the information at hand into account when preparing the operating budget. A new office building down the street, for example, may generate additional luncheon business that was not accurately anticipated, or planned advertising may bring in more customers than the manager had expected. Conversely, unexpected road construction outside a restaurant may cause a significant decrease in sales volume for some period of time, or a nearby manufacturing facility may close unexpectedly and bring about a loss of business.

To counteract the inherent shortcomings of fixed operating budgets, a manager can prepare a budget designed to project sales and costs for several levels of business activity. This is called a **flexible budget.** Flexible budgets are normally prepared for levels of business volume above and below the expected level. The idea is that if the level of sales is higher or lower than expected, management already has an new operating budget available with appropriate projections of costs for that sales level.

THE CONTROL PROCESS

Having discussed eight common control techniques used by owners and managers in food and beverage operations, we will now turn to the control process.

As indicated earlier in the chapter, control is defined as a process through which managers attempt to direct, regulate, and restrain the actions of people in order to achieve desired goals. This process consists of four steps:

1. Establish standards and standard procedures for operation.
2. Train all individuals to follow established standards and standard procedures.
3. Monitor performance and compare actual performances with established standards.
4. Take appropriate action to correct deviations from standards.

Sometimes investigation reveals that an established standard is actually unrealistic or inappropriate. If that is the case, then management should consider changing the standard.

To illustrate understand the relevance of the control process to food and beverage management, consider the following example. Imagine a restaurant owner who has taken great care to establish goals for his business. One of those goals is to serve the finest food in the area. To reach this goal, the owner has established standards and standard procedures that help define his meaning of the term "the finest." For one menu item—prime sirloin steak—the standard is made clear by the use of the term *prime,* which identifies certain specific characteristics in beef. The standards and standard procedures for his chef and steward reflect his wish that only prime beef is to be purchased for the production of this menu item. Those employees receiving deliveries of meat from purveyors have been trained to follow standard procedures that include checking the quality of beef delivered by examining it and verifying that the USDA (United States Department of Agriculture) grade stamp is present. The restaurant manager must monitor operations regularly, checking to see personally that the beef purchased meets the standards set. This could be done in any number of ways, one of which is by examining raw beef in the refrigerator. The manager knows that if operations are not monitored and this results in orders placed for a lower grade of beef, regular customers will notice the difference. Some will complain; most will not—they will simply find a restaurant that really has the prime beef promised by its menu. Therefore, whenever the manager finds that the quality of beef purchased deviates from the standards, appropriate remedial action is required if the owner's goal of offering the finest food is to be met.

There is a clear need for control in every phase of food and beverage operations. Control is one key to successful food and beverage management and must be established if success is to be achieved. Experience throughout the industry has long proven that establishing control means instituting the four-step process identified above.

CONTROL SYSTEMS

Control system is the term used to describe that collection of interrelated and interdependent control techniques and procedures in use in a given food and beverage operation. Historically, control systems in foodservice and related enterprises were heavily dependent on paper-and-pencil methods. Many required difficult and time-consuming calculations. In recent years, however, various time- and labor-saving devices have been introduced to decrease our industry's historical reliance on paper-and-pencil calculations and extensive paper records. Thankfully, these are disappearing from today's food and beverage operations. Many are now relying on electronic cash registers, for example, which are programmed to keep records of numbers of portions sold and to print out simple reports to management at the end of a day. Others are depending on computers with software designed to accumulate and summarize information that was simply not available in the past. Still others have invested in amazingly complex computer systems to assist in maintaining control over operations in ways that were not previously possible.

One of the primary reasons that the Graduate Restaurant has been able to control its costs so well is because it has a computer system with software designed specifically for restaurant operations. A schematic diagram of its layout is shown in Figure 2.4. A file server located in the manager's office serves as the hub of the computer network. Terminals with keypads and printers have been installed at two servers' stations. One workstation is on the manager's desk. Remote printers have been installed at the bar and at the cooks' station.

The control features for purchasing, receiving, issuing, producing, and selling described in the following chapters have been programmed into the software. Additionally, the system provides managers with full access to sales and cost information at any time.

Operations proceed along the following lines. Servers arriving for work change into uniforms on a lower level (not shown on the diagram), then proceed to their sidestands in the dining room. On each of the two sidestands is a small terminal with keypad and printer that dining room personnel use to log in. In other words, they record their arrival for work much as they would with a traditional time clock. Other personnel log in at the terminal in the manager's office.

Guests enter the dining room, leaving coats in the coat room. They are seated by the supervisor, who leaves menus at the table. A server greets the guests and takes their orders for drinks; the orders are written on a Captain's pad or an ordinary white pad rather than on a guest check. Having taken the orders, the server proceeds to a terminal and opens an accounts in computer memory. This account is equivalent to a guest check. The process requires that the server enter a personal identification code, the table number, the number

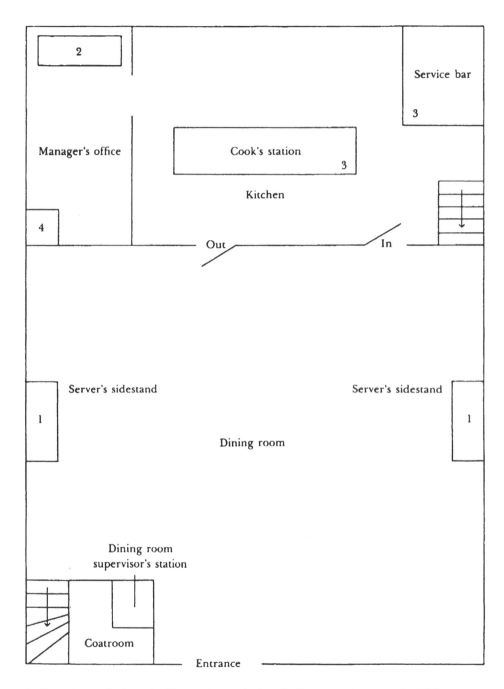

1. Server's terminals   2. Manager's terminal   3. Remote printers   4. CPU

FIGURE 2.4

of guests, and a special code used for creating a new account. With the account opened, the server uses a numeric code to enter the customers' orders for drinks. This information, together with the time of the order, is in computer memory, which has been programmed with correct prices for all drinks. The system is programmed to send the recorded drink orders to the bartender at the bar, where they are printed on a remote printer. The hard copy provided by the remote printer is an order for the bartender to prepare the drinks. This hard copy includes the server number, table number, and order time. The bartender removes the order from the printer, makes the drinks, and places the printed order on the tray with the drinks, thus eliminating questions about which drinks are for which server and what time the orders were entered.

At the appropriate time, the server follows similar procedures for placing food orders. Different codes are used for foods and drinks, and the computer is programmed to send food orders to the remote printers at the cooks' station. All ordered items are stored in computer memory, but the only items appearing on the remote printer at any preparation station are those appropriate to that station. Thus, food orders are not sent to the bar, and orders for coffee, handled by the servers themselves, do not appear on any remote printers.

After a diner has finished the meal, the server obtains the guest check by requesting one via the terminal and printer at the sidestand. With this system, the guest check is merely a hard copy of the data stored in the computer, accessed by table and server number. This hard copy is torn from the printer and given to the diner. In the Graduate Restaurant, each server acts as a cashier for his own checks, and settlement is recorded for each check as the server receives cash or a credit card. At the end of a shift, the server reports to the manager's office to turn in the cash, checks, and credit card vouchers for his sales. Jim Young sits at his terminal in the manager's office to obtain summary data showing charge and cash sales for that particular server. He collects cash and charge vouchers accordingly. Before changing out of uniform and leaving the premises, each server logs out, using the manager's terminal.

At any time of day Jim can monitor operations at will. Such data as gross sales volume, numbers of customers served, numbers of checks outstanding, sales mix, numbers of portions of particular items sold, and any number of other possibilities may be of special interest at given times throughout the day.

At the conclusion of business, Jim prints a detailed breakdown of the day's business. The software has been programmed to provide: total dollar sales categorized into cash sales and charge sales, with the charge sales divided by type of credit card; total dollar sales separated into food sales and beverage sales, with the food sales broken down into dollar sales by menu category or by individual menu items; average dollar sale per customer, per server, per seat, per table, or per hour, or any number of these; seat turnover; number of customers per server, per hour, per meal, and per day; number of orders of each food and beverage item sold (a reflection of the sales mix); total dollar sales per hour; sales in any category for the period to date; total payroll cost for the day, for any part of the day, or for the period to date; and a vast amount of food and beverage cost data, including standard costs.

Today, most food and beverage operators are using some type of computer control system as an aid to managing. For some, the computer system is simply a modern electronic cash register with features that earlier cash registers were not able to provide. In growing numbers of operations, however, the computer systems are increasingly complex and designed to provide both quick access to needed information and sophisticated managerial control over most or all operations in the restaurant.

COST/BENEFIT RATIO

One additional important concept must be introduced before proceeding. The concept is **cost/benefit ratio:** the relationship between the costs incurred in instituting and maintaining a single control or control system, and the benefits or savings derived by doing so. It should be obvious that no control measure can be instituted without some cost. Sometimes that cost is relatively insignificant. Sometimes it is much greater—great enough so that careful consideration must be given to the extent of the expected benefit before one feels justified in incurring the cost. Occasionally the cost may prove to be completely prohibitive. A relatively insignificant cost is required to institute one basic control measure: locking the front and back doors at night to prevent burglary. By contrast, relocating a restaurant cashier's desk to some position judged more suitable for preventing customers from leaving without paying the checks would cost somewhat more. Installing a sophisticated new time clock and hiring a new employee trained to operate it would require even greater, ongoing costs. Establishing a new control department, hiring a food and beverage controller and appropriate support staff, and supplying the staff with equipment and supplies would obviously require large—and possibly prohibitive—amounts of money.

In judging whether or not the cost of any control procedure is justified, one must take into consideration how long a period of time will be required for the savings to pay for the cost of the new procedure—the **payback period.** For example, purchasing and installing locks for food storage facilities to prevent employee theft costs a relatively small amount of money and could result in immediate savings. The payback period might be only one month or less and would clearly be justified. Relocating the cashier's station to a more suitable position might result in only minimal savings and might have a payback period of a year or longer. Establishing a new control department, and hiring a food and beverage controller and appropriate support staff might have annual costs that would exceed the financial savings, and thus, never justify the costs incurred.

One must keep clearly in mind the primary purposes of cost and sales control measures: to guard against excessive costs and to ensure that all sales result in appropriate income. In other words, some identifiable financial benefit must be obtainable from the introduction of any control device or control procedure or from the hiring of any staff member responsible for instituting controls. Benefits must always exceed costs. Before instituting any new procedures for control, management should first determine that the anticipated savings will be greater than the cost of the new procedures. Any manager must look critically at any new control methods and procedures to be sure they will save more than they will cost. If controls cost more than the benefits they deliver, their value is doubtful at best. In normal circumstances, it is not sensible to institute any controls that cost more than they save. Stated in other terms, one might say that one should not normally spend a dollar to save dollar. In numeric terms, one might say that the ratio of cost to benefit should always be less than 1/1.

Other Considerations

Before instituting any control procedure and incurring the consequent dollar costs, one should also look at the nonquantifiable effects. Some of these may be beneficial; others may not be. Control systems and procedures generally affect many aspects of the operation, sometimes in negative ways not anticipated by management. For example, a system designed to verify that all food transported by servers from kitchen to dining room is appropriately recorded on guest checks may slow down service, reduce seat turnover, and even result in cold food being served to guests. Similarly, the installation of a time clock to obtain accurate data for payroll purposes might cause resentment among longtime, loyal, and valued employees, some of whom might seek other employment rather than punch a time clock. Thus, management should carefully estimate the nonmonetary outcomes of any control system or procedure before putting it into effect.

CHAPTER ESSENTIALS

In this chapter, we established working definitions of the terms control, cost control, and sales control. We fixed responsibility for control and demonstrated that control is needed in all operating phases of a successful enterprise. We identified eight common control techniques, illustrated their use in foodservice, and explained their value to managers seeking to establish control. Particular emphasis was given to budgeting—the preparation and use of the operating budget—a control technique. We identified the four-step process of control and described its use in food and beverage operations. Finally, we defined cost/benefit ratio and explained the significance of this ratio in determining the extent to which proposed control measures are to be implemented.

KEY TERMS IN THIS CHAPTER

Budget
Control
Control process
Control systems
Cost/benefit ratio
Cost control
Flexible budget
Operating budget
Procedures
Quality standards
Quantity standards
Sales control
Standard cost
Standard procedures
Standards
Static budget

QUESTIONS AND PROBLEMS

1. Compare the quality standards one might use in a school cafeteria with those one might use in a fine-dining restaurant for one standard portion of roast turkey with dressing.

2. Would the quality standards for workers in a fine-dining restaurant be the same as those for workers in a school cafeteria? Why?

3. Is discipline the only control technique that has negative implications? Why?

4. The manager of Phil's Cocktail Lounge has purchased and directed bartenders to use a device that automatically measures the quantity of any alcoholic beverage poured. The bartenders were formerly permitted to mix drinks without measuring. What positive and negative effects do you think this will have on bar operations?

5. From your own experience, cite an instance in which a manager's

inconsistency in setting examples or giving directions has led to confusion in day-to-day operations.

6. How can budgets be used as control devices in food and beverage operations?

7. What is the purpose of cost control? Of sales control?

8. Imagine that you are the manager of a fine-dining restaurant. You are faced with the problem of a server who refuses to follow the service standards and techniques established by the owner. It is apparent to you that the server's techniques result in faster service, but they are clearly better suited to a diner. Two of the owner's goals are profitability and elegant service. Discuss the possible actions that you might take to bring the employee's performance into line with established standards and to work towards achieving the owner's goals.

9. One of the items on the menu in the Central Restaurant is chopped steak. Each cook has his own ideas about what a chopped steak is, and each prepares it differently. Using the four steps in the control process as the basis for your response, explain how a new manager might eliminate this problem.

10. The new manager of Jill's Joint has decided that all employees should be searched before they leave the premises each day because she believes this will reduce the problem of employee theft. Discuss the possible costs and potential benefits the manager should consider before instituting this policy.

11. The standard cost of a one-ounce drink (excluding mixer) in the Skyway Bar is $.25. The average cost per drink is actually $.27. Calculate the amount of excess cost in 32 drinks. What quantity of liquor does that additional cost represent?

12. Assume the standard cost of a one-ounce drink is $.40. If the real cost is $.43, calculate the excess cost in 32 drinks. What quantity of liquor does that excess cost represent?

13. If the standard cost of a one-ounce drink is $.30 and the real cost is $.35, calculate the additional cost in 32 drinks and the amount of the liquor the additional cost represents.

14. Calculate the standard costs of the drinks listed below if a one-liter bottle costs $6.76.
    a. 1 ounce.

      b. 1 1/4 ounce.

      c. 1 1/2 ounce.

15. Define standard procedures, and give two examples from your own experience.

16. The information below has been prepared by the manager of the Market Restaurant. It represents his best estimates of sales and various costs for the coming year. Using this information, prepare an operating budget for the Market Restaurant for the coming year, following the illustration provided in this chapter.

    Food sales: $820,000

    Beverage sales: $290,000

    Cost of food: 36.0% of food sales

    Cost of beverages: 24.0% of beverage sales

    Variable salaries and wages: 20.0% of food sales

    Fixed salaries and wages: $102,000

    Employee benefit: 25.0% of total salaries and wages

    Other controllable expenses: $95,000

    Depreciation: $65,500

    Interest: $55,000

    Occupancy costs: $56,000

17. In the current year, the manager of the Downtowner Restaurant has been following the operating budget reproduced below.

Sales:	
Food	$630,000
Beverage	140,000
Total sales	$770,000
Cost of sales:	
Food	$252,000
Beverages	35,000
Total costs	$287,000
Gross Profit	483,000
Controllable expenses:	
Salaries and wages	$173,250
Employee benefits	45,045
Other controllable expenses	82,000
Total controllable expenses	300,295
Income before occupancy costs, interest, depreciation and income taxes	182,705
Occupancy costs	64,000

Income before interest, depreciation,	
and income taxes	118,705
Interest	10,000
Depreciation	28,500
Restaurant profit	80,205

For the coming year, the following changes are expected:
a. Food sales will increase by 10%.
b. Beverage sales will increase by 6%.
c. Food cost percent and beverage cost percent will remain the same.
d. Fixed salaries and wages—$69,300 for this year—will increase by $8,000. Variable salaries and wages will be 16% of expected food sales.
e. Employee benefits will remain the same percentage of salaries and wages.
f. Controllable expenses will increase by $12,000.
g. Occupancy costs will increase by $5,000.
h. Interest and depreciation will remain the same.

Given these anticipated changes, prepare an operating budget for the Downtowner Restaurant for the coming year.

18. Referring to Question 17, assume that the operating budget you prepared for the upcoming year has been adopted. After the first six months of the year, financial records reveal the following:
a. Food sales have increased by 12% rather than by the 10% anticipated.
b. Beverage sales have increased by 5% rather than by 6%.
c. Food cost percent is 1% lower than budgeted, but beverage cost percent is 2% higher.
d. Variable salaries and wages is 14% of food sales, rather than the 16% anticipated.

Assuming that the trends evident in the first six months continue for the balance of the year and that both sales and costs are equally divided between the two halves of the year, prepare a revision of the budget for the second six-month period.

19. Define each of the following terms:
Budget
Control
Control process

Control systems
Cost/benefit ratio
Cost control
Flexible budget
Operating budget
Procedures
Quality standards
Quantity standards
Sales control
Standard cost
Standard procedures
Standards
Static budget

3

Cost-Volume-Profit Relationships

LEARNING OBJECTIVES

After reading and studying this chapter, you should be able to:
1. Explain the importance of the cost-volume-profit relationships to an understanding of cost control.
2. Solve problems to determine:
   a. Sales in dollars
   b. Sales in units
   c. Variable costs
   d. Fixed costs
   e. Profit
   f. Contribution rate
   g. Contribution margin
   h. Variable rate
   i. Break-even point
3. Define each of the Key Terms at the end of the chapter.

INTRODUCTION

Our discussion of costs, sales, and control would be incomplete without a chapter on cost-volume-profit relationships. It is not an easy topic to cover in one brief chapter. However, because an understanding of these relationships is the key to fully comprehending cost control in food and beverage operations, it is a necessary topic to include in a text of this nature. One principal objective of this chapter, then, is to provide an introduction to cost-volume-profit relationships. A comprehension of this topic makes an in-depth understanding of cost control possible.

In the introduction to Chapter 1, statements of income were provided for two comparable restaurants: the Rush Hour Inn and the Graduate Restaurant. It was apparent that profit earned in the Graduate Restaurant was substantially larger than that of the Rush Hour Inn for the period covered by the statements. In Chapter 1, we noted that the relationships of costs to sales in the Graduate Restaurant were somehow more favorable than those in the Rush Hour Inn. In fact, the food cost percentage, the beverage cost percent, and the labor cost percent in the Graduate Restaurant were about 7 percent lower than those in the Rush Hour Inn.

One cannot assume, however, that "good" cost-to-sales relationships automatically result in profit for a restaurant or that higher or lower cost percentages are necessarily desirable for a given restaurant. Indeed, it is possible that a higher food cost percentage—obtainable by lowering menu prices or by increasing food costs, thus giving each customer more for his money—may result in sufficient additional customers to increase profitability in spite of the higher food cost percent. It is also possible that lower cost percentages (achieved by raising menu prices or lowering costs) may result in many fewer customers and lower profits.

Another possibility is that lower menu prices will lessen profit because there are insufficient numbers of increased customers to offset the higher cost percentage. Nevertheless, it is obvious that the ratio of total costs—food, plus beverage, plus labor, plus all others—to total sales cannot exceed 100 percent if the operation is to be profitable. These possibilities are examined below and are based on the examples in Chapter 1.

SALES	$925,000	100.00%
COST OF SALES	309,875	33.5 %
COST OF LABOR	231,250	25.00%
COST OF OVERHEAD	277,500	30.00%
PROFIT	106,375	11.5 %

FIGURE 3.1 *The Graduate Restaurant*

SALES	$1,300,000	100.00%
COST OF SALES	520,000	40.00%
COST OF LABOR	390,000	30.00%
COST OF OVERHEAD	277,500	21.35%
PROFIT	112,500	08.65%

FIGURE 3.2 *The Graduate Restaurant*

At the given level of sales ($925,000) and costs ($818,625), satisfactory profit ($106,375) has been earned. However, it is also possible to earn acceptable profit at some sales level other than $925,000 even if prime cost, as percentage of sales, increases. Figure 3.2 illustrates this.

Although the costs and cost-to-sales ratios for the components of prime cost have increased (cost of sales from 33.5 percent to 40 percent, and cost of labor from 25 percent to 30 percent), a satisfactory profit was still realized because lowered menu prices resulted in many new customers and the number of dollars required for overhead was the same in both cases. Consequently, as sales volume increases, the number of dollars required for overhead has represented a smaller percentage of sales. Profit as a percentage of sales is considerably lower, but the dollar amount of profit is higher.

On the other hand, suppose that lowering menu prices resulted in relatively few new customers—only a sufficient number to maintain total sales at the given level of $925,000. In that case profit would be reduced to zero, as shown in Figure 3.3.

In the above illustration, total sales remained at the original figure, but prime costs expressed as a percentage of sales have increased because of lowered menu prices and increased labor cost to service the increased number of customers.

Now let us assume a decrease in sales in the restaurant, as illustrated in Figure 3.4.

In this instance, cost percents for the components of prime cost were the same as they had been in Figure 3.1. However, the operation shows a loss rather than a profit because of fewer customers. The fixed element for over-

SALES	$925,000	100.00%
COST OF SALES	370,000	40.00%
COST OF LABOR	277,500	30.00%
COST OF OVERHEAD	277,500	30.00%
PROFIT	0	0%

FIGURE 3.3 *The Graduate Restaurant*

SALES	$600,000	100.00%
COST OF SALES	201,000	33.5 %
COST OF LABOR	150,000	25.00%
COST OF OVERHEAD	277,500	46.25%
LOSS	(28,500)	04.75%

FIGURE 3.4 *The Graduate Restaurant*

head, still $277,500, now accounts for 46.25 percent of sales dollars, rather than the 30 percent it represented at the sales level illustrated in Figure 3.1.

A key lesson in the above examples, then, is that while percentages are very useful in comparing operations and judging a single operation, one should not be rely on them to provide all of the information necessary to judge profitability. Many restaurants operate with relatively high food cost percentages or beverage cost percentages, and at the same time are able to earn a satisfactory profit. Each operation must establish the cost percentages that are suitable for it.

The key to understanding cost/volume/profit relationships lies in understanding that fixed costs exist in an operation regardless of sales volume and that it is necessary to generate sufficient total volume to cover both fixed and variable costs. This is not to say, however, that ratios of variable costs to sales are to be ignored. In fact, if the ratio of variable cost to sales is very high, it may not be possible to generate sufficient volume to cover fixed costs. After all, the seats in a dining room can only be turned over a limited number of times in any given meal period. Conversely, if the ratio of variable cost to sales is too low, it may not be possible to generate adequate sales volume simply because potential customers perceive that prices are too high for the value they receive. If this is the case, they are likely to dine elsewhere.

THE COST/VOLUME/PROFIT EQUATION

From the foregoing, it should be apparent that relationships exist between and among sales, cost of sales, cost of labor, cost of overhead, and profit. In fact, these relationships can be expressed as follows:

Sales = Cost of sales + Cost of labor + Cost of overhead + Profit

Thus, in the Graduate Restaurant:

$925,000 = 309,875 + 231,250 + 106,375

Because cost of sales is variable, cost of labor includes both fixed and variable elements, and cost of overhead is fixed, one could restate this equation as follows:

$$\text{Sales} = \text{Variable cost} + \text{Fixed cost} + \text{Profit}$$

In fact, this is the basic equation of cost/volume/profit analysis.

Using the first letters of the terms to stand for those terms, this basic equation could be written as a formula:

$$S = VC + FC + P$$

Throughout this chapter, then,

$$S = \text{Sales}$$

$$VC = \text{Variable cost}$$

$$FC = \text{Fixed cost}$$

$$P = \text{Profit}$$

In proceeding with the chapter, the reader will do well to keep three points in mind:

1. Within the normal range of business operations, there is a relationship between variable costs and sales that remains relatively constant. That relationship is a ratio that is normally expressed either as a percentage or as a decimal.
2. By contrast, fixed costs tend to remain constant in dollar terms, regardless of changes in dollar sales volume. Consequently, whether expressed as a percentage or as a decimal, the relationship between fixed cost and sales changes as sales volume increases and decreases.
3. Once acceptable levels are determined for costs, they must be controlled if the operation is to be profitable.

Before we attempt a detailed discussion of cost/volume/profit relationships, it will be necessary to introduce and define some important concepts, abbreviations, and terms. These will be illustrated using figures from the statement of income for the Graduate Restaurant, reproduced in Figure 3.5.

Our first step will be to determine total variable cost for the Graduate Restaurant. Total variable cost consists of food cost, beverage cost, and the variable portion of labor cost. As discussed in Chapter 2, the cost of labor includes both a fixed element and a variable element. Figure 3.6 was taken from Chapter 2 and will be the basis for the following discussion.

By referring to Figure 3.5, one can determine that food cost is $275,187 and beverage cost is $34,688. The variable portion of labor cost will be 40 percent of total payroll expense (salaries and wages, plus employee benefits). Total

For the Year Ended December XXXX	
SALES	
Food	$786,250
Beverage	$138,750
Total Sales	$925,000
COST OF SALES	
Food	$275,187
Beverage	$ 34,688
Total Cost of Sales	$309,875
GROSS PROFIT	$615,125
CONTROLLABLE EXPENSES	
Salaries and Wages	$185,000
Employee Benefits	$ 46,250
Other Controllable Expenses	$138,750
Total Controllable Expenses	$370,000
INCOME BEFORE OCCUPANCY COSTS, INTEREST, DEPRECIATION, AND INCOME TAXES	$245,125
OCCUPANCY COSTS	$ 78,625
INTEREST EXPENSE	$ 13,875
DEPRECIATION	$ 46,250
RESTAURANT PROFIT	$106,375

FIGURE 3.5 *The Graduate Restaurant Statement of Income*

payroll expense is $231,250, and 40 percent of that total is $92,500. One can then determine total variable cost by adding the following three figures:

Food cost	$275,187
Beverage cost	34,688
Variable labor cost	92,500
Total variable cost	$402,375

The next step will be to determine total fixed cost for the restaurant. Total fixed cost includes all costs other than the variable costs. From Figure 3.1, these are the fixed portion of the labor cost (60 percent of $231,250, or $138,750), other controllable expenses ($138,750, by coincidence), occupancy costs ($78,625), interest ($13,875), and depreciation ($46,250). One can then determine total fixed cost quite simply by adding these five figures.

Fixed labor cost	$138,750
Other controllable expenses	138,750
Occupancy costs	78,625
Interest	13,875
Depreciation	46,250
Total fixed cost	$416,250

For the Year Ending December 31, XXXX	
FIXED COSTS	
Occupancy costs	$ 78,625
Other controllable costs	138,750
Fixed salaries and wages	111,000 (60% of $65,000 salaries and wages)*
Employee benefits	27,750 (25% of $39,000)
Interest	13,875
Depreciation	46,250
VARIABLE COSTS	
Cost of food	35.0% of food sales
Cost of beverages	25.0% of beverage sales
Salaries and wages	9.4% of food sales**
Employee benefits	25.0% of variable salaries and wages

*Salaries and wages are a semivariable cost, so they must be divided into their fixed and variable components. In the illustration, we have assumed that 60.0% of total salaries and wages is fixed, while the remaining 40.0% is variable.

**Variable salaries and wages are assumed to be associated only with food sales. Therefore, other salaries and wages will not increase or decrease with changes in the business volume. Variable salaries and wages—40.0% of $185,000, or $74,000—are 9.4% of food sales.

FIGURE 3.6 *Fixed and Variable Costs in the Graduate Restaurant*

Given the figures above, the basic cost/volume/profit equation for the Graduate Restaurant at the level of sales indicated is:

$$\text{Sales (\$925,000)} = \text{Variable cost (\$402,375)} + \text{Fixed cost (\$416,250)} + \text{Profit (\$106,375)}$$

or

$$\text{S (\$925,000)} = \text{VC (\$402,375)} + \text{FC (\$416,250)} + \text{P (\$106,375)}$$

VARIABLE RATE AND CONTRIBUTION RATE

Two additional terms must be introduced and defined before proceeding: **variable rate** and **contribution rate.**

Variable Rate

Variable rate is the ratio of variable cost to dollar sales. It is determined by dividing variable cost by dollar sales and is expressed in decimal form. It is similar to a cost percent.

$$\text{Variable rate} = \frac{\text{Variable cost}}{\text{Sales}}$$

Variable rate is normally abbreviated as VR, so the equation can be written:

$$VR = \frac{VC}{S}$$

In the example above, variable cost (VC) is $402,375, and sales (S) is $925,000. Therefore,

$$\text{Variable rate} = \frac{\text{Variable cost (402,375)}}{\text{Sales (925,000)}}$$

$$VR = .435$$

This is the same as stating that 43.5 percent of dollar sales is needed to cover the variable costs, or that $.435 of each dollar of sales is required for that purpose. As sales increase, the total dollars spent to cover these costs will increase, but the percentage will not change.

Contribution Rate

If 43.5 percent of dollar sales is needed to cover variable costs, then the remainder (56.5 percent) is available for other purposes. There are two other purposes:

1. Meeting fixed costs.
2. Providing profit.

As sales increase, an increasing number of dollars will be available to be used to meet fixed costs and provide increased profit. Thus, $.565 of each dollar of sales is available to contribute to covering fixed costs and providing profit. Indeed, one can easily see that if fixed costs were to remain the same, increased dollars resulting from the contribution rate of the increased sales would all be used to increase profit. This percentage (or ratio, or rate) is known as the **contribution rate,** and is abbreviated as CR. Thus,

$$CR = \text{Contribution Rate}$$

The contribution rate is determined by subtracting the variable rate from 1.

$$CR = 1 - VR$$

For the Graduate Restaurant, the CR is .565, determined by subtracting the VR of .435 from 1.

$$CR = 1 - .435$$

$$CR = .565$$

BREAK-EVEN POINT

One will recognize at once that no business enterprise can be termed profitable until all of the fixed costs have been met. If dollar sales volume is insufficient to cover both variable and fixed costs, the enterprise will clearly operate at a loss. If dollar sales are sufficient to cover both variable and fixed costs exactly, but insufficient to provide any profit (i.e., profit is zero), the business is said to be operating at the break-even point. Break-even point, usually abbreviated as BE, is defined as the point at which the sum of all costs equals sales, such that profit equals zero. Thus,

$$BE = \text{Break-even point}$$

COST/VOLUME/PROFIT CALCULATIONS FOR THE GRADUATE RESTAURANT

We now have the following information about the Graduate Restaurant:

Sales = $925,000
Variable costs = $402,375
Fixed costs = $416,250
Profit = $106,375
Variable rate = .435
Contribution rate = .565

An additional formula must be introduced at this point:

$$\text{Sales} = \frac{\text{Fixed cost} + \text{Profit}}{\text{Contribution rate}}$$

Which is abbreviated as:

$$S = \frac{FC + P}{CR}$$

This formula can be used to determine the level of dollar sales required to earn any profit that one might choose to put into the equation.

To prove that the formula works, one can substitute figures above in the formula, as follows:

$$\$925,000 = \frac{\$416,250 + \$106,375}{.565}$$

$$\$925,000 = \frac{\$522,625}{.565}$$

$$\$925,000 = \$925,000$$

To determine the break-even point for the Graduate Restaurant, the point at which profit would be equal to zero dollars, one would simply let $P = 0$, and solve the equation as follows:

$$S = \frac{FC + P}{CR}$$

$$S = \frac{\$416,250 + 0}{.565}$$

$$S = \$736,726$$

The calculations assume that the variable rate and the contribution rate will remain the same at the reduced sales volume. At that level of sales, variable costs (VC) will be 43.5 percent of sales, or $320,476. Thus, VC of $320,476 plus FC of $416,250 equals S, or $736,726, leaving no profit.

$$S\ (\$736,726) = VC\ (\$320,476) + FC\ (\$416,250) + P\ (0)\ \$736,726 = \$736,726$$

No profit-oriented business ever wants to operate at BE, and the Graduate Restaurant did not. The sales level achieved in the Graduate Restaurant was $925,000, which was $188,274 beyond BE. While there are no additional fixed costs to cover after the break-even point is reached, each additional dollar of sales does have variable costs associated with it. In the Graduate Restaurant, these were identified as $.435 for each dollar of sale, which is the same as saying that VR = .435. Variable cost can be determined by multiplying S (sales) by VR (variable rate).

$$VC = S \times VR$$

$$VC = \$188,274 \times .435$$

$$VC = \$81,899$$

If one multiplies dollar sales of $188,274 by VR .435, one determines that variable costs associated with those sales beyond BE is $81,899. If this $81,899 in variable costs is subtracted from sales of $188,274, the result ($106,375) is equal to the profit (P) for the period. It consists of $.565 of each dollar sale beyond BE.

$$P\ (\$106,375) = S\ (\$188,274) \times CR\ (.565)\ \$106,375 = \$106,375$$

It must be stressed that this is true only for sales beyond BE: Before BE, there is no profit.

CONTRIBUTION MARGIN

Each dollar of sales, then, may be divided imaginatively into two portions:

1. That which must be used to cover variable costs associated with the item sold.
2. That which remains to cover fixed costs and to provide profit.

The dollar amount remaining after variable costs have been subtracted from the sales dollar is defined as the *contribution margin* and is abbreviated as CM. Thus,

$$CM = \text{Contribution margin}$$

$$CM = \text{Total costs} - \text{Variable costs}$$

Thus, if a menu item sells for $12.00 and its cost is $5.00, the contribution margin is $7.00:

$$\$7.00 = \$12.00 - \$5.00$$

The above is true for each menu item and for the total of all menu items. When we look back at the statement of income for the Graduate Restaurant, food sales were $786,250 and food costs were $275,188. The contribution margin of food sales at the Graduate Restaurant was:

$$
\begin{aligned}
\text{Food sales} &= \$786,250 \\
-\ \text{Food costs} &= \underline{275,188} \\
\text{Contribution margin} &= 511,062
\end{aligned}
$$

The above figure is also referred to as **gross margin** and **gross profit on sales.**

When sales reach a level sufficient to cover all variable costs and all fixed costs, with an additional amount left over, that additional amount is obviously profit. Moreover, since contribution margin must go to cover fixed costs until break-even is reached, after break-even is reached, contribution margin becomes profit.

The importance of contribution margin in food and beverage management cannot be overemphasized. Clearly, any item sold for which variable cost exceeds sales price results immediately in a negative contribution margin, which is an immediate financial loss to the business. For example, a prime sirloin steak with variable cost of $4.00 must be sold for an amount greater than $4.00, or there will be such a loss. Furthermore, when one establishes a sales price for the steak, provision must be made for each sale to result in an adequate contribution margin. An adequate contribution margin is one that, when taken with all other contribution margins from all other sales, will be sufficient not only to cover fixed costs of operation, but also to provide for an additional amount beyond break-even that will be the desired profit.

Detailed discussion of the techniques for analyzing and evaluating the contribution margin for individual menu items will be found in Chapter 12.

COST CONTROL AND THE COST/VOLUME/PROFIT EQUATION

Earlier in the chapter, we emphasized that cost must be kept under control by the means discussed in Chapter 2 if operations are to achieve planned profits. It will be useful now to illustrate what happens to planned profits when costs are not kept under control. To illustrate, we will refer to the operating budget for the Graduate Restaurant for the coming year, developed in Chapter 2 and reproduced in Figure 3.7.

To determine the variable rate (VR) for the coming year, one must add the budgeted variable costs for food and beverages ($325,370) and the variable portions of salaries and wages and of employee benefits.

In the discussion of the budget for the Graduate Restaurant for the coming year in Chapter 2, it was stated that sales were expected to increase by 5 percent and that variable costs would remain the same percentages as before.

Therefore, the ratio of variable costs to sales (the variable rate, or VR), calculated as .435 from figures in the income statement earlier in this chapter, is budgeted to remain the same for the coming year. Since this is true, the contribution rate (CR), defined as 1 − VR, will also be the same: .565. Budgeted fixed costs for the coming year are:

Fixed salaries and wages	$115,400
Fixed employee benefits	$ 28,850
Other controllable expenses	$145,250
Occupancy costs	$ 80,625
Interest	$ 13,875
Depreciation	$ 46,250
Total fixed costs	$430,250

For the Year Ended December XXXX			
	Current Year	*Change*	*Upcoming Year*
SALES			
Food	$786,250	+$39,313	$825,563
Beverage	$138,750	+6,938	$145,688
Total Sales	$925,000	+$46,251	$971,251
COST OF SALES			
Food	$275,187	+$13,760	$288,947
Beverage	$ 34,688	+ 1,735	$ 36,423
Total Cost of Sales	$309,875	+$15,495	$325,370
GROSS PROFIT	$615,125		$645,880
CONTROLLABLE EXPENSES			
Fixed Sal. and Wages	$111,000	+$4,400	$115,400
Variable Sal. and Wages	$ 74,000	+3,603	$ 77,603
Employee Benefits	$ 46,250	+2,001	48,251
Other Controllable Expenses	$138,750	+6,500	145,250
Total Controllable Expenses	$370,000	+$16,504	$386,504
INCOME BEFORE OCCUPANCY COSTS, INTEREST, DEPRECIATION, AND INCOME TAXES	$245,125		$259,376
OCCUPANCY COSTS	$ 78,625	+$2,000	$ 80,625
INTEREST EXPENSE	$ 13,875		$ 13,875
DEPRECIATION	$ 46,250		$ 46,250
RESTAURANT PROFIT	$106,375		$118,606

FIGURE 3.7   *The Graduate Restaurant Statement of Income*

Assume that the new year has begun. The new budget has been adopted and is in effect. However, the manager has not been controlling variable costs adequately. Because of this, excessive variable costs are developing, largely through inefficiency and waste. Such problems as spoilage of raw materials and poor scheduling of staff are common causes of these excessive costs.

Now assume that these excessive variable costs have had the effect of increasing the variable rate from .435, a figure calculated earlier from figures in the income statement, to .515. This is the same as saying that the amount needed to cover variable costs has increased from a planned .435 to .515. Stated another way, the amount needed to cover variable costs has increased from a planned 43.5 percent of each sales dollar to 51.5 percent.

We will now use the formula developed earlier in the chapter to determine the sales level required to earn the $118,606 profit indicated in the budget (Fig. 3.7) if variable rate is .515.

Using the formula

$$S = \frac{FC + P}{CR}$$

we substitute numbers in the formula to find that:

$$S = \frac{\$430,250 + \$118,606}{.515}$$

$$S = \frac{\$548,856}{.515}$$

$$S = \$1,065,740$$

This indicates that an additional $94,489 ($1,065,740 − $971,251) in sales will be required to earn the target restaurant profit.

The reason these additional sales are required to earn the planned profit is simply that excessive variable costs have had the effect of increasing the variable rate unnecessarily. The planned profit could have been earned at the sales level of $971,251 if management had done a better job of controlling variable costs at the levels budgeted. And this could have been done, conceivably, without any change in quality or quantity standards and without raising prices.

This illustrates that an understanding of cost/volume/profit relationships is central to full comprehension of the need for cost control in food and beverage operations. For example, one must understand that lowering contribution margins will necessitate increasing volume in order to achieve a given target profit. Sometimes the higher volume may not be attainable in a given operation due to limited seating capacity, realistic turnover rates, or even the limited size of the market. On the other hand, higher contribution margins, while requiring fewer customers, may not be an adequate answer if it means raising sales prices beyond the capacity or willingness of customers to pay. Some establishments with low menu price and low contribution margins are very successful because they are able to maintain high volume. Some, with similar prices, contribution margins, and sales volume, may be unsuccessful because of their higher fixed costs. There are other food and beverage operations with high contribution margins and low sales volume, some of which are successful while others are not. The differences from one to another in their levels of profit and relative success can normally be traced to differences in their fixed costs. The ideal restaurant would have high contribution margins, high sales volume, and low fixed costs.

Once satisfactory levels have been determined for costs, sales, and sales volume, it is clearly necessary for management to control costs if the enterprise is to achieve the profit level planned in its budget.

FURTHER ANALYSIS

This chapter provides a brief introduction to some of the most basic concepts of cost/volume/profit analysis. There are several additional points that are important to break-even analysis—points that are not critical to the comprehension of material in the following chapters, but that can increase the depth of one's understanding of these topics. These are addressed in Appendix 1.

CHAPTER ESSENTIALS

In this chapter, we have shown that knowledge of cost/volume/profit relationships is important for those seeking to understand the need for control. We have given the basic formulas used in cost/volume/profit analysis and illustrated their use. We have defined several key terms, including break-even point, variable rate, contribution rate, and contribution margin. Finally, we have illustrated the effect of excessive or uncontrolled costs on profits.

KEY TERMS IN THIS CHAPTER

Break-even point
Contribution margin
Contribution rate
Cost/volume/profit equation
Variable rate

QUESTIONS AND PROBLEMS

1. Given the following information, determine total dollar sales.
   a. Cost of sales $46,500; cost of labor $33,247; cost of overhead $75,883; profit $3,129.
   b. Cost of sales $51,259; cost of labor $77,351; cost of overhead $42,248; loss $41,167.

2. Given the following information, find contribution margin.
   a. Average sales price per unit $13.22; average $5.78 variable cost per unit.
   b. Average sales price per unit $14.50; average .36 variable rate.
   c. Average sales price per unit $16.20; average .55 contribution rate.
   d. Average variable cost per unit $6.20; average .3 variable rate.

e. Average variable cost per unit $3.60; average .6 contribution rate.

(From this point on, we will eliminate the term average from the problems. This will affect neither the problems nor the solutions.)

3. Given the following information, find variable rate.
    a. Sales price per unit $19.25; variable cost per unit $6.70.
    b. Total sales $164,328; total variable cost $72,304.32.
    c. Sales price per unit $18.80; contribution margin $10.72.
    d. Sales price per unit $16.37; total fixed costs $142,408; total unit sales $19,364; total profit $22,952.80.

4. Given the following information, find contribution rate.
    a. Sales price per unit $18.50; contribution margin $10.08.
    b. Sales price per unit $17.50; variable cost per unit $6.95.
    c. Total sales $64,726; total variable cost $40,130.12.
    d. Sales price per unit $16.50; profit $33,381.80; total unit sales $18,440; total fixed costs $136,137.

5. Given the following information, find break-even point in dollar sales.
    a. Fixed costs $48,337.80; contribution rate .6.
    b. Variable rate .45; fixed costs $155,410.31.
    c. Variable cost per unit $5.85; sales price per unit $17.40; fixed costs $164,065.60.

6. Given the following information, find break-even point in unit sales.
    a. Fixed costs $113,231.64; contribution margin $2.28.
    b. Sales price per unit $17.22; fixed costs $215,035.68; variable cost per unit $6.98.
    c. Contribution rate .6; sales price per unit $18.20; fixed costs $219,423.16.

7. Given the following information, find dollar sales.
    a. Fixed costs $60,000; profit $18,000; sales price per unit $8.00; variable cost per unit $5.00.
    b. Variable rate .45; profit $21,578.10; fixed costs $58,382.
    c. Sales price per unit $16.60; profit $21,220; contribution margin $9.29; fixed costs $126,000.

8. Given the following information, find unit sales.
    a. Fixed costs $58,922; profit $9,838; contribution margin $3.82 per unit.

b. Profit $33,603; sales price per unit $17.00; fixed costs $97,197; contribution rate .6.

c. Variable cost per unit $5.30; profit equal to 18% of $211,000; sales price per unit $16.30; fixed costs $86,609.

d. Sales price per unit $16.20; fixed cost $129,425.36; variable rate .4; profit $44,000.

9. Given the following information, find fixed costs.
   a. Total sales $104,672; profit $18,000; variable rate .42.
   b. Profit $12,000; unit sales 32,392; variable cost per unit $4.63; sales price per unit $10.34.
   c. Sales price per unit $14.60; profit $34,000; unit sales 26,712; variable rate .35.
   d. Contribution rate .65; sales price per unit $18.40; unit sales 26,549; profit $33,000.

10. Given the following information, find profit.
    a. Fixed costs $82,449.40; total sales $167,543.20; variable cost $55,629.60.
    b. Variable rate .4; unit sales $26,412; fixed costs $193,764.40; sales price per unit $17.60.
    c. Total sales $190,830.66; variable cost per unit $5.64; fixed costs $75,919.70; sales price per unit $16.22.

11. The owner of the Barn Lodge Restaurant estimates that fixed costs for the coming year will be $360,000. Based on his investment in the business, he wants a profit of $120,000 for the year. Experience has shown that the average check is $12.
    a. If total variable cost is $720,000, what level of dollar sales will be required to earn the target restaurant profit?
    b. Given total variable cost and total sales figures above, what variable rate is the owner projecting?
    c. Given the variable rate calculated in Question 11b, determine the contribution rate.
    d. Given the contribution rate calculated in Question 11c, determine the average contribution margin based on a $12.00 average sale.
    e. At what level of dollar sales will the restaurant break even?

12. The following information is from the records of Daphne's Restaurant:

Sales	$800,000
Variable cost	$342,400
Fixed cost	$345,600

Assume that sales volume equals 40,000 covers.
  a. Calculate profit.
  b. Calculate average dollar sale.
  c. Calculate dollar sales required to earn a profit of $125,000, assuming variable rate does not change.

13. Define each of the following terms in this chapter:
Break-even point
Contribution margin
Contribution rate
Cost/volume/profit equation
Variable rate

Part II

Food Control

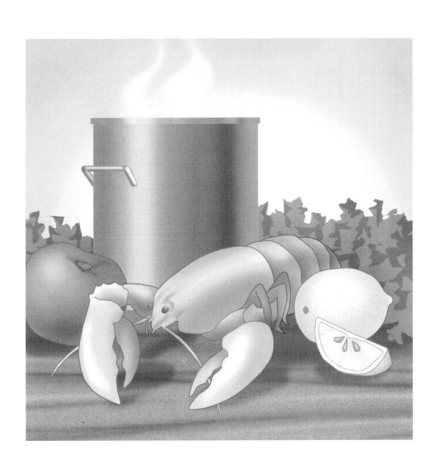

Having completed some general discussion of three topics central to the text—cost, sales and control—we now have a foundation to support discussion of some specific elements of food control. In this part of the text, we will look into various means of implementing the control process in order to guide the actions of employees who work with food, as well as to control, measure, and judge food costs and food sales. Our first step will be to discuss each of the several generally accepted steps in the chain of daily events that make up the foodservice business, from initial purchase of raw materials to the sale of the products prepared from those materials. Next, we will look into techniques for measuring food costs. Finally, we will investigate ways to judge food costs in relation to food sales and, from those judgments, to suggest approaches to improving performance.

We will begin with a discussion of the application of the control process to food purchasing.

4 Food Purchasing Control

LEARNING OBJECTIVES

After reading and studying this chapter, you should be able to:

1. Describe the application of the four-step control process to the purchasing function in a foodservice establishment.
2. Distinguish between perishable and nonperishable foods.
3. Describe how quality standards for food purchases are established.
4. Describe how quantity standards for perishable and nonperishable food purchases are established.
5. Write a standard purchase specification.
6. Describe the process used to determine the quantity of perishable foods to be purchased.
7. Compare and contrast the periodic and perpetual methods for purchasing nonperishable foods.
8. Determine order quantities using the periodic and perpetual inventory methods.
9. List the normal sources of supply for restaurant food purchases.
10. Describe the procedures for purchasing perishable and nonperishable foods at the most favorable prices.
11. List five methods for training employees responsible for purchasing foods.
12. Discuss the possible consequences of failure to train employees responsible for purchasing.
13. List and explain the advantages and disadvantages of centralized purchasing.
14. List and explain the advantages and disadvantages of standing orders.
15. Explain several computer application for food purchasing.
16. Define each of the Key Terms at the end of the chapter.

RESPONSIBILITY FOR PURCHASING

Responsibility for purchasing can be assigned to any one of a number of persons in foodservice operations, depending on organizational structure and management policies. It is not uncommon to find owners or managers taking the responsibility in some establishments, while the purchasing duties may be assigned to a chef or a steward in others. In some hotel/motel operations, foods may even be ordered by someone in a purchasing department who has responsibility for purchasing all supplies used in the property.

In order to facilitate discussion, we will arbitrarily assign responsibility for food purchasing to a steward. This does not mean that the authors believe that this responsibility should always be given to the steward; on the contrary, the determination of who should be assigned responsibility for food purchasing must be based on situations and conditions existing in a specific foodservice operation. The important point to be made here is that, for control purposes, the authority to purchase foods and the responsibility for doing so should be assigned to one individual. One individual can then be held accountable for the system of control procedures established by the food controller.

CONTROL PROCESS AND PURCHASING

In Chapter 2, control was defined as a process used by managers to direct, regulate, and restrain the actions of people so that the established goals of an enterprise may be achieved. The control process was identified as a four-step process, requiring that standards and standard procedures be established, that employees be trained to follow those standards and standard procedures, that employee output be monitored and compared to established standards, and that remedial action be taken as needed. This is a general process that can be applied to the control of any activity in foodservice or in any other business. Our objective in this chapter will be to apply the control process to the task of purchasing food.

PERISHABLES AND NONPERISHABLES

The types of foods to be purchased for any foodservice enterprise can be divided into two categories: perishables and nonperishables. Because there are significant differences between the approaches to purchasing foods in these categories, it will be important at this point to differentiate between them.

Perishables are those items, typically fresh foods, that have a comparatively short useful life after they have been received. Various kinds of lettuce and fresh fish, for example, begin to lose their quality very quickly. Some meats and cheeses will retain their quality for somewhat longer periods, but the quality of these perishables will begin to deteriorate much sooner than will the quality of nonperishables—cans of tomato puree, for example. Perishables, then, should be purchased for immediate use in order to take advantage of the quality desired at the time of purchase. If a steward is always careful to purchase the best quality available for intended use, then it would be wasteful and costly not to make use of that carefully selected quality.

Nonperishables are those food items that have longer shelf life. Often referred to as **groceries** or **staples,** they may be stored in the packages or containers in which they are received, often on shelves and at room temperature, for weeks or even months. They do not deteriorate quickly as long as they are unopened and kept at reasonable temperatures. They are typically purchased and stored in jars, bottles, cans, bags, and boxes; the storage area in which they are kept, usually called a **storeroom,** would resemble the shelves of a supermarket to the layman.

Because these foods do not deteriorate quickly, it is possible to keep a reasonable supply of each on hand, for use as needed. For example, a restaurant that used an average of four No. 10 cans of whole, peeled tomatoes daily (more than four cases per week) could keep a supply of eight cases on hand without running any risk of spoilage. Foods that typically fall into this category of nonperishables include salt, sugar, canned fruits and vegetables, spices, and flavorings.

DEVELOPING STANDARDS AND STANDARD PROCEDURES FOR PURCHASING

The primary purpose for establishing control over purchasing is to ensure a continuing supply of sufficient quantities of the necessary foods, each of the quality appropriate to its intended use, purchased at the most favorable price. Therefore, we will discuss purchasing from this point of view, first by establishing the essential standards and standard procedures for effective purchasing. Standards must be developed for the:

1. Quality of food purchased.
2. Quantity of food purchased.
3. Prices at which food is purchased.

ESTABLISHING QUALITY STANDARDS

Before any intelligent purchasing can be done, someone in management must determine which foods, both perishables and nonperishables, will be required for day-to-day operations. The basis for creating a list of these foods is the menu. However, this is not as easy as it may at first appear. For example, most restaurants use tomatoes and tomato products for a variety of purposes— as salad ingredients, as sauce ingredients, and so on. At the same time, tomatoes and tomato products are available for purchase fresh and processed, and in various grades. Before purchasing, one must make important decisions about brands, sizes, packaging, grades, and degree of freshness, among other things.

Developing a complete list of foods and their characteristics for a food-service operation is clearly a complex and time-consuming enterprise. It must be done, however, if one is to establish effective control over purchasing. If a restaurant is to produce products of consistent quality, it must use raw materials of consistent quality. Therefore, it is important that the food controller, in cooperation with other members of the management team, draw up the list of all food items to be purchased, including those specific and distinctive characteristics that best describe the desired quality of each. These carefully written descriptions are known as **standard purchase specifications.** These specifications are often based on grading standards established by the federal government or, in some instances, when federal grading standards are considered too broad, on grading standards common in the appropriate market. However, foodservice operators are not restricted to these possibilities. Many write specifications that are far more precise and thus more useful for indicating to purveyors the exact quality desired. Once these standard purchase specifications have been developed, they can be printed and distributed to potential purveyors to ensure that each fully understands the restaurant's exact requirements. Figure 4.1 gives five examples of standard purchase specifications.

Standard purchase specifications, if carefully prepared, are useful in at least six ways:

1. They force owners or managers to determine exact requirements in advance for any product.
2. They are often useful in menu preparation: it is possible to use one cut of meat, purchased to specifications, to prepare several different menu items.
3. They eliminate misunderstandings between stewards and purveyors.
4. Circulation of specifications for one product to several purveyors makes true competitive bidding possible.
5. They eliminate the need for detailed verbal descriptions of a product each time it is ordered.
6. They facilitate checking food as it is received. (The importance of this will be discussed in Chapter 5.)

Although specifications are written down at one particular time, they

Strip Loin	Bone-in 10″ cut.
	USDA Prime, upper half.
	Range #2, minimum 14 lbs., maximum 16 lbs.
	One-half to three-quarters of an inch fat except for seam fat.
	Moderate marbling, light red in color to slightly dark red.
	New York cut, chilled upon delivery.
	Free from objectionable odors, deterioration, and evidence of freezing or defrosting.
Flounder (grey sole)	Whole, dressed, fresh day of delivery.
	Minimum 2 lbs., maximum 4 lbs.
	Fish should be twice as long as is broad, with oval body.
	Flesh should be firm and elastic, meat should be white and slightly translucent, color should be bright and clear.
	Gills should be free from slime and reddish-pink in color, and scales should adhere tightly to the skin.
	No stale odors of ammonia.
	Yield of 40% to the fillet.
Grapefruit	Florida.
	Medium to large, 3-3/4″ to 4″ in diameter.
	Light yellow in color, approximately 12 to 14 sections, oval to round.
	Thin-skinned, tender, delicate flesh.
	No visible spotting or bruising on skins.
	Medium acidity and sweetness, faint bitterness.
	Packed 36 to a crate.
Canned Peaches	Yellow, cling halves, canned.
	US Grade A (Fancy), heavy syrup.
	19–24 Brix, minimum drained weight.
	66 ounces per #10 can.
	Count per #10 can: 30 to 35.
	Quote by dozen #10 can.
	Federal Inspector's certification of grade required.
Asparagus tips, frozen	Tips large, all green, frozen.
	US Grade A (Fancy).
	Packed in 2-1/2 lb. cartons, 12 cartons per case.
	Must be delivered at 10°F or below.
	Quote by pound net.
	Federal Inspector's certification of grade required.

FIGURE 4.1   *Standard Purchase Specifications*

need not be considered fixed for all time. If conditions change, they can be rewritten and recirculated. Stewards who use computers have an easier time rewriting specifications. They simply need to bring up a specification on the monitor and make the necessary changes.

This critically important step—the determination of quality standards and the development of standard purchase specifications—helps to ensure that all foods purchased will be of the desired quality for their intended use.

ESTABLISHING QUANTITY STANDARDS

Although purchase specifications can be established at one particular time and merely reviewed and updated on occasion, quantity standards for purchasing are subject to continual review and revision, often on a daily basis. All foods deteriorate in time, some more quickly than others, and it is the job of the food controller to put a system in place to ensure that quantities purchased will be needed immediately or in the relatively near future. In cooperation with the steward, the food controller does this by instituting procedures for determining the appropriate purchase quantity for each item to be purchased. These procedures are based principally on the useful life of the commodity.

For purchasing purposes, foods are divided into the two categories previously discussed: **perishables** and **nonperishables.** The procedures for determining purchase quantities differ from one another and will be discussed separately.

Perishables

The very nature of perishable products suggests the importance of always using up those already on hand before purchasing additional quantities. Therefore, the purchasing routine must provide for determining quantities already on hand. Decisions also must be made as to total quantities needed. Once these have been arrived at, the difference between them is the correct amount to order.

There is a term commonly used in industry for the quantity needed: **par,** or **par stock.** While it is generally acknowledged that par stock is a number of units related to usage and the time needed to get delivery, there is no general agreement on an exact definition of the term. Since the term is used in a variety of ways in the industry, one should be aware of some of its more common uses. In some places, par stock is taken to mean the maximum quantity of a given item that should be on hand after the most recent order has been received. In others, it means the quantity that should be on hand at all times. Still another possibility is to treat par stock as a range defined by maximum and minimum quantities between which the actual quantities on hand should vary. For purposes of this discussion, we will define **par** stock as **the quantity of any item required to meet anticipated needs in some specific upcoming period.**

A basic requirement of the purchasing routine is that the steward take a daily inventory of perishables. In some cases, this daily inventory may be an actual physical inventory. In others, it may be only an estimate based on physical observation. For example, the steward would probably count the actual number of ribs of beef, but might only estimate the quantity of chopped beef. Or the steward might count the avocados, but count only the cases of lettuce.

A very important and useful tool for the steward to use in taking this daily inventory is a standard form called the "Steward's Market Quotation List," illustrated in Figure 4.2. This form, generally available from stationers who cater to the hotel and restaurant industry, is a list of the most common perishables, arranged by types, with several blank lines provided for the special requirements of each restaurant. Restaurants that offer menus so specialized that this particular form is unsuitable, such as Chinese or Near Eastern restaurants, must devise their own and have them duplicated. Foodservice operators who have incorporated computers into the purchasing routine can readily prepare their own. Doing so makes it possible to limit the number of items on the form to those used by the establishment, and to easily add and subtract items as the need arises. If the forms are computer-generated, one could also have separate sheets for different food groups: one for meat, another for dairy, and so on.

To take the daily inventory of perishables, the steward goes through refrigerators and freezers with the form in hand and, next to the appropriate items in each category, fills in the column on the left marked "On Hand." After completing this survey, the steward has a relatively accurate inventory of perishable products.

The next step in the routine requires that determinations be made of anticipated total needs—in effect, par stocks—for each item, based on future menus and often on experience as well. Depending on the establishment, these determinations of total anticipated needs are determined by any of several key personnel—chef, manager, or steward, or by some combination of the three. If one is using the manual form illustrated in Figure 4.2, it is helpful to write this par stock figure for total anticipated needs in the "Article" column, just after the name of the item in question in the standard form.

Next, for each required item, the steward subtracts the amount on hand from the par figure to determine the proper order quantity. This difference is the amount that should be ordered to bring supply up to the total quantity required. This is written in the "Wanted" column at the right.

Referring to the Steward's Market Quotation List illustrated in Figure 4.2, for example, one assumes that legs of lamb are on the menu and that a total of twelve legs will be required to meet the anticipated demand. This number is recorded in the "Article" column, just after the name of the item. Since the daily inventory indicates two legs, written in the "On Hand" column, the quantity to be purchased is 10 legs, recorded in the "Wanted" column, and is found by subtracting the quantity on hand (2 legs) from the established par stock (12 legs).

On Hand	ARTICLE	WANTED	QUOTATIONS
	BEEF		
	Corned Beef		
	Corned Beef Brisket		
	Corned Beef Rump		
	Corned Beef Hash		
	Beef Chipped		
	Beef Breads		
	Butts		
4	Chuck	10	6
	Fillets		
	Hip Short		
	Hip Full		
	Kidneys		
	Livers		
	Loin, Short		
3	Strip	12	4
6	Shell Strip	15	9
	Ribs Beef		
	Shins		
	Suet Beef		
	Tails Ox		
	VEAL		
	Breast		
	Brains		
	Feet		
	Fore Quarters		
	Hind Quarters		
3	Head	8	
	Kidneys		
	Legs	5	
	Liver		
1	Loins	3	
	Racks	4	
	Saddles		
	Shoulder		
	Sweet Breads		

On Hand	ARTICLE	WANTED	QUOTATIONS
	Provisions (Cont'd)		
	Pig's Knuckles Fresh		
	Pig's Knuckles Corned		
	Pig, Suckling		
1	Pork, Fresh Loin	6	
	Pork, Larding		
	Pork, Spare Ribs		
	Pork, Salt Strip		
4	Pork Tenderloin	9	7
	Sausages, Country		
	Sausages, Frankfurter		
	Sausages, Meat		
	Shoulders, Fresh		
	Shoulders, Smoked		
	Shoulders, Corned		
	Tongues		
	Tongues, Beef Smoked		
	Tongues, Fresh		
	Tongues, Lambs		
	Tripe		
	POULTRY		
1	Chickens, Breast		
	Chickens, Roast		
	Chickens, Broilers		
	Chickens, Broilers		
	Chickens, Supreme		
	Cocks		
	Capons		
	Ducks		
	Ducklings		
	Fowl		
	Geese		
	Goslings		
	Guinea Hens		
	Guinea Squabs		
	Pigeons		
	Possums		

On Hand	ARTICLE	WANTED	QUOTATIONS
	FISH (Cont'd)		
	Carp		
	Codfish, Live		
	Codfish, Salt Boneless		
	Codfish, Salt Flake		
	Eels		
	Finnan Haddie		
	Flounders		
	Flounders		
	Flounders, Fillet		
	Flake		
	Haddock		
	Haddock, Fillet		
	Haddock, Smoked		
	Halibut		
	Halibut, Chicken		
	Herring		
	Herring, Smoked		
	Herring, Kippered		
	Kingfish		
	Mackerel, Fresh		
	Mackerel, Salt		
	Mackerel, Spanish		
	Mackerel, Smoked		
	Perch		
	Pickerel		
	Pike		
	Porgies		
	Pompano		
	Redsnapper		
	Salmon, Fresh		
	Salmon, Smoked		
	Salmon, Nova Scotia		
	Scrod		
	Shad		
	Shad Roes		
	Smelts		
	Sole, English		

On Hand	ARTICLE	WANTED	QUOTATIONS
	Vegetables (Cont'd)		
	Estragon		
	Egg Plant		
	Garlic		
	Horseradish Roots		
	Kale		
	Kohlrabi		
	Lettuce		
	Lettuce, Ice Berg		
	Lettuce, Place		
	Leeks		
	Mint		
	Mushrooms		
	Mushrooms, Fresh		
	Okra		
	Onions		
	Onions, Yellow		
	Onions, Bermuda		
	Onions, Spanish		
	Onions, White		
	Onions, Scallions		
	Oyster Plant		
	Parsley		
	Parsnips		
	Peppermint		
	Peas, Green		
	Peas		
	Peas		
	Peppers, Green		
	Peppers, Red		
	Potatoes		
	Potatoes, Bermuda		
	Potatoes, Idaho		
	Potatoes, Idaho		
	Potatoes, Sweet		
	Potatoes, New		
	Potatoes, Yams		
	Pumpkins		

On Hand	ARTICLE	WANTED	QUOTATIONS
	FRUIT (Cont'd)		
	Dates		
	Figs		
	Gooseberries		
	Grapes		
	Grapes		
	Grapes, Concord		
	Grapes, Malaga		
	Grapes, Tokay		
	Grapefruit		
	Grapefruit		
	Guavas		
	Lemons		
	Lemons		
	Limes		
	Limes, Florida		
	Limes, Persian		
	Muskmelons		
	Oranges		
	Oranges		
	Oranges		
	Peaches		
	Peaches		
	Peaches		
	Pears		
	Pears		
	Pears, Alligators		
	Pineapples		
	Plums		
	Plums		
	Pomegranates		
	Quinces		
	Raspberries		
	Strawberries		
	Strawberries		
	Tangerines		
	Watermelons		
	Watermelons		

FIGURE 4.2 *Steward's Market Quotation List*

MUTTON

Fore Quarters	
Kidneys	
Legs	
Racks	
Saddles	
Saddles, Hind	
Shoulder	
Suet	

LAMB

Breast	
Fore Quarters	
Feet	
Fries	
Kidneys	
Loins	IV 10
Legs	Y IV 10
Lamb, Spring	
Racks, Double	
Racks, Spring	
Saddles	
Shoulder	

PROVISIONS

Bacon	3 16
Bologna	
Bologna	
Crepinette	
Salami	
Hams, Corned	
Hams, Fresh	
Hams, Polish	✓
Hams, Smoked	6 4
Hams, Virginia	
Hams, Westphalia	
Head Cheese	
Lard	
Lyon Sausage	
Phil. Scrapple	
Smoked Butts	
Pig's Feet	
Pig's Head, Corned	

GAME

Squabs	✓
Turkeys, Roasting	8 6
Turkeys, Boiling	
Turkeys, Spring	
Birds	
Partridge	
Pheasant, English	
Rabbits	
Quail	
Venison, Saddles	

SHELL FISH

Clams, Chowder	
Clams, Cherrystone	
Clams, Little Neck	
Clams, Soft	
Crabs, Hard	
Crabs, Meat	
Crabs, Oyster	
Crabs, Soft Shell	
Crabs, Soft Shell Prime	
Lobsters, Meat	14
Lobsters, Tails	4 3
Lobsters, Chicken	
Lobsters, Medium	
Lobsters, Large	
Oysters, Box	
Oysters, Blue Points	
Oysters	
Scallops	
Shrimps	100 60
Turtle	

FISH

Bass, Black	
Bass, Sea	
Bass, Striped	
Blackfish	
Bluefish	
Bloaters	
Butterfish	
Soie, Boston	
Soie, Lemon	
Sturgeon	
Trout, Brook	
Trout, Lake	
Trout, Salmon	
Weakfish	
Whitebait	
Whitefish	
Whitefish, Smoked	

VEGETABLES

Artichokes	
Asparagus	
Asparagus	
Asparagus, Tips	
Asparagus, Fancy	
Beans	
Beans, Lima	
Beans, String	
Beans, Wax	
Beets	
Beets, Tops	
Broccoli	
Brussels Sprouts	
Cabbage	
Cabbage, Red	
Cabbage, New	
Carrots	
Carrots	
Cauliflower	
Celery	
Celery Knobs	
Chicory	
Chives	
Corn	
Chervil	
Cranberries	
Cucumbers	
Dandelion	
Escarole	
Endive	
Romaine	
Radishes	
Rhubarb, Fresh	
Rhubarb, Hot House	
Sage	
Shallots	
Sorrel	
Sauerkraut	
Spinach	
Squash, Crooked Neck	
Squash Hubbard	
Tarragon	
Thyme	
Tomatoes, New	
Tomatoes, Hot House	
Turnips, White	
Turnips, Yellow	
Turnips, New	
Watercress	

FRUIT

Apples, Cooking	
Apples, Baking	
Apples, Crab	
Apples, Table	
Apricots	
Bananas	
Blackberries	
Blueberries	
Blueberries	
Blueberries	
Cantaloupes	
Cantaloupes	
Honey Balls	
Melons, Casaba	
Melons, Honeydew	
Melons, Persian	
Melons, Spanish	
Cherries	
Cherries	
Cherries	
Currants	
Chestnuts	

BUTTER

Print	
Cooking	
Sweet	

EGGS

White	
Brown	
Mixed Colors	
Pullets	

CHEESE

American, Kraft	
American, Young	
Bel Paese	
Camembert	
Camembert	
Cheddar	
Cottage	
Cream	
Cream, Phila	
Cream, Phila	
Edam	
Gorgonzola	
Liederkranz	
Parmesan, Grated	
Roquefort	
Roquefort	
Roquefort, Broken	
Stilton	
Store	
Swiss	
Swiss, Gruyere	
Swiss, Gruyere	

Miscellaneous

FIGURE 4.2 (continued)

87

Nonperishables

While nonperishable foods do not present the problem of rapid deterioration, they do represent considerable amounts of money invested in material in storage. Obviously, cash tied up in nonperishables is not available to meet other operating expenses of the business. Therefore, one goal of the purchasing routine for nonperishables should be to avoid having excessive quantities on hand. Additional benefits to be derived from reducing quantities on hand include the elimination of some possibilities for theft, the reduction of storage space requirements, and possibly the reduction in the number of personnel required to maintain the storage area.

Fixing labels on shelves is one important step that should be taken in every storeroom. The purpose of doing so is to establish a permanent location for each item in the inventory. With locations for food products established in this way, no product should ever be found in more than one location at once. Without labels and fixed locations for products in storage, products are often stored in several different locations, which makes it more difficult for the steward to know the actual quantity on hand. When this is the case, there is a tendency to order additional quantities in the erroneous belief that stock is running low. Another benefit of identifying fixed locations for products is that this practice makes it easier to find things when regular personnel are off duty or when personnel change.

For the convenience of stewards, a form can be obtained from some stationers that lists nonperishables, just as the Steward's Market Quotation List itemizes perishables. It is not widely used, however, since lists of groceries are not as universally applicable as lists of perishables. Stewards prefer to make up their own lists of storeroom contents. These serve the same purpose: to list amounts to be ordered and competitive prices.

While there are undoubtedly a number of ways to maintain inventories of nonperishables at appropriate levels, most are variations on two basic methods:

1. Periodic order method.
2. Perpetual inventory method.

Both of these are discussed below.

PERIODIC ORDER METHOD. Perhaps the most common method for maintaining stores' inventories at appropriate levels is the so-called periodic order method, which, in contrast to methods for ordering perishables, permits comparatively infrequent ordering. Because nonperishables have longer shelf life than perishables, it is both possible and desirable to order them less frequently. By doing so, the steward has more time available to devote to ordering perishables, which typically require considerable attention. When the periodic order method is followed, a steward will normally establish, with the advice of management, regular dates for ordering with fixed intervals between them. Then, on a regular basis—once every week, every two weeks, or even once each month, depending on storage space available and the policies of management as to the amount of money to be tied up in inventory—the steward reviews the entire stock of nonperishable items and determines how much of each to order to ensure a supply sufficient to last until the next regularly scheduled order date. The calculation of the amount of each item to order is comparatively simple.

> Amount required for the upcoming period
> − Amount currently on hand
> + Amount wanted on hand at the end of the
> <u>   period to last until the next delivery   </u>
> = Amount to order

An example will help illustrate how the system works. In the Springfield Restaurant, where orders are placed on the first Monday of each month, one of the nonperishable items ordered is pineapple slices, purchased in No. 2 cans, packed 24 cans to a case. The item is used at the rate of 10 cans per week, and delivery normally takes five days from the date an order is placed. If the steward in this establishment found 12 cans on the shelf, anticipated a normal use of 40 cans during the upcoming period of approximately four weeks, and wanted 15 cans on hand at the end of that period, the calculation would be:

> 40 cans required
> − 12 cans on hand
> <u>+ 15 to be left at the end of the month</u>
> = 43 cans to be ordered on this date

However, since orders are normally placed for this item in cases rather than in cans, the steward would probably round the order up to the next highest purchase unit, placing an order for two cases, consisting of 48 cans. While rounding an order upwards in this way appears at first glance to be overpurchasing, in fact the steward is subtracting quantities on hand at the beginning of each period before placing the orders. Because of this, the small overpurchases resulting from rounding orders will be taken into account before order quantities are determined for the following period. In effect, the order for the next period is reduced by the amount of the small overpurchase in the current period.

One might ask how the steward would know the quantity of an item

ITEM Pineapple Slices						DESIRED ENDING INVENTORY 15		
Date	In	Date	Out	Date	Out	Date	Out	Balance
10/1								15
		10/2	2	10/4	2	10/6	2	9
		10/7	2					7
10/8	24							31

FIGURE 4.3   *Bin Card*

required for an upcoming period. Storerooms have hundreds of items, and it is impossible for a person to know, without records, the total quantity required for each item in the inventory. In some smaller operations, stewards simply guess, knowing that each subsequent order date will provide an opportunity to improve the accuracy of the figures. In others, experienced stewards get to know and remember the approximate quantities used in a period and keep this in mind when ordering. In some establishments that rely on a single supplier for most of their needs, stewards may seek help from the supplier, who keeps records of previous orders. With that information, the steward can look on the storage shelf and make an approximate determination of the amount used by subtracting the quantity remaining from the quantity last ordered. However, one must keep in mind that if orders are placed every time a salesperson calls, the order period will vary from item to item because salespersons do not all call with the same frequency.

While such methods are probably better than ignoring usage entirely, one must keep in mind that they all fail to take into account the amount on hand at the beginning of any period. Nevertheless, these informal methods are not uncommon in the food and beverage industry.

A more systematic method of determining usage requires that certain additional steps be taken. For establishments without computers, a desirable first step is to make shelf labels more useful by including additional information on them. For example, if the label were somewhat larger than standard size, it would be feasible in many establishments to record the quantities added to and taken from shelves right on this label. When used in this form, labels become known as **bin cards,** an example of which is shown in Figure 4.3.

As each delivery is received and placed on the shelf, both the date and number of units so placed are entered on the bin card. As quantities are issued for use, those dates and amounts are recorded as well. More spaces are provided for items issued than for items received, for the obvious reason that purchases are comparatively infrequent, but issues may occur daily. A balance column is provided so that a steward may determine and enter amounts on hand at any desired time, such as when a salesperson calls or when the periodic ordering date arrives.

At such times, it is quite simple to determine approximate usage by looking on the card for the balance on hand on the date the last order was placed, adding to that figure the number of units placed on shelves when the last order was received, and subtracting the balance currently on hand. The result will be the approximate usage in the most recent period, regardless of the length of that period. The assumption is made that this quantity was used productively, although this may not always be the case and should be considered in determining the amount to order for the next period. When such a system is followed, it is normally wise to compare the balance on the bin card with the number of units of the item actually on the shelves in order to be sure that all items issued have been suitably recorded. If a discrepancy exists, the balance shown on the bin card will not be entirely reliable as a measure of actual usage during the period, and the missing items, presumably issued, must be added to the derived usage figure to achieve a more accurate figure.

If the amount used in the preceding period were the amount ordered for the coming period, there is a strong possibility that no units of the item would be left on the shelf at the end of the coming period. Since this might make it impossible to produce some menu items or might make it necessary to obtain some emergency supply to last until the next delivery date, foodservice operators that follow the periodic method establish the quantity that should be on hand at the end of any period. That quantity should be an amount sufficient to last until the next delivery is received. Once established, this quantity, known as the **desired ending inventory,** is recorded on the bin card. Both delivery time and daily usage for the period must be used to determine the desired ending figure. Furthermore, it is advisable to include some additional quantity to serve as a safety factor, just in case the normal delivery is delayed or business volume is higher than expected in the coming period.

It should be obvious that a bin card system requires considerably more manual record-keeping than most operators would be willing to devote to one in today's foodservice world. It is doubtful that any have the time, the labor, or the trained personnel required to keep the bin cards up-to-date. Therefore, one will often see shelf labels in food storerooms, but may never see bin cards used for keeping records of foods received and issued.

In computerized foodservice operations, shelf labels are still useful for many of the purposes identified above but are not needed as bin cards. The information formerly recorded manually on bin cards is now an integral part of inventory records in the computer. As deliveries of any given item are received and placed on shelves, quantities are entered in the computerized inventory records. When units are removed from the shelf for use, those quantities are also entered. If the records are accurately maintained, a balance figure for each inventory item is readily available to the steward at all times and orders can be placed at the appropriate time.

Whether on cards or in a computer file, other useful information about inventory items can be maintained as well. The container size and the latest purchase price, for example, can be available as an integral part of the record. So can the current supplier. The ready availability of this information can help the steward prepare purchase orders quickly and with relative ease.

It is important for anyone planning to go into the foodservice industry to realize that those using the periodic order method must constantly review two quantities used in the formula: normal usage and desired ending inventory. After all, many changes occur in usage from period to period, and the steward or manager who fails to take changes into account is taking risks needlessly. For example, as the weather and menus change, some foods will be used in greater quantities. If demand for some menu items increases, usage for related inventory items will increase as well; the reverse would also be true. Thus, before one orders, it is normally advisable to compare usage in similar periods in preceding years. If menus and sales volume have changed as well, these, too, must be taken into account.

PERPETUAL INVENTORY METHOD.   The primary purposes of the perpetual inventory method are:

1. To ensure that quantities purchased are sufficient to meet anticipated need without being excessive, and
2. To provide effective control over those items that are being stored for future use.

The perpetual inventory method requires the maintenance of perpetual inventory records, similar in nature to that illustrated in Figure 4.4. Successful use of this method requires complete and accurate records. Some attempt to maintain perpetual inventories manually; more are likely to prefer computerized approaches. The primary difference is that those without computers must keep the records on paper cards and perform the calculations manually; computer users maintain the records on hard drives, with the computers doing all of the calculations.

Perpetual inventory cards, while similar to the bin card illustrated in Figure 4.3, include some additional information and are used differently. One very important difference is that the perpetual inventory card is not normally affixed to the shelf on which the covered item is maintained. It is kept in some location other than the storeroom and is maintained by someone who does not

ITEM	Pineapple Slices	COST	$9.84 per 12 can case
SIZE	#2½ can	PAR STOCK	32
SUPPLIER	ABC Co.	REORDER POINT	15
	18 120th St.	REORDER QUANTITY	24
	Springfield		

Date	Order #	In	Out	Balance
10/1	#222-24		2	15
10/2			2	13
10/3			2	11
10/4			2	9
10/5			2	7
10/6		24		31
10/7				
10/8				

FIGURE 4.4   *Perpetual Inventory Card*

work in the storeroom. The quantity of food purchased is recorded, and, as units of product are issued for use, those quantities issued are similarly recorded. If the quantities recorded accurately reflect the movement of items into and out of storage, it is possible at any given time merely to consult the perpetual inventory card to determine how much of an item is in stock at the moment. This system makes it possible to compare balances on the perpetual inventory cards with actual items on shelves to determine if any items are not accounted for.

The additional information, including the name and address of the supplier and the most recent purchase price for the item, facilitates ordering. Three additional terms used on the card—reorder point, par stock, and reorder quantity—are also of considerable use in facilitating purchase and require further discussion.

The **reorder point** is, quite simply, the number of units to which the supply on hand should decrease before additional orders are placed. Thus, if the reorder point for a given item is 22 cans, then no order for that item should be placed until the supply shown in the balance column has reached that number. To establish a reorder point for any item, it is necessary to know both normal usage and the time needed to obtain delivery. Furthermore, it is advisable to include in the calculations a certain additional amount to allow for delivery delays and for possible increased usage during that period. In effect, the re-order point in the perpetual inventory method is the equivalent of the desired ending inventory in the periodic method.

Reorder point is calculated in the following manner. If normal usage is two cans per day and it takes five days from date of order to get delivery, then the basic number of cans needed is ten. However, because delivery may be delayed, because usage may increase for unforeseen reasons, or because both of those possibilities may occur at once, it is advisable to increase that amount somewhat. The amount of the increase is a matter for management to decide. To some, 50 percent might be an appropriate amount. If that were so in this case, the reorder point would be set at 15 cans. Under the periodic method, the desired ending inventory would similarly be calculated as 15 cans.

The perpetual inventory card also provides for a **par stock** figure for each item in stock. Par stock was defined earlier in the chapter as the quantity of any item required to meet anticipated needs in some specific upcoming period. With nonperishables, that quantity can be determined only after carefully weighing the following considerations:

1. Storage space.
2. Limits on total value of inventory prescribed by management.
3. Desired frequency of ordering.
4. Usage.
5. Purveyors' minimum order requirements.

Because storage space is limited for all but a few very fortunate owners and managers, it is obviously necessary to calculate the maximum amount of space available for all nonperishable storage and then to allocate the use of that space carefully and wisely. For example, for those items normally purchased in comparatively large packages, such as bulk flour and sugar, it might be necessary to restrict space to that required for the storage of a one-week supply.

To the extent that management chooses to restrict the amount of cash invested in inventory, it becomes necessary to restrict the amount of any item that one can maintain on hand. If cash flow is a problem (that is to say, if the cash for meeting payroll and for paying outstanding bills is in comparatively short supply), then management is likely to restrict the size and value of inventory and to require rather more frequent ordering of smaller quantities. In some cases, it is possible to accomplish this by restricting only the purchase of the more expensive items in the inventory without effecting any change in purchase procedures for less costly products.

Obviously, management must determine how often foods should be ordered. In addition, while the foods involved are typically referred to as nonperishables, some are, in fact, more perishable than others, and this should be taken into account.

Determination of par stock should always take into account the relative quantities of an item used, which may change over time. If anticipated consumption of an item is expected to be high in a given period, then the par stock should be higher than at, say, another time or season when consumption is rather low.

Because most purveyors prefer to supply items in standard wholesale purchase units, such as cases and 50-pound bags, the minimum order requirements of purveyors must be taken into account.

Once all of these factors have been considered and a par stock figure has been established for each inventory item, it is entered on the appropriate perpetual inventory card.

The final consideration is the establishment of a **reorder quantity.** Reorder quantity is the amount that will be ordered each time the quantity of a particular item diminishes to the reorder point. The quantity ordered should be sufficient to bring the total inventory up to the par stock level. At first glance, that quantity would appear to be the difference between established par stock and reorder point. However, the difference between par stock and reorder point would fail to take into account normal usage between order date and delivery date—previously calculated as eight cans for the example in Figure 4.4. This quantity must be added. Therefore, the calculation of reorder quantity would be:

Par stock	32
− Reorder point	15
= Subtotal	17
+ Normal usage until delivery	8
= Reorder quantity	25

However, food is normally purchased in case lots of 6, 12, or 24, or some other quantity per case, depending on the item and size of container, and this must be taken into account. If the establishment needs 25 units of something packed 12 to the case, the order placed must be in some multiple of 12. In this case, the reorder quantity will be two cases, or 24 cans, rather than the 25 determined above. Upon delivery, the stock is brought to 31 units, or approximately to par.

Many establishments choose not to use either of these systems in precisely the forms described above. There are a number of reasons for this. Some appreciate the value of perpetual inventory records removed from the control of those who receive and issue food, but are unwilling or unable to place orders on the daily basis presupposed by pure perpetual method. Others fear the comparative absence of control in the periodic method. For these and other reasons, some have developed what amount to hybrid systems that selectively employ the more desirable features of both systems.

One such system is essentially a perpetual method, but with reorder points and par stocks set sufficiently high so that orders need not be placed at precisely the moment that reorder points are reached. Such establishments might use the reaching of a reorder point as a signal that a particular item should be ordered on the next regularly scheduled day for placing orders and would merely add the item to a list. If the reorder point were set high enough, there would be little danger of consuming the remaining quantity through normal usage prior to next delivery.

The final determination of a routine—one of those illustrated above or some variation—must be based on the needs of the individual operation and the policies established by management. The important point to be made is that the purchasing procedure must take into account the need for determining, on an ongoing basis, the quantity of each product that will be adequate for meeting anticipated demand. It must guard against **overpurchasing,** which is the purchasing of unneeded quantities. In the case of perishables, overpurchasing increases the possibilities for both spoilage and theft. In addition, it increases the possibilities for overproduction and consequent waste. In the case of nonperishables, overpurchasing clearly increases the possibilities for theft; it may increase the need for personnel, and it certainly can tie up unwarranted amounts of money in inventory. Because these are the very conditions that control systems are established to guard against, it is obviously important to set up procedures for determining appropriate quantities for ordering.

ESTABLISHING STANDARDS FOR PRICE

Having established purchase specifications so that purchasing personnel know the appropriate quality to buy, and inventory procedures so that they can determine the quantity to buy, one can turn to the question of price. Because it is desirable to buy products of the appropriate quality in adequate quantities at the lowest possible price, it is desirable to ensure that food purchases are made on the basis of competitive prices obtained from several possible suppliers.

The availability of sources of supply varies considerably from one location to another. Major metropolitan areas, for example, tend to offer the greatest number of possibilities, both in terms of different categories of suppliers and number of suppliers in each category. By contrast, remote rural areas tend to offer few possibilities; sometimes establishments in remote areas must be content with what they can get. In general, depending on ownership policy, availability of suppliers, and general market conditions, foodservice operators depend on suppliers who fall into the following general categories:

Wholesalers
Local producers
Manufacturers
Packers
Local farmers
Retailers
Cooperative associations

In most instances the foodservice operator will deal with several of these sources of supply to obtain the necessary foods. For example, a restaurant might turn to a local producer for dairy and bakery products, a packer for canned meats, a wholesaler for fresh meats, a different wholesaler for canned fruits and vegetables, and a local farmer for eggs.

In recent years there has been a trend for wholesalers to diversify their product lines in an attempt to better meet the needs of their restaurant customers. In some instances, one supplier may be able to provide virtually all of the food-related needs of a restaurant. In general, one will deal with as many as may be necessary to ensure the supply of foods of appropriate quality at the lowest prices.

To ensure that purchases are made at the lowest favorable price, the steward must obtain prices from several competing suppliers for each product that he or she intends to buy. The procedures differ for perishables and nonperishables.

MEANS OF OBTAINING PRICE QUOTATIONS

Today, purchasing stewards have several means of obtaining price quotations. They include:

1. Telephone.
2. Fax.
3. Quotation sheets obtained by mail.
4. Fax modem.
5. Information supplied by salespersons who call on customers.
6. Direct computer links with purveyors via the internet or dedicated telephone line.

Direct computer links with purveyors enable the purchasing steward to access price lists on a computer. Fax messages provide the advantage of obtaining written information very quickly. Fax modems enable one to obtain fax messages without a separate machine. Telephone quotations, obtaining quotes from salespersons who call at the establishment, and obtaining price lists by mail are the traditional means of obtaining information. However, as computers, fax machines, and modems become more common in restaurants, fewer establishments are relying on the traditional means.

Virtually all purveyors have fax machines to provide price quotations to customers and to receive orders. One expert has suggested that visits to customers by salespersons will shortly become a thing of the past because most foodservice operators are now relying on other means for obtaining information and placing orders.

Perishables

Because prices for perishables commonly change daily, it is necessary for the steward to contact several different suppliers by one or more of the means suggested above to determine current prices each time an order is to be placed. If copies of specifications have previously been sent to suppliers, the steward has reasonable assurance that each is quoting on products of comparable quality. The Steward's Market Quotation List, shown in Figure 4.2, provides columns for price quotations on each product, with space at the top of each column for the name of the supplier. Ideally, the steward will obtain prices from several suppliers for each item and will select the lowest price. In reality, other considerations should also be taken into account. These include delivery time, managers' preferences for particular dealers, the reliability of dealers in providing foods that meet specifications, and the number of individual items that can be ordered from any one dealer. Once price quotations have been obtained, the steward selects the most favorable and places the order with the chosen dealer. Normally it is placed with the lowest bidder. As the order is placed, the steward circles that particular price quotation next to the item to be supplied. Thus, when all perishables have been ordered, the steward has a complete record of products ordered as well as records of prices, quantities, and suppliers. As we shall see in the next chapter, this list will be valuable for checking purposes when the food is delivered.

Nonperishables

Procedures used to obtain competitive prices for nonperishables are somewhat different from those used for perishables. Stewards generally prefer to deal with fewer suppliers for nonperishables. In fact, many obtain extensive price lists from wholesale supply houses, each of which may be able to supply most of the nonperishable products that stewards are likely to order. With these lists in hand, stewards can compare prices and make selections at greater leisure than is ever possible with the purchase of perishables. Although a steward will normally select the lowest price consistent with the quality desired, there are exceptions here as well. For example, if dealer A were offering all but one item at a lower price than dealer B and dealer B's price for that one item were only $.02 per can lower, a steward would be likely to place an order for 12 cans with dealer A in spite of the higher price, the difference being only a matter of $.24. The expenditure would be more than justified by the simplification of the ordering. In addition, it is possible that dealer B might not accept an order as small as 24 cans of a single item because the profit might be more than offset by the cost of making the delivery.

TRAINING FOR PURCHASING

As everyone in the foodservice industry knows, formal training programs for food purchasers are not common. General food purchasing courses are taught in many schools, colleges, and universities, and seminars are conducted by such organizations as the National Restaurant Association. These are useful, but they cannot be considered substitutes for training workers to follow the standards and standard procedures established for an individual foodservice operation. The owner or manager is ultimately responsible for the training or lack of training of employees.

As discussed in Chapter 2, the second step in the control process is training employees to follow established standards and standard procedures. Having described such standards for food purchasing, we will turn to applying this second step in the control process.

Training employees means teaching them to perform a given job in the manner expected by management. Assuming that the employees have the ability and basic knowledge needed to do the work, training is easier if standards and standard procedures have been carefully and conscientiously developed. If these have not been formulated, training might be impossible. An example will illustrate this: One cannot train a server to wait on tables unless one has determined how the job is to be done: place settings must be standardized, service procedures must be developed, ordering procedures in the kitchen must be formalized, and so on. Unless there are standard procedures for servers to follow, each will perform the job in his or her own way. Some customers may be served quickly, while others wait for long periods; some may find teaspoons in their place settings, while others must request them of the server.

Purchasing personnel must also be trained, and the training is easier when the kinds of standards and standard procedures discussed earlier in this chapter are in place. For example, if management has established the periodic order method as the standard procedure for maintaining supplies of nonperishables, a manager can explain the method to a new steward and, if necessary, work with that steward when trying for the first time to use the method for determining correct order quantities. If neither the periodic order method nor any other method has been established as the standard and if each previous steward has done the job his or her own way over the years, it is difficult to imagine how someone in management could begin to explain the details of the job to a new steward.

To the extent that new employees bring specific knowledge of their field to a job, training is far easier. It may be possible to devote minimal time to training under these circumstances, merely acquainting such employees with their surroundings and explaining various general company policies and practices. However, when new employees with specific knowledge are not available and management is forced to hire those with little knowledge and experience, training becomes critical to the proper functioning and even to the survival of the enterprise. It will be the responsibility of management not only to explain general policies and procedures, but also to impart the basic knowledge and skills that a better-qualified employee would have brought to the job.

There are many acceptable methods for training employees, including classroom instruction, on-the-job training, simulation exercises, training manuals, and training films, to name but a few. Proper methods must be determined for each foodservice operation after careful review of the setting, the conditions, various budgetary considerations, and management's willingness to meet its responsibility for training. A detailed discussion of training methods is included in Chapter 20 of this book.

MONITORING PURCHASING PERFORMANCE

The third step in the control process is to monitor employee performance and compare it with established standards and standard procedures. Proper control cannot be established over the purchasing of foods without this third step, which is aimed at providing assurance that standards and standard procedures are being followed. For example, if management has directed that purchases of a given quality of beef be made at the lowest price, there can be no assurance that this policy is being followed unless the steward's purchasing performance is monitored.

Performance can be monitored in a number of ways. Some of these were discussed in general terms in Chapter 2, including observing and correcting employee actions and requiring records and reports. For example, management may require that the Steward's Market Quotation List be turned in daily with selected prices circled for daily verification. Another possibility would be to telephone purveyors from time to time to be sure that the prices written by the steward were accurate, or to compare the steward's record of prices with the actual prices on invoices received from suppliers. Many other monitoring techniques may be used as well—some daily and some periodically, depending on circumstances and management's perception of the need to monitor purchasing performance.

TAKING CORRECTIVE ACTION

The fourth step in the control process was defined in Chapter 2 as taking appropriate action to correct deviations from standards. It represents management's opportunity to do whatever may be necessary to ensure that employees' future performance will more nearly approximate established standards and standard procedures.

This fourth step may be very simple in some cases and far more difficult in others. For example, a willing and loyal employee may merely have forgotten one or more standards or may have been momentarily distracted while working. In such cases, a simple reminder may be the only corrective action needed. In other cases (those involving theft or drug abuse, for example), sterner measures are required.

It is important to remember that any deviation from established standards, no matter how slight, means that employee performance is not measuring up to the standards established by management. Such deviations will doubtless have a long-term negative impact on the overall performance of the enterprise, and many have noticeable short-term consequences, including production of inferior products for sale to customers. In extreme cases, if a steward has neglected to purchase some foods necessary for the production of the day's menu, it could mean no production of certain menu items. Corrective action would be warranted and mandatory.

CENTRALIZED PURCHASING

No discussion of purchasing procedures would be complete without some mention of **centralized purchasing systems,** which are widely used by chain operations and occasionally established by small groups of independent operators with similar needs. Under a centralized purchasing system, the requirements of individual units are relayed to a central office, which determines total requirements of all units and then purchases that total, either for delivery to the individual units by the dealer or for delivery to a central warehouse. This last method obviously requires that a whole system for distribution be maintained and operated by the organization doing the centralized purchasing. There are both advantages and disadvantages to these centralized systems that should be understood by anyone involved in food management.

Advantages

1. Foods and beverages can be purchased at lower prices because of volume.
2. Desired quality can be obtained more readily because the purchasing agent has a greater choice of markets.
3. Foods can be obtained that meet the purchaser's exact specifications.
4. Larger inventories can be maintained, ensuring reliable supply to individual units.
5. The possibilities for dishonest purchasing in individual units are greatly reduced.

Disadvantages

1. Each unit must accept the standard item in stock and has little freedom to purchase for its own peculiar needs.
2. Individual units cannot take advantage of local "specials" at reduced prices.
3. Menus are normally standardized, thus limiting the individual unit manager's freedom to change a menu.

Finally, it should be noted that decisions about whether or not to adopt a centralized purchasing system are normally made by top management, not by food controllers. However, there are times when food controllers are asked to provide their advice and opinions. To do so, they must understand the advantages and disadvantages of centralized purchasing.

STANDING ORDERS

Although it is desirable for the needed quantity of a given item to be determined with great care each time an order is placed, stewards commonly make arrangements with certain purveyors for the delivery of goods without specific orders. These arrangements are known as **standing orders** and typically take one of two forms.

One arrangement calls for the delivery of a specific quantity of a given item each day (for example, 12 loaves of bread). The number would remain constant unless specifically changed by the steward.

The second arrangement calls for the replenishing of stock each day up to a certain predetermined number. For instance, the steward might arrange with a dairy supplier to leave a sufficient quantity of bulk milk each morning, to bring the total supply up to a predetermined figure, such as 20 gallons.

While these arrangements are convenient, they do present a number of possibilities for both waste and excessive cost to develop.

COMPUTER APPLICATIONS

Today, many restaurants are using computers and computer systems for a variety of purposes, and increasing numbers will do so each year. One obvious use of a computer is to maintain information about the food inventory.

Assume that management elects to maintain supplies of nonperishables by the perpetual inventory method and that all relevant records are in a computer, including reorder point, reorder quantity, previous purchases and issues, and any other information that would be useful in making purchase decisions. With all such data available, management can quickly determine the current status of the entire inventory, including a list of those items at or below reorder point. In effect, the perpetual inventory card for each item would be a file in a computer database, rather than a card in a file drawer.

Using one of the programs currently available, one finds that it is comparatively simple to create an computer inventory for the nonperishable foods. Depending on the specifics of the software used, one can record such information as the items in the inventory, various vendors, purchase units, current prices, quantities purchased, and quantities issued. The purchases and issues for each item would be used to determine a quantity on hand, which can be compared to the reorder point, and a report can be generated listing those items for which the quantity on hand had reached the reorder point. In the case of an individual restaurant, this report would be used by the steward to place orders. In a chain organization, similar reports from all units can be transmitted electronically to a home office, where they would be used to generate one complete list of purchases to be made centrally for the entire organization, conceivably at considerable savings.

While there are many advantages to maintaining food inventories by computer, this approach is not without some problems. For example, perpetual inventory files in a computer must be kept current in the same basic manner as perpetual inventory cards in a file drawer: someone must be given responsibility for recording all purchases and issues. Unless this information is recorded with complete accuracy, the records will be useless for the purpose of making purchasing decisions. Also, recording data in a computer terminal requires as much time and concentration as recording this data on index cards. If management directs that computers be used as aids in record keeping and decision making, it must be prepared to accept an expense for the time one or more employees will spend at the computer terminal keeping the records current. Computer use is currently most common in larger restaurants and in chain organizations because it is still somewhat more difficult for small operators to identify sufficient tangible benefits to justify the cost.

The foregoing is but one example of the many possibilities offered by computers for more effective management of the purchasing function in foodservice.

CHAPTER ESSENTIALS

In this chapter, we described the application of the four-step control process to food purchasing. We discussed the need for fixing responsibility for purchasing, the establishment of appropriate quality and quantity standards, and a method for determining optimum purchase prices. Specific procedures for the purchase of perishable and nonperishable foods were outlined, including the two most common methods for purchasing nonperishable foods: periodic order method and perpetual inventory method. The most common sources of supply used by foodservice operators were listed, means of communicating with purveyors were discussed, and various considerations that affect selection of particular suppliers were described. We discussed the need for training purchasing personnel, as well as techniques for monitoring their performance and, when necessary, taking corrective action. We described centralized purchasing and discussed its advantages and disadvantages. We defined standing orders and discussed their use by some establishments, pointing out various risks associated with their use.

KEY TERMS IN THIS CHAPTER

Bin card
Centralized purchasing
Nonperishable foods
Par
Par stock
Periodic order method
Perishable foods
Perpetual inventory card
Perpetual inventory method
Reorder point
Reorder quantity
Standard purchase specifications
Standing orders
Steward's Market Quotation List

QUESTIONS AND PROBLEMS

1. List 10 items considered perishable and 10 considered nonperishable in the foodservice industry.

2. Write a standard purchase specification for each of the following:
   a. Leg of lamb.
   b. Fresh tomatoes.
   c. No. 10 cans of green beans.

3. Write a one-paragraph explanation of why the standard purchase specifications for eggs used for producing a breakfast menu would differ from the specifications for eggs used for producing baked goods.

4. Nestor's Restaurant uses the periodic order method, placing orders every two weeks. Determine the quantity of canned peaches to order today given the following:
   a. Normal usage is one case of 24 cans per week.
   b. Quantity on hand is 10 cans.
   c. Desired ending inventory is 16 cans.

5. Harvey's Restaurant uses the periodic order method, ordering once a month. Determine the proper quantity of tomato juice to order today given the following:
   a. Normal usage is one case of 12 cans per week.
   b. Quantity on hand is 6 cans.
   c. Desired ending inventory is 18 cans.
   d. The coming month is expected to be very busy, requiring 50 percent more tomato juice than normal.

6. The Midtown Restaurant uses the perpetual order method. One of the items to be ordered is canned pears. Determine reorder point and reorder quantity given the following:
   a. Normal usage is 21 cans per week.
   b. It takes four days to get delivery of the item.
   c. Par stock is set at 42 cans.
   d. Cans come packed 12 to a case.

7. The Last Chance Restaurant uses the perpetual order method. One of the items in the inventory is canned green beans. Determine reorder point and reorder quantity given the following:
   a. Normal usage is 2 cans per day.
   b. It takes five days to get delivery of the item.

    c. Par stock is 29 cans.

    d. Cans come packed 6 to a case.

8. Assume you have been hired as the purchasing steward of a new restaurant located in an area that is completely unfamiliar to you. You have never lived there before, and you have no friends or family in the area. How would you obtain information on sources of supply for perishable and nonperishable foods?

9. How can managers use computers to establish control over food purchasing?

10. Define each of the following terms:
    Bin card
    Centralized purchasing
    Nonperishable foods
    Par
    Par stock
    Periodic order method
    Perishable foods
    Perpetual inventory card
    Perpetual inventory method
    Reorder point
    Reorder quantity
    Standard purchase specifications
    Standing orders
    Steward's Market Quotation List

FOR COMPUTER USERS

11. Using any database program you choose, create a simple inventory file to incorporate the data provided in Figure 4.4.

12. Using the file initiated in Question 11 as a template, create another file for a second item in the inventory (whole, peeled tomatoes) for which information is provided below:
    Item: Tomatoes, whole, peeled
    Size: No. 10 can
    Supplier: EZ Foods
           41027 Fountain Avenue
           Chicago, IL
    Cost: $11.85 per case
    Par stock: 108
    Reorder point: 18
    Reorder quantity: 102

Record the following data in the proper fields, then determine from the file the proper date for reordering:

10/1—Balance in inventory: 37

10/1—Issued 7 cans

10/2—Issued 6 cans

10/3—Issued 6 cans

10/4—Issued 5 cans

5

Food Receiving Control

LEARNING OBJECTIVES

After reading and studying this chapter, you should be able to:

1. Identify the primary purpose of receiving control.
2. List and explain three standards established to govern the receiving process.
3. List and explain the six steps of standard receiving procedure.
4. Describe the duties of a receiving clerk.
5. Name the essential equipment and supplies needed for proper receiving.
6. Identify an invoice, and explain its use.
7. Explain the purposes of the invoice stamp.
8. Identify the Receiving Clerk's Daily Report, explaining its purpose and use.
9. Distinguish between directs and stores.
10. Describe a meat tag, list the information found on it, and explain how it is used.
11. Discuss the importance of training receiving personnel.
12. Explain the need for monitoring the performance of receiving personnel.
13. Describe one use of the computer in the receiving process.
14. Define each of the Key Terms at the end of the chapter.

INTRODUCTION

If great care is taken to establish effective controls for purchasing, but no attention is given to receiving controls, it is conceivable that all earlier efforts may have been wasted. After all, ordering specific quantities and qualities at optimum prices constitutes no guarantee that the products ordered will actually be delivered. Purveyors may deliver incorrect quantities of foods, foods of higher or lower qualities, foods with prices other than those quoted, or all three. Therefore, the primary objective of receiving controls is to verify that quantities, qualities, and prices of food delivered conform to orders placed.

In our discussion, we use the job title receiving clerk to identify the individual to whom management assigns the full responsibility for receiving food deliveries and carrying out the control procedures set up by the food controller. In larger operations, particularly those with complete food control systems, this is often the case. In smaller operations that deem the payroll expense of a receiving clerk unwarranted, food deliveries may be received by any of several individuals, including the owner, manager, chef, or steward. Although we use the job title receiving clerk extensively in this chapter, we are aware that others do receive deliveries. The point to be made here has nothing to do with the job title of the person doing the receiving; what is important is the development of a set of standard procedures for receiving food deliveries and verifying that these deliveries conform to orders in every respect.

As was illustrated in the preceding chapter, controlling any aspect of foodservice operation requires that one institute the four-step control process. In attempting to establish control over the receiving function, therefore, one should begin with the first step: establishing standards and standard procedures.

ESTABLISHING STANDARDS FOR RECEIVING

The primary purpose of receiving control is to verify that the quantity, quality, and price of each item delivered conforms to the order placed. To ensure that this is the case, it is necessary to establish standards to govern the receiving process, as follows:

1. The quantity delivered should be the same as the quantity listed on the Steward's Market Quotation List, and this should be identical to the quantity listed on the invoice, or bill, that accompanies the delivery.
2. The quality of the item delivered should conform to the establishment's standard purchase specification for that item.
3. The prices on the invoice should be the same as those circled on the Steward's Market Quotation List.

Quantity	Unit	Description	Unit Price	Amount
30	lbs.	Strip Steak	7.95	238.50
10	lbs.	Breast of Veal	4.65	46.50
				$285.00

Invoice
Market Price Meat Co.
300 Market St.
New York, N.Y.

TO   The Graduates Restaurant

DATE June 11

FIGURE 5.1 *Invoice*

THE INVOICE

Every time food is delivered to an establishment, it should be accompanied by some document that lists the items being delivered. For food, the document is normally an **invoice,** which is another word for a **bill.** A typical invoice is illustrated in Figure 5.1.

An invoice is usually presented to the receiving clerk in duplicate by the person making the delivery, who will expect the receiving clerk to sign and return the second copy. This serves as an acknowledgment to the purveyor that the establishment has received the products listed on the invoice. The original is, in effect, a bill that must be routed to the bookkeeper or other individual responsible for paying bills. This routing procedure will be dealt with later in this chapter.

Invoices not listing prices should be discouraged: Prices should be checked as the food products are received. Otherwise, it is possible that a purveyor might bill at the wrong prices, either by accident or by design.

ESTABLISHING STANDARD PROCEDURES FOR RECEIVING

Although the authors recognize that exact procedures and techniques for receiving vary from one establishment to another, it will be useful to examine one standard procedure that many managers have found appropriate for use in their establishments.

1. Verify that the quantity, quality, and price for each item delivered conforms exactly to the order placed.
2. Acknowledge that quantity, quality, and price have been verified by stamping the invoice with the rubber invoice stamp provided for that purpose.
3. List all invoices for foods delivered on a given day on the Receiving Clerk's Daily Report for that day, and complete the report as required, or enter appropriate information directly into a computer terminal.
4. Fill out meat tags for all appropriate items.*
5. Forward completed paperwork to proper personnel.
6. Move food to appropriate storage areas.

Each of the elements in this standard procedure will be discussed below.

Verifying Quantity, Quality, and Price

To carry out the verification procedure suggested above, the receiving clerk must have certain supplies and equipment available, including the following:

1. A permanent copy of the standard purchase specifications.
2. Appropriate equipment for determining weight, including such items as a hanging scale and a platform scale.
3. Certain paper forms, tags, rubber stamps, and related office supplies.

Quantity verification entails weighing, counting, or otherwise enumerating the quantity of a particular food delivered by the vendor and then checking to see that the same quantity appears on both the invoice and on the order (the Steward's Market Quotation List). In some larger establishments, a pur-

* Few establishments still use meat tags, so most will now disagree with this. However, no substitute for the meat tag has yet come into common use to provide the level and type of control that meat tags offered, as explained later in this chapter.

chase order might be used for staples in place of the Steward's Market Quotation List.

Quality verification requires knowledgeable inspection of delivered foods and careful comparison of perceived quality with the quality established in the standard purchase specifications. For example, the individual receiving strip loins of beef should be able to determine that the beef conforms to the restaurant's standard purchase specifications. Given the specification for strip loin illustrated in Figure 4.1, inspection should reveal prime beef, bone in, with weight ranging from 14 to 16 pounds, with fat limited to one-half to three-quarters of an inch except for seam fat, moderate marbling, and a light to slightly dark red color. Each item delivered should conform to the standard purchase specification written for it.

Price verification requires comparing the unit price appearing on an invoice with the price quote circled on a Steward's Market Quotation List, or a purchase order. Obviously, the price on the invoice should be the same as the listed purchase price used by the steward.

In the event that quantity, quality, or price of foods delivered does not conform to the orders placed, appropriate steps should be taken. Sometimes this will involve returning inferior foods with the delivery driver. Sometimes it may involve changing the quantities listed on the invoice and having the delivery driver initial the change. For purposes of this discussion, it is important only to note that each discrepancy should be noted and attended to at the time of delivery.

One difficulty frequently presents itself: Delivery drivers do not have the time to wait for verification to be completed. Therefore, it is important to maintain good working relationships with vendors so that any discrepancy found after the driver has left can be readily resolved by a telephone call or some other informal means. From time to time, some foodservice operators have found it necessary to put aside unacceptable food for return to the vendor at the earliest opportunity.

Stamping the Invoice

It is generally good practice to provide the receiving clerk with an **invoice stamp,** which is a rubber stamp to be used on all invoices.

This invoice stamp, a suggested form for which is illustrated in Figure 5.2, is used for a number of reasons. It provides for:

1. Verification of the date on which food was received.
2. The signature of the clerk receiving the food who vouches for the accuracy of quantities, qualities, and prices.

```
┌─────────────────────────────────────────────────────────────────┐
│  Invoice Stamp                                                     │
│                    ϑₙ Wilson              Date  6/11/XXXX          │
│  Received _____                                │
│                                                                   │
│  Steward _____                                 │
│                                                                   │
│  Prices and                                                       │
│  Extensions                                                       │
│  Verified _____                                │
│                                                                   │
│  OK for                                                           │
│  Payment _____                                 │
│                                                                   │
└─────────────────────────────────────────────────────────────────┘
```

FIGURE 5.2 *Invoice Stamp*

3. The steward's signature, indicating that the steward knows the food has been delivered.
4. The food controller's verification of the arithmetical accuracy of the bill.
5. Signatory approval of the bill for payment by an authorized individual before a check is drawn.

Listing Invoices on Receiving Clerk's Daily Report

For establishments that do not use a computer for keeping track of inventories, the Receiving Clerk's Daily Report is an important accounting document. For all establishments, food is divided into at least two different categories because some foods are purchased for immediate use, while others are purchased to be kept in inventory until needed. The former become part of cost immediately, while the latter are not included in cost until they are issued from the inventory. In food control, all foods that are charged to cost immediately are called **directs,** and all foods that are charged to cost when issued from inventory are called **stores.** An understanding of the differences between the two, as well as working definitions for both, will be increasingly important in future chapters.

Directs are those foods that, because of their extremely perishable nature, are purchased on a more or less daily basis for immediate use. The quality of these foods tends to diminish quickly and, if not used very soon after the time of purchase, become unusable for their intended purposes. Foods that typically fall into this category are fresh fruits and vegetables, fresh baked goods, and most dairy products. Ideally, the quantities of each purchased on any given day should be sufficient for that day alone. Therefore, since they are purchased for immediate use, they are considered to be issued as soon as they are received and are included in food cost figures on the day of delivery. The working definition will be that directs are those items that will be issued and charged to food cost as received.

Stores, on the other hand, are those foods that, while ultimately perishable, will not diminish significantly in quality if they are not used immediately. They can be held in storage and carried in inventory for a day or so or, in some instances, for considerable periods of time. Meats, for example, if stored under proper conditions, can be maintained for reasonable periods of time. So, too, can those grocery items that are purchased in cans, bottles, and boxes. All these items are purchased on the basis of anticipated needs, not necessarily immediate, and are kept in inventory until they are needed. When the need arises, they are released from inventory and issued to the kitchen. Since we have seen that cost occurs when food is issued or used, these items will be included in the food cost figures when they are issued for use. The working definition will be that stores are those items that will be charged to food cost as issued.

There are no industry-wide rules to indicate that any food item is always categorized with directs or with stores. The decision depends on how the item is stored and issued. In some establishments, for example, fresh fish is included with directs because it is purchased for use on the day of delivery. Other places may buy whole fish, which are cleaned and otherwise prepared for use the following day, and thus include fresh fish with stores. The food controller or manager in each establishment must decide how to classify foods in that particular establishment on the basis of use and then must consistently include each item in the predetermined category.

The Receiving Clerk's Daily Report, illustrated in Figure 5.3, is a summary of invoices for all foods received on a given day.

The Receiving Clerk's Daily Report is prepared by a receiving clerk, who merely copies data from each invoice to appropriate columns on the report and then enters the total for each invoice into one of the three columns under the general heading "Purchase Journal Distribution"—Food Direct, Food Stores, or Sundries. In the illustration, the invoice previously described in Figure 5.1 has been entered as the first invoice of the day, with the individual items and the totals copied. The total dollar value of food listed on that invoice, $285.00, has been recorded in the "Food Stores" column. This is because these items have been purchased for future use and will be held in inventory until needed, at which time they will be charged to cost. By contrast, the third invoice on the report, from Jones Produce and Fruit, totaling $40.75, is found in the "Food Direct" column because the listed items have been purchased for immediate use and will thus be charged to cost on the day they are received.

In computerized control systems, the information may be keyed into re-

Quant	Unit	Description	✔	Unit Price	Amount	Total Amount	Food Direct	Food Stores	Sundries
		Market Price Meats							
30	lbs.	Strip Steak	✔	7.95	238.50				
10	lbs.	Breast of Veal	✔	4.65	46.50				
						285.00		285.00	
		Ottman Meats							
15	lbs.	Pork Tenderloin	✔	2.50	37.50	37.50		37.50	
		Jones Produce & Fruit							
1	Crate	Lettuce	✔	12.50	12.50				
1	Bag	Onions		6.75	6.75				
1	Box	Grapefruit	✔	9.50	9.50				
1	Crate	Peaches	✔	12.00	12.00				
						40.75	40.75		
					363.25	363.25	40.75	322.50	

Receiving Clerk's Daily Report — NO. 1 — DATE June 11, XXXX — *Purchase Journal Distribution*

FIGURE 5.3 *Receiving Clerk's Daily Report*

cords directly as the goods are received. Alternatively, this information can be entered by the purchasing steward when the records of received goods reach him. It is still necessary to keep separate records of those foods treated as directs and those treated as stores, in order to facilitate the calculation of daily food costs.

Filling Out Meat Tags

In the majority of restaurants, meats, poultry, fish, and shellfish constitute the most costly group of foods on the menu. Because of this comparatively high cost, establishments with complete food control systems set up special controls for these items. One approach is to tag each package or piece received

```
┌─────────────────────────────────────────────┐  ┌──────────────────────────────┐
│              No. 20624                        │  │          No. 20624           │
│              DATE REC'D.   6/11               │  │  DATE REC'D.    6/11         │
│  ITEM   Strip Steak      GRADE   U.S. Prime   │  │  ITEM    Strip Steak         │
│  WEIGHT   15             LBS.   @7.95         │  │  WT.    15   LBS.    @7.95   │
│  DEALER   M P M          EXTENSION   119.25   │  │  EXT.    119.25              │
│                                               │  │  DEALER   M P M              │
│       DATE ISSUED _____    │  │  DATE ISSUED _____ │
│  William Allen & Co., N.Y. Stock Form 9247    │  │                              │
└─────────────────────────────────────────────┘  └──────────────────────────────┘
```

FIGURE 5.4 *Meat Tag*

before it is placed in storage. In general, the rule followed is that items typically purchased to be sent to the kitchen for immediate use are not tagged and are treated as directs; those that are typically held in inventory for one or more days before use are tagged and are treated as stores.

Figure 5.4 provides an illustration of a meat tag. Meat tags are printed on heavy card stock for durability and perforated into two parts for convenient separation. The tags are numbered sequentially, with the number appearing on both parts, and are used in numerical order. Because very few establishments still use meat tags, they are becoming increasingly difficult to find, although they can still be purchased from some of the stationers catering to the foodservice industry. The following describes the typical procedure adhered to by those who continue to use meat tags.

The receiving clerk fills in all information except date of issue, which cannot be filled in until meat is issued to the kitchen for preparation. After filling out the tag, the receiving clerk detaches the smaller part and sends it to the food controller. The larger part is either (a) attached securely to the piece or package of meat, or (b) sent to the steward. Both approaches have advantages and disadvantages, and there has never been any general agreement about which is preferable. The decision to follow one approach rather than the other is a matter for management to decide.

Forwarding Completed Paperwork

By the time all deliveries for the day are in, preferably as early in the day as possible, the receiving clerk will have stamped and signed all invoices and entered each on the Receiving Clerk's Daily Report, often referred to simply as the **receiving sheet.** This sheet, with the invoices attached, should then be sent to the steward, who signs the invoices and routes them to the food controller, who checks the arithmetical accuracy of each invoice. When the checking has been completed, the controller sends the receiving sheet and the invoices on to the accounting department, where the figures will be entered in the purchase journal.

However, while the food controller still has the receiving sheet, one very important total figure is recorded: the total cost of directs. Because directs are charged to the food cost as received, the food controller will need this figure in order to compute the daily cost of food sold. When we reach the chapter concerned with computing daily food cost (Chapter 10), it will be important to keep in mind that the daily cost of directs comes from the receiving sheet or from computer records.

Moving All Delivered Food

Once deliveries have been received in the manner described above, it is important that foods be moved to appropriate storage areas as quickly as possible, with those that will most quickly deteriorate at room temperature being put away first. The spoilage and theft that may occur between receiving and storing foods can be a major cause of excessive cost. Therefore, the food controller should check from time to time to be sure that foods are being moved to storage areas at optimum times.

The purpose of establishing control procedures for receiving is to ensure that the establishment receives food in the quantities ordered, in the qualities specified, and at the prices quoted. These steps are basic and should be common to all foodservice operations, regardless of size. More complex systems of control, operated as are with a greater number of personnel and more equipment and procedures for checking, obviously offer greater measures of protection, but do so at a greater cost. However, even the small, owner-operated restaurant should take these basic steps to guard against excessive costs that may develop from receiving improper quantities or qualities or charging improper prices.

In smaller establishments that do not have elaborate food control systems, some of the foregoing steps will be skipped, and the invoices are merely given to a bookkeeper by the person receiving the deliveries. However, this precludes a number of important possibilities for effective control. For example, such simplification makes it virtually impossible to compute a daily food cost. We will see that operating without knowledge of the daily food cost may be somewhat risky and possibly a great disadvantage.

TRAINING FOR RECEIVING

Establishing standards and standard procedures for receiving is merely the first step. This must be followed by employee training, or there is no reasonable way for management to expect that the established standards and standard procedures will be observed. At first glance, training for receiving does not appear to be difficult. After all, the routines for counting, weighing, and copying data from one paper to another can all be taught to an employee of reasonable intelligence. But there is more to receiving than routine clerical work.

The great problem faced by those who attempt to employ or train skilled receiving personnel lies with the vast amount of knowledge of foods these workers should have. They should be able to recognize whether or not particular items meet the established standard purchase specifications. They should be able to examine meats, for example, to determine grade, degree of freshness, and extent of trimming, among other considerations. With produce, they should be able to determine variety, degree of ripeness, and grade, at the very least. In other words, receiving personnel really need extensive knowledge if they are to do the proper job of checking quality. Anyone at all can be taught to weigh and count, but only a very few can make the necessary judgments as foods are received.

This may explain in part why so many restaurateurs do not require that receiving clerks check for quality as foods are delivered. They know that their receiving clerks do not have the knowledge. Instead, they rely on some other employee to check the quality after the receiving process has been completed. Some rely on a knowledgeable steward to do this. If the steward is unable, the chef may be required to do it. If the chef does not have the knowledge, the owner or manager may be forced to make the judgments personally. And if the owner or manager fails to make them, the judgments about food quality will finally be made in the dining room by the customers, probably with devastating results.

MONITORING RECEIVING PERFORMANCE AND TAKING CORRECTIVE ACTION

Even though counting, weighing, and transferring data from one form to another are comparatively simple routines, management must never assume that these tasks are necessarily being done and done correctly. Monitoring is required.

While the techniques used for monitoring vary from one establishment to another, there are some common points. Managers must occasionally be present when foods are received to be sure that receiving personnel are following established standard procedures. Since employees are more likely to do so when a supervisor is present, some managers prefer to wait until after the process has been completed and then quietly count or weigh one or two items and compare the results to the invoice. Managers do not do this every day with every delivery unless they find that employees are becoming lax. In that case, more frequent monitoring and appropriate corrective action will be required until receiving employees have improved their performance to the desired extent.

COMPUTER APPLICATIONS

If a single foodservice operation or a chain of restaurants is going to use a computer in back-of-the-house operations, using an inventory program, then it is necessary to input data indicating all items purchased as those items are received. This data is on the invoices checked by the receiving clerk. Management might designate some individual to input the data, thus keeping the quantities and prices recorded in the inventory up to date. In effect, this replaces work that could be done manually in those operations using perpetual inventory cards. Moreover, depending on the individuals involved and on the decisions of particular managers, it is possible to eliminate the Receiving Clerk's Daily Report because the essential information about purchase journal distribution and accounts payable is input at the same time the data about quantities and prices from invoices is input.

Another possibility might be to require that the steward placing orders take the additional step of recording in a terminal the items and quantities ordered and to provide the receiving clerk with a terminal for viewing or printing this information as deliveries are received. This would provide a means for comparing items and quantities ordered with items and quantities received. Depending on management policy, prices could also be compared by this means.

CHAPTER ESSENTIALS

In this chapter, we described the application of the control process to the receiving function in a foodservice enterprise, explaining why foods received should conform to orders placed in respect to quantity, quality, and price. We listed and explained common standards and standard procedures for receiving and then described various forms and pieces of equipment required for proper receiving, including the invoice, invoice stamp, Receiving Clerk's Daily Report, and meat tags. We distinguished between directs and stores and established useful working definitions for each. We described a procedure for tagging meats and other high-cost stores and pointed out the importance of effective receiving control in preventing excessive costs. We discussed the importance of training receiving personnel and pointed out their need for considerable knowledge of foods if they are to be effective. We indicated the importance of monitoring the performance of those who receive food and suggested several techniques that managers can employ for monitoring.

KEY TERMS IN THIS CHAPTER

Directs
Invoice
Invoice stamp
Meat tag
Purchase journal distribution
Receiving Clerk's Daily Report
Stores

QUESTIONS AND PROBLEMS

1. Explain several significant effects of improper receiving controls.

2. Why is each of the following necessary for effective receiving control?
   a. Platform scale.
   b. Hanging scale.

3. Assume you are a receiving clerk in a fine restaurant. Fifty pounds of strip steak have been delivered. The quality meets the restaurant's specification, but the quantity and price are different from those listed on the Steward's Market Quotation List. You have not yet signed the invoice, and the driver is still present. How would you deal with the apparent problems?

4. Why is it necessary for the receiving clerk to have a complete set of the establishment's standard purchase specifications?

5. What possible cost effects might there be if food deliveries all arrived at the same time?

6. Distinguish between directs and stores.

7. Is it possible for proper receiving to take place in the absence of standard purchase specifications? Explain your answer.

8. The manager of Rupert's Restaurant does not believe in using the Receiving Clerk's Daily Report form. Instead, she has her receiving clerk check each item delivered against the invoice. What are the

possible advantages and disadvantages of this alternative procedure?

9. The Uptowner Restaurant does not use meat tags, but treats meats as directs. What are the immediate effects of this procedure on food cost? What are the possible ultimate effects?

10. The receiving clerk in the Flammas Restaurant is also the dishwasher and has had no previous education or training in foods or in the food and beverage business. Discuss the possible effects on restaurant operations of having this individual responsible for receiving.

11. In many restaurant operations, the steward who purchases food also functions as the receiving clerk. What are some of the possible positive and negative effects of this procedure?

12. How can computers be used in receiving?

13. Define each of the following terms:
    Directs
    Invoice
    Invoice stamp
    Meat tag
    Purchase journal distribution
    Receiving Clerk's Daily Report
    Stores

FOR COMPUTER USERS

14. Using Figure 5.3 as a model, create a spreadsheet that could be used in place of the Receiving Clerk's Daily Report.

6

Food Storing and Issuing Control

After reading and studying this chapter, you should be able to:

1. List and explain three causes of unplanned costs that can develop while food is in storage.
2. List and explain five principal concerns that standards for storing food should address.
3. Identify optimum storage temperatures for the five classifications of perishable foods.
4. Explain the importance of establishing standards for each of the following:
   a. Storage temperatures for foods.
   b. Storage containers for foods.
   c. Shelving.
   d. Cleanliness of storage facilities.
   e. Assigned locations for the storage of each particular food.
5. Explain the principle of stock rotation as applied to foodservice.
6. Distinguish between issuing procedures for directs and those for stores.
7. Price and extend a food requisition.
8. Discuss the need for training those who store and issue food.
9. Describe the primary technique for monitoring the performance of those who store and issue food.
10. Distinguish between interunit and intraunit transfers, and give two examples of each.
11. Explain the significance of transfers in determining accurate food costs.
12. Explain the use of computers in establishing control over the storing, issuing, and transferring of foods.
13. Define each of the Key Terms at the end of the chapter.

INTRODUCTION

The two previous chapters were devoted to explaining the need for establishing control over purchasing and receiving and to describing the application of control process to ensure that the proper foods are purchased at optimum prices and that items purchased are received precisely as specified. When a foodservice operator selects particular qualities and quantities of food and places orders at particular prices, he or she is, in effect, creating and accepting the costs for food that will be served in the establishment. Eventually, these costs will be reflected in the income statement. Since the foodservice operator has accepted a particular level of cost, it is clearly in the operator's best financial interest to take all necessary steps to prevent the development of additional, unplanned costs before the foods are sold to customers. These unacceptable costs normally develop from spoilage, waste, or **pilferage** (the industry's term for theft). In this chapter, we will describe how the four-step control process can be applied to storing and issuing to reduce or eliminate the development of unplanned, unwarranted costs.

STORING CONTROL: ESTABLISHING STANDARDS AND
STANDARD PROCEDURES FOR STORING

In general, the standards established for storing food should address five principal concerns:

1. Condition of facilities and equipment.
2. Arrangement of foods.
3. Location of facilities.
4. Security of storage areas.
5. Dating and pricing of stored foods.

Each of these will be discussed separately.

Condition of Facilities and Equipment

The factors involved in maintaining proper internal conditions include temperature, storage containers, shelving, and cleanliness. Problems in any or all of these may lead to spoilage and waste.

TEMPERATURE.   One of the key factors in storing foods is the temperature of the storage facility. This is particularly important for perishables. Food life can be maximized when food is stored at the correct temperature and at the proper level of humidity. The food controller should occasionally check the temperature gauges on the refrigerated storage facilities to see that the appropriate temperatures are being maintained. The temperatures that follow are generally accepted as optimum for storing the foods indicated:

Fresh meats: 34 to 36°F.
Fresh produce: 34 to 36 degrees F.
Fresh dairy products: 34 to 36 degrees F.
Fresh fish: 30 to 34 degrees F.
Frozen foods: −10F to 0 degrees F.

If temperatures are permitted to rise above these levels, shelf life is shortened and the risk of food spoilage is increased for perishables.

Proper temperature can also be a key factor in preventing spoilage of nonperishables. Storage facilities for staple food products should usually be room temperature, approximately 65 to 70 degrees F. Sometimes, particularly in older establishments, staples are kept in facilities that are either too warm because of their proximity to hot stoves or steam pipes running through the ceiling, or too cold because they are located in unheated parts of a building. While the degree of risk is not as great with staples, it should be remembered that all foods are ultimately perishable and that the shelf life of food is increased by storage at proper temperatures.

STORAGE CONTAINERS.   In addition to maintaining foods at proper temperatures, care must be given to storing them in appropriate containers. In the case of staples, many are purchased in airtight containers. Some, however, are purchased in unsealed containers—paper bags, boxes, and sacks—which are susceptible to attack by insects and vermin. Whenever practical, products purchased in unsealed packages should be transferred to tight, insect-proof containers. In the case of perishables, both raw and cooked, care should be given to storing them in whatever manner will best maintain their original quality. Many raw foods, such as apples or potatoes, may be stored as purchased for reasonable periods; others, such as fresh fish, should be packed in shaved ice. In general, cooked foods and opened canned foods should be stored in stainless steel containers, either wrapped or appropriately covered.

SHELVING.   For perishable foods, shelving should be slatted to permit maximum circulation of air in refrigerated facilities. For nonperishables, solid steel shelving is usually preferred. At no time should any food product be stored on the floor. Appropriate shelving raised a few inches above the floor level should be provided for large and heavy containers that must occasionally be used in storerooms or refrigerators.

CLEANLINESS.   Absolute cleanliness is a condition that should be enforced in all food storage facilities at all times. In refrigerated facilities, this will prevent the accumulation of small amounts of spoiling food, which will give off odors and may affect other foods. In storeroom facilities, it will discourage infestation by insects and vermin. Storerooms should be swept and cleaned daily, and no clutter should be allowed to accumulate. A professional exterminator should be brought in on a regular basis to prevent rodents and vermin from reaching population levels large enough to cause damage and disease.

Arrangement of Foods

The factors involved in maintaining appropriate internal arrangement of foods include keeping the most-used items readily available, fixing definite locations for each item, and rotating stock.

KEEPING THE MOST-USED ITEMS READILY AVAILABLE.   It is usually helpful to arrange storage facilities so that the most frequently used items are kept closest to the entrance. Although it has no effect on spoilage and theft, this arrangement does tend to reduce the time required to move needed foods from storage to production and thus tends to reduce labor costs.

FIXING DEFINITE LOCATION.   Each particular item should always be found in the same location, and attention should be given to ensuring that new deliveries of the item are stored in the same location. All too often, one product is stored in several locations at once (for example, six cans on a shelf and two partially used cases in two other areas). This increases the chances for over-purchasing, spoilage, and theft. In addition, it makes difficult the monthly process of taking a physical inventory, which will be discussed in the next chapter. Incidentally, separate facilities for storage of different classes of foods should be maintained whenever practical and possible. Eggs, for example, should not be stored with fish, cheese, or other foods that give off odors because their shells are quite porous and they will absorb flavors from other foods. Fish should always be stored in separate facilities.

ROTATION OF STOCK.   The food controller must establish procedures to ensure that older quantities of any item are used before any new deliveries. The procedure used to do this is known as the **first-in, first-out** method of stock rotation, commonly called FIFO in the industry. The steward and staff must be held responsible for storing new deliveries of an item behind the quantities already on hand, thus ensuring that older items will be used first. This reduces the possibilities for spoilage. If this procedure is not followed and those who store foods are permitted to put new food in front of old food on shelves, the chances are increased that the older items will spoil before they are used. Insuring that stock rotation takes place is particularly important with perishables, but it should not be neglected with nonperishables.

Location of Storage Facilities

Whenever possible, the storage facilities for both perishable and nonperishable foods should be located between receiving areas and preparation areas, preferably close to both. Such locations facilitate the moving of foods from the receiving areas to storage, and from storage to the preparation areas. A properly located storage facility will have the effect of:

1. Speeding the storing and issuing of food.
2. Maximizing security.
3. Reducing labor requirements.

All too often, storage facilities are located in areas that are unusable for other purposes. This may not be a wise policy, particularly if temperature, security, and sanitary conditions are inadequate and problems develop that result in unwarranted costs.

Dry storage areas should be sealed to reduce the risk of infestation. Obviously, it is impossible to seal an area if its location is susceptible to rodents.

Security

Food should never be stored in a manner that permits pilferage. That is another reason for moving foods from the receiving area to storage as quickly as possible. Once in storage, appropriate security must be maintained at all times. A storeroom for staple food products should never be left unattended. Employees should not be permitted to remove items at will. Typically, a storeroom is kept open at specified times for specified periods well known to the staff and is otherwise closed to enable the storeroom clerk to attend to other duties. When the storeroom is closed, it should be locked, and the single key should be in the storeroom clerk's possession. In such cases, one additional "emergency" key is usually kept by the manager or in the office safe.

Security is also an important consideration in storing perishables, particularly in the case of high-cost items, such as meat and fish. The importance of security obviously increases with the value of the items stored. It is sometimes advisable to establish separate control procedures for steaks, liquor, and other high-cost items.

Dating and Pricing

It is desirable to date items as they are put away on shelves, so that the storeroom clerk can be certain of the age of all items and make provisions for their use before they can spoil. Of particular concern are items that are used infrequently. The storeroom clerk should visually check the stock frequently to ascertain which items are beginning to get old and then inform the chef, so that items can be put on the menu before they spoil.

In addition, all items should be priced as goods are put away, with the cost of each package clearly marked on the package. Following this procedure will greatly simplify issuing because the storeroom clerk will be able to price requisitions with little difficulty. If items are not priced as they are put away, the storeroom clerk will waste considerable time looking up prices when goods are sent to the kitchen. Computer users need not price goods if the program and inventory cards already have this information. As illustrated further on in this chapter, the latest prices are recorded on inventory records, enabling the steward to easily calculate the cost of goods issued.

ISSUING CONTROL: ESTABLISHING STANDARDS AND STANDARD PROCEDURES FOR ISSUING

In Chapter 5, definitions were given for directs and stores. Directs were defined as those foods charged to cost as received and stores as those carried in inventory and charged to cost as issued. That distinction is particularly important in a discussion of issuing.

There are two elements to the issuing process. The first is the physical movement of foods from storage facilities to food preparation areas; the second is the record keeping associated with determining the cost of the food issued.

Physical Movement of Foods from Storage Facilities

As described in the discussion of standards and standard procedures for storing, foods should be stored in fixed locations and under secure conditions in order to ensure that they will be available readily and in the purchased quantities when needed. When a cook needs a particular item, it must be removed from a storage facility and transported to the preparation area. Practices for doing this vary from one establishment to another. In some, all facilities are locked, and cooks must list all their needs on requisitions, which are turned over to a steward who sees to the issuing of the various items and their delivery to preparation areas. In others, storage facilities are unlocked, and any cook who needs an item simply goes to get it. In many, some of the storage facilities are locked (the storeroom and the walk-in refrigerators for meat, for example), while others are left unlocked (refrigerators containing produce or leftovers, for example).

There is no universal practice, but it should be obvious that establishments that take greater precautions tend to have greater control over unauthorized issuing. At the same time, it must be noted that these establishments tend to make issuing more time-consuming and thus costly by requiring written requisitions that must be filled by additional specialized personnel. In general, small establishments tend to follow more informal practices, while large organizations are more likely to rely on specific procedures requiring paper records and specialized staff. Standards and standard procedures for the physical movement of foods must be determined specifically for a given establishment, often on the basis of cost-benefit ratio.

Record Keeping for Issued Foods

DIRECTS.   Directs are charged to food cost as they are received, on the assumption that these perishable items have been purchased for immediate use. Theoretically, these foods will be moved to appropriate facilities in or near the kitchen and will be used entirely in food preparation on the day they are received. In practice, this is not normally the case. Some of the directs received on a given day are likely to be left over and used the following day; in fact, most establishments purposely purchase more than one day's supply of many directs. While this greatly simplifies the record keeping associated with determining the cost of directs, it does introduce some inaccuracy in the records maintained.

As we will see, establishments that determine daily food costs use the total dollar figure in the "Food Direct" column on the Receiving Clerk's Daily Report as one component of the daily cost of food. This is based on the presumption that all directs received on a given day have been consumed and should thus be included in food cost for the day. Since this is not strictly true, these daily costs tend to be artificially high on days when all directs received have not been consumed and artificially low on days when directs included in costs for previous days are actually being consumed.

For record-keeping purposes, then, directs are treated as issued the moment they are received, and no further record is kept of particular items. The alternative would be to follow an issuing procedure similar to that described below for stores, which would require significant additional time and labor. Finally, it should be noted that waste, pilferage, or spoilage of directs will result in unwarranted additions to food cost figures.

		Date	9/8,	XXXX

Supply   Main Kitchen _____ Dept.

Quantity	Description	Unit Cost	Total Cost
6	#10 Cans Green Peas		
50	Lbs. Sugar		
40	Lbs. Ground Beef		
6	Loins Pork		

Charge to __*Food*_____ Dept.

___*J J Lemon*_____
Chef

FIGURE 6.1 *Requisition*

STORES. The food category known as stores was previously described as one consisting of (a) staples, and (b) tagged items, primarily meats. When purchased, these foods are considered part of inventory until issued for use and are not included in cost figures until they are issued. Therefore, it follows that records must be kept of issues in order to determine the cost of stores. For control purposes, some system must be established to ensure that no stores are issued unless kitchen personnel submit lists of the items and quantities needed.

The Requisition. A requisition, illustrated in Figure 6.1, is a form filled in by a member of the kitchen staff. It lists the items and quantities the kitchen staff needs from stores for the current day's production. Each requisition should be reviewed by the chef, who should check to see that all required items are listed and that the quantity listed for each is accurate. If that is the case, the chef will sign and thus approve the requisition. It is next given to the storeroom clerk, who fills the order.

For computer users the requisition process may be slightly different. If the chef has a computer in her office, she may input the information directly into her computer and then send the requisition electronically to the storerc The quantity of each item requisitioned will automatically be deducted f inventory, and it will then simply be a matter of gathering the foods indic on the requisition.

Whenever practical, it is advisable to require that requisitions be submitted in advance to enable the storeroom clerk to prepare the order without haste. In some places, it has been found practical to insist on requisitions being submitted the day before food is needed. This has the desirable effect of forcing kitchen personnel to anticipate needs and plan for the following day's production.

It is also desirable, whenever possible, to set definite times for the storeroom clerk to issue food. The storeroom clerk, after all, has a number of other duties to perform, including keeping the storerooms and refrigerators clean, maintaining stocks of staples on shelves, rotating stock, and doing considerable paperwork. Some operations have achieved good results by restricting the times for issuing food to two hours in the morning and two in the afternoon. Naturally, such decisions must be left to management in any particular operation.

Pricing the Requisition. After stores have been issued from the appropriate storeroom, refrigerator, or freezer, it may be the storeroom clerk's responsibility to record on each requisition the cost of listed items and to determine the total value of the foods issued. If the requisition has been printed by the computer, prices should already be recorded. As will be discussed in Chapter 10, this information is necessary for a daily determination of food costs.

The items listed on requisitions fall into two categories:

1. Staples.
2. Meats and similar entree items.

Values for foods in these two categories are determined as indicated below.

1. Staples. The unit cost will come from one of the following, depending on the system in use:

a. The unit cost of each item is marked on each container as it is stored, making it readily available to the storeroom clerk.
b. A book or card file is maintained for all staple items, one page or one card per item. As prices change, the most recent purchase price is always entered.

c. The most recent purchase price is listed on a perpetual inventory card or in the computer for each item.

d. The storeroom clerk keeps a mental record of the orders placed and usually remembers the purchase prices because of constant use.

Computer users will use the third method. The first method is generally preferred for those still using a manual system. However, it unquestionably involves considerable labor and consequently is costly to maintain. Therefore, though preferred, it is not the method in general use. More often than not, prices come from the storekeeper's head. Although the accuracy of this "system" leaves much to be desired, it is the method requiring the least time and labor. Many have found that the resulting inaccuracies have no significant effect over the long run.

2. Meats and Similar Entree Items. The traditional method of obtaining the cost of pieces of meat and other tagged items issued was to detach the tag half as they were issued and to record the value on the requisition. If one requisition required the issuing of several pieces of meat, the tag values were totaled before a value was recorded. After meat tag values had been recorded, the tags were attached to the requisitions.

With the decreasing use of meat tags, it has become more difficult to determine the value of meats issued. One common approach is to weigh pieces as they are issued and then later to multiply the weight of each by its purchase price per pound, thus determining a value to record on the requisition.

Once the unit cost of each item on the requisition has been recorded, it becomes possible to determine the total value of the food issued. For each listed item, the unit value is multiplied by the number of units issued. This is called **extending the requisition.** Computer-generated requisitions are automatically extended.

Once the values of the various items on the requisition have been extended, each requisition is totaled, as illustrated in Figure 6.2. At the end of each day, all requisitions are sent to the food controller.

Thus, each morning the food controller will have figures available for the principal components of a daily food cost for the preceding day:

1. Cost of directs from the receiving sheet.
2. Cost of stores from the requisitions.

The importance of having accurate and timely data developed in this way will become apparent in Chapter 10, when we establish a method for determining daily food cost and discuss its significance.

As has been previously illustrated, the first step in the control process—

Quantity	Description	Unit Cost	Total Cost
		Date 9/8, XXXX	
	Supply Main Kitchen Dept.		
6	#10 Cans Green Peas	$2.79	$16.74
50	Lbs. Sugar	.39	19.50
40	Lbs. Ground Beef	2.59	103.60
6	Loins Pork (108 lbs. per tags)	2.39	258.12
			$397.96

Charge to _Food_ Dept.

H Lemon
Chef

FIGURE 6.2 *Requisition*

establishing standards and standard procedures—is the proper beginning, which must be followed by three additional steps. We will now direct our attention to those steps—training staff, monitoring performance, and taking corrective action as required—in storing and issuing control.

TRAINING FOR STORING AND ISSUING

The importance of training may best be illustrated by the following example. Let us suppose that the owner of a particular establishment hires inexperienced personnel to store and issue foods, pays them low wages, and restricts training to the barest minimum, merely telling people what their duties are in the most general way. Consider some of the possible problems that could arise:

- Foods could be stored in inappropriate containers or at improper temperatures, and quality could deteriorate very quickly.

- One single item might be stored in several locations, with quantities in one area spoiling because no one knew they were there.
- New deliveries might be stored in front of old, with the old spoiling while the new were being used.
- Pilferage could increase significantly if storage areas were not secured.
- The value of issues might not be readily identifiable because those issuing foods had not recorded item prices on the requisitions.

These are but a few examples; a complete list of the many such problems occurring in foodservice establishments that fail to train adequately would be considerably longer.

Fortunately, training for storing and issuing is not as difficult as training for purchasing. Purchasing personnel, after all, require considerable prior knowledge of food and the distinctions between food qualities. Storing and issuing personnel, on the other hand, can be taught the proper methods and procedures by a qualified trainer, one who knows the correct techniques for storing and issuing and can explain them clearly to new employees.

There are two elements at work here. First, correct storing and issuing techniques are not universally known. Frequently there are a few correct ways and an infinite number of wrong ways to store a given item. For issuing, it is important that older items be issued before newer ones. At best, new employees will learn the methods and procedures that they are taught. If the trainer is not qualified to teach correct methods, stored foods are not likely to be maintained for their maximum useful life, with obvious implications for cost. Second, those employed to store and issue foods are not normally hired specifically for their ability to train others, and they may not be able to explain the necessary information clearly to those they are expected to train. Misunderstandings resulting from the inability to convey knowledge clearly can also have negative impact on cost.

In the area of training, large organizations often have an advantage over their smaller counterparts. The large organization frequently has a sufficient number of new employees needing training to justify the expense of a training department staffed by professionals, while the small establishment must rely on the questionable training skills of regular employees to prepare new workers for their jobs.

Training employees to store and issue each food item properly is important to the successful operation of all foodservice establishments, large and small, and it is important that those who manage small operations recognize the training obstacles they face and seek to overcome these.

MONITORING STORING AND ISSUING PERFORMANCE AND TAKING CORRECTIVE ACTION

While properly trained employees are probably more reliable performers than they would be otherwise, it is not advisable for management merely to assume that they are correctly following the routines and procedures in which they were trained. Efforts must be made to monitor the actual performance of each employee, comparing it to the expected performance.

Perhaps the primary technique for monitoring the performance of those who store and issue food is to observe the results of their work. To monitor storing procedures, management must inspect the storage facilities on a regular basis to determine that facilities are kept clean and well organized, that refrigerators and freezers are operating at proper temperatures, that each food item is being stored in its assigned location, that stocks are being rotated, and that established security precautions are being maintained. To monitor issuing procedures, management must examine paperwork to verify that requisitions are being properly prepared, priced, and extended. From time to time, management must check to see that food is not being issued without requisitions.

To the extent that observation reveals that employees are not adhering to the standards and standard procedures they have been trained to follow, some corrective action will be required. In some instances, simple reminders will suffice; in others, more vigorous steps may be required. Finally, management must take the required corrective action as quickly as possible or else risk continuing failure to meet established standards in the affected areas.

FOOD AND BEVERAGE TRANSFERS

So far in our discussions we have assumed that a restaurant purchases, receives, stores, and issues food for use in one kitchen in which all production is accomplished. By doing so, we have quite purposely ignored the existence of a number of possible complications, which will be useful to consider at this point. For example, even in small restaurants, food production in the kitchen may require the use of certain beverage items, such as wines and liquors, not purchased specifically for kitchen use. Conversely, many establishments purchase some food items, knowing that they will be used at the bar for drink production. Whole oranges and lemons, as well as heavy cream, are good examples. In addition, in some large hotel and motel operations, more than one kitchen is in operation, and it may be necessary or desirable to transfer food from one kitchen to another. Transfers may also occur in chain operations, where one unit may produce such items as baked goods for other units in the chain or where one unit in the organization, running short of needed items, may be encouraged to secure them from another unit. In all of the above cases, a failure to record the value of transfers will result in a food cost that is inaccurate.

Since the goals of food control include determining food cost as accurately as possible and matching food cost with food sales, it is often necessary to maintain records of the cost of the food transferred. When the amounts involved are relatively insignificant and have little appreciable effect on cost and on the cost-to-sales ratio, they may be and usually are disregarded. But when the amounts become somewhat larger and have more significant effects, records of some type must be developed.

Intraunit Transfers

BETWEEN BAR AND KITCHEN.   Food and beverage transfers between the bar and the kitchen occur frequently in operations of all sizes. Many kitchens use such beverage items as wine, cordials, brandy, and even ale to produce sauces, parfaits, certain baked items, and rarebits. Occasionally, these beverages are purchased by the food department for use in the kitchen, kept in a storeroom until needed, and then issued on requisitions directly to the kitchen. In such cases, additional records are not required; the quantities and values listed on the requisition are sufficient to permit accurate calculations of cost. However, in most instances when these beverages are needed in the kitchen, appropriate amounts are obtained from the bar. After all, if sufficient supplies are already being maintained at the bar, it makes little sense to keep additional quantities for specific use in food production.

The same may be said of certain food items in the directs category used by bartenders in drink production. If supplies of oranges, lemons, limes, heavy cream, and eggs are already available in a kitchen, it makes little sense to purchase specific supplies of these items for exclusive use at the bar. It is far simpler merely to secure the needed items from the kitchen. When it becomes necessary or desirable to achieve a high degree of accuracy in determining costs to match with sales, records of these transfers between the food and beverage departments must be maintained. The form used to maintain these records is the Food/Beverage Transfer Memo, illustrated in Figure 6.3.

As transfers are made, items and amounts are recorded. These records are sent to the food controller, who can use them to adjust food cost figures to achieve greater accuracy, and then routed to the food controller and an accounting office, where the appropriate adjusting entries can be made in the financial records.

BETWEEN KITCHEN AND KITCHEN.   In some of the larger hotels that operate more than one kitchen and dining room, it is common practice to de-

Food/Beverage Transfer Memo

Date 9/8, XXXX

From Bar

To Main Kitchen

Quantity	*Description*	*Unit Price*	*Amount*
1	750 ml Sneed's Sherry	$3.95	$3.95
1	750 ml Red Wine	2.65	2.65
		Total	$6.60

Sent by Joe - bartender

Received by Paul - Chef

FIGURE 6.3 *Food/Beverage Transfer Memo*

termine food costs for each separately and to match the costs for each operating unit with the sales generated by that unit. When some food items are transferred from one kitchen to another, higher degrees of accuracy in determining food costs may be achieved by keeping records of items and amounts so transferred. In cases where, for example, one unit closes earlier than another and cooked foods may be conveniently transferred from a closing unit to one remaining open until a later hour, it would be possible to achieve a higher degree of accuracy in determining costs for each unit by crediting the cost of the early closing unit for the value of the items transferred and by adding that value to the cost for the later closing unit.

Even in cases where items are not so transferred but are merely returned to a central kitchen or commissary for reissue to the same or to other units on succeeding days, recording the value of the items returned on transfer memos or on other similar forms makes possible more accurate determination of food costs and consequently of cost-to-sales ratios for operating periods.

Interunit Transfers

The two examples that follow illustrate interunit transfers and the effect of such transfers on food costs.

In a number of instances, small chains produce some items (baked goods, for example) in only one unit and then distribute those items to other units in the chain. If the ingredients for the baked goods come from that particular unit's regular supplies, then some record must be made of the cost of the ingredients used. Failure to do so would result in overstating the food cost of the producing unit by the value of the ingredients used and in understating the food costs of the receiving units by the value of the foods they receive. In addition, if the matching principle is to be followed and if food sales are reported separately for each unit, then food cost figures that do not include the cost of all those foods sold, including the baked goods from another unit, cannot be said to be truly matched with sales. Under such conditions, if one of management's goals is to match costs and sales with a reasonably high degree of accuracy, it is necessary to use a transfer memo or some similar form to record the value of ingredients used to produce finished products that are to be transferred to other units.

With such records available, it is possible to credit cost of the producing unit. Appropriately increasing the food cost figures of the receiving units may pose more of a problem. If each unit receives an equal share of the goods produced, then one could simply divide the cost of the goods produced and credited to the producing unit by the number of units to which items had been transferred, and then increase the food cost of each by one equal share. However, if the total produced for distribution to the various units is not divided among them equally, then some more equitable means for apportioning cost must be found. One possible solution is to record the values of transferred items at standard costs. The question of calculating standard costs of production for this and for other purposes will be deferred to the next chapter.

Another problem involving the value of foods transferred from one unit to another may be seen in those chain organizations that permit or encourage unit managers to obtain foods from other units when their own supplies run low and when additional purchases are precluded by time.

When units are comparatively close to one another and offer identical menus, occasions may arise when one of the units nearly exhausts the supply of some important item and does not discover this shortage until it is clearly too late to purchase an additional amount. In some organizations, items are borrowed and returned within a day or so as a matter of course, and no complications arise as long as all borrowed items are returned. However, not all cases are quite so simple, as, for example, when a perishable item borrowed by one unit does not appear on the menu again for some considerable period of time. Rather than maintain records over long periods in order to ensure the return of borrowed items, it is often simpler to record such transfers of foods on transfer memos and to use the information so recorded to increase the cost of the unit that has borrowed and correspondingly to decrease the cost of the supplying unit.

An interesting problem that may arise in connection with this procedure is the extent to which it influences some managers purposely to maintain short supplies of some high-cost and perishable items. If the organization permits one to secure needed supplies from other units at the same prices one would pay in the market, some managers will be encouraged to reduce the possibilities for excessive costs due to spoilage and pilferage in their units simply by maintaining inadequate supplies. Under such conditions, discouraging managers from taking advantage might entail establishing a price for transfer purposes somewhat higher than the current market price.

In Conclusion

In this industry there is a reasonably large number of transfers of the various types discussed above, but there is also a large number involving comparatively small amounts of food of relatively insignificant value. Consequently, because the amounts involved are usually negligible in most places, records are often not used. However, if and when the amounts become significant, provision must be made for maintaining adequate records to ensure that food cost figures include the cost of beverages used in food preparation and exclude the cost of food items sent to the bar for beverage preparation, and that food cost figures for one unit of a large organization include the cost of food items sold in that unit. In every case, to the extent feasible, the cost of items sold in a department, division, or unit should include all items reflected in sales figures.

COMPUTER APPLICATIONS

In the previous chapter, the point was made that there are computer programs that can be used to record information about quantities purchased and received as well as purchase prices. It is also possible to establish codes for all storage locations, so that each particular item in storage is assigned a particular location. Before any food purchases are stored, one can determine from the program the exact storage location for each item, in order to help ensure that all available quantities of a given food item are consolidated in one particular location.

Issuing control offers many possibilities for computers. For example, rather than ask the chef to prepare handwritten requisitions and present them to a storeroom clerk, management can require that the chef record the same information at a workstation. By so doing, the chef is updating the inventory because the items are treated as issued when entered by the chef. If a **local area network** (LAN) is used, a printer installed in the storeroom can print the chef's "requisition," thereby making it instantly available to those who fill it. The requisition can be printed immediately or at some later time, making it possible to eliminate handwritten requisitions completely. Another desirable feature of this procedure is that the chef can review inventory data on a monitor to learn the quantities of particular items on hand. This has obvious benefits for menu planning.

Transfers may be processed in much the same way as requisitions. A bartender needing fruit or other directs for making drinks can input these needs in a terminal at the bar. They can be printed in the storeroom, and the storeroom clerk can then see to their delivery to the bar. Similarly, beverages required for food production can be entered by the chef and printed out at the bar. Food and beverage transfers so recorded can be available when needed for accurate food cost determination.

CHAPTER ESSENTIALS

In this chapter, we described the application of the control process to the storing and issuing functions in a restaurant. We explained that unwanted costs can develop from spoilage, waste, and pilferage, and listed the five principal concerns that standards for storing must address: conditions of facilities and equipment, arrangement of foods, location of facilities, security of storage areas, and dating and pricing of stored foods. Included were discussions of temperature, storage containers, shelving, cleanliness, food locations, and rotation of stock. We distinguished between issuing procedures for directs and stores and indicated the importance of the requisition and the meat tag in issuing stores. We discussed training, pointing out again the importance of proper training if standards and standard procedures are to be maintained, and we described some of the negative consequences of failing to train storing and issuing personnel adequately. We described the primary technique for monitoring the performance of those who store and issue foods. We defined food and beverage transfers and illustrated several types, pointing out the possible effects on food costs that such transfers may have. We described the means for maintaining records of transfers for the purpose of introducing greater accuracy into food and beverage cost determination. Finally, we indicated several ways in which computers can be used to help management establish control over the storing, issuing, and transfer of items in inventory.

KEY TERMS IN THIS CHAPTER

Extending a requisition
Food and beverage transfers

Interunit transfers
Intraunit transfers
Requisition
Rotation of stock
Unacceptable costs
Unplanned costs

QUESTIONS AND PROBLEMS

1. What are some of the possible problems implicit in allowing the chef, receiving clerk, or dining room manager to have keys to the storeroom?

2. Even with restricted access to storeroom keys, it is sometimes desirable to change locks. Under what specific conditions would you as a food controller advise a manager to change locks?

3. Explain how excessive food costs may be reduced by properly rotating stock.

4. List and explain the disadvantages of locating a storage area at some distance from the receiving and preparation areas. Are there any advantages?

5. If a new storeroom clerk discovers an item on the shelves still in good condition, but six months old, what, if anything, should be done about it? Why?

6. Referring to the price list provided in Figure 6.4, calculate the total value of each of the requisitions in Figures 6.5 through 6.8.

7. The Somerset Restaurant Company owns and operates three small units in one community. Gross food sales and food costs as recorded on the books of each unit are as follows:

	Unit A	Unit B	Unit C
Sales	$155,400	$98,300	$228,000
Food cost	80,808	30,473	77,520

The above figures do not include the values of food transferred from Unit A to the other two units. These are all baked goods used in the chain, which are produced in one bake shop located in Unit A. During the period, transfers from Unit A to the other two units totaled $20,000, of which $8,000 was sent to Unit B and the remainder to Unit C.

Item	Purchase Unit	Unit Price
Applesauce	#10 can	$2.10
Beets, sliced	#10 can	1.62
Carrots, diced	#10 can	2.63
Clams, minced	#10 can	4.29
Cocktail sauce	gallon	5.75
Coffee	pound	1.15
Corn, whole kernel	#10 can	2.13
Cranberry sauce	#10 can	1.89
Flour, all purpose	pound	.23
Fruit cocktail	#10 can	2.05
Garlic powder	pound	3.48
Ketchup	12 oz.	.48
Linguine, #18	pound	.32
Mushrooms, whole	#10 can	3.21
Mustard	8 oz.	.25
Olive Oil	gallon	3.72
Peaches, halves	#10 can	2.45
Pepper, black	pound	2.54
Pepper, white	pound	2.98
Pineapple, crushed	#10 can	1.89
Rice	pound	.18
Salt	pound	.10
Sauerkraut	#10 can	2.23
Sugar, granulated	pound	.39
Tomato puree	#10 can	1.98
Tomato, whole peeled	#10 can	1.49
Vinegar	gallon	2.58

FIGURE 6.4

    a. Calculate food cost percents before transfers are taken into account.

    b. Adjust food cost figures by the amounts of the transfers to determine more accurate food costs.

    c. Calculate food cost percents based on the costs determined in (b).

8. Food cost percent is often one of the elements used to judge a manager's ability to control food costs. Explain how failure to take the value of transferred foods into account before calculating food cost percents can affect the performance ratings of managers who send food items to other units and of managers who receive food from other units.

9. Lunch Inn is a small chain that operates four units in one city. Each

a. July 6

Quantity	Item	Unit Price	Extension
24—8 oz.	Mustard		
24—12 oz.	Ketchup		
20 lb.	Salt		
2 lb.	Black pepper		
5 gal.	Olive Oil		
5 gal.	Vinegar		
10 lb.	Sugar		

TOTAL: _____

AUTHORIZED BY: H. Sneed, Maitre D'

FIGURE 6.5

b. July 6

Quantity	Item	Unit Price	Extension
12—#10	Tomatoes, whole		
12—#10	Tomatoe puree		
10 lb.	Coffee		
2 lb.	White pepper		
50 lb.	Salt		
50 lb.	Flour, all purpose		
2—#10	Sauerkraut		
3—#10	Carrots, diced		
1—#10	Fruit cocktail		

TOTAL: _____

AUTHORIZED BY: P. Noir, Sous Chef

FIGURE 6.6

c. July 7			
Quantity	*Item*	*Unit Price*	*Extension*
3—#10	Corn, whole kernel		
6—#10	Beets, sliced		
3—#10	Peaches, halves		
2—#10	Applesauce		
25 lb.	Rice		
3—#10	Cranberry sauce		
1 gal.	Cocktail sauce		
2—#10	Mushrooms, whole		
AUTHORIZED BY: G. Chambertin, Chef		TOTAL: _____	

FIGURE 6.7

unit purchases for its own needs and produces for its own sales on premises. Each produces its own rolls, cakes, and pies. However, when one unit underproduces, the manager is encouraged to secure needed quantities from another unit in the chain before purchasing from the outside. One item, apple pie, costs $1.35 to produce in-house and is available outside for $2.75 from nearby bakeries. What would be an appropriate transfer price for apple pies sent from one

d. July 8			
Quantity	*Item*	*Unit Price*	*Extension*
2—#10	Clams, minced		
5 lb.	Linguine #18		
1 lb.	Garlic powder		
6—#10	Pineapple, crushed		
AUTHORIZED BY: P. Chardonnay, Relief Chef		TOTAL: _____	

FIGURE 6.8

unit to another? What effect would this transfer price have on the volume of transfers between units?

10. Why should food not be stored on the floor at any time? What may happen to food stored this way?

11. Explain how computers can be used in each of the following areas.
    a. Storing control.
    b. Issuing control.
    c. Control of transfers.

12. Define each of the following terms:
    Extending a requisition
    Food and beverage transfers
    Interunit transfers
    Intraunit transfers
    Requisition
    Rotation of stock
    Unacceptable costs
    Unplanned costs

FOR COMPUTER USERS

13. Create a simple spreadsheet to be used in place of the requisition illustrated in Figure 6.2.

14. Use the model spreadsheet developed in Question 13 to solve Question 6.

7

Food Production Control I: Portions

After reading and studying this chapter, you should be able to:
1. Explain the importance of standard portion sizes, standard recipes, and standard portion costs to foodservice operations.
2. Identify four methods for determining standard portion costs, and describe the type of food product for which each is used.
3. Calculate standard portion costs using each of the four methods.
4. Use cost factors derived from butcher tests and cooking loss tests to recalculate portion costs as market prices change.
5. Use yield factors derived from butcher tests and cooking loss tests to determine correct purchase quantities.
6. Discuss the levels of knowledge and skill needed by food production employees, and explain the effect of these on the approaches management takes to training food production workers.
7. Describe several ways that computers are used in controlling production.
8. Define each of the Key Terms at the end of the chapter.

INTRODUCTION

In a previous chapter, it was pointed out that a foodservice operation must be viewed as a complex array of interrelated systems, each of which has special goals. The purchasing system, for example, is designed to ensure the availability of an adequate supply of the ingredients required for food production, each of a carefully selected quality and acquired at an optimum price.

The best means for ensuring that the purchasing system will achieve its aims—that purchasing events will conform to plans—was shown to be instituting the control process. This is true not only for the purchasing system, but also for the systems designed for receiving, storing, and issuing foods. As we will see, it is equally true for the production system.

Following the pattern established in earlier chapters, we will now describe the application of the four-step process of control to the production phase of foodservice operation.

ESTABLISHING STANDARDS AND STANDARD PROCEDURES

The standards and standard procedures for production control are designed to ensure that all portions of any given item conform to management's plans for that item and that, insofar as possible, each portion of any given item is identical to all other portions of the same item. Portions of a given menu item should be identical to one another in four respects:

1. Ingredients.
2. Proportions of ingredients.
3. Production method.
4. Quantity.

In order to reach this goal, it is necessary to develop the following standards and standard procedures for each menu item:

1. Standard portion size.
2. Standard recipe.
3. Standard portion cost.

Standard Portion Size

One of the most important standards that any foodservice operation must establish is the *standard portion size,* defined as the quantity of any item that is to be served each time that item is ordered. In effect, the standard portion size for any item is the fixed quantity of a given menu item that management intends to give each customer in return for the fixed selling price identified in the menu. It is possible and desirable for management to establish these fixed quantities in very clear terms. Every item on a menu can be quantified in one of three ways: by weight, by volume, or by count.

WEIGHT.   Weight, normally expressed in ounces (or grams, if the metric system is used), is frequently used to measure portion sizes for a number of menu items. Meat and fish are two of the most common. Steak, for example, is served in portion sizes of varying weights, typically ranging from eight to sixteen ounces, with the particular size for a specific restaurant being set by management. The same is true of roasts, often served in four- or five-ounce portions. Vegetable, particularly those purchased frozen, are commonly portioned by weight as well.

VOLUME.   Volume is used as the measure for portions of many menu items. Liquids (soups, juices, coffee, and milk, to name but a few) are commonly portioned by volume expressed as liquid ounces (milliliters in the metric system). A cup of soup may contain five ounces, while a bowl of soup might contain eight; a portion of orange juice may be three or four ounces; coffee may be served in a five-ounce portion; a glass of milk may contain eight or ten ounces.

COUNT.   Count is also used by foodservice operators to identify portion size. Such items as bacon, link sausage, eggs, chops, shrimp, and asparagus are all portioned by count. Some foods are purchased by count, and this plays a major role in establishing portion size. Shrimp, for example, are purchased by number per pound (16 to 20 per pound is a common purchase size) and then portioned by number per shrimp cocktail (four or five to one order). Potatoes and grapefruit are purchased by count per purchase unit, which clearly serves as a determinant of portion size. Potatoes for baking, for example, can be purchased in 50-pound boxes with a particular number per box specified. The higher the count per box (120 rather than 90), the smaller the size of the portion served to the customer. Count is important even with some dessert items, such as pie, with the portion size expressed in terms of the number of slices of equal size to be cut from one pie.

An interesting variation occurs with those items portioned by means of such implements as scoops or slotted spoons. A portion size is stipulated to be one or more such measures, but the measuring device selected holds a particular quantity of the item to be portioned. In one sense, the item in question is portioned by count, while in another, it is portioned by volume.

Many devices are available to help the foodservice operator standardize portion sizes. Among the more common are the scoops and slotted spoons mentioned above, but there are many others, including ladles, portion scales, and measuring cups. Even the number scale or dial on a slicing machine, designed to regulate the thickness of slices, can aid in standardizing portion size: For example, a manager may stipulate a particular number of slices of some item on a sandwich and then direct that the item be sliced with the dial at a particular setting.

Standard portion sizes help reduce customer discontent, which should be viewed as a major cause of lost customers and lost sales. If standard portion sizes are established and served, no customer can compare his portion unfavorably with that of another customer and feel dissatisfied or cheated. In addition, repeat customers will be more inclined to feel they receive fair measure for their money on each visit.

Standard portion sizes help eliminate animosity between kitchen help and dining room personnel, which can lead to delays in service and make personnel antagonistic to patrons. When portion sizes are left to the whims of the kitchen staff, arguments can and do develop over whether or not some cook is giving larger portions to one particular server to give to his customers, thus ensuring larger tips, which can be shared with the cook.

Standard portion sizes also help eliminate excessive costs. Cost for any given item varies with the quantity served, so the cost for any item is closely linked to the quantity served to the customer. It stands to reason that an eight-ounce portion of anything costs twice as much as a four-ounce portion of the same item. If four ounces cost $2.40, eight ounces will cost $4.80.

Except in rare instances, selling prices do not vary with portion sizes. Prices are typically printed in a menu and usually are not changed until the menu is reprinted. Even when not printed, prices cannot be changed from customer to customer. If the menu price of an item is listed at $8.95 on a certain day, then each and every portion of that item will be sold for $8.95. If one customer receives a four-ounce portion costing $2.40, and a second customer receives an eight-ounce portion of the same item costing $4.80, it is apparent that costs are not under control. To anyone experienced in foodservice, it is equally apparent that there will be many dissatisfied customers and servers.

Serving portions of varying sizes can have a number of unpleasant consequences. Customers might complain, never return, or both. Servers argue with one another and with the customer, and some may quit. From a food controller's point of view, perhaps the most important undesirable consequence is that costs are not under control and excessive costs develop. In addition, under such conditions, contribution margins vary on sales of the same item. Using the example cited above, contribution margin is $6.55 on the sale to the first customer, and $4.15 on the sale to the second. As we shall see in a later chapter, permitting varying portion sizes, varying costs, and varying con-

Seafood Newburg (10 4-oz. portions)

1 lb. lobster meat	1 cup butter
1/2 lb. shrimps, raw, out of shell	salt and pepper to taste
1/2 lb. scallops	1 T. paprika
1/2 lb. filet of sole	1 cup sherry wine
1 cup heavy cream	6 egg yolks
3 cups cream sauce	extra sherry wine
	10 slices of toast

a. Sauté all seafood in the melted butter well.
b. Add a little sherry and simmer until wine is absorbed.
c. Add paprika and cream sauce; combine well and simmer for a while.
d. Beat egg yolks and cream and add slowly to pan; combine well.
e. Check for seasoning; pour into serving dishes and add toast points and sherry.

FIGURE 7.1 *Standard Recipe*

tribution margins makes it impossible to determine the relative profitability of one menu item over another.

Once standard portion sizes have been established for menu items, it is obviously important to see that each person producing portions of a given item knows the correct portion size for the item. Methods for accomplishing this vary. One effective way is to post charts conspicuously for ready reference at work stations or on kitchen walls. This approach is particularly effective in large establishments with high rates of employee turnover.

Standard Recipes

Another important production standard is the recipe. A **recipe** is a list of the ingredients and the quantities of those ingredients needed to produce a particular item, along with a procedure or method to follow. A **standard recipe** is the recipe that has been designated the correct one to use in a given establishment.

Standard recipes help to ensure that the quality of any item will be the same each time the item is produced. They also help to establish consistency of taste, appearance, and customer acceptance. Figure 7.1 provides an example of a standard recipe. If the same ingredients are used in the correct proportions and the same procedure is followed, the results should be nearly identical each time the standard recipe is used, even if different people are doing the work. In addition, returning customers will be more likely to receive items of identical quality.

Some people have the mistaken impression that standard recipes are those developed for use in schools, hospitals, and similar public institutions and that they use ingredients of poor quality and yield menu items of even lower quality. Such impressions are absolutely false. The term merely means a recipe that will produce an item of acceptable quality for a particular operation. Any recipe can be adopted as a standard recipe. Sometimes they are taken from cookbooks or magazines. Sometime they are developed by the chef in a given restaurant, then tested and modified until they result in the production of an acceptable product. At that point, the recipe becomes the standard—the recipe that will be used each time the product is to be made.

In many operations, these standard recipes are written or printed on cards intended to be used by kitchen workers. They are made readily available to any workers responsible for producing menu items. If handwritten, they must be clear and legible so that the standard recipes can be easily followed. Sometimes, they are printed on special cards that are then laminated in plastic for durability. Computer printed recipes are easily stored in the program and can be easily changed and reprinted. In some establishments, these recipe cards include either drawings or photographs of the finished products to illustrate for the production staff exactly how the final product should look when served to the customer. Because they help to provide uniform appearance for all portions of a given menu item, illustrated recipe cards are particularly important in restaurants that have photographs in their menus.

Standard recipes are also very important to food control. Without standard recipes, costs cannot be controlled effectively. If a menu item is produced by different methods, with different ingredients, and in different proportions each time it is made, costs will be different each time any given quantity is produced. Once standard recipes and standard portion sizes are established and steps are taken to ensure that personnel follow the standard preparation and portioning procedures, standard costs for portions can be developed.

Standard Portion Cost

A standard portion cost can be calculated for every item on every menu, provided that the ingredients, proportions, production method, and portion size have been standardized as discussed above. In general, calculating a standard portion cost merely requires that one determine the cost of each ingredient used to produce a quantity of a given menu item, add the costs of the individual ingredients to arrive at a total, and then divide the total by the number of portions produced. However, there are several techniques for doing this, each of which will be described in detail below.

Before we explain the several different ways of determining portion costs, it is very important for the student to understand that the portion costs determined by these techniques will be only calculated portion or planned portion costs. These indicate what portion costs should be. Real portion costs may be quite different. There are many possible reasons for this. For example, if the employee making shrimp cocktails gives customers seven shrimp rather than five (the number established by management as the standard), the real portion cost will be greater than the calculated or planned cost. On the other hand if the employee gives customers three, the real portion cost will be less than planned. Real portion costs for these shrimp cocktails may be either higher or lower than planned, depending on whether customers have been given too many or too few shrimp.

Real portion costs will also be different from planned costs if employees fail to use portion scales, use improper portioning devices, fail to follow standard recipes, or purchase ingredients other than those stipulated by standard recipes. If the seafood Newburg recipe illustrated in Figure 7.1 were prepared with pollack instead of lobster, it is quite clear that real portion costs would be lower than planned.

Calculated, or planned, portion costs are best known by the term **standard portion cost.** Standard portion cost is defined as the dollar amount that a standard portion should cost, given the standards and standard procedures for its production. The standard portion cost for a given menu item can be viewed as a budget for the production of one portion of that item.

There are several reasons for determining standard portion costs. The most obvious is that one should have a reasonably clear idea of the cost of a menu item before establishing a menu sales price for the item. For control purposes, there are additional reasons, including making judgments in the future about how closely real or actual costs match standard costs, as well as the extent to which operating efficiency can be improved. These topics will be discussed in later chapters.

Calculating Standard Portion Costs

There are several methods for calculating standard portion costs:

1. Formula.
2. Recipe detail and cost card.
3. Butcher test.
4. Cooking loss test.

Owners, managers, chefs, and others with responsible positions in foodservice should be familiar with and able to use all of these methods, each of which is discussed below.

FORMULA.   For many (perhaps even for a majority) of the menu items prepared in foodservice establishments, determining standard portion cost can be very simple. For a large number, one may determine portion cost by means of the formula:

$$\text{Standard portion cost} = \frac{\text{Purchase price per unit}}{\text{Number of portions per unit}}$$

For example, consider an establishment serving eggs on the breakfast menu, with two eggs as the standard portion. One could determine the standard cost of the portion by dividing the cost of a 30-dozen case of eggs—say, $27—by the number of two-egg portions it contained (180) to find standard portion cost to be $.15.

$$\frac{\$27 \text{ Purchase price per case}}{180 \text{ Standard portions per case}} = \$.15$$

This simple formula could also be used to find the standard cost of each of the additional items served in a typical standard breakfast, including the juice, bacon, toast, butter, and coffee. The sum of the standard costs of the individual items would thus be the standard cost of the whole breakfast, possibly offered in some particular restaurant as Breakfast Special #3, at a $4.95 menu price.

In many restaurants today, large numbers of menu items are purchased already portioned by vendors. Determining the cost of one portion of any of these items is very simple: One divides the purchase price by the number of portions. Frankfurters purchased 12 to the pound for $2.40 cost $.20 each. Frozen heat-and-serve entrees are often purchased in individual units, in which case the purchase price is the portion cost. Many frozen preportioned foods come packed in cartons marked to show the exact number of portions in the carton. In most fast-food restaurants, portion costs for the majority of menu items can be determined by means of this simple formula.

So determining the portion cost of a large number of menu items may be done rather easily, merely by applying a very basic formula. However, not all foods may be so simply portioned after purchase, and other techniques must be developed to determine the standard portion costs of more complex items, such as those prepared from standard recipes.

RECIPE DETAIL AND COST CARD.   For menu items produced from standard recipes, it is possible to determine the standard cost of one portion by using a form known as a **recipe detail and cost card.** A sample of that form is provided in Figure 7.2.

A standard recipe yields a predetermined number of standard portions.

	Recipe Detail and Cost Card				

Recipe Detail and Cost Card

ITEM: <u>Seafood Newburg</u>   MENU: <u>Dinner</u>

S.P.   <u>$8.50</u>
Cost   <u>$2.48</u>
F.C.% <u>29.2%</u>

Yield: 10 portions   Portion Size: 4 oz of Seafood, + sauce   Date 6/22/XXXX

Ingredients	Quantity	Unit	Cost	Ext.	Procedure
lobster meat	1 lb.	lb.	11.25	11.25	Sauté all seafood well in melted
shrimps	1/2 lb.	lb.	7.50	3.75	butter. Add sherry and simmer
scallops	1/2 lb.		6.00	3.00	until wine is absorbed. Add
filet of sole	1/2 lb.	lb.	4.50	2.25	paprika and cream sauce, then
heavy cream	1 cup	qt.	2.40	.60	combine and simmer. Beat egg
cream sauce	3 cups	—		.75	yolks and cream, add slowly to
butter	1 cup	lb.	2.00	1.00	pan, and combine well. Check for
salt and pepper				.05	seasoning, pour into serving
paprika	1 T			.10	dishes, and add sherry. Add
sherry wine	8 oz.	750 ml	3.20	1.01	toast points.
egg yolks	6 ea.			.42	
sherry wine	1 oz.			.13	
toast	10 slices			.50	
Total				24.81	

FIGURE 7.2   *Recipe Detail and Cost Card*

Thus, it is possible to determine the standard cost of one portion by dividing the number of portions produced into the total cost of preparing the recipe. To find the total cost, one lists each ingredient and quantity from the standard recipe on the recipe detail and cost card and then multiplies the quantity of each ingredient by the unit cost for that ingredient. In the example given, the second ingredient is one-half pound of shrimp. If one pound costs $7.50, then one-half pound costs $3.75; that figure is entered in the column on the right headed "Ext.," the abbreviation for extension.

Determining the cost of an ingredient can sometimes be rather complex. If, for example, a recipe called for three diced onions, it would be necessary to determine the number of average-size onions in a sack and then determine the price of one onion by dividing the total number into the price of the sack of onions. Multiplying the price of one onion by three gives the price for the onions in the standard recipe. If chicken stock were an ingredient, it would be necessary to refer to a separate recipe detail and cost card, to determine the cost of one measure of stock prepared according to that standard recipe.

For inexpensive ingredients used in small quantities, such as "a pinch of salt," it is not worthwhile to calculate the actual value. For such ingredients, the figure entered is some token amount, usually more than enough to cover the cost.

When fresh meat, poultry, or fish is used, it is sometimes necessary first to follow certain procedures involving butcher tests, cooking loss tests, or both of these, to determine ingredient costs. Butcher tests and cooking tests will be discussed later in this chapter.

Once the cost of each ingredient has been established, the total cost of preparing the recipe is determined by adding the costs of the individual ingredients. This total, divided by the number of portions produced (called the **yield**), gives the cost of one standard portion. As long as ingredients of standard quality are purchased as specified and at relatively stable market prices, this should be the cost of producing one standard portion, provided there is no waste. Measuring waste and other inefficiency in terms of the dollars involved will be covered in later chapters.

It must be recognized that standard costs of standard portions must be recalculated as market prices of the ingredients change. The frequency of the recalculations will depend largely on conditions in the market, as well as the availability of personnel to do the calculating. If market conditions and prices remain fairly constant, it should not be necessary to recalculate standard portion costs more frequently than every three or four months.

For some items (steaks portioned in house from wholesale cuts of beef, or portions of roast lamb, for example), neither the basic formula nor the recipe detail and cost card is useful for determining standard portion cost. For these items and for many like them, portion costs cannot be determined until after some processing has taken place. The processing may be trimming, butchering, cooking, or some combination of these. During this processing, fat, bone, and other inedible or unnecessary parts will be removed. In some cases, this is accomplished by cutting them away. In others (roasts, for example), fat is removed by melting during the cooking process.

Any such processing results in weight loss: the quantity available for portion determination weighs less than the quantity originally purchased. It should be apparent, then, that the true quantity available for portioning is not known until after the processing has been completed. The item to be divided into portions cannot be weighed to determine the quantity available for this step until after processing.

There are two special techniques used to determine standard portion costs for those items requiring the kinds of processing described above. They are known as **butcher test** and **cooking loss test,** each of which is discussed in detail below. In general, the butcher test is used to determine standard portion costs for those items portioned *before* cooking, while the cooking loss test is used for those items to be divided into portions *after* cooking. In some instances, both tests may be required to determine standard portion costs.

BUTCHER TEST.   When meat, fish, and poultry are purchased as wholesale cuts, the purchaser pays the same price for each and every pound of the item purchased, even though, after butchering, the resulting parts may have entirely different values. If, for example, a particular cut of beef is approximately half fat and half usable meat, the two parts clearly have different uses and different values, although they were purchased at the same price per pound because both were part of one wholesale cut. Among other purposes, the butcher test is designed to establish a rational value for the primary part of the wholesale piece.

A butcher test is usually performed under the supervision of a manager, chef, or food controller, who would ask a butcher to assist in testing a particular item. The butcher would use his special skills to break down the item into its respective parts, keeping the parts separate so that they could be weighed. As the butcher prepares to begin, the other individual records some basic information about the item being tested at the top of the butcher test card (Fig. 7.3).

Figure 7.3 indicates the results of a butcher test performed on a whole beef tenderloin, U.S. Choice, weighing 9 pounds 0 ounces, purchased at $6.11 per pound from the XYZ Meat Company on March 21st. The purchase price for the piece was $54.99.

As the butcher works, he keeps the parts separated so that their individual weights may be determined after the work is completed. The terms identifying the parts are recorded in the column at the left, marked "Breakdown," and the weights of the parts go into the next column to the right. Ideally, the total weight of the individual parts equals the total original weight. However, some small measure of weight is usually lost during the butchering, and it is common to find an entry in the "Breakdown" and "Weight" columns for "Loss in Cutting."

In Figure 7.3, the entries made in the "Breakdown" column are "Fat," "Loss in Cutting," and "Usable Meat." The weights for each have been written in the "Weight" column: 4 pounds 8 ounces for "Fat," and 4 pounds 4 ounces for "Usable meat." The weight for "Loss in Cutting," 4 ounces, is determined by adding the weights for the two known parts and then subtracting that total from the purchased weight.

ITEM Beef Tenderloin
PIECES One
TOTAL COST $ 54.99

Butcher Test Card
GRADE U.S. Choice
WEIGHING 9 LBS. 0 OZ.
AT $ 6.11 Per LB.

DATE 3/21/XXXX
AVERAGE WEIGHT —
SUPPLIER XYZ Meat Co.

| Breakdown | No. | Weight | | Ratio to Total Weight | Value Per Lb. | Total Value | Cost of Each Usable | | Portion | | Cost Factor Per | |
		Lb.	Oz.				Lb.	Oz.	Size	Cost	Lb.	Portion
Fat		4	8	50.0%	.13	.59						
Loss in Cutting			4	2.8%	-0-	-0-						
Usable Meat		4	4	47.2%		54.40	12.80	.80	8 oz.	6.40	2.0949	1.0475
Total		9	0	100.0%		54.99						

FIGURE 7.3 Butcher Test Card

158

Fat	4 lbs. 8 oz.
− Usable meat	4 lbs. 4 oz.
= Total	8 lbs. 12 oz.

Purchased weight	9 lbs. 0 oz.
− Total of parts	8 lbs. 12 oz.
= Loss in cutting	0 lbs. 4 oz.

The next column, labeled "Ratio to Total Weight," indicates the percentage of each part in relation to the whole. The ratio of each weight to the whole is calculated by following the formula:

$$\frac{\text{Weight of part}}{\text{Weight of whole}} = \text{Ratio to total weight}$$

$$\frac{4 \text{ lbs. 8 oz. (4.5 lbs.)}}{9 \text{ lbs. 0 oz. (9.0 lbs.)}} = .5 \text{ or } 50.0\% \text{ fat}$$

$$\frac{0 \text{ lbs. 4 oz. (0.25 lbs.)}}{9 \text{ lbs. 0 oz. (9.0) lbs.}} = .02777 = .028, \text{ or } 2.8\% \text{ Loss}$$

$$\frac{4 \text{ lbs. 4 oz. (4.25 lbs.)}}{9 \text{ lbs. 0 oz. (9.0) lbs.}} = .47222 = .472, \text{ or } 47.2\% \text{ Usable meat}$$

These ratios can be of particular interest to those attempting to compare similar cuts of meat supplied by two or more dealers. Performing butcher tests on pieces supplied by the dealers and then comparing ratios of usable parts may help determine which dealer offers better value. In addition, these ratios may be used to compare meats of different qualities to determine which is more economical to serve. This ratio is also known as a **yield percentage,** or a **yield factor.** Specific calculations using the yield percentage or yield factor will be discussed later in the chapter.

The "Value Per Lb." column appears mysterious, but is possibly the simplest to complete. The values per pound for all parts except the principal part—the need for which occasioned the original purchase—are merely the current prices that each of the parts would cost if purchased separately in the open market. In most instances, restaurants and other foodservice operations obtain these figures from one of their regular suppliers. The use of these market prices for the various parts is based on the fact that one would pay this price to buy each of the parts separately. Theoretically, the value recorded for each part thus represents a reasonable market value. No value per pound for the principal part is entered. That value will be derived after the total values for all other parts have been calculated and recorded in the next column, marked "Total Value."

The total value for each of the secondary parts is obtained by multiplying the value per pound by the weight. The total value of the primary part is determined by:

1. Adding the total values of the secondary parts, and
2. Subtracting that figure from the total cost indicated at the top of the form.

In Figure 7.3, the following calculations have been performed:

a. 4.5 lbs. of fat × $.13 per lb. = $.585 = $.59

b.   Total cost $54.99
    − Value of other parts   .59
    = Value of primary part (usable meat) $54.40

Thus, the sum of all total values will equal the total original cost.

With both the weight and total value of the principle part known, the cost of each usable pound and ounce—the next two columns to the right—can be determined by some simple division:

$$\frac{\text{Total value of usable meat}}{\text{Weight of Usable Meat}} = \text{Cost per usable lb.}$$

$$\frac{\$54.40}{4.25 \text{ lbs.}} = \$12.80 \text{ (Cost per usable lb.)}$$

$$\frac{\text{Cost per usable lb.}}{16 \text{ oz. per lb.}} = \text{Cost per usable oz.}$$

$$\frac{\$12.80}{16} = \$.80 \text{ (Cost per usable oz.)}$$

The standard portion size, typically stated in ounces, is entered in the next column, "Portion Size." This is obviously a quantity standard established by management. The portion cost is calculated by multiplying the portion size in ounces by the cost of each usable ounce:

Portion size × Cost per usable oz. = Portion cost
8 oz.   × $.80   = $6.40

The remaining two columns are used for recording the cost factors per pound and per portion, both of which will require explanation.

Cost Factors.   The market prices of meat, fish, and poultry change almost daily. As market prices change, the foodservice operator's usable pound costs and portion costs change as well. Therefore, it is good to have some simple means for calculating both usable pound costs and portion costs whenever market prices change, without having to complete a new butcher test form each time. The cost factors serve this purpose and are calculated in the following manner:

$$\frac{\text{Cost per usable lb.}}{\text{Purchase price per lb.}} = \text{Cost factor per lb.}$$

$$\frac{\$12.80}{\$\ 6.11} = 2.0949$$

$$\frac{\text{Portion cost}}{\text{Purchase price per lb.}} = \text{Cost factor per portion}$$

$$\frac{\$6.40}{\$6.11} = 1.0475$$

These factors are extremely useful. Suppose one were to learn that the dealer price per pound for beef tenderloin was expected to increase from the present $6.11 to $6.37. It is clear that this price increase would increase portion cost, but those in foodservice management must know more than this obvious truth: They must know the standard portion cost at the new, higher dealer price. One could, of course, proceed to complete a new set of butcher test calculations. But while that could be done, it would take some time. A simpler, faster method is to use the cost factors and the formulas provided below.

Cost factor per lb. $\times$ New dealer price per lb.
= Cost of a usable lb. at New dealer price

$$2.0949 \times \$\ 6.37 = \$13.\ 3445 = \$13.34$$

Cost factor per portion $\times$ New dealer price per lb.
= Cost of a portion of same size at New dealer price

$$1.0475 \times \$6.37 = \$6.672575 = \$6.67$$

By this means, one can determine quite specifically that the $.26 increase in the dealer price per pound will lead to an increase of $.54 in the cost of a usable pound and $.27 in the portion cost. Moreover, one can make all these determinations much faster than one could complete all the calculations required on the butcher test form.

The portion cost factor has one very serious shortcoming: It can be used only if the size of the portion for which one is determining cost is identical to that of the portion used to establish the cost factor. If the cost factor is based on a six-ounce portion and one is attempting to determine the cost of a five-ounce portion at a new market price, the portion cost factor cannot be used. It would be necessary to use the cost factor per pound to determine the cost of a usable pound at the new market price, divide that by 16 ounces to determine the new cost of one ounce, and then multiply that ounce cost by the number of ounces in the portion—a cumbersome business.

In order to make it easier to determine costs using factors, we recommend the derived formula given below, which can be used to determine the cost of a portion of any given size at any given market price, provided that one has previously determined cost factor per pound for the item.

Cost factor per pound × Portion size (expressed as a decimal)
× Dealer price per lb. = Portion cost at dealer price specified

The decimal equivalent of a given number of ounces is determined as follows:

$$\frac{\text{Number of ounces}}{16 \text{ (ounces in a pound)}}$$

Therefore,

$$\frac{8 \text{ oz.}}{16 \text{ oz.}} = .5 \text{ lb.}$$

The following is an example of the use of the cost factor per pound calculated in the butcher test in Figure 8.3. This new formula may be used to find the cost of the eight-ounce portion at the $6.37 dealer price, as follows:

2.0949 × .5 (8 oz. as a decimal) × $6.37 = $6.6722565 = $6.67.

While one can find the cost of the eight-ounce portion using the portion cost factor alone, it cannot be used directly to determine the cost of a seven-ounce portion. The new formula:

Cost factor per pound × Portion size (expressed as a decimal)
× Dealer price per lb. = Portion cost at specified dealer price

can be so used:

2.0949 × .4375 (7 oz. as a decimal) × $6.37 = $5.8382241 = $5.84

In fact, for all practical purposes, this single formula can be used to replace both formulas illustrated previously in the chapter that use cost factors to determine cost of a usable pound at the new dealer price and cost of a portion at a new dealer price.

These formulas provide owners, managers, and chefs with the means for determining new food costs as market prices change. At the same time, they enable one to determine when changes in menu sales prices may be required to maintain relatively stable cost-to-sales ratios.

In order to ensure the accuracy of figures derived by this method, it is necessary to perform butcher tests regularly on reasonable numbers of pieces. The test on one piece alone is not reliable because the piece may not be typical, even though it was purchased according to specifications. It is better to have test results on a number of different pieces in order to arrive at averages.

Establishments that do butcher tests find several other important uses for the results.

1. Butcher tests on pieces purchased according to specifications from two or more dealers give results that are useful in determining which dealer to buy from.
2. Butcher tests conducted periodically enable the manager to appraise the extent to which any one dealer is adhering to specifications.
3. Menu prices can be more intelligently planned because exact costs are known.

Those with experience in foodservice will recognize that comparatively few establishments do regular butcher testing today. That was not the case in years past, however. A primary reason for the change has been the availability from vendors of preportioned entrees: steaks, chops, and other items portioned before cooking. However, the butcher test is still extremely valuable to the manager who wants to compare the cost of a preportioned item purchased from a vendor with the cost of an identical item portioned in the restaurant. Typically, one would expect to find standard portion cost lower for the item portioned in the restaurant, but this figure would take into account only food cost for the item, not labor cost. On the other hand, the portion cost for the preportioned item purchased from a vendor would include the vendor's labor cost. Therefore, to make a valid comparison, management would have to determine labor cost per portion for items portioned in the restaurant.

Although the butcher test makes it possible for foodservice operators to determine portion costs for entree items portioned before cooking (steaks, chops, and filets), it is of no value for determining portion costs for one large group of menu items—those that cannot be portioned until after cooking. Consequently, portion costs for these items (typically roasts of beef, pork, lamb, and other meats) cannot be determined until after the cooking process is complete. A different procedure, known as the cooking loss test, is required.

COOKING LOSS TEST.   The primary purpose for the cooking loss test is the same as that for the butcher test: determining standard portion cost. The cooking loss test is used for those items that cannot be portioned until after cooking is complete. With these items, one must take into account the weight loss that occurs during cooking. Therefore, one cannot determine the quantity remaining to be portioned until cooking is completed and portionable weight can be determined. Cooking loss varies with cooking time and temperature, and it must be taken into account in determining standard portion costs. More-over, while the availability of preportioned meats has rendered the butcher test less common in recent years, the cooking loss test is as important and useful as ever.

Before we begin a detailed explanation of the cooking loss test, it will be useful to point out that the butcher test form and the cooking loss form have many similarities (see Fig. 7.4). A glance at the form shows that all the column headings are the same as those on the butcher test form. The major difference between the forms lies in the "Breakdown" column: on the butcher test form (Fig. 7.3), terms are written in this column as the butcher test progresses; on the cooking loss test form, they are preprinted ("Original Weight," "Trimmed Weight," and so on). It will be important, then, to learn the meanings of these terms if one is to understand the cooking loss test.

The cooking loss test is perhaps best explained by illustration. Referring to Figure 7.4, one will see a completed set of test results for one leg of lamb. As purchased, the lamb weighed 8 pounds 8 ounces. At a dealer price per pound of $6.38, the purchase price for the leg was $54.23. All this information is recorded on the first line of test form, "Original Weight." The leg of lamb required some butchering before it could be cooked. Presumably, it was given to a butcher who cut away unnecessary parts, primarily fat and bone, to pre-pare the lamb for roasting. After butchering, the leg was found to weigh 6 pounds 8 ounces. This weight is recorded on the line marked "Trimmed Weight."

Next, "Trimmed Weight" (6 lbs. 8 oz.) is subtracted from "Original Weight" (8 lbs. 8 oz.), and the difference (2 lbs. 0 oz.) is recorded on the line marked "Loss in Trimming." "Original Weight," then, represents the piece as purchased; "Trimmed Weight" represents the piece after in-house butchering, if any; "Loss in Trimming" represents the difference between the two.

At this point, the trimmed leg of lamb ("Trimmed Weight") is put into an oven to cook. After cooking for one hour and ten minutes at 385 degrees, it is removed from the oven and weighed. The weight, 5 pounds 8 ounces, is recorded on the line marked "Cooked Weight." Next, "Cooked Weight" (5 lbs. 8 oz.) is subtracted from "Trimmed Weight" (6 lbs. 8 oz.) to determine the entry for the following line, "Loss in Cooking"—1 pound 0 ounces.

Because the cooked piece includes cooked bone and cooked fat, all

COOKED __One__   HOURS __Ten__   Cooking Loss   DEGREES
                  HOURS ____   MINUTES AT __385__   DEGREES
                                   MINUTES AT ____

Breakdown	No.	Weight Lb.	Weight Oz.	Ratio to Total Weight	Value Per Lb.	Total Value	Cost of Each Usable Lb.	Cost of Each Usable Oz.	Portion Size	Portion Cost	Cost Factor Per Lb.	Cost Factor Per Portion
Original Weight		8	8	100.0%	$6.38	$54.23						
Trimmed Weight		6	8	76.5%		$54.23						
Loss in Trimming		2	0	23.5%		-0-						
Cooked Weight		5	8	64.7%		$54.23						
Loss in Cooking		1	0	11.8%		-0-						
Bones and Trim		1	8	17.6%		-0-						
Salable Weight		4	0	47.1%		$54.23	$13.58	$.847	4 oz.	$3.39	2.1285	.5313

Remarks:

ITEM: Leg of Lamb

PORTION SIZE: 4 oz.   PORTION COST FACTOR: .5266

FIGURE 7.4 *Cooking Loss Test Card*

5 pounds 8 ounces cannot be divided into portions. Usable meat must be removed from the bone and weighed to determine the quantity available for portions. The weight of the portionable meat is recorded on the line marked "Salable Weight"—4 pounds 0 ounces, in this instance. This is subtracted from the "Cooked Weight" (5 lbs. 8 oz.) to determine the amount of waste, noted on the line marked "Bones and Trim"—1 pound 8 ounces.

Having completed the entries in the "Weight" column, one can proceed to fill in the "Ratio to Total Weight" column. The percentage recorded on each line is the ratio of the weight of that part to the original weight of the piece as purchased. These ratios are calculated in exactly the manner described above in the discussion of the butcher test.

This is a most important step. These ratios may be used productively by managers and chefs to make various comparisons. For example, cooked weight ratios calculated for several pieces of meat may be compared to determine which of several available grades would yield the maximum quantity of salable meat of a desired quality. Similarly, cooked weight ratios may be used to compare the results of cooking several pieces at different temperatures or for different lengths of time, to determine the optimum cooking times and temperatures. Once optimum cooking times and temperature for a given type of roast has been determined, these may be established as the standards.

The "Value Per Lb." column is used only once in cooking loss tests. The only value recorded is that on the first line, "Original Weight." This is actually the dealer price per pound for the original piece as purchased.

The entries in the "Total Value" column on cooking loss test cards are conceptually different from those on butcher test cards. Note that the total value of the original purchase was $54.23 and that there was no change in the total value of the piece from time of purchase to time of portioning. The weight changed, of course, decreasing from the original, 8-pound 8-ounce purchase, to the raw, trimmed, 6-pound 8-ounce roast, to the cooked, 5-pound 8-ounce roast, to the 4 pounds of portionable meat, but the total value did not change. With each step in processing, the decreased weight assumes a greater value per pound, so that the costs of all nonportionable pounds are transferred to the salable weight. This clearly underscores the need for the cooking loss test. It is impossible to determine portion costs until cooking loss has been calculated and its value taken into account. Once the weight and value of the salable meat are recorded and the portion size is entered from the restaurant's chart or list of standard portion sizes, the remaining calculations are performed in the same manner as in the butcher test.

The foregoing discussion has been based on a piece of meat not requiring extensive butchering before cooking. However, in many instances, meats require considerable butchering (for example, in cases where the parts trimmed away have usefulness and value to the establishment). In these instances, the original and trimmed weights on the cooking loss test will appear as very different figures. This is because a butcher test has first been performed to determine weights and assign values to the secondary usable parts. The weight and value of the primary usable part become the weight and value entered on the cooking loss test as trimmed weight. The original weight and value remain that of the piece of meat as purchased.

Depending on the nature of the menu item, using one or more of the techniques described above will enable one to determine with reasonable accuracy the standard cost of one portion of any item on a menu. Once the standard cost of one portion is known, it is possible to set or adjust the menu sales price.

Using Yield Percentages

The **yield percentage** (or **yield factor**) is defined as the percent of a whole purchase unit of meat, poultry, or fish that is available for portioning after any required in-house processing has been completed. This percentage is calculated by dividing the portionable weight by the original weight of the purchase unit before processing. These calculations are included in the butcher test and cooking loss test calculations. On the butcher test, the yield percentage is found in the "Ratio to Total Weight" column on the line reserved for the usable meat. For example, in Figure 8.3, the "Ratio to Total Weight" for the usable meat is 47.2 percent. On the cooking loss test, the yield percentage is found in the "Ratio to Total Weight" column on the line labeled "Salable Weight." On the cooking loss test illustrated in Figure 8.4, the "Ratio to Total Weight" for the "Salable Weight" is 47.1 percent. The similarity of these ratios is pure coincidence.

Once determined, yield percentage can be used in a number of quantity calculations. The general formula for these is:

$$\text{Quantity} = \frac{\text{Number of portions} \times \text{Portion size (as a decimal)}}{\text{Yield percentage}}$$

As with any formula, it is possible to solve for any one of the terms, provided the other three are known. Thus, given quantity, portion size, and yield factor, one could determine the number of standard portions that should be produced from the given quantity. Or, given quantity, number of portions, and yield factor, one could determine the portion size that should be served to feed a given number of people with a given quantity of meat. The following are three variations on the basic formula:

$$\text{Number of portions} = \frac{\text{Quantity} \times \text{Yield percentage}}{\text{Portion size}}$$

$$\text{Portion size} = \frac{\text{Quantity} \times \text{Yield percentage}}{\text{Number of portions}}$$

$$\text{Yield percentage} = \frac{\text{Number of portions} \times \text{Portion size}}{\text{Quantity}}$$

While there are many, very practical uses for the basic formula and its variations, one illustration will suffice. It is possible to use the basic formula to determine the quantity of a given item that must be purchased to serve portions of a given size to a particular number of people.

Suppose that a steward wanted to buy the proper quantity of lamb to provide four-ounce portions of roast lamb to 32 people and that he had previously calculated the yield percentage given in the cooking loss test in Figure 7.4: 47.1 percent.

Using the formula provided above,

$$\text{Quantity} = \frac{\text{Number of portions} \times \text{Portion size (as a decimal)}}{\text{Yield percentage}}$$

the steward would calculate as follows:

$$\text{Quantity} = \frac{32 \text{ portions} \times .25 \text{ (4 ounces as a decimal)}}{.471 \text{ Yield percentage}}$$

Quantity = 16.985 lbs., rounded to 17 lbs.

To confirm the accuracy of the calculation, let us refer to the leg of lamb used for an example in the cooking loss test above, the calculations for which appear in Figure 7.4. Given similar legs of lamb, one can see that each leg would produce 16 portions because each portion weighs one-quarter of a pound and there are four pounds of usable meat. One can also see that if 32 portions were desired, one would need two legs of lamb, each yielding 16 portions. Two legs, each weighing 8 pounds, 18 ounces, or 17 pounds of raw lamb, would be sufficient. The minor discrepancy between this intuitive calculation and the mathematical calculation is due to the rounding of the yield percentage figure.

It is important to note that the above formula assumes that future purchases of lamb will provide the same yield as the tested leg. This means that the meat would contain the same relative amounts of bone, fat, and lean, and that it would be cooked at the same temperature for the same period of time so that shrinkage would be relatively the same as in the tested lamb. Calculations using yield percentages are only reliable if one is able to trust the accuracy of these assumptions in a given establishment.

TRAINING FOR PRODUCTION

Since we have established standards and standard procedures to control production, the next logical step, as illustrated in previous chapters, is to train staff members to follow the standards as they perform their jobs.

All job performance requires some combination of knowledge, skill, and experience. This is particularly true for food production jobs. The problems for the foodservice operator are, first, to determine the level of knowledge, skill, and experience required for the performance of a particular job and, second, to determine how much time and money can be spent to help employees acquire the necessary knowledge and skill on the job and, in the process, gain the experience.

A number of levels of knowledge and skill are needed in food production. At the lowest, an employee removes a preportioned item from a freezer, unwraps it if necessary, places it in a heating device, sets a timer, turns the unit on, and waits for an audible or visual signal to indicate that the item is ready to be served. This describes the work of substantial numbers of employees in the fast-food segment of the industry and of a good number of those employed in industrial and institutional foodservice. The knowledge and skill required are minimal and are easily learned in a job setting by most people. The experience required is also minimal.

At the highest levels of knowledge and skill, an employee may be expected to prepare a number of the classical grand sauces to accompany the exquisite dishes prepared and served in some of the world's finest hotels and restaurants. Extensive knowledge, high levels of skill, and some considerable experience are required to do this kind of work. At the extreme, a highly talented chef may be expected to create original recipes and present original dishes.

Between these extremes fall the majority of jobs in foodservice, each of which has a definable knowledge and skill quotient inherent in it. It is clearly the responsibility of an owner or manager to define this requirement for each job.

Having thus defined jobs in this special way, an owner or manager must then address the question of whether to institute comprehensive training for employees or to restrict hiring to those whose backgrounds include the knowledge, skill, and experience required for particular jobs. In general, managers tend to prefer selecting knowledgeable, highly skilled personnel for those positions requiring extensive knowledge and skill. One obvious effect of this approach is to keep training time and cost to a minimum.

For example, few managers would willingly attempt to train a newcomer to the industry as a pastry chef. Most would prefer to fill such a position with someone who has already acquired the proper knowledge and skill, such that training would consist largely of acquainting the newly hired employee with the equipment, recipes, portion sizes, and work routines of the particular establishment. On the other hand, managers often prefer to select inexperienced personnel for positions at the opposite end of the job spectrum. Innumerable examples of this can be found in fast-food operations. Managers who purposely hire the inexperienced must commit to spending the time and money necessary for training. Employees working at these lower levels can normally be hired at comparatively low wages, and managers often find that employee training can begin without having to break bad work habits or inappropriate work routines learned elsewhere. At the same time, many managers have found that hiring and training inexperienced workers is often the best means of ensuring that certain jobs will be done well, conforming to the standards established for the work. Sometimes inexperienced workers are the only ones available to take such jobs, and managers may have no choice but to hire and train them.

Regardless of the level of knowledge and skill that workers bring to their jobs, some amount of training is required for all production workers in food-service if the standards and standard procedures established to control production are to be met. If management has met its responsibility in establishing the necessary standards and standard procedures for production, employees must be made keenly aware of these standards. If portion sizes have been carefully set, employees must have instant access to the standard portion size for each menu item. It is normally insufficient simply to inform new employees of these standards; over time, employees tend to forget or distort the standards unless regular reinforcement is provided. An important aspect of training may be to make certain that each new production worker has access to a list of standard portion sizes, as part of a manual or as a wall chart for the kitchen, so that none need ever rely on memory alone to produce portions of the proper size. Failure to do this may result in the production of portions of varying sizes, with results as described early in the chapter.

A similar problem could develop if employees are not given adequate access to established standard recipes, leaving them little choice but to prepare menu items as they see fit, possibly by using their own recipes. At the minimum, the products prepared would be different from those defined by the standard recipes; their quality might be either better or worse than the standard products, and their costs would clearly be different from the established standard costs.

MONITORING PRODUCTION PERFORMANCE AND TAKING CORRECTIVE ACTION

Adherence to production standards can be monitored in a number of ways. Most commonly, the individual in charge of production—a chef or sous chef, in many restaurants—routinely observes production in progress, tasting as required, to be sure that resulting products conform to the planned products described by the standards. Sometimes managers monitor production—tasting various items, including finished products, weighing uncooked portions of some entree items, observing plated foods as they are about to be taken to the dining room, and so on.

In addition to these direct monitoring techniques, several indirect means are commonly used. Customers' reactions to products may indicate that one or more production standards are not being followed. If, for example, a customer complains about an item, the complaint should be investigated. If a number of guests complain about the same item during one meal, it is quite clear that something is seriously wrong with it. Sometimes it becomes necessary to stop serving the item for the duration of the meal.

Because many guests do not make formal complaints about products they find unacceptable, some managers make it a practice to observe plates being cleared from tables and sent to the dishwasher. If the customers are not eating a particular item, the cause may lie in improper production, and the manager who notices this is doing an excellent job of monitoring production performance.

If production performance does not adhere to the standards established, it is clearly important that some corrective action be taken. The first approach would normally be to bring the problem to the attention of the chef for investigation and correction. If the chef could not or did not correct the problem satisfactorily, additional action would be required, and the course of that action would depend on an assessment of the underlying problem.

COMPUTER APPLICATIONS

Production control is another area in which computer programs can play a very useful role. For those not interested in tailoring generic applications programs to their own particular purposes, there are increasing numbers of commercial programs designed specifically to accomplish many tasks related directly or indirectly to production control, including most of those suggested in this chapter.

Recipe costing is a common feature of these programs. Programmers have provided templates within many of these programs for users to input information—food ingredients and prices, for example—that are the basis for portion costs. When specific recipes are input, these programs use the ingredient and price information to determine and output recipe and portion costs automatically, at obviously great savings of time and labor over the manual methods of the past. While it is comparatively easy to make provision for cooking loss tests and even butcher tests in such programs, they are not as common as one might expect. This may stem from the fact that these tests are not as commonly used in industry as they could be.

Many computer programs designed to help food service managers control costs are advertised regularly in the trade journals catering to the foodservice industry, and can be seen at any of the various annual trade shows that have become so popular in recent years.

CHAPTER ESSENTIALS

In this chapter, we explained the application of the control process to the production phase of foodservice operations. We listed and discussed the standards and standard procedures required for control, including standardization of ingredients, proportions, production methods, and portion sizes. We described the importance of the standard recipe in maintaining standards and suggested a number of possible consequences of failing to maintain production standards. Having established basic production standards, we listed and explained in detail four methods for determining standard portion costs, including formula, recipe detail and cost card, butcher test, and cooking loss test. We described the procedures for calculating cost factor per pound, portion cost factor, and yield factor, and explained and illustrated their use in foodservice operations—for calculating portion costs as market prices change and for solving specific quantity problems faced by those who purchase food. We described management's need to determine the particular knowledge and skill levels required by employees in specific jobs and pointed out the common tendency of managers to provide extensive training for those whose jobs require the least knowledge and skill, while expecting those requiring the highest levels of knowledge and skills to have been trained before hiring. We explained several techniques used to monitor the performance of employees engaged in production and indicated the importance of the role that customers play in the process. We discussed the primary method used to take corrective action and suggested an alternative approach when that method is not successful. Finally, we indicated that growing numbers of computer programs can simplify the work associated with determining recipe and portion costs.

KEY TERMS IN THIS CHAPTER

Butcher test
Cooking loss test
Cost factor per pound
Portion cost factor
Recipe detail and cost card
Standard portion cost
Standard portion size
Standard recipe
Yield
Yield factor
Yield percentage

QUESTIONS AND PROBLEMS

1. In each of the following cases, determine selling price for one portion of a recipe yielding 30 portions, when the standard recipe cost and desired cost-to-sales ratio are as indicated below:

	Recipe cost	*Cost percent for one portion*
a.	$55.25	30.0%
b.	22.58	18.0%
c.	124.50	45.0%
d.	105.00	21.0%
e.	12.60	40.0%

2. Using the form illustrated in Figure 7.3, complete butcher test calculations on a beef tenderloin, U.S. Choice, from the information given below:
   Weight as purchased: 8 lbs. 8 oz.
   Dealer price: $4.19 per pound
   Portion size for filet mignon: 8 oz.
   Breakdown:
   Fat: 4 lbs. 12 oz.; Value per lb. $ 10
   Tidbits: 12 oz.; Value per lb. $2.49
   Filet mignon: 3 lbs. 0 oz.

3. Using cost factors from the butcher test in Question 2, determine:
   a. Cost of the eight-ounce portion if the dealer increases the price for beef tenderloin to $4.49 per pound.
   b. Cost of each usable pound at the $4.49 dealer price.
   c. Cost of a six-ounce portion at the $4.49 dealer price.

    d. The maximum number of ounces that can be served for a $5.55 portion cost after the dealer has raised the purchase price to $4.49 per pound.

4. Using the forms for butcher test and cooking loss test illustrated in Figures 7.3 and 7.4, complete butcher test and cooking loss test calculations for a rib of beef, U.S. Choice, weighing 38 lbs. 12 oz. and purchased from a dealer at $3.19 per pound.

BREAKDOWN:

Fat: 6 lbs. 8 oz.; Value per lb.: $ 10
Bones: 4 lbs. 4 oz.; Value per lb.: $.32
Short ribs: 3 lbs. 4 oz.; Value per lb.: $1.49
Chopped beef: 2 lbs. 8 oz.; Value per lb.: $1.59
Loss in cutting: 0 lbs. 4 oz.
Oven-ready rib: 22 lbs. 0 oz.
Cooked weight: 20 lbs. 4 oz.
Bones and trim: 1 lb. 4 oz.
Portion size for roast beef: 10 oz.

5. Records of cooking loss tests done on legs of lamb in the Hearthstone Restaurant provide the following factors for roast lamb:
Yield factor: .425
Pound cost factor: 2.1387

    a. Determine the number of pounds of uncooked oven-ready leg of lamb that must be purchased to produce 48 4-ounce portions of roast lamb.

    b. Determine the number of pounds of uncooked, oven-ready leg of lamb that must be purchased to produce 55 5-ounce portions of roast lamb.

    c. Determine the costs of the portions in Questions 5a and 5b if the dealer price per pound for leg of lamb is $3.19.

6. The information below, taken from records in the Circle Restaurant, provides the results of butcher tests on 10 legs of veal, U.S. Choice, purchased over the last several weeks from Middletown Meats, Inc. Veal legs are purchased to produce 5-ounce portions of veal cutlet. The restaurant paid $814.28 for the 10 legs, which weighed a total of 247 pounds 8 ounces as purchased:

BREAKDOWN:

Fat: 41 lbs. 8 oz.; Value per lb.: $.10
Bones: 56 lbs. 8 oz.; Value per lb.: $.38

Shanks: 19 lbs. 12 oz.; Value per lb.: $1.49
Trimmings: 47 lbs. 4 oz.; Value per lb.: $1.89
Loss in cutting: 2 lbs. 8 oz.
Veal cutlets: 80 lbs. 0 oz.

a. Given the information above, complete butcher test calculations to determine standard cost of the five-ounce portion, as well as yield factor, portion cost factor, and pound cost factor.

b. Find the cost of the standard five-ounce portion at each of the following dealer prices:
   1. $3.19 per pound.
   2. $3.39 per pound.
   3. $3.49 per pound.
   4. $3.89 per pound.

c. Find the cost of each of the following:
   1. A six-ounce portion, if dealer price is $3.19 per pound.
   2. A four-ounce portion, if dealer price is $3.59 per pound.
   3. A four-ounce portion, if dealer price is $3.69 per pound.

d. The owner of the Circle Restaurant wants portion cost for veal cutlet to be $2.65, regardless of variations in dealer price. Determine correct portion size if:
   1. Dealer price is $3.69 per pound.
   2. Dealer price is $3.03 per pound.

e. Develop a chart showing the costs of four-ounce, five-ounce, and six-ounce portions at dealer prices per pound of $3.00, $3.05, and so on in $.05 increments up to $4.00 per lb.

f. How many pounds of veal leg (as purchased) will be needed to prepare and serve five-ounce portions to 235 people?

g. Given the weight of the average leg of veal, as determined in the butcher test, how many legs should the steward order to prepare and serve five-ounce portions to 235 people?

h. Records show that the Circle Restaurant used 48 legs of veal last month. How many standard five-ounce portions should have been produced from these 48 legs?

i. The restaurant has a banquet for 500 people scheduled for tonight, and the manager has promised to serve veal cutlet as the entree. The steward neglected to order veal legs for this specific party, but there are 24 legs of veal in the house and veal cutlet is not on the regular dining room menu for tonight. Using these 24 legs of veal for the party, what size portion should be prepared so that all 500 people can be served?

7. The steward of Phil's Restaurant uses specifications to purchase

oven-ready legs of lamb, U.S. Choice. They are used to produce seven-ounce portions of roast lamb. Over a period of several weeks, records were kept of the original weights, cooked weights, and salable weights of 15 legs selected at random from the total number purchased. These records are summarized below:

Original weight (15 pieces): 135 lbs.

(Purchased @ $2.10 per lb. = $283.50)

Cooked weight: 120 lbs.

Salable weight: 75 lbs.

a. Using the data above, complete cooking loss test calculations for the 15 legs of lamb to determine yield factor, standard cost of the seven-ounce portion, portion cost factor, and pound cost factor.

b. Find the cost of the standard seven-ounce portion at each of the following dealer prices:
  1. $2.25 per pound.
  2. $2.49 per pound.
  3. $1.89 per pound.

c. Find the cost of each of the following:
  1. A six-ounce portion, if dealer price is $2.19 per pound.
  2. A five-ounce portion, if dealer price is $2.29 per pound.

d. Assume that dealer price increases to $2.25 per lb. and the manager of Phil's wants portion cost to be $1.65. What size portion should be served?

e. How many average-size legs of lamb should be purchased to serve six-ounce portions to 270 people?

f. Last month, this restaurant used 82 legs of lamb. How many standard seven-ounce portions should have been produced from these 82 legs?

g. If the standard portion size had been six ounces, how many portions could have been produced from the 82 legs of lamb used last month?

h. The restaurant has only 30 legs of lamb on hand today, and these must be used for a banquet function tonight for 350 people. What size portion should be served?

8. List and discuss three possible customer reactions to nonstandard portion sizes.

9. How can failure to follow standard recipes affect portion costs and quality of menu items?

10. Stella's Restaurant does not have standard cooking times and tem-

peratures for roast prime ribs of beef, one of the principal items on the menu. Two full standing ribs were roasted yesterday. One was well done, and the other was rare. Standard portion size is 10 ounces. Do 10-ounce portions cut from the rare roast have the same portion costs as those cut from the well-done roast? Why?

11. Using any standard cookbook, select one recipe that could be used as a standard recipe in a foodservice establishment. Following the form illustrated in Figure 7.2, use current market prices to determine the standard cost of one standard portion of the item. Determine an appropriate menu sales price for the item if the desired food cost percent is 35.0%.

12. Define each of the following terms:
    Butcher test
    Cooking loss test
    Cost factor per pound
    Portion cost factor
    Recipe detail and cost card
    Standard portion cost
    Standard portion size
    Standard recipe
    Yield
    Yield factor
    Yield percentage

FOR COMPUTER USERS

13. Following the form illustrated in Figure 7.2, create a spreadsheet to accomplish the same purposes: determining standard portion cost and, given a menu sales price, calculating food cost percent per portion.

14. Select one simple recipe of the type indicated in Question 11, then calculate standard portion cost for the item produced by that recipe, using the spreadsheet created in Question 13.

15. Using a word processing program of your choice, create a collection of 10 standard recipes, one to a file, and print them as individual documents, one to a page.

16. Using a spreadsheet program of your choice and following the forms illustrated in Figures 7.3 and 7.4, create worksheets to complete the

necessary calculations for butcher test and cooking loss test. Save the templates and use them to do Question 4.

17. Use the spreadsheet templates created in Question 16 to complete the test calculations required in Question 6a and Question 7a.

18. Using a spreadsheet program of your choice, create worksheets to complete the calculations required for the solution of Questions 6b through 6i and Questions 7b through 7h.

8
Food Production Control II: Quantities

LEARNING OBJECTIVES

After reading and studying this chapter, you should be able to:
1. Define the standard for controlling production volume and explain its importance.
2. List and describe three standard procedures that enable managers to gain control over production volume.
3. Define sales history and describe two methods for gathering the data from which a sales history is developed.
4. List three basic approaches to arranging data in a sales history.
5. Define popularity index.
6. Calculate popularity index for menu items.
7. Use popularity index to forecast portion sales.
8. Describe the production sheet, and calculate needed production for menu items.
9. Describe a void sheet and explain its use.
10. Complete a portion inventory and reconciliation.
11. Describe a procedure used for controlling high-cost, preportioned entrees.
12. Describe the use of computers in forecasting sales and controlling production quantities.
13. Define each of the Key Terms at the end of the chapter.

INTRODUCTION

In the preceding chapter, the focus of our attention was the portion—establishing control over the ingredients in a portion, the proportions of the various ingredients to one another, and the size of each portion. The reason for establishing control over these three was to be able to gain control over a fourth: portion cost.

In this chapter, we will assume that control has been established over individual portions and will shift our focus to the number of portions produced for each item on a menu for a given day or meal. After all, if the cost of a portion of some item is controlled at, say, $2.50 per serving and the establishment produces 100 portions but sells only 40, there will be 60 portions unsold. These may or may not be salable on another day. Even if they are salable, these portions are likely to be of lower quality than when first produced. It is also possible that they cannot be sold in their original form, but must be converted into some other item that will be sold at a lower sales price. Sometimes, if none of these possibilities are feasible, it may be necessary to throw the food away. In any case, there is excessive cost—either the cost of the food or the cost of additional labor that would not have been required if the establishment had produced 40 portions rather than 100.

The excessive costs suggested above can be reduced or eliminated by applying the four-step control process to the problem of quantity production.

ESTABLISHING STANDARDS AND STANDARD PROCEDURES

The standard for controlling production volume is to determine and produce, for any menu item, the number of portions that is likely to be sold on any given day. It is essential that foodservice establishments know this with some reasonable degree of accuracy so that intelligent plans can be made for purchasing and production. If, for example, it can be determined that 40 portions of an item are likely to be sold, this can readily be translated into a need to purchase the ingredients for producing that number of portions. Failure to set up procedures for establishing this can lead to excessive purchasing, with its obvious implications for cost.

In order to achieve any aim, one must establish appropriate standard procedures. To control production volume, several standard procedures are required. These include:

Maintaining sales history
Forecasting portion sales
Determining production quantities

Maintaining Sales History

A **sales history** is a written record of the number of portions of each menu item sold every time that item appeared on the menu. It is a summary of portion sales. In some establishments, sales histories are maintained for every item on the menu, from appetizers to desserts. In others, the only records are kept for entree items. In many instances, the extent and complexity of the sales history are related to the length and scope of the menu itself. In all instances, the best decisions on the nature of the sales history are based on the need for information that can be used to improve operations. Unless the information maintained is useful in leading to better control over costs, it cannot be justified.

Because a sales history records customers' selections, the basic information is gathered by those who record these selections: the sales staff, servers, or waitstaff. To see how the basic information is incorporated into the sales history, one must understand the two methods for recording customers' selections: manual and electronic.

MANUAL METHOD. Establishments that record customer selections manually are those that use the traditional guest checks—paper forms that become itemized bills given to customers at the conclusion of their meals. Essentially, there are two kinds of guest checks: single checks and checks that come in pads of 25, 50, or some other number. Servers commonly record customer selections on these checks manually, using pen or pencil, and the check is ultimately given to the customer as a bill to be paid. Payment is made to a cashier or to the server, and the check is retained by the establishment. Assuming that all selections have been recorded completely and legibly on the check, it is clearly a source document for the development of the sales history. The key is to set up a routine for abstracting the data from the check.

Abstracting of the information on the guest checks may be accomplished in any of several ways.

The simplest method involves maintaining a running count of portion sales as they occur. The work is often assigned to a cashier, who records information from the checks as they are presented by customers. The information may be recorded on a copy of the menu, on a special score sheet (Fig. 8.1), or on one of several types of mechanical counting devices widely available to the industry.

At the conclusion of a meal or at some other appropriate time, such as the end of the day, the information is given to the individual responsible for maintaining the sales history (manager, food controller, steward, dining room manager, or some other), so that it can be added to the accumulated records

DAY Tuesday	DATE 2/2/XXXX	MEAL Dinner
Item	*Number of Portions*	*Total*
A	‖‖‖ ‖‖‖ ‖‖‖ ‖‖‖ 111	23
B	‖‖‖ ‖‖‖ ‖‖‖ ‖‖‖ ‖‖‖ ‖‖‖ ‖‖‖ ‖‖‖ ‖‖‖ ‖‖‖ ‖‖‖ ‖‖‖	60
C	‖‖‖ ‖‖‖ ‖‖‖ ‖‖‖ ‖‖‖ ‖‖‖ 1111	34
D	‖‖‖ ‖‖‖ ‖‖‖ ‖‖‖ ‖‖‖ ‖‖‖ ‖‖‖ ‖‖‖ ‖‖‖	45
Total		162

FIGURE 8.1 *Portion Sales Breakdown*

previously developed. This method has the advantage of adding little or no cost to operations.

In some operations, where the cashier may be too busy to take on this extra work, the food controller or some other member of the management staff may take the guest checks after the meal or at the close of business and prepare an abstract of the portion sales, usually on a score sheet. While this method is time-consuming, it does present some advantages, which will be discussed in the chapter on sales control. A variation on this approach has the cashier giving the checks to someone from accounting who records the necessary information and forwards it to the individual responsible for maintaining the sales history.

ELECTRONIC METHOD.   As everyone knows, electronic terminals are becoming more common in foodservice establishments every day. Some interface with complex computer systems, while others are little more than electronic versions of the old mechanical cash registers. A number of these have the capacity to maintain cumulative totals of the numbers of portions of menu items sold.

Essentially, there are two methods for inputting portion sales data: by depressing a key marked with the name of the menu item selected or by depressing a two- or three-digit code for each menu item selected in a 10-key numeric keypad. In the first instance, if the customer ordered a cheeseburger, the server would depress a terminal key marked "cheeseburger." In the second, the server would translate "cheeseburger" into the code set up for that item (the three-digit number 472, for example) and then enter the code number in a terminal keypad. At the end of a day or a meal period, management can obtain a printout from the terminal listing all menu items available and the number of portions of each that were sold.

This portion sales data is added to the cumulative records developed to date. If the establishment used the manual methods described above, the data would be added to master records kept on file cards or in an analysis book. If electronic methods were used, the data might be transcribed annually on cards or in a book or added to a computer database or spreadsheet designed for this special purpose. Regardless of whether the portion sales records are stored manually or electronically, they are likely to be arranged in one of three ways:

1. By operating period, such as one week, so that all sales records for an entire operating period can be viewed together on one page, card, or screen (see Fig. 8.2).
2. By day of the week, so that all sales records for a given day (Tuesday, for example) for a period of several weeks can be compared.
3. By entree item, so that the degree of popularity of a given item can be seen over time.

Many have found it desirable to combine two of these systems in order to provide an overall picture of sales for the entire week at one glance. In addition, this approach provides some indication of the relative popularity of menu items compared to other items on the same menu. Figure 8.3 illustrates a sales history arranged in this way.

OTHER INFORMATION IN SALES HISTORIES.   It should be noted that sales histories often include provisions for recording additional relevant information—internal and external conditions that may shed light on sales data. One of the most common of these conditions is the weather. Most foodservice operators find that weather conditions have noticeable impact on sales volume. In many establishments, bad weather has clear negative impact on sales volume, so including some information about the weather each day will often help explain why sales were high or low on that day. Interestingly, hotels and motels in major metropolitan centers often find the impact of weather on sales to be the opposite of that experienced by neighboring restaurant operators: Bad weather seems to increase food and beverage sales in these properties, probably because it discourages guests from going out to nearby restaurants.

Special events can influence sales considerably and are often included in sales histories. The occurrence of a national holiday on a particular day or the presence of a particular convention group in a hotel can affect sales considerably. So can such varied conditions as faulty kitchen equipment, a torn-up street in front of the restaurant, or a major sale at a nearby store. In hotel

Weather	Fair	Snow	Cold	Fair	Fair	Fair	Cold	Cold										
Day	M	T	W	H	F	S	S	M	T	W	H	F	S	S	M	T	W	H
Date	1	2	3	4	5	6	7	8	9	10	11	12	13	14	15	16	17	18
Item																		
A	75	23	60	63	70	82	73	72										
B	60	60	55	65	62	58	61	65										
C	6	34	22	18	15	12	16	20										
D	159	45	140	149	150	161	154	155										
Total	300	162	277	295	297	313	304	312										

Sales History—Portions Sold—Month of February XXXX

FIGURE 8.2 *Sales History*

Sales History—Month of February XXXX

Item	Monday			Tuesday			Wednesday			Thursday			Friday			Saturday			Sunday	
	1	8	15	2	9	16	3	10	17	4	11	18	5	12	19	6	13	20	7	14
A	75	72		23			60			63			70			82			73	
B	60	65		60			55			65			62			58			61	
C	6	20		34			22			18			15			12			16	
D	159	155		45			140			149			150			161			154	
Total	300	312		162			277			295			297			313			304	

FIGURE 8.3 *Sales History*

185

Item	Portions Sold	Percent of Total Sales (Popularity Index)
A	23	14.2
B	60	37.0
C	34	21.0
D	45	27.8
Total	162	100.0%

FIGURE 8.4 *Popularity Index*

restaurants, the **house count,** or the number of people registered in the hotel on a particular day, is often included so that a determination can be made of the percentage of registered guests who are using the hotel's restaurants. With this, judgments can be made in the future as to numbers of portions to prepare for a given rate of occupancy. In general, one should include in the sales history any information about conditions and events that have affected sales and that should be considered in forecasting sales volume for a future period.

POPULARITY INDEX. In addition to keeping records of numbers of portions sold, many foodservice operators use the data to determine popularity index. **Popularity index** is defined as the ratio of portion sales for a given menu item to total portion sales for all menu items. This is illustrated in Figure 8.4.

The popularity index is calculated by dividing portion sales for a given item by the total portion sales for all menu items. The index may be calculated for any time period, even for a single meal. For example, the popularity index for Item A in Figure 8.4 is calculated as follows.

$$\text{Popularity index} = \frac{\text{Portion sales for Item A}}{\text{Total portion sales for all menu items}}$$

These ratios are of far greater use in determining an item's popularity than are the raw figures that simply indicate number of portions sold. For example, the sales history might show portion sales of Item B from a low of 12 portions to a high of 78. This would not be as useful as information indicating that, on the day 12 portions were sold, they had accounted for 35 percent of total portion sales and that, on the day 78 portions were sold, they had represented 39 percent. Given this information, as well as the information that Item B represented 37 percent of total sales on another recent day, one might conclude that this particular item accounted for approximately 37 percent of sales each time it appeared on the menu. If this were the case over a period of some weeks, the information should be useful for predicting the future. In many operations, particularly those with relatively stable menus, the popularity index is a key element in forecasting sales. The popularity index can also be useful in determining whether to continue offering a certain item on the menu. If an item consistently represents only 2 percent of total sales whenever it appears, serious consideration should be given to removing it from the menu and substituting a more popular item.

Forecasting Portion Sales

Forecasting is a process by means of which managers use data and intuition to predict what is likely to occur in the future. It amounts to intelligent, educated guesswork about future events. If one can predict the future with reasonable accuracy, appropriate plans can be made to prepare an enterprise for dealing with the predicted events. In the food industry, which deals with highly perishable products, predicting accurately and planning properly can be major factors in operating with a profit.

Forecasting is a principal element in cost control. If sales volume can be predicted accurately, then plans can be made for purchasing appropriate quantities of food to prepare for anticipated sales. Purchasing unneeded quantities can be avoided, thus reducing some of the possibilities for waste, spoilage, and pilferage. In addition, plans can be made for producing particular numbers of portions for sale on particular dates, thus reducing the possibilities for excessive costs to develop. Moreover, establishing control over purchasing can lead automatically to control over production: It is impossible to prepare a greater number of portions than necessary if the raw materials for overproduction do not exist.

A usual first step in forecasting is to predict total anticipated volume: total numbers of customers anticipated for particular days or particular meals. To arrive at a figure, one refers to the sales history to find the total number of sales recorded on each of a number of comparable dates in the recent past. When great differences are apparent, reasonable efforts must be made to determine the reasons for the differences. The causes are often revealed by information in the history relating to weather and other conditions that existed at the time of the sales. The effect of each of these conditions must be assessed — some increase sales, others decrease them.

When the effects of surrounding conditions have been evaluated, the next step is to judge the extent to which these conditions will exist and affect sales on the particular date or dates for which one is preparing the forecast. This may involve checking a local calendar for coming events, following weather forecasts, and looking into various other relevant sources of information.

After these steps have been taken, it is possible to estimate the total business volume that may be anticipated for the day or dates for which the forecast is being prepared. For example, if recent history indicated 275 to 300 sales for dinner on Tuesdays in pleasant weather, one could reasonably anticipate that the next Tuesday would bring approximately the same volume of business if good weather were expected. In this case, it would probably be safe to predict 300 sales.

The next step would be to forecast the anticipated number of sales of each item on the menu. This is simple to do when the menu is identical to the menus that have appeared on Tuesdays in the past. However, it can also be done for changing menus if the sales history is set up to reflect relative popularity of individual items compared to a changing variety of other items appearing on the same menu. This type of forecasting is more difficult, but by no means impossible.

If the sales history shows both portion sales and popularity index, the popularity index is the easier to use for predicting. For example, if Item M usually represents 20 percent of total sales on Tuesday evenings, it would be fairly safe to predict that, next Tuesday, Item M would also represent 20 percent of the anticipated 300 sales, or 60 portions. Thus, to forecast portion sales of a given item, one multiplies total forecasted portion sales by popularity index for the given item. After this has been done for every item that will appear on the menu, the result is a forecast of anticipated sales for a particular day or period. However, it must be recognized that this forecast must be considered flexible, subject to change as conditions change. A change in the weather forecast, for example, might indicate a need to change the forecast if there were sufficient time to do so.

After one member of the management team has developed the forecast, it should be reviewed by some other member of the team. Forecasting is educated guesswork, and two heads are usually better than one. The completed forecast represents management's best judgment of the sales volume anticipated, and the forecast should be shared with appropriate personnel. One staff member who needs this information is the manager responsible for developing a schedule for the waitstaff. With an accurate forecast in hand, the manager can make better plans for staffing. The aim is to have sufficient personnel on duty for each meal while keeping the total to the minimum necessary, thus maintaining control over labor costs. Perhaps the most important person with whom to share the forecast is the chef, who must be aware of anticipated volume, partly in order to anticipate labor requirements. In addition, with information about anticipated portion sales for each menu item, the chef is better equipped to advise the steward on the appropriate quantities of food to have on hand. If sales of 60 portions of Item M are forecasted for next Tuesday, the steward need not purchase a greater quantity of the perishable ingredients than is necessary. The consequent control of purchasing can be one of the most important factors in limiting excessive costs. When needed quantities are known, only those quantities should be purchased.

	Production Sheet	
DAY _Tuesday_ DATE _6/9/XXXX_		MEAL _Dinner_
	VOLUME FORECAST _305_	

Menu Item	*Forecast*	*Adjusted Forecast*
L	75	80
M	60	65
N	20	20
O	150	165
Total	305	330

FIGURE 8.5   *Production Sheet*

Determining Production Quantities

THE PRODUCTION SHEET.   A production sheet is a form on which one lists the names and quantities of all menu items that are to be prepared for a given date. Production sheets such as that illustrated in Figure 8.5 translate management's portion sales forecasts into production targets. Production sheets list menu items and quantities in terms that the chef and staff can use to in production. In some cases (with sirloin steaks, for example), quantity will be stated in portions. In others (beef stew and chicken noodle soup, for example), quantity may be stated in terms of total production rather than number of portions. The production sheet is best viewed as a tool used by management to control production and eliminate waste.

Production sheets vary in form and complexity from one kitchen to another. One very simple form appears in Figure 8.5. It would be filled out by a manager and forwarded to the chef as many days in advance as possible. Upon receiving it, the chef would have valuable information about both total anticipated volume for a particular meal and the number of portion sales anticipated for each item on the menu. With this information in hand, a chef is better equipped to determine needs for perishable foods, for which the steward would place orders, and for nonperishable foods, which would be requisitioned from the storeroom. Note that the form includes a column for adjusting the forecasted figure upwards or downwards on the basis of changes that may occur in weather or other conditions likely to affect sales.

Ideally, changes in the forecast will be minor. In any case, adjustments can be made immediately before the forecasted date—the night before or even

					Portions			
Menu Item	Forecast	Adjusted Forecast	Portion Size	Production Method	on Hand	Needed Production	Total Available	Left Over
L	75	80	6 oz.	Recipe #62	—	80	80	0
M	60	65	8 oz.	Recipe #4	5	60	65	5
N	20	20	4 oz.	Recipe #19	—	20	20	0
O	150	165	12 oz.	Broil	20	145	165	6
Total	305	330						

Production Sheet

DAY Tuesday   DATE 6/9/XXXX   MEAL Dinner

VOLUME FORECAST 305

FIGURE 8.6 *Production Sheet*

the morning of the date in question. The final figures in the "Adjusted Forecast" column are the final production goals for the chef for the date. With those goals in mind, the chef will proceed to produce the required quantities, seeing to it that leftover foods are used in meeting those goals whenever possible, provided that their use does not violate the establishment's quality standards.

In some operations, this very simple version of the production sheet would be considered inadequate. If additional control over production is necessary or desirable, a more elaborate form can be used. Such a form is illustrated in Figure 8.6.

This form establishes greater control in several ways. It restates the portion size for each item, thus continually reemphasizing management's concern that the size of each portion served be carefully controlled. This may be particularly important in those places that offer portions of different sizes for luncheon, for dinner, and for banquets. It also directs the kitchen staff in the production method to be employed, which can be important when several recipes exist for the same item and management chooses to specify one particular recipe.

The purpose of the "Portions on Hand" column is to induce the chef to take an inventory of leftovers from the previous day or meal before starting production. While this is inappropriate in some establishments because of their quality standards, it is perfectly permissible in others.

The figure in the "Total Available" column (the sum of leftover portions and additional portions produced) should equal the figure in the "Adjusted

Forecast" column. As an additional control, there is a column for portions left over. Whenever possible, this figure should be carried over to the production sheet for the next day or meal, in order to ensure that these leftovers will be sold. If portions of uncooked meats have been left over and the number recorded cannot be located the following day or meal, one can begin to suspect pilferage. If so, immediate steps can be taken to eliminate future possibilities.

Regardless of the degree of complexity of production sheets, their basic purpose is to establish control by setting goals for production. Controlling production eliminates a major cause of excessive cost. After all, the costs of unsold portions are included in cost figures, but have not increased in sales figures for the day. Therefore, to keep costs in line, controlling food production is necessary and desirable. Under ideal conditions, no unsold portions would ever be left over after a meal. Everyone recognizes that this is impossible, but it is a desirable goal nevertheless. If the number of unsold portions can be reduced or eliminated, food cost can be better controlled and excessive costs eliminated. It is with this goal in mind that managers use production sheets.

In most operations, the cost of entree items represents the major share of total food cost. Meats and fish, after all, usually account for the largest portion of food cost per customer served; thus, additional control procedures to isolate instances of waste and inefficiency are often concerned with entree items. Some of these additional control procedures will be covered later in the chapter.

TRAINING FOR PRODUCTION

For one to establish control over the number of portions produced, it is clearly important that complete and accurate information be obtained each day about the number of portions of each menu item sold. That information must be recorded accurately and reliably in a sales history and then used carefully to forecast future sales. Key elements in all this are the completeness and accuracy of the data recorded.

Management must take great care to train the waitstaff to record complete and accurate data. If manual techniques are used, then servers must be made aware of the need for legibility on all guest checks and of the special importance of recording all necessary data on each check. Someone other than the server will be reading these checks to abstract the data, and the data must, therefore, be complete and accessible. Poor handwriting and items remembered by the server but never recorded on the checks are clear impediments to developing the most useful sales history.

Although using electronic techniques does eliminate the problem of legibility, one must train servers to record all information and to do so accurately, or the data will not be as useful.

Many operators find it desirable to explain the goals of production control techniques to their employees, finding that the servers who understand the aims of the system are more likely to comply with management's directives concerning accuracy of input. The knowledgeable employee who understands his role in the collection of this important data can be among the most useful and reliable of employees, one who may be singled out for special managerial training over the long term.

Training personnel for forecasting requires selection of those with experience and judgment—both qualities essential to effective forecasting. It is unlikely that more than one or two persons on the staff can be trained to forecast sales and prepare production sheets. After all, these are special tasks clearly tied to the central functions of management; thus, they are usually reserved for the food controller, the chef, or, more commonly, the manager.

MONITORING QUANTITY PRODUCTION AND TAKING CORRECTIVE ACTION

There are two purposes for monitoring quantity production:

1. To determine whether the sales forecast has been reasonably accurate in predicting both the total number of customers and their individual preferences for particular menu items.
2. To judge how closely the chef has followed the production standards established on the production sheet. These will be discussed separately.

Monitoring Accuracy of Forecasting

To make judgments about the accuracy of a forecast, one must have detailed information about the forecast and about sales on the day for which the forecast was prepared. For the former, one need have only a copy of the forecast itself; for the latter, full details would be available in the sales history. Information from both sources could be recorded on a form such as that illustrated in Figure 8.7.

Examination of the specific information provided in Figure 8.7 indicates that the sales forecast differed from actual sales by only six portions. The total of actual portion sales was 98.2 percent of the total forecasted, a degree of accuracy that most foodservice operators would be likely to find acceptable. Examination of the figures for individual menu items suggests the following:

1. Item L was under-forecasted. Total portion sales were five over the number forecast, and one would question where these portions came from. It is possible that they were produced by reducing the size of other portions so that a number of customers ordering Item L received

DAY Wednesday		DATE 6/9/XXXX	MEAL Dinner
Item	Sales Forecast	Actual Sales	Difference
L	80	85	+5
M	65	60	−5
N	20	20	-0-
O	165	159	−6
Total	330	324	−6

FIGURE 8.7 *Comparison: Sales Forecast and Actual Sales*

less than the standard portion size. Alternatively, these five additional portions might have been produced from inventory, which might reduce inventory on hand for the following day to unacceptable levels.

2. Item N appears to have been perfectly forecasted. However, it is possible that the kitchen ran out of this item before the end of the meal period, and late customers who had wanted to order Item N were forced to make alternative selections. If this has been the case, then actual sales of Items L, M, and O may be higher than they would have been otherwise. It is important, therefore, that someone make an appropriate notation in the sales history about the time any item runs out so that this information may be taken into account when other forecasts are made in the future. In many restaurants, the host or hostess notes this kind of information in a log book that is kept in the dining room.

3. Items M and O, both of which sold fewer portions than were forecasted, indicate some need to improve the accuracy of forecasts. In addition, both suggest the possibility of excessive costs, depending on whether these items can be reused.

Judging Whether Production Standards Were Followed

It is important to keep in mind that the figures recorded in Figure 8.7 are not related to actual kitchen production in any useful way. Figure 8.7 merely compares numbers forecast to numbers sold. The next logical step is to monitor the performance of the kitchen staff to judge how closely the chef has followed the production quantity standards provided on the production sheet for the day. In order to do this, one must establish a procedure for keeping records of portions rejected by customers and returned from the dining room. Records of these may be kept on a form known as a void sheet, illustrated in Figure 8.8.

			Void sheet		
			DAY <u>Tues.</u> DATE <u>6/9/XXXX</u>		
Check #	*Waiter #*	*Item*	*Reason for Return*	*Authorization*	*Sales Value*
11031	6	O	Too well done	SJC.	7.95
11034	6	M	Dropped on floor	SJC.	6.95
11206	4	O	Too well done	SJC.	7.95
11227	3	O	Too well done	SJC.	7.95

FIGURE 8.8 *Void Sheet*

THE VOID SHEET.   Every restaurant offering steaks, chops, and other similar à la carte entrees has had some experience with portions being rejected by customers and returned from the dining room for one reason or another. Sometimes portions are returned by customers who are difficult or impossible to please. However, there are many occasions when portions are returned because some member of the staff was not listening carefully. Sometimes it is a careless server, sometimes an indifferent or overworked cook. In any case, regardless of who it was that failed to listen or why that was so, the item presented to the customer was returned. These returned portions are excellent examples of excessive cost and should not be ignored. Many restaurants record customer returns on a **void sheet.**

Whenever a portion is returned, some authorized individual, such as a kitchen supervisor or chef, records it on the void sheet, indicating the name of the item, the number of the check on which it appeared, and the reason for its return. These entries can be most revealing to an alert manager or food controller. For example, if one particular server appears on the list with greater than usual regularity, it is possible that he is not paying careful attention to customer orders. This can quickly lead to unwarranted and excessive costs for the restaurant and should be attended to quickly. On the other hand, it might be noted that the number of broiler items returned is far greater when one particular employee is working. This might suggest the need for the chef to observe this employee's job performance and, if warranted, take corrective action to improve the employee's performance. If the number of returns is consistently high and evenly distributed among job classifications, investigation might indicate general understaffing. This could suggest a need for additional personnel to improve customer service.

There are other important uses of the void sheet as well, particularly when efforts are being made to control portions by some method, such as the par stock control of preportioned entrees (described below). If all portions are not accounted for, kitchen personnel can easily claim that some were discarded after being returned by difficult customers. If all returned portions must be recorded on the void sheet and attested to by some member of the management team, it is more difficult for kitchen personnel to be careless with food. In addition, the recording of returned portions, taken with other techniques previously described, makes possible the reconciliation of kitchen records of portions produced and records of portions sold.

PORTION INVENTORY AND RECONCILIATION.   One useful means of determining how closely the chef has followed quantity production standards established for the day requires the use of the form illustrated in Figure 8.9. The procedure follows logically from the production sheet illustrated in Figure 8.6. In fact, Figure 8.9 might best be viewed as an elaboration on Figure 8.6.

Using this approach effectively requires that one follow a series of logical steps. First, each menu item should be listed on the form before kitchen production begins. Next, an inventory is taken of any portions left over from previous meals that may be used again. Reusing leftovers in this way is common in some establishments, but unacceptable in others.

If leftovers are to be used, the number of portions on hand is deducted from the quantity scheduled for production, and only the difference is prepared. That number is written in the "Portions Prepared" column. Additional quantities prepared, if any, are recorded in the next column. At the conclusion of the meal period, an inventory is taken of the portions on hand, with the information being recorded in the column headed "Closing Inventory." When these columns are completed, the form is given to a manager.

For each menu item, the manager adds opening inventory, portions prepared, and additional preparation to determine total available. Closing inventory is subtracted from total available to obtain number of portions consumed. Having determined the number of portions consumed according to kitchen records, the manager obtains from the cashier (or other source) the record of portion sales prepared for the sales history. These are recorded in the "Portions

Portion Inventory and Reconciliation						

DAY Wed.   DATE 10/8/XXXX

Portion Production:

Item	Opening Inventory	Portions Prepared	Additional Preparation	Total Available	Closing Inventory	Portions Consumed
AB	—	180		180	15	165
BH	5	60		65	5	60
CJ	—	110	10	120	14	106
DZ	20	145		165	8	157

Sales Reconciliation:

Item	Portions Sold	Portions Void	Total	Consumed (From Above)	Difference	Comment
AB	165	—	165	165		
BH	58	2	60	60		
CJ	103	1	104	106	2	2 missing checks
DZ	156	1	157	157		

PREPARED BY: _____
                              FOOD CONTROLLER

REVIEWED BY: _____
                              MANAGER

FIGURE 8.9   *Portion Inventory and Reconciliation*

Sold" column. The number of portions **voided,** or returned to the kitchen, is recorded in the "Portions Void" column and then subtracted from "Portions Sold." The result is entered in the "Total" column.

The next step is to determine the difference, if any, between the kitchen records and the portion sales records. That difference is written in the appropriate column. In the example given, kitchen records show the production of 106 cooked portions of CJ, while sales records indicate only 104 portions sold. The difference (2 portions) should be investigated immediately while events are still fresh in the minds of the personnel involved. Once the causes of the discrepancy have been identified, steps can be taken to eliminate them in the future.

While this technique is most useful to restaurants serving foods cooked to order, it can be helpful in other establishments as well. Its use requires that someone be able to estimate with some degree of accuracy the number of portions contained in, say, a steam table pan of beef goulash. The resulting information will not be as precise, but it can be useful for identifying problems.

If portion sizes are carefully controlled and standard portion costs known, the number of portions unaccounted for can be translated into dollars quite simply. In the previous example, if the missing portions of CJ have a standard cost of $3.35 each, then simple multiplication determines that the loss of these portions has increased costs by $6.70 on that particular day. Such an amount might not seem large, but if equal losses occur seven days a week throughout the year, this would amount to a weekly loss of $46.90 and an annual loss of $2,438.80, a substantial amount. The cost is excessive in every sense and should be eliminated. If the loss can be eliminated without increasing other costs, profits will be increased by the amount saved.

Two portions may seem a very small number to be concerned about. However, these two portions represent 1.9 percent of the portions of this item produced. The production of these portions has increased food cost figures. But, because they have not been sold, food sales figures have not increased by an appropriate amount. The net effect of this is an unwarranted increase in the food cost percent. Taking preventive steps seems advisable.

While this procedure for reconciling portion production and sales is useful, it does, after all, address itself only to entree items. In most instances, extending its use to cover other items on the menu would be unwieldy. Although it is true that entree items usually represent the greatest proportion of cost, this does not mean that the cost of other items can be ignored. Also, this reconciliation does not take into account the waste, if any, that occurred in the preparation of the number of portions that were finally listed on the form. It is possible, for example, that several steaks were improperly cut and discarded, never having been listed on the reconciliation form.

For these and other reasons, some large establishments, with the personnel and time necessary to complete the work, prepare various daily reports to determine the dollar difference between standard costs and actual costs. These topics will be discussed in Chapter 11.

Par Stock Control of Preportioned Entrees

Another useful technique for controlling the preparation of quantities of some specialized items is illustrated in Figure 8.10 and discussed below.

Steaks, chops, and other similar expensive entree items are either purchased already in portions or are divided into portions in the restaurant before cooking. These items are usually cooked to order and are typically held in a

Item	Portions Issued	Additional Issues	Total Issues	Returned to Steward	Portions Consumed
D	165	—	165	6	159

Day Tues.   Issues received *O. Jones*

Date 2/9/XXXX   Additional Issues _____

Returned portions received *Paul Smith*

Steward

FIGURE 8.10 *Control Sheet for Preportioned Entrees*

refrigerator close to the broiler or range. Under such circumstances, the cook will usually be responsible for putting the items on the fire when they are ordered.

Therefore, many managers and food controllers find it useful to make the cook fully responsible for these expensive items by requiring him to sign a form such as that illustrated in Figure 8.10. By signing, the cook acknowledges receiving the number of portions of each item indicated.

The number of portions that the steward issues should be equal to the number of sales forecasted for each item. In case the forecasted number is incorrect, provision is made for additional issues, for which the cook will also sign. At the conclusion of serving hours, the number issued can be totaled in the next column. The number of portions returned, if any, will be entered in the "Returned to Steward" column, and the steward will sign for the returns. "Total Issues minus Returns" equals the number of portions consumed, and the steward fills in this figure before giving the completed form to the manager.

One advantage of this procedure is that it makes the cook accountable for a particular number of portions. Knowing the certainty of being questioned about missing portions, a cook will be less likely to give any away to staff members.

The use of the form illustrated in Figure 8.9 will typically bring to light any discrepancies between management's plan for production (the forecast) and the actual production (the total of portions sold, returned, and left over). It is of obvious importance to determine the cause of any such discrepancies and to take action to reduce their number and extent in the future. In foodservice, some degree of inefficiency is normally tolerated in day-to-day operations, and management in a given operation must determine the level considered acceptable.

COMPUTER APPLICATIONS

Given the many electronic sales terminals available today, developing sales history data has become simpler and faster than it was in the past. With stand-alone sales terminals, it is comparatively easy at the end of a day or a meal period to print out a report of portion sales that can be added to a manually maintained history. With sales terminals integrated into a local-area-network, portion sales data may merely be stored for future reference in a file maintained in the server. It would be simple to create a database program for rendering the data in a form useful for forecasting.

With historical records of portion sales readily available in a computer file, forecasting might take the following form. The manager would access a forecasting screen at the terminal and record the projected menu. The menu items would be displayed in a column on the left side of the computer monitor. In columns to the right of each item, the manager would see numbers of previous sales from specific dates or the popularity index for each, depending on the specifics of the program employed. The cursor would appear on the top line at the right of the screen opposite the first menu item and would flash in that position until an entry had been made reflecting forecasted portion sales. Before making such an entry, the manager would obviously consider carefully all displayed records and make the necessary judgments about future sales.

As the manager recorded specific projections, the cursor would move from line to line until sales had been forecasted for each menu item. At that point, it would be simple to obtain a printout of the complete forecast, either as a simple forecast or in the form of one of the production sheets described earlier in this chapter. As many copies as necessary could be obtained, so that various key individuals in the establishment could be informed of anticipated future sales forecasts.

CHAPTER ESSENTIALS

In this chapter, we explained the application of the control process to the quantity production phase of foodservice operations. We described the standard for controlling production volume as determining and producing, for any menu item, the number of portions that is likely to be sold on any given day, and discussed techniques for establishing that standard. We defined sales history and described the two means of collecting the data included in a sales history. We illustrated several possible patterns for maintaining sales histories. We defined the popularity index and illustrated its calculation. We explained how the sales history and popularity index are used to prepare a forecast of portion sales. We identified the production sheet, explained its use, and illustrated two basic types commonly used in the industry. We described several techniques for monitoring performance: comparing the sales forecast to actual sales in order to make judgments about the accuracy of the forecast, and comparing production records to sales records to determine the extent to which kitchen production has matched that called for on the production sheet. We illustrated a technique for controlling and accounting for such preportioned items as steaks and chops. Finally, we discussed the use of computers in developing records for a sales history, for maintaining sales history, and for forecasting.

KEY TERMS IN THIS CHAPTER

Par stock control
Popularity index
Portion reconciliation
Production sheet
Sales forecast
Sales history
Void sheet

QUESTIONS AND PROBLEMS

1. Compute the popularity index for the following sales. Round each percentage to the nearest .1%.

   a. | Item | Portions Sold |
      |---|---|
      | A | 60 |
      | B | 20 |
      | C | 80 |
      | D | 40 |

   b. | Item | Portions Sold |
      |---|---|
      | A | 30 |
      | B | 42 |
      | C | 73 |
      | D | 115 |

   c. | Item | Portions Sold |
      |---|---|
      | A | 86 |
      | B | 113 |
      | C | 55 |
      | D | 44 |
      | E | 25 |

2. Using the popularity indexes calculated in Question 1a, predict the sales for each item if total sales for all items are expected to be 300.

3. Using the popularity indexes calculated in Question 1b, predict the sales for each item if total sales for all items are expected to be 150.

4. Using the popularity indexes calculated in Question 1c, predict the sales for each item if total sales for all items are expected to be 450.

5. Using the forecast developed in Question 2, assume that this forecast must be adjusted to indicate 20% fewer sales than had been forecasted originally. Using Figure 8.5 as a guide, prepare a production sheet showing both the original forecast and the adjusted forecast.

6. Using the forecast developed in Question 3, assume that this forecast must be adjusted to indicate 10% more sales than had been forecasted originally. Using Figure 8.5 as a guide, prepare a production sheet showing both the original forecast and the adjusted forecast.

7. List and discuss four possible causes of discrepancies between figures listed in the "Portions Consumed" and "Portions Sold" columns on the form illustrated in Figure 8.9.

8. Explain the value of having a sales history available when attempting a restaurant sales forecast.

9. What advantages and disadvantages do you see in using each of the two methods described in this chapter for gathering information for a sales history?

10. Describe the procedure identified in this chapter that is used for controlling high-cost preportioned entrees.

11. If a manager were looking for ways to reduce excessive food costs, would void sheets be of any use? Why?

12. What role can an electronic sales terminal play in developing a sales history?

13. Define each of the following terms:
Par stock control
Popularity index
Portion reconciliation
Production sheet
Sales forecast
Sales history
Void sheet

FOR COMPUTER USERS

14. Using any spreadsheet program of your choice,
    a. Reproduce the sales history illustrated in Figure 8.2.
    b. Insert columns as needed and calculate popularity index for each item on each date.
    c. Calculate popularity index for each item based on total sales for the eight days recorded in the sales history.

15. Using the popularity index calculated for each item in Question 14c, create a spreadsheet to generate a production sheet for the same menu items, given fair weather conditions and an expected total of 375 sales.

9

Monitoring Foodservice Operations I: Monthly Inventory and Monthly Food Cost

LEARNING OBJECTIVES

After reading and studying this chapter, you should be able to:
  1. Explain the importance of monitoring a foodservice operation to assess monthly performance.
  2. Describe the procedure for taking physical inventory at the end of the month.
  3. List and explain five ways to assign unit costs to a food inventory.
  4. State the formula for calculating cost of food consumed.
  5. Explain the effect on cost of each of five acceptable methods of assigning unit costs to a closing inventory.
  6. List and explain the adjustments made to cost of food consumed in order to determine cost of food sold.
  7. Distinguish between the terms opening (or beginning) inventory and closing (or ending) inventory.
  8. Explain the relationship between the monthly calculation of cost of food sold and the monthly income statement.
  9. Devise a simple monthly food cost report to management, given the necessary figures.
 10. Calculate cost of food consumed, cost of food sold, food cost percent, and food cost per dollar sale, given appropriate figures.
 11. Explain the possible shortcomings of a system in which judgments about operations are made exclusively on the basis of monthly food cost and food cost percent.
 12. Explain how computers are used to value inventories and to verify employee adherence to standard procedures for issuing foods from inventory.
 13. Define each of the Key Terms at the end of the chapter.

INTRODUCTION

In the preceding chapters, we have examined methods used to implement the control process through several phases of foodservice operation, including purchasing, receiving, storing, issuing, and production. In each chapter, we described techniques for monitoring the operations under discussion. Now, having addressed the establishment of control over some of the more critical phases of foodservice operation, we will turn to an examination of the techniques and procedures used by managers to monitor the totality of an operation, rather than specific phases. For purposes of classroom discussion, it is both useful and productive to engage in close examination of individual phases of an operation. However, although foodservice managers must be able to do that, they must also be able to look at the whole operation and monitor its overall performance. It should be obvious that the success of a foodservice operation is measured in terms of the whole, not one or more of its parts. Also, it is quite possible that a given operation may be very successful even though one or more phases of operation could be improved through better control.

The next three chapters will examine techniques and procedures for monitoring overall operations. The most common approach to monitoring is one requiring that various procedures and calculations be completed at the end of each month. The calendar month is a basic unit of time in the accounting process, and most of the procedures described in this chapter are actually accounting procedures designed to provide managers with monthly reports that measure the results of business operations. While they may not be sufficiently detailed to pinpoint specific problems in an enterprise, they can provide some reasonable estimate of overall financial health through the end of the most recent month. For example, a restaurant with food costs of 30 percent, labor costs of 35 percent, and overhead of 20 percent is clearly in better financial health than an establishment with food costs of 45 percent, labor costs of 45 percent, and other costs of 10 percent. The latter has difficulty, obviously, but one cannot tell from this limited information just which phases of operation are causing the difficulty. However, imprecise though they are, unless these basic monthly determinations are made, management will have no idea of the existence or the extent of difficulty until it is too late to undertake some form of corrective action.

In addition to providing management with information indicating the financial results of business operation, these monthly accounting procedures also provide information that can be useful for assessing the various control procedures established for the operation.

The purposes of the present chapter are to describe the procedures for determining monthly food cost and food cost percentage and to explain how these figures can be useful in helping to assess whether or not the operation is meeting its goals. To make these determinations, it is necessary to take a number of steps aimed at measuring performance. The first of these is taking physical inventory.

MONTHLY INVENTORY

Taking Physical Inventory

In most business establishments, including food and beverage operations, taking physical inventory is a universally accepted practice. Physical inventory is taken at the close of an accounting period, typically after the close of business on the last day of a calendar month. Taking physical inventory requires counting the actual number of units on hand of each item in stock and recording that number in an appropriate place. The whole purpose of this is to provide a list of goods on hand so that the value of the goods may be determined and recorded.

Physical inventory may be recorded in an inventory book, such as that illustrated in Figure 9.1, or in some other type of permanent business record. It is normally considered good practice to list the items in stock in a book set up for that specific purpose and to list them in the same order in which they are maintained in stock. Arranging the list in this way facilitates a procedure that can be long and tedious, depending on the number of products in the inventory.

Taking a physical inventory in a storeroom, for example, commonly requires two people: one to count the units on the shelves and the other to record the numbers in the inventory book. If the storeroom is arranged as suggested in Chapter 6, it is possible for the two to begin in one logical spot and work their way through the entire inventory in order, finding items on shelves in the same order as that listed in the inventory book.

Once the units in inventory have been counted and the count has been recorded, total values can be determined for the items listed. To determine these totals, one records the unit cost of each product and multiplies it by the number of units of that product in the physical inventory. Once the total value of each product has been determined in this way, these totals are added to find the total dollar value of all items in the inventory. This figure, known as **closing inventory for the period,** automatically becomes the opening inventory for the next period.

One of the principal difficulties in valuing an inventory is assigning the unit value for each item, since all purchases may not have been made at the same price. It is not uncommon for prices to change several times during the course of the month. Determining the proper value to assign to units remaining in inventory at the end of the month raises the question of which, if any, of

Month of	September, XXXX			October, XXXX			Novem...	
Articles	Quantity	Price	Amount	Quantity	Price	Amount	Quantity	Price
Brought forward	—	—	$743.82					
Tomato Paste #2½	16	1.24	19.84					
Tomato Paste #10	6	3.49	20.94					
Tomato Puree #10	8	3.29	26.32					
Tomato Juice, 46 oz.	24	.99	23.76					
Tomato Juice, 6 oz.	60	.29	17.40					
Tomato Sauce, #10	18	2.99	53.82					
Tomatoes, whole, peeled #10	15	2.89	43.35					

FIGURE 9.1 *Storeroom Inventory*

the various purchase prices should be assigned to the unit remaining in the inventory.

Valuing the Physical Inventory

There are at least five possible ways of assigning values to units of product in a physical inventory. Because each provides a value to the units remaining in inventory at the end of any given month, anyone planning a career in food-service management is well advised to become familiar with all five, any one of which might be selected by an accountant as appropriate for use in a particular establishment, given a particular set of circumstances.

Because it would be impossible to provide a complete set of inventory figures to illustrate each of the five, the discussion will be restricted to only one item in the stores inventory: No. 10 cans of fruit cocktail.

Inventory records for the month of May reveal the following:

Opening inventory on the 1st of the month:	10 cans @ $2.35 = $23.50
Purchased on the 7th of the month:	24 cans @ $2.50 = $60.00
Purchased on the 15th of the month:	24 cans @ $2.60 = $62.40
Purchased on the 26th of the month:	12 cans @ $2.30 = $27.60

A physical inventory on the 31st of the month showed that 20 cans remained in stock. From this one can deduce that 50 cans were consumed during the month, as follows:

Opening inventory	10 cans
+ Purchases during the month	60 cans
= Total available	70 cans
− Closing inventory	20 cans
(number of units still available)	
= Units consumed	50 cans
(number of units no longer available)	

Because both the value of the opening inventory ($23.50) and the value of the purchases ($150.00) are known, one can add the two values to determine the value of the total number of units available—$173.50. It should be obvious that one can determine the value of the units consumed only by determining the value of the units in the closing inventory and then subtracting that figure from the value of the total available. The following are five accepted methods for assigning values to units of the products in inventory.

ACTUAL PURCHASE PRICE METHOD.   Perhaps the most reasonable unit value to assign to the items in the closing inventory would be their actual purchase price. However, this can be done only if those prices are marked on the units. If the cans of fruit cocktail are marked with actual purchase prices, totaling their value is obviously a simple clerical job, requiring nothing more complex than addition. Assuming the cans were with the purchase prices indicated below, the value of the 20 cans would be determined as follows:

$$
\begin{array}{rl}
4 \text{ @ } \$2.35 = & \$\ 9.40 \\
12 \text{ @ }\ \ 2.30 = & 27.60 \\
\underline{4 \text{ @ }\ \ 2.60} = & \underline{10.40} \\
20 = & \$47.40
\end{array}
$$

However, if the actual purchase prices were not marked on the cans, some alternative procedure would be required.

FIRST-IN, FIRST-OUT METHOD (LATEST PRICES).   One alternative procedure is to assume that stock has been rotated properly during the period, such that the units consumed were the first to be placed on the shelf. In that case, those remaining on the shelf are those most recently purchased.

In order to establish the value for the units in closing inventory using this method, it would be necessary to know that the latest purchase on the 26th of the month was for 12 cans and that the next previous purchase on the 15th was for 24 cans. With that information available, it is possible to determine the value of the 20 cans as:

$$
\begin{array}{rl}
12 \text{ @ } \$2.30 = & \$27.60 \\
\underline{8 \text{ @ }\ \ 2.60} = & \underline{20.80} \\
20 = & \$48.80
\end{array}
$$

However, without some assurance that the stock on shelves had been properly rotated during the month, this could lead to inaccurate valuation. After all, it is based on an assumption about rotation that may not be valid.

WEIGHTED AVERAGE PURCHASE PRICE METHOD.   If there is no assurance that stock has been properly rotated and if large quantities of goods are involved, the weighted average purchase price method offers a reasonable alternative. One can determine a weighted average purchase price by multiplying the number of units in the opening inventory and in each subsequent purchase by their specific purchase prices, adding these values to determine a grand total for all units together and then dividing this grand total by the total number of units.

When one follows this procedure, the weighted average value of one unit could be determined by dividing 70 units into the $173.50 total value. The result would be a weighted average value of $2.48. Using that figure, the value of the closing inventory would be:

$$20 @ \$2.48 = \$49.60$$

It should be apparent that, while this procedure makes logical sense, its use requires access to detailed records of purchases. Except for those food and beverage operations that maintain computerized accounting records, the weighted average purchase price method is seldom used in food and beverage operations. Attempting the necessary arithmetic by manual means is simply too time-consuming.

LATEST PURCHASE PRICE METHOD (MOST RECENT PRICE). A simpler, faster, and more widely used approach is to use the latest purchase price for valuing the closing inventory. One justification for this approach is that, if it were necessary to replace the remaining cans, the cost of replacement at the present moment would likely be the latest price at which the items were purchased.

If this method were followed, as it frequently is in the food and beverage business, the value of the closing inventory of this item would be:

$$20 @ \$2.30 = \$46.00$$

LAST-IN, FIRST-OUT METHOD (EARLIEST PRICES). In certain specialized circumstances (when tax rates or inflation rates are particularly high, for example), management may choose to minimize profits on financial statements in order to decrease income taxes. To minimize profits, one might seek to maximize cost by minimizing the value of closing inventory. Doing this in periods of rising prices is easy: One merely values the units in the closing inventory by using the earliest purchase prices.

If this method were used, the value of the 20 cans would be:

$$
\begin{array}{r}
10 @ \$2.35 = \$23.50 \\
\underline{10 @ \$2.50 = \quad 25.00} \\
20 = \$48.50
\end{array}
$$

One should keep in mind that managers and food controllers do not normally determine the method to be used in valuing inventories. Although they may be asked to contribute to the discussion of which method to use, the decision would probably be made by an accountant.

In addition, once the decision is made, it is not normally changed; various accounting conventions and Internal Revenue Service regulations preclude frequent change.

COMPARISON OF METHODS.   If the prices of goods purchased were fixed, the selection of method for valuing a closing inventory would be of no importance: All methods would yield the same figure. However, in times of fluctuating prices, which, after all, describes most times in the food and beverage business, the selection of one method over another may be of considerable significance. A comparison of the values of the 20 cans in closing inventory described above illustrates the point:

1. Value based on actual purchase price method: $47.40.
2. Value based on first-in, first-out method: $48.40.
3. Value based on weighted average method: $49.60.
4. Value based on latest purchase price method: $46.00.
5. Value based on last-in, first-out method: $48.50.

Using the lowest value, $46.00, as a base, there is a difference of 7.8 percent between the highest value and the lowest value established for these 20 cans of fruit cocktail. And while the dollar differences for this single inventory item do not appear significant, the difference could be quite large if one were dealing with an entire inventory.

MONTHLY FOOD COST DETERMINATION

At this point, drawing on previous discussions in this and earlier chapters, it is possible to turn our attention to the monthly determination of cost of food sold and food cost percentage. The procedures discussed below are applicable to any foodservice enterprise, regardless of its size or of the nature and complexity of control procedures in effect.

The cost of food sold for any month is determined by the following formula:

$$
\begin{aligned}
& \text{Opening inventory} \\
&\underline{+\ \text{Purchase}} \\
&=\ \text{Total available} \\
&\underline{-\ \text{Closing inventory}} \\
&=\ \text{Cost of food}
\end{aligned}
$$

	Actual Purchase Price Method	*First-In, First-Out Method*	*Weighted Average Method*	*Latest Purchase Price Method*	*Last-In, First-Out Method*
Opening Inventory	$ 23.50	$ 23.50	$ 23.50	$ 23.50	$ 23.50
Purchases	150.00	150.00	150.00	150.00	150.00
Total Available	173.50	173.50	173.50	173.50	173.50
Closing Inventory	47.40	48.40	49.60	46.00	48.50
Cost of Food	126.10	125.10	123.90	127.50	125.00

FIGURE 9.2 *Comparison of Food Costs*

The explanation is rather simple. Opening inventory for any accounting period is, by definition, the same as closing inventory for the previous period. The figure is available from accounting records. To that, one adds the value of all directs and stores purchased during the period. The sources documents for this information are the invoices for the period, which are summarized on the Receiving Clerk's Daily Reports. Total available thus indicates the total value of all foods available during the period for the production of menu items. From this figure, one subtracts closing inventory, a valuation that is established by the means described earlier in this chapter. The result is a raw figure that indicates cost of food for the period. It includes the cost of all food, whether used productively or not.

It should be noted that the closing inventory figure does not include the value of any directs that have been purchased but not consumed. Thus, the food cost figure is somewhat higher than it should be. In practice, this is routinely ignored on the theory that any error in this procedure in one month will be offset the following month. In other words, some directs that will be used at the beginning of each month will have been included in cost for the previous month. However, since directs are purchased in small quantities for immediate use, the value of these should be fairly constant from month to month. In some large organizations, these directs are in a category termed **foods in process,** which is subtracted from total available along with the closing inventory.

At this point it will be useful to illustrate the effect of the various methods of establishing value of closing inventory on the cost of food for a period, using the values established earlier in this chapter for the No. 10 cans of fruit cocktail. These are summarized in Figure 9.2.

While the illustration shows only one item out of an inventory, it should be apparent that these effects would be cumulative over an entire inventory.

Thus, while the selection of the method to use for valuing the inventory in any one specific operation will be made by an owner and an accountant, a knowledgeable manager or food controller should be aware of the effects that the various inventory valuation methods will have on food cost.

Once food cost for a given period has been determined, food cost percentage may be calculated. For purposes of illustration, we will use the Pasta Pit, one of the units in a small chain operating in a large Eastern city. This particular unit is situated within walking distance of a large number of high-rent apartment buildings in one of the city's better residential neighborhoods. Financial records of the business reveal the following figures for the month of July:

Opening inventory	$ 2,000
Food purchases	6,000
Closing inventory	3,000
Food sales	15,000

Given these figures, we may now begin to determine the cost of food for March by using the formula stated earlier:

Opening inventory	$2,000
+ Food purchases	6,000
Total available	$8,000
− Closing inventory	3,000
= Cost of food	$5,000

Once the cost of food is known, food cost percent can be determined by using the formula identified in Chapter 1:

$$\frac{\text{Cost}}{\text{Sales}} = \text{Cost \%}$$

$$\frac{\$\,5,000}{\$15,000} = 33.3\,\%$$

Saying that food cost percent is 33.3 percent is the same as saying that the cost of food has been $.333 per dollar sale. As discussed in Chapter 1, these are merely two different ways of saying the same thing, and the two are used commonly and interchangeably in the industry.

At this point, it is important to recognize that, while the $5,000 figure is the cost of food, it is really the cost of food *issued*. This is not necessarily the same as the cost of food *consumed*. Determining the cost of food consumed may require that the cost of food issued be adjusted to account for a number of possible alternative uses of the food issued. A number of the more common adjustments are identified and discussed below.

Adjustments to Cost of Food Issued

TRANSFERS.   If there have been any transfers between the kitchen and the bar, adjustments must be made to take the value of the transfers into account. Similarly, if there have been transfers from units in a chain to other units in the same chain, these must be totaled and used to adjust the cost figures of all units concerned. In some large hotels, where separate cost records are kept for the several food outlets in the property, similar adjustments must be made for food items transferred from one outlet to another. There are various kinds of transfers.

Intraunit transfers (those occurring within a given property) include:

1. Transfers of alcoholic beverages from bar to kitchen, used in food preparation. The term **cooking liquor** is commonly used to refer to these.
2. Transfers of directs from kitchen to bar, where they will be used in drink preparation. The term **food to bar** (**directs**) is often used for these.

Interunit transfers (those between properties in a chain) may involve any foods or beverages. For obvious reasons, interunit transfers seldom involve properties that are distant from one another. They are more common among urban units in a chain that may be only a few blocks from each other.

Transfers are not the only possible adjustments to food cost figures. In order to achieve more accurate food costs, many operations make one or more of the adjustments discussed below.

GREASE SALES.   In many foodservice operations, particularly those that still butcher their meats on premises, raw fat is one of the normal by-products of kitchen operation. Most keep this raw fat under refrigeration until disposing of it. For some, this means paying to have it removed from the premises. For others, it means selling it to rendering companies, which convert it to industrial fats and oils. The sale of this fat at a small value per pound results in revenue recorded as **Other Income—Salvage and Waste Sales.** As such, it is treated as a credit in determining food cost.

STEWARD SALES.   In some establishments—primarily large hotels and motels and a very few restaurants—employees may be permitted to purchase food at cost and take it from the premises for their own personal use. Employees may take advantage of this for special occasions when, for example, they want a specific cut or grade of meat that is not normally available in their local markets. In those properties that permit steward sales, the amounts paid by employees are customarily treated as credits to cost rather than as revenue. In other words, steward sales are similar to reimbursements; they are considered cost reductions rather than revenue increases. If this is not done, the cost of any foods sold to employees are included erroneously in food cost figures for the period.

GRATIS TO BARS.   In many establishments, the kitchen staff is expected to produce various hot and cold hors d'oeuvres that are given free to customers at the bar. Since the purpose of this is to promote beverage sales, it seems logical to include the cost of these hors d'oeuvres in the cost of operating the beverage department. To do this, one must first adjust food cost by subtracting the value of the hors d'oeuvres, usually an estimated value, prepared for the bar.

PROMOTION EXPENSE.   In many properties, owners or managers entertain potential customers who are thought likely to bring in banquet business. In large hotels and other properties that depend on conventions and group bookings for a major part of their revenue, sales managers, marketing directors, catering managers, banquet managers, and other sales personnel routinely entertain potential clients. They may invite people to the property for luncheon or dinner and discuss hospitality products and prices during the course of the meal. Food is ordered from the menu and eaten. A server records it on a guest check, but sales revenue is not increased because no one pays the check. Since the purpose of this is to promote sales (food, beverages, rooms, or all of these), it seems logical to include the cost of the food consumed during these meals in the cost of operating a sales, banquet, or marketing department. To do this, one must first adjust food cost by subtracting the value of the food. Thus, management may credit food cost for the value of foods consumed for these purposes and charge the cost to another account, such as promotion expense.

Determining Cost of Food Consumed

If some or all of the adjustments described above are to be taken into account, the monthly determination of cost of food consumed is determined as follows:

> Opening inventory
> + Purchases
> = Total available for sale
> − Closing inventory
> = Cost of food issued
> + Cooking liquor
> + Transfers from other units
> − Food to bar (directs)
> − Transfers to other units
> − Grease sales
> − Steward sales
> − Gratis to bars
> − Promotion expense
> = Cost of food consumed

However, while this procedure does enable management to determine a food cost figure that is more accurate than one that ignores the possible need for adjustments of various kinds, it is still not sufficiently accurate for many. After all, some of the food consumed in many establishments does not produce sales revenue and is not intended to do so. In many operations, meals are provided on premises for employees as a matter of course. Typically, employees are not charged for the food they consume. Therefore, in order to determine a more accurate figure for food cost (cost of food sold), one must subtract the cost of employees' meals from the cost of food consumed.

COST OF EMPLOYEE MEALS.   While there are numerous techniques for determining the cost of employees' meals, some are in relatively common use in the industry, while others are comparatively uncommon. The four described below are among those in general use.

1. *Cost of Separate Issues.*   This technique requires that employees be given food other than that which is prepared for customers. All food used in the preparation of employee meals must be issued separately and listed on requisitions, which are kept separate from all other food requisitions used in the establishment. If the food issued is listed on separate requisitions, one can readily determine its cost: Some individual is assigned the task of pricing the requisitions, a procedure previously described in Chapter 6. For any given period, the total value of

the foods listed on these special requisitions is equal to the cost of food for employee meals for the period.

This technique is best suited to those operations large enough to maintain separate preparation and dining areas for their employees. Thus, it is used in a number of larger hotels but in comparatively few restaurants.

2. *Prescribed Amount Per Meal Per Employee.* A Somewhat more common approach is to direct the chef to give employees meals that will cost no more than a specific fixed amount per meal. For example, the fixed amounts established for meals might be $1.50 for breakfast, $2.50 for luncheon, and $3.50 for dinner. A procedure would be established to keep daily records of the number of employees consuming each of these meals. These totals would be added to cumulative figures for the period. The total cost of employees' meals for the period would be determined by multiplying the fixed amount per meal by the number of employees who consumed that meal during the period and then adding together the totals for the several possible meals. If employees have no choice of meals (if, for example, luncheon is the only meal they are permitted), this technique for determining the cost of employees' meals is comparatively easy to use.

3. *Prescribed Amount Per Period.* Because some find it difficult to keep records of the numbers of employees consuming meals each day, there is another technique that requires no such records. Management simply informs the chef of a fixed amount that will be credited to food cost for employee meals for each period, regardless of the number of employees who actually have meals on the premises. It is then up to the chef to estimate the number who may eat and either prepare food that will not exceed the cost guideline or offer employees food prepared for customers that does not exceed this permissible cost.

4. *Sales Value Multiplied By Cost Percent.* Another technique requires that each employee who eats records the selections on a check. This may or may not be the same as the guest check used in the dining room. The menu price is recorded next to each selection. The check is totaled, but the employee is not asked to pay it. The checks are totaled at the end of the period. This grand total is then multiplied by the average food cost percent in recent periods to arrive at a reasonable cost figure for employee meals for that period.

By means of these or other alternative techniques, it is possible to arrive at some reasonable figure for the cost of employee meals.

DETERMINING COST OF FOOD SOLD

Once the total cost of employees' meals for a period has been established, the figure should be subtracted from the cost of food consumed to determine the cost of food sold. This procedure provides one with a final figure that should be used for calculating food cost percent (the cost-to-sales ratio) and for evaluating performance. Those who calculate cost of food sold and food cost percent without taking employee meals into account are likely to have overstated food cost and distorted food cost percent.

When one uses all of the above adjustments, the calculation of cost of food sold in the month of July for the Pasta Pit, the restaurant previously described, is as follows:

Opening inventory		$2,000
+ Purchases		6,000
= Total available		$8,000
− Closing inventory		3,000
= Cost of food issue		$5,000
+ Cooking liquor	$200	
+ Transfers from other units	250	$ 450
= Subtotal		$5,450
Food to bar (directs)	$ 68	
− Transfers to other units	349	
− Grease sales	27	
− Steward sales	12	
− Gratis to bar(s)	72	
− Promotion expense	22	$ 550
= Cost of food consumed		$4,900
− Cost of employees' meals		300
= Cost of food sold		$4,600

Using the sales figure of $15,000 identified earlier in the chapter, one can now use this new and more accurate figure for cost of food sold to determine food cost percentage for the period:

$$\frac{\text{Cost of food sold}}{\text{Food sales}} = \text{Food cost \%}$$

$$\frac{\$\,4,600}{\$\,15,000} = .30666666 = 30.7\%$$

This is the same as stating that food cost in the period was $.307 per dollar sale, as discussed above.

	July XXXX	*June XXXX*
Food Sales	$15,000	$14,000
Net Cost of Food Sold	$ 4,600	$ 4,340
Food Cost %	30.7%	31.0%

FIGURE 9.3   *Food Cost Report*

Food cost percentage calculated with this more accurate figure, 30.7 percent, is actually 2.6 percent lower than that calculated before the adjustments were made. Similarly, cost per dollar sale was $.026 lower.

Although figures for food cost percentage and food cost per dollar sale may be interesting, they become useful when compared to figures for similar periods in the past. For example, if we knew that food cost percentage for June had been 38.0 percent, we could compare the two and determine that the figure for July was lower than the figure for June by 7.3 percent. Comparisons of this nature are easier to make when the figures for current and past figures are recorded side by side on reports to management.

REPORTS TO MANAGEMENT

Once cost of food sold and food cost percentage have been calculated, they are normally reported to management. The nature of the report must be determined individually for each establishment or unit in a chain. That will be based on management's need for information, as well as the availability of that information. If the food control system is extensive and complex, more detailed information is likely to be available. When it is, management is more likely to be better informed and thus better equipped to make decisions.

Although the specifics of reports to management differ from one foodservice operation to another, they tend to have some similarities. It will be worthwhile to identify these and to illustrate two simple types of reports that are reasonably common in foodservice establishments.

In some small establishments, where there are few formal control procedures and no specific control personnel, it may be impossible for anyone to prepare even the simplest reports without outside assistance. This assistance may be provided by a professional accountant who comes in once a month, between the first and the tenth of the month, to make the necessary entries in the financial records of the bussiness—the **books of account.** After the accountant has completed this work, the information required for preparing a basic report is available. After all, one only needs to know food sales and cost of food sold to determine food cost percentage and food cost per dollar sale,

	July XXXX	June XXXX
Food Sales	$15,000	$12,000
Net Cost of Food Sold	$ 4,600	$ 4,560
Food Cost %	30.7%	38.0%

FIGURE 9.4 *Food Cost Report*

as indicated above. A simple report can be prepared from that basic information. Report forms for foodservice operations are available from stationers catering to the industry. However, reports to management should always be based on management's need for specific information, rather than on the availability of a particular form. If no appropriate form can be obtained from a stationer, it is very easy to devise one that will meet the need for specific information in a particular establishment.

The form illustrated in Figure 9.3 is one of the simplest that can be devised for a report to management. Figures for the current period are in the first column, and those for the same period in the previous year are in the second. When both can be seen on one form, side by side, it is possible to compare them and to make some judgment about the relative effectiveness of current operations. Thus, if the 31.0 percent cost-to-sales ratio for the same period last year was within the range of acceptability, it is likely that the 30.7 percent figure this year would also be acceptable, provided there have been no significant changes in menu or operating procedure and no significant drop in sales.

In some instances, particularly when figures for previous periods have been unacceptable and corrective action has been taken to improve performance, it is desirable to have reports that make it easier to evaluate the effects of the corrective action. If the report were in a format that made it easy to compare the figures for two consecutive months (June and July, for example, as in Figure 9.4), one could readily make some judgment about whether or not the changes had produced the desired effect the following month.

If the manager of the Pasta Pit had judged the June cost-to-sales ratio of 38.0 percent unacceptable and had taken corrective actions aimed at bringing down the cost-to-sales ratio in July, this format would make it easy to compare the two months and to make some judgments about the effectiveness of the changes. In the current instance, it is likely that the reduction in the cost percentage from 38.0 percent to 30.7 percent would be considered acceptable. If so, the corrective actions taken to bring about the improvement would probably become the established standard procedures in the future.

In foodservice, cost percentage is often used as a means for monitoring operations and judging the effectiveness of control procedures. Managers routinely compare cost percent for one period to cost percentage for another. If the cost percentage for a current month is approximately the same as it has been in other recent months, it is likely that cost percentage for the current month will also be judged acceptable, provided that cost percentage in those recent months was judged acceptable and there have been no major changes in menu, purchase prices, or any of the other principal factors affecting food cost or food sales. However, if there have been no such changes, yet cost percentage for the current month is considerably higher or lower than in the recent past, management will normally want to identify the reasons for the change. Once the reasons are known, action can be taken aimed at insuring or preventing their recurrence, depending on whether or not the current cost percentage has been judged unacceptable.

Operating figures and comparisons between them are similar to the sightings taken by mariners. No one intending to sail a ship successfully across several thousand miles of ocean would consider setting a course on leaving port and taking no readings or sightings during the voyage. These readings and sightings are used by a mariner to make judgments about the position of a ship relative to its established course. If the captain of a ship failed to take readings and make the necessary judgments, the ship would be likely to end its voyage some considerable distance from the intended destination. During any voyage, readings are taken frequently to monitor the ship's progress. Judgments are made, and, when necessary, corrective action is taken to bring the ship back on course. The more frequently this is done, the closer the ship is likely to stay to its original course. If less infrequent readings are taken, there is greater likelihood that the ship will stray off course and that considerable time and money will be lost in reaching the intended destination.

Ideally, the readings used to monitor the progress of a ship or a foodservice operation will be both frequent and timely. For large numbers of foodservice managers, monthly food cost and food cost percentage are not truly useful for monitoring foodservice operations because they fail to meet the two following important criteria.

1. *Frequency.* In foodservice, many managers feel that monthly "readings" on the course of business are not frequent enough. A foodservice operation can stray quite far off course in one month. If that occurs, considerable difficulty and expense may be required to bring it back on course. Readings taken more frequently (daily or weekly, for example) provide managers with information that can be used to make course corrections during the current period.
2. *Timeliness.* The second important consideration is that information must be timely. One problem with relying exclusively on monthly figures for food cost and food cost percentage is that they are not timely.

That is to say that they do not become available until it is too late to determine the cause or causes of unacceptable results. One cannot normally look back over a period of three or four weeks to find explanations. It is difficult enough to remember the most recent two or three days; remembering what happened weeks ago may be impossible. And when causes cannot be identified accurately, taking corrective action may be impossible. In addition, even if monthly figures do enable one to identify causes and take corrective action, that corrective action cannot possibly have any positive effects on the past month. It is clearly too late for that. If food cost and food cost percent for June were completely unacceptable, for example, one would have to live with the June results forever. The best one could hope to do would be to make changes that would have a positive impact in July.

Because of the difficulties inherent in relying on monthly figures alone, many foodservice managers prefer to have food cost, food cost percent, and other operating figures calculated much more frequently (daily or weekly, for example). Daily or weekly calculations make it possible to prepare daily or weekly reports. The manager who can identify a problem that occurred yesterday has a better chance of identifying its causes and taking corrective action immediately. It is much easier to identify causes when the time span between the occurrence of a problem and its identification are minimal.

In general, the more frequent the reports and the more detailed the information they include, the better will be the opportunities they offer management to maintain control over operations and to ensure that the results conform to plans.

Procedures for the daily determination of food cost and food cost percentage and the preparation of reports based on these daily figures will be discussed in Chapter 10.

INVENTORY TURNOVER

It should be obvious that foodservice managers are responsible for insuring sufficient supplies of appropriate foods are available for use when needed. At the same time, they are expected to prevent the development of excessive quantities of foods. The stockpiling of quantities greater than needed can lead to any of a number of significant problems, including:

1. Excessive food costs due to the spoilage of food stored too long.
2. Excessive amounts of cash tied up in inventory.
3. Excessive labor costs to receive and store foods.
4. Excessive space required for storage.
5. Unwarranted opportunities for theft.

It is impossible to establish any valid industry-wide standards for the foods, the number of units of those foods, or the valuation of food that should be on hand in the foodservice enterprise. The particulars vary from one operation to another and are likely to be related to such considerations as menus, differences in size, sales volume, and financial health, among others. After all, larger establishments tend to need more storage space and greater quantities of food in storage than smaller establishments do. And many foodservice establishments have slow periods during the year when smaller-than-usual quantities of food are needed. Nevertheless, managers are expected to make judgments about whether or not appropriate, but not excessive, quantities of food are available for food preparation.

One technique commonly used to evaluate the adequacy of a food inventory is to calculate how often that inventory has been used and replenished during an accounting period. This varies from one establishment to another and is influenced by many factors, including the amount of cash available for such purposes, the space available for storage, and the time necessary to receive food once it is ordered. If one were to purchase sufficient food to last one full year, most reasonable people would agree that the quantity was excessive and would lead to waste, inefficiency, and higher costs than were warranted. On the other hand, if one were to purchase just enough food to last for one day, most would agree that more should be purchased and that savings could result by purchasing in larger quantities. Somewhere between these two extremes is an idealized amount of food to have on hand for a specific period. For most foodservice operations, an amount sufficient to last one or two weeks is considered normal, and we will use that range as our guide.

To measure how often a food inventory has been consumed and replenished during an accounting period, foodservice managers calculate a figure known as **inventory turnover,** or the **rate of inventory turnover.** The terms are used interchangeably. For example, if the Pasta Pit purchases, consumes, and replenishes its food inventory twice each month, its rate of inventory turnover would be 24 times each year. This is very close to the guideline cited above.

It is important to realize that literally every item in the inventory does not turn over exactly twice during the period. Some items in the inventory are likely to turn over more frequently than twice a month, while others may turn over much less frequently. As we will see, inventory turnover calculations are based on the dollar valuation of an inventory, not on the use of specific items in that inventory. Inventory turnover rates are calculated at the end of a month, soon after a value has been established for the closing inventory in the manner described earlier in the chapter.

Inventory turnover rate is calculated by means of the following formulas:

$$\text{Total inventory} = \text{Opening inventory} + \text{Closing inventory}$$

$$\text{Average inventory} = \frac{\text{Total inventory}}{2}$$

$$\text{Inventory turnover} = \frac{\text{Food cost}}{\text{Average inventory}}$$

Using three figures taken from previous discussion in this chapter, one can now proceed to determine inventory turnover for the Pasta Pit:

Opening inventory	$2,000
Closing inventory	$3,000
Food cost	$4,600

Next, one substitutes these figures in the formulas provided above, as follows:

$$\text{Total inventory} = \$5{,}000 \ (\$2{,}000 + \$3{,}000)$$

$$\text{Average inventory} = \$2{,}500 \ (\$5{,}000/2)$$

$$\text{Inventory turnover} = 1.84 \ (\$4{,}600/\$2{,}500)$$

If the rate were the same each month, the inventory turnover rate for the year would be 22.08 times, or once every 2.355 weeks, slightly higher than the guide indicated above—once every one or two weeks.

Some may question the accuracy of the average inventory figure calculated above, which is based on an assumption that the opening and closing inventory figures are truly representative of the levels of inventory on hand during the month. That is not always the case. Sometimes, when inventory value has been deemed too high early in the month, most purchasing may be stopped in order to bring overall inventory value down to an acceptable level before the end of the month. While this is not uncommon and does tend to distort the average inventory figure, the alternative to the procedure described above would be to determine the value of physical inventory more frequently. Most would find this too time-consuming and too costly to be considered a viable course.

COMPUTER APPLICATIONS

If inventory software is used and records of all foods received and issued have been entered in the computer terminal, it is easy to obtain a printout indicating the quantity of each item in inventory at any given time. The most appropriate time to obtain this report would be at the end of a month, the time when physical inventory is taken. This does not eliminate the need for physical inventory because the inventory software does not report actual quantities in inventory. Instead, the printout indicates quantities that should be found in inventory. This is an important distinction. If, for example, food has been taken from inventory without being recorded, then the number of units in the physical inventory will differ from the number on the computer printout. Therefore, if physical inventory is taken and compared item by item with computer records, management can determine the extent of unauthorized or nonstandard issues of food. This would be considered some measure of the extent to which employees were following the standard procedures established for operation.

A physical inventory provides information that can be used to update computer records of the inventory. With inventory records updated and current at the end of the accounting period, the software can attend to all calculations necessary for determining the value of closing inventory, regardless of which of the methods previously discussed has been selected. Once the calculations are complete, one can obtain a printout that provides all necessary information. It should be obvious that the calculation of closing inventory value can be completed much faster by computer than by manual means.

With the above information available, software presently available will calculate cost of food issued, cost of food consumed, and cost of food sold. It will also produce reports comparing figures for the current period with those for similar recent periods. The nature of these reports could range from the relatively simple variety illustrated in this chapter to any of a number of more extensive and detailed reports similar to those illustrated in the following chapter.

CHAPTER ESSENTIALS

In this chapter, we examined the simplest means of monitoring overall performance in foodservice. We described a series of monthly procedures used for this purpose in a large number of operations. We described the procedure for taking monthly physical inventory of food and identified five methods used to assign values to units of the products in an inventory. Having illustrated each of these methods, we showed the calculations necessary to determine food costs. We defined and differentiated among the terms cost of food issued, cost of food consumed, and cost of food sold. We described the procedure for calculating each of these and described various possible adjustments used in the calculations, including transfers, grease sales, steward sales, promotion expense, and employees' meals. We illustrated the monthly determination of food cost percent and food cost per dollar sale and showed how these figures are commonly reported to management and used for making comparisons with similar figures for other operating periods and for judging operational performance. We described and illustrated the calculation of inventory turnover and discussed its significance to foodservice managers. Finally, we indicated that software can help assess employee adherence to standard procedures for issuing food, calculate the value of closing inventory and the cost of food for the current period, and prepare comparative reports for managers.

KEY TERMS IN THIS CHAPTER

Actual purchase price method
Average inventory
Closing inventory
Cost of employee meals
Cost of food consumed
Cost of food issued
Cost of food sold
First-in, first-out method
Gratis to bar
Grease sales
Interunit transfer
Intraunit transfer
Inventory turnover
Last-in, first-out method
Latest purchase price method
Monthly food cost
Opening inventory
Physical inventory
Steward sales
Total available
Total inventory
Weighted average purchase price method

QUESTIONS AND PROBLEMS

1. The following figures for November have been taken from the financial records of three units in the Pasta Pit chain. Determine total food issues for each.

    a. Opening inventory $ 1,500.00
          Purchases $ 4,600.00
          Closing inventory   1,722.00

    b. Closing inventory $12,083.00
          Opening inventory   10,371.00
          Purchases   28,468.00

    c. Purchases $65,851.08

Closing inventory	18,335.10
Opening inventory	19,874.77

2. Given the figures below for three units in a chain of restaurants operated under the name Grandma's Kitchen, calculate cost of food issued and cost of food consumed for each.

   a.
Purchases	$ 8,300.00
Opening inventory	2,688.00
Closing inventory	2,540.00
Grease sales	76.00
Cooking liquor	94.00
Gratis to bar	119.00

   b.
Food to bar (directs)	$ 189.00
Closing inventory	6,647.00
Transfers to other units	339.00
Purchases	19,472.00
Steward sales	53.00
Transfers from other units	223.00
Opening inventory	6,531.00

   c.
Opening inventory	$ 6,622.40
Transfers from other units	47.35
Cooking liquor	253.65
Purchases	24,182.55
Closing inventory	6,719.30
Transfers to other units	347.60
Food to bar (directs)	337.40
Grease sales	91.85
Gratis to bar	177.35

3. For each of the following, determine cost of employees' meals.

   a. In the Meal Mall, employees were served 337 lunches and 381 dinners in March. Food cost is credited $.70 per meal for lunch and $1.10 per meal for dinner.

   b. In Monty's Restaurant, employees are required to record their food selections on checks and to enter the menu price next to each selection. The total sales value of employees' meals in September was $7,826.95. In recent months, food cost percentage has averaged 35%.

   c. In Bartholomew's Pub, the chef was directed to prepare food for the employees at a cost not to exceed $25 per day, regardless of the number of employees fed. In February, the restaurant was open six days per week, but closed on Mondays.

4. Given the following figures from the financial records of three units in a small restaurant chain in Centerville, determine the cost of food sold for each.

   a. Cooking liquor $ 210.50
      Steward sales   27.58
      Purchases   12,339.42
      Food to bar (directs)   201.38
      Gratis to bar   267.50
      Grease sales   95.60
      Closing inventory   4,278.37
      Opening inventory   4,031.19
      Employees' meals:
         328 lunches @ $.65 each
         449 dinners @ $.95 each

   b. Closing inventory $ 3,427.30
      Grease sales   92.60
      Purchases   11,230.45
      Opening inventory   3,012.80
      Transfers from other units   128.65
      Cooking liquor   298.40
      Gratis to bar   427.80
      Food to bar (directs)   312.45
      Transfers to other units   155.75
      Employees' meals:
      $2,576.45 sales value; recent average food cost percentage: 34.0%

   c. Purchases $68,543.36
      Promotion expense   81.17
      Grease sales   167.42
      Closing inventory   20,963.71
      Gratis to bar   58.73
      Transfers from other units   637.38
      Food to bar (directs)   296.35
      Opening inventory   22,687.40
      Transfers to other units   784.29
      Cooking liquor   543.18
      Employee meals:
         Executives: $1,833.75 sales value; recent average food cost percentage: 31.0%
            Other staff: 1,422 breakfasts @ $ .55
                            1,208 lunches   @ $ .80
                            1,012 dinners   @ $1.05

5. Using the figures for cost of food sold determined in Question 4, calculate food cost percent and food cost per dollar sale for each of the three restaurants, given the following sales figures.
   a. $ 26,173.55
   b. $ 25,819.45
   c. $191,405.95

6. The following information about one of the items carried in the food inventory of the Yellow Dog Restaurant is taken from inventory records for the month of January.

1/1 Opening inventory	12 units @ $1.05 each
1/5 Purchased	18 units @ $1.15
1/12 Purchased	18 units @ $1.20
1/19 Purchased	12 units @ $1.30
1/26 Purchased	6 units @ $1.40

   On January 31, the physical inventory indicated nine units remaining on the shelf. Determine both the value of the closing inventory and the cost of units issued, using each of the five methods identified in this chapter.

7. The information listed below has been taken from the May financial records of three restaurants in Springfield. Calculate inventory turnover for each.

a.	Opening inventory	$ 3,287.40
	Closing inventory	3,322.60
	Food cost	13,220.00
b.	Food cost	$18,448.30
	Opening inventory	6,327.65
	Closing inventory	6,581.75
c.	Closing inventory	$21,971.38
	Food cost	67,346.93
	Opening inventory	23,168.49

8. Determine inventory turnover for each of the three units in the Centerville chain identified in Question 4, using the information provided above and the cost of food sold figures you calculated.

9. List as many possible causes as you can for each of the following changes from one month to the next.
   a. Increase in the food cost percent.
   b. Decrease in the food cost percent.
   c. Increase in the inventory turnover rate.
   d. Decrease in the inventory turnover rate.

10. Define each of the following terms:
    Actual purchase price method
    Average inventory
    Closing inventory
    Cost of employee meals
    Cost of food consumed
    Cost of food issued
    Cost of food sold
    First-in, first-out method
    Gratis to bar
    Grease sales
    Interunit transfer
    Intraunit transfer
    Inventory turnover
    Last-in, first-out method
    Latest purchase price method
    Monthly food cost
    Opening inventory
    Physical inventory
    Steward sales
    Total available
    Total inventory
    Weighted average purchase price method

FOR COMPUTER USERS

11. Using any spreadsheet program you choose, create a worksheet for completing the calculations required in Question 4 and then use the worksheet to calculate cost of food sold for each of the three units.

12. Create a worksheet to calculate inventory turnover and then use it to solve Questions 7 and 8.

10

Monitoring Foodservice Operations II: Daily Food Cost

LEARNING OBJECTIVES

After reading and studying this chapter, you should be able to:

1. Calculate food cost for any one day and for all the days to date in a period.
2. Calculate food cost percent for any one day and for all the days to date in a period.
3. Prepare and explain a daily report of food sales, food cost, and food cost percent.
4. Determine book inventory value.
5. Explain the difference between book inventory and actual inventory.
6. Identify various causes for differences between book inventory value and actual inventory value.
7. Discuss the use of computers for generating daily food cost reports.
8. Define each of the Key Terms at the end of the chapter.

INTRODUCTION

One major problem with monitoring foodservice operations from monthly figures alone is the length of time between monthly reports. When the figures for one month reveal that problems have developed and corrective actions are taken to eliminate the problems, one must then wait one full month to see the next report and determine whether or not the corrective actions have been effective. If management has made erroneous judgments about the causes of excessive costs and the corrective actions taken have been based on those erroneous judgments, it will be a full month before the next report reveals that these corrective actions have not had the desired effect. This delay can be very costly. To avoid this delay and to make more timely figures available on which to base day-to-day operating decisions, a number of larger, better-organized foodservice operations use daily food cost calculations.

DETERMINING DAILY FOOD COST

It is possible to determine daily food cost for any operation if certain procedures discussed in previous chapters are used. Since all foods can be categorized as either *directs* or *stores* in food control, the total costs for these two are the two basic components of the daily food cost.

As discussed in an earlier chapter, directs are charged to food cost as received. Therefore, to determine food cost for any given day, one must know the total of directs received on that day. This figure is readily available if the Receiving Clerk's Daily Report or some similar form is completed each day. The sum of the entries in the "Food Direct" column on the report for any given day is the cost of directs for that day.

By contrast, stores purchases are added to inventory and charged to the food cost when issued. Therefore, one must determine the value of stores issued on a given day, each day, to obtain the second principal component of food cost for that day. If all foods issued from inventory are listed on requisitions, the determination is not difficult. One merely prices and extends each requisition for foods issued on that day and then adds the totals for all requisitions to obtain the total cost of stores issued.

In operations where transfers are made between the food and beverage departments, between units in a chain organization, or where any of the various other adjustments discussed in the previous chapters are used (promotion expense, employees' meals, and steward sales, for example), values for these should be determined daily and taken into account as well. For example, the values for any items received as directs, charged to food cost, but subsequently transferred to the bar for use in drink production would be credited to daily food cost, just as they are credited to monthly food cost. These items—oranges, lemons, limes, and heavy cream are some common ones—should be listed on transfer memos or some similar form. One would determine their value and then credit the daily food cost for that amount. Similarly, the value of any alcoholic beverages transferred from the bar to the kitchen for use in food preparation should be charged to food cost. These, too, should be listed on transfer memos. In addition, many establishments credit daily food cost for the value of employees' meals.

Thus, the daily cost of food can be determined in the following way:

Cost of directs (from the receiving clerk's daily report)
   + Cost of stores (from requisitions or from requisitions and meat tags, depending on the procedure followed)
   + Adjustments that increase daily cost (transfers from bar to kitchen; transfers from other units)
   − Adjustments that decrease daily cost (transfers from the kitchen to the bar: food to bar (directs), gratis to bar; steward sales; grease sales; promotion expense)
   = Cost of food consumed
   − Cost of employee meals
   = Daily cost of food sold

After one determines daily food cost, the next step is to obtain a daily sales figure, usually from accounting records. When both food cost and food sales figures are known, a daily food cost percent can be determined:

$$\frac{\text{Food cost}}{\text{Food sales}} = \text{Food cost \%}$$

By itself, the daily food cost percent for any one day may not be a very accurate figure. For example, many restaurants purchase directs every other day, and this will affect daily food cost, making it artificially higher on the days when directs are received and charged to food cost and correspondingly lower on the other days. In addition, some foods may be issued from stores one or more days before they will be used. Salt, flour, and various cooking oils, for example, may be issued to the kitchen once a week to avoid the need for daily requisitioning. In other instances, wholesale cuts of meat may be issued one full day in advance because of the times required for in-house butchering. These and any other similar examples will have the effect of raising food cost and food cost percent on the day of issue because the food is not reflected in sales until one or more days later.

To help overcome the problem of artificially high food cost percent one day and low food cost percent the next, most also calculate food cost percent to date. **Food cost percent** to date is defined as the cumulative food cost percent

Date	Directs	Stores	Adjustments Beverage to Food	Adjustments Food to Beverage	Cost Today	Cost to Date	Sales Today	Sales to Date	Cost % Today	Cost % to Date
3/1	50	100	—	—	150		500		30%	
3/2	25	75			100	250	250	750	40%	33.3%

FIGURE 10.1 *Daily Cumulative Cost Record*

for a period. It takes into account all food costs and all food sales for all days so far in the period. Thus, the food cost percent to date on the fourth day of a period would be based on the total food costs for the four days and the total food sales for the same four days. To determine this cumulative food cost percent (food cost percent to date), one divides cost to date by sales to date:

$$\frac{\text{Food cost \% to date}}{\text{Food sales to date}} = \text{Food cost \% to date}$$

Figure 10.1 is an example of the type of simple form that can be designed and inexpensively reproduced to give order and continuity to the procedure for determining daily food cost. In order to maintain simplicity for purposes of discussion, we have limited the number of adjustment columns to two: one for additions to cost and the other for subtractions. However, in practice there is no barrier to increasing the number of columns to whatever would be necessary for achieving the desired degree of accuracy in any particular operation.

The procedure may be followed on a daily and cumulative basis for any number of days, depending on the needs of management. In many cases, these cumulative figures are maintained on a weekly basis; in others, the basis is monthly.

Figure 10.2 is an example of an alternative form that could be used in establishments that still use meat tags in order to maintain separate figures for meats and other stores. Because meats and other tagged items normally represent the largest single element of food cost, this alternative form is useful for those who need a more detailed breakdown of where the food cost dollars are going. If meat tags are attached to requisitions, one can simply total the values of these meat tags and subtract that total from the total of the requisitions to obtain correct totals for the two categories.

The form illustrated in Figure 10.2 also makes provision for three additional columns at the right side of the form for purchases, issues, and balance. These columns are used to maintain a daily balance of stores inventory and are discussed in detail later in this chapter (see Figure 10.8).

| Date | Directs | Meat | Stores | Adjustments | | Total Cost | | Total Sales | | Food Cost % | | Food Inventory | | |
				Beverage to Food	Food to Beverage	Today	To Date	Today	To Date	Today	To Date	Purchases	Issue	Balance
10/15	500	275	100	20	10	885	885	2,000	2,000	44.3%	44.3%			
10/16	325	275	100	20	20	700	1,585	2,100	4,100	33.3%	38.7%			
10/17	400	300	125	25	20	830	2,415	2,200	6,300	37.7%	38.3%			
10/18	375	290	115	30	25	785	3,200	2,450	8,750	32.0%	36.6%			
10/19	490	450	105	30	30	1,045	4,245	3,400	12,150	30.7%	34.9%			
10/20	80	525	140	40	40	745	4,990	3,600	15,750	20.7%	31.7%			

FIGURE 10.2 *Daily Cumulative Cost Record, Using Meat Tags*

235

1	2	3	4	5	6	7	8	9	10	11
						Total				
Date	Day	Vegetables	Fruits	Dairy	Bakery	Directs	Beef	Poultry	Provisions	Other
10/1	Mon.	150.00	100.00	75.00	75.00	400.00	200.00	100.00	50.00	25.00
2	Tues.	100.00	50.00	25.00	25.00	200.00	100.00	50.00	40.00	10.00
3	Wed.	175.00	125.00	25.00	25.00	350.00	225.00	125.00	20.00	20.00
4	Thurs.	100.00	50.00	50.00	25.00	225.00	100.00	75.00	15.00	30.00
5	Fri.	175.00	100.00	75.00	75.00	425.00	250.00	125.00	25.00	50.00
6	Sat.	—	—	50.00	25.00	75.00	70.00	10.00	—	10.00
		700.00	425.00	300.00	250.00	1,675.00	945.00	485.00	150.00	145.00
10/8	Mon.	175.00	125.00	100.00	50.00	450.00	225.00	100.00	75.00	20.00
9	Tues.	100.00	75.00	25.00	25.00	225.00	100.00	75.00	—	10.00
10	Wed.	125.00	100.00	25.00	50.00	300.00	200.00	100.00	50.00	15.00
11	Thurs.	75.00	50.00	25.00	25.00		75.00	25.00	40.00	20.00
12	Fri.	200.00	100.00	100.00	25.00	425.00	250.00	150.00	40.00	—
13	Sat.	—	—	50.00	40.00	90.00	75.00	15.00	—	15.00
		675.00	450.00	325.00	215.00	1,665.00	925.00	465.00	245.00	80.00
10/15	Mon.	225.00	125.00	100.00	50.00	500.00	200.00	50.00	25.00	—
16	Tues.	100.00	100.00	75.00	50.00	325.00	100.00	125.00	25.00	25.00
17	Wed.	150.00	100.00	100.00	50.00	400.00	150.00	100.00	30.00	20.00
18	Thurs.	175.00	100.00	75.00	25.00	375.00	125.00	115.00	25.00	25.00
19	Fri.	200.00	150.00	115.00	25.00	490.00	225.00	150.00	75.00	—
20	Sat.	—	—	40.00	40.00	80.00	300.00	150.00	50.00	25.00
		850.00	575.00	505.00	240.00	2,170.00	1,100.00	690.00	230.00	95.00

FIGURE 10.3   *Food Cost Analysis/October, XXXX*

If there is a need for an even greater degree of detail than one can obtain from the form in Figure 10.2, it is perfectly possible to establish additional subdivisions for the categories. Because forms of greater complexity that provide greater detail also require additional time and staff to develop the detailed information that such forms include, one is unlikely to see these in any but the larger establishments. Few others have the personnel to compile the figures.

Figure 10.3 illustrates a form on which basic costs have been subdivided into additional categories. The cost of directs, for example, has been subdivided into four categories to provide detailed information about the daily cost of vegetables, fruits, dairy products, and baked goods. Similarly, the cost of meats has been subdivided into four categories to provide additional detail about the daily cost of beef, poultry, provisions, and other meats. Given an accountant's analysis pad with an appropriate number of columns or a computer and a spreadsheet program, any manager should be able to develop a reasonably detailed cumulative record of daily food costs, daily food sales, and daily food cost percents for any given operation. The specific subdivisions of the various

12 Total Meat	13 Total Store-room	14 Bar → Food Cooking Liquor	15 Food → Bar Directs	16 17 Total Costs		18 19 Total Sales		20 21 Total Costs	
				Today	to Date	Today	to Date	Today	to Date
375.00	135.00	—	10.00	900.00	900.00	2,000.00	2,000.00	45.0%	45.0%
200.00	150.00	—	—	550.00	1,450.00	1,500.00	3,500.00	36.7%	41.4%
395.00	145.00	20.00	10.00	900.00	2,350.00	2,700.00	6,200.00	33.3%	37.9%
220.00	120.00	5.00	20.00	550.00	2,900.00	1,800.00	8,000.00	30.6%	36.3%
450.00	240.00	20.00	10.00	1,125.00	4,025.00	3,600.00	11,600.00	31.3%	34.7%
90.00	135.00	25.00	25.00	300.00	4,325.00	1,300.00	12,900.00	23.1%	33.5%
1,730.00	925.00								
420.00	160.00	30.00	10.00	1,050.00	1,050.00	2,000.00	2,000.00	54.5%	52.5%
185.00	135.00	10.00	5.00	550.00	1,600.00	1,600.00	3,600.00	34.4%	44.4%
365.00	115.00	—	5.00	775.00	2,375.00	2,200.00	5,800.00	35.2%	40.9%
160.00	90.00	—	—	425.00	2,800.00	1,400.00	7,200.00	30.4%	38.9%
440.00	215.00	30.00	10.00	1,100.00	3,900.00	3,400.00	10,600.00	32.4%	36.8%
105.00	105.00	25.00	25.00	300.00	4,200.00	2,000.00	12,600.00	15.0%	33.3%
1,675.00	820.00								
275.00	100.00	20.00	10.00	885.00	885.00	2,000.00	2,000.00	44.3%	44.3%
275.00	100.00	20.00	20.00	700.00	1,585.00	2,100.00	4,100.00	33.3%	38.7%
300.00	125.00	25.00	20.00	830.00	2,415.00	2,200.00	6,300.00	37.7%	38.3%
290.00	115.00	30.00	25.00	785.00	3,200.00	2,450.00	8,750.00	32.0%	36.6%
450.00	105.00	30.00	30.00	1,045.00	4,245.00	3,400.00	12,150.00	30.7%	34.9%
525.00	140.00	40.00	40.00	745.00	4,990.00	3,600.00	15,750.00	20.7%	31.7%
2,115.00	685.00								

FIGURE 10.3   (continued)

categories would depend on specific needs identified in the particular operation.

DAILY REPORTS

When one uses the basic approach to monthly reports discussed in the preceding chapter, it is possible to design a report that:

1. Shows food cost, food sales, and food cost percent for any one specific day and for all the days to date in the period, and
2. Compares these figures to those for a similar period.

Figure 10.4 is an example of a simple report that accomplishes this.

This is a basic report that includes daily figures for food cost, food sales, and food cost percent. In addition, the report includes cumulative figures for the period for food cost, food sales, and food cost percent. These are aligned

| | Today | To Date | |
		This Week	Last Week
Food Cost	$ 745	$ 4,990	$ 4,200
Food Sales	$3,600	$15,750	$12,600
Cost %	20.7%	31.7%	33.3%

FIGURE 10.4   *Report to Management/10/20/XXXX*

with figures providing the same information about one or more recent periods. When the information is presented in this way, it is easier to monitor operations—to compare operating results for similar periods and to make judgments about the effectiveness of current operations. If results are judged undesirable and unsatisfactory, causes can be investigated while the events are relatively fresh in the minds of those concerned. In effect, by one's using readings or sightings taken daily, operational decisions can be made and corrective actions taken to get the operation back on course.

If, for example, investigation reveals that an undesirably high food cost percent is the result of the overpurchasing of directs, a decision can be made to use up quantities on hand before additional purchases are made. This corrective action will have an immediate impact on the daily cost of directs, which should be lower than normal for a few days or so. This, in turn, will tend to depress daily food cost percent and food cost percent to date for the balance of the period.

In another instance, investigation might reveal that the undesirably high food cost percent was the result of excessive issuing of foods from stores. If this were the case, a decision might be made that quantities previously issued were to be used up before any additional quantities would be issued. Corrective action of this nature would have an immediate impact by keeping down the cost of issues for several days. Thus, daily and cumulative food costs and food cost percents would tend to be lower than they might have been otherwise.

When food costs and food cost percents are determined daily and to date and used as monitoring devices, the effect of these kinds of measures can be assessed daily, with the expected effect that, by the end of the operating period, costs will be in line with management's goals. This is not always the case, but the likelihood is increased when food costs and food cost percents are determined daily.

Taking intelligent corrective action to eliminate undesirable effects is not possible until causes have been identified accurately. Occasionally, determining causes is simple. However, it is much more common to find that there is

	Today	Same Day Last Week	To Date	
			This Week	Last Week
Food Sales	$3,600	$2,000	$15,750	$12,600
Food Cost	$ 745	$ 300	$ 4,990	$ 4,200
Food Cost %	20.7%	15.0%	31.7%	33.3%
Cost Breakdown:				
Directs	$ 80	$ 90	$ 2,170	$ 1,665
Stores	$ 665	$ 210	$ 2,800	$ 2,495
Meats	$ 525	$ 105	$ 2,115	$ 1,675
Groceries	$ 140	$ 105	$ 685	$ 820

FIGURE 10.5 *Report to Management/10/20/XXXX*

more than one cause and that the causes are not readily determined from the information on the report illustrated in Figure 10.4. In many smaller operations, it may be possible to go into the kitchen and make a complete first-hand investigation of all possible causes. In major hotels and other large operations, this is not usually the case. To reduce the amount of time and effort required for identifying the causes of unacceptably high food costs, some foodservice managers rely on more complex reports. Figure 10.5 provides an example of a report designed with this aim.

A variation on this technique involves using the same form of report, but showing the cost breakdown in terms of ratios rather than dollar figures. Ratios are established between direct costs and sales, both today and to date, and the same is done for other costs as well. This can be a particularly useful approach in operations offering menus that seldom change.

In the example given in Figure 10.6, one can see that, while sales figures to date are considerably higher this week than last week, the ratio of cost components to sales has not changed dramatically. As percentages of sales, total directs are up by .6 percent and total meat is up by .1 percent, while total stores are down by 2.2 percent. While these percentages are useful, it is important to note how deceptive they can be. The 2.2 percent decrease in the ratio of cost of total stores to total sales is based on a comparatively small dollar decrease ($135), while the .1 percent increase in the ratio of cost of meats to total sales actually masks a comparatively large dollar increase ($440). In restaurants that use this type of report, the monitoring of operations is likely to include monitoring these ratios and watching for increases or decreases that appear to be too great. When some ratio varies considerably from its level in the recent past, causes can be investigated and corrective actions taken when warranted. If, for example, one noted an increase in the overall cost-to-sales ratio along with a dramatic increase in the ratio of meat cost to total sales while

DAY Saturday		DATE 10/20, XXXX		W/E 10/20, XXXX

| | | | To Date | |
Description	Today	This Week	Last Week	Same Week, Last Mo.
Food Sales	3,600	15,750	12,600	
Food Cost	745	4,990	4,200	
Food Cost %	20.7%	31.7%	33.3%	

Item	Vegetables	Fruits	Dairy	Bakery	Total Directs	
This Week	850	575	505	240	2,170	13.8%
Last Week	675	450	325	215	1,665	13.2%

Item	Beef	Poultry	Provisions	Other	Total Meat		Total Stores	
This Week	1,100	690	230	95	2,115	13.4%	685	4.3%
Last Week	925	465	245	80	1,675	13.3%	820	6.5%

Item	Cooking Liquor	Food to Bar (Directs)
This Week	165	145
Last Week	95	45

FIGURE 10.6 *Daily Food Cost Report*

DAY Saturday		DATE 10/20, XXXX		W/E 10/20, XXXX		
			To Date			
Description	Today	This Week	Last Week		Same Week, Last Month	
Food Sales	3,600	15,750	12,600			
Food Cost	745	4,990	4,200			
Food Cost %	20.7%	31.7%	33.3%			
Item		Vegetables	Fruits	Dairy	Bakery	Total Directs
This Week		5.4%	3.7%	3.2%	1.5%	13.8%
Last Week		5.4%	3.6%	2.6%	1.7%	13.2%
Item	Beef	Poultry	Provisions	Other	Total Meat	Total Stores
This Week	7.0%	4.4%	1.5%	.6%	13.4%	4.3%
Last Week	7.3%	3.7%	1.9%	.6%	13.3%	6.5%
		Cooking Liquor		Food to Bar (Directs)		
This Week		1.0%		.9%		
Last Week		.8%		.6%		

FIGURE 10.7 *Daily Food Cost Report*

other ratios remained approximately the same as they had been in recent weeks, the cause of the increase in the overall cost-to-sales ratio would be effectively localized. When seeking to identify a cause for the increase, one could disregard the costs of directs and stores and concentrate on possible problems in the meat category.

If one has the personnel and time available to do the work, it is perfectly possible to extend this approach by developing ratios of costs to sales for individual categories of foods, as illustrated in Figure 10.7.

This approach is even more useful for localizing problems and for facilitating more focused investigations than might otherwise be possible. In some instances, changes in these ratios may be traced to changes in the sales mix caused by changes in customers' behavior patterns for ordering. However, in cases where customer demand has remained constant and market prices relatively so, increases in these ratios are likely to be traceable to production problems—problems in kitchen operations. When problems are thus localized, they may be more easily identified and assessed so that appropriate corrective actions can be taken.

Date	Purchases	Issues	Inventory (Balance)
9/30			$6,305
10/1	273	510	6,068
10/2	946	350	6,664
10/3	498	540	6,622
10/4	734	340	7,016

FIGURE 10.8 *Daily Book Inventory Balance*

BOOK VERSUS ACTUAL INVENTORY COMPARISON

In Chapter 9 we identified and explained procedures for determining the value of closing inventory at the end of each monthly period and discussed the reasons for doing so. The closing inventory value determined in that way is the value recorded in the financial records and statements. The value is real, or actual. It includes the value of all items counted in the inventory—those that were physically present and thus could be found, identified, counted, and valued.

Some foodservice operators also determine what the value of the closing inventory should be, based on records indicating purchases and issues. This is defined as **book inventory.** Those who determine a book inventory value normally do so to compare it to the actual inventory value.

One method of establishing the value of the book inventory is readily available to those who maintain daily food cost figures in the manner illustrated in Figure 10.2. This form provides a means for maintaining cumulative book inventory figures for a period, as shown in Figure 10.8.

The closing inventory for any month is the opening inventory for the following month. Thus, in Figure 10.8, the closing inventory for September 30, $6,305, has become the opening inventory for October 1. To find a closing balance for October 1, one must add to the opening balance any stores purchases received on October 1 and then subtract any stores issued on that day. As discussed in previous chapters, the value of stores purchases for any given day comes from the Receiving Clerk's Daily Report for that day. The value of stores issues comes from the day's requisitions or from a combination of requisitions and meat tags in those establishments that continue to use meat tags. If the cost of meats and the cost of other issues from stores have already been recorded in the appropriate columns on Figure 10.2, one need only transfer the total of those two to the "Issues" column. Thus, to find the closing book inventory figure for any day, one merely starts from the closing inventory figure for the preceding day, adds any stores purchases, and subtracts any stores issues. This simple procedure can be followed daily through a period. If this is done daily for a calendar month, the final figure is the closing book value of the stores inventory for the month.

It is possible to determine the closing book value of the stores inventory in establishments that do not determine daily food cost figures, but only if some form of receiving report and daily issue requisitions are used. If so, book inventory value is determined as follows:

Opening inventory (Closing inventory for the preceding month)
  + Purchases (total stores purchases for the period, as listed on receiving
     reports)

  = Total available (total value of the stores available for use during the
     period)
  − Issues (total stores issues for the period, as listed on requisitions)

  = Closing book value of the stores inventory

Theoretically, the value of the book inventory should be identical to the value established for the physical inventory taken at the end of the month. This is never true, however. There are any number of reasons for this—some normally acceptable; others never acceptable. Some of the acceptable reasons include an occasional human error in costing out requisitions, the use of the most recent purchase price rather than actual purchase price in valuing the physical inventory, and the mismarking of actual purchase prices on items when that method is used. Reasons that are never acceptable include issuing stores without requisitions, allowing meats to age to the extent that they become unusable and must be discarded, and the theft of food.

Depending on the size of an operation and the volume involved, discrepancies of some small percentage between book inventory and physical inventory can often be attributed to acceptable causes and are of no further concern, except that discrepancies should be pointed out, if possible, to the employees whose errors have caused them. However, when discrepancies reach an unacceptable level, management has a responsibility to investigate, identify causes, and take corrective action aimed at ensuring that the variance will be significantly reduced in future periods. This may involve reviewing control procedures for purchasing, receiving, storing, and issuing food and revising those procedures where necessary. It also may involve reviewing the work habits of employees responsible for carrying out control procedures and taking appropriate steps to ensure that established procedures will be followed more closely in the future. In extreme cases, management may find it necessary to review all procedures and all employee work habits in order to find causes. Once identified, the causes will be the basis of appropriate corrective action by management.

Comparing book and actual inventory values at the end of an accounting period can be an important element in the control process. The actual inventory, while necessary for accurately determining cost of food sold at the end of each month so that proper financial statements can be prepared, provides a value that can be compared with the value of the book inventory, enabling management to assess the effectiveness of receiving, storing, and issuing procedures. Significant differences between actual and book inventory figures provide a signal that control procedures need investigating.

COMPUTER APPLICATIONS

In previous chapters, we discussed the possibility of using computers to maintain purchase and inventory records. Recording the data might be easier if numerical codes were assigned to all food items. For example, assume that every item were assigned a four-digit code. The first digit could differentiate between directs and stores; the second digit could be used to distinguish groups of foods within either category (such as fruits, vegetables, baked goods, and dairy products within the general category of directs); and the third and fourth digits might identify particular items (apples, bananas, grapefruit, and oranges, for example).

Using software to record all direct purchases as issues and thus as charges to food cost and all stores issues as charges to cost, would provide a daily food cost figure. This could be refined by entering any adjustments to cost each day, thus making possible a daily food cost report of the degree of accuracy required.

With the simple addition of sales terminals, managers can ensure that sales data is readily available as well. This information, summarized into daily sales figures and used with daily cost figures determined as above, would enable managers to obtain a daily food cost report of the type described earlier in the chapter.

By encoding further detail about food categories, possibly by the use of five-digit codes rather than four, generating a more detailed report along the lines of that pictured in Figure 10.3 would be entirely feasible. The format of the report could be similar to those illustrated in Figures 10.6 and 10.7. The summarized data could be very useful for monitoring operations and identifying problems.

CHAPTER ESSENTIALS

In this chapter we described procedures used in some operations to determine food cost and food cost percent both daily and cumulatively. This can be viewed as a basic management information system designed to provide data more frequently and in a more timely manner than that available from the monthly calculations described in the previous chapter. We illustrated and discussed various types of reports that provide basic information about the results of operations and that compare information about the current operating period to that from previous periods. We demonstrated how book inventory is calculated and explained how comparing book and actual inventory figures can be useful for evaluating the effectiveness of various control and reporting procedures. Finally, we described how computers can be used to prepare frequent and timely reports that provide quick and easy access to the information that managers require to make operating decisions.

KEY TERMS IN THIS CHAPTER

Actual inventory value
Book inventory value
Daily food inventory balance
Directs
Food cost percent to date
Food cost percent today
Food cost to date
Food cost today
Food sales to date
Food sales today
Gratis to bar
Grease sales
Promotion expense
Steward sales
Stores
Transfers from bar to kitchen
Transfers from kitchen to bar

QUESTIONS AND PROBLEMS

1. Following the format illustrated in Figure 10.1, use the information given below to determine food cost, food sales, and food cost percent today and to date for the Circle Diner for the first four days of May:

			Adjustments		
Date	Directs	Stores	Bar to Kitchen	Kitchen to Bar	Sales
5/1	$350	$350	-0-	-0-	$1,400
5/2	$250	$175	$25	-0-	$1,000

5/3	$135	$125	-0-	$10	$1,000
5/4	$ 75	$135	$10	$20	$ 500

2. Following the format illustrated in Figure 10.2, use the information given below to determine food cost, food sales, and food cost percent today and to date for the Magic Inn for the period September 4–19.

				Adjustments		
				Bar to	*Kitchen*	
Date	*Directs*	*Meats*	*Stores*	*Kitchen*	*to Bar*	*Sales*
9/4	$400	$350	$150	-0-	$50	$2,550
9/5	$150	$200	$125	-0-	-0-	$1,500
9/6	$350	$450	$100	$60	-0-	$2,850
9/7	$200	$250	$150	-0-	-0-	$2,850
9/8	$450	$300	$150	-0-	$40	$3,325
9/9	$ 50	$170	$120	-0-	$10	$1,300

3. Following the format illustrated in Figure 10.2, use the information given below to determine food cost, food sales, and food cost percent today and to date, as well as book inventory balances for Ravel's Restaurant for the period November 1–5. The opening inventory balance for November 1 is $9,330.

11/1:   Purchases: directs, $403; stores, $736
        Issues: meats, $320; other stores, $271
        Sales: $2,241
11/2:   Purchases: directs, $261; stores, $108
        Issues: meats, $282; other stores, $183
        Sales: $2,121
11/3:   Purchases: directs, $273; stores, $1,463
        Issues: meats, $491; other stores, $330; cooking liquor, $33; food to bar (directs), $24
        Sales: $2,740
11/4:   Purchases: directs, $521; stores, $281
        Issues: meats, $392; other stores, $552
        Sales: $4,063
11/5:   Purchases: directs, $334; stores, $372
        Issues: meats, $751; other stores, $470; cooking liquor, $19; food to bar (directs), $29
        Sales: $4,682

4. Use the information given below to determine the book value of the stores inventory on the morning of May 6:

Closing inventory for April: $11,353.40

Date	Stores Purchases	Stores Issues
5/1	$742.38	$621.80
5/2	$397.49	$516.76
5/3	$619.66	$472.51
5/4	$273.16	$845.26
5/5	$824.93	$725.77

5. In each of the following cases, determine the book value of the closing inventory for the month of October.

    a. Opening inventory: $ 3,748.00
        Purchases: 22,162.00
        Issues: 21,477.00

    b. Issues: $44,227.60
        Purchases: 42,191.40
        Opening inventory: 15,308.70

    c. Purchases: $10,601.58
        Opening inventory: 4,219.66
        Issues: 9,862.43

6. For each of the following examples, use the information given to find book value of the closing inventory and the dollar difference between book and actual inventory for the month.

    a. Opening inventory: $ 400.00
        Purchases: 1,200.00
        Issues: 900.00
        Actual value of closing inventory: 600.00

    b. Purchases: $ 6,327.00
        Issues: 6,498.00
        Opening inventory: 2,184.00
        Actual value of closing inventory: 1,912.00

    c. Issues: $12,395.62
        Opening inventory: 4,129.88
        Purchases: 11,623.71
        Actual value of closing inventory: 2,673.47

7. Using information from each of the examples in Question 6, determine the difference between book and actual closing inventory figures as a percentage of issues.

8. Given the dollar differences determined in Question 6 above and the percentages determined in Question 7, which of the three examples in Question 6, if any, bear closer examination by a manager? Justify your answer.

9. Assuming that one or more of the examples in Question 6 needs closer examination, explain in detail how that examination should proceed. If you were manager, what steps would you take?

10. What are some of the potential advantages of using daily and cumulative figures for food costs and food cost percents, rather than relying exclusively on end calculations?

11. Discuss the possible advantages and disadvantages of the kinds of complex computer-generated reports described in the chapter.

12. Define each of the following terms:
    Actual inventory value
    Book inventory value
    Daily food inventory balance
    Directs
    Food cost percent to date
    Food cost percent today
    Food cost to date
    Food cost today
    Food sales to date
    Food sales today
    Gratis to bar
    Grease sales
    Promotion expense
    Steward sales
    Stores
    Transfers from bar to kitchen
    Transfers from kitchen to bar

FOR COMPUTER USERS

13. Using a spreadsheet package of your choice, create a worksheet to calculate food cost, food sales, and food cost percent today and to date, as illustrated in Figure 10.1. Use the worksheet to solve Question 2.

14. Change the worksheet developed in Question 13 by adding three additional columns for book inventory, as illustrated in Figure 10.2. Use this new worksheet to solve Question 3.

11

Monitoring Foodservice Operations III: Actual Versus Standard Food Costs

INTRODUCTION

In previous chapters, considerable attention was devoted to methods for establishing control over the purchasing, receiving, storing, issuing, and production phases of foodservice operation. Discussion focused on the establishment of various standards and standard procedures for operation, including standard purchase specifications, standard receiving and issuing procedures, standard portion sizes, and standard production methods, among many others. Establishing these standards makes it possible to establish one additional and very important standard: the standard cost.

DETERMINING STANDARD COST

Standard cost was defined in Chapter 2 as the agreed-upon cost of goods or services used to measure other costs. In Chapter 7, standard portion cost was defined as the amount that a standard portion should cost, given the standards and standard procedures for its production. For example, one portion of filet mignon should cost $4.00 in a given restaurant, provided that the staff has followed all standards and standard procedures established for purchasing, receiving, storing, issuing, and producing the item. To the extent that these standards are not followed precisely, the actual cost of the portion is some amount other than what it should be—an amount that differs from the standard cost.

By using standard portion costs in ways that will be illustrated in this chapter, management can measure operating efficiency with a greater degree of accuracy than would otherwise be possible. Actual costs can be compared to standard costs, and any difference between them will be a useful measure of the extent to which the standards and standard procedures are being followed. This difference will indicate both the degree of inefficiency in day-to-day operations and the extent to which costs can be reduced without compromising or reducing standards.

COMPARING ACTUAL AND STANDARD COSTS

In general, there are two methods for comparing actual and standard costs. The first requires daily calculation of standard costs and actual costs for the day and for all the days thus far in the operating period—the week or the month. Daily reports are prepared to compare actual and standard costs to date, and the last of these in a given period is a final summary report for the period. The second method does not require daily calculation, relying instead on periodic determination of standard costs from records of actual portion sales in the period. Choosing one method over the other is a matter for the management of any given operation and should be based on the type of menu in effect, management's need for information, and the availability of personnel to prepare the needed information.

While the first method offers the advantage of immediacy and all its attendant benefits, it does require considerable staff time daily. The second method, while saving many hours of staff time, lacks immediacy. Because of considerable differences in the procedures they require, both methods will be discussed here.

DAILY COMPARISON

If standard costs and selling prices for standard portions are known and forecasts have been made, it is possible to determine in advance what food cost percent should be. Of course, this forecasted cost percent will not be accurate and reliable unless the forecast is entirely accurate and all personnel follow all established standards and standard procedures precisely.

At the end of the day or after the meal, when actual portion sales have been tallied to add to the sales history, this information can be used to determine standard cost and to calculate standard cost percent. In other words, management can use actual sales records to determine what food cost percent should have been.

Both of these procedures are accomplished on a form known as the "Menu Pre-Cost and Abstract," illustrated in Figure 11.1.

The Menu Pre-Cost and Abstract form is divided into two parts. The section on the left is based on a sales forecast prepared sometime before a day or meal. The section on the right is completed later, after the day or meal for which the forecast was prepared.

The Forecast

After sales have been forecasted, as described earlier, the food controller records in the first two columns on the form the names of the menu items and the number of portion sales forecasted for each. The entries in the third column, headed "Cost," are the standard portion costs for the items, as determined by means of the methods identified and discussed in Chapter 7: formula, recipe detail and cost card, butcher test, cooking loss test, and factors derived from tests. In the next column, headed "S.P.," the figures entered are menu sales prices. Each of these, obviously, is the amount to be collected from each customer ordering the item named on that line. In the next column, headed "F.C.%," the entry on each line is the ratio of cost-to-sales, given the standard portion cost and menu sales price identified for the item named on that line.

After all of these entries have been recorded, one makes entries in the

DATE Monday 11/1/XXXX

Menu Item	Number Forecast	Forecast					Number Sold	Actual				
		Cost	S.P.	F.C.%	Total Cost	Total Sales		Cost	S.P.	F.C.%	Total Cost	Total Sales
A	80	2.05	5.95	34.5%	164.00	476.00	75	2.05	5.95	34.5%	153.75	446.25
B	65	2.45	6.95	35.3%	159.25	451.75	60	2.45	6.95	35.3%	147.00	417.00
C	10	4.30	12.95	33.2%	43.00	129.50	6	4.30	12.95	33.2%	25.80	77.70
D	165	2.60	7.95	32.7%	429.00	1,311.75	159	2.60	7.95	32.7%	413.40	1,264.05
				33.6%	795.25	2,369.00				33.6%	739.95	2,205.00

FIGURE 11.1 *Menu Pre-Cost and Abstract*

next column, "Total Cost," by multiplying the number of portion sales forecasted for any given item by the standard portion cost of that item. Thus, referring to the line for Item A in Figure 11.1, one can see that the 80 portion sales forecasted have been multiplied by the $2.05 standard portion cost to determine a total cost of $164.00:

$$80 \times \$2.05 = \$164.00$$

Because $2.05 is a standard portion cost, $164.00 is really a total standard cost for producing the required quantity of Item A. This is the total that 80 portions of this item should cost. It presupposes that each of the 80 portions will be exactly as specified in terms of ingredients, proportions, production method, and portion size.

The same procedure is followed for each item listed, and the standard cost of producing the forecasted number of portions of each item is determined. All entries in the "Total Cost" Column are then added to determine the total standard cost for producing all on the menu.

Completing the "Total Sales" column requires the same general approach. One multiplies the number of portion sales forecasted for each item by the sales price of that item. Thus, referring again to the line for Item A in Figure 11.1, one sees that the 80 portion sales forecasted have been multiplied by the $5.95 sales price to determine total sales of $476.00. This is the total income that should result from selling 80 portions of this item after incurring costs projected at $164.00. Once total sales figures for all items have been determined in this way, the "Total Sales" column is added to determine total income that should be generated by the sales recorded in the forecast.

In this manner, one can arrive at anticipated totals for standard costs and sales, provided that the forecast reflects all items that will appear on the menu; the standard costs and sales prices of each are included as well. If, for example, the $12.95 sales price for Item C includes such side dishes as potato, vegetable, and salad, then standard costs for these items must be included in the standard portion cost.

Once total costs and total sales have been forecasted, a cost percent can be predicted by simply dividing cost by sales and multiplying the result by 100. In the example cited, the total cost of $795.25 has been divided by the total sales of $2,369.00, and the resulting decimal answer, .33569, has been multiplied by 100 to determine cost percent of 33.569 percent. This has been rounded to 33.6 percent.

$$\frac{\$795.25}{\$2,369.00} = .33569$$

$$.33569 \times 100 = 33.569\% = 33.6\%$$

Again, it must be emphasized that this is a standard cost percent. It will not correspond to actual cost percent except under ideal conditions. However, the difference between standard cost percent and actual cost percent gives some indication of the extent to which there are opportunities for improving operations.

The foregoing discussion has presupposed the existence of a menu scheduled for production for a particular day in the near future, as well as a need or desire to predict the standard costs and sales associated with that menu. However, the techniques described above have another important application for the foodservice operator who is considering changing or rewriting a menu. If accurate assessment can be made of customer demand for the items on a proposed menu, total standard costs and sales can be predicted. One can often avoid costly mistakes by preparing a forecast, such as that above for any new or revised menu. Customer demand for each item must be assessed and translated into the number of portion sales forecasted for each item. These numbers are then multiplied by carefully calculated standard costs and sales prices for the items. Totals for the individual menu items are then added to project total standard costs and total sales for the proposed menu as a whole. With these totals available, it is easy to project gross profit and standard cost percent. If the projections are judged satisfactory, the manager can send the menu to a printer. If they are not considered satisfactory, various changes can be made and their anticipated results assessed. Standard cost and sales figures may be raised or lowered, depending on which is desirable, by the following means:

1. Sales prices may be changed.
2. Standard portion costs may be changed by altering portion standards: sizes, ingredients, recipes, or some combination of these.
3. Menu items may be added or eliminated.

Conceivably, all of these means might be employed, and the final version of the new menu might bear little or no resemblance to that originally proposed. However, while the menu originally proposed might produce results that would have been undesirable or unacceptable, the new menu should not, provided that good judgment and careful calculations have gone into its preparation.

The Abstract

The abstract, or right-hand portion, of the form is prepared after the fact—after sales have taken place. The person preparing the abstract (a food controller or a manager) refers to the portion sales figures developed for inclusion in the sales history. These are recorded in the first column, headed "Number Sold." The next three columns, "Cost" (for portion cost). "S.P." (for sales price), and "F.C.%" (for food cost percent), are merely copied from the forecast section of the form. To complete the "Total Cost" column, one multiplies the number of portions sold for each item by the standard portion cost for that item. Next, one would add the column to determine total standard cost of the portions sold. One would complete the "Total Sales" column in similar fashion, multiplying the number of portions sold for each item by the sales price for that item and then adding the column to determine a total for all portions sold. A standard cost percentage based on actual portions sold is determined by dividing total standard costs by total sales.

The next step is to compare the cost percent determined on the forecast (left) side of the form with that determined on the abstract (right) side. Differences invariably exist, for many reasons. Sometimes a difference can be traced to a difference between total number of portion sales forecasted and actual number of portion sales recorded. Sometimes the difference is due to some menu items that have not sold as well as was anticipated.

Sometimes one sees that a menu item has sold in greater quantities than forecasted, which may raise questions about the extent to which the kitchen staff is following production schedules. Sales in excess of the number forecasted should always be investigated. Even though the sale of greater numbers of portions may have produced additional income, failure to follow production goals set by management indicates that at least one of the established control procedures is not working. Additionally, it is quite possible that the kitchen staff produced the quantity called for on the production sheet and that the extra portions were made by reducing portion size. This is clearly undesirable and may lead to loss of business because it really means that customers have been cheated.

Another important reason for comparing the forecasted cost percent with the percentage developed from the abstract is that any difference between the two indicates the extent to which the forecast was wrong, in terms of incorrect total volume, incorrect forecasted sales of particular items, or both of these. In addition, this difference will be an excellent indication of the extent to which one's forecasting techniques can be improved. The comparison is likely to suggest possibilities for improving forecasting performance, which may help bring future cost percents on abstracts more nearly in line with those from forecasts. After all, forecasted cost percents have received some measure of approval as acceptable goals and, therefore, should not be ignored.

A forecasted cost percent indicates the level of food cost that management will approve to achieve a given level of dollar sales. In addition, a forecasted cost percent reflects plans for achieving those sales, plans that can be seen in

Date	Standard Cost	Sales	Standard Cost %
	WEEK OF November 1–7, XXXX		
1	$739.95	$2,205.00	33.6%
2	601.50	1,800.95	33.5%
3	782.97	2,316.50	33.8%
4	771.15	2,288.25	33.7%
5	735.50	2,195.55	33.5%
6	825.66	2,435.60	33.9%
7	747.80	2,225.55	33.6%
Total Standard Cost	$ 5,204.53		
Total Sales	$15,467.40		
Standard Cost %	33.6%		

FIGURE 11.2   *Summary of Daily Abstracts*

the standards and standard procedures established for all phases of operation. So, to the extent that forecasted cost percents are not in line with those calculated after sales, overall performance, including forecasting, can be improved.

The cost percent calculated on the abstract side of the form indicates what the cost percent *should have been* if everything had gone according to plan. If the exact number of portions needed had been prepared in exact conformity to the standards and standard procedures established by management, then cost percent *should be* at this level. It suggests a level of dollar cost that should have been incurred to produce a particular level of dollar sales.

If the kinds of figures identified above are developed one meal at a time or even one day at a time and then put aside, it should be apparent that they are not being used as effectively as they might be. For example, it is possible and desirable to develop abstracts of standard costs and sales over a period of some days or weeks and then summarize the results. Taken together, the days or weeks can be considered a test period, with the results offering a good indication of an acceptable level for food cost percent over time. Figure 11.2 illustrates a method for summarizing figures developed over a seven-day test period.

In this case, the restaurant under consideration should generally operate with a food cost-to-sales ratio of 33.6 percent. Such figures can be useful in judging effectiveness of operations from week to week or month to month.

If standards are in effect for every item served, if the standard portion cost for every item is known, and if a Menu Pre-Cost and Abstract prepared daily reflects the total menu, it is possible to compare standard and actual food costs daily and to date regularly during an operating period of any given length. Actual food costs are determined from direct purchases and storeroom issues, as discussed in Chapter 10. The standard cost of all the portions sold is taken from the Menu Pre-Cost and Abstract. Food sales figures come from register readings or accounting department records. All figures are recorded on a form such as that in Figure 11.3.

Actual cost percent for any given day equals actual cost for that day divided by sales for that day. Actual cost percent to date on any day equals actual cost to date for all the days thus far in the period divided by sales to date for all the days thus far in the period. Similarly, standard cost percent for any given day equals standard cost for that day divided by sales for that day. Standard cost percent to date on any day equals standard cost to date for all the days thus far in the period divided by sales to date for all the days thus far in the period.

Typically, actual cost today and to date are greater than standard cost today and to date. The difference should be regarded either as waste or as its equivalent: excessive cost that can be reduced or eliminated if staff performance is improved. The raw dollar figures indicating that excessive costs have developed are not particularly useful for identifying specific causes of inefficiency or other operating difficulties. In order to determine specific causes, one must find ways to detect the areas in which waste and excessive costs have developed.

Potential Savings

Potential savings may be defined as the difference between actual costs and standard costs. Potential savings may be recorded as dollars, as percentages of sales, or as both. Regardless of which one is used, potential savings must be regarded as reflecting the differences between existing conditions and those that would exist if all standards and standard procedures were followed to perfection. No foodservice operation will ever achieve that perfection, of course, but it is usually possible to find ways to improve performance so that the future results will be somewhat closer to perfection.

Any number of problems can develop in day-to-day operations that will lead to differences between standard and actual costs. These include overpurchasing, overproduction, pilferage, spoilage, improper portioning, and failure to follow standard recipes, among many others. To the extent to which improvements are made and problems are reduced or eliminated, actual costs are likely to be closer to standard costs, thus reducing potential savings. In general, potential savings and waste are synonymous. Reducing potential savings means reducing waste and excessive cost.

When potential savings figures are available daily and to date during an operating period, it is possible to make daily investigations into the causes of

WEEK OF November 1-7, XXXX

Date	Actual Cost		Standard Cost		Sales		Actual Cost %		Standard Cost %		Potential Savings			
											Today		To Date	
	Today	To Date	Today	To Date	Today	To Date	Today	To Date	Today	To Date	$	%	$	%
1	786.00	786.00	739.95	739.95	2,205.00	2,205.00	35.6%	35.6%	33.6%	33.6%	46.05	2.1%	46.05	2.1%
2	612.33	1,398.33	601.50	1,341.45	1,800.95	4,005.95	34.0%	34.9%	33.4%	33.5%	10.83	.6%	56.88	1.4%
3	806.45	2,204.78	782.97	2,124.42	2,316.50	6,322.45	34.8%	34.9%	33.8%	33.6%	23.48	1.0%	80.36	1.3%
4	795.05	2,999.83	771.15	2,895.57	2,288.25	8,610.70	34.7%	34.8%	33.7%	33.6%	23.90	1.0%	104.26	1.2%
5	761.25	3,761.08	735.50	3,631.07	2,195.55	10,806.25	34.7%	34.8%	33.5%	33.6%	25.75	1.2%	130.01	1.2%
6	842.17	4,603.25	825.66	4,456.73	2,435.60	13,241.85	34.6%	34.8%	33.9%	33.7%	16.51	.7%	146.52	1.1%
7	759.05	5,362.30	747.80	5,204.53	2,225.55	15,467.40	34.1%	34.7%	33.6%	33.6%	11.25	.5%	157.77	1.0%

FIGURE 11.3 Summary of Actual and Standard Food Costs, Food Sales, and Potential Savings

differences between the two. Understanding that the difference can be traced to instances in which actual performance is producing results other than those anticipated by established standards and standard procedures, a manager should be able to make hundreds of comparisons and judgments daily. Many believe that good managers can profitably spend many of their working hours comparing what they see with what they should be seeing and making judgments about the differences, if any. Many avoid spending time in offices, preferring to be out in those areas where staff employees are working. This, they feel, gives them opportunities to see where and how actual performance differs from the standards established and to begin planning corrective actions.

It will never be possible completely to eliminate discrepancies between actual and standard costs. Instead, management must make intelligent judgments about the extent to which reductions are possible and must be ready to accept some small discrepancy between the actual and standard costs. There are no industry-wide figures to use as guides. However, once management has established a reasonable figure for the acceptable variance, exceptions can be noted quickly and investigation can begin at once. After all, an immediate investigation is more likely to uncover causes than will one undertaken days or weeks later. As soon as causes are identified, one can take remedial action in the hope of correcting problems before their effects become pronounced. Immediate discussions with chef, steward, and key personnel will often reveal causes and suggest simple corrective measures.

PERIODIC COMPARISON

In establishments where daily calculations of standard costs and potential savings are impractical or impossible, it is often possible to adopt an alternative method that relies on periodic calculations for determining potential savings. Like the daily method described in the preceding section, the periodic method presupposes that standards and standard procedures have been established for all phases of operation, that sales histories are maintained, and that standard portion costs are known. Under these circumstances, one can calculate standard cost for a test period (one week, for example) and compare that figure to actual cost for the same period to determine the extent of potential savings. This can be done for a period of any length, long or short, depending on the need for information and the time available for the work.

Using a form such as that illustrated in Figure 11.4, one records menu items and portion sales for the test period. This information can be found in the sales history. Standard portion costs are entered as well from records of calculations based on formulas, recipe detail and cost cards, butcher tests, cooking loss tests, and cost factors. The total standard cost of the number of portions sold of a given item is found by multiplying the number of portions by the

FOR TEST PERIOD 7/8 TO 7/22 , XXXX			
Item	# Sold	Portion Cost	Total Standard Cost
A	520	$2.25	$1,170.00
B	731	3.85	2,814.35
C	322	4.10	1,320.20
D	903	1.85	1,670.55
E	611	2.45	1,496.95
			$8,472.05
Sales for Test Period:		$25,416.15	
Actual Cost		8,877.45	
Standard cost		8,472.05	
Potential Savings		$ 405.40	
Actual Cost %		34.9%	
Standard Cost %		33.3%	
Potential Savings as a % of Sales		1.6%	

FIGURE 11.4 *Periodic Potential Savings Worksheet*

portion cost. Thus, for Item A, one multiplies 520 portions by the $2.25 standard portion cost to determine total standard cost of $1,170.00:

$$520 \times \$2.25 = \$1,170.00$$

The total of standard costs for all items sold in the period is determined by adding the entries in the "Total Standard Cost" column. Actual costs for the period are determined from records of direct purchases, storeroom issues, and any adjustments, obtained from the accounting office. If the foodservice operation is already following the daily costing procedures described in Chapter 10, actual cost figures for the period will be readily available.

With the necessary total figures for actual and standard costs for the test period recorded on the form, the difference between the two can be determined by subtracting. This difference can be stated in dollar terms and as a percentage of total sales for the test period. If the test period is truly representative of day-to-day operations, one can take the difference between actual and standard costs to indicate the extent of inefficiency or improper performance in the enterprise. When necessary, one can also institute appropriate corrective actions intended to improve actual performance before the end of the next test period.

It is usually advisable to select test periods at random, after the fact. The figures developed tend to be more truly representative than they might be if employees knew in advance that a certain week were being used as a test period. In the latter case, employees would be likely to pay more careful attention to both the standards set by management and their own performance with respect to those standards. While the results of their efforts might be entirely desirable, the comparison of actual versus standard costs for the period would clearly present distorted pictures of operations and of potential savings.

Once a valid standard cost percent for an operation, it may be compared to actual cost percents and used to evaluate day-to-day operations in the intervals between test periods. Thus, one has a reasonable means for making judgments about the efficiency of operations on a regular basis. For example, if actual cost percents are developed on a weekly basis, it could be much more useful to make comparisons with a recently calculated standard cost percent than with an actual cost percent from the previous week. This, of course, assumes there have been no significant changes in menu contents, portion costs, or sales prices since the test period. To the extent that there had been significant changes in any of these, the results of comparisons between actual cost percent and standard cost percent would be less useful than otherwise would have been the case. The important point to remember is that a comparison of actual cost percent for any given period with actual cost percent for an earlier period may provide no useful information about whether or not there are excessive costs in an operation. That determination can be made only by comparing actual cost with standard cost or actual cost percent with standard cost percent.

One final word about potential savings is in order. To the extent that savings can be achieved without incurring other costs, profits will be increased. If, for example, some portion of the potential savings figure can be traced to overproduction, then by eliminating the overproduction while keeping other costs in line, one should see a reduction in excessive costs and an increase in profit. Furthermore, the increase in profit should be equal to the reduction in excessive costs. This is illustrated by the following:

	Actual	*Standard*
Sales	$10,000	$10,000
Food cost	3,800	3,400
Gross profit	$ 6,200	$ 6,600

It should be immediately apparent that a $400 reduction in actual food costs, bringing actual food cost in line with standard food cost, will bring an identical increase in gross profit. If this reduction can be achieved without increasing any other costs (for example, the cost of labor), then literally every dollar saved will be an additional dollar in profit. This fact, perhaps more than any other, should point out the importance of comparing actual cost to standard cost on a regular basis, determining the causes of any excess of actual cost over standard cost and taking appropriate corrective actions. These, obviously, should be aimed at bringing actual performance into line with that anticipated by established standards and standard procedures and, by this means, reducing or eliminating excessive costs.

COMPUTER APPLICATIONS

As we have seen, appropriate applications programs enable one to calculate standard portion costs and to prepare forecasts. Similarly, even the most basic spreadsheet program makes it reasonably simple to prepare a Menu Pre-Cost and Abstract, a form that was always a time-consuming nuisance to complete manually. As computers become more common in foodservice operations, the Menu Pre-Cost and Abstract could become much more widely used than it is currently. It is a comparatively simple worksheet to develop, provided that one has access to sales prices, standard portion costs, forecasts, and the sales history. The **left,** or **pre-cost, section** could be displayed on a monitor or printed before the forecasted date and then circulated to appropriate members of the management team for adjustment before the fact. The **right,** or **abstract, section** would be completed after the fact. The sales data could be keyed in either manually or through the use of an integrated software system, automatically input from the sales history. Formulas in the worksheet would quickly calculate any number of figures, including total standard cost, total sales, and standard cost percent, among others.

Once calculated, the standard cost for an operating period could be readily compared with the actual cost for that same period, determined by computer in the manner suggested in Chapter 10. With both actual cost and standard cost for a period available, comparisons could be made on an expanded version of the worksheet identified above. This could include formulas for inserting actual cost and standard costs in appropriate columns, for subtracting standard costs from actual costs to determine potential savings and for determining potential savings as a percentage of sales. If collected on a daily basis, the data could be filed and reported both daily and cumulatively for a period on a worksheet resembling the form illustrated in Figure 11.3. Alternatively, the data might be input daily but reported only periodically, possibly once a month, timed to coincide with the end of the accounting cycle.

CHAPTER ESSENTIALS

In this chapter, we presented two methods for determining total standard cost for a given operating period. We explained the Menu Pre-Cost and Abstract, providing a step-by-step method for completing the form, and discussed various important information that can be obtained from it. We described how the Menu Pre-Cost and Abstract can be used to project and evaluate the consequences of offering a new or revised menu and identified three means that can be used to change projected costs or sales. We defined potential savings, equated potential savings with waste and excessive costs, and explained how reductions in excessive costs result in increased profits. We explained how comparing actual and standard costs for a period can reveal any number of inefficiencies in day-to-day operations, including poor forecasting, overproduction, failure to follow standard recipes, and overpurchasing, to name just a few. Finally, we identified computers and spreadsheets as useful tools for preparing the Menu Pre-Cost and Abstract and for comparing actual and standard costs for an operating period.

KEY TERMS IN THIS CHAPTER

Actual cost
Actual cost percent
Forecasted sales
Menu Pre-Cost and Abstract
Potential savings
Standard cost
Standard cost percent
Standard portion cost
Standard procedures
Standards

QUESTIONS AND PROBLEMS

1. List and discuss five problems that can lead to differences between actual cost and standard cost for an operating period, pointing out how each increases potential savings.

2. It has been said that potential savings, taken as a percentage of sales, can be used as one possible measure of operating efficiency. Do you agree or disagree? Why?

3. Discuss the advantages and disadvantages of calculating and comparing standard and actual costs by the daily method rather than by the periodic method.

4. Using the figures below, determine actual cost percent, standard cost percent, and potential savings as a dollar figure and as a percentage of sales:

	Sales	Actual Cost	Standard Cost
a.	$ 400.00	$ 120.00	$ 100.00
b.	$ 860.00	$ 318.20	$ 301.00
c.	$ 3,486.00	$1,394.40	$1,324.68
d.	$11,198.00	$3,919.30	$3,695.34

5. Using the form illustrated in Figure 11.3, prepare a summary of actual and standard food costs, food sales, and potential savings for a four-day period given the following figures:

	Actual Cost Today	Standard Cost Total	Sales Today
Monday	$110	$100	$300
Tuesday	$160	$145	$450
Wednesday	$175	$160	$505
Thursday	$185	$175	$520

6. With the form illustrated in Figure 11.2 for a guide, prepare a Menu Pre-Cost and Abstract given the following information:

Item	Portions Forecasted	Portion Cost	Sales Price	Number Sold
A	60	$2.50	$6.00	55
B	20	$3.25	$8.50	18
C	80	$2.25	$5.00	80
D	40	$2.70	$6.50	30

7. Use the following information to prepare a Menu Pre-Cost and Abstract:

Item	Portions Forecasted	Portion Cost	Sales Price	Number Sold
A	30	$3.70	$8.50	28
B	42	$3.00	$6.80	42
C	73	$2.75	$6.00	70
D	115	$2.50	$5.50	106

8. In an essay of approximately 300 words, compare and contrast the Menu Pre-Cost and Abstract to the Portion Inventory and Reconciliation (Chapter 8) as a method for controlling costs.

9. The owner of the Red Fox Inn has developed a new menu for use in her establishment. Each menu item represents a complete meal. She has calculated standard cost for each item and has kept careful records of sales for the month of March as shown below:

Menu Item	Number Sold	Standard Portion Cost
A	310	$5.50
B	270	7.80
C	540	3.80
D	425	5.25
E	175	8.70
F	340	6.50
G	510	5.70
H	480	4.20

Food sales for March totaled $50,028.50.

Using the information provided, calculate total standard cost for the period.

10. The following figures are from the accounting records of the Red Fox Inn, the restaurant identified in Question 9.

Opening inventory	$ 7,414.80
Closing inventory	6,327.35
Food purchases	17,642.80
Transfers: beverage to food	443.00
Transfers: food to beverage	226.00
Employees' meals	837.00

   a. Calculate cost of food sold for the month of March.
   b. Using information from Question 9, calculate each of the following:
      1. Actual cost percent.
      2. Standard cost percent.
      3. Potential savings in dollars.
      4. Potential savings as a percentage of sales.

11. Why might the increased use of computers in foodservice make the Menu Pre-Cost and Abstract more commonly used than has been the case?

12. Define each of the following terms:
    Actual cost
    Actual cost percent
    Forecasted sales
    Menu Pre-Cost and Abstract
    Potential savings
    Standard cost
    Standard cost percent

Standard portion cost
Standard procedures
Standards

FOR COMPUTER USERS

13. Using a spreadsheet program of your choice, prepare a Menu Pre-Cost and Abstract, using the information provided in Question 6.

14. Use the worksheet developed for Question 13 to prepare a Menu Pre-Cost and Abstract, using the information provided in Question 7.

15. Develop worksheets to solve Questions 9 and 10.

12

Controlling Food Sales

After reading and studying this chapter, you should be able to:

1. List and explain the three goals of sales control.
2. List and discuss eight determinants of customer restaurant selection.
3. Describe the two principal means of maximizing profits.
4. Explain the three most common methods of establishing menu prices.
5. Describe the two principal means of selling products effectively in a restaurant.
6. List and explain the five most important elements of menu preparation.
7. Explain attempts by management to maximize profits by establishing sales techniques for use by the sales force.
8. Explain the importance of menu engineering as an analytical tool.
9. Complete a menu engineering worksheet, interpret the results, and suggest various possible changes to improve profit.
10. Explain the importance of revenue control.
11. List and explain the three standards established to achieve the goals of revenue control.
12. List and describe five standard procedures for controlling revenue.
13. Describe two ways in which computers are used in revenue control.
14. Define each of the Key Terms at the end of the chapter.

INTRODUCTION

For many, the term **sales control** is merely a synonym for revenue control, a collection of activities designed to ensure that each order placed by a customer results in appropriate revenue for the enterprise. Revenue control is, of course, critically important to the financial health of any enterprise, and it will be treated in detail in this chapter. However, revenue control is only one part of sales control.

THE GOALS OF SALES CONTROL

In our view, foodservice requires an interpretation of sales control that is somewhat broader than mere revenue control. In Chapter 2, control was defined as a process used by managers to direct, regulate, and restrain the actions of people so that the established goals of an enterprise may be achieved. Revenue control is clearly an important goal of sales control, but it is not the only one. There are at least two others.

A second goal of sales control is to optimize the number of sales—to undertake those activities that are likely to increase numbers of sales or customers to a desired level. To some, this desired level may be nearly impossible to reach, even if the enterprise is open 24 hours a day, seven days a week, and commonly has long lines of potential customers waiting to get inside. To others, the desired level may be considerably lower: no lines and leisurely and unobtrusive service so that the staff may prepare and serve each menu item perfectly and each diner will consider the meal a memorable occasion.

A third goal of sales control is to maximize profit. Profit maximization requires two essential activities: pricing products properly and selling those products effectively. Selling products effectively has two essential requirements: a carefully crafted menu and some sales techniques to be used by the staff.

In this broad sense, then, there are three principal goals of sales control:

1. Optimizing number of sales.
2. Maximizing profit.
3. Controlling revenue.

These will be discussed individually.

OPTIMIZING NUMBER OF SALES

There are probably no restaurants that operate at desired sales levels at all times. Most experience both high- and low-volume periods. Sometimes both are evident on the same day; at other times, entire weeks of high volume may be followed by long periods of comparatively low volume. Sometimes the high- and low-volume periods coincide with the seasons of the year; sometimes sales volume is high or low for an entire year.

At one time or another, most owners and managers are faced with the problem of a sales volume that is higher or lower than the desired level. Consequently, most are engaged at one time or another in attempting to regulate sales volume—to either increase or decrease volume to the desired level. The most productive efforts to do either are made by those who understand the determinants of customer selection of restaurants. The following are the most important for most people:

Location
Menu item differentiation
Price acceptability
Decor
Portion sizes
Product quality
Service standards
Menu diversity

All customers have their own important reasons for patronizing restaurants, and these change under varying circumstances. To some, food quality is the single most important reason for patronizing a particular restaurant. However, when time is short, the determining factor for these same individuals might be convenient location. To be successful, a restaurant must meet a sufficient number of these needs to appeal to a large enough market so that sales volume will be sufficient to cover costs and provide profit. It will be useful to examine these eight determinants individually.

Location

If one were to take a given population center and draw concentric circles around it, each one an additional mile from the center, and then place a restaurant on each of these concentric circles, as shown in Figure 12.1, one could judge the effect of location in relation to the population center. Other things being equal, customers will normally choose the most convenient restaurant. In addition, there is a maximum time and distance that any customer will travel to reach any particular restaurant.

One would expect Restaurant A to have more customers than Restaurant B at any given time. Similarly, one would also expect Restaurant C to have

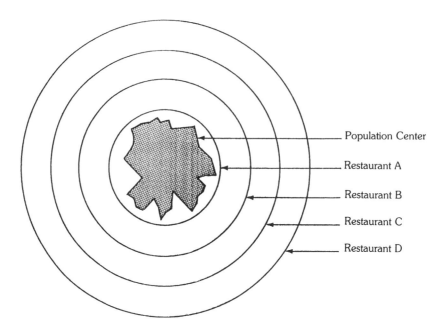

Population Center

Restaurant A

Restaurant B

Restaurant C

Restaurant D

FIGURE 12.1

fewer customers than Restaurant B and more than Restaurant D. Generally, the greater the distance from the population center, the fewer the customers a restaurant owner can reasonably expect to attract from that population center. On the one hand, it should be obvious that a restaurant in California situated in the center of Death Valley would tend to attract very few customers from Los Angeles because of the distance from that population center. Most people would be unwilling to travel that far to reach a restaurant, no matter how fine its reputation. On the other hand, the only Italian restaurant in a city of 100,000 can expect to do quite well, even if its product quality or its prices are not particularly attractive to potential customers. Similarly, restaurants located in New York City's financial district do excellent luncheon business on weekdays, but many are not open for dinner for lack of business. By contrast, large numbers of restaurants in midtown Manhattan do excellent dinner business. Having a good location is usually necessary for volume business. The operators of fast-food restaurants have always recognized the importance of location. The managers of national fast-food chains know precisely the number of customers that can be expected to patronize one of their units located in a given population center. That helps explain the fact that one seldom hears of the failure of any of the units in these major national chains.

Menu Item Differentiation

Economists characterize goods and services as homogeneous or differentiated. This distinction is based on how similar or different goods or services are from one another. A **homogeneous** product or service is one that is so similar to another that customers do not have a preference and will purchase whichever costs less. Therefore, there is a general "market price" for homogeneous goods and services, and no individual operator can raise prices without the risk of losing some or all customers. In the grain market, for example, a farmer can sell an entire crop of grain for the "market price," but cannot sell any of it at a price one penny higher. This is because his grain is a homogeneous product, and no buyer will pay higher than market price.

Differentiated goods or services, on the other hand, are sufficiently different from others in their class that customers develop preferences for them. Customers may actually consider differentiated products unique. The uniqueness can be real or imagined. As long as customers prefer one product or service over another, whatever their reasons for preference, that product or service is differentiated.

There are comparatively few products and services that can truly be labeled homogeneous. Most are differentiated, some more so than others. Differentiation is a matter of degree for most products and services, and the greater the degree of differentiation, the greater the degree of customer loyalty one can detect among those seeking the type of product or service.

The terms homogeneous and differentiated are useful for classifying menu items. To the extent that the foodservice operator can develop and include in the menu products that are differentiated, potential customers seeking those products are likely to be willing to travel greater distances and pay higher prices to obtain them. If Restaurant D in Figure 12.1 offers menu items that customers in the population center consider both desirable and unique, the operator of the restaurant will have little difficulty increasing sales volume.

Unique menu items created for this purpose are called **signature items.** Signature items are often specially named for a restaurant, a chef, or a locality. Waldorf salad, for example, was originally a signature item, created and served in one of New York's most famous hotels. Many restaurants operators create signature items in order to attract greater numbers of customers.

Price Acceptability

One of the most important factors in customer selection of one restaurant over another is price. Given three food service establishments exactly alike in every respect except for menu prices, the one with the lowest prices will have the greatest sales volume. Of the restaurants in Figure 12.1, Restaurant A could be expected to have the highest sales volume, unless one of the others (Restaurant C, for example) lowered menu prices significantly. With lower prices, one would expect Restaurant C to increase volume by drawing some customers from Restaurants A, B, and D.

Restaurant menu items tend to be **price sensitive,** meaning that there is a relationship between sales price and sales volume. As the price of a menu item is increased, it can be expected that fewer customers will order that item. In the food and beverage business, the more homogeneous a menu item, the more price sensitive it is. By the same token, the more differentiated the item is, the less price sensitive it is. This helps to explain why so many of the well-known national chains charge approximately the same prices for inherently similar or homogeneous menu items.

In order for a menu item to sell, the menu sales price must be acceptable to the customer. The customer must judge that the value received, including the food and all the other items that go to make up the restaurant product, is sufficient to justify acceptance of the stipulated menu price. Obviously, every individual has a different perception of price acceptability. The challenge to the foodservice operator is to establish menu prices that will be acceptable to those who make up the market segment to which the establishment is targeted.

Decor

There is an old saying that "Beauty is in the eye of the beholder." This is particularly true with restaurant decor. Decor helps to differentiate one restaurant from another. Each establishment attracts customers who prefer—or at least accept—its decor. However, decor that some customers may find pleasing is likely to be less so to others. Family groups, for example, tend to prefer informal, light, bright, and cheerful interiors; those patronizing restaurants offering gourmet cuisine are likely to expect a more formal setting. A restaurant's decor helps determine not just the type of customer, but the number of customers as well. One key to restaurant success, then, is to select decor that will appeal to a sufficiently large segment of the targeted market and thus will help maximize the number of customers.

Portion Sizes

The quantity of the product given a customer must be appropriate to the clientele that a food and beverage operator wishes to attract. Young, active people are more likely to prefer larger portions, and some may select those restaurants that are the most generous with servings. Some older adults, on the other hand, prefer smaller portions. They may avoid restaurants offering large portions because they feel wasteful paying for food they will not consume. It is clearly false to say that large portions always attract the greatest numbers of customers. Customers want value for their money, and portion size is only one of the factors they consider when determining whether or not any given establishment offers value. Portion sizes must satisfy the clientele that a foodservice operator seeks to attract. If portions are too small, business will be lost. If they are larger than necessary, food will be wasted, food costs will be higher than necessary, and profits will be lower than they might have been.

Product Quality

Quality is a term that conveys different meanings to different people. Those with particularly refined tastes—people sometimes referred to as gourmets—are more likely to seek perfection in food and may be inclined to accept nothing less. For them, this may mean that the quality of restaurant food must meet a long list of criteria: All ingredients must be fresh rather than canned or frozen, soups must be prepared from freshly made stocks, vegetables must be cooked only until just tender, and so on. Unless the food products offered in a particular restaurant meet their exacting quality standards, they will not patronize it. By contrast, most foodservice customers do not have the rigid standards of the gourmet; most are perfectly willing to consume and enjoy food products of a quality that might not meet the tests of the gourmet. At the same time, there are some who appear to be completely indifferent to all the quality standards for foodservice products that the majority appear to insist on. For them, food is food—a necessity similar to fuel for an engine. They seem perfectly prepared to accept foodservice products of very low levels of quality—so low that most others would find that quality unacceptable. Their reasons for patronizing restaurants do not appear to be related to product quality defined in terms that the majority would accept.

In any given population, various segments demand food products of various levels of quality. It is the responsibility of management to assess the market and then to offer products of an appropriate level of quality such that they will appeal to a large enough segment of the market to ensure the level of sales volume required for profitability.

Service Standards

Anyone who has patronized restaurants and other foodservice operations can recognize that a number of different types of service are available. Some is of very high quality; some much less so. Fast-food restaurants and cafeterias tend to provide comparatively little service beyond the basic requirements, while some classic hotel dining rooms and large numbers of fine restaurants offer extraordinary levels of service, with some appearing to have more staff than customers. In establishments offering extensive service, it is sometimes of the very highest quality—swift, unobtrusive, and approximating an art form. More commonly, however, the service is likely to be indifferent—slow, disorganized, intrusive—with the servers obviously untrained.

Each individual diner has a personal view, consciously or unconsciously, of the standards of service that he considers appropriate for any given occasion when a meal is consumed outside the home. Whenever possible, the customer will tend to select a restaurant offering a type and level of service that he finds appropriate to the occasion. If the individual's time is strictly limited, he is likely to select a restaurant with limited service—one that allows a customer to eat within the limited time available. This individual may select one of the nationally known fast-food chains or a popular local cafeteria.

On the other hand, there are customers for whom time is of no concern. Sometimes they are celebrating some special occasion. For them, the pleasure of the dining experience, including food and service of the very highest quality, is of paramount importance. They may be entirely willing to travel some distance to reach a well-known and widely respected restaurant renowned for offering the finest food and service in the region.

Additionally, there are many customers who are well aware that service means leaving tips for the servers, which they prefer not to do. Many on low or fixed incomes cannot afford to tip. They may find it necessary to use their limited means to pay for menu selections.

Managers who seek to optimize restaurant sales should he aware of the extent and quality of service that their customers want. With that in mind, they may find it comparatively easy to adjust some aspects of service in ways that will increase customer satisfaction. For example, a full-service restaurant may find it desirable to reduce the amount of service by creating a salad bar and training servers to direct customers to the salad bar between the appetizer and entree courses. This might make it possible to reduce the size of the waitstaff and at the same time satisfy the needs of customers wanting to consume their meals as quickly as possible. It would have the added benefit of increasing turnover rate during peak dining hours.

Menu Diversity

With the exception of those offering relatively homogeneous products that are commonly accepted and consumed in vast quantities because of their comparatively low prices, most restaurants find it necessary to have a broad range of items on the menu. A menu that includes only 2 or 3 entree choices is clearly of more limited appeal than one offering 12 or 15. Any given diner would be more likely to find an acceptable entree on the longer menu. In restaurants that depend heavily on repeat business, a limited menu could have a significant negative impact on the number of times any given customer would return within a specific period of time.

The number and range of items on any menu are governed by several important considerations, including the equipment available in the kitchen, the culinary abilities of the kitchen staff, and the cost considerations that arise when the large number of items offered result in considerable leftover food. As a general rule, the greater the scope of the menu consistent with these other considerations, the larger the segment of the market to which the menu will appeal and the more likely the restaurant will be to succeed.

It is probably impossible for anyone to plan and operate a restaurant that would be ideal in terms of meeting the various considerations discussed above. After all, no location is perfect, and it is likely to be impossible to plan a menu consisting only of differentiated products offered at prices acceptable to all customers and to do so in a setting that all will find pleasing. However, for a restaurant to succeed, management must keep all these considerations in mind, taking care to satisfy as many as possible of the preferences of the greatest possible number of potential customers. Failure to take these considerations fully into account increases the risk that one will fail to attract a sufficient share of the foodservice market to cover costs and establish a successful and profitable enterprise.

MAXIMIZING PROFIT

There are two principal means for maximizing profit:

1. Pricing products properly.
2. Selling those products effectively.

These will be discussed separately.

Pricing Products Properly

Restaurants normally have standard sales prices for the menu items they offer. The sales prices for menu items are usually established by restaurant owners or managers and are communicated to customers via printed menus or conspicuously posted signs. Because the sum of the prices paid by all customers for their menu selections is the total food revenue for a restaurant, it should be evident that these sales prices are critically important in determining the degree of profitability for any restaurant.

Cost is normally the most significant consideration in establishing the sales price for any menu item. In any given restaurant, higher-cost items typically have higher sales prices than lower-cost items. Steak, for example, usually commands a higher sales price than spaghetti because the portion cost is higher. However, cost is not the only determinant of price.

Another important consideration is the desire to maximize sales. Restaurants with highly differentiated products have more flexibility to raise or lower menu prices than those with homogeneous products. For example, an exclusive French restaurant that increases menu prices may have very little adverse reaction from customers if they perceive the restaurant's products as highly differentiated. By contrast, if there were two similar hamburger restaurants offering relatively homogeneous products in one mall and one raised its prices substantially while the other did not, the one raising prices would be likely to lose a substantial number of customers. In fact, it is likely that the increase in prices would result in decreases in both total revenue and profit.

It is important for foodservice managers to have some understanding of the relationship between the sales price of a menu item and the number of portions sold. If changes in the sales price of a given menu item result in changes in the number of portions sold, then the item is said to be price sensitive. To identify an item as price sensitive is to say that the number of portions sold will be influenced by changes in sales price.

Some menu items are more price sensitive than others. And while homogeneous products are clearly more price sensitive than differentiated products, there are variations within each classification. In other words, among products characterized as homogeneous, some are more price sensitive than others, and the same is true of differentiated products. Finally, price sensitivity is a function of the customer's attitudes, perceptions, and ability to purchase a given product. Therefore, price sensitivity tends to be of greater significance in some restaurants and neighborhoods than in others. In neighborhoods where the majority of residents have low incomes, price sensitivity tends to be a more important consideration than those where incomes are high. In any given restaurant, the proper sales price for a menu item is that which will produce an acceptable number of sales and yield an acceptable level of profit.

Sometimes changing conditions force changes in pricing policies. For example, a certain restaurant in New England had an excellent location on a major highway and catered primarily to interstate travelers. Menu prices were comparatively low, and the restaurant served more than 1,000 customers each day. A new interstate highway was built a short distance from the restaurant, and interstate traffic no longer drove past the restaurant. The number of customers immediately decreased to about 250 per day, and the restaurant could not operate profitably with low menu prices and low volume. The owner attempted to attract the local population by offering products of higher quality at higher menu prices. His efforts were successful. Profit margins were considerably higher, and the restaurant again became a profitable operation, although with fewer customers than before.

There are a number of methods for establishing menu prices. Many of these, however complex they may appear, are variations on three basic approaches:

1. Matching competitors' prices.
2. Calculating prices from costs and cost percents.
3. Adding desired contribution margins to portion costs.

These will be discussed individually.

MATCHING COMPETITORS' PRICES. Perhaps the most widely used approach to menu pricing is one that might best be described as "follow the leader"—establishing prices that meet those of competitors. This is an approach commonly employed by those who have little or no idea of the costs of the items they sell. Many of those adopting this approach believe that, if a nearby competitor manages to stay in business by, say, selling hamburgers for $2.25, then they can do the same. When they later discover they are nearing bankruptcy, they can never quite understand why.

The use of this imitative approach is not restricted to those who lack the knowledge to do otherwise; it is not uncommon among seasoned and successful operators. Many restaurateurs believe that if their prices are higher than those of nearby competitors, they will lose business to the competition. Tacitly, they are defining their products as homogeneous rather than differentiated. In many cases, they are correct: They are offering price-sensitive, homogeneous products. Restaurants featuring such common items as pizza, fried chicken, or hamburgers can be very much alike in products, services, and prices. Decor may be the only element that renders one different from another. In such cases, accessibility to the market—location—is likely to be the primary determinant of the number of customers and sales. If that is the case, any increase in price over that charged by the competition may effectively destroy the small advantage offered by location and lead to an unacceptable loss in sales.

While a policy of pricing to meet the competition may be satisfactory for some operators in some markets, it can lead to disastrous consequences for others. If menu prices are low, so are contribution margins; therefore, greater numbers of customers are required to cover fixed costs and provide a given level of profit. Every restaurant in a given area cannot maintain the necessary volume to survive when all are offering low menu price. If that is the case, only the most able operators survive, and the failure rate for restaurants in the area will be abnormally high.

CALCULATING PRICES FROM COSTS AND COST PERCENTS.   The second approach to menu pricing, calculating prices from costs and cost percents, has two variations. In both cases, portion costs must first be determined by means of the techniques discussed in Chapter 7. The first variation proceeds as follows. Given portion cost for any menu item, one can calculate a menu price such that the portion cost will be some fixed percentage of that price. If, for example, a restaurateur wanted food cost-to-sales ratio to be 40 percent, he could set a menu price for each item merely by dividing .4 into the portion cost and adjusting the resulting answer to some suitable amount to print in a menu. Thus, a figure such as $8.24 would be adjusted to $8.25, a more common menu price. If this approach were followed with literally every menu item, the cost percent for operation for any period would be 40 percent, provided that the staff followed all established standards and standard procedures for purchasing, receiving, storing, issuing, and producing food. The food cost percent figure to use could be determined by subtracting profit, fixed cost, and labor cost as percentages of sales from 100 percent.

The second variation is slightly different. With portion costs known, a manager sets tentative menu prices and then forecasts sales volume for an upcoming period. Projected figures for total cost, total sales, and food cost percent may be determined by using the Menu Pre-Cost and Abstract illustrated and discussed in Chapter 11. If the projected cost percent is judged unsatisfactory, then portion costs, menu prices, and even the forecast itself can be adjusted until a realistic and satisfactory potential result is achieved. If the forecast has been reasonably accurate and if the staff has observed the standards and standard procedures established for all phases of operation, the resulting cost percent for operation should conform to management's plans.

ADDING CONTRIBUTION MARGINS TO PORTION COSTS.   The third approach, adding contribution margins to portion costs, is becoming more common in the industry. This approach requires that the foodservice operator determine the average contribution margin required to cover costs other than food and to yield the desired level of profit at the expected level of sales volume.

This average contribution margin is then added to the portion costs of menu items to determine their menu prices.

The use of this approach can be illustrated from figures abstracted from the statement of income for Julio's, a very successful restaurant adjacent to the largest shopping mall in the region. The statement of income indicates the following for a period during which 30,000 customers were served:

Food sales	$500,000
− Cost of sales	200,000
Gross profit	$300,000
− All other costs	250,000
Profit	$ 50,000

Each customer in this example spent an average of $16.67 and contributed an average of $10.00 to covering costs other than food and providing profit.

This method would suggest that each menu item be priced at $10.00 above portion cost, regardless of the item. For example, a steak with a portion cost of $8.00 would be priced at $18.00, and a pasta item costing $ 2.50 would be priced at $12.50. If this approach were followed and if sales volume matched or exceeded forecasts, the minimum acceptable dollar profit would be assured, provided that costs were kept strictly under control in all areas.

In addition, many might consider this a more equitable pricing method. Assuming that no significant difference exists in the cost of producing menu items, each customer is bearing only his fair share of costs and profits.

Selling Products Effectively

Essentially, a restaurant has two principal means available for selling products effectively:

1. The menu.
2. The sales techniques used by the staff.

These will be discussed individually.

THE MENU. The menu is the primary sales tool in most restaurants. Because of this, one is inclined to turn to the menu to shed light on the numbers of sales of the various items offered. Those items that are presented most favorably (featured on the menu, for example) typically outsell other items. Conversely, those that are least favorably presented tend not to sell as well as they might. Since menu items normally have differing costs, contribution margins, and cost precents, the foodservice operator has an opportunity to exercise some level of control over cost percent and gross margin by preparing menus that achieve maximum sales volume. It is quite clear that one would want to maximize sales volume for those items deemed to be the most profitable.

Menu preparation is a complete subject in itself, which renders full coverage beyond the scope of a text in food, beverage, and labor cost control. However, because the menu is such a key ingredient in efforts to maximize profits, anyone planning a career in foodservice should have some general knowledge of the most important elements in menu preparation, which are:

1. Layout and design.
2. Variety.
3. Item arrangement and location.
4. Descriptive language.
5. Kitchen personnel and equipment.

Layout and Design. It should be apparent that the entire physical menu (the paper, the color, the printing, and so on) should suit the character and style of the restaurant. One would not, after all, expect an elaborate menu printed in raised type on parchment stock in the average roadside diner, nor would one expect to see the menu of a high-priced and exclusive Continental restaurant printed poorly on the cheapest paper available. Appropriate menu layout and design for a restaurant are essential factors in satisfying the clientele and achieving maximum revenue.

Anyone unfamiliar with the principles of menu layout and design would be well advised to consult one or more of the several excellent books on the subject and to have one's initial attempts reviewed by an expert before having a menu printed.

Variety. For a menu to have maximum public appeal, it should offer a suitable variety of foods, preparation methods, and prices. Variety will satisfy the needs of a broad market and will help the restaurant operator capture the largest possible number of customers. Even in specialty restaurants and those offering ethnic foods, variety is important. After all, even the fast-food restaurant chains offer their customers choices.

Various authors and restaurant specialists have suggested that a good general menu should include among the entrees several different types of meat, fish, poultry, and pasta dishes. One highly respected consultant has suggested that five is the minimum number of entrees acceptable for a restaurant menu and that the number should include at least one of each of the general types of dishes mentioned above. Additionally, restaurant patrons are increasingly conscious of the nutritional value of their meals. More and more restaurants are including low calorie and low fat items on their menus.

In general, menus should also reflect various cooking methods. Some items should be sautéed, some roasted, some boiled, and so on. This not only ensures acceptance by customers with various preferences, but also adds variety in the appearance of foods reaching the customers' tables.

Appearance of foods is of great importance. The number of combinations of foods that may appear together on plates is vast, and some are more interesting and attractive than others. The possibilities for providing pleasant and appropriate contrasts in color, contour, and texture are always in the mind of the experienced menu writer. It may sound trite to say that people eat first with their eyes, but it is true nevertheless and should be considered by anyone writing a menu.

It is also desirable to include a reasonable range of entree prices. Not every potential customer is willing and able to purchase the most expensive items, and most restaurants risk losing customers if their prices do not appeal to a broad market. This is particularly true in restaurants that cater to families and depend on repeat business for survival.

Item Arrangement and Location.   One of the most significant menu-making principles is the physical arrangement of items on the menu. Items on the menu seen first by customers tend to be ordered more frequently than those seen later. It is generally agreed that patrons' eyes are first focused on the center of a menu. And unless their attention is otherwise directed, items listed first and at the top of a list are seen first and make the greatest impression. It stands to reason that those items will sell in the greatest quantities or at least will sell in greater quantities than if they were placed at the bottom of the list.

Another way of bringing customers' attention to a particular menu item is to feature it in larger type than the items surrounding it. Sometimes a different typeface can have the same effect. In some cases, not only is the type different, but the item is given its own featured spot on the menu. In addition, many restaurants use color pictures, drawings, or photographs of some menu items to capture attention and to build sales volume for the pictured items.

The significant point is that the items management wishes to sell in the greatest quantities should be the featured items. These may be those items in greatest supply in the kitchen on a particular day, those with the most favorable cost-to-sales ratios, or those that provide the greatest contribution margins. In some instances, the featured items are those whose sale would most greatly enhance the restaurant's reputation and thus help build sales volume. Many operators place items with greatest contribution margins in the most prominent places on the menu and relegate those with lesser contribution margins to less conspicuous spots. On such menus, high-cost, high-price items will be more prominent, often appearing first on a list of entrees. Other operators may feature items that require extensive preparation and cannot be used up as leftovers. On such menus, less perishable à la carte items, such as steaks cut and cooked to order, will be far less prominent.

On a well-prepared menu, foods will appear in just those physical locations and with just those degrees of prominence that will induce customers to order what management wants to sell.

Descriptive Language.   The dining experience begins well before customers taste the food they have ordered. It may begin with the first impression of the food operation, when the restaurant is first described by a friend, when potential customers read a review or an advertisement, or when they first enter the premises. The physical appearance of the establishment and its staff and the attitude of the staff toward customers will make or reinforce an initial impression or change it.

The menu itself and the language used to describe menu items may make a good impression and induce customer orders. The descriptions of foods may make the customer hungry and may help to increase the number of sales to a level that might otherwise have been impossible. On the other hand, a menu that describes available items poorly may actually decrease sales. A food and beverage operator can exercise great influence over the amount of the average check by using written descriptions that make menu items sound interesting. Customers tend to react positively to foods that are appealingly described and negatively to those that are not.

Appropriate adjectives tend to increase customer satisfaction because they lead to higher levels of expectation. As long as the foods meet expectations, customers obtain greater satisfaction from foods that verbal description has suggested will be good. The successful operator knows that a menu item simply labeled "Broiled Steak" has considerably less appeal to the customer than one described as "U.S. Prime Sirloin Steak, Aged to Perfection and Prepared to Your Taste, Garnished With the Chef's Special. . . ." And after all, "Deep-Fried Maryland Chicken, Southern Style" does conjure up a different image for the diner than the simple "Fried Chicken."

Kitchen Personnel and Equipment.   Over the years, there have been many horrible examples of foodservice operators adding various items to their menus that were completely beyond the culinary skills of the kitchen staff. There have been instances of foodservice consultants creating menus with items requiring higher levels of culinary skill than were available in the local labor market. Also, everyone knows of at least one case of a specific chef who was preparing menu items that were perfect delights to a restaurant's customers and then quitting and leaving behind a staff that was unable to prepare the items satisfactorily.

Anyone writing a menu should have a clear, unbiased view of the culinary abilities of the present staff and should be entirely realistic about the possibility of replacing any staff member with another of equal skill. At the same time, the menu writer should be aware not only of the equipment needed to prepare the foods on the menu, but also of the kinds of equipment available in the kitchen and its general condition. Before including some dish requiring precise oven temperatures to prepare, for example, one should be sure that oven thermostats are in proper working order. And before deciding to include French fries with every order, one should be sure of having adequate staff and equipment to prepare the needed quantity.

In many kitchens, particularly large hotel kitchens, employees are given workstation assignments and specific responsibilities. One individual may be assigned to the broiler, one to sautéing, one to a garde-manger station, another to vegetable preparation, and so on. If this is the case, the menu writer must be sure that each station is likely to have a reasonable amount of work, so that none of the employees or workstations are either overloaded or underworked. If an analysis of an existing menu suggests that the amount of work in the kitchen is not suitably balanced among employees or workstations, one should consider rewriting the menu, adjusting the number of employees at each work-station, providing additional equipment, or attending to some combination of these. If situations of this nature are permitted to develop or continue, the turnover rate for kitchen personnel may increase significantly.

By taking these basic elements of menu preparation carefully into account, a menu writer can substantially increase the possibility of developing a menu that will produce an appropriate level of sales volume and a growing number of satisfied customers.

SALES TECHNIQUES.   The second means for selling products effectively is to develop appropriate sales techniques to be used by servers, who are, after all, a restaurant's sales force. In many instances, the customer's decision to order an item (or not to order it) is influenced by the server. Because of the important role that servers play in influencing customers' selections, restaurant managers are usually interested in developing appropriate sales techniques for their servers and in providing some basic sales training.

In many restaurants, managers hold daily meetings with servers just be-fore opening time. Managers often use this time to go over the day's menu with servers to be sure they can describe each item to any customer, naming the principal ingredients and identifying the preparation method. The time can also be used to go over new menu items, to enumerate the specials of the day, and to identify any dishes that servers are expected to make special efforts to sell.

Daily meetings normally have positive outcomes for management, for customers, and for the servers themselves. For management, these meetings help ensure that the sales force will have a thorough knowledge of the products they sell, a prime requirement for sales personnel in all businesses.

For customers, these meetings increase the likelihood of being able to obtain immediate and accurate answers to questions about menu offerings. It is a distinct advantage to be able to learn from a knowledgeable server any information one needs or wants to know about a dish before it is ordered. This helps customers make realistic decisions about what to order or not to order, and it helps reduce the number of orders sent back to the kitchen by customers who made incorrect assumptions about food items.

For servers, daily meetings increase the likelihood of them being able to provide correct answers to questions arising from the menu. Most servers quickly comprehend that these meetings improve their ability to provide each customer with a satisfactory dining experience and that this leads to increased income from tips.

The adoption of standard sales techniques can play an important role in increasing and maximizing sales. If properly used by the servers, standard sales techniques not only help build sales volume, but also provide customers with more personal attention than they might otherwise receive.

One useful sales technique that many successful restaurateurs train their personnel to use is to suggest menu items or courses to customers that they might not otherwise consider ordering. Common examples include drinks before dinner, soups, wine to accompany a meal, and cordials after the meal. If the server takes orders for drinks before dinner, he is not just increasing sales revenue for the restaurant, but is also providing customers with some means of occupying their time while their orders are being prepared. Servers are often trained to suggest appetizers, salads, and desserts—courses that customers might not order unless servers suggest them.

A slight variation on this technique is to train servers to suggest specific menu items. In some restaurants, servers make suggestions for every course; in others, servers make suggestions for the main course alone. For example, if the chef has prepared a limited quantity of a particularly desirable fresh fish item that is not normally on the menu, servers may be asked to suggest that item to customers to help ensure the sale of every portion. These suggestions, if made in an appropriate manner, can add a pleasant, personal touch to customer service, while increasing sales at the same time.

It is normally not difficult to secure employee cooperation in making suggestions to customers, particularly if the personnel are aware that customer tips are typically a percentage of the total check and that higher dollar sales tend to increase tips.

In restaurants that hold daily meetings with servers and train personnel to use standard sales techniques, management normally engages in some sort of periodic review and evaluation of staff performance. Performance can be assessed in a number of ways. One common method is to determine gross sales per employee or average sale per employee for a given period (a week, for example). Those with performance levels significantly lower than those of their colleagues may need some coaching or some additional training.

If management takes the steps described above to price products properly and sell those products effectively, there is a greater likelihood that sales revenue and numbers of sales in a restaurant will be maximized and that sales records will indicate increases in the number of sales of those items that produce the highest contribution margins and greatest profits.

CONTROLLING REVENUE

Throughout the discussion of food control in previous chapters, we have made numerous references to food sales. With all these references, there has been an unstated assumption that all food sales have been accurately recorded and that all have resulted in appropriate revenue to the establishment. While accurate recording of sales and inflows of appropriate revenue are both desirable and necessary to the successful operation of a restaurant, neither can be assumed.

There are many possibilities for errors to occur in the recording of sales. Some are accidental; other are not. Sales may be incorrectly recorded; incorrect prices may be charged; checks may be lost, stolen, or simply not used at all; sales that have been correctly recorded may not always bring revenue to an establishment because of the actions of dishonest employees or customers. While these are but a few of the many possibilities, they serve to suggest the need for establishing some control over revenue.

After reading the previous chapters on food control, one should be keenly aware of the proper method for establishing control over any phase of operation: instituting the four-step control process first discussed in Chapter 2. To control sales or revenues, then, one must institute the process, beginning by establishing standards and standard procedures. Standards and standard procedures for revenue control are aimed at one clear and simple goal: to ensure that all food served produces the appropriate revenue for the enterprise. For any menu item served to a customer, appropriate revenue is the price stipulated in the menu; for food served to an employee at the discretion of management, appropriate revenue may be a menu price, a discounted price, or no price at all, depending on management's policies. In any case, all food served must be accounted for in some appropriate manner. If one fails to account for all food served to customers and employees, the result will be distortion of the cost-to-sales ratio. This may lead management to believe erroneously that cost control procedures are not working as planned. In addition, without proper revenue control, an establishment may be a financial failure even with excellent cost controls. This point is best illustrated by example. Imagine that the cost controls in the Fidelity Restaurant are so successful that actual food cost for one week, $3,500, is nearly identical to standard cost for that period. Given a planned food cost-to-sales ratio of 35.0 percent, this food should produce sales of approximately $10,000. Without appropriate sales control procedures, it is quite possible that sales for the week might be recorded as $09,000, rather than $10,000, resulting in a food cost-to-sales ratio of 38.9 percent. If so, gross profit on sales would be reduced by $1,000, and food cost percent would be 3.9 percent higher than would have been the case if all sales had been recorded correctly.

If this were the case, additional cost controls and additional efforts aimed at improving employee performance will not be effective. The real need would be for standard procedures intended to control revenue. It is important for anyone planning a career in foodservice management to understand the nature of these procedures and be prepared to establish them in any foodservice enterprise.

Establishing Standards and Standard Procedures for Revenue Control

To achieve effective control over revenue, management must establish standard procedures intended to insure that food sales are documented, priced correctly, and both checked and verified daily.

The specifics required to achieve the necessary level of control are the following:

1. Documenting food sales.
2. Using numbered checks.
3. Checking and verifying food sales.
4. Recording revenue.

A great many systems and procedures for controlling food sales are currently in use in the industry. The larger the organization, the more complex these are likely to be. Sometimes the standard procedures used to control revenues in one restaurant appear to differ markedly from those used by another. On closer inspection, however, one is likely to find that they are merely variations. In the following pages, we will describe the basics that one is likely to see used in foodservice operations of various kinds throughout the industry.

DOCUMENTING FOOD SALES.   One of the most basic steps in food sales control is to require that each menu item ordered be recorded in some way. The traditional method for attending to this has been to require that servers record guests' menu selections and the menu prices of those selections on paper forms called **guest checks** or **sales checks.** Guest checks, used almost universally in the past and still very common today, are used to:

1. Help servers remember the specifics of guests' orders;
2. Give itemized bills to guests;
3. Maintain written records of portion sales to add to a sales history;
4. Prove the accuracy of cashiers' work;
5. Verify the accuracy of prices charged;
6. Provide the records required for tax purposes.

Many years ago when handwriting was considered an art and schools spent considerable time teaching children to write legibly, handwritten guest checks were normally easy to read. In recent years, however, with the number of instructional hours for penmanship declining, handwritten checks have become much more difficult to read. Thus, they have lost much of their former value for meeting the needs identified above.

Today, because of technological advances, many foodservice operators have been able to end their dependence on the traditional guest check. In a number of fast-food operations with limited menus, for example, servers at counters record guests' selections at computer terminals by depressing keys marked with the names of menu items. Even in restaurants dedicated to fine dining, servers can be observed recording guests' selections in small terminals located at sidestands, using three-digit or four-digit codes assigned to the menu items. In both fast-food and fine-dining establishments, additional features automatically look up correct menu prices for the items selected and then calculate both tax and total, printing itemized checks, or bills, for guests.

Although electronic advances have made it easy to eliminate the use of many paper forms in the industry, many operators continue to prefer the traditional guest check to its alternatives. Some find a measure of continuing security in familiar ways. Others are not familiar with computers and are somewhat reluctant to use them. Still others prefer systems that use paper forms, including guest checks, which are less costly than computer systems. Growing numbers, however, are finding computers appealing as well as efficient and cost effective for many of the control-related tasks that required many hours and hundreds of repetitive calculations in years past. In fact, the control possibilities discussed below are all far easier to accomplish in the "checkless" restaurant—the one that uses a computer system for control, rather than paper guest checks.

While the use of handwritten guest checks provides some measure of control over sales, those who use them agree that numbering the guest checks sequentially increases the extent of the control they provide.

USING NUMBERED CHECKS.   Those still using guest checks purchase them from printers or stationers. When placing orders, they are careful to specify that the checks be serially numbered. In fact, many take care to specify the first number to print on the first check in the new order. This is normally the next number in a long sequence and is determined by looking at the last number on the last check from the previous order.

Essentially, there are two kinds of numbered guest checks: padded and unpadded.

Padded: Some operators buy sequentially numbered guest checks in pads of 25, 50, or some other number. The first check might be numbered 0001, followed by 0002, and so on through the last in the pad, 0025. One pad of checks will be assigned to one server, who will be held accountable for all the checks in that pad. Padded checks are more common in restaurants that are somewhat less formal, where seat turnover tends to be higher and servers tend to use greater numbers of checks in any one day.

Unpadded: Other operators buy sequentially numbered checks unpadded. These checks are assigned to servers one at a time, such that a server is held accountable only for the specific check assigned to him or her. Unpadded checks are more common in restaurants where the style of service is more formal, where seat turnover tends to be lower and a server will tend to use fewer checks during a shift.

Whether padded or unpadded, numbered checks make it possible to assign responsibility for specific checks to particular employees. In most cases, this is done by requiring personnel to sign for checks. Servers are typically required to sign for a pad of checks before a serving period and return it at the end, recording the serial numbers of the checks used. Figure 12.2 illustrates one type of signature book used for this purpose.

An alternative procedure, often used in restaurants serving haute cuisine from à la carte menus, is to require that personnel sign for individual checks as needed. Figure 12.3 shows a sample of one type of server's signature book used in this kind of operation.

Although some establishments fail to take full advantage of them, there are a number of benefits to using sequentially numbered checks. For example, with the use of numbered checks, it is possible at the end of any meal period to reassemble the checks in numerical order to see if any are missing. If a check is missing, it is easy to look at the signature book to determine which server signed for it, and then to question the server.

There are any number of explanations for missing checks, none of which are acceptable. Missing checks can be indications that a waiter or a cashier is

			Date 10/1/XXXX			
			Checks			
Date	Waiter No.	Book No.	From	To	Closing No.	Signature
10/1	1	7	700	799		T J Jones
10/1	2	8	800	899		S.S. Smith

FIGURE 12.2 *Server's Signature Book*

	H. Martin Cashier			9/3/XXXX
Check No.	Waiter No.	No. Served	Table No.	Waiter's Signature
100	1	4	2	D. Smith
101	2	2	3	P. Jones
102				
103				
104				
105				
106				
107				
108				
109				
110	3	2	7	J. Gawley
111	4	3	8	B. Miller
112				
113				
114				
115				
116				
117				
118				
119				

FIGURE 12.3 *Cashier's Record of Checks Distributed to Servers*

dishonest, destroying checks and pocketing the money. A missing check can also be a sign that some customer has taken the check from the restaurant and failed to pay for the food. In most establishments using numbered checks, there is an immediate investigation made whenever any check is missing, and someone is held accountable. In some restaurants, the server to whom the check was assigned is required to pay a flat amount in cash for any missing check.

Assigning responsibility for specific individual checks or pads of checks makes it possible to monitor other elements of servers' work as well. Essentially, foodservice managers are concerned with two additional aspects of hand-prepared guest checks:

1. Legibility. If guest checks provide the raw data that must be summarized before being added to a sales history, then it is obviously important that management be able to read the guest checks. For this purpose, illegibility is likely to mean inaccuracy.

   While legibility for sales history purposes is important, it is equally important for purposes of determining whether or not employees are accurately recording the menu items ordered by customers. For example, when management insists on legibility, it is much more difficult for a server to get away with giving friends expensive entrees while charging them only for dessert and coffee.

2. Accuracy. Busy servers can make errors. Incorrect prices may be charged for menu selections, and incorrect selections can be written on checks. Errors of this nature are normally accidental; sometimes they are purposeful. A price of $19.95 might be written for a sirloin steak, for example, that is listed at $29.95 on the menu. Or the $29.95 steak order might be written on the check as a chopped steak with a menu price of $14.95.

   In addition to verifying the accuracy of menu prices, managers are usually interested in the accuracy of the arithmetic on guest checks: the accuracy of the subtotal determined by adding individual menu prices, the tax calculated as a percentage of that subtotal, and the grand total for the check.

It is normally advisable to monitor employee performance by conducting routine reviews of handwritten guest checks on a regular basis, checking the legibility of handwriting and verifying the accuracy of menu prices charged and arithmetic. Some managers take the additional step of analyzing checks periodically. This involves examining all guest checks for one day, noting the nature and extent of each error, as well as the name or number of the server responsible. Pricing errors and errors in addition and in calculation of taxes can be called to the attention of the individual servers. Sometimes the list of errors is posted on an employee bulletin board. Few people like seeing their errors posted for all to see, and this is often an inducement to improve.

CHECKING AND VERIFYING FOOD SALES.   Years ago, in order to elimi-nate some of the many possibilities for problems to develop in the area of sales control, many restaurants (especially hotel restaurants) employed personnel who were known as **food checkers.** Food checkers were assigned to work at stations in the kitchen, near doors leading to dining rooms. The food checker's job was to verify that each food item leaving the kitchen was recorded on a guest check. In some establishments, menu prices were recorded on guest checks by food checkers, not by servers, and the entries on the guest checks were made mechanically with a register similar to a cashier's register. This approach provided an extra measure of control because at the end of any serv-ing period the total of the readings in the checker's register would equal the total of cash and charge sales recorded by the cashier, with allowance made for taxes and tips. When the total recorded in the food checker's register ex-ceeded that in the cashier's register, management would investigate the cause of the discrepancy. One advantage of this system was that the independent recording of menu prices by the food checker provided some measure of pro-tection against servers giving away food or undercharging for menu items purposely in a misguided effort to obtain larger tips.

While some managers found some benefits from using food checkers, there were so many disadvantages that this approach to sales control has dis-appeared. One serious disadvantage was that lines tended to form at the food checker's station during busy periods. Consequently, service to customers slowed, turnover decreased, some customers were served cold food, and they were dissatisfied. In addition, labor costs were obviously higher with food checkers than without them, and this has normally been a powerful induce-ment in foodservice to reconsider. In some cases, attempts were made to com-bine the jobs of food checker and cashier, but with little success. Today, all control measures provided by food checkers in the past are available to those who have selected appropriate control-oriented computer systems from the growing numbers on display at hotel and restaurant trade shows and in the pages of the many foodservice periodicals.

In order to retain some of the desirable qualities of the food checker sys-tem while eliminating some of the problems, many restaurants follow a stan-dard procedure that is usually referred to as the **dupe system.** "Dupe" is an abbreviation of the word "duplicate." A standard requirement of this system is that a duplicate copy be made of each order. There are several means of doing this. One is to provide servers with pads of guest checks, each of which produces a second copy, usually on a paper of a different color and texture. Whenever a server records an order on a guest check, a duplicate copy of the order is made on this second copy. This is not the only way of producing the duplicate; there are several others. The important point is that this duplicate copy, the dupe, must be given to personnel in the kitchen before any food will be prepared or issued. Management usually instructs kitchen personnel to give servers only the food items recorded on the dupes in the quantities indicated. When food has been picked up by servers, the dupes are left behind in the kitchen. In some restaurants, these are then deposited in locked boxes to prevent their reuse. At the end of a serving period, dupes bearing the same numbers as the original checks may be matched against the checks to locate any discrepancies.

Although it is conceivable that dupes could be used for all food orders in some kitchens, it is not usually the case. In most instances, dupes are used only for entree items and certain other high-cost items (shrimp cocktails, for example) over which management wants to exercise control.

When dupes are used, many establishments match the duplicate to the original check to verify that nothing was given out from the kitchen without an original and that the cashier received all original checks. Because this is a time-consuming task, some establishments take additional measures to simplify the verification procedure. One method is to require that servers write food orders, but no prices, on checks and dupes as the orders are taken. Then, on the way to the kitchen to place the orders, each server records prices on the checks with a machine similar to a cash register. The register dispenses a printed receipt, which is attached to the dupe before kitchen personnel will issue any food. When this procedure is followed, it is possible at the end of a meal period to compare the readings from the kitchen register with the cashier's register and to locate missing amounts.

RECORDING REVENUES.   Traditionally, most restaurants employed cashiers who were assigned responsibility for taking payments from customers and recording sales as the customers left the restaurants. They were usually stationed near restaurant exits, although some worked in other locations. These cashiers are still very much in evidence in the restaurant business today. Many establishments have upgraded the equipment that cashiers use to record sales (cash sales, charge sales, and portion sales for a sales history), but continue to place cashiers at the familiar workstations adjacent to the front door. Although today's equipment is different, the basic requirements of the job are not. Restaurant cashiers today are following the same general principles established by restaurant managers in years gone by.

Check #	Waiter #	# Covers	Food Sales	Tax	Tips	Cash	Charge	Detail
101	6	2	4.00	.48		4.48		
102	3	5	20.00	1.60	5.00		26.60	Diners'
103	2	1	3.00	.24	1.00		4.24	Amex
104	2	2	7.00	.56		7.56		
105	6	4	12.50	1.00		13.50		
Totals		14	46.50	3.88	6.00	25.54	30.84	

FIGURE 12.4 *Restaurant Sales Control Sheet*

For proper revenue control, sales were always recorded in a register, and each guest check was endorsed in the register as the sale was recorded. This meant that each check had to be inserted in the register as the sale was being recorded so that the amount recorded was printed on the check. Thus, all guest checks were endorsed, regardless of how they were settled. The printed endorsement helped differentiate between guest checks that had been settled and those that had not. In many restaurants, management required that any guest checks settled with cash be clearly identified as such, and cashiers were often required to use a rubber stamp to mark these guest checks "Paid." Some even required cashiers to deposit all paid guest checks in a locked box as soon as the cash has been collected. The purpose of both procedures was to prevent the reuse of paid guest checks, a practice that sometimes occurs when a dishonest server and a dishonest cashier collaborate to steal.

It is still common practice to require cashiers to record the breakdown of checks into appropriate categories (food sales, taxes, and tips, for one example; cash sales and charge sales, for another). While this is no longer done on paper—mechanical cash registers, electronic cash registers, and now computers are used to do the breakdown —the results are perhaps best illustrated by the traditional control sheet shown in Figure 12.4.

In this illustration, one should note that the total of food sales, taxes, and tips is equal to the total of cash sales and charge sales. Thus:

$$\$46.50 + \$3.88 + \$6.00 = \$56.38$$

$$\$25.54 + \$30.84 = \$56.38$$

Traditionally, in restaurants using forms of this nature, cashiers were required to list the guest checks in numerical order so that missing numbers would be readily apparent. If any were, the servers to whom the checks had been assigned were questioned immediately.

Today, there has been an increase in the number of restaurants requiring that servers also act as cashiers. It is interesting to note that at the end of a day's work, many individual servers are determining their net receipts for the day from computer printouts. These printouts provide information similar to that provided in Figure 12.4. In many instances, the printouts resemble that form.

These are but a few of the methods and procedures that knowledgeable managers employ in their efforts to establish effective revenue control procedures. The net effect of these efforts should be an accurate accounting of all sales so that undesirable food cost percentages will not be attributed to improperly recorded sales.

MENU ANALYSIS

A useful topic to introduce at this stage of the discussion is **menu analysis.** Although menu analysis is not covered by the definition of sales control identified earlier in the chapter, it does provide a means for monitoring the effectiveness of efforts to maximize profits. In addition, it offers some general guidelines that are useful for increasing the profitability of a menu.

The menu analysis technique discussed below was developed by Michael L. Kasavana and Donald I. Smith and was described in a book published in 1982. Known as **menu engineering,** the technique is now widely known and respected and has been the subject of numerous papers and articles. While some people do not agree entirely with the conclusions drawn by Kasavana and Smith, their approach to menu analysis is both interesting and revealing.

Space does not permit full exposition of their method, which can best be obtained from their book. Within the limited confines of this chapter, we will offer a brief introduction to menu engineering and then relate it to the problem of profit maximization discussed earlier in this chapter.

The first step in this introduction will be to present an example of a menu engineering worksheet, illustrated in Figure 12.5. Initially, one notes many similarities to the Menu Pre-Cost and Abstract form illustrated and discussed in Chapter 11. Such column headings as "Menu Item," "Number Sold," "Item Food Cost," "Item Sales Price," "Menu Cost," and "Menu Revenue" give one a sense of familiarity. Although the terms differ slightly, these are much the same as those used on the Menu Pre-Cost and Abstract form. Specifically, the menu engineering worksheet closely corresponds to the right, or Abstract, side of the form in Chapter 11. The sources of the data and the required computations are exactly the same.

Several additional columns distinguish the menu engineering worksheet:

RESTAURANT: Sturnley's   **PERIOD:** March 3–9, XXXX

A Menu Item Name	B No. Sold (MM)	C Menu Mix %	D Item Food Cost	E Item Sales Price	F Item CM (E-D)	G Menu Costs (D*B)	H Menu Revenues (E*B)	L Menu CM (F*B)	P CM Category	R MM Category	S Menu Item Classification
Broiled Chicken	375	18.8%	$3.00	$6.50	$3.50	$1,125.00	$2,437.50	$1,312.50	L	H	Plowhorse
Strip Steak 12 oz	330	16.5%	$5.50	$13.00	$7.50	$1,815.00	$4,290.00	$2,475.00	H	H	Star
Strip Steak 16 oz	125	6.3%	$6.50	$15.00	$8.50	$812.50	$1,875.00	$1,062.50	H	L	Puzzle
Stuffed Shrimp	160	8.0%	$5.00	$12.50	$7.50	$800.00	$2,000.00	$1,200.00	H	H	Star
Scrod	90	4.5%	$3.50	$7.00	$3.50	$315.00	$630.00	$315.00	L	L	Dog
Lobster 1/4 lb.	130	6.5%	$7.50	$16.00	$8.50	$975.00	$2,080.00	$1,105.00	H	L	Puzzle
Veal Piccata	135	6.8%	$5.50	$14.00	$8.50	$742.50	$1,890.00	$1,147.50	H	L	Puzzle
Roast Prime Ribs	405	20.3%	$6.00	$13.00	$7.00	$2,430.00	$5,265.00	$2,835.00	H	H	Star
Pork Chops	170	8.5%	$4.00	$9.00	$5.00	$680.00	$1,530.00	$850.00	L	H	Plowhorse
Salisbury Steak	80	4.0%	$3.50	$7.00	$3.50	$280.00	$560.00	$280.00	L	L	Dog
COLUMN	N					I	J	M			
TOTALS	2,000	100.0%				$9,975.00	$22,557.50	$12,582.50			

ADDITIONAL COMPUTATIONS			
	$K = I/J$	$O = M/N$	$Q = (1/\text{no. of items} \times 70\%)$
	$\dfrac{\$9,975.00}{\$22,557.50} = 44.2\%$	$\dfrac{\$12,582.50}{2,000} = \$6.29$	$\dfrac{1}{10} \times .7 = 7.0\%$

FIGURE 12.5 *Menu Engineering Worksheet*

(C)"Menu Mix %"; (F)"Item CM"; (L) "Menu CM"; (P) "CM Category"; (R) "MM Category"; and (S) "Menu Item Classification." At the foot of the worksheet, there are several additional computations. Both the additional columns and the computations require some explanation.

Column C: Menu Mix Percent

The menu mix percent for each item is calculated by dividing the number of units sold by the total number of units sold for all items. For example, broiled chicken accounted for 375 portions out of the total portion sales for all items 2,000. The menu mix percent for this item is calculated as:

$$\frac{375}{2000} = .1875, \text{ or } 18.8\%$$

The menu mix percent for each of the other items is calculated in the same way.

Column F: Item CM

You student will recall from discussion in previous chapters that contribution margin (CM) is defined as sales price minus variable cost per unit. For simplicity and for purposes of this analysis, food cost is treated as the only variable cost. Therefore, the CM for broiled chicken is determined by subtracting the portion cost for the item from its sales price, as follows:

Sales price	$6.50
− Food cost	$3.00
= CM	$3.50

The CM, of course, is the amount available from each sale to contribute toward meeting all other costs of operation and, when those costs have been met, to provide profit for the owner.

Column L: Menu CM

The menu contribution margin is found by multiplying the number of units sold for each menu item by its contribution margin. Thus, for broiled chicken:

375 Units sold × $3.50 CM = $1,312.50 Menu CM

This calculation indicates the total of contribution margins provided by the particular menu item. The sum of all the individual totals is found in box M.

Box O

The figure in Box O is the average contribution margin, determined by dividing the total in Box M by the total number of units sold, found in Box N. For the illustrated worksheet, the calculation is:

$$\frac{\$12{,}582.50 \text{ Total CM (Box M)}}{2{,}000 \text{ Units sold (Box N)}} = \$6.29$$

This is merely a variation on the calculation of average contribution margin, described in Chapter 3.

Box Q

The figure in Box Q requires careful consideration. This is the percentage of an entire menu represented by each item on that menu, multiplied by 70 percent.

There are ten items on the menu used for Figure 12.5, so each is one-tenth, or 10 percent, of the menu. Similarly, if there were five items on the menu, each would be one-fifth, or 20 percent, of the total. The figure in Box Q is calculated by dividing one menu item by the total number of items on the menu and then multiplying the result by .7 (70 percent). Thus:

$$\frac{1}{10} \times .7 = .07, \text{ or } 7.0\%$$

This figure will be used when making entries in column R, as discussed below.

Column P: CM Category

The entries in this column, L for "low" and H for "high," are made after comparing the contribution margin for each menu item (Column F) with the average contribution margin for the menu (Box O). If the contribution margin for a given menu item is lower than the average contribution margin, the entry for that item in Column P is L for "low." If the contribution margin is higher than average, the entry is H for "high." For example, the contribution margin for broiled chicken is $3.50, which is considerably lower than the average contribution margin for the menu, $6.29. Thus, the entry for that item in Column P is an L for "low."

Column R: MM Category

The entries in Column R (L and H for "low" and "high," respectively) are determined by comparing the menu mix percentage for each item in Column C with the figure in Box Q. For example, the menu mix percentage for broiled chicken is 18.8 percent. Compared to the 7.0 percent figure in Box Q, this is high, so the entry for broiled chicken is the letter H. The menu mix percentage for Salisbury steak is 4.0 percent and, because this is lower than the 7.0 percent in Box Q, the letter L has been entered.

Because all entries in Column P and Column R must be one of two letters (either H or L), there are four possible combination of letters: H/H, L/L, H/L, and L/H. These four possible combinations are used to identify menu items and, in the special language of menu engineering, each has been given a name:

H/H is a **Star.** A star is a menu item that produces both high contribution margin and high volume. These are the items that foodservice operators prefer to sell when they can.

L/L is a **Dog.** A dog is a menu item that produces a comparatively low contribution margin and accounts for relatively low volume. These are probably the least desirable items to have on a menu.

L/H is a **Plowhorse.** A plowhorse is a menu item that produces a low contribution margin but accounts for relatively high volume. These items have broad appeal to customers, but contribute comparatively little profit per unit sold.

H/L is a **Puzzle.** A puzzle is a menu item that produces a high contribution margin, but accounts for comparatively low sales volume.

Because it provides a graphic demonstration of the extent to which each menu item contributes to profitability, the menu engineering worksheet is a tool that can be of great use to restaurateurs interested in maximizing profit. Having completed the worksheet as described above, a restaurateur can use the general guidelines offered below to analyze a list of menu offerings and then determine the changes, if any, that would improve the menu.

Dogs: Because dogs are both unprofitable and unpopular, they should be removed from the menu and replaced with more profitable items unless (a) there is a valid reason for continuing to sell a dog (as with an item that promotes other sales), or (b) its profitability can somehow be increased to an acceptable level. This will require that the item be changed in some way. One way of changing an item from a dog to a puzzle is to increase contribution margin per unit, which might be done by increasing sales price.

Plowhorses: Plowhorses are popular but relatively unprofitable. They should be kept on the menu, but attempts should be made to increase their contribution margins without decreasing volume. One possibility would be to decrease standard portion size slightly and at the same time improve the appearance of the product.

Puzzles: Puzzles are comparatively profitable but relatively unpopular. They should be kept on the menu, but attempts should be made to increase their popularity without decreasing their profitability substantially. There are any number of ways to do this, including repositioning items to more favorable locations on the menu, featuring items as specials suggested to diners by servers, and changing appearances or menu descriptions of these items to increase their appeal.

Stars: Stars are both profitable and popular and should normally be left alone, unless there is some valid reason for change. Because of the popularity of stars, it is sometimes possible to increase their menu prices without affecting volume, thus increasing their profitability.

Some examples of the application of these general guidelines will be useful. For purposes of illustration, we will refer to Figure 12.6, which reflects changes made by management to the menu represented in Figure 12.5.

The changes were made in accordance with the general guidelines provided above. The specific changes and their effects are as follows:

1. Scrod, a dog, was replaced with broiled trout, an item with a higher contribution margin. While sales volume did not change, the higher contribution margin changed the classification of the item from dog to puzzle. In addition, total revenues, total contribution margin, and average contribution margin were all increased.
2. Broiled chicken, a plowhorse, was increased in price by $.50. Volume was not affected because of the popularity of the item, its relatively low sales price, and the minimal price increase. While the item remains a plowhorse, total revenues, total contribution margin, and average contribution margin were all increased.
3. Veal piccata, a puzzle, was repositioned on the menu and suggested to customers by servers. This resulted in an increase in sales volume, reclassifying the item from puzzle to star. This change had some negative impact on the sales of stuffed shrimp, although this item remains a star. However, the higher contribution margin and higher sales price for veal piccata, compared to stuffed shrimp, produced an overall increase in total revenue, total contribution margin, and average contribution margin. Thus, the net effect was desirable.

The effects illustrated above show clearly the value of menu engineering as an analytical tool that can be used for many purposes. In terms of the present chapter, the most significant of these is profit maximization.

RESTAURANT: Sturnley's **PERIOD:** March 10–17, XXXX **DATE** 3/20/XXXX

A Menu Item Name	B No. Sold (MM)	C Menu Mix %	D Item Food Cost	E Item Sales Price	F Item CM (E-D)	G Menu Costs (D*B)	H Menu Revenues (E*B)	L Menu CM (F*B)	P CM Category	R MM Category	S Menu Item Classification
Broiled Chicken	375	18.8%	$3.00	$7.00	$4.00	$1,125.00	$2,625.00	$1,500.00	L	H	Plowhorse
Strip Steak 12 oz	330	16.5%	$5.50	$13.00	$7.50	$1,815.00	$4,290.00	$2,475.00	H	H	Star
Strip Steak 16 oz	125	6.3%	$6.50	$15.00	$8.50	$812.50	$1,875.00	$1,062.50	H	L	Puzzle
Stuffed Shrimp	150	7.5%	$5.00	$12.50	$7.50	$750.00	$1,875.00	$1,125.00	H	H	Star
Trout	90	4.5%	$4.30	$11.00	$6.70	$387.00	$990.00	$603.00	H	L	Puzzle
Lobster 1/4 lb.	130	6.5%	$7.50	$16.00	$8.50	$975.00	$2,080.00	$1,105.00	H	L	Puzzle
Veal Piccata	145	7.3%	$5.50	$14.00	$8.50	$797.50	$2,030.00	$1,232.50	H	H	Star
Roast Prime Ribs	405	20.3%	$6.00	$13.00	$7.00	$2,430.00	$5,265.00	$2,835.00	H	H	Star
Pork Chops	170	8.5%	$4.00	$9.00	$5.00	$680.00	$1,530.00	$850.00	L	H	Plowhorse
Salisbury Steak	80	4.0%	$3.50	$7.00	$3.50	$280.00	$560.00	$280.00	L	L	Dog
COLUMN	N					I	J	M			
TOTALS	2,000	100.0%				$10,052.00	$23,120.00	$13,068.00			

ADDITIONAL COMPUTATIONS

$$K = I/J$$
$$\frac{\$10,052.00}{\$23,120.00} = 43.5\%$$

$$O = M/N$$
$$\frac{\$13,068}{2,001} = \$6.54$$

$$Q = (1/\text{no. of items} \times 70\%)$$
$$\frac{1}{10} \times .7 = 7.0\%$$

FIGURE 12.6 *Menu Engineering Worksheet After Changes*

COMPUTER APPLICATIONS

Computers play a key role in controlling revenue. For example, the sales history developed with the aid of a sales terminal can provide a valuable body of information about customer preferences. Properly used, this information can lead to the development of menus that exclude food items that are unpopular with the clientele of a particular restaurant. This, of course, is only one simple and obvious use.

Another possibility is a sales terminal capable of generating sales reports quickly while sales are in progress (halfway through the dinner hour, for example). It would obviously benefit a manager to be able to compare actual sales during the dinner hour with the forecast of sales, the basis for many purchasing and production decisions. If sales for some item were far lower than had been forecast, the manager might want to make some judicious efforts to increase sales (as opposed to orders taken) for the item, possibly by offering some inducement for the servers to "sell" the item. If successful, this type of mini-campaign could have many beneficial outcomes, including a decrease in leftover food, lower food costs, and possibly an increase in dollar sales.

Perhaps the most important use of the computer as a sales control device may be illustrated by its capacity for eliminating the need for the traditional guest check and dupe. With the computer control system described in Chapter 2, the server first records guests' selections on a simple pad of white paper. Next, the server signs into a terminal using an individually assigned code and follows a step-by-step program, using codes to record the table number, the number of diners, and their food selections. By doing this, the server is opening a numbered "check" in computer memory, where it will remain until the server requests a printed copy after the diners have completed their meals. As the menu selections are entered, they are transmitted to the various stations of the kitchen, where they are displayed on printers. By this means, various stations are advised of orders placed, including the number of portions, the name or number of the server placing the order, and the time the order was placed. Servers pick up orders at suitable times for delivery to diners. Additional menu selections for other courses are similarly recorded in the terminal, until the guests have finished their meal and requested a check. At that time, the waiter orders a copy of the check, which is printed at the terminal. The check is stored in memory until the check is settled with cash or credit card. If the check is not settled by the close of business, management will learn of it from a printed report, which will show table number, number of guests, name or number of the server, and the outstanding amount. If needed, a duplicate copy of the check can be printed.

This particular system offers a number of benefits to managers. First, it helps speed service in the dining room and increase seat turnover by eliminating the need for each server to walk to the kitchen to place each order. Next, it completely eliminates the need to maintain traditional guest checks, verify the accuracy of each, and conduct a daily audit to ascertain that none are missing. Finally, by means of the printers at various kitchen stations, it becomes possible to ensure that each food item ordered and picked up has actually been ordered by a guest in the dining room.

CHAPTER ESSENTIALS

In this chapter, we explained the scope of sales control and listed its three goals: optimizing the number of sales, maximizing profit, and controlling revenue. We listed eight determinants of customer restaurant selection and explained how an understanding of these can help to optimize the number of sales. We discussed two primary means for maximizing profits: pricing products properly and selling products effectively. We described the three most common approaches to menu pricing and identified the two principal means for selling products in a restaurant: the menu and sales techniques used by the staff. We discussed one useful technique for menu analysis, menu engineering, and explained how it could be used as an aid to profit maximization. We listed the goals of revenue control and explained the most common standard procedures used to achieve the goals. Finally, we illustrated some uses of computers as sales control tools.

KEY TERMS IN THIS CHAPTER

Differentiated product
Dupe system
Guest check
Homogeneous product
Menu engineering
Menu mix percent
Plowhorse
Price sensitive
Puzzle
Revenue control
Sales control
Sales control sheet
Signature book
Signature item
Star

QUESTIONS AND PROBLEMS

1. Distinguish between sales control and revenue control.

2. List and explain the three goals of sales control.

3. Given two restaurants offering similar products at similar prices, one of which is located in a city center while the other is in a rural setting, which would you expect to achieve greater dollar sales volume? Why?

4. How can the portion sizes offered by a restaurant affect both the number and type of customers it attracts?

5. Distinguish between homogeneous and differentiated products.

6. List and explain the determinants of customer restaurant selection.

7. Describe the two principal means used by food service operators to achieve profit maximization.

8. List and explain the five most important elements of menu preparation.

9. Describe the three most common methods for establishing menu prices.

10. What sales techniques might management suggest that sales personnel use to:
    a. Improve gross revenue and average check?
    b. Increase tips?
    c. Sell a menu item prepared in excess quantity that must be thrown away if not sold?

11. For each of the following number of covers, calculate the average sale.

Number of Covers	Total Sales
20	$ 70.00
87	$ 372.40
142	$ 863.45
463	$2,309.00

12. Why would each of the following adversely affect the average sale in a restaurant?
    a. Deterioration in service standards.
    b. Customer dissatisfaction over food quality.
    c. Inadequate sales promotion.
    d. Changes in portion sizes.

13. Show by example how improper recording of sales affects food cost percent.

14. a. The owner of Foster's Restaurant projects labor costs of 36% and fixed costs of 28%, and wants to plan for profit of 12%. What food cost percent should be projected? (Assume no alcoholic beverages are served.)

    b. Using the food cost percent from Question 14a, what menu sales prices would be suitable for each of the following?

	Portion Cost
Item A	$1.94
Item B	$2.26
Item C	$4.40
Item D	$2.88
Item E	$2.42

15. The owner of Gideon's Restaurant realizes that her establishment is offering homogeneous products that are extremely price sensitive. Given present costs and sales, the business is unprofitable, and she wants to take steps to turn the business around. What suggestions could you make to help this owner make the business profitable?

16. The new manager of Frisbee's Restaurant has learned that there is always a waiting line of customers on Friday and Saturday nights. Because of the apparent need to serve customers as quickly as possible so that seating can be made available to those waiting in line, to what extent should this new manager suggest the use of selling techniques that tend to prolong service and result in customers spending additional time at tables?

17. Given the following information, determine an appropriate contribution margin to use in setting menu prices and then determine suitable menu prices for each of the items listed.

Gross sales:	$300,000
Cost of food sold:	$100,000
Number of customers served:	50,000

	Portion Costs
Item A	$1.85
Item B	$2.60
Item C	$3.50
Item D	$6.28
Item E	$4.12

RESTAURANT: Smuggler's Inn **DATE:** March/9/XXXX

A Menu Item Name	B No. Sold (MM)	C Menu Mix %	D Item Food Cost	E Item Sales Price	F Item CM (E-D)	G Menu Costs (D*B)	H Menu Revenues (E*B)	L Menu CM (F*B)	P CM Category	R MM Category	S Menu Item Classification
Fried Chicken	175		$3.00	$7.00							
Sirloin Steak	190		$5.50	$13.00							
Baked Ham	40		$4.00	$8.00							
Stuffed Sole	45		$7.00	$13.00							
Broiled Swordfish	80		$8.00	$15.00							
Lobster	60		$7.50	$16.00							
Veal Marsala	90		$5.50	$14.00							
Roast Prime Ribs	145		$6.00	$13.00							
Lamb Chops	125		$6.00	$9.00							
Beef Burgundy	50		$3.50	$7.00							
COLUMN TOTALS	N 1,000					I	J	M			
ADDITIONAL COMPUTATIONS						K = I/J		O = M/N	Q = (1/no. of items × 70%)		

FIGURE 12.7   *Menu Engineering Worksheet*

18. **a.** Complete the menu engineering worksheet reproduced in Figure 12.7, filling in the missing information.
    b. Which items, if any, should be removed from the menu? Remain unchanged? Increased in price? Featured or repositioned on the menu? Why?

19. Define each of the following terms:
    Differentiated product
    Dupe system
    Guest check
    Homogeneous product
    Menu engineering
    Menu mix percent
    Plowhorse
    Price sensitive
    Puzzle
    Revenue control
    Sales control
    Sales control sheet
    Signature book
    Signature item
    Star

FOR COMPUTER USERS

20. Using any spreadsheet software you choose, prepare a menu engineering worksheet following the form illustrated in Figure 12.6.

21. Use the worksheet prepared for Question 20 to complete the menu engineering worksheet illustrated in Figure 12.7.

22. Use your spreadsheet program to set up the restaurant sales control sheet illustrated in Figure 12.4 as a worksheet.

Part III

Beverage Control

In previous chapters, the need for food, beverage, and labor control procedures was discussed, and specific control principles and procedures for food were described. In the following five chapters, specific control principles and procedure for beverages will be described.

Beverage control is similar to food control in many ways. It requires that standards and standard procedures be developed for purchasing, receiving, storage, issuing, production, and sales. The standards and standard procedures of beverage control are akin to those used for food control. The principal differences between food controls and beverage controls can be traced to differences in the nature of the products: In general terms, foods tend to be more perishable than beverages, many of which can be kept indefinitely.

Beverage control is as important as food control because of the nature of the product. The possibilities for excessive costs to develop because of some form of theft are probably greater with beverages than with food. Interestingly enough, although everyone recognizes the need for beverage control, it is an area where only limited controls can be successfully instituted.

13 *Beverage Purchasing Control*

After reading and studying this chapter, you should be able to:

1. List and describe the three principal classifications of beverages.
2. Identify two broad classifications of beers and distinguish between them.
3. Identify the three color classifications of wines.
4. Describe the fermentation process, and explain its significance in the making of alcoholic beverages.
5. Explain the purpose of the distillation process.
6. Distinguish between call brands and pouring brands.
7. List the primary purposes for establishing beverage purchasing controls.
8. Identify the principal factors one must weigh before establishing quality standards for beverages.
9. Identify eight principal factors used to establish quantity standards for beverages.
10. Distinguish between license states and control states.
11. Identify the two principal methods for determining order quantities, and calculate order quantities using both methods.
12. Describe one standard procedure for processing beverage orders in large hotels and restaurants.
13. Describe the use of computers to determine order quantities for beverages.
14. Define each of the Key Terms at the end of the chapter.

CONTROL PROCESS AND PURCHASING

In Chapter 2, **control** was defined as a process used by managers to direct, regulate, and restrain the actions of people so that the established goals of an enterprise may be achieved. The control process was described as having four steps: establishing standards and standard procedures, training staff to follow those standards and standard procedures, monitoring staff performance and comparing it with established standards, and taking remedial actions as needed.

Previous chapters illustrated the application of this process to the significant phases of foodservice operations: purchasing, receiving, storing, issuing, producing, and sales. In this part of the text, the process will be applied to these phases of beverage operations. This chapter will focus on the application of the control process to beverage purchasing.

BEVERAGE TYPES

The term **beverage** requires some definition. Technically, any liquid intended for drinking is a beverage, a word derived from French and Latin verbs meaning to drink. In a sense, all beverages can be divided into two groups: those that contain some measure of alcohol and those that contain no alcohol at all.

Alcoholic Beverages

Alcoholic beverages, obviously, are those that contain alcohol. They contain one particular type of alcohol, ethyl alcohol, which is produced naturally in the process of making alcoholic beverages. Other types of alcohol are unsuitable for human consumption. The amount of alcohol contained in alcoholic beverages varies considerably from one to another. Some have a very small percentage, as little .5 percent. Most have substantially more.

There are three classifications of alcoholic beverages: beers, wines, and spirits. These are substantially different from one another, and anyone planning a career in food and beverage management should be able both to describe them and identify their differences.

BEERS. **Beers** are beverages produced by the fermentation of malted grain, flavored with hops. The grain used is normally barley. **Malted grain** is grain that has been mashed and then steeped in water. **Hops** are the dried blossoms of the hop vine and are used to impart the typical bitter flavor to beer. Hops may be either domestic or imported; imported hops are commonly considered superior to domestic.

Fermentation is a natural process resulting from the addition of yeast to a liquid containing malted grain and hops. The starches in the liquid are converted to sugars by complex chemical processes. These sugars, in turn, are converted to carbon dioxide and alcohol. The carbon dioxide is dispersed, while the alcohol remains in the liquid. This liquid containing the alcohol is strained and then stored for varying periods of time to mature and develop flavor. Because natural carbonation is seldom retained during the storage process, most beers are carbonated just before being bottled, canned, or kegged.

Beer does not keep well unless steps are taken to eliminate the bacteria and natural impurities that can cause spoilage. Essentially, there are two methods for doing this: high filtration and pasteurization. Pasteurized beer tends to last longer, but most agree that pasteurizing harms flavor. Regardless of the method used to improve shelf life, most beers should be refrigerated as soon as they are received. Low temperatures help retain flavor and lengthen the shelf life of beers.

While the term **beer** suggests that all products so named are much the same, this is not the case. Beers are normally divided into two broad classifications: **lager beers** and **ales.** These differ from one another in taste, alcohol content, body, and processing method. Lager beer, the type most commonly consumed in the United States, is a category that includes the popular brands of regular and light beer—Budweiser, Miller, Coors, and many others. Bock beers and malt liquors are also classified as lager beers. Compared to lager beer, ale is typically stronger and has a higher alcohol content. Porter and stout, more popular in Europe than in the United States, are both ales.

Nonalcoholic beers are comparatively new products that are produced in much the same way as regular beer, but most of the alcohol is removed. Their popularity is growing faster than most would have thought possible a few years ago. In any event, these nonalcoholic beers should be stored and served like other beers.

WINES. **Wines** are beverages normally produced by the fermentation of grapes, although various other fruits and one grain (rice) are also fermented to produce comparatively small quantities of wine.

The fermentation process for wine differs considerably from that for beers. Traditionally, grapes are crushed and then placed in tanks where the yeasts occurring naturally on the grapes begin the fermentation process. By natural chemical processes, the sugars in the crushed grape mixture are converted to carbon dioxide and alcohol. Left unchecked, this conversion will continue until the level of alcohol reaches 14 percent, at which point the yeast is killed by the alcohol and the process ceases.

Grapes contain varying amounts of natural sugar, depending on the type of grape and the degree of ripeness when picked. Grapes with less natural sugar produce wines that are not as sweet as those with more natural sugar. The difference has to do with the amount of sugar, if any, remaining in the mixture when the yeasts are killed. If sugar remains unprocessed in the resulting wine, the flavor will have a certain sweetness to it. If no sugar remains, the wine will be dry, a term used to describe wines that lack sweetness.

When fermentation ends, the resulting liquid is drawn off and stored in fresh wood casks. During the time it is stored, any residue will settle in the cask so that the new wine will be clear. When the wines have "cleared" sufficiently, they are removed from the wood casks and placed in other containers to mature. The nature of these containers and the length of time required to reach maturity vary from one wine to another. When the new wine is mature, it is filtered and then bottled. Once bottled, the wine is either shipped for immediate consumption or stored under carefully controlled conditions, or aged, for a period of time. The type of wine produced will determine whether it is shipped or aged and, if aged, the length of time appropriate for aging.

The above is an oversimplified description of the traditional method for making wine, used today primarily by those wineries producing high-quality, expensive wines. It should be noted that some makers, typically those producing large quantities of inexpensive wines for mass markets, use modern adaptations of traditional methods, such as producing wines in vast steel tanks rather than individual wood casks. Some pasteurize their wines, a process the traditional wine maker would never consider.

Wines are normally classified as red, white, or rosé. The color of a wine is determined by the variety of grape used and the manner in which is it processed. Red wines tend to be drier than white wines, and range from hearty and full-bodied to light and fruity. By contrast, white wines tend to be lighter-bodied than reds, and range from very dry to very sweet. Red wines, normally served at room temperature, are often considered better accompaniments to red meat, while white wines, typically served chilled, more commonly accompany fish, poultry, and veal. Rosé wines, usually served chilled, may be used to accompany any entree. These are general rules, commonly quoted in texts and practiced by a number of wine connoisseurs. Today, however, most agree that individuals should follow their own tastes, and it is not uncommon to see restaurant customers ordering white wines to accompany beef.

The color classifications discussed above are not the only means for identifying wines. The four terms listed below are commonly used as well:

1. **Varietal:** A varietal wine is one named for the variety of grape that predominates the wine. Chardonnay, Zinfandel, Cabernet Sauvignon, and Pinot Noir, for example, are varieties of grapes that lend their names to wines—varietal wines.

2. **Brand name:** A brand name wine is one known primarily by the name of the producer. Many wine makers produce wines under their own names. Some are superior, while others are less so. These are normally blended wines, carefully produced so that their characteristics are the same from bottle to bottle, year after year. Lancers Vin Rosé is an excellent example.

3. **Geographic:** A geographic wine is one named for its place of origin. Many wines are named for the specific locations where they are produced. The location may be as large as a region or a district or it may be as small as a particular vineyard, known in France as a chateau. Producers are normally required to follow standards and regulations established by some authority, usually a governmental agency, to insure that the wine named for the area has identifiable and presumably desirable characteristics, given the climate and soil in the region. One example of a geographic wine is Chateau Margaux.

4. **Generic:** A generic wine is named for a well-known wine-producing region but is not produced in that region. Generic wines take their names from geographic areas, most commonly in France or Italy. Generic wines attempt to replicate the characteristics of the better-known geographic wines after which they are named. For example, a number of wines produced in California are known as burgundy, a name borrowed from the Burgundy region of France. A generic wine may be excellent, very poor, or anything in between. One must taste the wine to determine.

There are several types of wines and wine-based beverages with characteristics that are sufficiently different to warrant separate discussion:

Sparkling wines: Sparkling wines are carbonated. The carbonation may be natural or artificial, and the wines may be red, white, or rosé. Champagne, Asti Spumante, and sparkling burgundy are three well-known examples of sparkling wines.

Fortified wines: Fortified wines are wines to which small quantities of brandy or spirits have been added to increase the alcoholic content. Port and sherry are the two best-known examples.

Wine coolers: Wine coolers are blends of wine and fruit juice. Consequently, wine coolers have comparatively low alcoholic content—commonly about 5 percent. With the growing trend to lighter drinks, wine coolers are becoming increasingly popular.

Blush wines: Blush wines are characterized by their slightly pinkish color. They are comparatively new to the market. One way to make blush wines is to ferment red and white grapes together in order to produce a wine similar in appearance to a rosé. Blush wines tend to be light-bodied and sweet and are growing in popularity with Americans.

Distilled Beverage	Primary Ingredient
Bourbon	Corn
Brandy	Grapes
Gin	Any grain
Rum, dark	Molasses
Rum, light	Sugar cane
Rye	Rye
Scotch	Barley
Vodka	Potatoes; any grain

FIGURE 13.1   *Primary Ingredients in Distilled Beverages*

SPIRITS.   **Spirits** are alcoholic beverages produced by the distillation of a fermented liquid. The fermented liquid may be made from grain, fruit, or any of a number of other food products, including sugar cane and potatoes. A complete list of the possibilities would be almost endless. Most spirits, however, are produced from the food products listed above. Figure 13.1 lists some of the major alcoholic beverages produced by distillation and the primary food ingredients used to produce them.

Distillation is the process by means of which alcohol is removed from a fermented liquid. The process takes place in a device known as a **still.** In the still, the fermented liquid is heated to change the liquid alcohol to a gas. The gas is then cooled, and the result is a condensed distillate that is principally alcohol, but with various impurities that are important in giving spirits their essential character. The nature of the final product is determined primarily by:

1. The basic food ingredient from which the fermented liquid was prepared.
2. The alcoholic content of the distillate.

The alcoholic content of a distillate is stated in terms of proof. In the United States, proof is measured on a scale from 0 to 200, with 0 being the complete absence of alcohol and 200 being pure alcohol. One proof is equal to .5-percent alcohol. Thus, a beverage described as 80 proof is 40-percent alcohol. The higher the proof of a distillate, the purer it is and the fewer the impurities it contains. Higher-proof distillates are also more clear than those of lower-proof; a 200-proof distillate would have the appearance of water, but would actually be pure alcohol. A distiller can control the proof of a distillate by regulating the temperature, duration, and other elements of the distillation process. In general, the lighter and clearer the final product, the higher the proof of the distillate. To produce vodka, for example, the process must be regulated so that the proof of the distillate is 190 or higher; by contrast, the proof of the distillate for bourbon is normally between 110 and 130.

With the exception of vodkas and some gins, spirits are stored in wooden barrels for some period of time before being bottled. This aging mellows and brings out the flavor of the final product. The longer the aging, the better and more costly the final product. Thus, 12-year-old scotch is considered better than 6-year-old scotch and is more expensive. Just before bottling, all spirits are diluted, or cut, with distilled water to lower the proof and thus reduce the potency of the bottled product. When bottled, most spirits are between 80 and 100 proof. Once spirits are bottled, they can be stored at normal temperatures indefinitely.

One particularly interesting group of spirits is that known as **liqueurs,** or **cordials.** Liqueurs are spirits, typically brandies or neutral spirits, that have been sweetened and combined with flavoring agents. Some, such as Drambuie, come from carefully guarded recipes; others, such as creme de menthe, are produced from well-known recipes by numerous distillers. Because liqueurs are sweet, they are commonly consumed as after-dinner drinks or are combined with other ingredients in cocktails. Grasshoppers and Brandy Alexanders are examples of cocktails in which liqueurs are vital ingredients. The proof range for liqueurs is wider than spirits, ranging from a low of about 30 proof to a high of over 100.

Nonalcoholic Beverages

Nonalcoholic beverages include those normally found listed in restaurant menus under the beverage category: coffee, tea, and milk, as well as a host of others, some carbonated and some not. Carbonated nonalcoholic beverages include seltzer, club soda, tonic, ginger ale, and a wide range of other flavored beverages known as soda or pop in various places. Nonalcoholic beverages that are not carbonated include fruit and vegetable juices, such as orange juice and tomato juice.

Many of the nonalcoholic beverages are used to dilute alcoholic beverages and to produce a vast number of drinks with a wide variety of flavors. When so used, nonalcoholic beverages are called **mixers.** A list of the most common mixers includes club soda, ginger ale, lemon-lime soda, cola, tonic, orange juice, tomato juice, and grapefruit juice.

For purposes of these chapters, we will use the term **beverage** alone to refer to alcoholic beverages and the term **mixers** to refer to nonalcoholic beverages that are typically used with alcoholic beverages to produce mixed drinks. Some mixed drinks, usually produced from recipes, require additional items, and they will be referred to simply as other ingredients. These typically include olives, pearl onions, sugar, cream, and two juices that are a bit too strong to be used as mixers: lime juice and lemon juice.

RESPONSIBILITY FOR BEVERAGE PURCHASING

The nature and size of an operation often dictate who is responsible for purchasing beverages. In small, owner-operated establishments, the responsibility normally is that of the owner. In others, it may be that of the manager. In some large operations, purchasing responsibility may be delegated to a purchasing agent, a steward, or a beverage manager. The job title of the individual responsible for beverage purchasing is of little consequence. The important point is that one individual should be given responsibility and held accountable for all beverage purchasing. For control purposes, it is desirable to assign the responsibility to someone who is not directly engaged in either the preparation or sale of drinks.

THE PURPOSES OF BEVERAGE PURCHASING CONTROLS

The primary purposes of beverage purchasing controls are:

1. To maintain an appropriate supply of ingredients for producing beverage products.
2. To ensure that the quality of ingredients purchased are appropriate to intended use.
3. To insure that ingredients are purchased at optimum prices.

As always, the key to successful control is to establish suitable standards and standard procedures.

ESTABLISHING STANDARDS FOR BEVERAGE PURCHASING

For beverage purchasing, standards must be developed for:

1. Quality.
2. Quantity.
3. Price.

These will be discussed individually.

Quality Standards

Alcoholic beverages purchased for bars may be divided into two classes according to use: **call brands** and **pouring brands.** A call brand is one used only if the specific brand is requested by a customer; a pouring brand is one used whenever a customer does not specify a call brand. If a customer simply orders a "scotch and soda," he would be given the pouring brand. By contrast, if a specific brand of scotch is ordered (Dewar's White Label, for example), the customer is given the call brand specifically requested, assuming it is available. The usual practice is for management to designate one low- to medium-priced brand in each category of spirits as the pouring brand. The specific brands selected as the pouring brands will vary with the clientele and the price structure. Once pouring brands have been identified, all other brands become call brands. The selection of pouring brands is an important first step in establishing both quality and cost standards. Before establishing quality standards for alcoholic beverages, one must first weigh a number of considerations, including product cost, customer preferences, and product popularity. Most people will agree on the extremes—that certain 25-old scotches are of high quality and that particularly inexpensive gins are of very low quality—but between these extremes there is a vast area for legitimate differences of opinion.

The extent of the need for each of the three different types of alcoholic beverages must be determined before any purchase decisions can be made. Needs will differ from place to place, depending on clientele and inherent differences in the nature of operations. Some neighborhood bars cater to customers whose tastes run primarily to domestic beer, inexpensive wines, and comparatively few whiskies. By contrast, cocktail lounges serving an upper-middle-income business clientele commonly offer imported beers, a large assortment of spirits, and a few fine wines, while some expensive restaurants are widely regarded for their specialized wine lists that include the finest of imported wines. And these are but a few of the many possibilities. Because all alcoholic beverages are comparatively expensive, defining customer taste carefully is particularly important. By doing so, management attempts to eliminate the purchase of beverages that will not sell.

Purchasing beverages requires the expenditure of cash for merchandise that must be carried as inventory until sold. It is usually undesirable to maintain an inventory of items that move very slowly. Once an operation is open and control procedures are in place, a manager can identify slow-moving items and restrict or eliminate their purchase. However, this is a partial solution at best. It is of great importance to restrict initial purchases to items that are likely to meet customer tastes. Thus, deciding on the specific alcoholic beverages and brands that are of suitable quality for the expected clientele is the responsibility of management in each operation.

Quantity Standards

Because beverage products are not highly perishable if stored properly, beverages can be purchased far less frequently than perishable foods. This is not to say that beverages are nonperishable, however. Canned and bottled beers should be used within approximately three months of packaging. Draft beers should be consumed within one month. Some wines have comparatively limited lives, while others, those that improve with age, can and should be stored for some period before use. Most spirits can be stored almost indefinitely. Thus, perishability is not a critical factor in establishing quantity standards for beverages. Other factors are far more significant.

The principal factors used to establish quantity standards for beverage purchasing are:

1. Frequency with which management chooses to place orders.
2. Storage space available.
3. Funds available for inventory purchases.
4. Delivery schedules set by purveyors.
5. Minimum order requirements set by purveyors.
6. Price discounts for volume orders.
7. Price specials available.
8. Limited availability of some items.

Some of these considerations are often more important than others. Most establishments, for example, have limited storage space, and this is clearly a limiting factor in establishing quantity standards. So is the number of times that management will permit orders to be placed. It would be foolish to place orders for any item too frequently, so quantity standards must be such that the number of orders placed over time is kept to a minimum. Availability of funds can be another severely limiting factor: Beverage purchases require relatively large cash outlays, either at the time of delivery or very soon thereafter, depending on local regulations. Thus, if the necessary cash is not normally available for purchasing large quantities, it may be necessary to purchase smaller amounts and place orders more frequently. And while management may choose to order a given item frequently, the purveyor may not be willing to deliver more often than once every other week. In addition, purveyors may establish minimum order quantities for some items. Wines, for example, must often be purchased by the case.

It is sometimes possible to obtain discounted prices for alcoholic beverages or to receive merchandise dividends by purchasing quantities somewhat larger than one would normally order. From time to time, some beverage products are available at discounted prices for limited periods, and it is sometimes desirable to increase a current order beyond the normal order quantity so that one can take advantage of the discount. Sometimes, some beverage products, especially wines, may not be readily available in the market, and it may be necessary to purchase a very large quantity when the item is available if one is to ensure an adequate supply for continuing needs.

To establish quantity standards for beverages, then, management must take a number of considerations into account. This is best done by those who have considerable experience with beverage management and are fully informed about all aspects of the beverage operation, including its financial status.

Standards for Price

Assuming that quality standards have been established and appropriate purchase quantities are known, the next step is to ensure that all beverage purchases are made at the optimum price. Any discussion of price standards is complicated somewhat by laws that vary from state to state.

In general, states may be divided into two groups:

1. **License states,** where beverage wholesalers (and sometimes manufacturers and distributors as well) are permitted to sell alcoholic beverages directly to hotels, restaurants, and similar operations. This often results in competitive pricing of brands in the market.
2. **Control states,** where the state government actually sells some or all alcoholic beverages through its own network of stores, thus exercising complete control over prices. The practices of control states vary considerably from one to another. Some sell all alcoholic beverages through state outlets; others sell spirits and wines through state outlets, but permit beer to be sold through private beer distributors. In others, beer and wines are sold in private retail outlets, and state outlets sell spirits as well as wine. In control states, by the way, it is typically illegal for hotels and restaurants to purchase alcoholic beverages out of state.

Obtaining optimum price for spirits is simple in a control state. There is only one price for each brand: the price set by the state. Because all available brands are sold by the state outlet, one need only determine whether or not to buy a particular brand at the established price. Control states do offer special prices on some items from time to time, and beverage buyers usually watch for these.

By contrast, obtaining optimum price in a license state can be more complicated for the buyer. In license states, hotel and restaurant operators can purchase beverages from wholesalers. This may or may not induce price competition, depending on state laws and on such complicating factors as exclusive distributorships granted by some companies that produce alcoholic beverages.

In general, anyone responsible for purchasing alcoholic beverages must be familiar with the laws, restrictions, and industry practices in effect in the area. If competitive pricing is the rule, the buyer should clearly take full advantage of it. If competition is minimal or nonexistent, the buyer must simply accept the fact and watch for special offers, if any, on appropriate beverages.

ESTABLISHING STANDARD PROCEDURES FOR BEVERAGE PURCHASING

After one has established standards for purchasing beverages, the next step is to establish standard procedures. In beverage purchasing, standard procedures are needed:

1. To determine order quantities.
2. To process orders.

Determining Order Quantities

There are two basic methods for determining order quantities. The first, known as the **periodic order method,** is based on fixed order dates and variable order quantities; the second, the **perpetual order method,** uses variable order dates and fixed reorder quantities. These are discussed separately below.

PERIODIC ORDER METHOD.   The periodic order method requires that order dates be fixed so that there are equal operating periods between order dates. Ordering may be done weekly, biweekly, or on any other regular schedule, depending on the decisions of management with respect to such considerations as frequency of ordering, storage space to be devoted to beverages, and funds available for inventory purchases, as well as on purveyors' delivery schedules and anticipated consumption of beverages.

Determination of anticipated consumption is a key element: The person who sets order quantities must have some reasonable knowledge of the quantity of each beverage that is likely to be consumed in the interval between fixed order dates. There are two ways to determine this. The first and by far the best is to have records of the quantity of each beverage consumed during one such period. If bar requisitions of the type discussed in the following chapter are used, it is comparatively easy to determine quantities consumed. Without bar requisitions, some appropriate record-keeping system must be set up for one period. The second method is simply to estimate consumption, based on one's experience in the particular operation, experience in other similar operations, or both of these.

Having established for each beverage the anticipated consumption for one period, one increases that number by some amount that will allow for such unanticipated occurrences as increases in business volume, time required to receive delivery, and possible delay in receiving delivery. Some multiply the

```
ITEM: Relska Vodka
SIZE: 1 liter


Par Stock:              Usage:
   72                      48
(6 cases)               (4 cases)
```

FIGURE 13.2   *Shelf Label*

usage figure by 150 percent; others use some other percentage. Many round the results to whole case lots for pouring brands and any other beverages accounting for high volume. In the periodic system, the number so determined for each beverage item is defined as the **par stock** for that item—the maximum quantity of the item that should be on hand at any given time.

There are now two figures established for each beverage: anticipated usage and par stock. For each item in the inventory, both of these figures should be recorded on a label affixed to the shelf where the item is kept in the beverage storeroom. An example of such a shelf label is illustrated in Figure 13.2.

On the established date for placing orders, the individual responsible for determining purchase quantities reviews the entire beverage inventory in an orderly manner to determine the correct purchase quantity for each item in the inventory. This is done by means of the following standard procedure:

1. Count the inventory (the number of units on the shelf).
2. Subtract the inventory from the par stock figure on the shelf label.
3. Obtain the purchase quantity, which is the result of the above subtraction.

Referring to the information provided on the shelf label in Figure 13.2, if there were 24 units of Relska Vodka on the shelf, that number would be subtracted from the par stock figure, 72, to determine the proper order quantity: 48 units, or four cases.

Par stock	72
− Current inventory	24
= Purchase quantity	48

If the actual usage is the same as the usage figure on the label, the purchase quantity determined in this manner will be the same as the usage figure. If the subtraction results in a purchase quantity that is substantially different from the usage figure on the label, this is the signal that actual usage is not as anticipated and that the figures on the shelf label must be reviewed for possible change. For example, if one finds 42 units of vodka on the shelf, the order quantity would appear to be 30. However, the fact that there are 42 units on the shelf means that usage has been considerably less than anticipated; thus, one should assess the need for a par stock of 72. Unless the decrease in the number of units consumed is a temporary phenomenon, par stock and usage figures on the label should be changed for future periods. In general, if the number of units in inventory on a given order date differs markedly from the difference between par stock and usage, the adequacy of these two figures for purchasing purposes must be reviewed.

PERPETUAL ORDER METHOD. The perpetual order method requires fixed purchase quantities and variable order dates. Its use depends on the establishment of a perpetual inventory system for beverages, with paper perpetual inventory cards on which all purchases and issues are recorded carefully and in a timely manner. Today, perpetual inventory records are more likely to be in a computer database. The perpetual inventory is normally maintained in some location other than the beverage storeroom. However, as an alternative, some managers attach perpetual inventory cards to the shelves on which the beverages are stored.

For one to use the perpetual order method, several key figures must be established and recorded on the cards: **par stock, reorder point,** and **reorder quantity. Par stock** is the maximum quantity that may be on hand at any given time. It takes into account the storage space to be allocated to the item, the desired frequency of ordering, the anticipated usage, and a safety factor to cover such considerations as unanticipated increases in quantities consumed. **Reorder point** is the number of units to which inventory should decrease before an order is placed. It must take into account the time required to obtain delivery of the order. **Reorder quantity** is the amount that should be ordered each time an order is placed. It is calculated by subtracting reorder point from par stock and adding the number of units consumed between order date and delivery date.

Figure 13.3 illustrates a perpetual inventory card for a pouring gin in a restaurant open seven day per week. The card indicates that this gin is consumed at the rate of approximately five bottles per day. Management has determined that orders are to be placed at approximately two-week intervals, and experience has shown that it takes five days to obtain delivery. Therefore, par stock is calculated as follows:

5 bottles per day $\times$ 14 days $\times$ 150% (to include a safety factor) = 105 units

This is rounded to 108 bottles—an even nine cases. Reorder point is determined by multiplying the number of units used in the five days required

ITEM	Greys Gin		PAR STOCK			108 (9 cases)
SIZE	1 liter		REORDER POINT			36 (3 cases)
			REORDER QUANTITY			96 (8 cases)

Date	Order #	Quantity	In	Out	Balance
8/25	# 7	108			
8/31			108		108
9/1				5	103
9/2				5	98
9/3				4	94
9/4				5	89

FIGURE 13.3   *Perpetual Inventory Card*

for delivery—25—by 150 percent to include a safety factor and rounding to the nearest whole case. Reorder quantity is determined by subtracting reorder point from par stock and then adding the number of units used in the five-day period before receiving delivery.

The standard procedures suggested above for determining order quantities assume that supplies of the needed items are readily available. While this is normally true for all mixers, most spirits and beers, and many wines, it is not universally true for all beverages. There are a number of complicating factors. For example, some wines (especially vintage wines, both imported and domestic) may be unavailable at any given time, and this unavailability may be either temporary or permanent. In some control states, supplies of various items may not always be adequate to fill an order completely, thus making adjustments necessary. The beverage buyer must be prepared to meet contingencies as they arise and must be able to deviate from established purchasing procedures when required. Sometimes one can anticipate problems, as with particular wines that one knows will be available at an appropriate price for only a short time. This is sometimes the case with fine wines. In such instances, one must be prepared to place one order for the total amount required over a very long period, possibly several years.

Processing Orders

Whenever practical, it is advisable to establish a purchasing routine that requires formal written purchase orders. In most large hotels and many large

Quantity	Item	Bottle Size	Purchase Unit	Supplier
6	Old Crow bourbon	750 ml	case	A&C Suppliers
2	Beefeater gin	750 ml	case	A&C Suppliers

REQUESTED BY _____   APPROVED BY _____

DATE _____   DATE _____

FIGURE 13.4   *Purchase Request Form*

restaurants, formal purchase requests serve as the basis for ordering. In a large hotel, the purchasing routine might be the following: a wine steward, as the person in charge of maintaining the beverage inventory and stockroom, would prepare a purchase request similar to that illustrated in Figure 13.4 just after the first of the month.

The purchase request would be prepared in duplicate, with the original being forwarded to the purchasing agent in the accounting department. In some establishments, the purchasing agent would be required to secure the manager's written approval on the purchase request before placing any order. The order placed would be recorded on a form known as a **purchase order,** illustrated in Figure 13.5.

The purchase order would be made up in quadruplicate. The four copies would be distributed as follows: the original would be sent to the firm from which the beverages had been ordered; one copy would be sent to the wine steward to confirm that the order had been placed; another copy would be sent to the receiving clerk so that hé would know what deliveries to expect and would be able to verify that the quantities and brands delivered were correct; and the final copy would kept by the purchasing agent.

Obviously, not all establishments follow such detailed purchasing routines for beverages. However, because written records reduce misunderstandings and disputes, it is advisable in all instances to maintain some written record of purchases, preferably on a purchase order, to verify the accuracy of deliveries received. Written purchase orders eliminate disputes over brands and quantities ordered, prices quoted, and delivery dates. Because the purchase of alcoholic beverages involves the outlay of considerable amounts of

```
HENRY HILSON HOTEL
NEW YORK, NY 10098                                    DATE:   10/1/XXXX

TO:   A&C Suppliers                                   ORDER #:    C 267
      907 West 38th Street
      New York, NY 10090

PLEASE SHIP THE SUPPLIES LISTED BELOW VIA:        Your truck
```

Quantity	Purchase Unit	Bottle Size	Item	Unit Price	Total Amount
6	case	750 ml	Old Crow bourbon	$155.40	$932.40
2	case	750 ml	Beefeater gin	179.40	358.80
				TOTAL	$1,291.20

ORDERED BY _____

FIGURE 13.5 *Purchase Order*

cash, it is wise to establish a system (the purchase order method or some other)—to reduce or eliminate the possibilities for error.

In establishments located in states where the practice is permitted, salespersons may make site visits to meet with those who place the orders for beverages. It is not uncommon for purchase requests to be made on the basis of these meetings. In some states, dealers offer special discounts from time to time, and buyers can frequently save considerable amounts by taking advantage of them. In addition, in locations where prices are not set by government, this kind of procedure may enable a buyer to list a quoted price on the purchase request. By listing a particular dealer's name, in states where this is possible, some of the purchasing work is simplified.

TRAINING FOR PURCHASING

Training means teaching an employee to perform a job in the manner expected by management. It should be obvious that this cannot be done properly until standard procedures for the job have been established. It is, after all, comparatively easy to train someone to follow established procedures; it is virtually impossible to train someone if there are no procedures to follow.

If management has established standard procedures for the beverage purchasing (the periodic method, the perpetual method, or some other method more suitable for a given operation), it should not be difficult for an intelligent manager to explain the standard procedures to the employee who is to follow them. In most operations, this must be done at the work site during the course of the normal working day; few but the largest corporations can set up extended training periods for employees away from their jobs. The training must be carried out on the job, but some time must be set aside when trainer and trainee can concentrate on the task.

The following represents one typical approach. On a day when beverage orders are to be placed, trainer and trainee work together in the beverage storage area to determine the proper quantities of the various beverages to purchase. The trainer explains in general terms how the job is to be done and then determines purchase quantities for the first few beverages. This is done slowly, with each step explained in detail. The trainee is encouraged to ask as many questions as necessary; as the trainer answers the questions, he uses them to evaluate the extent of the trainee's comprehension. When the trainer judges the trainee to be ready, the trainee is asked to determine the purchase quantity for the next beverage. The accuracy of the trainee's determination and the trainer's judgment about the trainee's progress dictate the next step. The trainer might have the employee continue with the work; hé might also explain one or more steps again. Finally, the trainer and the trainee arrive at a point at which both are confident of the latter's ability to perform the job as required. This might take a comparatively short time or a very long time, depending on the intelligence, ability, and previous experience of the employee. It is conceivable that the trainee may even be unable to master the job.

Training employees to follow the standard procedures established for jobs can be tedious and time-consuming. However, unless adequate time and effort are devoted to training, managers have no assurance that employees are able to perform their jobs in the stipulated manner.

MONITORING PURCHASING PERFORMANCE AND TAKING CORRECTIVE ACTION

Once training has been completed and the employee begins to do the job for which he has been trained, management must monitor performance. With beverage purchasing, there are a number of possibilities for monitoring.

One simple method of monitoring (not recommended, by the way) is to assume that the employee is performing the job correctly unless something occurs to indicate the contrary. If, for example, the bartender reported that supplies of the gin identified as the pouring brand had completely run out, this could be taken as a clear sign that standard procedures for beverage purchasing were not being followed, at least for pouring gin. Most managers would agree that some better method of monitoring could have prevented this.

If the periodic order method has been established as the standard procedure for beverage purchasing, a manager has several means of monitoring employee performance. One possibility would be to create a form for the employee to use when taking inventory on the regular day for determining order quantities and placing orders, as described previously. The employee would be asked to record the number of bottles on hand for each beverage identified on the form, which would be turned in to management. The use of this form would provide some reasonable assurance that the employee had counted units in inventory before determining purchase quantities. This approach could be refined to the development of a worksheet showing, for every item in inventory, par stock, normal usage, amount on hand, and quantity ordered. After orders were placed, the employee would give this worksheet to the manager, who could quickly evaluate the order quantities. These are but a few of the possibilities for monitoring performance using the periodic order method.

The perpetual order method also provides many possible means for monitoring. The simplest is to consult the perpetual inventory cards to see that orders have been placed for the proper quantities as items reached their reorder points. A check of the perpetual inventory cards at any time during the course of an operating period will quickly reveal an employee's adherence to the standard procedures established.

To the extent that employees are not following the standard procedures established for their jobs, action is required to improve performance. The proper action to take will depend on the nature of the problem. The possibilities include explaining one or two small points that the employee may have misunderstood; completely retraining an employee who misunderstood the entire procedure; and laying off or otherwise disciplining an employee who wilfully ignored some or all of the standard procedures established for the job. It is the responsibility of a manager to determine the appropriate action to take in a given situation. However, some steps must be taken to improve employee performance or the job will not be done in a manner consistent with the standards and standard procedures established.

COMPUTER APPLICATIONS

Computers can eliminate much of the tedious work associated with determining purchase quantities for beverages. There are many possibilities, de-

Beverage Inventory GINS	Par Stock	Normal Usage	Quantity on Hand	Order Quantity
Beefeater's	18	12	6	12
Booth's	12	8	6	6
Gilbey's	108	72	42	66
Gordon's	54	36	12	42
Plymouth	12	8	8	4
Tanqueray	18	12	2	16

FIGURE 13.6 *Flagg's Bar/Beverage Purchasing Worksheet*

pending on the nature of the standard procedures established for beverage purchasing.

If the periodic method is used, it is easy to use any standard spreadsheet program to develop a worksheet for calculating purchase quantities. As illustrated in Figure 13.6, the worksheet requires five columns, the first of which lists all the beverages in inventory. The second and third columns have the par stock and normal usage figures for the listed beverages. The fourth is used to record the quantity on hand for each beverage, as counted on the order date. The fifth column indicates the proper order quantity for each beverage, calculated as column 2 minus column 4. One then prints the worksheet and examines the figures carefully to be sure that the figures in column 3 approximate those in column 5. Significant differences between these two may indicate the need for future adjustments to par stock, usage, or both.

If the perpetual method is used, the first step would be to set up a complete perpetual inventory and then add such required data as par stock, reorder point, and reorder quantity. A database program would be excellent for this. With the perpetual inventory established, some individual would be assigned to input all quantities received and issued to keep the inventory balance for every beverage up to date. Each day, after current data had been input, one would print a report identifying the beverages that had reached reorder point. These would be the items for which orders would be placed.

Regardless of whether one uses the periodic or perpetual method, one can use a computer to maintain records of purchases and to print reports showing, for example, total purchases of each beverage in inventory in units, dollars, or both of these, or totals for categories of items, such as gins or Italian wines, and so on. These kinds of reports are of great value for analysis and planning.

While spreadsheets can be very useful for these purposes, database programs provide greater numbers of options for maintaining records and are generally considered superior by those who have used them. While they take more time and effort initially to construct, they consume no more time for daily entries than the spreadsheet and yet produce output that is more useful by far.

Rather than use generic spreadsheet or database programs, most managers interested in using computers today are inclined to adopt one of the growing number of programs specifically written as tools for beverage purchasing and inventory control. However, some managers who have tried using these programs have found that the time and effort required to maintain the records are greater than warranted by any advantages they may offer. Thus, the use of beverage control software is not as widespread as one might expect.

CHAPTER ESSENTIALS

In this chapter, we defined beverages, distinguished between alcoholic and nonalcoholic beverages, and classified beverages into four categories: beers, wines, spirits, and mixers. We described basic methods for producing each of the three classes of alcoholic beverages and described the differences among them. We discussed the quality, quantity, and price standards required to establish control over beverage purchasing and identified the principal factors governing the establishment of these standards. We described two common standard procedures for determining purchase quantities and identified the most common standard procedure for processing purchase requests. We discussed one typical approach to training purchasing employees and several methods for monitoring performance. We outlined several possible means for improving performance and correcting deviations from standards. Finally, we described several possible uses for computers in beverage purchasing.

KEY TERMS IN THIS CHAPTER

Aging
Beers
Beverage
Blush wines
Brand-name wines
Call brand
Control state
Distillation
Fermentation
Fortified wines
Generic wines
Geographic wines
License state

Liqueur
Mixer
Par stock
Periodic order method
Perpetual order method
Pouring brand
Proof
Reorder point
Reorder quantity
Sparkling wines
Spirits
Varietal wines
Wine coolers
Wines

QUESTIONS AND PROBLEMS

1. What are the three classifications of alcoholic beverages?

2. What are the two broad classifications of beers, and how do they differ from one another?

3. What are the three color classifications of wines?

4. Of what significance is the fermentation process in the making of alcoholic beverages?

5. What is the distillation process?

6. In the United States, what percentage of alcohol is found in 100-proof vodka? In 90-proof gin? In 86-proof bourbon?

7. How do liqueurs differ from other spirits?

8. Explain the importance of assigning responsibility for beverage purchasing.

9. Distinguish between call brands and pouring brands.

10. What are the primary purposes of establishing beverage purchasing controls?

11. What considerations should be taken into account by those responsible for establishing quality standards that will be used when beverages are purchased for a particular hotel, restaurant, or bar?

12. List and explain the principal factors used to establish quantity standards for beverage purchases.

13. Distinguish between a license state and a control state.

14. Name the two principal methods used in beverage purchasing to determine order quantities and identify the principal differences between them.

15. **a.** Given the following information, determine the proper order quantity for each item if the periodic order method is used:

Item	*Par Stock*	*Usage*	*Quantity on Hand*
Smirnoff Vodka	72	48	24
Gordon's Gin	36	24	3
Jack Daniels	5	3	4
Canadian Club	9	6	4
Dewar's White Label	36	24	10

   b. Should any adjustments to par stock or usage figures be considered for any of the beverages listed in Question 15a? Which? Why?

16. The new manager of the Philby Hotel plans to do the beverage purchasing for the property using the perpetual inventory method. She wants to reorder the items listed below approximately every two weeks and plans to use a safety factor of 50% for calculating par stock and reorder point. Delivery requires six days. Storage space is ample. Given the daily usage figures below, determine par stock, reorder point, and reorder quantity for each item.

Item	*Daily Usage*
Gilbey's Gin	4
Relska Vodka	8
Ron Rico Light Rum	2
Cutty Sark Scotch	3
Bushmill's Irish	1

17. The New Amsterdam Hotel uses the perpetual inventory method for purchasing beverages. The training director is about to teach a new employee how to fill out purchase request forms (as illustrated in Figure 13.4) daily for those beverages that have just reached reorder point. The employee has been trained as a bartender but has never before worked with a perpetual inventory.
   a. Describe in detail one suitable step-by-step procedure for the training director to follow.

    b. How could the manager monitor the job performance of this new employee after the training period?

18. Define each of the following terms:
Aging
Beers
Beverage
Blush wines
Brand-name wines
Call brand
Control state
Distillation
Fermentation
Fortified wines
Generic wines
Geographic wines
License state
Liqueur
Mixer
Par stock
Periodic order method
Perpetual order method
Pouring brand
Proof
Reorder point
Reorder quantity
Sparkling wines
Spirits
Varietal wines
Wine coolers
Wines

FOR COMPUTER USERS

19. Using any spreadsheet program you choose, develop a worksheet to solve Question 15a.

20. Develop a worksheet to solve Question 16.

14

Beverage Receiving, Storing, and Issuing Control

LEARNING OBJECTIVES

After reading and studying this chapter, you should be able to:

1. Identify the objectives of controls for receiving, storing, and issuing beverages.
2. List and explain the various standards necessary for establishing control over beverage receiving, storing, and issuing.
3. Describe the standard receiving procedure for beverages.
4. Identify the beverage receiving report, and explain its use.
5. Describe two means for maintaining security in beverage storage facilities.
6. Describe the procedures used to organize beverage storage facilities.
7. Describe the effects of temperature, humidity, light, handling techniques, and storing methods on the shelf life of beverages.
8. List the three types of bars, and describe their differences.
9. Define a requisition system, and describe its use in beverage control.
10. Compare the techniques for receiving, storing, and issuing beverages used in small restaurants and bars with those used in large hotels and restaurants.
11. Compare methods used for training employees for beverage receiving, storing, and issuing in large and small properties.
12. List and describe three means of monitoring the performance of employees responsible for receiving, storing, and issuing beverages.
13. Discuss the use of computers in beverage receiving, storing, and issuing control.
14. Define each of the Key Terms listed at the end of the chapter.

INTRODUCTION

As discussed and illustrated in preceding chapters, establishing control over any phase of operations requires the four-step control process. One begins by establishing standards and standard procedures. The previous chapter presented some of the common standards and standard procedures for beverage purchasing. The use of these helps to ensure that adequate quantities of beverages of the proper quality are purchased at optimum prices.

Management in a beverage operation identifies quality standards by selecting particular brands, determines needed quantities of those brands, and places orders at optimum prices. By doing so, one is, in effect, identifying the cost of the beverages that will be served in the establishment. By placing orders, one is tacitly accepting those costs, which may then be viewed as planned or budgeted costs. It is, therefore, clearly in the interest of the enterprise to take appropriate steps to ensure that no unwarranted, unbudgeted costs develop before the beverages are sold to customers.

This chapter focuses on the application of the control process to three critical areas of beverage operations in which excessive costs can develop: receiving, storing, and issuing. Standards and standard procedures for each of these areas are identified below.

RECEIVING

Establishing Standards

The primary goal of receiving control is to ensure that deliveries received conform exactly to orders placed. In practice, this means that beverage deliveries must be compared to beverage orders with respect to quantity, quality, and price. The standards established for receiving are quite simple.

1. The quantity of an item delivered must equal the quantity ordered. Verifying this normally requires examining bottles, to be sure they have been filled and sealed, and then simply counting bottles or cases. It can also involve weighing kegs of beer to confirm the standard of fill or examining containers to confirm that those received conform to the order.
2. The quality of an item delivered must be the same as the quality ordered. For all spirits, wines, and beers, one would check to be certain that the brand delivered was the same as the brand ordered. For wines, verification may also require checking vintages or the bottling dates of wines that are best when young. For beers, it may require checking bottling or canning dates to ascertain freshness.

3. The price on the invoice for each item delivered should be the same as the price quoted or listed when the order was placed.

Because the basic standards for the job are rather clear and simple, any honest individual of suitable intelligence and ability can be trained to receive beverages correctly.

Establishing Standard Procedures

Standard procedures must always be established to ensure that standards will be met. The steps identified below are generally considered those that make up a basic standard procedure for receiving beverages.

1. Maintain an up-to-date file of all beverage orders placed. Depending on the operation, these orders may be formal, informal, or some combination of the two. Major hotels, for example, commonly use formal purchase order systems. By contrast, the only record of an order placed by a small neighborhood restaurant may be some notes taken during a telephone conversation between the owner and a salesperson. Regardless of the size of an establishment, there can be no effective receiving procedure without written records of the orders placed, and the individual responsible for receiving must have these records available.
2. Remove the record of the order from the file when a delivery arrives, and compare it to the invoice presented by the delivery driver to verify that quantities, qualities, and prices on the invoice conform to the order. Figure 14.1 illustrates a typical beverage invoice.
3. Complete the following before the delivery driver leaves the premises:
   a. Check brands, dates, or both, as appropriate, to verify that the quality of beverages delivered conforms to the invoice.
   b. Count or weigh goods delivered to verify that the quantity received also conforms to the invoice.
4. Compare the invoice to the order to verify that goods received conform to the order placed.
5. Call to the attention of both management and the delivery driver:
   a. Any broken or leaking containers.
   b. Any bottles with broken seals or missing labels.
6. Note all discrepancies between delivered goods and the invoice on the invoice itself. Call any discrepancy between an order and the delivery to management's attention immediately. Any such discrepancy may require a decision from management as to whether or not to accept delivery of the questionable items.

Item No.	Quantity Ordered	Quantity Shipped	Purchase Unit	Bottle Size	Description	Unit Price	Total Price
3628	6	6	case	750 ml	Old Crow bourbon	$155.40	$932.40
27,441	2	2	case	750 ml	Beefeater gin	179.40	358.80
						TOTAL	$1,291.20

A&C SUPPLIERS
907 WEST 38TH STREET
NEW YORK, NY 10090

TO: HENRY HILSON HOTEL
1066 WEST 41ST STREET
NEW YORK, NY 10098

INVOICE NO.
639-A142

DATE: 10/3/XXXX   ORDER NO. C267   ACCOUNT NO. H108   TERMS C.O.D.   SHIP VIA TRUCK

FIGURE 14.1   *Beverage Invoice*

7. Sign the original invoice to acknowledge receipt of the goods, and return the signed copy to the driver. Retain the duplicate copy for internal record keeping.
8. Record the invoice on the *beverage receiving report*.
9. Notify the person responsible for storing beverages that a delivery has been received.

In many establishments, a form known as a **beverage receiving report** is filled out daily by the individual responsible for receiving beverages. A basic beverage receiving report is illustrated in Figure 14.2.

There are any number of variations possible because forms of this nature are developed to the specifications of management in a given operation. As a rule, beverage receiving reports summarize the invoices for all beverages received on a given day. They include columns for listing quantities received and their values, and for dividing purchases into essential categories (wines, beers, spirits, and mixers) for appropriate distribution in purchase journals. The need for separating purchases into these categories will be evident in Chapter 16, on costs and management reports. In states requiring deposits on

HENRY HILSON HOTEL
BEVERAGE RECEIVING REPORT DATE: 10/3/XXXX

Distributor	Item	Quantity Received	Purchase Unit	Size	Unit Cost	Total Cost	Purchase Journal Distribution			
							Wines	Beers	Spirits	Mixers
A&C Sup.	Old Crow	6	case	750 ml	$155.40	$ 932.40			$932.40	
A&C Sup.	Beefeater	2	case	750 ml	$179.40	$ 358.80			$358.40	
Blue Dist.	Budweiser	12	case	375 ml	$ 11.95	$ 143.40		$143.40		
Canada Dry	Tonic	7	case	250 ml	$ 9.00	$ 63.00				$63.00
Krumpf Imp.	Moselle	4	case	750 ml	$ 60.00	$ 240.00	$240.00			
Krumpf Imp.	Chateau Rue	2	case	750 ml	$105.00	$ 210.00	$210.00			
TOTAL						$1,947.60	$450.00	$143.40	$1,291.20	$63.00

PREPARED BY

FIGURE 14.2   *Beverage Receiving Report*

bottles and cans of beers and mixers, beverage receiving reports are likely to include columns for recording the charges and credits attributable to the deposits.

Filling out a beverage receiving report is a rather simple matter, merely requiring that essential data be transferred from an invoice to the report. The process for doing this can be readily inferred from a careful comparison of Figures 14.1 and 14.2. Because the beverage receiving report is an accounting document, its specific makeup will vary considerably from one beverage operation to another, depending on the nature and the degree of complexity of the accounting practices in effect. It is generally advisable to require a receiving report for beverages that is separate and distinct from that for food and to design a form tailored to an individual establishment's needs.

It is generally considered good practice to require not only that the individual receiving the beverages sign the beverage receiving report each day, but also that the individual responsible for storing the beverages (the wine steward, for example) sign it. By so doing, this individual acknowledges receiving the beverages listed on the report for addition to the beverage inventory.

STORING

Establishing Standards

Storing control is established in beverage operations to achieve three important objectives:

1. To prevent pilferage.
2. To ensure accessibility when needed.
3. To preserve quality.

In order to accomplish these objectives, standards must be established. The following standards are critical to effective storing control.

1. To prevent pilferage, one clearly must make all beverage storage areas secure. To establish the proper degree of security, one must restrict access to storage areas to authorized individuals, and take steps to guard against unauthorized use of beverages by those who are permitted access to the storage areas.

    Alcoholic beverages are among the items in hotels and restaurants that are most prone to theft by those who are inclined to steal. Unless appropriate steps are taken, beverage products will disappear. There are many reasons for this, including the dollar value of the products, addiction to alcohol, and irresponsible, impulsive behavior, among others.

2. To ensure accessibility of products when needed, the storage facility must be organized so that each individual brand and product can be found quickly when needed. In practice, this means assigning a specific storage location (shelf or bin number) to each item in the beverage inventory.

Once appropriate supplies of beverage products have been purchased, it is important that they be stored in such a way that they can be found quickly in order to be issued when needed.

3. To maintain product quality, one each item in the beverage inventory, must be stored appropriately under conditions that will maximize its shelf life. This requires taking into account such important elements as temperature, humidity, and the manner in which items are stored.

While the quality of spirits will not be adversely affected in storage under most conditions, wines and beers are subject to rapid deterioration if improperly stored.

Establishing Standard Procedures

Standard procedures must always be established to ensure that standards will be met. The standard procedures required to achieve control over the storing of beverages normally include those discussed below.

PROCEDURES TO MAKE BEVERAGE AREAS SECURE.   All beverages must be stored in secure facilities. Because beverage products are prone to theft, it should be obvious that keeping them in a secure facility is an urgent requirement.

There are two ways to maintain the necessary degree of security. The first is to assign the responsibility for security of the stored items to one person alone. This can mean literally keeping watch over them. In many hotels and some large restaurants, a steward may be assigned to work in the storage facility, maintaining the stock and issuing beverages as needed. Typically, this steward is the only person permitted in the facility, except for authorized managers. In operations that are open for long hours, this responsibility may be shared by two or more stewards working different shifts. Alternatively, the hours for storing and issuing beverages may be restricted so that one person can be held accountable for the beverage inventory.

The second way to maintain security is to keep the beverage storage facility locked and to issue a single key to one person who will be held accountable for all beverages in the inventory. The person with the key would be required to open the lock and issue the needed beverages. Some alternative provision would be made for issuing the needed beverages in the absence of this one individual: A procedure would be established through which some manager could gain access to the beverage storage facility.

The difficulty with both of these procedures is, of course, that the individual assigned responsibility for the beverage inventory is not likely to be available 24 hours a day. At some point, the storage facility would be inaccessible, and no one would be able to obtain items that might be urgently needed. One way to prepare for this eventuality is to place a second key in a safe or some similar secure location and require that anyone using it sign for it and write a short explanation of the need for its use. Some managers would require both an explanation and a list of the items removed from the facility. However, making a second key available reduces both the degree of security and the possibility of holding one individual accountable for all beverages in the inventory. In general, the common standard procedure is to keep the number of keys to the minimum that management deems appropriate for efficient operation and maximum security. If there is more than one key or if more than one person has access to the single key, it is normally advisable to change locks regularly to minimize the possibility that some persons may obtain and use duplicate keys. It is also advisable to change locks whenever a worker with access to the beverage storage facility leaves the employ of the establishment.

Some hotels and large restaurants take the additional precaution of installing closed-circuit television cameras to keep various facilities under observation. These would include the doors to beverage storage areas. A security guard in some remote area would be responsible for monitoring traffic into and out of the area on a television screen. As an alternative, activity in the area might be monitored by means of a videotape recording that could be viewed by the security staff at some later time.

Another means of monitoring is to install special locks that print on paper tape the times that the doors on which they are installed are unlocked and relocked. The times printed on the tape inform management exactly when the door to a facility was unlocked and how long it remained so. This is a less costly alternative to a closed-circuit television system, but it provides less information.

Maintaining the security of the beverage inventory is a clear imperative for any hotel or restaurant, requiring continual vigilance and careful monitoring.

PROCEDURES TO ORGANIZE THE BEVERAGE STORAGE FACILITY. Ensuring accessibility means storing beverage products in an organized manner, so that each stored item is always kept in the same place and thus can

ITEM Old Crow				STOCK NUMBER 153			
Date	*In*	*Out*	*Balance*	*Date*	*In*	*Out*	*Balance*
10/1			4				
10/3		1	3				
10/7		1	2				
10/11		1	1				
10/12	4		5				

FIGURE 14.3 *Bin Card*

be found quickly when needed. The physical arrangement of a storage area is important. Similar items should be kept close to one another. All gins, for example, should be kept in one area, rye whiskies in another, and scotch whiskies in a third. This kind of arrangement simplifies finding an item when needed. It is helpful, too, for a floor plan of the storage area to be affixed to the door or the facility, so that authorized personnel can easily locate items.

One way of ensuring that items will always be found in the same location is to institute the use of bin cards of the type illustrated in Figure 14.3.

Bin cards can be affixed to shelves and serve as shelf labels. When properly used, bin cards include essential information (type of beverage, brand name, and bottle size, for example). They may also include an identification number for beverages. Some establishments assign a code number from a master list to each item in the beverage inventory and record that code number on the bin card. Figure 14.4 provides an example of the kind of numbering code often used for wines, spirits, and beers in a beverage inventory.

In many establishments, indelible ink is used to stamp this code number on each bottle received. This technique serves several purposes. In the case of wines, the names of which can be difficult to pronounce and spell, code numbers eliminate the problems faced by customers ordering wines and employees seeking to fill the orders. In many instances, wine lists are printed with bin numbers. This can lead to an increase in wine sales, which can be highly profitable. Stamping code numbers on bottles of alcoholic beverages also provides an added measure of control: The stamped number on a bottle identifies that bottle as the property of the hotel or restaurant. This makes it impossible for an employee to claim that such a bottle is personal property if one is found in his possession. In addition, empty bottles can be checked for numbers before they are replaced by full bottles, thus ensuring that no one is bringing empty

---

Sample Numbering Code for Wines, Spirits, and Beers

American Whiskies: 100 series
    Blended Rye: 100–139
    Straight Rye: 140–149
    Bourbon: 150–179
    Sour Mash: 180–189

Imported Whiskies: 200 series
    Scotch: 200–239
    Canadian: 240–249
    Irish: 250–259
    Other: 260–269

Gins and Vodkas: 300 series
    Gins: domestic 300–320
          imported 330–349
    Vodka: domestic 350–379
          imported 380–399

Rums and Brandies: 400 series
    Rum: 400–449
    Brandy: domestic 450–459
          imported: 460–479
    Cognac: 480–499

Cordials and Liqueurs: 500 series

Red Wines: 600 series

White wines (still): 700 series

Other Wines: 800 series
    Sparkling, Rosé, Dessert, Aperitif

Beers and Ales: 900 series

FIGURE 14.4 *Illustration of Beverage Code Numbers*

bottles into the establishment and using them to obtain full bottles from the establishment's inventory.

The use of bin cards also enables a wine steward to maintain a perpetual inventory record of quantities on hand. By using this card carefully to record the number of units received as they are placed on the shelves, as well as the number of units issued as they are given out, the wine steward has a way of determining the balance on hand without counting bottles. In addition, the wine steward who carefully maintains such records has a way of determining that bottles are missing, so that this can be brought to management's attention immediately.

Internally, the storage area should be kept free of debris that can pile up as the result of emptying cases and stocking shelves. Once opened, cases should be completely emptied. All units in a case should be stored on the appropriate shelf and the empty carton removed at once. In addition, care must be taken to ensure that some individuals do not purposely remove cartons that are not completely empty.

PROCEDURES TO MAXIMIZE SHELF LIFE OF STORED BEVERAGES. Procedures for maximizing the shelf life of stored beverages may be divided into two categories:

1. Those dealing with temperature, humidity, and light in the storage facilities.
2. Those dealing with the manner in which bottles and other containers are handled and shelved.

These will be discussed separately below.

Temperature, Humidity, and Light in Storage Facilities. For every beverage product, there is a temperature range appropriate for storage that will tend to preserve quality and shelf life. For some, the range is extremely broad; for others, it is very limited. Spirits, for example, can be stored indefinitely at normal room temperatures without harming product quality. If necessary, they can be stored well above or well below room temperatures for considerable periods. As long as the storage temperature does not become extreme, spirits will not suffer loss of quality. By contrast, carefully controlled storage temperatures are critical for maintaining the quality of beers and wines. The problem of maintaining product quality for these items is complicated by the fact that various wines and beers require different treatments, depending on how they were made and the containers in which they are purchased.

It is normally advisable to learn from the maker, brewer, or distributor of each specific brand the temperature range recommended for the proper storage of the product. As a general rule, red wines should be stored at about 55°F. White wines and sparkling wines should be kept at slightly lower temperatures. Pasteurized beers can be stored for limited periods at normal room temperature without great harm, but they are normally kept under refrigeration, closer to the temperature at which they will be served. However, beer that has once been chilled should be kept chilled thereafter to maintain quality. Unpasteurized beers, including all draft and some bottled and canned beers, should be stored at about 40°F to reduce the risk of deterioration.

The degree of moisture in the air is of significance only for those beverages purchased in corked bottles. In general, wines are the beverages typically purchased in corked bottles, and the better the wine, the more likely the bottle is to have a cork rather than a screw top. Low humidity will cause corks to dry out, thus permitting air to reach the product. Air is likely to harm product quality. Therefore, wines should be stored either in rooms that are naturally cool and damp or in special facilities, such as refrigerated rooms, where both temperature and humidity can be controlled.

Bottled wines and beers should be kept away from light, which adversely affects product quality. Natural light is more harmful than artificial light, but any light will affect these products.

Vintners and brewers package their products in colored glass bottles, commonly dark green or dark brown, to minimize the negative effects of light. However, while the dark glass reduces the impact, it merely slows the inevitable deterioration that light will cause if these products are not properly stored.

Shelving and Handling Bottles and Other Containers. Spirits can be stored upright on horizontal shelves for unlimited periods. By contrast, wines and other corked beverages cannot safely be stored in an upright position. If they are to be kept for any length of time, they must be stored on their sides, parallel to the floor. There are special racks designed to store wines in the proper position. In this horizontal position, the beverage in the bottle is kept in constant contact with the cork, helping to keep the cork moist and thus keeping the bottle tightly sealed.

Canned and bottled beers are usually not shelved at all. They are delivered in cases and are stored in those cases. The cases are typically stacked in the storage facility to save space. Handling is an important factor in maintaining the quality of beers and wines. They should be handled with great care as they are being positioned in wine racks and later, as they are being removed to fill customers' orders. Many wines, especially fine reds, develop a natural sediment that settles in the bottle. If the bottle is improperly handled, this sediment will be dispersed through the wine, destroying its clarity and making it unpalatable to those who appreciate and order fine wines. For all practical purposes, the wine becomes unusable until the sediment has resettled. Sparkling wines—those containing natural or artificial carbonation—must also be handled carefully for obvious reasons. Beers require careful handling as well. They are carbonated beverages and shaking will cause them to foam excessively.

ISSUING

Establishing Standards

Issuing control is established in hotel and restaurant beverage operations to achieve two important objectives:

1. To ensure the timely release of beverages from inventory in the needed quantities.
2. To prevent the misuse of alcoholic beverages between release from inventory and delivery to the bar.

It is important for managers to control the quantities of alcoholic beverages issued and to take all necessary steps to insure that quantities issued reach their intended destinations.

To achieve these objectives, managers must establish two essential standards for issuing beverages:

1. Issue quantities must be carefully set.
2. Beverages must be issued to only authorized persons.

Authorized persons means those who have been assigned responsibility for the security of the issued beverages and will be held accountable for their disposition.

Establishing Standard Procedures

In order to ensure that the essential issuing standards identified above will be met, it is necessary to establish appropriate standard procedures for issuing beverages. There are two:

1. Establishing par stocks for bars.
2. Setting up a requisition system.

ESTABLISHING PAR STOCKS FOR BARS. As used in bar operations, the meaning of the term **par stock** is somewhat different from the definition used in wine cellar or liquor storeroom operations. In storeroom operations, par stock means the maximum quantity that may be on hand at any one time; it is a limit that the quantity on hand should never exceed. In bar operations, on the other hand, par stock is the precise quantity, stated in numbers of bottles or other containers, that must be on hand at all times for each beverage at the bar. For example, the stock of gin at a bar should be listed by brand name with bottle size, and an exact number of bottles that should be at the bar at all times. One particular brand of gin, stocked in 750 ml. bottles, might have a par stock of five bottles at a certain bar. This implies that someone could check the stock at any time and expect to find five bottles of that particular brand on hand. Not all would necessarily be full, but at least the number of bottles would be under control.

Essentially, there are three kinds of bars:

1. **Front bars,** where bartenders serve the public face to face.
2. **Service bars,** where customers' orders are given to the bartender by the waitstaff, who serve the drinks to the customers.
3. **Special-purpose bars,** usually set up for one particular event, such as a banquet.

Par stocks vary greatly from one establishment to another. In every case, however, the par stock for any particular beverage should be related to quantities used and should be changed from time to time as customer demand changes. Drinks may go in and out of fashion for seasonal as well as for other reasons, and par stocks at the bar should be adjusted to meet customer demand without being overstocked. In addition, since storage space at a bar is limited, the quantity of any item should be limited to the amount necessary to meet no more than two to three days' demand.

For front bars and service bars, specific par stocks should be established for each bar. However, this is not possible in the case of special-purpose bars, which present unique problems. When these bars are set up, sufficient stocks must be issued to meet anticipated demand for the length of time the bar is to be open. Typically, the quantities established are greater than needed, and the remainder is returned to the beverage storeroom at the conclusion of the event. In effect, a new par stock is established for a special-purpose bar each time one is needed for an event.

Setting Up a Requisition System.   A **requisition system** is a highly structured method for controlling issues. In beverage control, a key element in the system is the **requisition form,** on which both the names of beverages and the quantities of each issued are recorded. No bottles should ever be issued without a written requisition signed by an authorized person, often the head bartender. A simple requisition form is illustrated in Figure 14.5. In the majority of beverage operations, one type of requisition form is normally sufficient for maintaining the desired degree of control over issues. In more complex beverage operations, such as those found in many hotels, several kinds of requisitions may be required for specialized bars.

The requisition form is filled out by either a head bartender or some other authorized person who determines the quantities needed at the bar to replenish the par stock. For a special-purpose bar, the quantities would be those established as the par stock for the specific occasion. The signed and dated requisition is given to a wine steward or beverage storeroom clerk—jobs and titles vary from one operation to another. This individual is responsible for obtaining the listed items and quantities from inventory shelves and issuing them to the person authorized to receive them—normally the person who has signed the

Quantity	Description	Unit Cost	Total Cost
			DATE 10/5/XXXX
3	Old Crow Bourbon		
6	J & B Scotch		
5	Relska Vodka		

REQUISITIONED BY _____

ISSUED BY _____

RECEIVED BY _____

FIGURE 14.5 *Bar Requisition*

requisition. In some establishments, the worker who receives the beverages is required to sign the requisition to acknowledge receipt of all listed items.

Later, after the beverages have been issued, the unit value of each beverage is entered on the requisition, and these individual values are extended. This means that each unit value is multiplied by the number of units issued to determine the total value of the quantity issued. A total value is obtained for all the beverages listed on the requisition by adding the total values of the individual items.

The majority of establishments take the further precaution of requiring that each requisition from a front bar or a service bar be accompanied by empty bottles from the bar, to ensure that the units issued are actually replacing quantities the bartender has used. When this system is used, a par stock can be maintained at the bar. For example, suppose that the par stock of a particular brand of scotch is five bottles. When one bottle is emptied, the bartender puts it aside. At the end of the night, the bartender lists it on a requisition form along with all other bottles emptied in the course of the evening. This form is left for the morning bartender, who takes all empty bottles and the requisition on which they are listed to the wine steward. The wine steward checks each bottle against the requisition and then sends full bottles of those items—including that particular scotch—to the bar before the beginning of business. This would bring the stock of the bar—including the scotch—back up to par. Such a system ensures a constant supply of beverages at the bar. Occasional comparisons of numbers of bottles at the bar with the par stock list would ensure that items are not missing from the bar. This affords an additional measure of control.

FUNCTION Lions Club				BARTENDER Joe			
LOCATION Green Room				DATE 10/15/XXXX			

Item	Quantity	Original Issue	Additional Issue	Returns	Con-sumed	Unit Cost	Total Cost
Scotch	2	2					
Gin	2	2					
Vodka	2	2					
Bourbon	1	1					
Canadian	1	1					
S. Vermouth	1	1					
Dry Vermouth	1	1					

REQUISITION BY _B. Berry_

ISSUED BY _____

RECEIVED BY _____

RETURNS CHECKED BY _____

FIGURE 14.6 *Banquet Bar Requisition*

Establishments that operate more than one bar must prepare separate requisitions for each, so that bars may be controlled separately. For example, special banquet requisitions are often used that make provision for all bottles issued, whether consumed or returned. An example is illustrated in Figure 14.6.

In hotels and catering establishments, requisitions of this type are often made out by a banquet manager. They are given to a wine steward, who issues the items listed in time for the bar to be set up for an event. Provision is made for recording additional issues that may be required. At the end of the event, some other individual (a beverage controller, for example) checks that all full, empty, and partially used bottles are accounted for. Thus, the correct dollar amount can be recorded for the quantities actually consumed, and unused quantities can be returned to stock. Perpetual inventory and bin card entries can be made from the "Consumed" column on the banquet requisition.

Many hotels and restaurants in which most wines are sold by the bottle, rather than by the glass, establish additional control procedures. In some, small

DATE 10/5/XXXX		TABLE # 8		CHECK # 1230
Code #	Description	Quantity	Size	Cost
602	Chateau LaGrim	1	Full	$95.00
		SERVED BY	D. FEAT	
		ISSUED BY		

FIGURE 14.7   *Full Bottle Sales Slip*

supplies of the most popular wines are maintained at a front bar or service bar to eliminate the need for a trip to the wine cellar each time a bottle is ordered. Once the bottle of wine is taken from the bar and served to a customer in a dining room, it is effectively removed from the bartender's control. The bartender may not have an empty bottle to turn in with the requisition on the following day to bring the stock of the wine back to the par level. Therefore, many establishments maintain additional control over full-bottle sales by requiring that a form be filled out each time a bottle of wine is removed from the bar for service at a table. One example is illustrated in Figure 14.7.

Such a form is also useful in hotels that serve full bottles of wines and spirits to guests in their rooms, as well as in situations where par stocks of wines are not maintained at the bar and each bottle must come directly from the wine cellar. The full-bottle sales slip serves as a requisition in such instances. When such a form is used, it is important to require that the server fill it out completely before the bottle is issued to guard against potential problems. When used correctly, the form provides an excellent means for verifying each sale of a full bottle. It is possible to compare full-bottle sales slips to the guest check numbers indicated and to hold the servers accountable for errors.

TRAINING FOR RECEIVING, STORING, AND ISSUING

In an establishment that offers both food and beverage products for sale, one normally finds fewer employees involved with beverages than with food. In some beverage operations, only one person (an owner or manager, in many cases) is responsible for all aspects. In such operations, the establishment of control procedures in the usual sense is not a critical concern; the owner or manager, by taking responsibility for all purchasing, receiving, storing, issuing, production, and sometimes sales, is eliminating the need for those control procedures that would be critical to the success of a larger establishment. In the small operation, there may be no training because there are neither employees to train nor control mechanisms. When the size of an establishment increases to the point at which an owner or manager can no longer perform all tasks alone and he or she must hire an employee to help, it becomes desirable to set up certain basic work routines. If the new employee can be assigned responsibility for certain specific tasks, the owner can devote time to other tasks that are more important, more appropriate, or more complex.

An owner might decide to make the new employee responsible for all beverage receiving, storing, and issuing. The obvious next step would be for the owner to explain the methods and procedures for accomplishing these tasks in an organized manner and in sufficient detail so that the employee could do the work as required. However, if there were no organized methods and procedures in use, it would be necessary first to establish a certain minimum number so that the new employee could follow them and thus perform the job correctly. Without some basic standards and standard procedures, little useful training is possible. At the same time, it is clearly unreasonable to expect an employee to perform a job for which no adequate training has been provided.

Before an owner or manager can train anyone, there must be a clear job definition. In small operations, the job definition is likely to exist only in the owner's mind, if at all. In large, formal organizations, it is probably committed to writing and is called a **job description.**

A job description is a formal definition of a job, including a summary of work to be performed, often accompanied by a list of specific tasks and duties. The more complete the job descriptions, the simpler the task of training because both trainer and trainee have access to detailed information. Further discussion of job descriptions will be found in Chapter 19.

Large organizations typically establish standards and standard procedures in all areas of operation, including the receiving, storing, and issuing of beverages. A number of national and large regional organizations have departments responsible for developing training programs that include manuals with job descriptions, standard procedures, examples of forms that employees will be expected to use, and other pertinent information. The larger and more complex the organization, the more likely it is that the new employee will be provided with full information about responsibilities and the employer's expectations.

Regardless of the size of an organization, training cannot proceed effectively without carefully conceived standards and standard procedures. Once these have been established, appropriate training programs can be designed to ensure that employees are prepared to carry out tasks associated with their jobs. For receiving, these are likely to include maintaining up-to-date files of beverage orders; verifying that quantities, qualities, and prices of beverages received conform to the orders placed; and recording appropriate information on a beverage receiving report. For storing, these tasks may include organizing the beverage storage facility, storing the beverages appropriately to maximize their shelf life, and maintaining security in the beverage storage facility. For issuing, the tasks will include filling requisitions properly.

MONITORING RECEIVING, STORING, AND ISSUING PERFORMANCE, AND TAKING CORRECTIVE ACTION

Unless employees' performance is monitored, managers will have less than the desirable amount of information about the extent to which standards and standard procedures are being followed. If, for example, the individual responsible for receiving wines fails to count bottles and cases, to check labels and vintages, and to compare invoice prices with order prices, some beverages received may not be the same as those ordered, and some invoice prices may be incorrect. If wines and beers are improperly stored, their shelf life may be minimized, resulting in unsalable beverages and excessive costs. If improper quantities are issued, bars may be inadequately supplied, leading to lost sales. On the other hand, if excessive quantities are issued, pilferage may occur.

It is not wise for a manager simply to assume that all employees are performing their jobs correctly. Some amount of auditing is both necessary and desirable. If work is being done carelessly or improperly, it is important that this be discovered as quickly as possible. Even in establishments where managers have found employees to be entirely trustworthy and reliable, it is desirable to verify regularly that this continues to be the case.

There are many possible means for monitoring employees' performance. The selection of one rather than another depends on many factors, including the size and complexity of an enterprise, the specific standards and standard procedures established, and the availability of personnel to do the monitoring. However, a number of specific techniques for monitoring beverage receiving, storing, and issuing activities are fairly common.

One technique that is all but universal in organized beverage operations is a monthly physical inventory of stored beverages. A primary purpose for taking this inventory is to determine cost of beverages sold for the month. At the same time, a manager can monitor adherence to standard procedures for receiving, storing, and issuing by verifying quantities received and issued, reviewing the organization of the storage facility, and evaluating such considerations as the temperature and cleanliness of the storage area and the manner in which the beverages are stored. Checking performance in these areas monthly is basic. Most well-managed operations take additional steps.

The many other possible monitoring techniques for receiving include spot-checking the work of the employee responsible by directly overseeing the work, observing the employee over closed-circuit television, or verifying receiving records before beverages are sent to storage. Similar methods can readily be devised for monitoring storing and issuing by anyone familiar with the physical layout of an establishment and its standards and standard procedures.

In beverage operations, corrective action must be taken immediately if monitoring reveals any deviations from the standards.

COMPUTER APPLICATIONS

Increasing numbers of managers are recognizing the value of computers for essential record keeping in food and beverage operations. Effective beverage management requires regular maintenance of numerous important records, including orders placed and deliveries anticipated, beverages received and stored, and beverages issued. Computers are particularly useful for these purposes.

Once deliveries have been received and verified, the quantities received and stored must be added to the perpetual inventory. This can be done from invoices or from the daily receiving report, depending on the system and the procedures established in a given operation. Data from beverage requisitions indicating issues from inventory must also be recorded. If all data are recorded in a timely manner, it is simple to check the current quantity of any particular beverage item by looking at the appropriate file on a computer monitor. If necessary, one could print the record for a particular beverage or the perpetual inventory records for all beverages.

No perpetual inventory, whether manually or electronically maintained, is of any value unless the data recorded is both accurate and timely. Any decision to maintain a computer-based perpetual inventory must be accompanied by a commitment to providing the time and staff necessary to update the records regularly and carefully. Daily updates are the most desirable; every other day might be acceptable to some. Infrequent updating tends to make for inaccurate records, which are useless.

CHAPTER ESSENTIALS

In this chapter, we examined the application of control process to the receiving, storing, and issuing phases of beverage operations. We identified management's objectives in establishing control over these three phases and described the standards and standard procedures commonly employed to achieve the stated objectives. For receiving, deliveries received must conform to orders placed in three critical areas: quality, quantity, and price. Standard receiving procedure includes maintaining records of orders placed, verifying that beverages received conform to those ordered, and making necessary entries on a beverage receiving report. For storing, the objectives are to prevent pilferage, to ensure product accessibility when needed, and to maintain product quality. Standard storing procedures include assigning responsibility to one person, keeping the storage facility locked when unattended, organizing the storage facility, and maintaining appropriate conditions for temperature, humidity, and light in the facility. For issuing, the objectives are to ensure the timely release of needed quantities and to prevent their misuse in the interval between their issue from inventory and their delivery to a bar. Standard issuing procedures include establishing par stocks for bars and setting up requisition systems to replenish the par stock.

We discussed the extent of training in operations of various sizes, indicating the principal differences between small and large establishments. We identified several approaches to monitoring the performance of employees responsible for receiving, storing, and issuing. Finally, we discussed the updating of data in computer-based perpetual inventory systems as part of receiving, storing, and issuing procedures.

KEY TERMS IN THIS CHAPTER

Beverage receiving report
Beverage requisition
Bin card
Front bar
Full-bottle sales slip
Job description
Par stock for bars
Requisition system
Service bar
Special-purpose bar

QUESTIONS AND PROBLEMS

1. What is the primary goal of receiving control in beverage operations?

2. List and explain the three standards for beverage receiving.

3. Identify the steps in the standard procedure for receiving beverages,

and explain the importance of each in achieving the primary goal of beverage receiving control.

4. List and explain the three objectives of storing control in beverage operations.

5. Discuss the importance of storeroom security, storeroom organization, and appropriate storage conditions in achieving the objectives of beverage storing control.

6. Describe two methods for maintaining security in the beverage storeroom.

7. What are the purposes of bin cards in beverage storerooms?

8. Explain the reasons for using beverage code numbers.

9. Of what importance is each of the following in a beverage storage facility:
    a. Temperature?
    b. Humidity?
    c. Light?

10. Why should corked wine bottles normally be stored on their sides?

11. What are the immediate effects of shaking:
    a. A bottle of fine red wine?
    b. A container of beer?
    c. A bottle of spirits?

12. Identify the two objectives of issuing control in beverage operations.

13. What standards must be established for issuing beverages to achieve the objectives identified in Question 12?

14. List and describe the three types of bars.

15. Define the term par stock as it is used in bar operations. How does this differ from the definition of par stock used in a beverage storeroom?

16. What is a requisition system?

17. Why are written requisitions considered necessary in beverage control?

18. What is a full-bottle sales slip? Why are they used?

19. How might training for beverage receiving, storing, and issuing in

a small, owner-operated bar differ from training in a major hotel or restaurant organization?

20. List and describe three means for monitoring the performance of employees responsible for receiving, storing, and issuing beverages.

21. Define each of the following terms:
Beverage receiving report
Beverage requisition
Bin card
Front bar
Full-bottle sales slip
Job description
Par stock for bars
Requisition system
Service bar
Special-purpose bar

FOR COMPUTER USERS

22. Using any spreadsheet program you choose, develop a worksheet to be used in place of the receiving report illustrated in Figure 14.2.

15
Beverage Production Control

INTRODUCTION

Having established standards and standard procedures for purchasing, receiving, storing, and issuing beverages, the next logical step is to establish appropriate standards and standard procedures to control beverage production—the making of drinks. It should be apparent that failure to establish control in this area could lessen the overall impact of the standards and standard procedures carefully designed to establish control in the other areas. In addition, neglecting to establish control over drink production can lead to customer dissatisfaction due to improperly prepared drinks, as well as to any number of unwarranted costs. Sales, profits, and the number of customers may all be decreased if management fails to establish control over production.

OBJECTIVES OF BEVERAGE PRODUCTION CONTROL

Control over beverage production is established to achieve two primary objectives:

1. To ensure that all drinks are prepared according to management's specifications.
2. To guard against excessive costs that can develop in the production process.

Specifications for drink production must take into account both the tastes of expected customers and management's desire to prepare drinks of appropriate quality and size. After all, customers who order drinks commonly have preconceived ideas of how the drinks will taste. A customer ordering a daiquiri, for example, may remember enjoying taste sensations experienced in the past from the subtle blending of lime juice, sugar, and rum by skillful bartenders. A customer who is served a cocktail that does not meet expectations maybe dissatisfied and complain or simply not return. Therefore, any establishment selling drinks to the public must recognize and accept certain standards of customer expectation and drink preparation and should establish procedures to ensure that these standards will be met.

In order to achieve the two primary objectives cited above, managers must establish appropriate standards.

ESTABLISHING STANDARDS AND STANDARD PROCEDURES FOR PRODUCTION

Standards must be established for the quantities of ingredients used in drink preparation, as well as for the proportions of ingredients in a drink. In addition, drink sizes must be standardized. When standards are set for ingredients, proportions, and drink sizes, customers can have some reasonable assurance that a drink will meet expectations each time it is ordered. Once these standards have been established and procedures have been developed for training employees to follow them, they can be adhered to even in the face of a high rate of employee turnover.

By establishing and maintaining these standards, managers also establish a means for controlling costs. When drinks are prepared by formula and served in standard portion sizes, one portion of any drink prepared (a daiquiri, for example) should cost the same as every other portion of that same drink. In addition, because the sales prices for drinks are fixed, the cost-to-sales ratio for one portion of any drink should be the same as the cost-to-sales ratio for every other portion of that drink. If this is true, the cost-to-sales ratio for the overall operation should be reasonably stable, provided that the sales remain relatively constant.

Simply stated, once standards and standard procedures for beverage production have been established, it becomes possible to develop a standard cost percent for operation to which the actual cost percent can be compared. This will be discussed in greater detail in the next chapter.

Establishing Quantity Standards and Standard Procedures

As suggested above, one of the first steps in establishing control over beverage production is to standardize the quantities of the most costly ingredients used: the alcoholic beverages. The quantities used by the bartender must be controlled. To do so, one must determine in advance the specific quantities to be used for the production of drinks and then provide the bartender with a means of measuring those quantities.

The majority of drinks prepared with spirits are a combination of one kind of liquor and a mixer. Scotch and soda, gin and tonic, rye and ginger ale, and rum and Coke are all examples of this type of drink. A manager must determine in advance the specific quantity of the expensive ingredient—the liquor—that a bartender should use to prepare any drink. The amount varies from bar to bar, but most have identified quantities that fall between two extremes—as little as three quarters of an ounce in some bars to as much as two ounces in others. This quantity standard is established in advance by the manager and is the fixed quantity that will be given to a customer in return for the fixed sales price of a drink. Once the quantity standard is established, managers must provide bartenders with some means for measuring this quantity each time a drink is prepared. One must keep in mind that wines, spirits and some mixers are purchased in metric units, but bartenders preparing drinks measure the ingredients in ounces.

DEVICES FOR MEASURING STANDARD QUANTITIES. Four measuring devices are commonly used by bartenders: shot glasses, jiggers, pourers, and automated dispensers. Each of these is discussed below.

The Shot Glass. In some establishments, bartenders are provided with small glasses, called **shot glasses,** that are used for measuring. There are two kinds of shot glasses: plain and lined.

A **plain shot glass** holds a predetermined quantity when filled to the rim. Plain shot glasses are available in a number of sizes, from fractions of an ounce to several ounces. In any given bar, all should be the same size. In many of the establishments that use shot glasses, bartenders are told to fill the shot glass and pour the exact measure into the drink. In others, bartenders are provided with shot glasses that hold slightly less than management is willing to give (three-quarters of an ounce, for example, if one ounce is the standard measure). Bartenders are instructed to fill the shot glass, pour the three-quarters of an ounce into the drink, and then, in full view of the customer, pour an additional small amount directly from the bottle into the glass. Some believe there is positive psychological impact to this: Customers think they are getting more than they are entitled to.

A **lined shot glass** is similar to a plain one, but a line is etched around the glass below and parallel to the rim. In some bars, the standard of fill is to the line, which is in full view of both the customer and the bartender. Some bars use shot glasses with deceptive lines such that when the bartender fills to the line on the inside of the glass, it appears to the customer to go above the line on the outside. This is an optical illusion, but it can give the customer a sense of getting something for nothing. Another variation on the lined-glass approach is to use glasses that hold the standard measure when filled to the rim, but have lines etched in the glass at some level below the rim. These are used for the same psychological reasons.

The Jigger. A **jigger** is a double-ended stainless steel measuring device, each end of which resembles a shot glass. The two measuring devices that make up the jigger are of different sizes—one may hold 1 ounce and the other 1½ ounces. Many believe the jigger is necessary for the accurate measuring that ensures perfect cocktails. It can be used for measuring straight shots as well, but is more useful for preparing cocktails that call for varying quantities of ingredients. For measuring the ingredients required for these complex drinks, shot glasses are inappropriate. Some cocktails call for such varied measures as 1 ounce of one ingredient and 1½ ounces of a second. To measure exact quantities of each ingredient, one must use the jigger.

The Pourer.   A **pourer** is a device fitted on top of a bottle that measures the quantity poured from a bottle, limiting that quantity to a predetermined amount. This is another way to control the quantity of liquor used in preparing drinks. A number of different types of pourers are available, but all operate on the principle of controlling the quantity poured each time the bottle is used. In an establishment where one ounce is the standard measure, all bottles can be fitted with devices that dispense just one ounce. Each time the bartender tips the bottle to pour, exactly one ounce is dispensed. The psychological effect, if any, of these pouring devices is widely disputed. Some feel that the customer is given the illusion of the bartender pouring freely; others argue that customers may feel a certain resentment towards an establishment that neither trusts the bartender nor permits an extra drop to be dispensed to a customer. Still others feel that pourers are useful at service bars, which customers never see, but should not be used at front bars, where customers watch bartenders mixing drinks.

The Automated Dispenser.   Many companies have developed and success-fully marketed various automated devices for dispensing predetermined mea-sures of liquor. These range from comparatively simple systems for controlling only the pouring brands, to elaborate electronic control systems that not only control ounces but also mix drinks at the push of a button. These systems, costing many thousands of dollars, are usually linked to cash registers in such a way that each sale is recorded on a guest check as the drink is prepared. In addition, meters record the quantities used, and this makes accurate inventory control possible. Many believe that these systems are best used in settings where bartenders have little or no direct supervision. Others feel that such systems should be used in service bars but never at front bars, except in cases where repeat customers are rare, as in the case of an airport bar.

FREE POUR.   Another means of measuring quantity is to allow bartend-ers to **free pour.** This is a method by which bartenders pour without using any device to measure quantity other than their own judgment or eyesight. In some cases, bartenders are taught to count silently to measure the duration of the act of pouring, which is clearly related to the quantity dispensed. More often than not, however, managers are relying on experienced bartenders to use that experience to gauge the quantities poured. Free pouring is very common. It is usually defended on the grounds that bartenders can prepare drinks at a faster rate by free pouring than they can with any of the measuring devices available.

Although many experienced bartenders can free pour with considerable accuracy, the procedure clearly reduces a manager's control over bar operations. In addition, in bars that suffer from high rates of employee turnover, managers may find that they have no control at all over bar operations. In any bar operation, free pouring is likely to be abused by all but the most dedicated employees. Free pouring makes it possible for dishonest bartenders to operate more for their own advantage than for the general good of the business. However, many owners who permit free pouring seek to offset its costs by raising sales prices to ensure the desired level of profit.

GLASSWARE.   In addition to controlling the quantity of liquor used in preparing each drink, it is desirable to control the overall size of the drinks. Standardizing the glassware used for service makes this comparatively simple. It is the manager's responsibility to establish the standard portion size for each type of drink and to provide bartenders with appropriate glassware.

Beverage glassware is available in a wide variety of shapes and sizes. Therefore, it is very easy to furnish the bar with particular glassware for particular drinks. In the Middletown Inn, for example, stemmed cocktail glasses holding four ounces have been identified as the standard glassware for all cocktails. Because bartenders cannot fill glasses above the rim, it is impossible for them to serve a portion size greater than four ounces unless they use the wrong glassware or give the customer an extra measure known as a "dividend." By furnishing the bar with four-ounce cocktail glassware, directing that all cocktails be served in these glasses, and declaring that no dividends may be given to customers, managers can effectively control portion sizes.

Many fine hotels and restaurants consider the four-ounce cocktail glass too small. In these establishments, management is willing to give more generous portions in return for the higher sales prices charged. Thus, bartenders are instructed to use lined cocktail glasses holding five ounces, with lines etched around the glass, indicating a 4½ ounce measure.

In order for managers to establish effective portion control, then, it is important to purchase glassware in appropriate sizes. Managers must determine the kinds of glassware that will be needed based on present or anticipated customers and their preferences and then determine portion sizes. The glassware purchased should be matched to the portion sizes established by the manager, and bartenders must be instructed which glasses to use for serving specific drinks.

While a neighborhood bar may be able to get by with just four or five types of glasses of as many sizes, a fine restaurant cannot do so. Neither can a hotel. Beverage service in these may require as many as 10 to 15 different types of glassware in as many sizes. Fine hotels and restaurants often require an array of glassware similar to that listed in Figure 15.1.

Samples of common glasses are pictured in Figure 15.2.

STANDARD GLASSWARE	Sturnley's	Restaurant

Item	Size	Par Stock at Bar
Shot Glass	1.25 oz.	72
Cordial	2 oz.	36
Cocktail	3.5 oz.	72
Cocktail	4.5 oz.	72
Champagne	4.5 oz.	72
Sour	5.25 oz.	72
Rocks	5.5 oz.	144
Brandy	5.5 oz.	36
Wine	8.5 oz.	72
Wine	6.5 oz.	72
Hi-Ball	8 oz.	48
Hi-Ball	10 oz.	144
Pilsner	10 oz.	72

FIGURE 15.1

Thus, managers standardize portion sizes by purchasing specific glass-ware to be used for the service of specific types of drinks and then training bar personnel to serve drinks in the proper glasses. While standardization of portion sizes helps control beverage costs, that alone is insufficient. It is useful to stipulate that a gin and tonic is to be served over ice in a 12-ounce glass, yet this alone does not tell bar personnel what part of the standard portion should be gin and what part mixer. This consideration is particularly important in cost control because, after all, the cost of gin is greater per ounce than the cost of tonic water, and the relative amounts of each used in making the drink will affect the cost. The following two examples clearly show the difference in the cost of ingredients effected by changing proportions:

Cost of gin: $.45/oz.
Cost of mixer: $.04/oz.

Gin and tonic A		Gin and tonic B	
Gin—2 oz.	= $ .90	Gin—1 oz.	= $.45
Mixer—6 oz. =	.24	Mixer—7 oz. =	.28
Total	$1.14	Total	$.73

In both cases, the result is eight ounces of gin and tonic. However, because the proportion has been changed, the cost of Gin and tonic B is far less than that of Gin and tonic A. If this particular drink were to be offered at a standard sales price of $4.00, there would be considerable difference between the

Shot Glass
1¼ oz.

Cordial
1¼ oz.

Whiskey Sour
4½ oz.

Brandy
6 oz.

Cocktail
6 oz.

Old Fashioned
6½ oz.

White Wine
7¾ oz.

Hi-Ball
8 oz.

Rocks
8¼ oz.

Red Wine
9 oz.

Footed Pilsner
8 oz.

Tulip Champagne
9 oz.

FIGURE 15.2 *Standard Glassware for Bars*

cost-to-sales ratios as well: 28.5 percent for drink A versus 18.25 percent for drink B.

Establishing Quality Standards and Standard Procedures

STANDARD RECIPES.   It should be clear that, to control costs, one must establish control over the ingredients that go into each drink, as well as over the proportions of the ingredients to one another. In other words, standard recipes must be established so that bar personnel will know the exact quantity of each ingredient to use in order to produce any given drink.

Generally speaking, bartenders prepare and serve two kinds of drinks that require liquor: straight shots with mixers, such as the gin and tonic identified above, and mixed drinks or cocktails, many of which involve a number of ingredients that must be combined in a specific way for the drink to be right.

For straight shots with mixers, the standard drink is controlled by providing the bartender with appropriate glassware of predetermined size, as well as a jigger or other device for measuring the liquor. The standard quantity of liquor for the drink is measured and poured over ice in the proper glass, and the glass is then filled with the mixer. In effect, this constitutes the standard recipe. Each time a customer orders a scotch and soda, the bartender places a certain number of ice cubes in a glass of the proper size, adds one standard measure of the pouring brand of scotch, and fills the glass nearly to the rim with soda. Every scotch and soda prepared in this way will be the same. The customer's second drink will be the same as the first, and, if he returns to the bar in two weeks and orders a scotch and soda, he will be served the same drink for the same price, barring changes in management policy. Preparing drinks that are consistently the same is a major factor in establishing customer satisfaction and developing repeat business.

With mixed drinks and cocktails, establishing control over ingredients, proportions, and cost while providing drinks that are consistently the same is somewhat more complex. There are normally two or more recipes for making any given cocktail, and the resulting cocktails are often quite different from one another. For example, the two recipes below for a cocktail known as a Manhattan have been taken from two different drink mixing guides:

Manhattan #1	Manhattan #2
2½ oz. blended rye whiskey	1½ oz. blended rye whiskey
¾ oz. sweet vermouth	¾ oz. sweet vermouth
Dash of bitters	Dash of bitters

While mixing the listed ingredients in the prescribed manner will produce a Manhattan cocktail in either case, there are substantial differences between

MANHATTAN   S. P. _____
2-1/2 ounces blended rye whiskey
3/4 ounce sweet vermouth
dash of bitters
4 ice cubes
stem cherry

Combine the whiskey, vermouth, and ice cubes in a mixing glass and stir well. Strain into a 4-ounce stem cocktail glass. Garnish with a cherry.

BRANDY ALEXANDER   S. P. _____
3/4 ounce brandy
3/4 ounce Creme de Cacao
3/4 ounce heavy cream
3 ice cubes

Combine all ingredients in a cocktail shaker and shake vigorously. Strain into a 4-ounce cocktail glass.

FIGURE 15.3 *Standard Drink Recipes*

them. In cocktail #1, the ratio of whiskey to vermouth is more than 3 to l; in #2, it is 2 to 1. In addition, recipe #1 produces a drink that is one ounce larger than that produced by recipe #2. Finally, recipe #1 costs more to make because it contains one additional ounce of blended rye whiskey.

It is apparent that management must identify which of several recipes will be the standard recipe used to prepare the Manhattan. Similar decisions must be made for all cocktails. While the most common solution is to adopt one of the standard bartender's recipe guides for use at the bar, it is by no means uncommon, particularly in chain operations, to find a book of standard recipes specifically prepared for company-wide use. In every case, the standard recipe includes not only the measures of alcoholic beverages to be used in preparation, but the quantities of all other ingredients, including garnishes, as well as mixing and serving instructions. In some cases, pictures of the drinks are provided to ensure uniformity, particularly in the face of high rates of employee turnover. Figure 15.3 gives examples of typical standard recipes for two common cocktails: the Manhattan and the Brandy Alexander.

Adopting a book of standard recipes also makes it possible for a bartender to prepare various unusual cocktails that are requested only on rare occasions. Although a number of professional bartenders are able to mix virtually any drink requested, many have few occasions to mix cocktails as unusual as a Taxco Fizz, an Opal, or an Earthquake. Thus, a standard recipe guide can help ensure the satisfaction of the customer requesting the unusual drink.

Although standard bar recipes are a necessity for control purposes, many bartenders and some managers dislike them. In some establishments, therefore, any discussion of standard recipes is likely to result in a heated debate.

It is theoretically possible to establish a standard recipe for every drink served by any bar, indicating the size of the drink and the specific quantity of each ingredient the drink should contain. As a practical matter, it is not possible to enforce the use of standard recipes in all instances at all bars. One illustration of the problem should suffice.

Most people are familiar with the martini, a cocktail made with gin and dry vermouth, stirred with ice, strained into a cocktail glass, and served garnished with an olive. For some, the best mixture for a three-ounce martini is two ounces of gin to one ounce of vermouth; for others, it is three ounces of gin to one drop of vermouth. And there is an infinite number of variations. Because much of the success of a bar depends on satisfying customer tastes, it is very difficult—many would say impossible—for a bar manager to establish an inflexible standard recipe for a martini. One single standard recipe might satisfy some customers but displease others. Many bar managers feel that bartenders must be permitted a certain amount of freedom to alter standard recipes to suit the tastes and requests of customers. Some believe that the standard recipe should be a kind of average of all the martinis mixed in a particular bar over a period of time.

With standards and standard procedures established in the form of standard recipes and standard portion sizes, it is possible to calculate the standard cost of any drink.

Establishing Standard Portion Costs

STRAIGHT DRINKS. The cost of straight drinks, served with or without mixers, can be determined by first dividing the standard portion size in ounces into the number of ounces in the bottle to find the number of standard drinks contained in each bottle. This number is then divided into the cost of the bottle to find the standard cost of the drink.

With the introduction of the metric system for beverage packaging, it has become necessary to convert the metric contents of bottles into their ounce equivalents. A conversion table is illustrated in Figure 15.4.

For example, the standard portion size for the pouring brand of scotch in the Broadway Bar is 1.5 ounces. The bar uses 750-ml. bottles of scotch. Figure 15.4 indicates that a 750-ml. bottle contains 25.4 ounces. Dividing the 1.5-ounce standard drink into the 25.4 ounces in the 750-ml. bottle, one determines that each bottle contains 16.9 drinks, rounded to the nearest tenth:

$$\frac{25.4 \text{ oz.}}{1.5 \text{ oz.}} = 16.9 \text{ Drinks}$$

	Distilled Spirits		
Old Sizes		*Standard Metric Sizes*	
U.S. Standards of Fill	*U.S. Ounces*	*Liters*	*Milliliters*
Gallon	128		
Half-Gallon	64		
	59.2	1.75	1,750
	33.8	1.00	1,000
Quart	32		
Fifth	25.6		
	25.4	3/4 liter	750
3/4 Quart (Cordials)	24		
	17	1/2 liter	500
Pint	16		
4/5 Pint	12.8		
3/4 Pint (Cordials)	12		
Half Pint	8		
	6.8	1/5 liter	200
1/4 Pint	4		
1/8 Pint	2		
	1.7	1/20 liter	50
1/10 Pint (Miniature)	1.6		

FIGURE 15.4 *Relationship of Approved Metric Sizes to U.S. Standards of Fill*

Because there is a small amount of spillage and evaporation in all bar operations, this can be safely adjusted to an average of 16.5 drinks per bottle. If the purchase price of the bottle is $13.85, then the standard cost of each of the 16.5 drinks it contains can be determined by dividing the bottle cost, $13.85, by the number of drinks it contains, 16.5:

$$\frac{\$13.85}{16.5 \text{ oz.}} = \$.839, \text{ or } \$.84 \text{ rounded to the nearest cent}$$

Old Sizes U.S. Standards of Fill	Wines U.S. Ounces	Standard Metric Sizes Liters	Milliliters
4.9 Gallon	627.2		
3 Gallon	384		
1 Gallon	128		
Jeroboam (4/5 Gallon)	102.4		
	101	3	3,000
Half-Gallon	64		
Magnum (2/5 Gallon)	51.2		
	50.7	1.5	1,500
	33.8	1	1,000
Quart	32		
Fifth	25.6		
	25.4	3/4 liter	750
Pint	16		
4/5 Pint	12.8		
	12.7	3/8 liter	375
1/2 Pint	8		
Split (2/5 Pint)	6.4		
	6.3	3/16 liter	187.5
4 Oz.	4		
	3.4	1/10 liter	100
3 Oz. Miniature	3		
2 Oz.	2		

FIGURE 15.4   (continued)

This bar would normally offer a number of call brands of scotch as well, and the same technique would be used to determine the standard cost of one standard drink of each call brand. For a premium scotch costing $18.15 per 750-ml. bottle, the standard cost of each drink is somewhat higher:

Bottle Code	Item	Size ml.	Size oz.	Bottle Cost	Ounce Cost	Drink Size	Drink Cost
201	Old Bagpipe	750	25.4	$12.95	$.51	1.5 oz	$.77
206	Highland Hiatus	750	25.4	14.95	.589	1.5 oz	.88
302	Gimby's Gin	1000	33.8	11.95	.354	1.5 oz	.53

FIGURE 15.5 *Standard Costs for Straight Drinks*

$$\frac{\$18.15}{16.5 \text{ oz.}} = \$1.10$$

An alternative procedure for finding the standard cost per drink requires that one divide the cost of the bottle by the number of ounces it contains to find the cost per ounce and then multiply the ounce cost by the standard drink size. For example, if the pouring brand of gin costs $16.90 per liter, the equivalent of 33.8 ounces, each ounce would cost $.50:

$$\frac{\$16.90}{33.8 \text{ oz.}} = \$.50$$

This ounce cost, multiplied by the standard 1.5-ounce drink size for gin in the Broadway Bar, yields a standard cost for the standard measure of $.75, as indicated below:

1.5-ounce Standard size × $.50 per Ounce = $.75 per Drink

Some who use this method prefer to subtract one ounce from the true number of ounces contained in a bottle to allow for evaporation and spillage. Using this approach, one would treat a 750-ml. bottle as 24.4 ounces, and a one-liter bottle as 32.8 ounces.

The selection of one method rather than another depends on the preferences and those performing the calculations. Once these calculations have been completed, a common practice is to record the results on a form similar to that illustrated in Figure 15.5. These are updated regularly, whenever dealer prices change. In this way, up-to-date cost figures are readily available for managers to use in several ways. One use is to calculate the cost of mixed drinks and cocktails.

ITEM: Martini		BAR RECIPE #: 53

DRINK SALES PRICE: $4.00
DRINK COST: $ .85
COST PERCENT: 21.3%

Ingredients	Quantity	Cost
Gimby's gin	2 oz.	$.71
Old Modesto dry vermouth	1/2 oz.	.10
cocktail olive	1 ea.	.04
TOTALS	2-1/2 oz.	$.85

GLASSWARE: 3 oz. cocktail

PROCEDURE: Pour gin and vermouth into glass shaker. Add cracked ice.

Stir gently. Strain into 3 oz. cocktail glass. Add olive and serve.

FIGURE 15.6 *Standard Recipe Detail and Cost Card*

MIXED DRINKS AND COCKTAILS. It is particularly important to determine the standard costs of cocktails and other mixed drinks. These drinks, typically prepared from standard recipes, normally have several ingredients and may require two or more alcoholic beverages. Consequently, mixed drinks are usually more expensive to make than straight drinks. Knowledge of the cost per drink is important for making intelligent pricing decisions.

To simplify the task of determining standard costs of cocktails and other mixed drinks and maintaining records of the calculations, many bar managers obtain supplies of recipe details and cost forms similar to those illustrated in Figure 15.6 and Figure 15.7.

Both forms are in common use, and both can be made up by a printer or by office workers with access to computers and photocopiers.

The first step in determining the standard cost of a drink is to record on the form all the information from the standard recipe for the drink. It is essential to take into account all ingredients used by the bartender in preparing the

ITEM: __Maurice cocktail__		BAR RECIPE #: __77__	
Date	*9/11/XXXX*		
Drink sales price	$3.95		
Drink cost	$.65		
Cost percent	16.5%		
BOTTLE DATA ingredient	Gimby's gin		
bottle size	1 liter		
bottle cost	$11.95		
DRINK DATA Juice of 1/4 orange	$.08		
1/2 oz. sweet vermouth	.10		
1/2 oz. dry vermouth	.10		
1 oz. gin	.35		
dash of bitters	.02		
TOTAL	$.65		
GLASSWARE: __4 oz. cocktail__			
PROCEDURE: __Combine all ingredients in glass shaker. Add cracked ice. Stir.__ __Strain into cocktail glass.__			

FIGURE 15.7 *Standard Recipe Detail and Cost Card*

drink. The cost of a drink should include the cost of any nonalcoholic ingredients used in its preparation. Fruit juices, eggs, and heavy cream are but a few of the possibilities for other ingredients that must be included in the cost of a drink. In addition, any garnish for a drink must be included. Garnishes can include olives, stem cherries, cocktail onions, and slices of various fruits. To arrive at the true cost of a drink, one must add the cost of all other ingredients to the cost of the basic alcoholic ingredients.

Both of the forms illustrated make provision for including the standard preparation procedure and the standard glassware. With this information recorded, management has a complete set of the standard bar recipes for ready reference. Depending on the type and size of paper used, these can be kept in either a looseleaf notebook or in a card file. For ease of use, one might be better advised to rely on a computer.

After the standard recipe has been recorded on the recipe detail and cost card, the next step is to determine the cost of each ingredient, both alcoholic and nonalcoholic. Determining the cost of alcoholic ingredients is easier if someone has previously completed a form such as that illustrated in Figure 15.5, which indicates the standard costs of straight drinks. If this information is not available, additional calculations are required. To do them, one must have access to bottle costs and bottle sizes. In many hotels and large restaurants, someone in an accounting office may have perpetual inventory records that include bottle sizes and costs. Alternatively, the individual responsible for beverage purchasing may keep the information in an up-to-date price book.

In smaller bars and restaurants, managers may find it necessary to obtain the information from invoices, receiving sheets, or inventory books. For non-alcoholic ingredients, such as the food items transferred from the kitchen, it may be necessary to refer to transfer memos. Alternatively, one might ask the steward for the most recent purchase prices. Exact procedures vary considerably from one place to another. In general, the exact procedure followed is of no particular significance, so long as it results in the correct cost figures for each item in the recipe.

For each of the two forms illustrated, the techniques for recording the data differ slightly. For that in Figure 15.6, one must determine the cost of the specific quantity used before making any entry on the form. In the example given, the cost of the two ounces of gin is recorded as $.71. This is determined by referring to the chart in Figure 15.5, which shows that one ounce of the pouring brand costs $.354. This, multiplied by the two ounces in the recipe and rounded to the nearest cent, gives the cost of the gin in the drink.

If a form similar to Figure 15.7 is used, the first step is to record the size and cost of a bottle of the pouring brand. In the example shown, the 33.8-ounce bottle of gin is recorded as costing $11.95. The next step is to divide the number of ounces into the cost of the bottle and to multiply the result by the number of ounces of gin in the recipe. This is essentially the calculation required for developing the data included in Figure 15.5.

The principal advantage of the form shown in Figure 15.7 is that it provides additional columns that can be used to recalculate drink costs as ingredient costs change. Those who adopt this form, as opposed to that in Figure 15.6, find that it can be used for a relatively longer period of time before it becomes necessary to prepare a new card.

Once the costs of all ingredients in a drink have been determined, the figures are totaled. The result is the standard cost for a drink prepared according to the standard recipe. This cost is recorded on the line provided and divided by the sales price to determine the cost-to-sales ratio for the drink. This is recorded as the cost percent for the drink. If sales prices have not yet been determined, the cost per drink should certainly be one of the chief considerations used to set reasonable sales prices. Even if sales prices have been set before costs are calculated, all these prices should be reviewed in the light of the newly developed costs.

Establishing Standard Sales Prices

Once standard costs for standard drinks are known and listed, a list of standard sales prices should be established. One obvious reason for this is so that sales prices can be posted at the bar or listed in a menu, depending on the type of establishment. It is generally considered good practice to maintain a complete list of current standard sales prices in the manager's office. Success with some of the techniques to be discussed in Chapter 16 requires that one have access to an accurate list of sales prices.

The techniques for maintaining up-to-date lists of standard sales prices are many and varied. As in so many other cases, the simplest is often the best. Many recommend that current sales prices for cocktails and mixed drinks be maintained on the recipe detail and cost cards and that those for straight drinks be kept on an expanded version of the list first shown in Figure 15.5. This expanded version is illustrated in Figure 15.8.

It is absolutely essential in any bar operation that the sales price be standardized for each drink sold, for straight drinks as well as for cocktails and other mixed drinks. When sales prices are standardized, customers can be properly charged for the drinks they order, and the prices will not vary from day to day. The possibilities for customer satisfaction are increased: The customer who has been charged $3.50 for a particular drink on Tuesday has reasonable assurance that an identical charge will be made for the same drink on Wednesday. In some places, a list of standardized drink prices can be found posted on a sign over the bar. In others, they may be printed in the menu. These signs and menus eliminate many possible arguments over drink prices.

Perhaps the most important purpose behind the standardization of sales prices is to maintain a planned cost-to-sales ratio for each drink. The drink costing $.90 when prepared from a standard recipe and selling for $4.50 has a cost-to-sales ratio of $.90 to $4.50—20 percent. The sale of one of these drinks results in the addition of $4.50 to daily sales and $.90 to daily cost, the net effect being a gross profit on the sale of $3.60. For the drink in question, this is the desired, preplanned effect of each sale. It is not a matter of chance or a bartender's whim; it has been planned by the manager. Ingredients (and consequently costs) are planned. With costs established, sales prices are set that yield acceptable cost-to-sales ratios. Product cost has a known relationship to prod-

Straight Drinks: Scotch		Bottle Size						
Bottle Code	Item	ml	oz	Bottle Cost	Ounce Cost	Drink Size	Drink Cost	Drink S.P.
200	Nessie's Blended	1,000	33.8	$11.95	$.354	1.5 oz.	$ .53	$2.50
201	Old Bagpipe	750	25.4	12.95	.51	1.5 oz.	.77	3.25
203	Purple Heather	1,000	33.8	14.95	.442	1.5 oz.	.66	2.95
206	Highland Hiatus	750	25.4	14.95	.589	1.5 oz.	.88	3.50
207	Grant's	750	25.4	15.95	.628	1.5 oz.	.94	3.50
210	Teacher's	750	25.4	16.95	.667	1.5 oz.	1.00	3.95
212	Dewar's	750	25.4	16.95	.667	1.5 oz.	1.00	3.95
213	Bell's	750	25.4	15.95	.628	1.5 oz.	.94	3.50

FIGURE 15.8 *Standard Costs and Sales Prices*

uct sales price. In addition, each sale has a known impact on gross profit. In effect, the increase in gross profit attributable to each sale is planned when management establishes the cost and sales price of a drink. Thus, it becomes possible to plan for and maintain acceptable levels of profit.

TRAINING FOR PRODUCTION

After management has attended to the first step in the control process by establishing the standards and standard procedures necessary for controlling production, it is important to devote appropriate time and energy to the second step: training bartenders to follow the standards and standard procedures.

For the purposes of the following discussion, we will assume that any bartenders hired have become qualified for their positions by some combination of training and experience. Thus, it will not be necessary to teach them basic bartending skills. Training will be restricted to the specific standards and standard procedures used in the establishment. It should be noted that most new employees, including bartenders, bring to their new jobs the methods and procedures they learned in previous jobs. To the extent that these are inapplicable, managers must see that the necessary retraining is done.

A suitable first step in training in most operations is to conduct an appropriate orientation to working in the establishment, including a tour of those areas the new employee would find relevant to his work. Actual training would take place at the specific work station to which the new employee would be assigned. Here, the trainer, often the manager, would devote an appropriate amount of time to showing the employee the locations of supplies and equipment. He might then spell out the standard procedures established for replenishing supplies. Next, the trainer would explain the standards and standard procedures for producing drinks, covering such important details as pouring methods, mixing methods, call brands and pouring brands, standard drink recipes, standard drink sizes, standard glassware for drinks, and standard garnishes. Additional topics covered would be likely to include serving techniques, opening and closing procedures, inventory procedures, and specific rules for registering sales and handling cash. This training would be conducted at a time when it would not interfere with normal business, and the bartender would be given ample opportunity to ask questions.

One difficulty with this approach to training is its heavy dependence on the memories of both the trainer and the trainee. The trainer may forget to include some topics; the trainee may not remember all of the details covered in the short training period. In an effort to eliminate these problems, many large organizations employ specialized personnel to prepare training manuals and operation manuals that specify the standards and standard procedures established for every job in the organization. In such organizations, a manual is given to the new employee as the job is explained, and the employee keeps the manual for study and reference. This approach reduces the need for quick memorization on the part of the trainee and helps eliminate the possibility that important topics may be neglected during training. Such manuals provide the additional advantage of helping the manager to standardize both training and job performance in all units of the organization.

MONITORING PRODUCTION PERFORMANCE AND TAKING CORRECTIVE ACTION

Once standards and standard procedures for beverage production have been established and employees have been suitably trained, managers are able to institute the final steps in the control process: monitor employee performance, and take corrective action as needed.

Before discussing the specifics of monitoring employee performance in this area, we must note that bar operations present unique opportunities for employees to deviate from established standards and standard procedures without management becoming aware until well after the fact. For example, a bartender instructed to pour 1¼ ounces for a straight shot may instead pour 1½ ounces for many customers for as long as a month (one full accounting period) before management would obtain data revealing that excessive beverage costs had developed. The bartender might have simply misunderstood instructions or might have been pouring the larger shots purposely to increase tips. In either case, beverage costs would be higher than warranted, but this would not be known until beverage costs for the month had been determined and an investigation had uncovered the cause. And this is just one simple example of dozens of possible deviations from standard procedures that can occur at a bar. Discussion of other possible deviations and methods for detecting them will be found in Chapter 16.

One common approach to monitoring beverage production is to observe bartenders as they proceed with their daily work. The frequency of the observations may range from continual to occasional, depending on a given manager's perception of need. Some employees—those whose honesty, ability, or receptivity to training is questionable—should probably be observed rather frequently. In making these observations, a manager would attempt to determine the type of corrective action, if any, that could lead to improved performance. Other employees whose loyalty, interest, honesty, and willingness to follow standards and standard procedures have been demonstrated amply in their daily work need not be observed so frequently. At most, the manager would probably spot check their work to confirm previous evaluations. If, from time to time, a spot check were to suggest that some individual's performance had fallen below its previous acceptable level, the manager would be wise to focus attention more closely on the particular employee and increase the frequency of observation.

A basic precursor to monitoring beverage production is selecting the means to be used for observing employee performance. Essentially, there are four possibilities:

1. A manager can personally observe bar operations on a regular basis.
2. A designated employee, such as a head bartender, can observe others working at the bar and report unacceptable performance and problems to management.
3. Individuals unknown to the bartenders can be hired to patronize the bar, observe the employees, note problems, and report to management.
4. Closed-circuit television systems can be installed to permit observation of bartenders and bar operations from some remote location.

By using one or more of these approaches, managers have some reasonable means for assessing employee performance and uncovering operating problems. However, this is not to suggest that the manager of any bar operation can maintain perfect control merely by adopting these approaches. As Chapter 16 will show, the opportunities for employees to purposely deviate from established standards are too many and too varied to be discovered by mere observation.

COMPUTER APPLICATIONS

Computers can be used in beverage production control to maintain standard drink recipe files and to determine standard costs for drinks. If maintaining standard recipes files were the only objective, one could do so with any simple word processing program. One approach would be to treat each standard drink as a document, give it a file name, and save it on a hard disk or a diskette. The individual files could be loaded, edited if necessary, and then filed or printed, depending on need. Alternatively, all standard recipes could be filed as one document, which would make it easier to print them for use in training. A more practical approach would be to maintain the standard recipes with one of the two more flexible programs: spreadsheet or database. Both would permit the user to print the recipes for training and would offer such other useful possibilities as determining standard costs of drinks and updating standard costs when ingredient costs change. With both the spreadsheet and database programs, information could be filed and printed selectively. For example, managers would certainly want bartenders to have the recipes, but would probably not want to give them cost data. Using the "report" function common to spreadsheet programs, the computer could be directed to print that section of the spreadsheet containing the recipe, but not the section containing the cost information. Using a database program would permit an even greater degree of flexibility.

Today, with the substantial number of software programs specifically written for beverage control, few managers are willing to devote the time energy required to institute control with generic spreadsheet and database programs. Growing numbers of managers are simply adopting one or another of the beverage control programs currently advertised in trade magazines and demonstrated at hotel and restaurant trade shows. Today's software is designed to accomplish far more than one could expect from any generic spreadsheet or database package.

CHAPTER ESSENTIALS

In this chapter, we identified the two primary objectives for establishing beverage production control: to ensure that all drinks are prepared according to managers' specifications and to guard against the development of excessive beverage costs in the production phase of operation. We described the standards and standard procedures commonly established to achieve these objectives, including measuring devices, pourers, and other dispensing devices, and standard recipes. We identified methods for determining standard costs for straight drinks and for mixed drinks, including cocktails, and explained the importance of determining standard costs as one basis for establishing sales prices. We described common methods for training bartenders to follow established standards and standard procedures and discussed the importance of monitoring employee performance. We identified four methods for monitoring employee performance at bars and discussed the problems inherent in relying on these as the sole means for controlling production. Finally, we suggested several ways that computers are being used to aid in production control.

KEY TERMS IN THIS CHAPTER

Cocktail
Free pouring
Jigger
Lined shot glass
Mixed drink
Mixer
Pourer
Shot glass
Standard drink cost
Standard drink recipe
Standard selling price
Straight drink

QUESTIONS AND PROBLEMS

1. Identify the two primary objectives of beverage production control.

2. List four devices used to standardize quantities of alcoholic beverages used in beverage production.

3. Identify the primary purposes for establishing standard drink recipes.

4. Why are standard sales prices necessary?

5. The cost of the pouring brand of scotch is $.58 per ounce, and the cost of club soda is $.04 per ounce. Determine the cost of a scotch and soda from each of the following standard recipes:
   a. One ounce of scotch and six ounces of club soda.
   b. One and one-half ounces of scotch and seven ounces of club soda.
   c. Two ounces of scotch and six ounces of club soda.

6. In each of the examples in Question 5, determine sales price if the desired liquor cost percent is:
   a. 20%.
   b. 25%.
   c. 18%.

7. In Fleezee's Bar, the standard measure for a straight shot is one ounce. How much does a straight shot of blended rye cost if the price of a one-liter bottle is $13.50?

8. In the cocktail lounge at Fribble's Hotel, a straight shot of Irish whiskey is 1½ ounces. The purchase price for a 1-liter bottle of the pouring brand is $16.95. If the desired cost-to-sales ratio is 20%, what should be the sales price for the drink?

9. In the Midway Bar, a straight shot of Canadian whiskey is 1¼ ounces. The purchase price for a one-liter bottle of the pouring brand is $14.95. If the desired cost-to-sales ratio is 20%, what should be the sales price for the drink?

10. In the Airport Lounge, a straight shot of scotch whiskey is one ounce. The purchase price for a one-liter bottle of the pouring brand is $15.95. If the desired cost-to-sales ratio is 20%, what should be the sales price for the drink?

11. What steps can a manager take to institute portion control in a bar operation?

12. Why is production control necessary in bar operations? What are some of the measures that can be taken to institute control?

13. Select recipes for any four common drinks from a book of drink recipes, obtain current market prices for the ingredients, and then determine the standard cost of one portion of each drink.

14. Describe two approaches commonly used to train beverage production employees to follow established standards and standard procedures.

15. Why is frequent monitoring of bar operations essential?

16. List four techniques for observing the performance of bartenders.

17. Assume that you are manager of a cocktail lounge. The bar register is an electronic sales terminal with automatic pricing. There is no other register in the establishment. It is 5:00 P.M. on a busy Friday afternoon, and the terminal has just become inoperable. What pro-

cedures would you direct the bartender to use to record sales until the terminal could be repaired?

18. Define each of the following terms:
Cocktail
Free pouring
Jigger
Lined shot glass
Mixed drink
Mixer
Pourer
Shot glass
Standard drink cost
Standard drink recipe
Standard selling price
Straight drink

FOR COMPUTER USERS

19. Using any spreadsheet program you choose, develop a worksheet similar to Figure 15.6 for determining the standard portion costs for mixed drinks and cocktails.

20. Using the worksheet developed in Question 19 as a template, calculate the standard portion costs for any six drinks selected from a bartender's guide. Obtain current market prices to use in your calculations.

16 *Monitoring Beverage Operations*

LEARNING OBJECTIVES

After reading and studying this chapter, you should be able to:

1. Identify the three general approaches to monitoring beverage operations.
2. Calculate value of liquor issued to a bar, bar inventory differential, and cost of liquor consumed.
3. Calculate cost of beverages sold and beverage cost percent, both daily and monthly.
4. Calculate daily and monthly costs and cost percents for wines, spirits, and beers separately.
5. Determine standard beverage cost for a given period.
6. List five possible reasons for differences between actual and standard beverage costs.
7. Calculate potential sales value per bottle for beverages sold by the straight drink.
8. Determine a mixed drink differential, and use it to adjust potential sales values.
9. Calculate potential sales values by the average sales value method.
10. Calculate potential sales values by the standard deviation method.
11. Calculate beverage inventory turnover, and discuss its interpretation.
12. Identify two types of computer programs that can be used in monitoring beverage operations.
13. Name the beverage monitoring methods for which computers are most necessary.
14. Define each of the Key Terms at the end of the chapter.

INTRODUCTION

One important aspect of the control process is regular monitoring of operations to determine whether results conform to the manager's plans. In previous chapters, techniques and approaches for the regular monitoring of the performance of employees engaged in beverage purchasing, receiving, storing, issuing, and production were illustrated and explained. Clearly, the monitoring of individual performance is necessary. However, one must also assess the overall effectiveness of control procedures that, taken together, constitute the control system. In other words, one must evaluate the entire control process— the standards and standard procedures established, the training methods employed for the staff, and the monitoring techniques used by the manager—to determine whether the controls instituted are producing the desired results.

There are three general approaches to monitoring beverage operations. The first is based on cost: determining the cost of beverages sold, and comparing that figure with either actual cost or standard cost. The second is based on liquid measure: comparing the number of ounces of beverages sold with the number of ounces consumed. The third is based on sales values: comparing the potential sales value of beverages consumed with the actual sales revenue recorded. Deciding which to use depends on the size and scope of operations. Many operators use just one method; some use more than one. All three methods will be discussed in detail below.

THE COST APPROACH

Cost Percent Methods

MONTHLY CALCULATIONS. It is useful to compare cost and sales figures on a regular basis to see if the planned cost-to-sales ratio is being maintained. Methods for doing this vary considerably from one operation to another, so it will be useful to look at several that might be used in operations of different sizes.

Small operations, often owner-managed and with few employees, do not have beverage controllers. The task of determining the cost-to-sales ratio normally falls to the owner. In many places, the owner attends to this monthly, with or without the help of an accountant. Beverage cost is determined from inventory and purchase figures in the following manner.

A physical inventory of the storage area is taken after the close of business on the last day of the month. The number of bottles of each item in stock is counted, and its value is determined by means of one of five methods for inventory valuation: actual purchase price method; first-in, first-out method; weighted average purchase price method; latest purchase price method; last-in, first-out method. The specifics of these five are described in detail in Chapter 9.

When the value of each item in stock is known, these values are added, and the result is the total dollar value of the closing inventory for the period. Because the closing inventory figure for any period is, by definition, the opening inventory for the following period, it is necessary to look back at the records to determine the closing inventory for the preceding period. To this opening inventory valuation, one adds the cost of all purchases for the month, obtained from financial records. Opening inventory plus purchases equals the value of beverages available for sale during the period. To illustrate, consider the case of Shelly's, a small bar and restaurant located in a city in Rhode Island. The following are figures taken from the financial records of Shelly's:

Opening beverage inventory	5,000
+ Beverage purchases this month	8,000
= Total available for sale this month	$13,000

Of the total available for sale, some has been issued to the bar and some has not. To find the value of the beverages issued to the bar, the closing inventory figure for the current month is subtracted from the total available:

Total available for sale this month	$13,000
− closing inventory this month	6,000
= Value of beverages issued to the bar	$ 7,000

While this $7,000 figure is the value of liquor issued to the bar, it is not necessarily the cost of beverages sold at the bar. To determine the cost of beverages sold, the $7,000 must be adjusted by the change in the value of inventory at the bar from the beginning to the end of the month. To illustrate:

Bar inventory value at the beginning of month	$1,500
− Bar inventory value at the end of the month	800
= Bar inventory differential	$ 700

To determine the cost of beverages consumed in the month, one must take this bar inventory differential into account. In this case, $700 must be added to the $7,000 figure for issues. Thus:

Value of beverages issued to the bar	$7,000
+ Inventory differential	700
= Cost of beverages consumed	$7,700

If the bar inventory differential is positive, as in this case, it is added to the value of beverages issued to the bar. If it is negative, it is subtracted.

After the cost of beverages consumed at the bar has been determined, it is possible to calculate the beverage cost percent, or cost-to-sales ratio. The financial records of Shelly's indicate beverage sales for the month to be $29,389.30. The calculation of beverage cost percent is as follows:

$$\text{Beverage cost percentage} = \frac{\text{Beverage cost}}{\text{Beverage sales}}$$
$$= \frac{\$\ 7,700}{\$29,389.30}$$
$$= .262 = 26.2\%$$

This procedure can be used by the owners and managers of even the smallest bars because it entails a minimum of paperwork and calculation. The basic requirements are simple records of beverage purchases and a par stock at the bar. This par stock can be maintained rather easily by issuing full bottles in exchange for empties, as discussed in the preceding chapter. From the point of view of a beverage controller, it is not the ideal approach, but it does enable the owner or manager of an establishment to determine beverage cost percent for a period even if there is no staff member available to keep extensive daily records of issues.

Many managers find that these simple procedures result in beverage costs and beverage cost percents that are not sufficiently accurate for their particular operations. They feel a need to take into account some or all of the adjustments described below. By doing so, they derive beverage cost figures of the degree of accuracy they require.

ADJUSTMENTS TO BEVERAGE COST.   There are various possible adjustments to beverage cost, as identified below:

Food and Beverage Transfers.   One reason that some do not consider the beverage cost figures above sufficiently accurate is that they do not include the cost of all ingredients used in drink production. They argue that accurate beverage costs would include the cost of such food items as oranges, lemons, eggs, and heavy cream, which are commonly used to make drinks but are typically purchased by the food department and transferred to the bar. The cost of these items can be significant and should be included in beverage cost, not food cost. To do so, one keeps records of the transfer of these food items from the kitchen to the bar. At the end of the accounting period, the total value of these items is added to beverage cost and subtracted from food cost. For those food items issued directly from food stores to the bar, such as olives, cocktail cherries, and pearl onions, separate bar requisitions are prepared, typically on paper of a different color from that used for food requisitions. When these additional records are maintained, provision must be made for adding the cost of these items to the beverage cost as well. The effect of their use is reflected in beverage sales, so their cost should properly be reflected in beverage cost.

In many hotels and restaurants, alcoholic beverages are used as ingredients in food production. It is rare to find supplies of these beverages kept in a kitchen. Instead, appropriate quantities of these ingredients are simply obtained from the bar when needed. If the value of the quantities used is deemed significant, separate records of these transfers are maintained as well. In a restaurant featuring a different parfait each day and using some quantity of a liqueur from the bar to prepare it, records of the liqueurs used and their values could be kept on transfer memos. These values would be subtracted from beverage cost figures and added to food cost.

Other Adjustments.   Other possibilities for additions to cost include:

1. Any foods used in beverage preparation, but not included in transfer memo.
2. Cost of mixers, if not included as transfers.

Possibilities for subtractions from cost include:

1. Cost of any drinks consumed by managers that should more properly be charged to entertainment or to business promotion. In the event that sales revenue has been recorded for such drinks, this revenue should probably be subtracted from beverage sales and written off.
2. Cost of the beverages used in other promotional activities, such as free drinks to couples celebrating 50th wedding anniversaries, complimentary drinks offered to diners ordering before 5:30 P.M., and so on.

Taking into account a variety of the adjustments described above, the cost of beverages sold would be determined as illustrated in Figure 16.1.

For Shelly's, beverage cost percent equals adjusted beverage cost of $7,640.00 divided by beverage sales of $29,389.30, or 26.0 percent.

Once the beverage cost percent for a period has been calculated, it may be compared to the beverage cost percent for other, similar periods to evaluate the extent to which current results measure up to past results. If, for example, the beverage cost percent for the current period is 26.0 percent and records indicate that the beverage cost percent for each of the last six months has been between 25.8 percent and 27.0 percent, a manager would be likely to conclude that the results for the current period were satisfactory, provided that the past results had been considered satisfactory. However, if there had been some dramatic change in the beverage cost percent (an increase of 5 percent, for

COST OF LIQUOR CONSUMED		$7,700
ADD:		
Food to bar (Directs)		220
Storeroom issues		105
Mixers		525
	Subtotal	$8,550
LESS:		
Cooking liquor		335
Officers' drinks		110
Special promotions		465
COST OF BEVERAGES SOLD		$7,640

FIGURE 16.1   *Calculation of Cost with Adjustments*

example) and the change were both unexpected and undesirable, the manager would try to find the reasons for the change. If causes can be identified, appropriate corrective actions can be taken to bring beverage costs back into line by the end of the next accounting period and to keep them in line in the future.

COST CALCULATIONS BY CATEGORY.   A number of managers believe that one single figure for beverage cost is too general to be of maximum value for their operations. They prefer to separate the beverage cost figure into its three components: cost of spirits, cost of wines, and cost of beers. By doing so and by similarly separating beverage sales figures, one can calculate individual cost-to-sales ratios for these three categories. The cost-to-sales ratios for these three may differ significantly from one another, and changes from one period to another may not be apparent in a single cost percent figure that includes all three. Given appropriate data, a form such as that illustrated in Figure 16.2 may be used both to distribute cost and sales figures for these three major categories and to facilitate adjusting costs in the manner previously discussed.

In Chapter 15, in the discussion of standard drink recipes and standard costs for drinks, the point was made that standard costs were useful for determining sales prices for drinks. If, for example, prices for drinks made with spirits had been determined with a target cost percent of 20.0 percent, the single 26.0 percent cost-to-sales ratio identified earlier in this chapter would not be useful for evaluating whether or not that cost percent was being achieved. However, if the costs, sales, and adjustments for all wines and beers can be factored out, as in Figure 16.2, one can determine the cost percent for spirits alone for a period—in this case, 20.3 percent. A comparison of this figure to the 20.0 percent target suggests that the actual cost of drinks made with spirits nearly conforms to planned cost. Determining component cost percents makes

Beverage Sales:			
	Sales	*Adjustments*	*Net Sales*
Spirits	$20,572.50	$260.00	$20,312.50
Wine	5,877.80	50.00	5,827.80
Beer	2,939.00	50.00	2,879.00
Total sales	$29,389.30	$370.00	$29,019.30

Cost of Beverages Sold:				
	Spirits	*Wines*	*Beer*	*Total*
COST OF ISSUES	$3,496.30	$3,250.00	$953.70	$7,700.00
Adjustments:				
ADDITIONS				
Food to bar (Directs)	220.00	—	—	220.00
Storeroom issues	105.00	—	—	105.00
Mixers	525.00	—	—	525.00
Subtotal	850.00	- 0 -	- 0 -	850.00
SUBTRACTIONS				
Bar to kitchen	45.00	220.00	70.00	335.00
Officers' drinks	65.00	25.00	20.00	110.00
Special promotions	105.00	360.00	—	465.00
Subtotal	215.00	605.00	90.00	910.00
NET ADJUSTMENTS	635.00	(605.00)	(90.00)	(60.00)
NET COST OF SALES	4,131.30	2,645.00	863.70	7,640.00
COST PERCENT	20.3%	45.4%	30.0%	26.3%
COST PER DOLLAR SALE	$.203	$.454	$.30	$.263

FIGURE 16.2 *Cost Calculation by Category*

these kinds of comparisons possible and facilitates evaluation of the effectiveness of the cost control measures instituted.

DAILY CALCULATIONS. Analyzing the beverage cost-to-sales ratio just once each month presents some problems. The normal month is an accumulation of 30 or 31 yesterdays, and by the time the results of all those yesterdays are summarized in monthly cost and cost percent figures, it is too late to do anything about them. By the time monthly figures reveal that operating results for a previous month were disastrous, nothing can be done to change those results. If, for example, the results for October have been terrible, the best a manager can hope to do is to show improvement in November and December and thus offset the poor results for October. It may be possible to offset the effects to some extent over the course of a year by striving for improved results in upcoming months, but nothing can be done to change the past.

It would clearly be preferable to have some indication of the probable beverage cost-to-sales ratio before the end of a period so that efforts could be made to improve operations while there was still time for the improvements to affect the figures for the current period. This is the aim of procedures for the daily calculation of beverage cost and cost percent.

If a manager obtained cost and cost percent figures for the first 10 days of a month and these figures indicated unsatisfactory operating results, corrective actions could conceivably be taken in time to have a positive impact on the final figures for the period. In some large operations with staff to maintain the necessary records, beverage cost and cost percent are calculated daily. It is not difficult to do: If beverages are issued to the bar daily on the basis of requisitions that accompany the empty bottles, it is rather easy to determine beverage costs daily. After beverages have been issued, unit costs are recorded on the requisitions, which are then extended and totaled to determine the cost of the issues for one day. This figure is recorded as the cost of beverages sold on the preceding day. After a beverage sales figure for the day is obtained, beverage cost and sales figures are used to determine a beverage cost percent for the day.

It is obvious that the figures obtained in this way are less than completely accurate. After all, an assumption has been made that every ounce in every empty bottle was sold on the preceding day; this does not account for the possibility that the contents of a bottle were probably sold over a period of several days. The daily cost percentage is therefore unreliable. However, if figures for the cost of daily issues are accumulated daily for all the days thus far in a period and if the same procedure is followed with daily sales, it becomes possible to determine beverage cost percent for all the days thus far in the period. This new cost percent, **beverage cost percent to date,** is a more accurate and reliable figure. Cumulative cost and sales figures developed in this way tend to reduce the degree of inaccuracy inherent in figures for one single day. This approach, illustrated in Figure 16.3, provides a reasonably reliable picture of overall operations.

A more accurate picture of daily operations could be obtained if management could take daily inventory of the stock at the bar and determine a daily bar inventory differential analogous to the monthly differential discussed earlier in this chapter. If one could subtract a closing bar inventory for a given day from an opening bar inventory for that day, the daily bar inventory differential obtained could be added (or subtracted, in the case of a negative figure) to the daily issue figure to determine daily cost with greater accuracy.

If daily bar inventory differentials were used, it would be necessary to add two more columns to the form illustrated in Figure 16.3. These would be inserted between the two columns headed "Date" and "Cost Today" and would be headed "Beverage Issues" and "Bar Inventory Differential". With the addition of these, "Cost Today" would become a net figure, incorporating daily

Date	Cost		Sales		Cost %	
	Today	To Date	Today	To Date	Today	To Date
11/1	$300		$900		33.4%	
11/2	240	$ 540	970	$1,870	24.8%	28.4%
11/3	220	760	920	2,790	23.8%	27.3%
11/4	225	985	995	3,785	22.6%	26.0%
11/5	170	1,155	930	4,715	18.3%	24.5%
11/6	190	1,345	920	5,635	20.7%	23.9%

FIGURE 16.3 *Daily Cost Calculations*

issues and bar differential. This would yield a greater degree of accuracy in the figures for beverage cost percent for the day and for the period to date.

Cost percent to date reflects the net effect of all costs and all sales for the number of days thus far in the period. It is reasonable to compare this figure to cost percents to date for equivalent periods in the recent past. If this comparison reveals unsatisfactory performance in the current period, corrective action can be initiated to improve performance in the days remaining in the period. If this is done, it is possible that the final figures at the end of the period will be more acceptable than they might have been otherwise.

Adjustments to Cost. Just as a number of adjustments can be made to monthly figures, so, too, can daily figures be adjusted by those who prefer more precise numbers. If the records required as the basis for adjustments are available (transfer memos, sales checks, and the like), the form illustrated in Figure 16.3 could be expanded to that illustrated in Figure 16.4.

Figure 16.4 makes provision for adjusting the daily cost of beverage issues. It can be increased by recording such items as transfers of direct purchases (directs) from the kitchen to the bar, mixers purchased directly for the bar, and food storeroom issues to the bar in the "Additions" column. If bar inventory were taken daily, positive bar inventory differentials would be in-

Date	Beverages Issued	Additions	Subtractions	Total Cost		Sales		Cost %	
				Today	To Date	Today	To Date	Today	To Date
11/1	$300	$10	$35	$275		$900		30.6%	
11/2	$240	$20	$25	$235	$ 510	$970	$1,870	24.2%	27.3%
11/3	$220	$10	$20	$210	$ 720	$920	$2,790	22.8%	25.8%
11/4	$225	$ 5	$10	$220	$ 940	$995	$3,785	22.1%	24.8%
11/5	$170	$10	$15	$165	$1,105	$930	$4,715	17.7%	23.4%
11/6	$190	$ 5	$ 5	$190	$1,295	$920	$5,635	20.7%	23.0%

FIGURE 16.4 *Daily Cost Calculations with Adjustments*

cluded in this column. In the "Subtractions" column, one would include transfers of beverages to the kitchen (cooking liquor), the cost of drinks attributable to entertainment or promotion, and the cost of complimentary drinks used for special promotions. Negative bar inventory differentials could be included in this column. If desired, individual columns for all of these adjustments could be inserted in place of the two columns illustrated.

Using one or another of these forms, a manager can monitor bar operations, note significant deviations from acceptable norms, and then take corrective action while events are still fresh in the minds of participants and investigations are feasible.

Standard Cost Method

In all of the methods discussed so far, the objective has been to obtain current cost figures to compare with historical figures (the cost percent for the current period with that for a previous period, for example). Actual costs are determined in any of several possible ways, and actual sales figures are used to determine actual cost percents. Judgments made are based on the acceptability of figures for the previous period and on the degree to which current figures match past figures. This is certainly the most common approach to monitoring and controlling beverage costs, but it is not necessarily the most desirable. After all, while current figures may compare favorably to figures for a number of previous periods, there is no adequate way of evaluating the figures for previous periods. Figures for previous periods may reflect any number of unknown problems, and the comparison of current to past figures may merely confirm that past problems continue to exist. There is a clear need for a method that can be used to determine the extent to which problems exist. In short, some more reliable means for evaluating current costs is needed.

The standard cost method is a better means for evaluating beverage costs and judging the effectiveness of control procedures. By using this method, managers can compare actual cost for a period with standard cost for that period. It can be used only by those who have established standard recipes and have calculated standard costs for all drinks. The standard cost method requires very detailed records of drink sales and considerable calculation.

To calculate standard cost for a given operating period, one would need records of the number of sales of each specific drink sold during the period, as well as the standard cost of each drink. For example, the records of spirit sales would have to show type of drink and brand of liquor. Types of drinks would include cocktails, mixed drinks, and straight shots. Records of beer sales would have to show both bottle sales and draft sales by brand. Equivalent detailed records of wine sales would also be needed. One would also need to know the standard cost of each.

Item	Number Sold	Standard Cost	Total Standard Cost
BOTTLED			
Miller	1,178	$.65	$ 765.70
Budweiser	1,483	.65	963.95
Coors	674	.70	471.80
DRAFT			
Miller	2,005	$.40	$ 802.00
Budweiser	2,361	.40	944.40
		TOTAL	$3,947.85

FIGURE 16.5 *Determination of Standard Beverage Cost: Beer*

With the necessary sales records and standard cost figures available, one could proceed to determine standard cost of beverages sold for the operating period. The first step would be to multiply the number of sales of each type of drink by the standard cost of that drink to find total standard cost for each type of drink. This would be done for each specific type of drink sold during the period. Next, the total standard costs for all drinks would be added to determine total standard cost for the period. In Figure 16.5, the standard cost for one category of drinks, beer, is calculated in this way. The same procedure would be used to calculate standard cost for each of the other categories of drinks.

Once total standard cost for a period has been determined, it can be compared to actual cost for the same period. For example, assume that the actual cost of beer sold in March, was $4,098.90, while standard cost for beer for the period was $3,947.85, as calculated in Figure 16.5. Comparison of the two indicates a difference between actual and standard cost. The amount of the difference can readily be determined by subtraction:

Actual cost	$4,098.90
− Standard cost	3,947.85
= Difference	$ 151.05

It is clear that actual cost is greater than it should be by $151.05. This difference is excessive cost—cost that is greater than warranted given the standards, standard procedures, and standard costs established. Knowing that the cost of beer sold was excessive, a manager could immediately begin to investigate in order the determine the cause. Some of the possible causes include breakage, pilferage, improper storage and handling of draft beers, and failure to record revenue from sales. It is important to identify the causes so that corrective actions can be taken. Corrective actions would obviously be expected to result in improved performance in future periods.

Excessive cost is readily translated to everyday language as wasted money. After all, the excess cost determined above ($151.05) should not have been required to produce these beer sales. This amount could have been used for some other purpose and would have been available for that purpose if employee performance had more nearly matched that anticipated by the standards and standard procedures established by management.

THE LIQUID MEASURE APPROACH

Ounce-Control Method

Another technique for beverage control is the **quantity-** or **ounce-control method.** As practiced some years ago, it required taking daily physical inventory of bar stock, determining the number of ounces consumed each day, and calculating the number of ounces sold each day from detailed sales records. Ideally, of course, the number of ounces consumed should equal the number of ounces sold; in practice, they never equalled one another because of spillage, evaporation, breakage, and any number of other reasons. However, when bar operations were strictly controlled and bar personnel closely followed the standards and standard procedures established by management, the difference was kept to a minimum.

In this form, the ounce-control method has completely disappeared. One obvious reason is that the labor costs associated with it far outweigh the benefits that can be derived. However, modern technology has made possible the reappearance of ounce-control procedures in a variety of forms. Some use meters attached to bottles to measure the quantities used daily. Others require the use of complex and expensive computerized devices that dispenses ingredients, mix drinks, record sales, and maintain bar inventory records automatically. Because complex equipment of this nature generally becomes comparatively less expensive with growing acceptance and use, it is not surprising that a greater numbers of hotels and restaurants are taking advantage of it, particularly for use at service bars.

THE SALES VALUE APPROACH

Another approach to controlling beverage operations is to determine the sales revenue that should be generated by each full bottle of each of the various liquors issued from the storeroom. For example, if the standard drink of gin is one ounce and the pouring brand of gin is issued in one-liter bottles, then each

Bottle Code	Item	Bottle Size	Drink Size	Drinks per Bottle	× Drink Price	= Sales Value per Bottle
301	Dover gin	1 liter	1 oz	33.8	$3.00	$101.40
107	Old Kentucky rye	1 liter	1 oz	33.8	3.00	101.40
217	Loch Ness scotch	750 ml	1 oz	25.4	3.00	76.20
352	Lenin vodka	1 liter	1 oz	33.8	2.75	92.95
456	Burble's brandy	750 ml	1 oz	25.4	3.50	88.90

FIGURE 16.6 *Calculation of Bottle Sales Values*

bottle potentially contains 33.8 drinks. If the sales price for the standard one-ounce drink is $3.00, then the potential sales value of each bottle of the pouring brand issued is equal to 33.8 drinks times $3.00 per drink, or $101.40. Hypothetically, then, each bottle of this gin issued should produce $101.40 in sales. Given standard drink sizes and standard sales prices, it is possible to determine the total revenue that should be generated by the issue of one bottle of any item kept at the bar. Therefore, when an empty bottle of any item is turned in with a requisition for replacement, it should be possible to find the potential sales value for that empty bottles reflected in actual sales. In a simple, hypothetical bar, for example, using only liter bottles and serving only straight drinks in one-ounce shots for $3.00 per drink, the consumption of one bottle each of gin, rye, and scotch should produce $304.20 in sales:

$$3 \text{ bottles} \times 33.8 \text{ oz.} \times \$3.00 = \$304.20$$

Theoretically, one should find $304.20 in sales recorded in the register for the day.

As illustrated in Figure 16.6, it is possible to develop a chart of the standard sales values of bottles sold only by the straight drink.

In practice, such a chart would necessarily include all brands sold at the bar and would obviously be considerably longer than the chart illustrated. However, most bars do not sell spirits only in straight shots. Beverage operations are seldom quite this simple. In most bars, cocktails and other mixed drinks account for some portion of sales, and such drinks require varying quantities of spirits and other ingredients. Therefore, if a control process is to be devised that uses the potential sales values of bottles, some way must be found to account for the complications that result from the production of mixed drinks. The potential sales values of bottles must be adjusted by means of some formula that takes into consideration variations in quantities of spirits used and in sales prices.

In fact, control procedures involving potential sales values are generally quite complex and require considerable time and calculation. For these and other related reasons, they are not commonly used, except in some very large operations. However, some basic understanding of these procedures is necessary for anyone seeking to acquire a complete overview of beverage control. The major problem is to establish the sales values. Three different methods for doing so will be discussed here.

The first requires that potential sales values be established on the basis of sales of straight shots only and then adjusted daily or periodically by the means of a so-called mixed drink differential. These adjustments to the values of bottles issued and consumed are made after sales have taken place. The second method requires analyzing sales for a test period and determining weighted average values for bottles in advance, based on historical sales records. The third method is really a modification of the second and is generally easier and more practical to use. However, it is sufficiently different from the second to warrant separate discussion.

Actual Sales Record Method

If standard recipes are used to prepare drinks and detailed sales records are available, one can calculate the sales value of the ingredients in each type of drink sold. For example, the preparation of a screwdriver may require one ounce of vodka. Assume that vodka as a straight drink is sold in one-ounce measures for $2.75, and the screwdriver sells for $3.50. The sales value of the vodka is $2.75. The difference, $.75, is known as a **mixed drink differential.** Each time a screwdriver is sold, sales revenue will be $.75 greater than it would have been if the one ounce of vodka had been sold as a straight shot. Mixed drink differential is defined as the difference between the sales price of a given drink and the sales value of its primary ingredient if sold as a straight shot.

Once the sales value of the primary ingredient in a drink has been determined, it is possible to determine the mixed drink differential for that drink: subtract the sales value of the primary ingredient from the sales price of the drink. Assume that gin is the primary ingredient in a martini and that the sales value for the 1 1/2 ounces of gin in the martini is $4.50 as a straight drink of gin. The sales price of the martini is $4.00. Therefore, the mixed drink differential for a gin martini is a negative $.50. Each sale of that particular drink decreases potential revenue by $.50. That is to say, each time a martini is sold,

Bottle Code No.	Item	Bottles Consumed	Sales Value per Bottle	Total Sales Value
301	Gin	3	$101.40	$304.02
107	Rye	2	101.40	202.80
352	Vodka	2	92.95	185.90
			TOTAL	$692.90

Mixed Drink	Primary Ingredient	Ounces of Primary Ingredient	Straight Drink Price	Mixed Drink Price	Mixed Drink Differential	Number Sold	Total Differential
Martini	gin	1.5	$4.50	$4.00	− $.50	5	− $ 2.50
Screw driver	vodka	1	$2.75	$3.50	+ $.75	18	+ $13.50
Martini	vodka	1.5	$4.13	$4.00	− $.13	3	− $ .39
						TOTAL	+ $10.61

SALES VALUES ADJUSTED BY DIFFERENTIALS

SALES VALUES OF EMPTY BOTTLES FROM BAR $692.90
ADJUSTMENT FOR MIXED DRINK DIFFERENTIALS   +   10.61
                                                                              + $703.51

FIGURE 16.7   *Daily Analysis of Potential Sales Values*

the sales revenue is $.50 less than it would have been is the gin in the martini had been sold as a straight drink.

Thus, to determine potential sales value of the quantity of gin sold, one must subtract $.50 for each martini sold. The differential for each type of drink must be calculated and recorded for frequent reference.

Each day, after sales have been analyzed—either from guest checks or from the register—the number of drinks of each type sold is multiplied by the differential for that drink, and the total bottle sales value for spirits consumed is increased by the total of all positive differentials and decreased by the total of all negative differentials.

Figure 16.7 illustrates the use of the method for calculating potential sales values. Bottle code numbers, item names, and numbers of bottles consumed are taken from the bar requisition. Sales values per bottle are taken from a chart similar to that shown in Figure 16.6. Total sales values for the bottles consumed are determined by multiplying the number of empty bottles of each primary ingredient by the potential sales value per bottle. These are totaled to

PRIMARY INGREDIENT: gin					
Drinks	*No. Sold*	*Ounces/ Drink*	*Total Ounces*	*Drink Price*	*Total Sales*
Martini	90	1.5	135	$4.00	$360.00
Straight shots	150	1	150	$3.00	450.00
		TOTALS	285		$810.00

FIGURE 16.8   *Analysis of Actual Sales (Gin)*

find sales values of the empty bottles from the bar. Next, this total is adjusted for mixed drink sales, as shown in the lower half of the form. Mixed drink differential for each type of drink is multiplied by the number sold to determine total differential per item. These, in turn, are added. In some instances the differential is negative and is subtracted. The net of these two figures is the differential for the day, which is combined with the sales values of empty bottles to obtain an adjusted potential sales value. This adjusted potential sales value should be very close to the actual sales figure recorded in the bar register.

Determining potential sales values by this method requires considerable work each day. Although it results in highly accurate figures to use for evaluating actual sales data, it is somewhat cumbersome for day-to-day use in most establishments. Many who formerly used it have concluded that some simplification of this very complex method would make it more feasible to use. Therefore, a method was developed that used average potential sales values instead of potential sales values adjusted for actual mixed drink sales.

Average Sales Value Method

This method eliminates the need for daily sales analysis and daily calculation of a net mixed drink differential. Instead, it depends on results determined during a test period when careful records are kept of the number of drinks sold of each type. These records serve as the basis for determining the average potential sales value of each bottle. Figure 16.8 illustrates the method used to analyze drink sales for the test period.

Assuming that actual drink sales during the test period truly represent the sales mix, a determination of the average sales value for one ounce of gin can be made by dividing 285 ounces sold into $810.00 total sales. In this case, the average sales value for one ounce of gin is $2.84. Because this primary ingredient is purchased and used by the liter, the average sales value of each liter is 33.8 ounces multiplied by the average sales value of each ounce, or $95.99. In some operations, the individual doing these calculations would use a figure one ounce less than the actual number of ounces in the bottle (32.8 for

Bottle Code	Item	Bottle Size	Average Potential Sales Value
301	Dover gin	1 liter	$95.99
107	Old Kentucky rye	1 liter	97.38
217	Loch Ness scotch	750 ml	82.60
352	Lenin vodka	1 liter	92.57
456	Burble's brandy	750 ml	85.75

FIGURE 16.9 *Chart of Average Potential Sales Value of Bottles*

the one-liter bottle, for example) in order to account for unavoidable spillage and evaporation. Many feel that this approach results in average sales values that are more realistic.

Once these calculations have been completed for all primary ingredients consumed during the test period, a chart is prepared showing the average sales value of each bottle used in the bar. Figure 16.9 illustrates a chart of this type.

This would be used in place of the chart of standard sales values of bottles sold only by the straight drink, illustrated previously in Figure 16.6. Once these average potential sales values have been established, it is comparatively easy to determine the potential sales value of the bottles consumed at the bar each

Bottle Code	Item	Bottles Consumed	×	Sale Value per Bottle	=	Total Sales Value
301	Dover gin	3		$95.99		$287.97
107	Old Kentucky rye	2		97.38		194.76
352	Lenin vodka	2		92.57		185.14
					TOTAL	$667.87

FIGURE 16.10 *Procedure for Determining Total Sales Value*

day. One simply multiplies the number of empty bottles of each brand by the potential sales value per bottle, as shown on the chart. Figure 16.10 illustrates a form that can be used to organize the work required to determine a daily total.

Once determined, this total potential sales figure for the day would be compared to actual sales for the day, as previously discussed. The manager making the comparison would be watching for any significant difference between actual and potential sales that would suggest some deviation from the standards and standard procedures established for bar operation.

Although the average potential sales value method is more common than the method requiring the calculation of mixed drink differential, its use is by no means universal. Although simpler to use, the average potential sales value method still requires a great many calculations and is not practical unless the work involved can be assigned to one individual who has the time to do it each day. Most establishments lack the staff to do it. In addition, the average potential sales value method is useful only if the sales mix at the bar remains relatively stable. Major changes in the sales mix because of changing times and changing customer preferences make the calculated averages inaccurate. When this is the case, new average potential sales values must be calculated from data collected during a new test period.

Standard Deviation Method

In the interest of further simplifying and eliminating frequent and time-consuming sales analyses of the types discussed, some managers have adapted one of the basic tools of statistics for beverage control purposes. The result is the method described below that appeals to many beverage managers because it is comparatively simple to use.

Use of this method requires the establishment of a test period during which the manager takes all appropriate steps to ensure strict employee adherence to all standards and standard procedures for bar operation. In addition, all phases of bar operation are kept under close observation during the period to ensure compliance. At the conclusion of the test period, the number of bottles consumed is determined from records of inventory, purchases, and issues. Next, a potential sales value is determined for each type and brand of beverage issued. This potential sales value is based on bottle contents sold as straight drinks. The procedure for determining potential sales value is the same as that explained earlier in the chapter: If drinks are sold in one-ounce shots for $3.00 per shot, then the sales value of a one-liter bottle containing 33.8 ounces is $101.40. Next, the total number of bottles of each type and brand consumed during the test period is translated into total potential sales values by multiplying the number of bottles by the potential sales value of the bottle.

After determining a total for each type and brand, these totals are added to determine a total potential sales value for all bottles consumed during this test period. The next step is to compare this figure to the actual sales revenue for the test period. Typically, the potential sales figure is greater than actual sales, and the difference between the two is assumed to reflect the sale of cocktails and other mixed drinks, as well as the normal spillage to be expected at the bar. Because the bar operation has been under careful observation throughout the test period, this difference is taken as a standard difference, which can be used in the future for purposes of comparison. The difference is divided by the potential sales figure to determine, as a percentage, the extent of the deviation from the potential. If, for example, potential sales value were $10,000 and actual sales were $9,500, the $500 difference would be divided by $10,000 to determine that the difference amounted to 5.0 percent. Expressed in another way, one could say that actual sales during the test period were 5-percent less than potential sales. By reducing the potential sales figure by 5 percent to account for normal spillage and the sale of cocktails and other mixed drinks, one can develop an adjusted potential sales figure, which can be used to monitor bar operations in the future as long as the sales mix remains fairly constant.

Using this approach, one can calculate potential sales values for bottles consumed, adjust for the standard difference determined during the test period, and use the resulting figures to determine the extent to which bar operations are measuring up to expectations. As long as the sales mix does not change significantly, this approach makes it possible to monitor operations without dealing with extensive and elaborate calculations of the sort described earlier in the chapter. However, if there are major discrepancies between actual sales revenue and adjusted potential sales values of bottles consumed, using one of the more complex methods may be required to determine the causes.

One important advantage to this method is that, when necessary, the differential can be recalculated with comparative ease. As customers' tastes change and the sales mix changes accordingly, it is comparatively simple to establish a new test period and calculate a new differential to use for monitoring operations. Also, as costs or sales prices change, this differential as a percentage of potential sales should remain relatively constant.

Regardless of the techniques involved in their calculation, potential sales figures can be useful for monitoring bar operations. When compared to actual sales figures, they provide a means for measuring the extent to which actual operations are meeting management's expectations. For example, if actual sales of $14,000 are compared to potential sales of $15,000, it is apparent that the actual falls short of the potential by $1,000, or 6.7 percent. It is the responsibility of the manager in a particular beverage operation to determine how great a difference is to be tolerated. Assuming that a potential sales figure is reasonably reliable, a difference between that and the actual sales figures is likely to mean that employees are not using beverages—the raw materials of drink production—in the manner prescribed by the manager. It could also mean that sales are being recorded incorrectly or that sales are not being recorded at all. The difference between actual and potential sales figures reflects operational problems of all sorts, including failure to mix according to standard recipes, excessive spillage, errors in filling orders, overpouring, general waste, and even outright theft. Every one of these problems should be of concern to a manager, who should be taking steps to eliminate them. In most operations, however, some difference between actual and potential sales figures is inevitable. The question becomes one of determining the extent of the difference that can be tolerated. This will vary considerably from one beverage operation to another. In some, a difference of 1 percent between actual and potential sales may cause extreme concern and lead to careful and detailed analysis of all phases of the operation. In others, a 3 percent difference may be considered within the limits of tolerance. In general, managers are usually less tolerant of differences arising from failure to record sales. Poor pouring and mixing techniques may be a result of the pressures of business at the bar. But failure to record sales commonly indicates an intention to steal. For this reason, bar managers do not normally see it as an acceptable reason for the difference between actual and potential sales.

INVENTORY TURNOVER

While it is obviously important to monitor bar operations by one or another of the means identified above, no manager can afford to focus on these alone. Most managers would agree that it is important to monitor the size, value, and use of the beverage inventory on a regular basis. After all, one would not want to maintain a beverage inventory that was too large for the sales volume generated. A beverage inventory can easily reach excessive size and excessive value if beverage purchases are not suitably matched to beverage issues.

If beverage purchases are greater than warranted by beverage issues and sales volume, the value of a beverage inventory can quickly become excessive. When too much money has been spent to purchase unwarranted quantities of beverages, it should be quite clear that money has been expended unproductively. The funds could have been used more productively for other purposes.

On the other hand, if the beverage inventory is not large enough, more frequent ordering of comparatively small quantities may be necessary, and this often means paying higher unit prices. Such ordering can also result in higher labor costs and increased costs for processing orders. Moreover, if the stock of some beverages is allowed to run too low, it may result in lost sales.

Suppose, for example, that the manager of Queezee's Bar has records indicating that consumption of Lesser Lager, a popular local beer, amounts to approximately 60 cases per month. Because this brand is known to have a very limited shelf life, it is apparent that an inventory of 600 cases would be too large. However, an inventory of 2 cases would clearly be too small unless daily delivery was possible.

Beverage managers require some routine procedure for monitoring the adequacy of beverage inventories. The normal method for doing this is to determine a turnover rate for the beverage inventory each month and to watch for significant changes.

The turnover rate for a beverage inventory is calculated by means of the same formulas used for calculating turnover rate for a food inventory. These were identified and discussed in detail in Chapter 9. The formulas are as follows:

$$\text{Turnover rate} = \frac{\text{Cost of beverages sold for a period}}{\text{Average inventory for the period}}$$

$$\text{Average inventory} = \frac{\text{Opening inventory} + \text{Closing inventory}[1]}{2}$$

For example, given opening inventory of $4,800, closing inventory of $5,600, and cost of beverages sold of $5,720, turnover rate would be calculated as follows:

$$\text{Average inventory} = \frac{\$4,800 + \$5,600}{2}$$

$$= \frac{\$10,400}{2}$$

$$= \$5,200$$

$$\text{Turnover rate} = \frac{\$5,720}{\$5,200}$$

$$= 1.1$$

This calculation yields the turnover rate for one month. One can infer from this that the average inventory is being consumed at the approximate rate of 13.2 times per year—just under once a month. Some individual items are consumed at higher rates, while the rate for others would be lower. However, on average, the overall inventory is being turned over 1.1 times per month.

---

[1]For accuracy, both opening inventory and closing inventory figures should include the values of all beverages in the beverage storeroom and at the bar.

While many beverage managers use this single turnover rate, calculated for the beverage inventory in its entirety, others find it useful to calculate separate turnover rates for the three principal components of the beverage inventory: spirits, beers, and wines. Generally accepted monthly turnover rates for spirits and beers are:

Spirits—1.5
Beers—2.0

For a spirits inventory, a monthly turnover rate of 1.0 or less normally indicates an inventory larger than necessary for the current volume of business. This suggests that too many dollars have been used to purchase unneeded quantities of spirits—dollars that might better have been used for some other purpose. Some will disagree, of course, arguing that if it is possible to obtain a sufficiently large discount by increasing the size of purchases, it may be perfectly appropriate to increase purchase quantities and temporarily to accept a lower than normal turnover rate.

If the monthly turnover rate is 2.0 or higher, it is quite possible that the inventory is smaller than it should be, which could lead to frequent purchasing, possibly at higher prices than might have been obtained by purchasing larger quantities.

Because beers are perishable products that lose quality with age, monthly turnover rates for beers should be higher. Many beverage managers prefer to purchase beers weekly, a system that results in higher turnover rates with fewer dollars committed to inventory at any one time. Most would find a monthly turnover rate of 2.0 to be acceptable.

There is no accepted monthly turnover rate for wines. Some hotels and restaurants maintain extensive inventories of vintage wines, purchased young and stored in wine cellars until they reach maturity; others offer more common wines, purchased for immediate use and turned over frequently; still many others stock a great variety of wines—some very fine and others simple table wines. The range of possibilities is too great for any accepted turnover rate to be determined.

COMPUTER APPLICATIONS

Virtually any of the methods for monitoring beverage operations illustrated and discussed in this chapter may be integrated into a computer-based control system. In fact, many chain organizations, franchises, and independent operators use computers to one extent or another to monitor bar operations. Some merely monitor sales, a topic that will be discussed in Chapter 17. Growing numbers of others use computers to monitor the cost of beverage operation.

Some managers maintain computer-based perpetual inventories of beverages, as discussed previously. This may be done by means of a generic database program or the function may be incorporated into a beverage control package. A large chain might hire a programming firm to develop a database for its specific needs; a large, individually owned hotel or restaurant might purchase one of the beverage inventory programs that one sees at the hotel and restaurant trade shows. A small individual operator might simply use one of the generic database programs. Assuming timely and accurate data entry for purchases and issues during a period, a printout of the perpetual inventory could be obtained to compare to the monthly physical inventory. Differences would show the extent of deviations from standard control procedures.

To determine monthly cost, one must value the monthly physical inventory, a time-consuming task if done manually. However, any standard spreadsheet program can be used to maintain perpetual inventory and to value the physical inventory. So, too, can several of the beverage control packages available today from various software developers.

Spreadsheets can also be used for calculating daily cost percents in the manner illustrated in Figures 16.3 and 16.4. Once the spreadsheet is set up, one merely records figures daily for issues, adjustments, and sales. The next logical step, printing a daily report for management, is easy. The standard cost methods for monitoring beverage operations would be particularly difficult to use if one did not have a computer-based file of standard drink recipes and their costs, along with detailed records of sales showing the number of drinks of each type sold daily and for the period. The latter is best obtained from a computerized sales terminal.

The ounce-control and sales value methods, which have seldom been used in recent years because of the considerable time and high labor costs they require, may return to favor with the increasing use of computers for beverage control. Manual calculations consumed far too many hours to justify the adoption of these methods, but growing acceptance of beverage control software substantially improves the outlook for their increased use.

CHAPTER ESSENTIALS

In this chapter, we identified the three general approaches to measuring the effectiveness of beverage controls: cost, liquid measure, and sales values. We described and illustrated calculations for several cost-based methods, including monthly cost and cost percent, daily cost and cost percent, and standard cost. We illustrated the ounce-control method and discussed its limitations. We explained three methods for using potential sales values to monitor beverage operations: actual sales record method, average sales value method, and standard deviation method. We demonstrated the determination of beverage inventory turnover rate and discussed its use as a monitoring device.

Finally, we discussed computer-based applications of the various methods illustrated in the chapter and pointed out the impracticality of attempting several of the methods without computers.

KEY TERMS IN THIS CHAPTER

Actual beverage cost
Actual sales record method
Average inventory
Average potential sales value
Average sales value method
Beverage cost percent
Food and beverage transfers
Inventory differential
Inventory turnover
Inventory turnover method
Mixed drink differential
Ounce-control method
Potential sales value
Primary ingredient
Standard cost method
Standard deviation method

QUESTIONS AND PROBLEMS

1. Given the information below, determine beverage cost in each of the three bars.

Storeroom Inventory Data

	Opening Inventory	Purchases	Closing Inventory
Art's	$5,000	$ 8,000	$7,000
Ben's	$8,325	$10,666	$9,327
Carol's	$4,872	$ 7,454	$3,856

Bar Data

	Opening Inventory	Closing Inventory
Art's	$1,000	$1,000
Ben's	$2,325	$2,050
Carol's	$1,867	$1,988

2. Using the costs determined in Question 1, calculate beverage cost percent if:

a. The sales figure in Art's is $20,000.
b. The sales figure in Ben's is $41,412.50.
c. The sales figure in Carol's is $29,817.85.

3. Using the figures from Questions 1 and 2, as well as the adjustments given below, calculate adjusted cost of beverages sold following the format provided in Figure 16.1 and then calculate beverage cost percent based on adjusted costs.

Arts

Food to bar (directs)	$200
Issues from food storeroom	150
Mixers	475
Cooking liquor	110
Managers' drinks	120
Special promotions	160

Ben's

Mixer's	$925
Food to bar (directs)	500
Cooking liquor	335
Special promotions	320

Carol's

Special promotions	$285
Issues from food storeroom	235
Managers' drinks	165
Mixers	695
Cooking liquor	185

4. Use the information given below to prepare a report showing costs, sales, and adjustments by category, using the form illustrated in Figure 16.2.

Total beverage sales: $42,320, of which 10% represents beer sales, 18% represents wine sales, and the balance represents spirits sales.

Total adjustments to sales: $424, of which 8% is allocated to beer sales, 12% to wine sales, and the balance to spirits sales.

Total cost of issues: $10,500, of which 55% is allocated to spirits, 35% to wines, and the balance to beer.

Mixers	$865
Food to bar (directs)	305

Bar to kitchen   440
Special promotions   520

Mixers and food to bar (directs) are all adjustments to spirits alone, but figures for bar to kitchen and special promotions must be allocated as follows:

Bar to kitchen: 70% to wines, 10% to beer, and the balance to spirits.

Special promotions: 60% to wines and 40% to spirits.

5. Using Figure 16.3 as a guide, prepare a cumulative and daily cost-to-sales ratio chart given the following information.

Date	Cost	Sales
10/1	$250	$ 910
10/2	225	850
10/3	270	920
10/4	290	1,070
10/5	240	900

6. Using the figures in Question 5, prepare a chart in the form illustrated in Figure 16.4 to include the following additional information.

Date	Food Transferred to Bar	Liquor Transferred to Kitchen
10/1	$15	$25
10/2	$10	$30
10/3	$12	$45
10/4	$20	$10
10/5	$ 8	$18

7. Determine the potential sales values of the bottle issues listed below, assuming that only one-ounce shots were poured, one-liter bottles were issued, and the sales price for all straight shots was $2.95.

Liquor	Number of Bottles Issued
Gin	5
Scotch	3
Canadian	4
Rye	3
Vodka	4
Bourbon	2

8. During the period covered by the issues identified in Question 7, the following mixed drinks were served:

Gin martinis:	20
Vodka martinis:	10

Manhattan cocktails
(prepared with rye whiskey):   25
Whiskey sours: 13
Rob Roys: 16

The sales price for each of these mixed drinks was $3.00. However, all martinis and Manhattans contain 1½ ounces of liquor, and all whiskey sours and Rob Roys contain 2 ounces of liquor. Use this information and any additional information required from Question 7 to prepare an analysis of potential sales values in the form illustrated in Figure 16.7.

9. a. Using the sales data provided below, prepare a chart in the form illustrated in Figure 16.8.

Drinks Prepared	Number Sold	Ounces per Drink	Drink Price
Martinis	20	2	$4.95
Straight shots	120	1.5	$3.00

   b. Using the average sales value method determine the potential sales value of 12 one-liter bottles of gin.

10. a. Compute the deviation from potential sales, as described in the text, given the following information for a recent test period:
        Actual sales for period = $12,000
        Potential sales based on straight shots = $12,500
    b. What should actual sales be if the potential sales based on straight shots in Question 10a were $9,000?

11. Refer to the figures provided in Question 1. Using this information, calculate inventory turnover for each of the three bars. Be sure to take both bar and storeroom inventories into account when determining average inventory.

12. According to the chapter, there are three general approaches one can take to monitoring beverage operations. List the three, and discuss each briefly.

13. Most bar managers are interested in their monthly cost percents. Why? For what purpose is the figure used?

14. Why is it necessary to take bar inventory differential into account when calculating the cost of beverages sold?

15. The beverage manager of the Smart Hotel uses a single beverage

cost percent for the entire month to monitor beverage operations. What are the disadvantages of relying exclusively on this figure as a means for monitoring operations?

16. Would you advise a bar manager who relied wholly on the monthly cost percent as a monitoring device to consider adopting a daily method? Why? What would be the advantages and disadvantages of the daily method, compared to the monthly?

17. Compared to the cost percent methods, would you consider the standard cost method more useful or less useful for monitoring operations? Why?

18. Compare and contrast the advantages of the average sales value method with those of the standard deviation method for measuring the effectiveness of beverage controls.

19. Define each of the following terms:
    Actual beverage cost
    Actual sales record method
    Average inventory
    Average potential sales value
    Average sales value method
    Beverage cost percent
    Food and beverage transfers
    Inventory differential
    Inventory turnover
    Inventory turnover method
    Mixed drink differential
    Ounce-control method
    Potential sales value
    Primary ingredient
    Standard cost method
    Standard deviation method

FOR COMPUTER USERS

20. Using any spreadsheet program of your choice, prepare a worksheet using the dollar values and the format of Figure 16.4.

21. Use the worksheet template prepared for Question 19 to solve Questions 5 and 6.

17

Beverage Sales Control

LEARNING OBJECTIVES

After reading and studying this chapter, you should be able to:

1. List and explain the three goals of beverage sales control.
2. Identify five explanations given by customers for patronizing establishments that serve drinks.
3. Describe the specific steps that bar managers can take to attract particular market segments.
4. Describe two methods that can be used to maximize profits in beverage operations.
5. Identify two important factors normally taken into account when establishing beverage sales prices.
6. Name 10 work practices considered unacceptable at bars because they inhibit the ability of bar managers to institute effective revenue controls.
7. Identify the two basic operating patterns for bars that help determine management's approach to revenue control.
8. Describe the essential features of a pre-check system.
9. List the advantages and disadvantages of automated bars compared to more traditional methods of mixing and pouring drinks.
10. Describe one common computerized beverage sales control system.
11. Define each of the Key Terms at the end of the chapter.

413

INTRODUCTION

In previous chapters, we pointed out that establishing control over any phase of food and beverage operations requires that one have some understanding of management's objectives. Any controls established must be carefully designed to ensure that they facilitate reaching these objectives. This is true for the standards and standard procedures developed for sales control. A good beginning point, then, is to identify the objectives of beverage sales control.

THE OBJECTIVES OF BEVERAGE SALES CONTROL

In the discussion of food sales control in an earlier chapter, it was pointed out that many consider that food sales control has a single objective—revenue control—ensuring that each individual sale to a customer results in appropriate revenue to the establishment. In the earlier discussion, our position was that sales control is much more than a mere synonym for revenue control. Revenue control is clearly a critical objective of sales control, but it is not the only one. Sales control is a broad topic and has at least two other objectives. In this chapter, discussion will focus on three objectives of beverage sales control:

1. Optimizing the number of sales.
2. Maximizing profit.
3. Controlling revenue.

While these objectives give the initial appearance of being identical to those of food sales control, there are special considerations in bar operation—some legal, some ethical and moral—that lead to significant differences. For example, in food sales control, one of the means of maximizing profit is to increase sales to individual customers, to use any of several possible approaches to induce the average customer to purchase greater numbers of products. Obviously, this is an approach that no reasonable beverage manager would ever attempt. At the same time, bar operators who attempt to optimize the number of sales in this way will find their efforts restricted by various local, state, and federal laws and regulations affecting such considerations as customer age, hours of operation, and perhaps most important, society's growing level of concern over those who drive while under the influence of alcohol. And a number of other special concerns also give rise to differences in the meanings of sales optimization and profit maximization in beverage sales control.

OPTIMIZING THE NUMBER OF BEVERAGE SALES

In beverage operations, optimizing the number of sales means engaging in activities that will increase the number of customers to the desired level, as defined by the individual operator. However, anyone seeking to increase beverage sales volume in this way must first understand why people patronize establishments that serve alcoholic beverages, including both restaurants and bars. At first glance, it might appear that people patronizing these establishments are usually motivated by a desire to consume alcoholic beverages. While this may be true for some customers, it is probably not the principal reason that people buy drinks in establishments serving the public. After all, alcoholic beverages can be obtained for home consumption in most communities, and drinking at home is considerably cheaper than drinking in a bar. It is necessary, then, to understand some of the many other possible reasons for a customer to decide to patronize bars and restaurants that serve alcoholic beverages.

People patronize these establishments for the following reasons:

1. Socializing.
2. Conducting business.
3. Eating.
4. Seeking entertainment.
5. Killing time.

Socializing

Perhaps the most significant factors motivating those who patronize beverage operations are social: meeting other people and engaging in conversation. There are endless numbers of examples: seeing colleagues after work, meeting neighbors after dinner, and making new friends. The alcoholic beverages consumed are almost incidental; they are simply an accepted and expected element in the social setting. The incidental nature of the drinking may help to explain the trend to drinks with lower alcohol content, including wine, spritzers, wine coolers, and light beers.

Conducting Business

Considerable business is conducted in bars, cocktail lounges, and similar settings. For some people, discussing business in this type of setting is easier than it would be in a formal business office around a conference table. Many find that even the formal cocktail lounge in an elegant center city hotel is more informal than a conventional office. The use of bars and lounges for business discussion is probably most common with sales personnel, who commonly depend on establishing personal relationships with their clients. The bar setting can be an excellent one for the sales representative and the client to get to know one another.

Eating

Many customers patronize food and beverage establishments primarily to eat. They order alcoholic beverages as desirable enhancements to their meals. Beverage orders with restaurant meals include cocktails, mixed drinks, aperitifs before meals, beer or wine to accompany meals, and such after-dinner drinks as brandy, liqueurs, and dessert wines. The primary motivation for patronizing the establishment comes from the desire for food, and the food purchased can range from the hearty fare of pubs to the elegant cuisine of the finest restaurants and hotel dining rooms. The beverage purchases may even be incidental. For some customers, however, the availability of beverages may be an important factor in selecting one restaurant over another, and most successful restaurants would probably lose considerable business volume if they did not serve alcoholic beverages as accompaniments to luncheon and dinner.

Seeking Entertainment

Many people go to bars, clubs, and other establishments offering alcoholic beverages for sale because they seek various forms of entertainment. Many of these people consume alcoholic beverages while enjoying the entertainment. In general, there are two types of establishments that offer entertainment: those deriving their primary revenue from beverage sales and providing entertainment to attract customers to buy the beverages, and those deriving their primary revenue from the entertainment and providing beverages to satisfy the expectations of customers. The former include nightclubs, discos, and piano bars—establishments that offer entertainment to increase the number of customers and thus to increase beverage sales volume. The latter include sports facilities, gaming casinos, many legitimate theaters, and some concert halls—estasblishments that offer alcoholic beverages as a convenience, albeit a profitable one—to patrons.

Killing Time

There are many occasions when people waste time, either because they choose to or because they have no other useful option. It is common to hear of people doing this described as "killing time." Many of them are waiting: for boarding time at airports, for train arrivals at rail stations, for the appearance of a friend or business associate for lunch, for curtain time at a theater, and so on. Time must be passed—some number of hours or minutes must somehow be consumed. For many people, a bar is a suitable place to wait while time passes. So, many bars are conveniently located, offering shelter, a place to sit, a television set to watch, and something to do: drink. Bars and cocktails lounges at airports are examples of establishments that cater almost exclusively to those who must pass time while they wait for flights to arrive or depart.

Clearly, anyone who operates an establishment that serves beverages should understand the beverage market and the various subgroups within that market. These should be taken into account by anyone attempting to make plans designed to maximize sales by increasing the number of customers to the necessary level.

Any customer may be included in one subgroup of the beverage market one day and another subgroup the next. An individual's reasons for patronizing a beverage establishment may change from day to day. For example, the person who patronizes a neighborhood bar for social reasons one evening may be killing time in an airport bar the following afternoon and then going out to dinner in the evening to celebrate some special occasion.

Each of these subgroups is called a **market segment.** The owner or manager of a beverage operation must determine which market segment or segments he intends to attract, or target. Once the target segments have been identified, numerous decisions must be made as to brands and types of drinks, portion sizes, selling prices, entertainment, lighting, decor, ambiance, dress codes, giveaways, advertising, promotions, hours and days of operation, extent of service, classifications of employees, and suitable uniforms, among others. The decisions made will have a significant impact on whether or not the target market will be attracted to the establishment in sufficient numbers to achieve the desired level of sales. For example, the owner of a bar attempting to attract a late afternoon clientele of office workers might decide to offer moderately priced, large drinks made with high-quality liquor: to maintain an informal atmosphere: to provide free hot and cold hors d'oeuvres: to advertise by means of handbills distributed through neighboring office buildings: and to make a conscious effort to learn and use customers' names. By contrast, the management of a fine hotel, targeting a different market segment for the late afternoon cocktail hour, might prefer to offer expensive, high-quality drinks in a more elegant atmosphere, with formal service, and to provide such amenities as soft piano music and elegant hors d'oeuvres, while restricting advertising to small, tasteful signs in the elevators and guest rooms.

It should be apparent that optimizing the number of sales is a complex process, requiring not only substantial time and effort, but also considerable experience in the beverage business and some reasonable knowledge of both marketing and the techniques of market research.

MAXIMIZING PROFITS

In the chapter dealing with food sales control, one element of profit maximization was identified as increasing customer purchases. This approach is of very limited use to those interested in maximizing profits from beverage sales. It is important to understand the reasons for this.

Today, the majority of people appear to reject the notion that the amount of alcohol an individual consumes is wholly his own affair. They point out that those who have consumed excessive amounts of alcohol frequently behave in ways that have adverse, sometimes lethal, effects on others. Drunk drivers are the most common examples. As a consequence, there is a growing tendency to hold both the consumer of alcohol and those responsible for serving that consumer accountable for any harm the drinker may do as a result of excessive drinking. Many states have passed relevant laws, known as **dram shop laws,** that hold the serving establishment and the server financially liable for damages if any employee in the establishment has served an alcoholic drink to an intoxicated person who, in turn, causes harm to a third party. In some states without dram shop laws, third parties can still recover damages under common-law liability. In addition, some states have now passed laws to eliminate the use of the term "happy hour" and to prohibit such practices as offering two drinks for the price of one. Because of changes in society's outlook and the passage of various laws, it is both advisable and necessary for beverage operators and their employees to restrict customers' purchases of alcoholic beverages, rather than to attempt to increase them in the manner common with food sales. Beverage operators can, however, adopt various merchandising techniques to influence the customer to select one drink (a drink with a greater contribution margin) rather than another.

In beverage operations, **profit maximization** is accomplished by:

1. Establishing drink prices that will maximize gross profit.
2. Influencing customers' selections.

These must be discussed separately.

Establishing Drink Prices

Unlike food sales prices, the costs of ingredients and labor are not the primary determinants of drink prices. Beverage ingredient costs and labor costs per dollar sale are both significantly lower than those for food, so they are not as important in establishing sales prices. This is not to say that labor costs can or should be wholly ignored; in fact, many operators tend to charge more for drinks that require more labor to produce. However, the ingredient and labor costs associated with a particular drink tend to be similar from one operation to another. Other considerations are of greater importance in establishing drink prices. These include overhead costs (occupancy, insurance, licenses, and entertainment, to name a few) and significant market considerations.

Overhead costs for a beverage operation typically account for a large percentage of total costs. This is true regardless of differences in location, sales volume, and specific dollar costs. For example, rents for airport locations tend to be very high, inducing beverage operators to set higher sales prices for drinks than would otherwise be necessary. By contrast, neighborhood bars in low-rent areas can charge considerably lower prices and still be profitable. Insurance premiums vary dramatically from one area to another, depending in part on the legal climate in the region. The passage of dram shop laws, for example, normally increases the cost of liability insurance for a bar owner. The costs associated with purchasing and maintaining licenses are considerably different from one place to another.

Establishments that offer live entertainment must either charge drink prices that are high enough to cover these costs or to cover the cost of entertainment in some other way. There are also market considerations that must be taken into account before operators set sales prices for drinks. Chief among these is the clientele targeted. Many operators rely heavily on regular customers—those who patronize an establishment frequently, often because they live or work close by. Such customers tend to be concerned with the prices charged, and operators serving this kind of clientele are usually careful to charge prices their customers consider reasonable and to avoid price increases unless absolutely necessary. By these means, they attempt to maintain as large a base of regular customers as possible, thus maximizing profits. By contrast, other beverage operations cater to transient, rather than regular, customers. The transient customer may have no practical choice of establishments (at an airport, for instance), and the choice may be limited to paying the high price charged by the only bar available or not drinking. Some transient customers are traveling on expense accounts and may be unconcerned about the specific prices charged for drinks. In general, bar operators serving transient customers can charge high drink prices.

Other market considerations that a beverage operator must take into account in establishing drink prices include average income in the area served, prices charged by the competition, special advantages offered by a specific location (such as the top floor of the world's tallest building), and even a manager's desire to maintain exclusivity through pricing. For these and many other reasons, each individual operator must establish sales prices for drinks after carefully weighing both the cost structure and relevant market considerations for that specific establishment.

No discussion of drink prices could be concluded without bringing up pricing differences between **call brands** and **pouring brands.** Call brands, selected by the customer, are normally considered to be of higher quality. They are typically of higher cost. It is, therefore, logical that they are given higher sales prices. Pouring brands, selected by the bar operator for the customer who expresses no preference, are commonly of somewhat lower quality and less costly, and are therefore given lower sales prices than call brands. In general, the contribution margins of drinks made with pouring brands are likely to be lower than those of drinks made with call brands. While it is to the operator's advantage for customers to request specific call brands, most customers do not.

Influencing Customer Selections

As with food products, contribution margins for beverage products vary greatly from one drink to another. For the bar operator, it is obviously desirable to sell more drinks with high contribution margins and fewer drinks with low contribution margins. If a customer were having difficulty deciding which of two drinks to order, it would clearly be to the bar operator's advantage for the customer to select the one with the higher contribution margin. In fact, under these circumstances, a bar operator might want the employees to help the customer make a decision in favor of the drink with the higher contribution margin.

Some bar operators attempt to maximize profits by featuring and promoting selected drinks, often drinks specially created for the purpose. These drinks may be given enticing names, be served in unusual ways (in hollowed fruits or with exotic garnishes, for example), or be made from unusual combinations of ingredients. These special drinks are normally sold for higher-than-average prices, and they normally have higher-than-average contribution margins.

Another technique for influencing customer selections is to produce a carefully designed beverage menu that includes pictures (color photographs or artists' drawings) of the drinks management would prefer to sell, along with appropriate descriptive language to entice customers. Customers' orders would not necessarily be restricted to the listed drinks, but the drink menu would include only those drinks management preferred to sell.

Understanding and using the many creative possibilities for influencing customer selections are key elements in maximizing profits that is too often ignored by some bar operators and used wisely and to full advantage by others.

CONTROLLING REVENUE

Revenue control consists of those activities established to ensure that each sale to a customer results in appropriate revenue to the operation. In beverage operations, the opportunities for revenue control are often somewhat limited.

In general, effective control procedures in business are likely to depend on division of work among several employees, but the possibilities for dividing work in this way do not exist in most bars. In many, one employee—the bartender—is responsible for virtually all of the work: taking orders from customers, filling those orders, recording the sales, and collecting cash or obtaining signatures on charge vouchers. This dependence on one individual tends to minimize the possibilities for instituting and maintaining control. In addition, it often sets the stage for the development of a number of control problems.

One common means for determining whether or not control problems exist in a particular establishment is to assess the work practices of the bartender. Most of those listed below are considered unacceptable in most well-managed bars because the owners or managers are aware of the kinds of control problems that are likely to develop:

1. **Working with the cash drawer open.** This practice makes it possible for dishonest employees to make sales transactions without recording the sales in the register. This is a serious problem if the bartender is held responsible at the end of the shift for only those sales recorded on the register tape.
2. **Under-ringing sales,** either as "No Sale" or as some amount less than the actual sale. Doing so enables an employee to steal the difference between the cash in the register drawer and the sales recorded on the tape.
3. **Overcharging customers,** but ringing correct amounts in the register. This practice, too, provides a dishonest employee with a source of cash equal to the difference between the amounts collected and amounts recorded in the register.
4. **Undercharging customers.** This may be done to accommodate a bartender's personal friends or to increase tips. It may be done in various ways, including using call brands but charging for pouring brands, or by overpouring.
5. **Overpouring.** Giving customers more than they pay for, often through failure to measure, typically results in unfavorable cost-to-sales ratios and in reduced profits from operation.
6. **Underpouring.** This technique is sometimes adopted by bartenders who selectively overpour. If they overpour for some customers (those who tip well, for example), they may be able to avoid being detected by underpouring for others. One may offset the other. Also, the bartender who keeps track of the extent of underpouring may later use the reserved amounts to prepare drinks. These drinks may then be given to friends or sold to customers, with the sales revenue going to the bartender rather than to the bar.

7. **Diluting bottle contents.** This practice involves pouring out some of a bottle's contents to reserve for later use and replacing it with an equal amount of water. The liquor poured out and reserved is typically used later to make drinks that are sold to customers. However, the revenue for those drinks goes directly to the bartender's pocket rather than to bar revenue.

8. **Bringing one's own bottle into the bar.** This practice enables a bartender to become a "silent partner" in the bar operation. He can prepare drinks using his own liquor and take the sales revenue without his performance being detected through changes in the figures used to monitor bar operations.

9. **Charging for drinks not served.** By charging a customer or a group of customers for drinks that were never served, a bartender can then serve equivalent drinks to other customers and steal the sales revenue.

10. **Drinking on the job.** In addition to the unprofessional appearance and performance this practice is likely to cause, an employee who is drinking is more likely to make mistakes in pouring, mixing, and recording sales than one who does not drink on the job.

In order to reduce the number of control problems, management must establish standards and standard procedures for bar operation. Effective revenue control requires that employees adhere strictly to these standards and standard procedures and that the performance of bartenders be monitored by management.

GUEST CHECKS AND CONTROL

Some bars use guest checks. Others do not. It is important to understand the fundamental differences between these two approaches because of the impact they have on management's ability to establish effective control over sales revenue.

Bars Without Guest Checks

Many bars, especially small, owner-operated neighborhood bars, do not use guest checks. Customers pay cash. The bartender is often the owner, who collects all cash personally. This owner-bartender does not perceive any revenue control problem and sees no need for guest checks. Some owner-bartenders require each customer to pay for each drink as it is served; others serve customers more than one drink without requiring payment and somehow remember what each customer has consumed. Cash is collected after each customer has finished his last drink. This system offers the advantage of simplicity, saves time that would be required to prepare guest checks, and is clearly less expensive than alternatives. It works well enough as long as the owner is also the bartender.

If the owner does not tend the bar and collect the cash personally, someone else must be hired to work behind the bar. This individual must do the work that the owner would otherwise have done, including making the drinks and collecting the cash. But the hired bartender may be guilty of some or all of the unacceptable work practices identified above. If so, sales revenue will be recorded incorrectly or not recorded at all. To reduce the number of errors, accidental or intentional, the owner will be likely to spend some amount of time at the bar observing the bartender. Someone other than the owner could also be stationed at the bar to monitor the bartender, with or without the bartender's knowledge. This approach, with some variations, works well in many establishments. However, if there is no one available to monitor the bartender, some other operating procedure must be found.

Bar With Guest Checks

When the visual monitoring methods described above are impossible or impractical, some degree of control is made possible by the use of numbered guest checks. A standard procedure is established that requires that all drink orders be recorded on numbered checks. If all employees follow the procedure, records of all sales are available for daily audit. In its simplest form, such an audit would consist of verifying that no numbered checks were missing, that correct prices were charged for all drinks, and that total sales recorded on the checks equaled the total of cash and charge revenues recorded in a register or a sales terminal. With sales records available, it becomes possible for an owner or manager to monitor revenue by conducting a simple audit of the type described above.

The system has some disadvantages. Essentially, there are two. First, recording orders on guest checks takes time and tends to make customer service slower than would otherwise be the case. Second, the standard procedures must be followed if the revenue control system is to be effective. However, if there is no one available to monitor the bartender, it is conceivable that he will purposely fail to follow those procedures. This is especially true of bartenders who demonstrate some or all of the poor work practices described above. Guest checks are used in a variety of ways. Two of the most common are:

Pre-check systems
Automated systems.

```
┌──────────────────────────────────────────────┐
│ REGISTER #1                      6-12-XXXX     │
│                                                │
│ Liquor            $375.00                      │
│ Beer                45.00                      │
│ Wine                30.00                      │
│ Tax                 18.00                      │
│ Tip                  5.00                      │
│    Total                         $473.00       │
│                                                │
│ Cash              $420.00                      │
│ Charge              42.00                      │
│ Voids               11.00                      │
│    Total                         $473.00       │
└──────────────────────────────────────────────┘
```

FIGURE 17.1 *Cash Register Reconciliation*

PRE-CHECK SYSTEMS.   There are registers available that enable bartenders to record sales as drinks are served and to accumulate the sales to any one customer on one check. The use of such registers makes it feasible to require that a guest check be placed in front of each customer at the bar. When the customer is ready to leave, the check is inserted into the register or terminal and the total sales to the customer are recorded as cash or charge, depending on how the customer settles the check. At the end of the day's operation, the total drink sales recorded in the terminal, plus taxes, should equal the total of cash and charge sales. Readings taken from the terminal at the end of a day would be similar to those illustrated in Figure 17.1.

A void key would be used to record such cases as drinks rejected by customers or unserved because customers walked out. An accountant or bookkeeper would reduce beverage sales figures by the total of the voids before making entries in the accounting records for the day's sales.

AUTOMATED SYSTEMS.   Another approach to controlling revenue, particularly when close supervision by a manager is either impossible or impractical, is to install an automated bar. An automated bar is both an electronic sales terminal and a computerized dispensing device for beverages. The dispensing device is controlled by the sales terminal. Bottles are inverted, with flexible tubing connecting the bottles to a dispensing device. The automated bar apparatus may be in full view of the customers or in some nearby location, out of sight. In either case, the bartender cannot pour directly from the bottles; their contents may be dispensed only by depressing keys on a sales terminal.

When a customer orders a drink, the bartender places the proper glassware under the dispensing device, inserts a guest check in the terminal or in a separate printer controlled by the terminal, and depresses the terminal key with the name of the drink on it. When the key is depressed, the name of the drink and its preassigned sales price are printed on the check. Simultaneously, the terminal signals the release of the proper quantities of the correct ingredients, which are automatically dispensed. Both the drink and the check are given to the customer or to a server who delivers them to the customer, depending on the type of bar.

At the end of each day, management obtains a report showing the number of each type of drink sold and the total dollar sales recorded in the terminal, as well as other information. With some systems, a type of perpetual inventory is maintained for beverages connected to the system, and the number of ounces in the inventory is reduced appropriately with each drink order recorded.

Automated systems are available in a variety of sizes and configurations. Some hold a comparatively small number of bottles and can prepare only a limited number of drinks. Others can accommodate many bottles and produce hundreds of different drinks.

There are some significant advantages to automated systems over traditional methods of preparing drinks. The proportions of ingredients are exactly the same each time a given drink is prepared, and the drinks are, thus, of uniform quality, prepared according to the standard recipes programmed; the quantity of each ingredient is measured exactly; and the sizes of all drinks of any given type are uniform. However, it must be noted that these systems only reduce the possibilities for the development of excessive costs through pilferage, spillage, and various bartender errors. The possibilities for charging incorrect prices are greatly reduced.

There are also some important disadvantages to these systems. Most cannot accommodate customers' requests for drinks made according to recipes other than the standard recipes programmed. Because of this, they are more commonly used at service bars than at front bars. At front bars, many customers have negative reactions to automated bars. They are accustomed to watching the bartender go through the ritual of drink mixing—many are accomplished artists who enjoy displaying their showmanship. For these customers, having drinks prepared by a machine takes something away from the "atmospherics" of the experience. In addition, traditional methods of drink preparation often give customers the impression that the bartender is giving them more than the standard measure—a dividend, so to speak. This may or may not be true, depending on the bar and the bartender, but the customer who believes that it is true may not react well to machine-prepared drinks. This customer is likely to feel that the measure is miserly.

COMPUTER APPLICATIONS

While any effective computerized sales control system must be designed to meet a particular establishment's needs, one relatively common system is described below.

The server takes orders for drinks from customers at tables, records the specific orders on a pad of plain paper, and then proceeds to a small computer terminal located on a sidestand. There the server enters a personal passcode number to gain access to the computer and follows a menu-driven program to identify the number of guests, record their table number, and place their drink orders. This is normally done with preassigned code numbers for all drinks. By using code numbers, hundreds of varying drinks may be identified with three- or four-digit code numbers. The drink orders recorded in the terminal are printed on a small printer at the service bar, thus notifying the service bartender of the drinks to be prepared. After a suitable interval, the server picks up the drinks from the service bar and proceeds to serve customers their drinks. When the customers request a check, the server uses the terminal on the sidestand to request a printed check from the computer. The check is printed on a small printer located on the sidestand adjacent to the terminal. The server gives the customer the check and either collects cash or receives and processes a credit card. In either case, the check balance in the computer is appropriately credited and brought to zero. At the end of the day, the bar manager prints a report showing sales summaries for all servers and indicating the total cash and credit card vouchers that must be turned in by each server. Before leaving for the day, each server turns in the totals indicated on his printout.

Although no system guarantees that all sales will result in appropriate revenue for the establishment, any sensible system designed to take into account the realities and needs of a particular operation will provide some desirable measure of control.

CHAPTER ESSENTIALS

In this chapter, we defined the scope of beverage sales control and explained essential differences between food sales control and beverage sales control. We identified the three goals of beverage sales control as optimizing the number of sales, maximizing profit, and controlling revenue. We pointed out various special considerations in beverage operations that lead to significant differences in the interpretation of these goals. We identified the principal reasons that customers patronize establishments that offer alcoholic beverages for sale. We discussed some of the market segments that beverage operators attempt to target and suggested some specific steps that management can take to reach these target markets. We identified the two means considered appropriate to maximizing beverage profits: setting suitable drink prices and influencing customer selection of drinks. We listed a number of poor work practices that bartenders may exhibit and explained how these limit management's ability to institute revenue controls. We identified two basic operating patterns for beverage revenue control and described variations on both. Finally, we described a common computerized sales control system for beverage operations.

KEY TERMS IN THIS CHAPTER

Automated bar
Beverage profit maximization
Beverage sales control
Dram shop laws
Market segment
Pre-check system

QUESTIONS AND PROBLEMS

1. What are the three goals of beverage sales control?

2. Why is selling the maximum number of drinks to each customer an inappropriate goal for a bar operator?

3. List and explain five possible reasons for a customer to patronize an establishment that offers alcoholic beverages for sale.

4. Identify two ways in which profit can be maximized in a beverage operation.

5. How do dram shop laws typically affect bar operation?

6. What are the principal factors considered by managers when establishing beverage sales prices?

7. Select one beverage operation in your area, list the primary target market it attempts to reach, and describe features of the operation that attract that market. If possible, identify specific steps that management has taken to increase the appeal of the operation for that market.

8. Select a beverage operation in your area, and list the market considerations that have been taken into account by management in establishing sales prices for drinks.

9. Two months ago Fred Sneed became the owner of a small bar in

Springfield. When he assumed ownership, beverage cost percent was 24.5%. Since Fred assumed ownership, beverage cost percent has increased to 29.5%, although there have been no increases in purchase prices and the sales mix has not changed. The bartender has been employed in the establishment for the last eight years. Fred has concluded that the increase in beverage cost percent is somehow related to the bartender and has decided to observe his performance closely. Given the list of poor work practices identified in this chapter, rank in order of importance the five that he should watch for as he observes the bartender at work.

10. If the owner of a bar does not mandate the use of guest checks, how can he establish some degree of control over revenue?

11. What are the essential features of a pre-check system?

12. List the possible advantages and disadvantages of automated bars as compared to traditional methods for pouring and mixing drinks.

13. What are the advantages of a computerized beverage sales control system as compared to a manual system using guest checks?

14. Define each of the following terms:
    Automated bar
    Beverage profit maximization
    Beverage sales control
    Dram shop laws
    Market segment
    Pre-check system

Part IV

Labor Control

Anyone who visits restaurants and other foodservice operations has witnessed situations that suggest a need for control. Sometimes it seems nearly impossible to get any service; the few servers in sight clearly have more customers to serve than they can possibly handle, and even when a customer has managed to place an order, it seems an eternity before the food is served. At other times, there appears to be more servers on duty than there are customers in the dining room, and one wonders how the management can afford to have so much help around when there is no business to support it.

In the first example, one can readily imagine the number of customers who walk out in disgust without ordering at all, as well as those who silently resolve never to return after waiting 15 minutes or more to order and another 45 minutes to be served. The total sales for the day are undoubtedly less than they might have been if adequate service had been provided; total sales for future days may also be affected because of customers who have decided to take their business elsewhere.

In the restaurant where more staff members are on duty than are warranted by current business, the wages paid to unnecessary staff increase payroll costs. At the very least, this will lead to owner dissatisfaction on the one hand and, on the other, to dissatisfaction among those employees whose incomes depend largely on the tips they receive from customers.

In either case, one certain effect will be the reduction of net profit from current operations, from lower sales in the first instance and from increased costs in the second. Clearly there is some need to manage staffing levels and control payroll costs in such a way as to maximize sales while minimizing costs.

Labor control represents an attempt to obtain maximum efficiency from staff without compromising standards of operating performance. As we will see, it is most difficult to achieve because of the relative unpredictability of the number of customers in a restaurant at any given time, and other factors. These will be discussed in the following chapters.

18 *Labor Cost Considerations*

After reading and studying this chapter, you should be able to:

1. Define employee compensation, and list the principal types of compensation common in food and beverage operations.
2. Distinguish between direct and indirect compensation.
3. Explain why each of the following is a determinant of labor cost or labor cost percent:
   Labor turnover rate
   Training
   Labor legislation
   Labor contracts
   Use of part-time staff
   Outsourcing
   Sales volume
   Location
   Equipment
   Layout
   Preparation
   Service
   Menu
   Hours of operation
   Weather
   Competent management
4. Explain why labor costs and labor cost percentages vary from one establishment to another.
5. Explain why the minimizing of dollar wages is not the same as labor cost control.
6. Define labor cost control.
7. Define each of the Key Terms listed at the end of the chapter.

INTRODUCTION

In hotels, restaurants, and all other related food and beverage establishments, the cost of labor accounts for considerable amounts of money. Taken as a percentage of sales, labor cost typically ranges from 15 percent to 45 percent. In some instances, labor cost percents are as high as 60 percent, although this tends to be true only in establishments operated on a not-for-profit basis. Because labor cost is such a major consideration in the typical food and beverage enterprise, an ability to deal with it effectively is an important requirement for food and beverage managers.

The objective of this and subsequent chapters is to provide an introduction to the elements of labor cost and some of the procedures and techniques for controlling labor cost in food and beverage establishments. However, any discussion of labor cost control must be preceded by some basic introduction to the following:

1. Employee compensation.
2. The determinants of total labor costs and labor cost percents.

EMPLOYEE COMPENSATION

Because **labor cost,** or **employee compensation,** consumes such a major share of sales dollars in food and beverage operations, it is important to understand the various components of labor cost before proceeding to the discussion of labor cost control.

The term **compensation** is used to refer to all forms of pay and other rewards going to employees as a result of their employment. In the hospitality industry, employees receive two forms of **current compensation, direct** and **indirect,** as well as **deferred compensation.**

Current Compensation

DIRECT COMPENSATION.   Direct compensation includes salaries, wages, tips, bonuses, and commissions. Traditionally, the term **salary** is used to refer to a fixed dollar amount of compensation paid on a weekly, monthly, or annual basis, regardless of the actual number of hours worked. **Wages,** by contrast, always take the actual number of hours worked into account: Wages for a given employee are calculated by multiplying the employee's hourly rate by the number of hours worked, up to the number of hours at which overtime rates apply. At that point, the hourly rate increases, but the same procedure is followed to calculate overtime wages.

Tips, also known as **gratuities,** while not paid from an employer's funds, are also compensation in the eyes of the law and are so treated by federal and state agencies for purposes of calculating such taxes as income tax, Social Security tax, and Medicare tax. Many workers in the hospitality industry earn more from tips than from wages.

Bonus is a term that refers to dollar amounts over and above an employee's regular wages or salary given as a reward for some type of job performance. **Commissions,** on the other hand, are dollar amounts calculated as percentages of sales. Travel agents and some banquet managers commonly earn commissions on their sales.

INDIRECT COMPENSATION.   Indirect compensation may include paid vacations, health benefits, life insurance, free meals, free living accommodations, use of recreational facilities operated by the employer, discounts on accommodations at other properties within a chain, and many other possibilities.

The paid vacation is among the most common forms of indirect compensation available to employees in the hospitality industry today. Paid vacations are typically linked to length of service with the employer. In many instances, employees are awarded a basic vacation period with pay amounting to two weeks per year. Those whose length of service reaches some predetermined number of years (five, for example) are given an additional week with pay, so that they will be able to take three weeks off with pay each year. Another approach is to give each employee 2 days of paid vacation per year of service, up to a maximum of 20 days for 10 years of service.

Health benefits, including medical, dental, and optical insurance, are among the most sought after forms of indirect compensation. They are also among the most costly. Health benefits are commonly in the form of some or all of the costs of insurance being paid by the employer, who also assumes the entire cost of administering the health insurance plan, hiring personnel in the human resources office to process forms, maintain records, and generally attend to the myriad details associated with any of these plans.

Life insurance coverage, another popular form of indirect compensation, provides protection for the families of covered employees, thus saving these employees the considerable costs that can be associated with life insurance coverage.

Many establishments provide meals to employees during their working hours. Thus, foodservice employees assigned to work from 7:00 A.M. to 3:00 P.M. may be permitted to have breakfast and lunch on premises. In hotels and other large properties where this is permitted, special facilities may be set up to be used by employees. In some cases, one or more members of the kitchen staff may be assigned exclusively to the preparation of employees' meals. Including meals in the hospitality compensation package is generally very popular with employees who gain from this very tangible benefit.

In some lodging properties, part of the employees' compensation package may include living accommodations. This is particularly true in resort hotels, but is not uncommon in some large transient hotels. In the former, living accommodations may be available to all employees; in the latter, accommodations would likely be limited to some of the managerial staff who are expected to be on call 24 hours a day.

Many resort properties include in their employees' compensation packages the rights to use various recreational facilities during the hours they are off duty. Thus, employees at ski resorts may have access to the slopes, while those at beach resorts may be able to use special beaches and such equipment as water skis and sailboats during their off hours.

Many hotel and motel chain organizations offer their employees special discounted rates on accommodations. Those who choose to travel during their vacation periods find this an extremely useful and valuable form of indirect compensation.

Deferred Compensation

Deferred compensation is defined as compensation received by an employee after the conclusion of his period of employment. Two of the most important forms of deferred compensation are **pension benefits** and that collective group of benefits generally known by the term **Social Security.** The employer is required by law to match the amounts withheld from employees' paychecks.

It is obviously important for the owners and managers of food and beverage operations to have broad and comprehensive knowledge of the various forms of compensation found in the industry, all of which have some impact, direct or indirect, on the overall cost of labor in an establishment.

DETERMINANTS OF TOTAL LABOR COSTS AND LABOR COST PERCENTS

The cost of labor is affected by a number of important considerations. Some of these are within the scope of a manager's control; others are not. Each plays some role in determining total cost of labor and labor cost percent in food or beverage operations. Each can, therefore, be described as a determinant of labor cost or labor cost percent.

The determinants discussed below are those that have a direct effect on the total cost of labor or on the cost of labor expressed as a percentage of sales. some affect both. The significance of each varies from one establishment to another. Although the following discussion treats each briefly and singly, one must keep in mind that these determinants are so interdependent that managers do not normally have the luxury of dealing with them one at a time in this fashion.

Labor Turnover Rate

Labor turnover rate, a ratio relating the number of departing employees to the total number of employees on the staff and usually expressed as a percentage, has traditionally been very high in the foodservice industry. It has been commonly measured at 100 percent per year across the industry, with some establishments having rates as high as 300 percent. This does not compare favorably with turnover rates in American industry in general, which tend to range between 10 percent and 20 percent.

When jobs become vacant and managers decide that those jobs must be filled, some individual manager must be assigned responsibility for recruiting, interviewing, selecting, and hiring replacement personnel. Large organizations often have human resource personnel to attend to much of this work, but small restaurants do not. Instead, the work must be done by restaurant managers, possibly with help from assistant managers, chefs, stewards, dining room managers, and others. It can be time-consuming work, depending in part on the level of skill and experience required in the new employee. If a manager is engaged in recruiting and hiring, he must defer some other tasks. If personnel work consumes a great portion of the manager's time, it may become necessary to hire some assistance for him. If turnover is so great that it becomes necessary to hire a human resource manager to fill vacancies, the additional cost is obvious.

High labor turnover rates generally result in higher labor costs. It has been estimated by some authorities that the cost of replacing a hospitality employee may be as high as $2,500—for advertising, interviewing, checking backgrounds and references, training, and so on. Using this figure, it is easy to calculate that the potential expense to a restaurant with 50 employees and a turnover rate of 100 percent could be as high as $125,000 per year.

Training

The need for some degree of training exists in all foodservice establishments. Managers, after all, are not typically able to find employees with complete and accurate knowledge of the jobs for which they are hired. All require some level of training. On the most elementary level, training may entail merely showing a new dishwasher the location of the dish machine and explaining the operation of the controls. With an experienced cook, training may involve a meeting to familiarize him with the nature of the menu or the preferences of the restaurant's clientele. On another level, training may include daily meetings with servers to make sure that each understands the menu fully and is aware of which items it is most beneficial to sell. Then again, training may mean taking completely inexperienced people and teaching them everything they need to know to perform particular jobs. This may be done on the premises or in facilities provided by such outside agencies as unions, public schools, community colleges, or proprietary schools.

Training can be a key factor in reducing the labor turnover rate in a restaurant. Over the years, many studies have shown some relationship between extent of training and turnover rate. Generally, restaurants with training programs that are both extensive and effective tend to have employees who report greater job satisfaction than those in restaurants where training is ignored. In restaurants with good training programs, customers often report that they receive better service and that staff members appear to be friendlier and more attentive. Where this is the case, the working environment is more pleasant, which in turn makes for lower turnover rates.

Detailed discussion of training will be found in Chapter 20. For purposes of the present chapter, it is sufficient to state that the extent of training carried on in any particular establishment is an important determinant of the overall cost of labor.

Labor Legislation

Labor legislation differs considerably from state to state, and thus the net effect of legislation on labor cost for any particular food operation must be discussed in terms of the legislation in effect in the particular state where the operation is located. However, it is possible to generalize a discussion of a significant area covered by legislation in all states: minimum wages and provisions for overtime.

A **minimum wage** is the least dollar wage before deductions that an employer is permitted to pay each employee in a covered category. It is usually expressed as an amount per hour. In addition, minimum-wage legislation normally defines a maximum permissible number of hours per day for work at that hourly wage; beyond that number of hours, an overtime rate must be paid. Also, a maximum number of consecutive working days per week is specified, and the overtime rate must be applied beyond that maximum.

In the United States, the Congress has established a federal minimum hourly wage for all covered employees. State legislatures have the power to mandate higher minimum wages for employees in their jurisdictions, and some have done so. None, however, may pass legislation permitting a minimum wage lower than that mandated by Congress. As a labor-intensive industry, the foodservice industry has traditionally employed a large number of unskilled individuals, many of whom have been paid the prevailing minimum wage. Thus, as state legislatures have steadily increased minimum wages, labor cost in the restaurant industry has been significantly affected.

Federal and state legislation also mandates other costs that affect total labor cost. These include old age survivors' insurance (Social Security, as discussed above), Medicare/Medicaid insurance, workers' compensation, and unemployment insurance. Federal requirements are uniform, while state requirements vary. For example, some states meet the cost of unemployment insurance by levying a tax on an employer's gross dollar payroll. This often takes the form of a percentage of that payroll, and the percentage is governed by an experience factor such that the higher the employee turnover rate, the higher the percentage that must be paid. Because the foodservice industry traditionally experiences a higher rate of employee turnover than almost any other industry, this extra expense has been a significant part of overall labor cost. In an effort to reduce the percentage levied against gross payroll, some employers have made special efforts to reduce the rate of employee turnover and thus reduce at least one aspect of labor cost.

Labor Contracts

The presence or absence of labor contracts will always be an important factor affecting labor cost. Where employees are organized (i.e., members of unions) and labor contracts exist, wages for each category of employee are likely to be higher than they would be in the absence of a union. In addition, such fringe benefits as vacation pay, sick pay, employees' meals, and health insurance are more likely to be found where union organizations and contracts exist.

Although the effects of wages and fringe benefits on labor cost are apparent in situations where labor contracts exist, there are often other factors that also have a significant effect. Of primary concern are provisions in labor contracts that limit management's freedom to change work rules. Such contracts typically restrict management's ability to arbitrarily alter the duties of an employee in a particular job category. One effect of this may be to force the employer to hire someone for a job when existing employees may have the time and ability to do it. This would obviously increase total labor cost.

Use of Part-time Staff

The use of part-time staff in place of full-time staff can have a significant impact on labor cost. The extent of the impact depends, obviously, on the difference between the full-time wage and the part-time wage for specific types of work and on the extent to which part-time help is used. One example will be sufficient to illustrate the point. Suppose the Circle Diner has five full-time cooks on duty in the kitchen daily, seven days each week. To cover these 35 shifts (five per day multiplied by seven days), the manager employs seven full-time cooks, each of whom works five shifts. The prevailing wage in the area for full-time cooks is $15.00 per hour, plus the cost of a package of employee benefits amounting to an additional 20 percent. The labor cost for these seven full-time cooks would be calculated as:

Wages: 7 Cooks × 35 Hours × $15 per Hour = $3,675

Benefits: $3,675 × 20%   = $ 735

Total labor cost   = $4,410

Now suppose the manager decided to cover some of the shifts by hiring part-time cooks with adequate skills at $10 per hour, plus the cost of a smaller package of employee benefits: an additional 10 percent. If it were possible to lay off three full-time cooks, to keep four full-time cooks to cover 20 shifts, and to hire part-time cooks to cover the remaining 15 shifts, the new labor cost would be calculated as follows:

Full-time cooks

Wages: 4 Cooks × 35 Hours × $15 per Hour = $2,100

Benefits: $2,100 × 20%   =   420

Part-time cooks

Wages: 15 Shifts × 7 Hours × $10 per Hour = $1,050

Benefits: $1,050 × 10%   = $ 105

New total labor cost   = $3,675

Thus, it would be possible for the manager of the Circle Diner to reduce labor cost from $4,410 to $3,675 (16.7 percent) by reducing the number of full-time cooks from seven to four and hiring part-time cooks at lower hourly wages to cover the 105 hours previously covered by full-time cooks. If, in the manager's judgment, part-time cooks were able to produce work equal to that of full-time cooks, there are likely to be some staffing changes in the Circle Diner. In the foodservice industry today, a large number of managers are hiring growing numbers of part-time employees to keep labor costs lower than they would be if all work were done by full-time personnel. Thus, the use of part-time staff is another determinant of labor cost.

Outsourcing: The Use of Outside Services

Arranging to have work done on a contract basis by outside organizations rather than by full-time employees also affects labor cost. Some establishments, for example, no longer rely on full-time employees to clean the premises at night, after the close of business. Instead, the owners and managers have engaged firms that contract to offer night cleaning services for a fixed amount per month. Similarly, many foodservice organizations now use contract services to calculate payrolls and prepare paychecks, rather than have the work done by their own employees. Others no longer employ skilled kitchen personnel to prepare such items as baked goods, desserts, and ice carvings. Still others are purchasing frozen, portioned entrees, rather than hiring high-cost chefs. Many are finding it less costly to rely on outside contractors for various goods and services that were commonly provided by in-house personnel in years past. Where this is the case, there is a significant effect on labor cost.

Sales Volume

For a restaurant of any given size, increases in sales volume will result in increased productivity per employee up to his maximum capacity to perform. For example, in a certain restaurant selling only hamburgers and employing only one cook, 100 hamburgers are typically prepared and sold during one busy hour of the lunch period. During the slack period of the afternoon, the same cook prepares only 10 hamburgers during a one-hour period. If the cook is being paid $8 per hour, the labor cost per unit produced during the peak period is equal to the hourly wage of $8 divided by the 100 hamburgers produced during that period, or $.08 per unit. On the other hand, the labor cost per unit for hamburgers prepared during the slow period is equal to the $8 wage divided by the 10 hamburgers sold, or $.80.

It is clear from the foregoing that the cook in question is working at less than his proven capacity during the slack hour, obviously because of the absence of customers. We can see that, as the sales volume increases, the cook's labor is used more efficiently. At the same time, as his efficiency increases, the cost of labor per unit produced actually decreases. Therefore, it is apparent that an increase in sales volume results in greater employee efficiency at lower labor cost per unit.

In the previous example, one employee is the minimum number that can be hired for that particular job. However, in larger establishments that require greater numbers of employees as the minimum, it is possible to better schedule employees for greater efficiency, thus keeping each employee busy a greater amount of time. It is desirable to schedule fewer employees during slack periods and more during busy periods, thereby increasing individual efficiency.

In addition, large restaurants are often able to take advantage of the economies of large-scale production. In simplest terms, this might also be described as the division of labor, assigning individuals to the tasks they are best qualified to complete and paying each a wage commensurate with level of ability and training. For example, the single cook cited above might be required as part of his job to wash dishes, keep the counter clear, or act as cashier, all for the single wage of $8 per hour. In effect, the jobs of cook, dishwasher, counterman, and cashier are all being paid $8 per hour. Furthermore, the particular individual in the job may not be very good at the side jobs assigned, and his performance at those tasks may be less efficient than that of someone hired at a lower hourly wage but specifically trained for the job. The small restaurant can usually do nothing about this, but the large restaurant frequently can hire dishwashers and countermen at considerably lower wages.

In large establishments where there is enough work to keep a specialist in any category busy most of the time, it is usually cheaper to hire the specialist at the prevailing wage for the job category, thus reducing the labor cost per unit produced. As an illustration, if the hamburger restaurant cited above were large enough, it could hire cooks at $8 per hour, dishwashers at $5 per hour, and a counterman at $4.50 per hour, thus resulting in a reduction of the overall labor cost per unit produced. As an additional benefit, each of the specialists should be more efficient at his job and capable of performing higher-quality work. In the long run, this should reduce the labor cost per unit still further.

Location

It is well known that labor costs vary from one part of the country to another. In many rural areas, particularly those where jobs are scarce and competition for those jobs is intense, employers can often pay comparatively lower hourly rates and so keep labor costs down. This same condition often can be noted outside rural areas, particularly in depressed areas and in areas where living costs are low. However, while such conditions as these may result in lower labor costs in dollars, labor costs as percentages of sales may not be lower at all. The reason for this may be the lower menu prices in effect in such areas.

By contrast, the opposite effect often can be noted in metropolitan areas where living costs are greater and wage scales higher. Under such conditions, labor costs in dollars may be quite high by some standards, but, as percentages of sales, they may be identical to those found in rural and depressed areas. To illustrate, one might consider a certain item produced in a kitchen in one area at a labor cost of $1.50 and sold at a menu price of $5, contrasted with that same item produced in another area at a labor cost of $3 and sold for $10. In the second instance, the labor cost in dollars is twice what it is in the first. In both cases, the relationship between labor cost and sales price is the same.

Equipment

Given such tasks as peeling potatoes, washing dishes, and slicing meats, lower labor costs can often result from doing this work with modern equipment, rather than by traditional hand methods. For example, a machine can peel 100 pounds of potatoes in less than 20 minutes, while the same job done by hand might require many hours. Slicing a round of beef with modern slicing equipment may take less than 5 minutes, while doing the same job manually could require more than 15 minutes. Chopping cabbage for coleslaw by hand might require four to six times the amount of time needed to do the job with up-to-date machinery. In addition, old equipment in poor condition often requires more time to accomplish a given job than equipment that is newer or in better condition. In general, from the point of view of one seeking to control labor cost, doing work by machine is cheaper than doing it by hand, and doing a job with good equipment is cheaper than doing it with poor equipment. The amount of equipment in use, as well as its variety and condition, has a considerable effect on labor cost.

Layout

Labor cost is directly affected by the manner in which space is used. Within the work area, the equipment must be arranged to facilitate, rather than impede, the employees' ability to perform their tasks. In new establishments, the equipment and facilities can be suitably arranged during construction; in converted properties, the arrangement is often less than satisfactory because of walls that cannot be moved, plumbing that cannot be readily moved, and room sizes that are less than ideal for a given purpose. If equipment is poorly arranged, employees may have to walk excessive distances. In extreme cases, it may even be necessary to hire employees who might not have been required had the equipment and facilities been arranged better. For example, if the person working at the broiler does not have ready access to a reach-in refrigerator, he may have to walk a considerable distance each time a broiler order is placed. If the broiler were extremely busy, it might be necessary to assign one person to bring items from a refrigerator when they were required at the broiler station. In some older hotels, the kitchen is so far removed from the dining room that a larger-than-necessary staff of servers is required.

In all of the above instances, equipment and facilities have been poorly or improperly arranged, with the effect of raising labor costs to higher levels than would otherwise be possible. It is not a question of the workers being inefficient; the poor layout of the restaurant virtually forces them to be so.

Preparation

Theoretically, one could rate all foodservice operations on a scale of 0 to 100 to reflect the amount of preparation required on the premises. At the "0" end of the scale would be any establishment that purchased all items pre-cooked, fully prepared, and preportioned, thus requiring minimal preparation beyond reheating prior to sale. At the opposite end would appear those establishments that prepared everything on the premises, including such basic ingredients as mayonnaise and catsup. In places falling near the "0" end of the scale, labor costs could clearly be kept minimal. Foods could be served in the disposable packages in which they were purchased, thus eliminating the need for dishwashing. Clearly, this type of establishment would require largely unskilled personnel in the kitchen. "Cooking" would merely be a matter of reheating, and the services of a traditional chef would not be required. Conversely, restaurants at the other end of the scale would require kitchen personnel with special talents for comparatively complex and conceivably elaborate preparations, probably under the expert guidance of a highly trained and highly paid executive chef. In addition, such an establishment would require additional personnel to take charge of the many responsibilities involved in the purchasing, receiving, storing, and issuing of the expensive and highly perishable basic ingredients required for many of the preparations.

While few, if any, restaurants would appear at either absolute end of such a scale, a reasonable number would be near either end. Typical fast-food restaurants would appear at the lower end, and traditional restaurants offering haute cuisine would appear at the higher end. Clearly, fast-food restaurants have considerably lower labor costs than those offering continental dishes to customers who have gourmet tastes.

Service

Foodservice establishments could also be charted on a scale of 0 to 100, based on the amount of service offered to the customer. At the lower end of the scale, one would find vending machine operations offering no service. At the other end are continental establishments that offer French service, which includes some cooking as an element. Typically the finishing of entrees and some other items is accomplished in the dining room by highly trained staff on specialized trolleys known as **gueridons.** In the middle range, one could find typical American restaurants where food is plated in the kitchen and served by a server, whose station includes a number of tables.

For those establishments at the lower end of the scale, labor costs for service tend to be minimal. On the other hand, establishments near the opposite end of the scale require not only considerable numbers of skilled servers, but also appropriate personnel to properly prepare and plate food. Labor costs would clearly be lower in restaurants in the former category and higher in those in the latter category.

Menu

From the point of view of a manager interested in controlling labor cost, it is less costly to prepare 300 portions of one item than it is to prepare 30 portions each of 10 different items. This is especially true if those 10 items require several types of preparation, such as braising, broiling, baking, roasting, and boiling. This is because one employee could conceivably prepare all 300 portions of the single item, but the preparation of 10 different items by several different methods would probably require employees in several different job categories, particularly if all portions were needed at one time, as in the case of a banquet. This is one of the primary reasons that many establishments restrict their menus to only a few items. In the case of some fast-food operations, the menu may even be structured around one basic entree: the hamburger. Clearly, the limiting of the numbers and varieties of menu items is one factor of considerable importance in the control of labor cost.

Hours of Operation

Obviously, the number of hours that a restaurant operates will have a significant impact on labor cost. A restaurant open only for dinner will have lower labor costs than that same operation open for three meals each day. However, decisions concerning numbers of hours of operation involve more considerations than the mere cost of labor.

Every operation has overhead costs that exist regardless of whether the restaurant is open or closed. These typically include rent or mortgage payments, salaries not based on hours of work (managers' salaries as distinguished from those of service personnel paid hourly wages), insurance premiums, depreciation, property taxes, and so on. These fixed costs are independent of business volume. As a general rule, as long as additional revenue gained by staying open is greater than the additional cost incurred during that period of time, remaining open is desirable from a financial viewpoint.

For example, assume that a restaurateur is trying to determine whether to extend the dinner hours from 9:00 P.M. to 10:00 P.M. He calculates that additional wages for that hour will be $148; heat and light are estimated at $11. These additional costs can be considered fixed once the decision to remain open for the extra hour is made. Variable costs, including food, beverages, linen, and miscellaneous, are estimated at 38 percent of each dollar of sale. Thus, from the formulas in Chapter 3:

$$\text{Break-even (BE) for the additional hour} = \frac{FC}{CR \text{ (equal to } 1 - VR)}$$

$$BE = \frac{\$159}{.62}$$

$$BE = \$256.45$$

If management can project sales volume in excess of $256.45, it will be financially advantageous to remain open. Thus, assume sales volume of $350 for the additional hour. Costs for that period would include the $159 previously cited plus 38 percent of $350, or $133. Total costs for the additional hour at the projected sales level would be $292, leaving a net revenue of $58 ($350 − $292) that would be available to cover overhead costs of the restaurant and additional profit. Management must decide if the additional $58 of net revenue is worth the time and effort required. Employee morale and long-term effects on overall sales volume must also be considered.

Weather

Of all the determinants of labor cost, weather is clearly one that is completely beyond any manager's control. However, it can have a significant impact on labor cost percentages. Weather often affects sales volume, which in turn affects staffing levels in our industry. Bad weather, such as heavy rain or snow, deters potential customers from venturing out to restaurants. Interestingly, identical weather conditions typically increase sales volume in hotel dining rooms for the very same reason: those who might have gone out to other restaurants remain in the hotel to avoid the weather.

To the extent that one can obtain accurate weather forecasts, one can plan staffing levels suitable for anticipated demand. The problem, of course, is that weather forecasts are not always accurate, and unforeseen weather changes may render planned staffing levels inappropriate. When this occurs, it is often too late to modify the employee schedule. Sometimes employees can be sent home early if the restaurant is overstaffed, although this may have negative consequences, particularly on employee morale, labor turnover, and performance. On the other hand, weather changes that render planned staffing levels inadequate may cause other types of problems, including poor service and even lost sales, as well as an overworked staff. These consequences can sometimes be avoided by maintaining a list of part-time employees willing to come to work on call. Some managers keep "on-call" lists of students enrolled in nearby culinary arts or foodservice and lodging management programs who are willing to fill in at the last minute.

To the extent that a restaurant is unable to adjust staff schedules quickly to accommodate unforeseen changes in the weather, labor cost percents will be affected.

Competent Management

The cost of labor is always affected by management's ability to plan, organize, control, direct, and lead the organization in such a way that the desired level of employee performance is obtained at the appropriate level of cost. Competent management requires, among other things, that managers have clear conceptions of a number of important elements of the work at hand, including the nature of the work to be done; the number and types of employees required to do it; the measurement of suitable performance; scheduling employees to optimize performance levels; the training, facilities, equipment, and other materials required; and how, when, and in what quantities these resources are to be utilized. The manager's ability to motivate, direct, and lead will determine the quality of work and level of performance.

This might be summed up by saying that good management will have positive effects on labor costs, while poor management will have negative effects. A good manager, merely by being a good manager, will create a work environment conducive to optimal performance at minimal cost.

Conclusion

In the light of the foregoing discussion of the determinants of labor cost, it is apparent that each of these must be taken into account in analyzing labor costs. Moreover, because of the many differences that are readily apparent from one establishment to another within this vast industry (which includes operations ranging from hot dog stands to the finest hotels, and from fast-food chains to award-winning gourmet-style restaurants), it is impossible to arrive at industry-wide standards or averages for a particular manager to use as guides for his own establishment.

Each owner or manager must base the desired and optimal labor cost and labor cost percentage for an operation on an array of relevant factors, and must recognize that labor cost in a particular operation will be affected to a greater or lesser extent by the various determinants discussed above: labor turnover, training, labor legislation, labor contracts, outsourcing, sales volume, location,

	Restaurant A		Restaurant B	
	Dollars	Percentage	Dollars	Percentage
Sales	$300,000	100%	$300,000	100%
Fixed Costs	90,000	30%	90,000	30%
Semivariable Costs	60,000	20%	105,000	35%
Directly Variable Costs	120,000	40%	75,000	25%
Profit	30,000	10%	30,000	10%

FIGURE 18.1 *Cost Comparison: Two Restaurants*

equipment, layout, preparation, service, menu, hours of operation, weather, and competent management. Clearly, the impact of each of these varies considerably from one establishment to another.

Indeed, two identical restaurants located in different areas do not and probably should not have the same labor costs or the same labor cost percentages. In fact, two such restaurants will normally be found to have significantly different cost structures for food, beverages, and overhead, as well as for labor.

It is worthwhile, at this point, to restate an important point made in the first section of this text, namely that the basic categories of cost (fixed, directly variable, and semivariable, also identified previously as overhead, food, beverages, and labor) must add up to a figure that is less than total sales if the operation is to show a profit: These costs must total less than 100 percent of sales. Therefore, the proportion of total sales that must be allocated to cover each of the three types of costs partly depends on the proportion required to cover the other two. Figure 18.1 illustrates this point.

In the illustration, fixed costs account for equal percentages of sales in both restaurants, as well as for equal numbers of dollars. Profits are equal as well. The differences between the two restaurants are to be seen in the dollars and percentages attributable to semivariable costs (labor) and to directly variable costs (food and beverages). In Restaurant A, food and beverage costs and cost percents are comparatively high, which means that labor costs must be kept comparatively low for the restaurant to earn the 10 percent profit. By contrast, food and beverage costs and cost percents are comparatively low in Restaurant B, meaning that labor costs can be comparatively higher than in Restaurant A, without causing profit to be lower than 10 percent.

Whenever directly variable costs account for a high percentage of the income dollar, semivariable costs (primarily labor costs) must be kept down. By the same token, if fixed and directly variable costs are comparatively low, semivariable costs can be proportionally higher.

It should be obvious that an increase in the percentage of sales attributable to any cost category will have an effect on the remaining cost categories, on profit, or on both. If the semivariable cost of labor increases from 20 percent to 25 percent, then a manager must somehow reduce the percentages for the remaining costs or be prepared to accept a decreased percentage of profit. Similarly, if the percentage of variable costs increases, then the manager must be prepared to exercise some restraining influence on fixed or semivariable cost percentages if the percentage of profit is to be held constant.

In the final analysis, all restaurant owners and managers must control combined food, beverage, and labor costs so that their operations will earn satisfactory levels of profit. The combined costs of these three typically should not exceed 60 percent to 70 percent of sales if establishments are to cover overhead and earn profits.

Having addressed the elements of employee compensation and some major determinants of labor cost and labor cost percent, it will now be appropriate to turn our attention to the primary subject of this part of the text: labor cost control.

LABOR COST CONTROL
Labor Cost Control Defined

Labor cost control is a process used by managers to direct, regulate, and restrain employees' actions in order to obtain desired levels of performance at appropriate levels of cost. To the inexperienced, labor cost control is sometimes mistakenly taken to suggest the mere reduction of payroll costs to their irreducible minimum. This can be achieved by employing a bare minimum number of people paid the minimum legal wage. But there is much more to labor cost control than just minimizing dollar wages, a fact sometimes ignored by owners and managers who take the short-term view of operations, thinking only of immediate profits and not taking into account the long-term effects of their policies and actions.

Short-term policies geared strictly to minimizing immediate costs may have undesirable long-term effects, including decreased dollar sales, increased operating costs, and even business failure. For example, hiring a full staff of employees at minimum wage may minimize immediate labor costs, but may also lead to poor-quality products, high labor turnover, customer dissatisfaction, decreasing sales volume, and a host of other long-term problems. Obviously, management should pay the wage rates necessary to attract and retain qualified personnel, but not more. To overpay may make for an operation that cannot be profitable.

Appropriate performance levels differ from establishment to establishment. For some (fast-food restaurants serving frozen, portioned products that need only be heated and served by comparatively unskilled labor), desired levels of performance may be such that minimum-wage employees are appropriate; for others (fine restaurants attempting to offer the finest food, wines, and service in their areas), appropriate levels of performance may be such that wages considerably above those prevailing in the area may be required.

But level of performance is not simply a function of wage rates. Unskilled employees in fast-food establishments cannot perform at appropriate levels unless they are provided with appropriate equipment, given suitable training, placed in a working environment conducive to getting work done, and supervised in a manner that will inspire them to work and remain on the staff. This is also true for highly skilled employees in the finest restaurants. Suitable wage levels do not guarantee appropriate performance. Many other factors are involved in ensuring suitable levels of performance.

The Purpose of Labor Cost Control

The primary purpose of labor cost control is to maximize the efficiency of the labor force in a manner consistent with the established standards of quality and service. Ideally, each employee's services will be utilized as effectively as possible. There should be a sufficient numbers of dishwashers working to ensure that dishes are washed as efficiently as possible, but there should be no time when dishwashers stand around with no work to do. Similarly, a sufficient number of servers should ensure that all customers are served as quickly as possible while standards of service are maintained, but at no time should there be more than a sufficient number to serve the customers then in the restaurant.

Control Process

Before one proceeds to the topics to be discussed in the remaining chapters on labor cost control, it will be useful to review the four-step control process identified and discussed at length in Chapter 2 and used as the focus for Parts II and III of the text. This process comprises the following steps:

1. Establish standards and standard procedures for operation.
2. Train all individuals to follow established standards and standard procedures.
3. Monitor performance, and compare actual performance with established standards.
4. Take appropriate action to correct deviations from standards.

These four steps are as important to labor cost control as they are to both food cost control and beverage cost control. They will provide the framework for the discussion of labor cost control that occupies the chapters that follow.

CHAPTER ESSENTIALS

In this chapter, we discussed the elements of employee compensation; identifying direct, indirect, current, and deferred compensation; and distinguishing between the terms **salary** and **wages.** We listed and explained 16 major determinants of labor costs and labor cost percentages: labor turnover rate, training, labor legislation, labor contracts, use of part-time staff, outsourcing, sales volume, location, equipment, layout, preparation, service, menu, hours of operation, weather, and competent management. We explained why labor costs and labor cost percentages vary from one establishment to another by illustrating the comparative cost structures of two common types of restaurants. We defined labor cost control and explained that minimal labor costs are not necessarily optimal labor costs. Finally, we reviewed the four steps in the control process, which are the themes of the following chapters on labor cost control.

KEY TERMS IN THIS CHAPTER

Bonus
Commission
Compensation
Control process
Current compensation
Deferred compensation
Direct compensation
Directly variable cost
Fixed cost
Gratuities
Indirect compensation
Labor cost control
Labor turnover rate
Minimum wage
Outsourcing
Salary
Semivariable cost
Tips
Wages

QUESTIONS AND PROBLEMS

1. Distinguish between direct compensation and indirect compensation.

2. Distinguish between current compensation and deferred compensation.

3. List five forms of indirect compensation.

4. Distinguish between salaries and wages.

5. List and discuss four hidden costs of labor turnover.

6. In a short paragraph, discuss the possible effects on labor cost of a newly negotiated labor contract.

7. Select and describe a reasonably well-known restaurant in your area, and then discuss the effect of each of a minimum of five of the determinants identified in this chapter on that specific establishment's labor cost.

8. Research the following types of dining room service: American, French, Russian, and cafeteria. Rank them according to the extent of labor cost normally associated with each, and justify the rank of each.

9. Discuss considerations that a restaurant owner or manager should take into account before deciding between the following alternatives: purchasing an expensive piece of equipment to make hamburger portions of uniform size, or employing people on hourly wages to do the same work, buying inexpensive portion scales for them to work with.

10. Identify several laws affecting labor cost in your region. What is the specific effect of each?

11. The Alibi Restaurant is normally open for business until 8:00 P.M. Recently, business has been getting better during the time period just before closing, and the manager is attempting to determine the viability of remaining open until 9:00 P.M. She estimates her additional costs for the extra hour as follows:
    Labor = $75
    Heat, light, and gas = $12
    Variable cost of food, beverage, etc. = 40% of sales
    a. What additional sales are necessary for the manager to break even exactly on the extra hour of opening?

    b. If the manager were able to obtain $280 in sales volume for the extra hour, what income could be applied to normal overhead expenses?

12. A restaurant's income statement shows the following cost and sales structure:

Sales	$450,000
Fixed costs	$135,000
Directly variable costs	$120,000

    What must the semivariable cost figure be if the restaurant is to show a profit of $30,000?

13. In Erphalene's Restaurant, fixed costs are 30% of sales, while directly variable costs are 25%. What percentage of sales should semivariable costs be if the restaurant is to show a 10% profit?

14. Rank the foodservice operations listed below in order of probable labor cost percent, from low to high. Justify the rank you have assigned each establishment.
    a. An industrial cafeteria using only convenience foods.
    b. A seafood restaurant using only fresh fish.
    c. A continental restaurant specializing in tableside cookery.

15. A restaurant selling hamburgers employs only one cook. During the peak lunch hour, he is able to produce 120 hamburgers per hour. During the slack afternoon period, he produces only 30 hamburgers per hour. If each hamburger sells for $.60 and the cook is paid $8 per hour, calculate the labor cost per hamburger for one hour during each of the two periods described.

16. Define each of the following terms:
Bonus
Commission
Compensation
Control process
Current compensation
Deferred compensation
Direct compensation
Directly variable cost
Fixed cost
Gratuities
Indirect compensation
Labor cost control

Labor turnover rate
Minimum wage
Outsourcing
Salary
Semivariable cost
Tips
Wages

19 *Establishing Performance Standards*

LEARNING OBJECTIVES

After reading and studying this chapter, you should be able to:

1. Discuss the meaning and significance of quality and quantity standards in labor control.
2. Identify the three steps used to establish standards and standard procedures for employees.
3. Explain the need for an organizational plan.
4. Describe an organization chart.
5. Define the term job description.
6. Define the term job analysis, and explain its importance in developing job descriptions.
7. Identify the three parts of a job description.
8. Define the term job specification, and explain its importance in making employment decisions.
9. Distinguish between variable cost personnel and fixed cost personnel.
10. Discuss the use of records of business volume in scheduling personnel.
11. Distinguish between the scheduling of variable cost personnel and the scheduling of fixed cost personnel.
12. Prepare an hourly schedule for variable cost personnel from records of business volume.
13. Discuss the development of performance standards based on judgments of performance during test periods.
14. Determine appropriate staffing levels for an establishment given a table of standard staffing requirements and a sales forecast.
15. Explain the use of computers and electronic cash registers in developing records of business volume.
16. Define each of the Key Terms listed at the end of the chapter.

INTRODUCTION

Discussion in the previous chapter of the considerations affecting labor cost suggests that job categories and numbers of personnel involved vary greatly from one foodservice establishment to another. That is true: as the extent of preparation increases, the numbers of job categories and the degrees of specialization increase as well. In addition, as the nature and extent of service increase, on a continuum from self-service to elaborate continental service, the number of personnel and the degree of expertise required also increase. Regardless of the extent of preparation and the type and extent of service, managers should work to ensure that every employee is performing as effectively as possible. This is best accomplished by establishing standards and standard procedures.

ESTABLISHING STANDARDS AND STANDARD PROCEDURES

In Chapter 2, standards were defined as rules or measures established for making comparisons or judgments. Management establishes standards for many reasons, one of which is to determine the extent to which the results of organizational activities match those anticipated by plans. Other chapters illustrated the importance of standards for judging the effectiveness of food and beverage cost controls. Now it will be appropriate to discuss using standards for evaluating employee performance and controlling labor costs.

Earlier chapters explained that there are three kinds of standards used in cost control: quality, quantity, and cost. These three are also used in labor cost control. Quality standards and quantity standards are discussed below. The discussion of cost standards will be deferred to the end of the chapter.

Quality Standards

Before developing quality standards for employee performance, a manager must first have a clear and detailed understanding of the establishment, including the quality standards for food and beverage products. With these clearly in mind, a manager can then begin to establish quality standards for employee performance. For example, a manager would be better equipped to establish quality standards if he or she knew that the restaurant would be serving sandwiches to a clientele consisting of workers and shoppers wanting to eat quickly. The standards would be quite different than they would be in a restaurant commonly required to serve such elegant menu items as steak Diane to corporate executives celebrating their successful closing of a multi-million dollar deal. The quality standards for employee performance in the first instance need not be as exacting as those in the second: sandwiches typically do not require the same polished service as that appropriate for serving steak Diane.

Quantity Standards

Once appropriate quality standards have been established, corresponding quantity standards must be developed. The manager must determine the number of times that a task can be performed within a certain time period at a given level of quality. The typical time period is the same as that used for payroll purposes, the hour. In effect, the manager must determine the quantity of performance to be expected per hour and, by extension, per meal and per day from employees in each job classification.

In other industries, various sophisticated techniques have been developed for establishing performance standards. These have been successfully used by those scheduling personnel for factory and office jobs that are essentially repetitive in nature. On an assembly line, for example, one person is typically responsible for one task and can reasonably be expected to perform that task a certain number of times per hour. Time and motion studies can be used to analyze each job. A time and motion study breaks a job down into component parts and specific body movements to find the most efficient way of doing the work. This must be clearly defined and taught to the workers. The key to this approach lies in the repetitive nature of the tasks to be performed and in the fact that management has the ability to control the rate of production.

In a typical manufacturing business, production is normally linked to demand in the long run, but not on a day-to-day basis. A factory can turn out items that can be stored in inventory for appreciable periods. In the long run, management must schedule production in such a way that the supply of an item produced does not exceed demand, which can be done by increasing and decreasing (or even by ceasing) production for a period of time. Food and beverage managers do not have this luxury. In our business, production must be linked to immediate demand.

Some fast-food chains have made significant progress in defining jobs and scheduling production so that they come close to approaching the efficiency of many manufacturing operations. For example, several nationally known fast-food chains produce various menu items for anticipated demand based on ongoing business volume records. These items are stored in inventory for a very short period, usually not more than 10 minutes, after which they are discarded.

While industrial approaches could be used in the food and beverage industry, they have not been widely applied. A time and motion study could be used to determine appropriate techniques that a cook might use to make omelettes of acceptable quality at peak efficiency for one hour. Such a study might result in a determination that the cook could produce 30 omelettes per hour by following certain carefully specified procedures. However, this would be of little use unless the cook actually had to produce 30 omelettes per hour for each hour of work. Generally, this is not the case.

In the restaurant business, production must be linked to immediate customer demand, not to long-term demand, as is commonly the case in manufacturing businesses. In part, this is due to the perishable nature of food and beverage products, most of which can only be stored for very limited periods before sale. Some items (soft-boiled eggs, or soufflés, for example) cannot be stored at all.

The products of restaurant kitchens are highly perishable. In addition, their rate of production must take into account both the perishable nature of the product and fluctuations in customer demand. Further, unlike typical factory workers, restaurant personnel do not usually repeat the same tasks hour after hour, day after day. The cook who makes an omelette one minute may be called on to produce some other item the next. If and when the menu changes, the tasks assigned to the cook may change as well. If omelettes are no longer on the menu, the cook will be producing some other item.

Some fast-food operators and a number of food processing firms that cater to fast-food restaurants have been able to take advantage of production techniques used in typical manufacturing enterprises and have used time and motion studies and other related techniques to establish quantity standards. Certain preproportioned fast-food items can be produced, frozen, and stored by a food processing firm or by a fast-food operator. In some instances, such items as hamburgers can be produced by employees doing repetitive assembly line jobs. These cooked products can then be stored for limited periods. If not sold within a predetermined period, they are discarded. However, the majority of foodservice operators are not able to use these assembly line techniques. Even those that do use them to some limited extent find that they are applicable only to a very limited number of products. Therefore, in our industry, other ways must be found to establish quantity standards.

Establishing standards and standard procedures for employees requires three steps:

1. Organizing the enterprise.
2. Preparing job descriptions.
3. Scheduling employees.

ORGANIZING THE ENTERPRISE

Few activities designed ultimately to control labor cost can be undertaken sensibly until management has devoted the appropriate time, thought, and energy to organizing the operation, establishing jobs, and identifying the relationships between them. Properly organizing an enterprise normally requires that one design a rational organizational plan.

Establishing an Organizational Plan

Creating an organizational plan requires the owner or manager to first develop a clear picture of the nature of the operation. This would include the type of clientele, the nature of the products offered, and the extent and type of service rendered, as discussed earlier in this chapter. In addition, the picture should include some reasonable estimate of the number of meals to be prepared and served. Once the owner or manager has developed this basic idea of the nature and scope of the operation, he or she can begin to think in terms of specific jobs that must be performed.

As an illustration, consider a very small establishment serving fast foods from a limited menu and offering counter service rather than table service. The manager could order a comparatively small selection of frozen, preportioned foods and oversee the simple preparation of these items by a small number of cooks of limited ability, who could also serve as counter help. If the serviceware—plates, cups, and so on—were all disposable paper and plastic, the services of a dishwasher might not be needed. And if the manager were able to work the cash register, no cashier would be needed. The restaurant could exist with only two categories of employees: manager and cook/counter worker. With that understanding clearly in mind, the manager could begin to think of hiring a staff.

By contrast, a large restaurant offering continental cuisine prepared from fresh ingredients by highly skilled kitchen personnel and served by a highly professional dining room staff would require a comparatively large staff consisting of a number of specialists. The kitchen staff would include several types of skilled professionals, carefully trained in the arts of butchering meats, preparing soups and sauces, decorating cold platters, and doing other jobs appropriate to such a restaurant. Typically, one individual could not attend to managing such an enterprise while covering one of the workstations (that of cashier, for example). Operating this type of establishment successfully requires the services of any number of specialists, including receiving clerks, stewards, storeroom clerks, hosts, cashiers, and many others.

In addition to establishing the general categories of employees needed to operate an establishment, a manager must also think in terms of the relationships that should exist between and among employees in the various job classifications. In essence, the manager must decide which employees will be responsible for overseeing the work of other employees. The manager must determine, for example, that an executive chef will have complete responsibility for the production of food items and that, to carry out this responsibility, the chef will be placed in charge of a number of specialists who will serve under his or her direction and guidance, including sous chef, saucier, légumier, and garde manger, among others. In turn, the executive chef must know and understand that he or she reports to the manager and works under the manager's direction. The chef and the steward must realize that a special working relationship must exist between them, that they are equals in the organizational structure, and that they must cooperate fully if the best interests of the restaurant and its customers are to be served.

Preparing an Organization Chart

So that all of these distinctions and relationships may be seen in their proper perspective, the owner or manager of a restaurant is usually well advised to set them down on paper in the form of an **organization chart,** like that illustrated in Figure 19.1. Such a chart shows the positions and describes reporting relationships within an organization.

The lines drawn from one position to another signify the lines of authority. An unbroken line from one position to another indicates that the person below reports to and takes direction from the person immediately above on the chart. The dotted lines show communication and cooperation between the two positions, but one does not have authority over or the responsibility for the actions of the other. The lateral dotted line between the executive chef and the chief steward shows that the two are expected to cooperate in every possible way in accomplishing their respective tasks, but that neither takes direction from the other.

PREPARING JOB DESCRIPTIONS

Once the organization chart is completed and accurately reflects the organizational plan of the owner or manager, particularly with respect to the job titles needed for successful operation, it is necessary to gather the information required to prepare an appropriate job description for each job title on the chart. The term given to the process of gathering this information is **job analysis.**

Job Analysis

Organizing an enterprise is much more complex than simply listing the various job titles commonly used in food or beverage operations and determining the number of workers needed in each. Instead, it requires that one identify the nature of each job, as well as the skills, the level of education, and any other specific qualifications required to perform them. For example, plan-

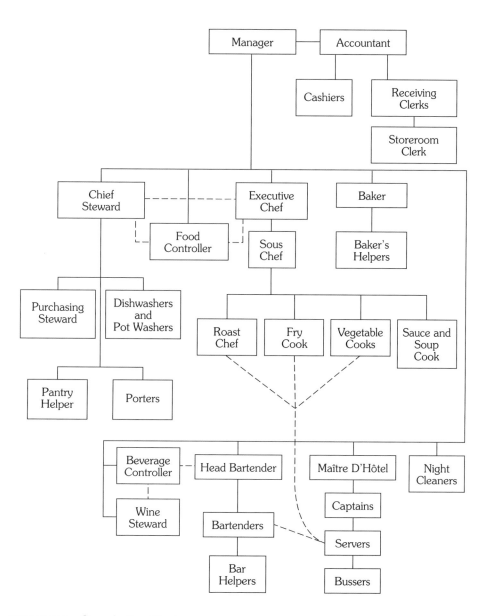

FIGURE 19.1 *Organization Chart*

ning for personnel in the kitchen of a restaurant is more complicated than simply determining that there will be one fry cook on duty for every eight-hour shift, every day of the week. One must also know and understand the nature of the fry cook's job in that particular restaurant, the specific duties assigned to that job, the skills required to carry out those duties, and any other qualifications or attributes that an individual holding the job should possess or demonstrate.

Job analysis is the first step in preparing job descriptions. The information necessary to complete job analysis may be gathered in any of several ways. In new food and beverage operations, the information tends to be based on a manager's previous experience in the industry. In existing operations, the two most common methods are:

1. Interviewing workers and supervisors to obtain the information.
2. Observing workers on site as they perform the jobs.

Complete analysis requires effective use of both methods. One approach is to conduct in-depth interviews with workers and supervisors during the course of a normal work day. These interviews are typically conducted on the premises in a reasonably quiet area, somewhat removed from the actual work-site. In some instances they are videotaped to facilitate review. Each interview is carefully structured to elicit the specific information required for the job analysis. Later, interviewers will observe both workers and supervisors, taking extensive notes to supplement those taken during the interviews. The interviews and observations are designed to provide information about the following:

1. Job objectives.
2. Specific tasks required to achieve objectives.
3. Performance standards.
4. Knowledge and skills necessary.
5. Education and experience required.

In addition to the information gathered through interviews and observations, the manager must have thorough knowledge of the standards and standard procedures established for the purchasing, receiving, storing, issuing, preparing, selling, and serving all menu items—foods and beverages—as discussed in Chapters 4 through 17. For example, in the chapters dealing with food production and beverage production, the concept of the standard recipe and its importance for cost control was stressed. Now, in analyzing jobs to determine the nature and extent of skills needed for such jobs as cook and bartender, one must take into account the need for individuals in those jobs to be able to read and follow the standard recipes developed.

Unless job analysis is thorough, any resulting job description and job specification will not accurately indicate the specific duties of a job and the qualifications required to perform it. If job analysis does not uncover a need for reading and following standard recipes, the job description and job specification resulting from the faulty analysis will not accurately reflect the real duties of the job and the qualifications needed by the job holder.

The information gathered in job analysis is reported in the form of **job descriptions,** used for informing employees of their duties and for developing training plans, and **job specifications,** used for making employment decisions.

Job Descriptions

Once job analysis is completed, job descriptions can be written. As the term implies, job descriptions are detailed written statements that describe jobs. They can be very detailed. In some instances, job descriptions list very specific duties and directions for performing jobs. Job descriptions for particular jobs should answer three important questions:

1. What is to be done?
2. When is it done?
3. Where is it done?

Today, growing numbers of experts in the field of human resources development advocate including performance criteria in job descriptions. **Performance criteria** are statements that describe an acceptable level of job performance. Included in performance criteria are standards of job performance that should be known and understood by each job holder because each is likely to be evaluated on the basis of these standards. For example, if the job description for a server includes some such statement as, "Customers are greeted and dealt with in a polite and helpful manner at all times," then there is a standard established that can be used as a basis for evaluating servers' behavior towards customers. A job description typically has three parts.

1. A heading that states the job title and the department in which the job is located. In some organizations, the heading may include such information as the number of positions with that particular job title, the specific hours, days, or shifts worked by those with the job title, and the supervisor to whom those with that job title report.
2. A summary of the duties of the job, typically written in paragraph form. The summary enables the reader to quickly gain some basic understanding of the nature and purpose of the particular job. By reading the summaries of all the jobs in a particular department, one could

obtain a great deal of information about the department in a very short period. This could be of great benefit to a new manager, for example.

3. A list of the specific duties assigned to the job. These will be as detailed as possible, to the point that well-written job descriptions can be used as step-by-step instructions for doing the specific work required of those holding these jobs. As we will see, having detailed job descriptions of this nature can be of great value to those charged with appraising employee performance.

A job description is particularly important for prospective employees. Because they have access to detailed descriptions of the duties assigned to particular jobs, job applicants and newly hired workers have a means of knowing the work that is to be done by someone holding a particular job.

Job descriptions are also very important for employers. They enable employers to hold employees accountable for doing the specific work assigned to a particular job. Employees who have read job descriptions but fail to perform the assigned work cannot successfully use the age-old excuse, "Nobody ever told me I had to do this."

Job analysis and the resulting job descriptions have the added benefit of forcing managers to assign specific work to each job holder. If all the normal duties of a department are identified within specific job descriptions, the department will be better organized and will operate more smoothly.

Figure 19.2 is an example of the kind of job description that one might find in a foodservice enterprise. Note the degree of specific detail provided. Job descriptions that include this level of detail can be of great assistance to those responsible for developing employee training programs.

Job Specifications

A job specification outlines the qualifications needed to perform a job. It is a second outcome of job analysis. A job specification describes the specific skills needed for a given job and the kinds and levels of education and experience required. The job specification is an important standard that can and should be used by anyone assigned to interviewing applicants for employment and making judgments about their suitability for particular jobs. Job specifications typically include minimum qualifications that are used to determine which applicants have the qualifications needed to fill particular positions and which do not. Applicants who possess the qualifications indicated in the job specification are normally considered suitable for further consideration; those who lack the listed qualifications are not.

With the foregoing discussion of job analysis, job descriptions, and job specifications as background, we will turn our attention to another important

JOB TITLE: Server   SUPERVISOR: Dining Room Manager
WORKING HOURS: Schedule for week posted each Friday. Hours and days vary each week.
JOB SUMMARY: Servers greet seated guests, take orders, serve food and drinks, present checks with last service, and clear/reset tables.

Duties:

1. Report to supervisor one hour before meal period to assist in preparing dining room for opening.
2. Pour water; take food and drink orders; place orders in kitchen and bar; pick up and serve food and drink; present checks to guests; clear and reset tables.
3. Follow standard service procedures: serve food from guest's left; beverages from right. Remove all china, glassware, and silver from guest's right.
4. Attend daily briefing 15 minutes before the scheduled opening of the dining room to learn about daily specials, service techniques, and other matters of importance.
5. Pool all tips: 10% of the tip pool goes to bartenders; remainder is divided equally among servers. Tips are distributed the following day.
6. Provide own uniform, as follows. Black pants or skirt; white dress shirt with long sleeves and buttoned cuffs; black bow tie; polished black shoes with flat heels. No high heels. Servers will be given an allowance of $5.00 per week to care for their uniforms.
7. Standards for personal appearance:
   Showered or bathed prior to work;
   underarm deodorant required;
   clean fingernails;
   hair clean and neat;
   no excessive jewelry.

Males:

   a. Clean shaven preferred. Moustache permitted if neat and trimmed.
   b. No facial or ear jewelry.
   c. Hair cannot extend beyond shirt collar.

Females:

   a. No excessive jewelry, makeup, or perfume.
   b. Long hair must be in hair net.
   c. No long false nails.

FIGURE 19.2   *Job Description*

element in developing standards and standard procedures for labor: scheduling.

SCHEDULING EMPLOYEES

One popular scheduling method is that commonly used in operations where menus seldom vary and sales change little from week to week. Managers routinely review staffing levels in the most recent weeks. Purely on the basis of recollection, they decide whether or not the level of staffing was sufficient to meet customers' needs. Then, to the extent to which previous schedules were adequate, they are repeated, thus making these schedules standards of sorts. If the manager's recollection suggests that staffing was excessive or inadequate, changes are made and a new schedule is prepared. It should be noted that this entire scheduling process depends on the manager's remembering the details of past performance; intuitive judgment is the essential factor in determining increases or decreases in the number of scheduled work hours.

Because this approach fails to recognize essential differences between fixed cost and variable cost personnel and neglects to take sales records into account, it does not normally provide the most effective labor cost control. Improved labor cost control can be obtained by taking these factors into account.

Labor Classifications for Control Purposes

It is important for any manager attempting to develop schedules for employees and to control labor costs to recognize that there are two classifications of employees:

1. Variable cost personnel.
2. Fixed cost personnel.

Because the scheduling of these categories of employees differ from one another, they are discussed separately below.

VARIABLE COST PERSONNEL.   **Variable cost personnel** are those whose numbers are linked to business volume. As business volume increases, it becomes necessary to hire more personnel in this category. As a consequence, the total labor cost increases for this category of employees. The reverse also should be true: as business volume decreases, it is possible to decrease the number of employees in this category and thus to decrease the total labor cost for this category of employees. Typical examples of variable cost employees are servers and bussers. When business volume reaches a peak, as it typically does during normal meal hours, more of these workers are needed. During non-peak times—the middle of the afternoon, for example—reduced levels of business volume can be handled with comparatively fewer servers, bussers, and other such variable cost employees. For this category of employees, the total cost of labor is higher during peak hours than it is during non-peak hours. Other examples of variables cost employees are dishwashers and certain food preparation personnel. As business volume increases, so does the volume of work for these employees.

It is interesting to note that the hours of work for some variable cost employees correspond to the hours of peak sales, while the work hours of others may not. For example, preparation personnel are needed in comparatively large numbers before the hours of anticipated peak sales so that food will be ready when needed. By contrast, a time lapse normally exists between the onset of peak sales in the dining room and the beginning of peak dishwashing needs in the kitchen. Moreover, the period of peak dishwashing usually continues for some time after peak food sales have ended. In general, an increase or decrease in business volume will dictate the need for an increase or decrease in the number of variable cost personnel, but their hours of work will not necessarily coincide with the hours of peak business volume.

It is important to recognize that the points made in the foregoing discussion also apply in those establishments that experience periodic or seasonal changes in business volume. During slow periods, fewer variable cost personnel are needed to handle reduced business volume; as volume increases during busier periods, more of these employees must be hired. One typical example is a restaurant at a well-known eastern seashore resort, which does comparatively little business during the winter months, but operates at near capacity during the summer. The number of variable cost personnel is kept to a minimum during the slow season and is greatly expanded during the busy summer season.

FIXED COST PERSONNEL. **Fixed cost personnel** are those whose numbers are unrelated to business volume. Although business volume in a given establishment may increase or decrease, the number of these employees remains relatively constant. Because of this, the cost of their services tends to remain relatively constant. Typical examples of fixed-cost personnel include managers, bookkeepers, chefs, and stewards, as well as maintenance personnel and cashiers.

Regardless of the increases and decreases in business volume, there will be only one manager. The same is true of the chef. As business volume changes, it becomes necessary to vary the number of personnel working under the chef's jurisdiction, but the chef, whose job as a result will vary in difficulty, will be the single constant factor in the kitchen. The same is usually true of the bookkeeper. During a slow period, the sales figure recorded in the accounting records of the business might be only $1,000 for a given day, but it takes neither more nor less time to make that entry than it does to enter a sales figure of $10,000 for a single day during a busy period. Depending on the particular duties assigned to the bookkeeper, preparation for making the bookkeeping entry may take longer in the case of $100,000 in sales, but it is highly unlikely that any additional bookkeeping help will be hired during busy periods.

Keeping and Using Records of Business Volume

One very important step that managers should take before scheduling employees is to keep records of business volume. These typically are in the form of tallies of numbers of covers served. For best results, these tallies should be made both daily and hourly.

DAILY TALLIES.   Several techniques are commonly used for determining the number of covers served daily. Perhaps the simplest is to take the information from records being prepared for a sales history, as discussed in Part II of this text, the section dealing with food control. If a cashier, for example, is developing records of the number of portions of each entree served in the dining room, one could determine the total number of covers served by totaling the number of portions served for all items on the menu. In small restaurants, where sales histories are not developed but where guest checks are used, it is reasonably simple to determine the number of persons served from information on the checks after the close of business. A third approach, becoming the most common in the industry today, is to use electronic means to record sales. This may be done with either computers or their close relatives, electronic cash registers. Either of these provides up-to-the-minute data, indicating the number of persons or covers served. In the last analysis, each restaurant manager must find a technique appropriate to his operation to determine the number of covers served daily.

Any manager or owner is in a better business position if he can determine today what conditions and sales volume are likely to be encountered in a future period. Forecasting is an attempt to make these determinations. Since experience has shown that history tends to repeat itself in food and beverage operations, any owner or manager can use historical records to predict what is likely to occur in the near future. As discussed in previous sections of the text, such forecasts enable a manager to exercise some degree of control over food and beverage purchasing and production, for example, and thus to gain some control over food and beverage costs. Similarly, a manager can exercise greater control over labor costs if he is able to predict the establishment's labor requirements with some reasonable degree of accuracy. This can be accomplished if he can predict business volume and then schedule an appropriate number of variable cost personnel on those days and times when they are needed.

With data collected over a suitable period, business volume can be forecasted with some reasonable degree of accuracy. Many restaurants have found, for example, that the number of customers served varies from day to day during the week. Many have found that Monday is normally slower than Friday. Knowing this in advance, a manager is able to schedule an appropriate number of employees for each of the days, with fewer on Mondays and more on Fridays.

In addition to helping forecast the appropriate numbers of employees needed to meet anticipated sales volume on various days of the week, such records also enable a careful manager to spot such situations as seasonal variations in business volume, which should always be taken into account in scheduling staff. Obviously, nontypical days and weeks resulting from such unforeseen circumstances as bad weather, strikes, and road construction must be dealt with as they occur. A graphic illustration of business volume by day of the week appears in Figure 19.3.

HOURLY TALLIES.   The daily record of business volume described above helps in controlling labor cost by enabling the manager to schedule employees' workdays and days off in accordance with anticipated needs. However, it does not help with problems posed by hourly fluctuations in demand. Many establishments, for example, find that the middle of the afternoon is a very slack period between two periods of peak volume: the luncheon and dinner hours. In such cases, the maximum number of dining room personnel on duty are clearly necessary during the luncheon and dinner hours. However, from the standpoint of a manager attempting to keep labor cost at the optimum level, it is undesirable for the dining room personnel on duty during the busy lunch hour to be idle through the slack afternoon while waiting for the start of a busy dinner hour. This is the kind of problem that can sometimes be reduced or eliminated by more efficient scheduling. However, improved scheduling is possible only if the manager can forecast with reasonable accuracy busy times and comparatively slow times. This can be done from hourly records of business volume, the key to designing employee schedules intended to maximize employee efficiency and minimize excessive labor cost.

There are several manual means for developing hourly records of business volume. One common way is to require the dining room manager to count and record the number of customers seated in the dining room every hour on the hour. While this is by far the simplest system, it is not the most accurate. Many customers order several cocktails before ordering food, and others linger over coffee after eating. In either case, the hourly count does not accurately reflect the number of covers served during any particular period. To the extent that this count is used to schedule preparation personnel as well as dining room personnel, it may be misleading and may result in the preparation of inefficient work schedules.

To offset the inadequacy of this hourly counting procedure, some managers have instituted a system requiring that each guest check or dupe be time-stamped in the kitchen as the order is given to cooks. The checks or dupes are

WEEK ENDING 4/3

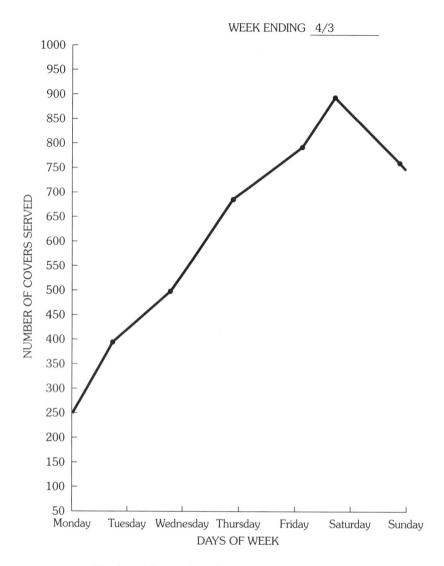

FIGURE 19.3   *Number of Covers Served Per Day*

then analyzed at the end of the day. These results more accurately reflect the times when service personnel take orders, as well as when preparation personnel receive them.

A third system for developing records of hourly volume of business requires that the cashier in the dining room record the number of covers served as customers settle guest checks. Each guest check reaches the cashier as the customer leaves the restaurant. Therefore, a simple system can be instituted to

WEATHER Clear		DATE 4/1

EXTERNAL CONDITIONS AFFECTING SALES Strong Breeze; cool

Hourly Period		Number of Covers
11:00 to Noon	ℍℍℍℍℍℍℍℍℍℍℍℍ 111	33
Noon to 1 PM	ℍℍℍℍℍℍℍℍℍℍℍℍℍℍℍℍ ℍℍℍℍℍℍℍℍℍℍℍℍℍℍ ℍℍℍℍ	90
1PM to 2PM	ℍℍℍℍℍℍℍℍℍℍℍℍℍℍℍℍ ℍℍℍℍℍℍℍℍℍℍℍℍℍℍℍℍ ℍℍℍℍ	89
2PM to 3PM	ℍℍℍℍℍℍℍℍℍℍℍℍℍℍℍℍ ℍℍℍℍ 1	51
3PM to 4PM	ℍℍℍ 1	6
4PM to 5PM	ℍℍℍ 11	7
5PM to 6PM	ℍℍℍℍℍℍℍℍℍℍℍℍℍℍℍℍ ℍℍℍ	45
6PM to 7PM	ℍℍℍℍℍℍℍℍℍℍℍℍℍℍℍℍ ℍℍℍℍℍℍℍℍℍℍℍℍℍℍ 111	78
7PM to 8PM	ℍℍℍℍℍℍℍℍℍℍℍℍℍℍℍℍ ℍℍℍℍℍℍℍℍℍℍℍℍℍℍℍℍ ℍℍℍℍℍℍ	95
8PM to 9PM	ℍℍℍℍℍℍℍℍℍℍℍℍℍℍℍℍ ℍℍℍℍℍℍℍℍℍℍℍℍℍℍℍℍ ℍℍℍℍℍℍ	95
9PM to 10PM	ℍℍℍℍℍℍℍℍℍℍℍℍℍℍℍℍ ℍℍℍℍℍℍℍℍℍℍℍℍ 111	73
10PM to 11PM	ℍℍℍℍℍℍℍℍℍℍℍℍℍℍℍℍ ℍℍℍ 111	48

FIGURE 19.4 *Tally of Covers Served Per Hour*

have the cashier record covers on a form such as that illustrated in Figure 19.4.

When the guest check has been settled and the transaction is completed, the cashier determines how many covers are reflected on the check and records that number in the space on the form for the one-hour period then current. This system is not as accurate with respect to preparation and service as is the one involving time stamps in the kitchen, but it has the advantage of being relatively simple and inexpensive.

It must be noted that manual means for developing hourly customer counts are rapidly being rendered obsolete by the growing use of sophisticated computer systems in foodservice. Detailed discussion of one typical system was included in Chapter 2.

By one or another of these means, the owner or manager can quickly accumulate a useful set of figures reflecting the hourly volume of business in his establishment. By developing and maintaining this information on a regular basis, he can better schedule variable cost employees and thus control labor cost more effectively, as described below.

The first step in using this information is to tabulate the hourly volume of business for a given day, as has been done in Figure 19.4. These tabulated figures are shown on the graph in Figure 19.5.

In this graph, the degree of fluctuation in hourly volume of business for this particular restaurant is readily apparent. However, this graph represents only one day—a certain Friday in April—and no manager could safely assume that one specific day was typical. Clearly, it would be unwise to base general scheduling on such limited information. Therefore, it is necessary to accumulate similar data for other Fridays and for other days of the week as well. The broader picture of operations that would emerge would provide a better basis for making scheduling decisions. A second step in scheduling is to tabulate the hourly volume data for a series of days (Fridays, for example) on a form similar to that shown in Figure 19.6.

Charts of this nature may be prepared for each day of the business week. Taken together, they present a history of the hourly volume of business that management can use to plan future schedules and thus to improve control over the cost of labor. One of the keys to labor cost control is effective scheduling, and it is very important to schedule labor according to anticipated requirements, based on experience.

An important third step in scheduling is to translate the raw numbers, such as those in Figure 19.6, into a graph that reflects the hourly volume experienced over a reasonable period. The graph shown in Figure 19.7 is a picture of the hourly volume of business for Fridays in the month of April.

The figures on the vertical axis show volume of business, and those on the horizontal axis show hourly periods of the operating day. Three lines are plotted on the graph to show various levels of volume for each hour. The upper dotted line shows the maximum volume experienced at each hour during the period covered by the graph. The lower dotted line shows the minimum. These are the extremes to which the hourly volume has gone during the period covered. The solid middle line shows the median.

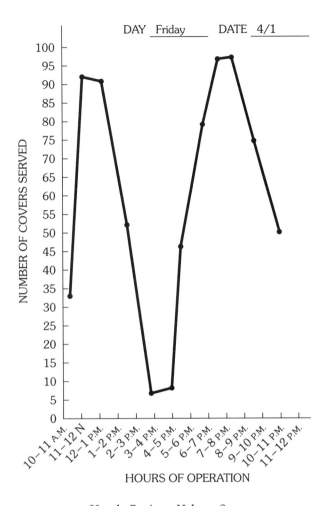

DAY _Friday_ DATE _4/1_

NUMBER OF COVERS SERVED

HOURS OF OPERATION

FIGURE 19.5 *Hourly Business Volume Summary*

The **median** is the value of the middle item in a group. It is not an arithmetic average, but a middle point. Figure 19.7 shows that business volume on the five successive Fridays between the hours of noon and 1:00 P.M. ranged from 85 to 107 covers. The numbers of covers during that hour for the five days, taken in ascending order, were 85, 90, 100, 105, and 107. From this list of five days, the two with the highest values were the days when the figure reached 105 and 107 covers per hour. The two days with the lowest volume were those on which it was 85 and 90 covers per hour. By eliminating the two highest and two lowest values, one is left with the value in the middle—the median. If the list of values had covered 15 days, one could identify the median by eliminating the seven highest and seven lowest values.

Hourly Volume of Business (number of covers): Fridays					
	Dates				
Hourly Time Periods	*4/1/XXXX*	*4/8/XXXX*	*4/15/XXXX*	*4/22/XXXX*	*4/29/XXXX*
11 A.M. to Noon	33	30	50	40	60
Noon to 1 P.M.	90	85	105	100	107
1 P.M. to 2 P.M.	89	85	105	100	105
2 P.M. to 3 P.M.	51	50	63	60	65
3 P.M. to 4 P.M.	6	5	15	10	18
4 P.M. to 5 P.M.	7	5	12	10	18
5 P.M. to 6 P.M.	45	45	55	50	60
6 P.M. to 7 P.M.	78	75	96	90	100
7 P.M. to 8 P.M.	95	95	100	100	105
8 P.M. to 9 P.M.	95	85	95	95	100
9 P.M. to 10 P.M.	73	70	77	75	85
10 P.M. to 11 P.M.	48	45	55	50	60

FIGURE 19.6 *Tabulation of Hourly Data*

The advantage of determining the median number of covers served during an hour rather than the arithmetic mean, commonly known as the **average,** is that the median shows the central tendency, unaffected by either high or low extremes. For example, if the number of covers served between 1:00 P.M. and 2:00 P.M. on five successive Fridays were 65, 66, 68, 71, and 25, the arithmetic mean, or average, would be the total of 295 divided by the five periods represented, or 59 covers. The median is 66, however, which is clearly more representative of the typical number of covers served. In this case, the average is weighted too heavily by the one extremely low number of covers served on one particular day. Since these figures are to be used for staff scheduling, it would be far safer to plan on the basis of the median rather than on the arithmetic average. The presence on the graph of both the maximum and minimum numbers served, as discussed above, provides the manager with a complete picture of the hourly volume of sales: the typical number of covers served, as well as the maximum and minimum extremes.

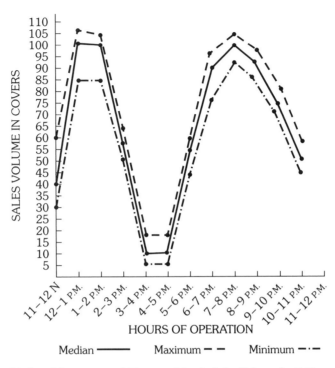

Median, Maximum, and Minimum Hourly Sales Volume for Fridays
1 Month Period Ending 4/31/XXXX

FIGURE 19.7 *Graph of Hourly Volume*

Developing Schedules for Employees

With appropriate information obtained from records of daily and hourly business volume, a manager is then prepared to develop schedules for employees, an important element in controlling labor costs. Because of marked differences in the scheduling of variable cost employees and fixed cost employees, the two categories described above (scheduling techniques and procedures for employees in these groups) will be discussed separately.

VARIABLE COST EMPLOYEES. Referring to limited data in Figure 19.3, one notes a greater daily volume of business on Friday and Saturday than on Monday and Tuesday. If the graph represented the historical record of median volume over an appropriate period, it would be advisable to plan a schedule for variable cost employees geared to the data in the graph, assuming that similar conditions were expected for the week to be scheduled. A manager

Hours of Operation	Anticipated Sales Volume in Covers	Staff Required
10 A.M. to 11 A.M.	—	2
11 A.M. to Noon	40	2
Noon to 1 P.M.	100	5
1 P.M. to 2 P.M.	100	5
2 P.M. to 3 P.M.	60	3
3 P.M. to 4 P.M.	10	1
4 P.M. to 5 P.M.	10	1
5 P.M. to 6 P.M.	50	3
6 P.M. to 7 P.M.	90	5
7 P.M. to 8 P.M.	100	5
8 P.M. to 9 P.M.	95	5
9 P.M. to 10 P.M.	75	4
10 P.M. to 11 P.M.	50	3
11 P.M. to 12 P.M.	—	2

FIGURE 19.8   *Staffing Table for Servers—Friday, September 2, XXXX (Based on Median Sales)*

should also use the records of hourly volume to plan schedules that have adequate numbers of variable cost employees on duty at appropriate times through the work day. Their working hours should be staggered to meet anticipated hourly demand.

A preliminary step in the scheduling of variable cost employees is determining the types and numbers of employees needed at given levels of business volume. These are used to develop staffing tables. Staffing tables for variable cost employees are estimates of the numbers of these employees required at various levels of business volume, given the quality and quantity standards established for their work. Each manager must make judgments about the number needed in each job classification affected by hourly volume. For servers, he must determine the number of covers that each can serve in a given hour while maintaining the established service standards. For dishwashers, he must determine the quantity of dishes that each can process in an hour. Similar judgments must be made for each job category.

Determining the number of employees required at various levels of business volume is typically an intuitive process, based on a manager's experience. Figure 19.8 is a staffing table for servers in a given restaurant. To develop it, the manager first had to use intuitive means to set the number of covers that each server could reasonably be expected to serve per hour. Having set that number at 20, he then referred to Figure 19.7, indicating the number of covers served per hour on Fridays. She assumed that the expected number of customers for the coming Friday would be approximately the median number served on previous Fridays. As the figure indicates, the median number of covers served between noon and 1:00 P.M. was 100. If one server can serve 20 covers per hour, then 5 servers should be needed for any hour when 100 customers must be served. The balance of the staffing table is prepared from similar estimates for the other hours of the day.

With records available of the daily and hourly volume of business and with staffing tables developed from those records, a manager is suitably equipped to schedule variable cost employees for a specific Friday.

The manager can then prepare a schedule showing the total number of servers needed for that day and the time periods they will work. Figure 19.9 is an hourly schedule for servers for a particular Friday.

In the illustration, the manager has scheduled two servers to begin work one hour before opening and two to remain one hour after closing to clean up and prepare for the following day. To increase efficiency, he has also scheduled some part-time workers. It is apparent that seven servers are needed for the day, three of them part-time and four full-time, of whom three are working split shifts. Other possible schedules could be devised. For example, employee B could become a full-time employee by working his normal shift and, in addition, taking on the shift of employee G. This would reduce the number of servers from seven to six.

By following this procedure for all days and hours of operation during the work week being planned, while keeping in mind the number of days and hours that each employee could or would work, the manager could develop a work schedule based on both anticipated sales volume and judgments about servers' abilities to provide each customer with the established level of service quality. In addition, because the schedule would be based on realistically anticipated needs, it could be set up to keep labor costs at a suitable level for the forecasted number of covers. Once complete, a schedule such as that illustrated in Figure 19.10 would be prepared and posted for employees, so that each would know his scheduled work hours for the coming week.

FIXED COST EMPLOYEES. While the scheduling of variable cost employees is linked directly to daily and hourly records of business volume, the scheduling of fixed cost employees is not.

Before fixed cost personnel can be scheduled with any degree of certainty, the manager must determine the specific requirements of the job that should be taken into account in scheduling. For a storeroom clerk, such requirements might include a need to have the storeroom open during hours of preparation, so that food supplies can be issued to the production staff, or a need for the

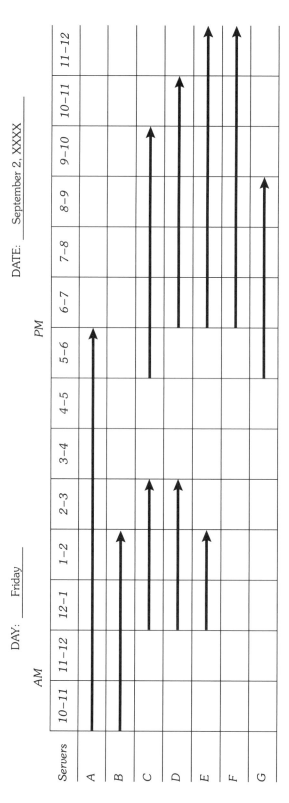

FIGURE 19.9 *Sample Schedule Worksheet: Hourly Schedule for Servers*

Server	Mon.	Tues.	Wed.	Thurs.	Fri.	Sat.	Sun.
A	Off	Off	10–6	10–6	10–6	10–6	10–6
B	Off	10–6	10–2	10–2	10–2	10–2	10–2
C	Off	Off	12–3 5–10	12–3 5–10	12–3 5–10	12–3 5–10	12–3 5–10
D	12–3 6–11	Off	Off	12–3 6–11	12–3 6–11	12–3 6–11	12–3 6–11
E	10–2 5–9	10–2 5–9	Off	Off	12–2 6–12	12–2 6–12	12–2 6–12
F	10–6	6–12	Off	Off	6–12	6–12	6–12
G	Off	5–9	5–12	5–12	5–9	5–9	Off
H						6–10	

FIGURE 19.10   *Sample Schedule for Servers*

storeroom clerk to be available to accept food deliveries taken in by the receiving clerk. These details should be considered before establishing the work
schedule for the job.

When all such requirements have been considered, a manager can establish and post a schedule for fixed cost personnel that would resemble that
illustrated in Figure 19.11.

While schedules for fixed cost employees tend not to change from one
week to the next, major changes in business volume for protracted periods
may cause management to reassess both schedules and costs for fixed cost
personnel. Substantial decreases in business volume, for example, may suggest
the need for a substantial decrease in labor costs generally, including a reduction in the number of fixed cost personnel. When such a step is necessary, it is
important to see that any reduction in staff does not lead to a decrease in
operating efficiency.

The foregoing is a very basic approach to labor cost control commonly
used by many food and beverage managers. It establishes performance standards for staff, but does so informally. Because the resulting performance standards are based on a manager's recollections about the adequacy of performance, they are not sufficiently accurate and reliable to meet the needs of
managers in highly structured organizations. In these kinds of organizations,
management has found that the intuitive approach to establishing performance
standards is not sufficient. A better approach is to base one's standards on

Employee	Mon.	Tues.	Wed.	Thurs.	Fri.	Sat.	Sun.
Purchasing Steward	9–5	9–5	9–5	9–5	9–5	9–5	Off
Storeroom Clerk	Off	8–4	8–4	8–4	8–4	8–4	8–4
Receiving Clerk	7–3	7–3	7–3	7–3	7–3	7–3	Off
Porter	Off	12–8	12–8	12–8	12–8	12–8	12–8
Vegetable Preparer	Off	8–4	8–4	8–4	8–4	8–4	8–4
Cashier 1	Off	5–12	10–5	10–5	10–5	10–5	10–5
Cashier 2	5–12	Off	5–12	5–12	5–12	5–12	5–12

FIGURE 19.11   *Sample Schedule for Fixed Cost Employees*

written evaluations of performance accumulated over a period of time. The results will be more objective and are likely to be better suited to monitoring performance.

Managers in large organizations are better equipped to establish performance standards for work in this way and to use the resulting standards for evaluating the degree of efficiency with which managers of individual units schedule employees. In such organizations, standards of employee performance have been established and various means have been found to compare these performance standards with actual performance. Preliminary aspects of this approach to establishing standards will be discussed below.

PERFORMANCE STANDARDS BASED ON TEST PERIOD

Performance standards developed from records kept during a test period take both quantity and quality standards for work into account. A test period of a particular number of days or weeks is established for gathering data. During this period, detailed sales records are kept, indicating the number of covers served per day or per meal, depending on the type of establishment being analyzed. Managers also record the number of staff members on duty in each fixed and variable cost job and reviews each, making judgments about sufficiency of staff and efficiency of employee performance. These judgments are key to establishing standards for use in future periods.

			Noon Meal 11:00 A.M.–2:00 P.M.				
Date	*5/1*	*5/2*	*5/3*	*5/4*	*5/5*	*5/6*	*5/7*
No. of Covers Served	275	450	400	350	400	425	500
Servers Scheduled	7	7	7	7	7	7	7
Efficiency of Performance	Poor— Only 5 Servers Needed	Excellent	Very Good	Poor— Only 6 Servers Needed	Very Good	Excellent	Poor—8 Servers Needed
Warewashers Scheduled	3	3	3	3	3	3	3
Efficiency of Performance	Poor— Only 2 Needed	Excellent	Good— Some Inefficiency	Poor— Only 2 Needed	Good— Some Inefficiency	Excellent	Poor— Overtime Required
Preparation Personnel Scheduled	4	4	4	4	4	4	4
Efficiency of Performance	Poor— Only 3 Needed	Excellent	Good— 1 Less Needed	Not Good— 1 Less Needed	Good	Excellent	Excellent

FIGURE 19.12 *Evaluation of Employee Efficiency*

Variable Cost Personnel

Figure 19.12 relates numbers of variable cost personnel to sales volume in covers for a particular test period and shows one manager's judgments about staffing during that period. As the chart shows, with sales of 275 covers and seven servers scheduled for lunch on May 1, the manager judged performance to be highly inefficient because of overstaffing and recorded his observations for future reference. As the one-week period progressed, he continued to note his estimates of labor efficiency, relating the number of servers working to the total number of covers served. While Figure 19.12 has been set up to record estimates of labor efficiency for an entire meal period, it would be possible to do this on an hourly basis if a more detailed view were required.

Fixed Cost Personnel

It also is feasible to prepare a similar chart that relates numbers of fixed cost personnel to numbers of covers sold for a period and to make provision for the manager to estimate employee efficiency by the day or meal or even by the hour. However, as has been noted, the nature of the work of fixed cost personnel is such that the numbers on duty in any category cannot be varied in normal circumstances. Under extraordinary conditions (when sales increase or decrease abnormally for protracted periods, for example), such charts could reflect the need for increasing staff or for laying off staff and combining jobs. However, under normal circumstances, such volume/staffing review charts are prepared only for variable cost personnel.

STANDARD STAFFING REQUIREMENTS

Once appropriate charts have been prepared for a test period and the manager has a record of sales volume, numbers of variable cost employees working, and his own personal estimates of the employees' efficiency, it is time to take the next logical step: to develop a table of standard **staffing requirements,** traditionally known as **manpower requirements,** for variable cost personnel at several levels of business volume. Figure 19.13, a typical example, shows standard staffing requirements for variable cost personnel in each category. It is apparent from a comparison of Figures 19.12 and 19.13 that this manager judged seven servers excessive for serving 275 covers on May 1 and therefore set five as a more appropriate number. Similarly, he judged seven as insufficient for serving 500 covers on May 7 and determined that this number of covers could be satisfactorily served by eight servers. Thus, by judging performance carefully and recording these judgments over a period of time, a manager can set standards for staffing. Referring to these two tables of standard labor requirements and to forecasts of anticipated sales for a coming week, the manager can establish better control over labor cost by scheduling the number of personnel necessary to meet the preparation and service standards of the establishment.

This technique can be further refined. Records may be analyzed to establish hourly standards for performance, and suitable tables may then be developed. When hourly tables are used, the manager can achieve an even greater degree of control over payroll. Clearly, hourly records of the sort discussed

Covers	200–299	300–399	400–499	500–599
Servers	5	6	7	8
Warewashers	2	2	3	4
Preparation Personnel	3	3	4	4

FIGURE 19.13 *Standard Staffing Requirements: Luncheon*

earlier in this chapter and tables of standard labor requirements developed from these hourly records would offer a more complete and detailed means for scheduling staff efficiently.

STANDARD WORK HOURS

Before we attempt to describe an approach to improving labor efficiency, it is necessary to introduce another way of looking at standards for labor productivity. We will discuss **standard work hours:** the number of employee work hours required to perform a given volume of work. The term is normally related to the work of those in specific job categories, such as servers, dishwashers, or cooks. If, for example, eight servers are needed to serve 500 covers in a three-hour luncheon period, the standard work hours required for servers would be calculated as follows:

$$8 \text{ servers} \times 3 \text{ hours} = 24 \text{ work hours}$$

The 24 work hours would become the standard for serving 500 covers over a luncheon period. Given a forecast of 500 covers, the scheduling of any number of servers' work hours in excess of 24 would be an indication of poor scheduling. Fewer than 24 would also be an indication of poor scheduling and would further suggest that unsatisfactory levels of service quality would be provided to customers. Varying numbers of standard work hours would be established for varying levels of sales volume, and it would be the responsibility of management to establish these standards.

The number of standard work hours required would not necessarily vary directly with changes in the volume of business. In the previous example, 24 work hours for servers was the standard for 500 covers during the luncheon period. For the three-hour time period, this is 20.83 covers per standard work hour. At a lower level of sales volume (300 covers, for example), six servers equaling 18 standard work hours might be established as the standard. This is 16.7 covers per standard work hour, suggesting less efficiency than that at the higher volume level. High levels of efficiency are more difficult to achieve at lower volume levels.

By employing the techniques previously discussed, management can develop tables of standard work hours for all job categories at various levels of business activity. Figure 19.14 illustrates a table of standard work hours for variable cost personnel for one particular restaurant. Used in conjunction with forecasts of sales volume, these figures are helpful both in forecasting work hours required and scheduling employees as efficiently as possible. For example, assume that the manager of a given restaurant, after referring to the establishment's sales history, has forecast 500 covers for a given luncheon period. Given that level of sales volume, one can determine from the chart illus-

Number of Covers	Service Personnel	Warewashing Personnel	Preparation Personnel
200–299	15	6	9
300–399	18	6	9
400–499	21	9	12
500–599	24	12	12

FIGURE 19.14 *Standard Work-Hour Requirements Variable Cost Personnel: Luncheon*

trated in Figure 19.14 that the standard work hours required for that level of sales are as follows:

Service personnel: 24
Warewashing personnel: 12
Preparation personnel: 12

Forecasts would be made for each meal or day, depending on the nature of the operation, and the number of standard work hours required at those levels of volume would be determined. The standard work hour requirements would form the basis for developing work schedules for employees, following the procedures discussed earlier in this chapter. Obviously, all this would be done far enough in advance so that employees would have appropriate notice of their work schedules for the week.

STANDARD COSTS

The development of standard work hours makes possible the development of standard labor costs. This may be done by simply multiplying the number of standard work hours required to perform a given volume of work by the hourly wage paid those performing the work. For example, assume that servers were paid $4.00 per hour and that 24 standard work hours are required to serve 500 covers in a three-hour luncheon period, as indicated in Figure 19.14 and described above. Standard cost for this can be calculated by multiplying the number of standard work hours by hourly wage[1] as follows:

24 hours × $4.00 per hour = $96.00 standard cost

Thus, the standard cost for servers serving 500 covers in a three-hour period is $96.00. Similar calculations would be used to determine standard

[1]Note that standard cost calculated in this way takes only the hourly wage into account and not the cost of various payroll taxes and fringe benefits.

costs for other categories of employees (cooks, dishwashers, and others). Calculated standard costs are useful for evaluating the efficiency of scheduling, a subject that will be addressed in Chapter 21.

As discussed previously in so many ways in this text, a principal requirement for gaining control over cost in food and beverage operations lies in establishing the standards to be used for making comparisons and judgments. Quality standards and quantity standards have been cited as critical standards that had to be established before management could begin to control costs. Quality and quantity standards for labor are established by the means described above: organizing an enterprise, preparing job descriptions, and scheduling employees. Having established these standards, one can turn to the second step in the control process: training all individuals to follow standards and standard procedures. This will be the subject of the next chapter.

COMPUTER APPLICATIONS

Chapters 2 and 12 included descriptions of computer terminals located at sidestands in a dining room and used by servers for a variety of purposes, including sending orders to kitchens and service bars. The time at which any order is placed is automatically recorded. It is also possible to record both the time at which any party placed its first order and the time at which it settled the check. With this computer-generated information available, analyzing business volume by day, by meal, or by hour is simply a matter of referring to a printout of the data. This data can be used to develop a staffing table for servers and others and would aid management in scheduling variable-cost personnel.

CHAPTER ESSENTIALS

In this chapter, we identified three steps used to establish standards and standard procedures for staff. The first of these is organizing an enterprise, which includes identifying the types of jobs needed and designing an organization chart that shows the relationships of jobs within the enterprise. The second step is preparing job descriptions based on job analysis, which makes possible the development of job specifications. The third step is scheduling employees, which requires developing hourly, daily, or weekly records of business volume. We distinguished between variable-cost and fixed-cost personnel and discussed basic approaches to preparing schedules for both. We discuss the importance of developing performance standards, both as guides to efficient scheduling and as means for judging performance. Finally, we described how computers could aid in keeping records of business volume used to develop staffing tables.

KEY TERMS IN THIS CHAPTER

Fixed-cost personnel
Job analysis
Job description
Job specification
Median
Organization chart
Organizational plan
Performance criteria
Standard labor cost
Standard staffing requirements
Standard work hours
Variable cost personnel

QUESTIONS AND PROBLEMS

1. List the three steps used to establish standards and standard procedures for personnel.

2. What does an organization plan include? Why is it necessary to develop one?

3. Describe an organization chart.

4. Distinguish between variable cost personnel and fixed cost personnel.

5. Define the term job analysis, and explain its importance in developing job descriptions.

6. Define the term job description. What are the three elements of a job description?

7. What are performance criteria? What purpose do they serve?

8. Using the appropriate chapters from the food control or beverage control section of this text as reference, develop a job description for a receiving clerk.

9. What is a job specification? For what primary purpose are job specifications used?

10. The chart below is an hourly record of business volume for a typical day in a nearby restaurant. Servers are expected to attend to 25 customers per hour, and each server is scheduled for an eight-hour work day whenever possible. Part-time help is often used, and split shifts

are permitted. Two servers are always scheduled to come in one hour before the 11:00 A.M. opening to set up the dining room, and two remain from 10:00 P.M. to 11:00 P.M. for cleanup.

Time Period	Covers Served
11:00 A.M.–Noon	50
Noon–1:00 P.M.	200
1:00 P.M.–2:00 P.M.	100
2:00 P.M.–3:00 P.M.	25
3:00 P.M.–4:00 P.M.	10
4:00 P.M.–5:00 P.M.	10
5:00 P.M.–6:00 P.M.	60
6:00 P.M.–7:00 P.M.	150
7:00 P.M.–8:00 P.M.	100
8:00 P.M.–9:00 P.M.	50
9:00 P.M.–10:00 P.M.	20

    a. Prepare a chart similar to Figure 19.5, showing a record of the volume of business per hour on a typical day.

    b. Prepare an hourly schedule for servers similar to that in Figure 19.9.

11. Refer to the record of the volume of business per hour in Question 10. Assume that the restaurant is open seven days per week and that the first five days follow the pattern of business indicated above, but the last two days of the week normally have business volume equal to 50% of that on other days. Full-time servers work a five-day week, part-time servers work four-hour days, and the manager prefers to use as few part-time servers as possible. Given this information, prepare a weekly schedule for servers similar to that found in Figure 19.10.

12. Developing work schedules for variable-cost personnel requires taking into account some considerations that are quite different from those used in developing work schedules for fixed-cost personnel. List and discuss two such considerations.

13. Of what value are performance standards in controlling labor costs?

14. List and describe the methods for establishing performance standards.

15. Which of the methods identified in Question 14 would be most practical for most foodservice establishments? Why? Which would be the least practical for small operations? Why?

16. Why might managers of small restaurants decide not to adopt the standard work hour approach to controlling labor cost?

17. Many object to the standard work hour approach to labor cost control on the grounds that it ignores the human relations element in the workplace. What do you believe they mean by this? What possible drawbacks are inherent in the standard work hour approach?

18. Assume that the figures in Figure 19.13 are applicable to a foodservice establishment that you are managing. Prepare a list of staffing requirements for the five days forecasted below:
Monday, June 7—200 covers
Tuesday, June 8—350 covers
Wednesday, June 9—450 covers
Thursday, June 10—475 covers
Friday, June 11—575 covers

19. Define each of the following key terms:
Fixed cost personnel
Job analysis
Job description
Job specification
Median
Organization chart
Organizational plan
Performance criteria
Standard labor cost
Standard staffing requirements
Standard work hours
Variable cost personnel

20 *Training Staff*

After reading and studying this chapter, you should be able to:

1. Define training, and distinguish between training and education.
2. Identify the purpose of training.
3. Discuss the relationship of training needs assessment to the development of a training plan.
4. List and discuss the 10 elements commonly covered in a training plan, including objectives, approach to training, training method, instructional timetable, location, lesson plan, trainer preparation, trainee preparation, training session(s), and evaluation.
5. Discuss the advantages and disadvantages of centralized and local training for multi-unit organizations.
6. Identify the four content areas normally included in training manuals.
7. Discuss two computer applications that can provide assistance to trainers.
8. Define each of the Key Terms listed at the end of the chapter.

INTRODUCTION

As previously discussed, the second step in the control process is training employees to follow the standards and standard procedures established. This is a critical step in the successful control of labor cost: Employees who are properly trained will be more efficient, enabling management to keep labor costs to their practical minimum. This should result in better financial performance for the establishment.

Improved financial performance is not the only benefit of training. It must be pointed out that training has additional benefits beyond the immediate goal of controlling labor cost. Properly trained employees will be more effective. They will be able to do their jobs in the manner that presents the establishment in its most favorable light. For example, properly trained servers will make favorable impressions on guests both by their approach to guest relations and by their professional use of proper serving techniques. They will speak to guests in the manner intended by management, suggest appropriate items to guests, take orders efficiently, and serve food using proper techniques. In general, well-trained personnel will create a more satisfactory dining experience for a guest. Finally, experience shows that well-trained employees are more likely to continue working for the employers who have provided their training, thus keeping the labor turnover rate lower in establishments with effective training programs.

A DEFINITION OF TRAINING

Training is a process by means of which individuals acquire the skills necessary to perform particular tasks. For the present discussion, we will assume that these tasks are job related and that the individuals acquiring the skills do so for employment purposes. Many are given training by their employers; some seek training to become qualified for employment in some specific job.

Training is narrowly focused on particular skills and tasks. It normally includes some education, but it is not the same as education, which is a broader-based term. The objectives of education include increasing one's knowledge of a given subject and developing the capacity of the mind to address complex topics and to analyze critically.

THE PURPOSE OF TRAINING

The primary purpose of training is to improve job performance. Many employers provide training for this specific purpose: to improve their employees' on-the-job performance. Some only provide training for new employees so that each newcomer will learn the specifics of the job he is expected to do, as well as the performance criteria associated with the job. Others also provide training for long-term employees so that each will have an opportunity to maintain or improve the skills required in that specific job. One particularly important step in training, most would agree, is that of developing a healthy climate for training. In some organizations, management has devoted considerable time and attention to developing an organizational climate that treats training as a necessary and important element for its health and well being. Training is considered a positive factor in achieving organizational and personal goals, and employees learn early in their careers to look forward to the training that will increase their skills inventories and enhance their ability to contribute to the organization.

Whether it is done properly or improperly, training does consume resources in any organization: It requires time and money. Because training is costly, one must take care to develop an approach and a program that will meet the needs of the organization. The training program starts with an assessment of needs.

THE TRAINING PROGRAM
Assessing Training Needs

Training needs should be based on assessments of:

1. Present staff.
2. New staff.

For present staff members, one should be concerned about their current ability to carry out their tasks and to meet the standards and standard procedures established for their jobs. In addition, one must bear in mind that the purchase of new equipment, the development of new standards and standard procedures, or both of these may lead to the need for additional training of present staff. Often, employers find that employees who have been at their jobs for some time require some training. Long-term employees may need training to work with new equipment that is purchased and new methods and procedures that are developed. For example, a foodservice operator who has purchased a complex computer system to be used for dining room and kitchen operation must spend considerable time training servers and others to use the system.

Another consideration for some employers is the extent of the need to institute **cross training.** Cross training is defined as teaching a worker to perform the duties of some job or jobs other than his own. Some employers consider it important to provide cross training so that employees are prepared to perform the duties of those who are absent or ill or so that jobs can be combined during slow periods. Sometimes employees are reassigned to jobs for which they have been cross trained so that they will not lose their new skills. In some cases, employers have found it desirable to reassign employees in this way to help prevent the feelings of boredom that those with routine jobs can develop. Employees may be reassigned for several weeks and then either returned to their regular jobs or reassigned again. The process of periodically reassigning employees to other jobs is known as **job rotation.**

In well-managed organizations, training is generally required of all new employees, even those who come to an organization with considerable experience. Every foodservice operation has its own way of doing things—its own methods for performing tasks and accomplishing work. It is very important that people who already know how to perform a job be shown the specific methods and procedures used by the organization for which they have just started to work. For those who are inexperienced, more formal training is likely to occur.

Every new employee needs some amount of training in the methods and procedures of the foodservice operation. This can range from a mere tour of the establishment for a highly skilled and experienced professional to urgently required basic skills training for some newcomers to the industry. Once an assessment has been made of the nature and extent of the training that will be required, a plan for undertaking the training can be developed.

Developing Training Plans

A **training plan** is a series of elements that constitute a method for teaching a specific employee the skills required to perform a job correctly and in the manner anticipated by management when the standards and standard procedures for the job were developed.

While the specifics of training plans vary from one organization to another, the elements most commonly included are those discussed below:

1. Objectives.
2. Approaches to training.
3. Training methods.
4. Instructional timetables.
5. Location.
6. Lesson plans.
7. Trainer preparation.
8. Trainee preparation.
9. The training session(s).
10. Evaluation.

OBJECTIVES.   Training objectives identify the skills, tasks, and behaviors that a specific employee will have mastered by the time training is complete. These skills, tasks, and behaviors are the basis for developing lesson plans for training, as described below.

Training objectives are developed from a job analysis and from a carefully developed job description that lists the duties of a job and the performance criteria for that job. Each job description should identify the specific duties and performance criteria associated with a particular job. Given the specific duties and performance criteria, one must determine the specific skills, manual and otherwise, that each job holder will require to carry out the duties of his job. Once these skills have been identified, training becomes possible.

In a food and beverage operation, there are many different kinds of jobs, and management must devise one set of training objectives for each job title for which training is to be done. For example, the most basic training objectives for a dishwasher would include the ability to:

1. Start the equipment at the beginning of the day.
2. Operate the equipment properly, in accordance with manufacturer's directions.
3. Shut down the equipment at the end of the day, cleaning it in accordance with manufacturer's directions and local health codes.
4. Load soiled china, glassware, and flatware properly to avoid breakage.
5. Unload clean china, glassware, and flatware properly, stacking and storing in accordance with company rules.

Some managers would be inclined to add many other training objectives to the short list above. These could include some related to personal hygiene, foodservice sanitation, and others.

APPROACHES TO TRAINING.   One must consider several approaches to training before selecting one or another of the training methods available. These approaches are characterized and described below.

On-the-job versus Off-the-job.   Training can be done on the job or off the job. On-the-job training is more commonly used with experienced workers who need to be shown only the methods used by the hospitality operation. For example, a new cook may be put to work immediately under the guidance and instruction of an experienced cook who will show the new cook how to fill out requisitions for supplies, how orders are placed for menu items, and how the establishment garnishes plates of food going into the dining room.

For inexperienced employees, on-the-job training can be used effectively in situations where the work they do can be easily monitored and corrected before it has a negative impact on guests or where a new employee can work side by side with an experienced worker. For example, a new dishwasher can be trained effectively if assisted by an experienced dishwasher. The experienced dishwasher can show the new dishwasher the normal routine for preparing the dishwashing machine for operation. He can show the new dishwasher the best way to place dishes, glassware, and other pottery and glass to be washed in the dish racks, as well as how to do all the other tasks that go into washing dishes. The experienced dishwasher can monitor the work performed by the new dishwasher, correct mistakes, and suggest those improvements that will ensure that the work is done in the most efficient manner possible without damage or breakage to the machine or dishes and glassware. Other related uses for on-the-job training include apprenticeships and internships, although these are somewhat more common in Europe than in North America.

Sometimes the type and level of job for which training is required is such that off-the-job training is more suitable. While this would not be the case with a dishwasher, it might be for a loyal kitchen worker who management wanted to train to be a cook. Rather than attempt the training in-house, management might enroll the worker in one of the culinary programs offered by community colleges, proprietary schools, or under the sponsorship of hotel and restaurant unions in some major cities.

Structured versus Unstructured. Training may be done on a structured or an unstructured basis. Structured training is characterized by a formal approach to instruction. The structured approach requires extensive planning, with considerable time and attention being given to the nature of each formal step in the specific training plan being undertaken. It may be characterized by lesson plans, manuals, training films, and videotapes developed specifically for use in the structured training program. By contrast, unstructured training is commonly undertaken with relatively little thought being given to the specifics of the training. It is quite informal and is often characterized by a trainee being directed to follow and carefully observe an experienced worker doing the job.

The unstructured approach tends to work well in situations where high levels of skills training are not required. For example, a garde manger newly hired to replace a retiring employee and coming to the job with extensive skills honed over a period of many years might be able to gain all the training needed by working closely with the retiring garde manger for a period of several days. He would come to the job with all the requisite skills and would have to learn only the standards and standard procedures established by the new employer. This approach would be unproductive if a trainee came to the job without garde manger skills.

Individual versus Group. Training can be done on an individual basis, as described above, or it may be done in groups. Individual training is undoubtedly the most effective. However, in terms of cost per person trained, it is very expensive: The trainer must devote time to training only one person at a time. By contrast, some of the major foodservice organizations rely heavily on group training sessions because of the large number of employees requiring training.

There are many specific methods used for training employees. Some of those described below are more commonly used to train groups. Others are best suited to the training of individuals. Some are equally effective in either setting, provided that suitable adjustments are made.

Decisions as to approaches and methods vary from one establishment to another and include such considerations as the type and level of the jobs for which training is to be done; the number of individuals to be trained; the number of trainers available; time, space, and funds available for training purposes; and many others.

TRAINING METHODS. There are any number of training methods available for those seeking ways to institute employee training. Some of the more common methods are identified and described below:

1. Lecture/demonstration.
2. Role playing.
3. Individual assignments.
4. Field trips.
5. Seminars.
6. Case studies.
7. Panels.
8. Programmed instruction.

Lecture/Demonstration. The **lecture/demonstration method** requires that a trainer explain a subject or task to one trainee or to a group of trainees, demonstrate the skills involved, and respond to questions during or after the lecture/demonstration. For example, a trainer may explain to new servers the proper procedures for taking orders and serving food and then demonstrate those procedures to trainees. The lecture/demonstration method typically has limited effectiveness unless combined with other training methods that provide students with opportunities immediately to practice the techniques and standard procedures explained and demonstrated.

Role Playing.   **Role playing** can be a very effective method of training, particularly when coupled with the lecture/demonstration approach. Role playing enables each learner to play a part in a scene created by the trainer. For example, servers can be divided into small groups, with each member of the group taking a turn at practicing the various serving techniques that a trainer has previously demonstrated.

Seminars.   **Seminars** are group discussions of particular subjects led by trainers. They are the most useful for management training, where the input of the trainees is an important part of the learning process. Significant questions are typically raised by the seminar leader, and each member of the group is asked for his opinions. For example, a foodservice chain may hold a seminar on guest relations for restaurant managers. Participants could be asked to discuss the best way to handle guest complaints about food quality or service in the dining room. Each manager would be expected to participate actively in the seminar, and each individual's expressed point of view would be discussed by the others, enabling all present to benefit from the thoughts of their colleagues. These types of training sessions can be extremely valuable when conducted as part of an ongoing training program.

Individual Assignments.   **Individual assignments** constitute a very effective means for undertaking the training of employees for particular types of jobs at or near the management level. This method is most effective for trainees who are comfortable with self-paced learning, a characteristic this method shares with programmed instruction.

The individual assignment method actually includes a broad array of techniques, including assigning specific readings, requiring research into a specific topic, directing that one observe experienced personnel performing their tasks and duties in a specified setting, and requiring that one practice the skills and techniques learned via one of the other methods. Many have found that this method works best when preceded by more formal training delivered via one of the other methods. It is frequently used with the seminar method and makes it possible, for example, for the seminar participants to gain firsthand experience and to verbally share their experiences with others attending the same seminar.

Field Trips.   **Field trips** offer an excellent means for individuals or groups to observe others at work and to study the standards and standard procedures they follow in carrying out their job assignments. Group field trips are preferred by many because of the opportunities they afford for a leader to call attention to key points and to ensure that all participants note the particular elements they are expected to observe. In addition, the leader can also serve as a discussion leader, effectively linking the field trip method to the seminar method in a very useful way.

Field trips for single individuals, rather than groups, offer a valuable means for a learner to observe settings, standards, and processes as they normally occur: Group observation can sometimes disturb the normal work environment, in which case participants in a group field trip may get a somewhat distorted view of the work behavior of those being observed.

Case Studies. The **case study method** bears some similarity to the seminar method, except that the participants are asked to read a prepared case involving a real or hypothetical situation. The case should provide sufficient information so that the participants can discuss the particulars of the case, providing their personal views about the meaning, significance, or importance of all that has occurred. In addition, all participants are commonly expected to develop or to assist a group in developing solutions to the problems posed by the case.

The case method is best suited to use in management training and is often used to assist managers attempting to learn how to deal with such common problems as dealing with difficult guests and settling interpersonal disputes among employees.

Panels. **Panels** consist of groups of experts called in by trainers to express their opinions on specific questions for the benefit of an audience of trainees, usually management trainees. The panel members are typically asked to comment on timely subjects under discussion. They may agree with each other or provide differing and contrasting opinions, thus giving trainees the benefit of hearing several views.

Like the seminar method, the panel method offers an excellent means of eliciting the opinions of participants. However, the opinions are those of the panel members, not those of the trainees. In some instances, especially with management training groups, trainees are encouraged to question members of the panel and to challenge their views.

Programmed Instruction. The **programmed instruction method** is considered by its supporters to be among the most effective means of providing individual training. Programmed instruction can be accomplished via books or dedicated equipment. Study guides and workbooks are good examples.

These are commonly designed to accompany texts and thus to help students acquire more knowledge and understanding than might otherwise be possible. Computers provide additional examples. Today, much programmed instruction is delivered by computer. The tutorials that normally accompany computer software are among the common examples of programmed instruction. The learner is presented with information, walked step-by-step through a process, and then asked to demonstrate that they have acquired the knowledge and skills that the programmed instruction was designed to teach. If the learner is unable to complete the necessary task satisfactorily, the program will so indicate and then conduct the learner through instruction once again.

One obvious advantage of programmed instruction is that it provides immediate feedback to the learner. Another is that instruction is totally under the control of the programmer, effectively preventing the learner from straying beyond the bounds written into the program. In addition, the program can be repeated endlessly by the learner until he has acquired the knowledge or skills that the program was designed to teach.

Each of the above methods of training may be used for any of several different levels of training. In addition, their purposes vary slightly from one method to another. Lecture/demonstration and role playing are excellent for teaching specific skills. Seminars, case studies, and panels are fine methods to use in programs designed for employee development, to improve levels of job performance and to qualify participants for higher levels of responsibility within the hospitality organization. Depending on their particular uses in a given setting, individual assignments, field trips, and programmed instruction are also excellent methods for assisting individuals and groups to learn about and follow the standards and standard procedures established for successful hospitality operation.

From the several approaches to training and the array of training methods available, one must select those that can best be employed for achieving the training objectives established. For example, to teach a new employee how to perform the job of a dishwasher, one would probably choose the individual rather than the group approach, as well as the lecture/demonstration method. One might combine this with the role playing method or with the individual assignment method, both of which would serve to reinforce the valuable lessons imparted during the lecture/demonstration. If role playing or individual assignment were selected, one would clearly elect to supervise the trainee's activity so that incorrect behaviors would be subject to timely corrective action.

INSTRUCTIONAL TIMETABLES.   Once a suitable training method has been selected, it is necessary to assess the amount of time training will take—the number of days, hours, or minutes that should be allotted to each phase of training, as well as the overall length of time required to complete the training.

There is a limit to the amount of new material that can be absorbed by learners in a given training session. While the amount varies with the nature of the material to be presented, the capabilities of the trainer, and the degree of concentration required of the learners, any qualified trainer understands that this limit exists and takes great care not to attempt to go beyond it in any one session. This limit, known intuitively by experienced trainers, helps to determine both the length of a given training session and the number of sessions required to achieve a specific training objective.

Provision for the development of suitable instructional timetables is a major requirement in training plans.

LOCATIONS.   Training locations should be determined by the nature of the training to be done. The nature of the training to be done is key to selecting a training method, which helps determine the type of location that will be most suitable for training.

On-the-job training typically requires that trainees be present at the job site during normal business hours. Off-the-job training carries no such requirement and enlarges the list of potential training locations. The structured approach to learning is more likely to require that specific locations be set aside for regular use as instructional sites. By contrast, the informality of the unstructured approach can make this unnecessary. Similarly, the individual approach is not as likely as the group approach is to require the assignment of a classroom or similar specific site for training activities. For the individual approach, the job site is often the proper location for training.

Determining the proper location for training is often a very simple exercise. For example, if one intends to train servers, it would be sensible to undertake some of the training in a setting that resembles the area in which they will work: a dining room. Some of the training could take place in a classroom setting, but clearly a great deal of it should be done in a dining room. Similarly, most—possibly all—of the training for a dishwasher should be done at the dish machine and should be specifically directed at learning to load, start, run, stop, unload, and clean the machine properly.

Finding suitable space for training can be a severe problem in some organizations and may play some role in determining the hours when training can take place. If servers should be trained in a dining room, then the specific times set aside for training must coincide with the hours when the room is closed to the public. If a dining room normally opens at 11:00 A.M. and the staff members preparing the room for opening begin their work at 10:00 A.M., then training sessions for servers may be restricted to the hours between 7:00 A.M. and 10:00 A.M. If these hours are unsuitable for any reason, then some other location may have to be identified. This could be another part of the building that could be made to resemble a dining room, or it could be a suitable space located in another unit, in the case of a chain establishment. In fact, some chain organizations prefer to schedule training in centralized locations, as will be discussed later in this chapter.

LESSON PLANS. With training objectives clearly established and with appropriate decisions made as to approach, method, instructional timetable, and location, it becomes possible to devise a lesson plan that will ensure that the appropriate training takes place.

A lesson plan is a written, step-by-step description of the training required for a specific job, including an objective, detailed notes about content, the instructional timetable, and any items that may be required during instruction, including specific pieces of equipment, materials, and other audiovisual aids. The objective of the lesson plan is to ensure that a trainee learns to accomplish the skills and tasks that make up the job. Ideally, the lesson plan will be so complete and detailed that any qualified trainer will be able to follow it and deliver the necessary instruction to some individual or group. Figure 20.1 is a lesson plan for training a server, based on the job description for a server illustrated in Chapter 19.

Without lesson plans, training sessions tend to be less effective than intended. Trainers working without lesson plans are more likely to lose sight of the particular objectives of training and to neglect specific points that ought to be covered in training a given individual to perform a specific task. In general, the absence of a lesson plan makes for highly informal and largely ineffectual presentations that are less likely to meet the carefully defined training objectives.

TRAINER PREPARATION. With considerable effort having been devoted to establishing training objectives, creating job descriptions, writing job breakdowns, developing performance criteria, determining suitable approaches and methods, developing lesson plans, establishing timetables, and choosing locations, the essentials for training are in place.

At that point, it becomes the responsibility of the trainer to make sure that all is ready for training to begin. Many points are likely to require attention. Lesson plans must be available to the trainer. Arrangements must be made for individual employees to be available for training at specific times. Transportation arrangements from job site to training site may sometimes be

OBJECTIVE: Training servers to perform all duties of job.
LOCATION: Dining Room.
TIMETABLE: 8 hours of instruction, divided into 5 training sessions delivered over 24-hour days, with 15-minute breaks between sessions.
TRAINING METHODS: Lecture/Demonstration and Role Playing
MATERIAL AND EQUIPMENT: The following for each trainee: one complete place setting (placemat, napkin, china, flatware, and glassware), service tray, tray stand, guest checks, coffee carafe, and water pitcher.

Session I: Introduction to Training and Introduction to the Establishment–2 Hours
1. Introduction of supervisory staff: dining room manager, chef, and restaurant manager.
2. Discussion of payroll matters, handling of tips, employee parking, work schedules, station assignment, health benefits, employee meals, vacation, sick leave, and employee evaluation.
3. Uniforms and standards for personal appearance.
4. Rules for behavior while on the job.
5. A tour of the facility, including employee locker rooms and kitchen.
6. Location of supplies and equipment needed by serving staff.
7. Off-limit areas for serving staff.

Session II: Pre-opening Duties–1 Hour
Preparation of dining room for opening. Table settings and mis en place.

Session III: Taking Initial Orders for Drinks and Food–1 Hour
1. Approaching the guest's table.
2. Taking drink order.
3. Placing drink order at service bar.
4. Explaining menu and describing specials.
5. Taking food order.
6. Placing food order in kitchen.
7. Role playing. Trainees will be divided into groups of 3, taking turns as guests placing food and drink orders and server taking the orders.

Session IV: Attending Guests During the Meal: Service–2 Hours
1. Serving food.
2. Serving beverages.
3. Wine service.
4. Server conduct during meal.
5. Removing plates, glassware, and flatware.
6. Taking dessert orders.
7. Dessert service.
8. Totaling and presenting guest check.
9. Handling guest complaints.

Session V: Role Playing–2 Hours
The trainees will be divided into teams of 3 and will each take turns being guest and server, going through entire sequence. Role playing will continue until trainer is satisfied trainees are fully prepared to be servers.

FIGURE 20.1 *Lesson Plan—Server Training*

required. Some checking may be required to see that a given worker has been informed that he will be "shadowed" by a less experienced worker on Thursday mornings for the next two weeks. In some cases, it may mean that a particular room set aside for training must be made ready for a scheduled session: Items must be taken to the room and placed on the chairs that trainees will occupy, for example. In others, it may mean that specific pieces of equipment must be prepared for use during a training session or that particular supplies must be taken to a training site for the use of trainees. Sometimes it means that special workstations must be made ready for trainees to use during a training session. Sometimes it may be important to gather paper, pencils, chalk, felt-tip markers, or other similar materials required for a training session. It may even mean checking to see that lights are on and air conditioning equipment is working properly in some room being used as a training site.

These are a few simple examples of the many details for which trainers are commonly responsible. Most are mere details, seemingly minor, but each can be a critical factor in determining whether or not a training session meets the objectives established for it.

TRAINEE PREPARATION.   After particular employees have been selected and are at the point of beginning their training, it is important to take some preliminary steps before the training begins. Adults learn best when they understand the need for learning and both the personal and organizational benefits that will result from it. These can usually be communicated to learners in an introduction to training that explains:

1. The objectives of the training.
2. The instructional method being used.
3. The skills the employees will learn.

Most employees have some degree of apprehension when faced with any kind of change. This may show itself as reluctance or fear and can be an impediment to successful training. An introductory explanation by a skilled trainer can have several positive effects on learners' attitudes. It can:

1. Help change employees' negative feelings.
2. Reduce their fears of inability to complete the training or to learn new skills.

Thus, trainee preparation plays an important role in improving the climate for learning and skills improvement.

THE TRAINING SESSION(S).   With objectives, approach, method, instructional timetable location, and lesson plan all established and with the trainer and trainee prepared to begin, the actual training process can start. The trainer is expected to follow the lesson plan, proceeding at a reasonable pace. A good trainer will normally respond to any question raised by a trainee and will sense trainees' concerns, spoken or unspoken. Additionally, good trainers help trainees feel at ease during training sessions, speaking clearly and distinctly, using words and phrases appropriate to the language level of the trainees, correcting helpfully, and praising appropriately for good work. Under these conditions, the training is more likely to achieve its intended goals. Under less suitable conditions, this is less likely to be the case.

EVALUATION.   After training of any kind has taken place, it is important to evaluate the training, to see if established training objectives have been met and to learn whether those trained are able to meet the performance criteria for their positions. After all, men and women trained as servers should be able to work as servers in a dining room, meeting the performance criteria established by management for servers.

It is normally advisable to begin the testing of trainees during their training period to make some assessment of learning as it progresses. This can take place at various stages of training and may be accomplished by various means. In general, one seeks to determine the extent to which the trainee is making progress towards acquiring the skills required by a worker in the position for which he is being trained. Some of the practical testing techniques used by trainers include oral questioning, written examinations, supervised practice of newly acquired skills, and requiring demonstration of those skills.

However, unless their training has taken place in an entirely realistic work environment, one cannot fully evaluate the future ability of trainees during training. The ability of individuals to meet established performance criteria cannot be fully tested until they take their places in the workforce, working alongside others similarly trained and performing the same duties under the same pressures.

CENTRALIZED VERSUS LOCALIZED TRAINING

Many multi-unit organizations, including chains of company-owned and franchised units, face very complex training problems. Some of these organizations have hundreds of units and must find some means of providing employees across the organization with the training they need. In addition, it is important that each individual in a given job title receive training that will enable him to meet the same performance criteria as others in very distant locations.

Many large organizations employ professional human resources personnel to develop training programs that can be implemented throughout the organization. Essentially, there are only two alternatives available for any company-wide program:

1. Send trainers to the individual units, either to train the staff at their normal work site or at some appropriate site nearby.
2. Send trainees to a central training facility, often located at the national or regional headquarters of the organization.

The first of these is more commonly used to train servers and others in similar capacities. The latter is more common for management personnel.

The first alternative is a good choice when many individuals in a single unit all require the same training. It is clearly less costly to send one trainer to the unit than to send all the employees to a distant training location. By contrast, the second alternative is a better choice when numerous individuals in various locations all require the same training. Rather than send the trainer on a tour of the locations to provide costly one-on-one training to numerous individuals, it is quicker and probably less expensive to bring all those needing the training to one central location to receive their training together.

While each of these alternatives offer excellent means to ensure that personnel with particular job descriptions receive appropriate training, each must be employed in those situations to which it is most suited.

TRAINING MANUALS

Many large organizations also employ human resources professionals to develop training manuals for use throughout the organization. These can be used any time training is required, regardless of whether the training is done centrally or locally. Under optimum conditions, an organization will develop a training manual for every job that is common to all units in the organization. Any time training is required, it will be based on the information printed in the training manual. This approach provides for standard training and standard results in all units. In addition, the existence of a training manual makes it unnecessary to "reinvent the wheel" each time training is required.

Training manuals take different forms, depending on the intended audience. Some are written as guides for trainers and give the trainer specific information and tips that will help to provide the best possible training sessions for staff. Others are aimed at trainees and are designed to give the trainee the information required even if there is no trainer available to provide instruction.

Some of these might better be termed **programmed instruction aids** than training manuals.

Some training manuals are little more than collections of typewritten paragraphs, mimeographed or photocopied and then stapled together. Others are more attractive booklets, produced with modern desktop publishing techniques and containing written materials and useful illustrations. Still others could best be described as books, printed at great expense by managers who believe that providing training to staff is one of management's most important functions.

While the specific contents of training manuals vary, most attempt to include information that can be categorized in four areas:

1. *General background:* The manual should include some introduction to the organization, to its principal goals and objectives, to its philosophy, and to its view of the role of the individual within the organization. In addition, it should provide some introduction to the specific job, indicating the particular role the job plays in the organization and the position of the job within the unit structure. This is normally the first section in a training manual.

2. *Specific duties of a job:* The manual should include a detailed list of the duties of the job taken from the job description, as well as the performance criteria established for each task. In order for a trainee to be able to understand the duties clearly, these should be described in great detail and in comprehensible language. Any terms that the trainee might not know should either be avoided or carefully and fully explained. Sometimes the manual will include questions designed for trainees to self-test as they use the manual. When such questions are included, answers are provided so that the trainee can have immediate feedback.

3. *Specific procedures for carrying out the duties:* The manual must list all standard procedures established for performing the duties and tasks assigned to the job. If possible, the standard procedures should be listed with the duties, tasks, and performance criteria associated with the job. It should be obvious that separating these would make learning more difficult for the trainee. In some instances, complexity or limitations of space may make it impossible to list all of these together. If so, it is of great importance that the arrangement be such that it not impede learning by the trainee. Whenever feasible, line drawings, diagrams, and even cartoons can be included to illustrate and thus to clarify the standard procedures for the trainee. Here, too, questions and answers for self-tests can be an important learning aid for the trainee.

4. *Summary:* This section of the manual normally reemphasizes critical

points made in the earlier sections, including the importance of the job, of major duties associated with the job, and of those specific and distinctive standard procedures that render the proper performance of the job critical in the organization. In addition, the Summary often restates and thus reinforces for the trainee the organization's commitment to him as a developing long-term member of a very important team.

COMPUTER APPLICATIONS

Given today's technology, programmed learning aids can be employed to provide employee training on premises. In an establishment with a major computer system, several workstations can be permanently installed for regular and ongoing training. In smaller establishments without computer systems, management can take advantage of decreasing prices for increasingly complex technology to purchase and install computers and related devices for programmed learning. At the same time, growing numbers of interactive programs for training are coming into the market. Some of these use multimedia techniques, and there will be growing numbers that simulate real conditions to add new dimensions to training. In addition, any organization choosing to do so today can develop and print training manuals and other learning aids, using one of the many desktop publishing programs available. If such materials are published in-house, they can readily be revised and reprinted at far lower cost than would have been the case before the advent of desktop publishing.

CHAPTER ESSENTIALS

In this chapter, we provided a definition of training, distinguished it from education, and identified its purpose. We discussed the assessment of training needs, the first step in training. We listed and discussed 10 elements commonly covered by training plans, including objectives, approaches to training, training methods, lesson plans, instructional timetables, location, trainer preparation, trainee preparation, training sessions, and evaluation. We discussed the alternatives faced by organizations engaged in centralized and localized training, and we described the typical contents of training manuals. Finally, we identified several computer applications of specific value for training.

KEY TERMS IN THIS CHAPTER

Centralized training
Cross training

Job rotation
Localized training
Off-the-job training
On-the-job training
Training
Training manual
Training objectives
Training plan

QUESTIONS AND PROBLEMS

1. Define training.

2. Distinguish between training and education.

3. What is the primary purpose of training?

4. Why is it important to complete a training needs assessment before developing a training plan? What does a training needs assessment examine?

5. Define cross training. Why might a manager want staff members cross trained?

6. What is job rotation? Why might a manager institute job rotation?

7. What do training objectives identify?

8. Identify and distinguish between the following approaches to training:
   a. On-the-job versus off-the-job.
   b. Structured versus unstructured.
   c. Individual versus group.

9. List and explain eight methods that can be employed in training. Which are best suited to use with groups? With individuals? For structured training? For unstructured training?

10. Given the following jobs, identify appropriate locations for training staff to accomplish each:
   a. Dishwasher.
   b. Server.
   c. Bartender.
   d. Host/hostess.
   e. Manager.

11. What is a lesson plan? What should a lesson plan include?

12. What is the purpose of trainee preparation? What positive effects can an introductory explanation by a skilled trainer have on learners' attitudes towards training?

13. List five performance characteristics of a good trainer that help make employees feel at ease during a training session.

14. Why should training be evaluated? Against what two criteria should training be measured?

15. Identify four practical testing techniques that trainers can use to evaluate the progress being made by trainees.

16. Distinguish between centralized and localized training. Which approach would be more commonly used to train management personnel? Which for servers?

17. The information included in training manuals can be categorized into four areas. Identify the four, and describe the material typically covered in each.

18. Identify two computer applications that are of specific value for training.

19. Define each of the following key terms:
    Centralized training
    Cross training
    Job rotation
    Localized training
    Off-the-job training
    On-the-job training
    Training
    Training manual
    Training objectives
    Training plan

21

Monitoring Performance and Taking Corrective Action

LEARNING OBJECTIVES

After reading and studying this chapter, you should be able to:
1. Define the term monitoring, as used in labor cost control.
2. Distinguish between direct and indirect monitoring of employee performance.
3. Identify the two types of direct monitoring, and provide examples of each.
4. List and discuss four sources of information used for indirect monitoring.
5. Identify the five-step approach to problem-solving used to identify the specific cause of some deviation between actual and standard performance.
6. List and discuss the three general causes of discrepancies between actual performance and that anticipated by standards.
7. Define each of the Key Terms listed at the end of the chapter.

INTRODUCTION

In the preceding chapters, we discussed the application of the first two steps in the control process: establishing standards and standard procedures for operation, and training all individuals to follow these established standards and standard procedures. This chapter will be devoted to the remaining steps: monitoring performance, comparing actual performance with established standards, and then taking appropriate action to correct deviations.

Training employees to follow established standards and standard procedures does not guarantee that they will always work as trained. There are any number of reasons for this. Some trained employees will follow their training initially, but they may begin to forget after some weeks or may begin to be influenced by the poor work habits of some long-term employees whose training dates from sometime in the distant past. Some merely become indifferent to details after they have done one particular job for too long a time. And there are many other reasons as well. Because there is a strong possibility that employees' work will not always conform to the established standards, it must be monitored to assess whether or not it meets those standards.

MONITORING PERFORMANCE

To **monitor** the performance of employees is to gather information about their work and the results of that work. This is the necessary third step in the control process—the step that enables managers to make those judgments about performance that will suggest whether or not corrective action will be required. Employees' work may be monitored directly, indirectly, or by some combination of the two, as discussed below.

Direct Monitoring

Direct monitoring of employee performance normally means the direct observation by a manager or supervisor of an employee at work or the direct examination of the results of that employee's work by a supervisor or manager. The host in a hotel dining room normally spends some time in direct observation of the servers assigned to work in the room to determine the extent to which each is observing the standards and standard procedures established for servers and covered during their training (serving plates of food from the left and removing soiled dishes from the right, for example). Similarly, the steward in a foodservice operation will watch those that he is responsible for supervising to be sure they are doing their assigned work correctly—putting away deliveries of frozen food as quickly as possible after they have been received, for example.

While direct observation often takes place in this manner—as an employee is actually attending to a task—this is not always the case. Another possibility is for the supervisor to examine the results of the work and make a judgment about it immediately after it has been done. This would be the approach adopted by a chef who waited until after a cook finished plating an entree and handing it to a server to examine the appearance of the plate. Similarly, a steward would be unlikely to watch an employee storing cans of food on shelves in a storeroom. He would be more likely to monitor the employee's performance by examining the storeroom after the food had been put away.

Many examples of direct monitoring of employees' performance can be seen everyday in any food and beverage operation, such as any time there are supervisors on hand and time available for direct monitoring. The extent to which direct monitoring can take place is dependent on the number of employees working under the jurisdiction of a supervisor and how closely the supervisor is able to monitor each employee. For example, supervisors in most dining rooms seldom have the ability to closely watch all the movements of servers under their jurisdiction. They typically cannot listen to the greetings given customers by an individual server, nor can they hear explanations to customers of the methods used to prepare particular menu items. Dining room supervisors (and most supervisors in food and beverage operations, for that matter) have limited ability to monitor employees directly. To a greater or lesser extent, supervisors must rely on indirect monitoring.

At the same time, there are many examples of establishments with other kinds of supervisory problems (inadequate numbers of supervisors or supervisors with inadequate training, for example). In such establishments, it may be difficult or impossible to adequately monitor employees' performance by direct means. Indirect monitoring becomes necessary.

Indirect Monitoring

Indirect monitoring of employees' performance refers to that array of procedures through which managers obtain information about operations without directly observing those operations. The purpose of this is to determine the need, if any, for corrective action to bring actual performance into line with standards.

Indirect monitoring is accomplished by developing a variety of means or methods for assessing work without directly observing it. This approach to monitoring is very common in food and beverage operations. The various sources that provide the information needed for indirect monitoring include the following:

1. Customers.
2. Employees.
3. External agencies/organizations/groups.
4. Managers.

CUSTOMERS.   It is interesting to note that restaurant customers typically have little to say to dining room servers and dining room supervisors about the high or low quality of food or service. They have very little to say when food quality and service exceed their expectations, and they seldom complain to dining room servers or supervisors when they receive poor service or when food quality does not meet their expectations. Even when questioned by supervisors upon leaving restaurants, customers frequently will not admit that their dining experience was poor. And they seldom take the time to write positive or negative letters to management, although occasionally some individual will write a letter of complaint if an experience with restaurant food or service was extremely bad. Instead, customers typically accept the level of service or food quality, good or bad, and then pay their bills and leave. Privately, their innermost reactions are likely to determine whether or not they ever return.

By contrast, in conversations with co-workers, neighbors, and friends, people describe many of their dining experiences in great detail. They are particularly inclined to describe the good ones and the bad ones, not the indifferent, and they will dwell on those that have been particularly bad. These are described endlessly, and the impressions they create are carried orally throughout the community. In fact, the overall reputation of a restaurant may actually be little more than the sum of statements and comments, positive and negative, made about that restaurant by its customers in conversations with their friends, relatives, neighbors, and co-workers.

When comments about service quality and food quality are made by customers, management must take them seriously. When the comments are complaints, they are frequently indications that other more serious problems exist.

Complaints or compliments may result from questions customers are asked by employees or supervisors. These may be verbal or written. Most servers today are trained to ask customers some question similar to "Is everything all right?" at some time during a meal. Asking this question has several primary purposes, including showing interest in and concern for the customer's dining experience and determining whether or not the meal is progressing satisfactorily. Sometimes the answer to the question may be "No." A server asking the question may learn that the soup is not hot, that some desired condiment is missing from the table, or that the meat is too well done. A supervisor asking the question may be told that the service is too slow, the room too cold, or the server misinformed about the nature of a dish. However, negative re-

We need your help. By responding to the several questions below, you can help us maintain the levels of service and food quality you look forward to when you come to *Our Place*.
On the basis of the following scale:
  5 = excellent
  4 = very good
  3 = average
  2 = poor
  1 = unacceptable

Circle one of the numbers below to rate each of the following:

	5	4	3	2	1
1. The host's greeting	5	4	3	2	1
2. The appearance of the table	5	4	3	2	1
3. The service	5	4	3	2	1
4. The food:					
appearance:	5	4	3	2	1
quantity:	5	4	3	2	1
quality:	5	4	3	2	1
5. The drinks	5	4	3	2	1
6. Your overall impression of *Our Place*	5	4	3	2	1

Any comments you may choose to write below will be carefully considered and greatly appreciated:

_____

_____

_____

Thanks for all your help.

The Fibney Family

FIGURE 21.1 *Customer Satisfaction Survey for* Our Place, *a local restaurant*

sponses to such questions are rare in most establishments, even if service quality or food quality are not up to customers' expectations. Customers will typically say "Everything is fine" even when it is not. This is because many are unwilling to express their real views openly. Some customers undoubtedly are self-conscious, perhaps embarrassed to complain; others do not want to be labelled "complainers." Thus, the accuracy of these comments solicited from customers is questionable.

Because a relatively small percentage of customers will state their true views to servers or dining room supervisors about the quality of food and service, many foodservice establishments ask their customers to formally evaluate the quality of their service and food. They ask customers to write answers to specific questions. Figure 21.1 is an example of the kind of form that customers are often asked to complete. Forms of this nature are available for customers to complete at the conclusion of a meal. Many recommend that they be coded or marked in a way that will facilitate identifying particular servers and particular menu items. Customers frequently are more willing to answer questions honestly when presented with a form of this nature because their responses are anonymous and because they know that they will be gone by the time the form is read.

EMPLOYEES.   Another means for indirect monitoring comes from reports about co-workers from their fellow employees. Good managers encourage all employees to care about the establishment and to want to maintain established standards and standard procedures. When loyal employees see that co-workers are not maintaining standards, some will suggest to their colleagues that they return to accepted methods for doing the work, as they were trained to do. Others may be more inclined to alert their supervisors.

When reports about co-workers come to supervisors, it is important that they be carefully considered. Supervisors must make judgments about the individuals providing the information and their reasons for doing so. Frequently the report is based on the loyal employee's deep concern for the best interests of the establishment—a true concern that standards and standard procedures are not being met. Sometimes other motives prompt such a report. For example, it is not uncommon for an employee to exaggerate or to make a false report about some co-worker's behavior because of a personal quarrel or a genuine dislike. In all instances, it is important that information be verified before corrective action is taken.

EXTERNAL AGENCIES/ORGANIZATIONS/GROUPS.   In many areas, one finds an array of external agencies, organizations, and groups engaged in monitoring the performance of employees. While a complete list of these can be quite extensive, some are much more common than others. The following comprise the most common.

1. **Government agencies:** Various agencies can be found inspecting food and beverage operations to assess their adherence to the standards and standard procedures established by government for foodservice operation. In effect, they are monitoring performance with respect to government standards that should be incorporated into the establishment's own standards and standard procedures. Local fire departments, for example, routinely inspect restaurants, bars, and related operations to verify compliance with local laws designed to protect the lives of customers and employees. They commonly check to see that fire extinguishers are available and suitably charged, that

grease filters over cooking equipment have been cleaned as required by law, and that fire exits are neither locked from the inside nor blocked by stored materials. If job descriptions list the tasks and responsibilities related to fire safety and if training adequately prepares employees to carry out those tasks and responsibilities correctly, fire inspections should not be matters of great concern: Monitoring in the form of a fire department inspection should merely confirm that standards and standard procedures are being followed. The same can be said of inspections carried out by representatives of any number of other agencies—local, city, county, state, or federal. These may include health and safety inspectors from a Health Department or from Occupational Safety and Health Administration (OSHA). All are engaged in monitoring adherence to various standards and standard procedures.

2. **Chain organizations:** Many foodservice chains employ inspectors to perform a monitoring service by visiting and inspecting units in the chain. These units may be company owned, franchised, or both of these. The aim is to verify that every unit bearing the corporate name and logo is following the standards and standard procedures established by headquarters. The nature and extent of these inspections vary. They may be announced or unannounced. They may be brief, or they may take several days. They may be confined to tasting the food and beverage products prepared in the kitchen, or they may be extended to include observation of actual preparation.

3. **Food critics:** Another kind of monitoring of performance is carried out by food critics—those who patronize foodservice operations as customers and then inform the public at large about their professional views of these establishments. Some write for the daily press, some for magazines, some comment on radio, and others report on local television news or on syndicated cable programs. All are interested in the quality of food, beverages, and service, and many notice decor, cleanliness, and other conditions in the establishment. The results of their monitoring can have powerful positive or negative impact on the success of a restaurant, so both owners and managers of the establishments that these powerful people are likely to visit are normally careful to be ready for such a visit at any time.

4. **Rating organizations:** The better foodservice enterprises are likely to have annual visits from representatives of organizations that are in the business of rating restaurants and publishing their ratings. There are any number of these, from local agencies serving major cities, to national organizations covering the entire United States, Canada, as well as many international organizations. These, too, are monitoring and

rating the performance of all employees in a given establishment and publishing their views in some appropriate book or periodical.

All of these provide monitoring services that, although conducted by a variety of external entities, help to provide management with some means of verifying that the established standards and standard procedures covered in employees' training are being carried out in day-to-day operations.

MANAGERS.   Managers at all levels may be the most important of those engaged in monitoring the performance levels of staff. There are any number of means by which this may be accomplished, the most significant of which is to require the preparation of records and reports that reflect employee performance. The basic daily reports discussed in the food and beverage sections of this text provide some indication of the performance of all employees working as a group. Suppose, for example, that a daily report is prepared that shows that food cost percent to date for the first four days of this week is 53.6 percent, compared to 45.3 percent for the similar period last week. Assume that other data reveals approximately the same menu mix, number of covers, and dollar sales for the two weeks. If 45.3 percent is considered an acceptable level of cost under the circumstances, it is likely that the 53.6 percent level will be considered less than acceptable. The results of the two weeks are determined by a form of monitoring designed to keep management abreast of employee performance. When monitoring reveals unexpected and negative results, management normally begins to look for some explanation. Further investigation may lead to explanations rooted in inadequate employee performance: improper portioning of foods, excessive preparation of foods, or failure to follow standard recipes, to name but a few possibilities.

Another important consideration that requires regular monitoring is labor cost. In fact, many managers find today that labor cost requires more careful monitoring than food and beverage cost. As with all costs, the key to control lies in establishing standards.

In Chapter 19 we described several methods for establishing quality, quantity, and cost standards for labor. If a way could be found to compare actual performance with established standards for performance developed by management, differences could be noted, particularly those that reflect inefficiencies in labor productivity. Once these differences, or variances, were identified, it would be possible for management to seek some explanation for each and to work towards eliminating them in the future, to bring labor productivity up to established standards.

Once standards for work hours have been established, it becomes possible to make judgments about the number of actual work hours used in an estab-

Number of Covers	Service Personnel	Warewashing Personnel	Preparation Personnel
200–299	15	6	9
300–399	18	6	9
400–499	21	9	12
500–599	24	12	12

FIGURE 21.2 *Standard Work-Hour Requirements Variable Cost Personnel: Luncheon*

lishment, given an actual level of business volume for a period (hour, meal, day, or any other). This may best be illustrated by an example. Figure 21.2, a duplicate of Figure 19.14, provides a list of standard work-hour requirements at various volume levels for three classifications of variable-cost personnel (in service, warewashing, and preparation categories) in a particular restaurant.

Assume that a sales forecast has been prepared for the coming week, which includes Tuesday, June 4. According to the forecast, 500 covers are expected to be served during the normal three-hour luncheon period on that date. Given that forecast, the manager has consulted the chart of standard work-hour requirements and prepared an appropriate schedule.

Sometime after the June 4 luncheon period, it becomes possible to compare the actual number of employee hours worked with the number that should have been worked based on the number of covers actually served. For example, on June 4, with a forecast of 500 covers, 24 work hours were scheduled. If 24 standard work hours were scheduled and 500 covers were actually served, then management's standards for service and cost would have been met. However, assume that the actual number of covers served were 400 instead. According to the chart, the number of standard work hours appropriate for serving 400 covers is 21. Because of faulty forecasting, a managerial responsibility, too many standard work hours were scheduled. In fact, if the manager had been able to prepare a more accurate forecast, only 21 standard work hours need have been scheduled, which would have resulted in labor cost savings. Given the wage rate of $4.00 per hour for servers, 24 work hours would cost $96.00 in wages, while 21 hours would cost $84.00. The three extra hours would amount to $12.00 in excessive labor cost for servers alone in this single three-hour luncheon period.

To some, this amount does not seem to be large enough to be concerned about. However, $12.00 is 14.3 percent of $84.00, indicating that this small segment of labor cost for the day was 14.3 percent higher than necessary to provide the standard of service established by management. In addition, this

	Actual	Standard		
Personnel	Work Hours	Work Hours	Difference	Explanation
Service	24	21	3	Covers fewer than forecast
Warewashing	12	9	3	Covers fewer than forecast
Preparation	12	12	0	- - - - - - -

DAY: Tuesday   DATE: 6/4/XXXX   MEAL: Luncheon
                                              WEATHER: fair

Number of covers:
    FORECAST: 500   SOLD: 400

PREPARED BY _____

FIGURE 21.3 *Reconciliation of Standard and Actual Work Hours, Based on Actual Covers Served*

excessive cost of $12.00 per luncheon period multiplied by 365 days per year amounts to $4,380.00 in unnecessary costs for servers alone, without considering the amount of such other costs as payroll taxes and fringe benefits.

To the extent that more work hours than the standard have been utilized, it is apparent that greater efficiency is possible. It is also desirable: Greater efficiency will translate to a lower payroll cost. If fewer work hours than the standard have been utilized, it would be likely that the quality of service had been less than standard.

The next step would be to prepare a report that assesses the efficiency of labor utilization by period—the same period used for forecasting volume and scheduling work hours. In some establishments, this will be by meal period; in others, it will be by the day. In the present instance, because forecasting and scheduling was by meal period (luncheon), the assessment report should also be by meal period. An appropriate report would be similar to that illustrated in Figure 21.3.

Note that the report shows both the forecasted number of covers and the actual number of covers for the meal period, which facilitates making judgments about the accuracy of the forecast. If the forecast was quite close to the actual number of covers, one can ignore any difference. However, if there is a considerable difference between forecast and actual covers, it will be desirable to make some attempt at explanation. If a satisfactory explanation can be found, it may be possible to develop more accurate forecasts in the future.

The number of hours in the standard work-hour column require some explanation. The number of standard work hours recorded for each job category are those required for the actual number of covers, not the forecasted number. If there is a significant difference between the forecasted number of covers and the actual number, then the standard work hours recorded in the standard work-hour column will be somewhat different from the actual number of hours worked by employees.

In the present instance, it is quite apparent that, while scheduling has been efficiently accomplished on the basis of the forecast, a degree of inefficiency resulted from the overscheduling of personnel. If the above result were repeated frequently, the owner or manager might have to find ways to improve the accuracy of the forecasts. Other possible reasons for differences between standard work hours and actual hours worked might be unforeseen variations in weather and in other conditions affecting sales, such as repairs to the street in front of the restaurant, improper attention to standard work-hour charts (resulting in poor scheduling), and absenteeism. The important point is that management now has some means of monitoring the efficiency of labor.

As a result of the kinds of monitoring methods, techniques, and procedures described and discussed above, managers are given information that must be evaluated, normally by a capable, experienced manager. Increasingly, this is someone who has completed coursework in a post-secondary institution and has acquired the knowledge and skill to make the necessary judgments. Judgment is the key word here. Today, a foodservice manager must be able to read financial and statistical reports, evaluate related data, make judgments about the significance of the information, and determine which of various possible courses of corrective action to pursue in order to improve operational performance in the near term and over the long term.

TAKING CORRECTIVE ACTION

If actual performance brings results that deviate significantly from those anticipated by established standards and standard procedures, some corrective action must be taken to bring actual performance into line with the standards. Once evaluation reveals some discrepancy between actual performance and that anticipated by standards and standard procedures, there is a generally accepted five-step approach that can be used to identify the cause and find a suitable solution to the problem:

1. Meet with appropriate staff to point out the problem and to determine its cause.
2. Identify all appropriate corrective measures that might be adopted.
3. Select the best corrective measure from among the alternatives.
4. Institute the selected measure.
5. Monitor performance to be sure that the corrective measure has the desired effect.

The initial difficulty, of course, lies in identifying the reasons for the discrepancy. Essentially, there are three possibilities:

1. Inadequate performance.
2. Unsuitable standards.
3. Inappropriate organization.

Each of these is discussed below.

Inadequate Performance

If the reason for the discrepancy is identified as inadequate performance, one must seek the cause. There are any number of possibilities, some of which are attributable to employees, while others are not. In fact, some may even be traceable to poor management performance manifesting itself as poor employee performance.

A complete list of all the possibilities would be impossible to produce: It would be as long and as varied as the list of names of those working in foodservice operations. Some of the more common possibilities include: improper materials provided to workers; lack of the equipment or tools required; need for additional training; inadequate management or supervision; poor union/management relations; personal problems away from the job; difficulties with interpersonal relations on the job; inadequate compensation, compared to other jobs or employers; illness, including substance abuse and addiction; poor working conditions, including improper heat, light, or ventilation; and improper work schedules. And this is just the beginning. A more complete list would be very long—indeed, beyond the scope of this and most other texts.

For those contemplating careers as foodservice managers, it is probably distressing to learn that the list of possibilities is so long. It will be equally distressing to learn that there is no single best approach to dealing with any one of the causes on the list. Treating any of these causes requires the attention of an experienced manager, who must take great care in determining the proper approach to take in a given instance. It will depend on the particular situation and the specific personalities involved.

Unsuitable Standards

If standards and standard procedures for staff have been established by knowledgeable and experienced managers, one would expect that these would be well suited to the operations in which they were designed to be used. However, this is not always the case. Sometimes conditions change and render the standards and standard procedures inappropriate. This might be the case in an establishment adopting a new menu and new service techniques to accompany renovations in the physical plant. Sometimes the managers who develop standards for a given operation are not as experienced at doing so as they might be, and their efforts result in standards that are not well suited to the operation for which they were developed. In other instances, consultants may develop standards and standard procedures that are wholly unrealistic for the staff members who will be expected to work with them.

When evaluation and analysis reveal that standards and standard procedures are unrealistic, it would make no sense to waste time and effort attempting to bring employee performance up to the level anticipated by the standards. It would make obvious sense simply to change the standards so that they would be better suited to an operation and its staff.

Inappropriate Organization

It would be impossible to compose a complete list of the conditions that have led restaurant owners and managers to conclude that their basic organization structures had been rendered inappropriate. Those with experience in food and beverage management are quick to agree that many have decided to reorganize their establishments. In most cases, the conditions that have led them to do so include increases in costs, decreases in sales, or both of these.

We will address the need for the reorganization and consequent restructuring of the labor force, on the assumption that all other possibilities have been ruled out. This will enable us to make certain points about reorganization in general, as well as to continue pertinent discussion of labor cost control.

Any manager planning reorganization must have some clear, basic objectives in mind. Without these, it is difficult to imagine how one could proceed in any logical, orderly fashion. Just as in every other area of human endeavor, basic objectives give direction to activity and provide benchmarks against which to measure and judge any plans for change. For purposes of the following discussion, we will assume that the primary objective of reorganization is a reduction in labor cost, and we will use this objective to judge the effectiveness of the reorganization that will be proposed below.

The techniques for reducing labor costs as part of a reorganization program do not differ markedly from those employed by managers seeking to reduce costs temporarily. These include combining jobs, hiring part-time rather than full-time employees where possible, adding duties of variable-cost employees to the normal work of fixed-cost personnel, and making appropriate use of various preprepared food and beverage items to reduce the labor cost of preparation.

The chief differences between a temporary reduction of labor cost and a permanent reduction through reorganization typically involve a degree of

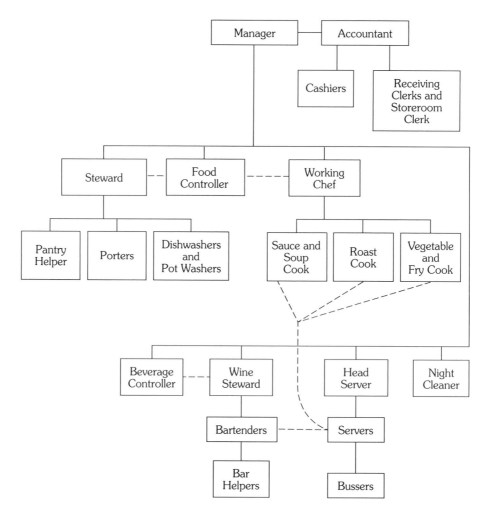

FIGURE 21.4   *Organization Chart after Reorganization*

change, as well as the impact on the labor force as a whole and on particular jobs. Clearly, the manager who decides in favor of reorganization is reacting to a situation that has become untenable—one that dictates the need for a steady and reasoned reversal from unacceptable financial statements to an acceptable level of profit. The manager knows what must be done: reduce the cost of labor to the extent necessary to ensure profit, particularly if there can be no increase in revenue. To the extent to which the manager can do this, each dollar reduction in the labor cost should be a dollar increase in profit, assuming there is no change in overall dollar sales.

As an example of what might be done, Figure 21.4 shows the effect of reorganization on the organization chart of the restaurant first described in Chapter 19 and pictured in Figure 19.1.

It will be noted that reorganization has had a major impact on a number of positions in the kitchen. For example, the sous chef has been eliminated, and the executive chef is now a working chef. In addition, the work of the purchasing steward has been taken over by the chief steward. Both the fry cook and the vegetable cook have been eliminated and replaced by a new worker whose duties include those of both the former job titles. The entire baking department has been eliminated, occasioned by a decision to buy rather than make baked products. These and other changes have resulted in a net reduction of five fixed-cost employees, as well as an indeterminable number of variable-cost employees. This reorganization represents an annual payroll saving of thousands of dollars, by which amount net profits should be increased.

It will be noted in the foregoing that management decided to eliminate the jobs of both the fry cook and the vegetable cook in favor of creating a new position for a combination vegetable/fry cook. This new worker probably could not perform all the duties of the former employees, so management would need to undertake another important aspect of reorganizing: writing new job descriptions. As a result of the reorganization and the consequent elimination of some jobs and combining of others, new areas of responsibility have been created, and it is important that each be covered clearly and concisely by job description.

COMPUTER APPLICATIONS

Many fast-food chains are using computers to monitor the sales performance of servers. Various in-house computer systems now in use make it possible to easily determine various rates for each server per hour or per shift. These include such basic ones as dollar sales and covers and may extend to such possibilities as appetizers or desserts or bottles of dinner wine per server. Computers are superior at maintaining detailed records and may be used to determine which servers, for example, are meeting predetermined sales targets and identifying those who fail to meet the targets. Management can then focus on improving the performance of those who fail to meet the targets.

CHAPTER ESSENTIALS

In this chapter we defined the term monitoring as it relates to labor control. We distinguished between direct and indirect monitoring and identified and discussed various sources of the information used for indirect monitoring. We identified a generally accepted five-step approach that can be used to determine the cause of a discrepancy between actual and standard performance and to find a suitable solution to the problem. Finally, we listed and discussed three possible reasons for these discrepancies, including inadequate performance, unsuitable standards, and inappropriate organization.

KEY TERMS IN THIS CHAPTER

Direct monitoring
Indirect monitoring
Monitoring
Reorganization
Standard procedures
Standards

QUESTIONS AND PROBLEMS

1. Define the term *monitoring* as used in labor cost control.

2. Distinguish between the two types of direct monitoring identified in the chapter, and provide examples of each.

3. Distinguish between direct monitoring of employee performance and indirect monitoring.

4. List the four sources of information used in indirect monitoring of employee performance.

5. Do the majority of foodservice customers readily and voluntarily provide management with useful information about the quality of food or service? Why?

6. Suppose you are manager of a foodservice operation. One of the employees reports to you that another employee does not do his work correctly except when you are watching. What should you say to the employee making the report? What should you do about it?

7. Identify three government agencies that inspect and report on foodservice operations. What kinds of information do the agencies provide? How does this help managers monitor employee performance?

8. "Food critics are not valuable sources of information that management can use to monitor employee performance!" Do you agree or disagree? Why?

9. Develop a customer questionnaire along the lines suggested by Figure 21.1 for a college foodservice operation or for some specific food-

service operation of which you are an employee or a customer. How would the data developed from the use of this form help management monitor employee performance?

10. In a certain restaurant the manager has determined that six servers are needed for between 320 and 380 covers over a three-hour luncheon period; seven servers are needed for between 381 and 440 covers; eight servers are needed for between 441 and 520 covers; and nine servers are needed for between 521 and 600 covers. Prepare a table of standard work hours along the lines suggested by Figure 21.2.

11. Using the data from Question 10, prepare a report along the lines suggested by Figure 21.3 for servers only, assuming 520 covers forecast and 420 covers actually served during the three-hour luncheon period on Tuesday, June 11.

12. Define each of the following key terms:
Direct monitoring
Indirect monitoring
Monitoring
Reorganization
Standard procedures
Standards

Afterword

Our aim in developing this text was to provide a structured introduction to food, beverage, and labor controls for the individual planning a career in the hospitality industry. We strongly believe that anyone planning a career on any level of management in this industry should be familiar with the principles of control. Moreover, anyone planning such a career should be prepared to translate these principles in judicious practice whenever and wherever conditions warrant. The operative phrase here is, of course, judicious practice.

In our teaching experience, both of us have encountered students who were planning to impose some predetermined control system on any operations they were hired to manage. They have been warned, by us and by others, of the impossibility of doing so. Most have heeded the warnings; some have not. Those who have not have been the ones to reconfirm, through their own hard experiences, the problems inherent in imposing preconceived ideas about control systems in operations where no control systems have previously been used or, alternately, in changing existing systems to match some preconceived ideas of the kinds of controls that should be used. A few have even been surprised to discover that most establishments have no food controller and no beverage controller and that, in fact, any control procedures put into effect in the average foodservice operation must be both instituted and supervised by the manager, who, in effect, becomes food controller, beverage controller, or both.

Those beginning their careers in hospitality management should be aware from the outset that comparatively few of the many thousands of foodservice operations maintain anything like complete control systems. Many large establishments, including some of the chains, do have reasonably complex systems. Some individually owned and managed operations attempt to institute controls in some parts of an enterprise, but a substantial number have no concept of the principles or techniques of control. This last item may help to explain why the business failure rate among restaurants and other food and beverage enterprises continues to be so high.

To attempt to impose complex control techniques and procedures on all foodservice operations surely is not the answer. To do so would certainly be costly, and the results obtained would be worth less than the costs incurred. On the other hand, carefully and judiciously selected techniques used in certain phases of the operation would probably benefit many foodservice operations.

This is what we hope that graduates entering the industry will recognize. We hope, for example, that they will see the importance of reasonable portion control measures in most situations and will be able to suggest or institute portion control in some specific kitchen without feeling obligated to insist on a complete precost, precontrol system. We hope that each will be able and feel free to modify and adapt the principles, techniques, procedures, forms, devices, and suggestions from this text to use in particular industry settings. If our readers across the years are able to do this, the industry will have been well served.

Appendix

COST-VOLUME-PROFIT IN-DEPTH ANALYSIS

The analysis in Chapter 3 was based on certain assumptions that an owner or manager must understand before attempting cost-volume-profit analysis. The assumptions were that:

1. Costs in a particular establishment can be classified as fixed or variable with reasonable accuracy.
2. Variable costs are directly variable, as defined in Chapter 1.
3. Fixed costs are relatively stable and will remain so within the relevant range of business operations.
4. Sales prices will remain constant for the period covered by the analysis.
5. The sales mix in the restaurant will also remain relatively constant for the period.

To the extent that these assumptions are not valid in a particular establishment, the analysis attempted for that particular establishment will yield results that are not accurate. However, even if the results are not entirely accurate, the analysis can be useful. For most establishments, inaccuracies within the normal business volume range do not seriously inhibit the general value of the results.

An owner or manager attempting cost/volume/profit analysis is likely to be seeking answers to questions along the lines of the following:

* What profit will the establishment earn at a given sales level?
* What level of sales will be required to earn a given profit?
* How many sales (or covers) will be required in order to reach the break-even point?

The questions to be answered by cost/volume/profit analysis can be sorted into two general categories:

1. Those requiring answers stated in terms of money.
2. Those requiring answers stated in terms of numbers of sales.

Questions in the first category can be answered by performing various calculations with some so-called **dollar formulas;** those in the second require unit formulas. The various formulas and their uses are illustrated below.

Dollar Formulas and Calculations

The formula for determining the dollar sales level required to earn any planned or targeted profit, given a dollar total of fixed costs and an expected variable rate is:

$$S = \frac{FC + P}{1 - VR} \text{ (or CR)} \qquad \text{(Formula \#1)}$$

This formula can also be used to find the break-even point, merely by letting $P = 0$.

Algebraically, this formula may be restated in several ways as listed below, to solve for any unknown component:

$$CR = \frac{FC + P}{S} \qquad \text{(Formula \#2)}$$

$$P = (S \times CR) - FC \qquad \text{(Formula \#3)}$$

$$FC = (S \times CR) - P \qquad \text{(Formula \#4)}$$

These formulas have a number of useful applications in food and beverage management and control. For example, suppose that an owner projects fixed costs and sales for a given restaurant and has a particular profit target in mind. He wants to determine what variable rate must be maintained to achieve the targeted profit. Assume the following figures:

Fixed costs = $160,000.
Sales = $500,000.
Profit target = $40,000.

Using Formula #2, one can determine a projected CR:

$$CR = \frac{FC\ (\$160,000) + P\ (\$40,000)}{S\ (\$500,000)}$$

$$CR = \frac{\$200,000}{\$500,000}$$

$$CR = .4$$

Since CR = 1 − VR, then VR must be .6. This is the same as saying that variable costs may not exceed 60 percent of the projected figure, or that $.60 out of every dollar of sales is the maximum that can be used to cover variable costs.

Using figures selected from those above, we might then use Formula #3 to solve for potential profit in a restaurant with fixed costs of $160,000, projected sales of $500,000, and a projected variable rate of .6. Thus:

$$P = (S\ \$500,000 \times CR\ .4) - FC\ (\$160,000)$$

$$P = \$40,000$$

Using Formula #4 to solve for FC, we see that:

$$FC = (S\ \$500,000 \times CR\ .4) - P\ \$40,000$$

$$FC = \$200,000 - \$40,000$$

$$FC = \$160,000$$

The cost/volume/profit calculations above and the questions they answer all relate to dollars: dollar costs, dollar sales, or dollar profits. However, there are times when owners and managers are interested in finding answers to questions relating to numbers of sales (covers) or customers required to achieve a given goal. For these, unit formulas and calculations are used.

Unit Formulas and Calculations

In general, determining the numbers of sales needed to cover fixed costs is possible if one also knows the average dollar sale and the average variable cost per sale. As discussed in Chapter 1, the average dollar sale may be determined by dividing the total dollar sales for a period by the number of customers served. This figure is also known as the **average sale per customer, average cover,** or **average check.** It is also known as **average sales price.** We will let the abbreviation SP stand for sales price in the balance of this appendix. The average variable cost may be determined by dividing total variable costs by this same number of customers. For example, if the financial records of a small restaurant known as Ma's Place indicated sales of $48,000 and variable costs of $18,000 in a period when 3,000 customers were served, then:

$$\frac{\$48,000 \text{ Sales}}{3,000 \text{ Customers}} = \$16.00 \text{ Average dollar sale}$$

Similarly

$$\frac{\$18,000 \text{ Variable cost}}{3,000 \text{ Customers}} = \$6.00 \text{ Average variable rate}$$

Using this information, it is possible to determine average contribution margin (CM), defined previously as average sale minus average variable cost. Thus:

Average SP	$16.00
Average VC	− 6.00
Average CM	$10.00

Before using this figure to complete calculations to determine required unit sales levels, one important limitation on its use must be noted. An establishment with a stable sales mix will obtain more reliable data from the following calculations than will one with large fluctuations in the sales mix. Fluctuations in the sales mix typically cause the average sale and the average variable cost to change. These changes typically produce inaccurate results. Mathematically, unit sales (the number of sales) required to reach the break-even point may be calculated by means of the following formula:

$$\text{Unit sales} = \frac{\text{Fixed costs}}{\text{Contribution margin per unit sale}}$$

For example, suppose that Ma's Place, the small restaurant referred to above, is offering just one item on its menu. The sales price for the item is $16.00, and the variable cost is $6.00. The establishment has total fixed costs of

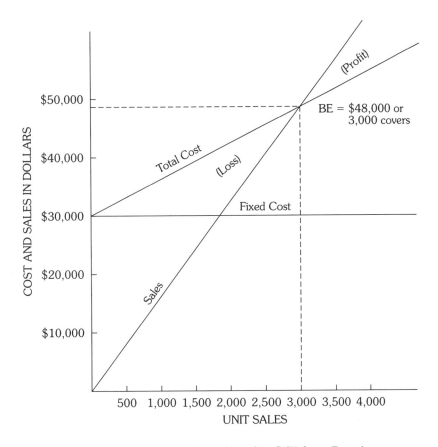

FIGURE A1.1 *Graphic Representation of Cost/Profit/Volume Equation*

$30,000. Each time one order of this item is sold, the sale generates a contribution margin (sales price−variable cost) of $10.00. Therefore, in order to meet the $30,000 fixed cost, the restaurant must sell 3,000 units of the item, each producing its $10.00 contribution margin. This may be calculated as follows:

$$\text{Unit sales required} = \frac{\text{FC } \$30,000}{\text{CM } \$10.00}$$

$$\text{Unit sales required} = 3,000$$

This is further illustrated in Figure A1.1, a graphic representation of the cost-volume-profit equation, often referred to as a break-even graph.

Note that dollar costs and sales are plotted on the vertical axis, while **sales volume,** or **unit sales,** are plotted on the horizontal axis. Note that the line for fixed costs is a perfectly horizontal line because fixed costs do not change as sales volume increases or decreases. Note, too, that the line for total cost is the sum of all fixed and variable costs at each level of sales volume covered by the graph. At volume level zero (if such a level were possible), there would theoretically be no variable costs. Total costs would be the same as fixed costs. As volume level increases, variable costs increase accordingly. These are added to fixed costs and result in the diagonal total cost line. The sales line begins at zero. As sales volume increases, dollar sales obviously increase. At each sales level illustrated in the graph, the dollar sales are equal to the unit sales multiplied by the average dollar sale. If the average dollar sale is $16.00, then 1,000 sales are plotted as $16,000, and 3,000 sales are plotted as $48,000.

The point at which the sales line and the total cost line meet is the break-even point, previously defined as the point at which total costs equal total sales, with neither profit nor loss resulting. In the present case, break-even occurs at $30,000 in sales, with 3,000 units sold. Sales volume of fewer than 3,000 units will result in loss, while sales volume greater than 3,000 units will result in profit. Note that the amount of the loss at each level of sales volume below break-even is represented by the space between the total cost and the total sales lines to the left of the break-even point. The amount of profit at each level of sales above break-even is represented by the space between the same two lines, but to the right of the break-even point.

Calculating Average Variable Rate

It is apparent that food and beverage operations do not offer one product, as in the preceding example. Instead, they offer a number of products with varying sales prices and costs. Consequently, each product's contribution margin is different from that of the other products on the menu. The application of cost-volume-profit analysis to restaurant operations is, therefore, somewhat more complex than the foregoing discussion leads one to believe.

One key to applying cost/volume/profit analysis to foodservice operations is to establish an average variable rate for an individual establishment. The following will illustrate a method for doing this.

As an example, let us use the Springfield Inn, a small restaurant without a liquor license that sells four items: steak, scallops, chicken, and spaghetti. The variable costs, sales prices, and variable rate for these four menu items are provided in Figure A1.2.

In order to determine an average variable rate for the establishment, one must know the sales mix, defined in Chapter 1 as the ratio of number of unit sales of a given item to total unit sales for all items in the same category. This can normally be determined from past records of sales. If none are available, estimates must be made. Assume sales records in the Springfield Inn indicate that each of the four items has accounted for 25 percent of unit sales in the

	VC	SP	VR
Steak	$10.00	$16.00	.625
Scallops	6.00	12.00	.5
Chicken	4.00	10.00	.4
Spaghetti	2.00	8.00	.25

FIGURE A1.2 *Variable Costs, Sales Prices, and Variable Rates for the Springfield Inn*

past. We will also assume that will hold true in the future. If so, then the relationship between total dollar sales attributable to any item and total dollar sales for all items will hold constant, regardless of whether the restaurant has 40, 200, or 300 customers in a given period. To illustrate at 40-customer level:

* Ten will order steak at a total variable cost of $100.00 and total sales of $160.
* Another 10 will order scallops at a total Variable Cost of $60.00 and total Sales of $120.00.
* Still another 10 will order chicken at a total Variable Cost of $40.00, bringing total Sales of $100.00.
* The final 10 will order spaghetti at a total Variable Cost of $20.00, bringing total Sales of $80.00.

Total variable costs and total sales for all items are illustrated in Figure A1.3.

Since VR equals VC/S, given the sales and costs above, one can determine that average variable rate is .478, calculated as follows:

$$\frac{\$220 \text{ VC}}{\$460 \text{ S}} = \text{Average variable rate}$$

Estimated Unit Sales	Item	Unit VC	Unit SP	Total $ VC	Total $ S
10	Steak	$10.00	$16.00	$100.00	$160.00
10	Scallops	6.00	12.00	60.00	120.00
10	Chicken	4.00	10.00	40.00	100.00
10	Spaghetti	2.00	8.00	20.00	80.00
40				$220.00	$460.00

FIGURE A1.3 *Extended Data for the Springfield Inn*

	Total revenue	PSTS
Steak	$160.00	.3478
Scallops	120.00	.2609
Chicken	100.00	.2174
Spaghetti	80.00	.1739
Total	$460.00	1.0 = 100%

FIGURE A1.4 *PSTS for Menu Items, Springfield Inn*

If the total number of customers were to increase from 40 to 200 and the sales mix were to remain unchanged, one can calculate that the total variable cost would be $1,100 and total sales $2,300. These figures also yield an average variable rate of .478.

Another way of determining the average variable rate is to determine the percentage of total dollar sales represented by sales of each menu item. Thus, if steak has produced $160.00 in sales when total sales for all items have been $460.00, as in Figure 3.8, then 34.78 percent of total sales is attributable to steak sales. Taking this approach, one can determine the **proportional share of total sales** (PSTS) attributable to each item, as shown in Figure A1.4.

The individual variable rate of each item may then be multiplied by the PSTS represented by each item. The resulting figures are then added to determine the total average variable rate (see Fig. A1.5).

Using the formula illustrated earlier in the chapter, one can use this derived average variable rate to determine a break-even point (BE). For example, assume that the Springfield Inn had fixed costs of $128,656. Rounding the average variable rate to .478, one could determine the break-even point as follows:

$$\text{BE} = \frac{\$128{,}656}{1 - .478}$$

$$\text{BE} = \$246{,}467.43$$

If the break-even point for the Springfield Inn is $246,467.43, sales above that level will be profitable, while sales below that level will result in a loss.

Once the break-even point has been calculated, it is comparatively simple to determine the number of customers required to reach that break-even point. In Figure A1.3, there were 40 customers spending a total of $460.00, so the average check was $460.00 divided by 40, or $11.50.

Given this figure, one would divide sales of $246,467.43 by the average check of $11.50 to determine that 21,432 customers would be required for the

	VR		PSTS		Weighted VR
Steak	.625	×	.3478	=	.2174
Scallops	.5	×	.2609	=	.1305
Chicken	.4	×	.2174	=	.0870
Spaghetti	.25	×	.1739	=	.0435
				VR Total Average	.4784

FIGURE A1.5 *Total Average Variable Rate, Springfield Inn*

establishment to break even. This can be further broken down into the average number of customers required per month or per week to reach the break-even point. Management can then determine whether or not the potential market exists to reach the necessary sales level.

Changing the Break-even Point

Unquestionably, there are times when analysis indicates that management's expectations cannot be reached—when the potential market is too small or the required volume level is beyond the capacity of the restaurant. At such times, management must be prepared to make adjustments that will result in a change in the break-even point. Food and beverage managers tend to look first at two basic possibilities:

1. Increase menu prices.
2. Reduce variable costs.

Figure A1.6 illustrates the effect of adjusting menu prices upwards, using the information previously illustrated in Figure A1.1. Let us assume that the price of the single item on the menu in Ma's Place, the small restaurant mentioned earlier in the chapter, was raised from $16.00 to $18.00. No change is made in fixed costs ($30,000) or in variable cost ($6.00). Break-even is determined as follows:

$$VR = \frac{\$6}{\$18} = .3333$$

$$BE = \frac{\$30,000}{1 - .3333}$$

$$BE = \frac{\$30,000}{.6667}$$

$$BE = \$44,997,75$$

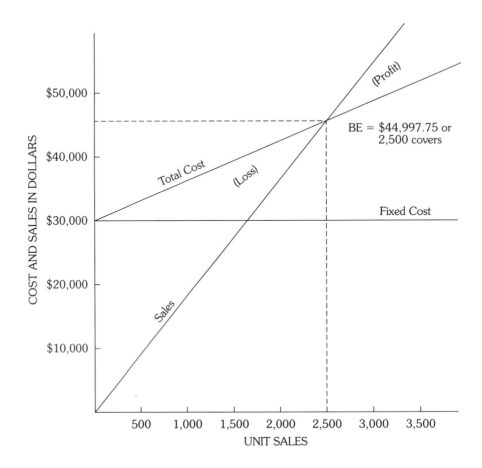

FIGURE A1.6 *Breakeven, with Menu Prices Adjusted Upwards*

This represents approximately 2,500 customers, a decrease of 500 in the number of customers necessary to reach the break-even point.

As illustrated in Figure A1.6, raising the sales price has had the effect of changing the slope of the sales line and shifting the break-even point downwards and to the left. If the business were able to maintain its previous level of unit sales (3,000), a profit of $6,000 could be achieved. This is calculated as 3,000 sales multiplied by an additional $2.00 per contribution margin.

Figure A1.7 illustrates the effect of reducing variable costs. If the owner of Ma's Place decides, instead, to reduce portion size or to take other measures to reduce the cost of the portion served by $.50, a new break-even point is calculated as follows:

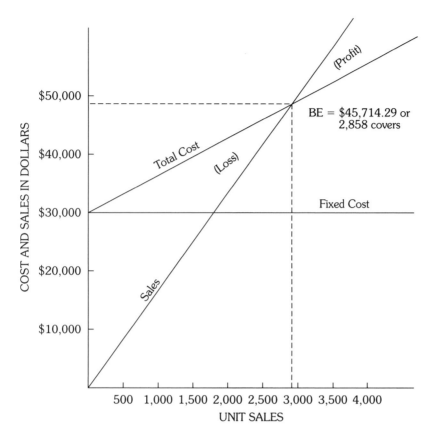

FIGURE A1.7 *Breakeven, with Variable Costs Reduced*

$$VR = \frac{\$5.50}{\$16.00} = .34375$$

$$BE = \frac{\$30,000}{1 - .34375}$$

$$BE = \frac{\$30,000}{.65625}$$

$$BE = \$45,714,29$$

This represents approximately 2,858 customers, a decrease of 142 in the number of customers required to break even. Lowering costs has the effect of changing the slope of the total cost line, and again shifting the break-even point downwards and to the left.

Some Final Words

Restaurant managers typically do not attempt just one of the two ways described above to change a break-even point. They often attempt both of them at the same time: raising prices a bit while reducing costs somewhat, hoping that current customers will not react adversely.

Sometimes both of the alternatives suggested above are poor choices. In some specific situations, it may not be possible either to raise menu prices or to decrease costs by any of the traditional means. Some other approach may be required. There are at least two possibilities worth considering:

1. Increasing sales volume.
2. Reducing fixed costs.

There are various ways to go about increasing sales volume, including increasing one's advertising and other promotional efforts, among a number of other possibilities. However, one must recognize that these and other efforts aimed at increasing sales volume commonly lead to increases in costs. If costs increase, the break-even point will be changed, and the change will normally mean an increase in the number of sales required to reach break-even. If these efforts do not result in profits greater than the additional costs they occasion, then the restaurant will be in a worse position than it was before attempting to increase sales volume.

Some fixed costs are controllable (advertising and repairs and maintenance, for example). When one reduces or eliminates expenditures in these categories, fixed costs can quickly be reduced, although not without some potential difficulty. Other fixed costs are noncontrollable, but in extreme cases one might want to attempt to change one or more of these (by renegotiating a lease or mortgage or by seeking tax relief from local government, for example).

One primary objective in a commercial food and beverage enterprise is to make a profit, not just to break even. Many food and beverage managers treat profit as a fixed cost and thus take profit into account when determining a break-even point. The amount of profit to be added to fixed costs is a discussion outside the scope of this text and includes such considerations as rate of return on investment capital, desire to build sales volume, and alternative investment opportunities.

Summary

In this Appendix, we have illustrated various dollar calculations, showing how the basic cost-volume-profit equation may be used to solve for any of several possible unknowns. We have explained several unit calculations, including the computation of average sale, average variable cost, and average contribution margin. We have shown how the break-even point may be represented graphically. We have calculated the average variable rate for a restaurant serving a variety of menu items with various costs and sales prices. Finally, we have explained and graphically illustrated two fundamental means of changing the break-even point to achieve more desirable results.

KEY TERMS IN THIS APPENDIX

Average cover
Average dollar sale
Contribution margin
Proportional share of total sales (PSTS)
Variable cost
Variable rate

Questions and Problems

1. Given the following information, determine the break-even point in unit sales:
   a. Fixed costs $240,000; contribution margin per unit $8.20.
   b. Fixed costs $337,192; contribution margin per unit $8.91.
   c. Contribution margin per unit $4.27; fixed costs $88,722.48.

2. Given the information below, determine the break-even point in dollar sales:
   a. Fixed costs $512,400; variable rate .39.
   b. Average sale $16.25; average variable cost per unit $5.38; fixed costs $266,427.40.
   c. Fixed costs $114,827.

Menu Items	% of Revenue	VR
A	40	.45
B	25	.60
C	35	.50

   d. Fixed costs $221,617.43; contribution rate .443.

3. Determine the dollar sales needed to achieve each of the following:
   a. Annual restaurant profit of $20,000 in an operation with fixed costs of $95,422 and an average variable rate of .545.
   b. Annual restaurant profit equal to 12% return on invested capital of $500,000 in a restaurant with fixed costs of $247,387 and a contribution rate of .415.
   c. Annual restaurant profit equal to 11% return on invested capital

of $750,000 in an operation with fixed costs of $356,725, and that offers a simple menu of the following items.

Menu Item	% of Return	VR
A	30	.60
B	20	.45
C	35	.35
D	15	.25

4. Determine the unit sales volume needed to achieve each of the following:

   a. Annual restaurant profit of $44,000 in a restaurant with fixed costs of $132,000, an average sale of $17.22, and an average contribution margin of $9.25.

   b. Annual profit before taxes equal to 14% return on invested capital of $300,000 in an establishment with fixed costs of $144,500, an average sale of $18.40, and an average variable rate of. 625.

5. In a certain restaurant with fixed costs of $324,000 and a projected average sale of $16.00, the owner wants to earn a restaurant profit equal to a 10% return on $750,000 of invested capital. The owner is projecting 35,000 unit sales for the coming year. What average variable rate will be required to accomplish this? What will be the average contribution margin?

6. Given the following figures, answer (a) through (c):

   Fixed cost = $120,000.
   Variable cost per unit = $8.00.
   Sales price = $20.00.

   a. Determine the break-even point in dollar sales.

   b. Determine the break-even point for the above establishment if the variable cost per unit is reduced by $1.00.

   c. Determine the break-even point for the establishment in (a) if the sales price is increased to $22.00 per unit.

7. The Granite Hills Restaurant has fixed costs of $96,400 annually. The restaurant operates at an average variable rate of .45. The average check is $15.00. For the upcoming year, management plans to decrease the variable rate to .4 and at the same time to adjust menu prices upward so that the average check will be $16.50.

   a. What was the break-even point in dollar sales for the year now ending? In unit sales?

   b. What will the break-even point be in the upcoming year in dollar

sales and in unit sales if management makes the changes described above?

   c. Prepare break-even graphs to illustrate both Question 20a and
Question 20b.

   d. If management's target restaurant profit for the upcoming year is
$30,000, how many unit sales will be needed to achieve it?

8. The Beach House Restaurant offers a simple menu to the public as
follows:

Menu Item	% of Revenue	Variable Rate
A	15	.30
B	20	.35
C	28	.42
D	18	.55
E	19	.48

Fixed costs total $201,010.

   a. Determine the break-even point in dollar sales.

   b. At an average check of $16.50, determine the break-even point in
unit sales.

   c. Prepare break-even graphs to illustrate both Question 21a and
Question 21b.

   d. If the Beach House Restaurant achieves 24,500 unit sales, how
much dollar profit should result?

   e. If only 20,000 unit sales are achieved, what will be the dollar
amount of the loss?

9. Define each of the following terms from Appendix 1:
Average cover
Average dollar sale
Contribution margin
Proportional share of total sales (PSTS)
Variable cost
Variable rate

Glossary

The definitions included in the text and collected in the following glossary tend to be those common in food and beverage operations. Some will point out that many of the terms have broader applications than suggested by these definitions. While this is clearly true, we have chosen to restrict the definitions to those specific to food, beverage, and labor cost control and to this text. Thus, they are intentionally limited.

Actual beverage cost   The cost of beverages sold as determined from inventory and purchase figures, with adjustments, if any, taken into account.

Actual cost percent   The ratio of actual cost of sales to total sales for a given period.

Actual food cost   The cost of food sold, as determined by adding the cost of direct purchases to the cost of issues from inventory, calculated either from requisitions or from valuation of inventory. At the discretion of management, actual food cost may also take various adjustments into account.

Actual inventory value   The total value of the physical inventory, determined by pricing each item in that inventory.

Actual purchase price method   A method used for determining the value of a physical inventory that requires that each unit be valued at the price at which that particular unit was purchased.

Actual sales record method   A method for monitoring bar operations that translates quantities of alcoholic beverages consumed into potential sales values, taking into account actual numbers of various drinks sold.

Aging   A process for improving the flavors of alcoholic beverages by storing the beverages under carefully controlled conditions for periods of time that vary from one beverage to another. Also, a process for improving the flavor and texture of meat, especially beef.

Automated bar   A computerized device for dispensing beverages and simultaneously registering sales.

Average contribution margin   The difference between average sale and average variable cost; the amount remaining after average variable cost is subtracted from average sale.

Average cover   See *average sale per customer*.

Average dollar sale   Total dollar sales for a period divided by the number of sales. Also referred to as *average cover, average sale per cover*, and *average sale per customer*.

Average inventory   The sum of opening and closing inventory for a period, divided by two.

Average potential sales value   The calculated sales value of a bottle of liquor based on detailed records indicating actual sales in a test period.

Average sale per cover   See *average sale per customer*.

Average sale per customer   Total dollar sales for a period, divided by the number of customers served in that period; an average dollar figure representing the average amount spent by customers.

Average sale per server   Total dollar sales attributable to a particular server in a given time period, divided by the number of customers served.

Average sales value method   A method for monitoring bar operations that calculates the potential sales value of all bottles of liquor consumed, based on the number of empty bottles at the bar multiplied by the average potential sales value of each bottle.

Average variable cost   Total variable cost for a period divided by the number of customers served in that period.

Average variable rate   The ratio of average variable cost to average sale, normally expressed in decimal form.

Beers   Alcoholic beverages produced by the fermentation of a malted grain flavored with hops.

Beverage   Any liquid intended for drinking. There are two general classifications of beverages: alcoholic and nonalcoholic.

Beverage cost   The expense to an establishment for beverages consumed, regardless of the reason. Beverage cost includes the cost of beverages sold, given away, stolen, and spilled.

Beverage cost percent   The ratio of beverage cost to beverage sales, expressed as a percent.

Beverage profit maximization   An approach to maximizing beverage profits by 1) establishing drink prices that will maximize gross profit, and 2) influencing customers to purchase those drinks with the highest contribution margins, rather than attempting to sell greater number of drinks to customers.

Beverage receiving report   A form used to summarize the invoices for all beverages received on a given day, indicating both quantities received and their values and providing columns for dividing purchases into essential categories (wines, spirits, beers, and mixers) for purchase journal distribution. See *receiving clerks daily report*.

Beverage requisition   A form used to record the names and quantities of beverages ordered or issued from inventory.

Beverage sales control   The sum of various processes used by managers to optimize the number of sales, maximize profits on sales, and ensure that all sales result in appropriate revenue to the establishment.

Bin card   A card, label, or other device affixed to a storage shelf, used for recording the number of units of a particular item added to and issued from inventory, and for determining the inventory balance that should be found on the shelf.

Blush wines   Wines named for or described by their distinctive pale reddish color.

Bonus   Dollar amounts over and above an employee's regular wages or salary, normally given as a reward for some type of job performance.

Book inventory value   The value of an inventory determined as follows: opening inventory, plus purchases, minus issues.

Brand-name wines   Those wines that are given identifying names (sometimes unusual names) by their producers, often to differentiate the wine. Blue Nun is an example.

Break-even point   The point at which the sum of all costs is equal to sales, such that profit equals zero.

Budget   A realistic statement of management's goals and objectives, expressed in financial terms.

Budgeted cost   A planned cost included in the financial plan, or budget, of an enterprise.

Butcher test   A procedure used to determine the standard cost of one standard portion of a product portioned before cooking. It is used for products that cannot be portioned as purchased, but that require some further processing before portions are produced. Butchering is an example of the kind of processing required. The butcher test is also used to determine yield factors and cost factors.

Call brand   An alcoholic beverage that a customer must specifically request by brand name.

Centralized purchasing   A system used by chains, franchises, and groups of independent operators that results in purchases for all participating units being made by one central office.

Centralized training   Training that takes place at a central training facility, rather than at a given trainee's job location. Central training facilities are often located at the national or regional headquarters of an organization.

Closing inventory   The physical inventory at the end of a period, expressed in terms of units, value, or both.

Cocktail   A drink consisting of the appropriate measures of two or more alcoholic beverages.

Commission   Compensation calculated as a percentage of sales.

Compensation   All forms of pay and other rewards going to employees as a result of their employment.

Contribution margin   The amount resulting from the subtraction of variable cost from sales price.

Contribution rate   The percentage (expressed as a decimal) of the sales dollar available to cover fixed costs and profit. It is calculated by subtracting the variable rate from 1 (1 − variable rate).

Control   A process used by managers to direct, regulate, and restrain the actions of people so that the established goals of an enterprise may be achieved.

Control process   The means employed by managers to institute control, consisting of four essential steps.

Control state   A state in which some or all alcoholic beverages can be purchased only in state-owned stores.

Control system   The term used to describe that collection of interrelated and interdependent control techniques and procedures in use in a given food and beverage operation.

Controllable cost   A cost that can be changed by management in the short term. Examples include food cost, beverage cost, and labor cost.

Cooking loss test   A procedure used primarily to determine the standard cost of one standard portion of a product that is portioned after cooking. It is used for products that cannot be portioned uncooked. The cooking loss test is also used to determine yield factors and cost factors.

Cost   The expense incurred for goods or services when the goods are consumed or the services rendered.

Cost-benefit ratio   The relationship between costs incurred in instituting and maintaining a single control or control system and the benefits or savings derived from doing so.

Cost control   The process used by managers to regulate costs and guard against excessive costs.

Cost factor per pound   The ratio of the cost of a usable pound of edible product to the dealer price per pound for the product as purchased. Cost factor per pound is obtained from butcher test or cooking loss test calculations and is used to update standard costs when dealer prices change.

Cost of employee meals   The dollar value of foods used for employees' meals. This dollar amount is used as an adjustment when calculating cost of food sold.

Cost of food consumed   The cost of food issued plus or minus all adjustments, except employees' meals.

Cost of food issued   The sum of opening inventory and purchases, less the value of closing inventory.

Cost of food sold   Cost of food consumed, less the cost of employees' meals.

Cost per dollar sale   The cost percent expressed as a dollar figure, or the ratio of cost to sales expressed as a dollar figure.

Cost percent   The ratio of cost to sales, expressed as a percent.

Cost/volume/profit equation   An equation stating that sales is equal to the sum of variable costs, fixed costs, and profit (or loss).

Cover   A diner; one customer who has purchased food in a restaurant, regardless of the number of items purchased.

Covers per hour   The average number of diners per hour of operation; total covers, divided by the number of hours of operation; usually calculated for particular meal periods (i.e., breakfast, luncheon, dinner).

Cross training   Teaching a worker to perform the duties of some job or jobs other than his or her own.

Current compensation   Direct and indirect compensation received by an employee while he is employed.

Daily analysis of business volume   A record of the number of covers served each day in a given period.

Daily food inventory balance   The inventory book value of food at the close of business on a given day.

Deferred compensation   Compensation received by an employee after the conclusion of his period of employment.

Differentiated product   A product that is sufficiently different from other similar products so that customers may consider it unique and develop a preference for it.

Direct compensation   Salaries, wages, tips, bonuses, and commissions.

Direct monitoring   Direct observation of employee performance at work, or direct examination of the results of employee work.

Direct purchases   See *directs.*

Directly variable cost   A cost that varies directly with sales volume, such that every change in sales volume brings a corresponding change in that cost.

Directs   Those foods (typically perishables) charged to cost on the day they are received.

Distillation   A process by means of which alcohol is evaporated from a fermented liquid and then condensed and collected as a liquid.

Dog   A term used in menu engineering to describe a menu item for which both contribution margin and sales volume are judged low.

Dram shop laws   State statutes that hold the serving establishment and the server financially liable for damages to third parties resulting from the serving of alcoholic beverages to intoxicated customers.

Dupe   An abbreviation of the term *duplicate.*

Dupe system   A system for recording customers' orders that provides for two copies of each order, one on a guest check for the customer and the other on a "dupe" used by the server to place the order in the kitchen. Additional uses of the "dupe" are possible.

Extending a requisition   A two-step process for determining the total value of all items listed on a given requisition. The first step is to multiply the quantity of each item listed by its unit price to determine a total value of the quantity issued. The second step is to add these individual totals to determine a grand total for the requisition.

Fermentation   A natural chemical process by means of which sugars in a liquid are converted to ethyl alcohol and carbon dioxide.

First-in, first-out method   A method for determining the value of a physical inventory, based on the assumption that units are used in the order of purchase, such that those remaining in the physical inventory are the units most recently purchased. The values of these can then be determined from recent invoices or other records of recent purchases.

Fixed cost   A total cost that is normally unaffected by changes in sales volume; a fixed cost does not increase or decrease significantly as business volume changes and thus is said to have little direct relationship to the volume of business.

Fixed-cost personnel   Those employees whose numbers do not normally change because of increases and decreases in the volume of business. Changes in their numbers are unlikely unless there are extraordinary changes in volume over an extended period.

Flexible budget   A budget prepared for more than one level of business activity.

Food and beverage transfers   Foods or beverages received by one cost center from another. The value of the foods or beverages transferred are normally recorded and these values used later for end-of-period adjustments.

Food cost   The expense to an establishment for food, incurred when food is consumed for any reason. Food cost includes the cost of food sold, given away, stolen, or wasted.

Food cost percentage today/food cost percentage to date   The daily and cumulative ratio of food cost to food sales as shown on various reports to management.

Food cost today/food cost to date   The daily and cumulative cost of food sold as shown on various reports to management.

Food sales today/food sales to date   The daily and cumulative dollar sales of food as shown on various reports to management.

Forecasted sales Predictions of unit sales, dollar sales, or both of these, normally based on historical data.

Fortified wines Wines to which small quantities of brandy or other spirits have been added to increase alcoholic content. Sherry and port are examples of fortified wines.

Free pouring A technique for pouring alcoholic beverages that permits a bartender to "measure" the quantity poured visually, without such physical devices as jiggers or shot glasses. Quantities poured thus depend on the judgment of the individual doing the pouring.

Front bar A fixed counter for beverage service, open for business on a regularly scheduled basis and directly accessible to customers. A front bar includes various facilities for beverage production and is staffed by a bartender to whom customers have direct access.

Full-bottle sales slip A special beverage requisition form used to record the issue and sale of full bottles of beverages.

Generic wine A wine that take its name from a specific geographic area. California burgundy is an example.

Geographic wine A wine produced in a specific location and named for that location. Chateau Latour is an example.

Gratis to bar(s) The dollar value of foods given away without charge at the bar that have been previously added to food cost. This dollar amount is used as an adjustment when calculating cost of food consumed.

Gratuity Another word for tip. A gratuity is a form of direct compensation—an amount voluntarily given to employees by customers for services rendered.

Grease sales The dollar value of fats and oils sold to rendering companies. This dollar amount is used as an adjustment when one calculates cost of food consumed. Grease sales are cost recoveries and thus decrease food cost.

Guest check A special type of invoice used in restaurants and other similar food and beverage operations to provide customers with itemized bills for their menu selections/purchases. The guest check lists the specific items sold to the customer, identifying quantity and sales price for each, and indicates the total amount the customer is to pay. The total includes any applicable sales tax.

Historical cost A past cost that has been documented in business records.

Homogeneous product A product that is so much like other similar products that customers have no preference for any one over the others and will purchase the one with the lowest price.

Hourly analysis of business volume   A record of the number of covers served each hour of one or more business days.

Indirect compensation   All current compensation that is not direct compensation. Examples of indirect compensation include paid vacations, health benefits, life insurance, meals, accommodations, use of recreational facilities operated by the employer, and use of company automobiles.

Indirect monitoring   Obtaining information about employees' performance or the results of their performance by some means other than directly observing the employees.

Interunit transfer   A food or beverage transfer between units in a chain.

Intraunit transfer   A food or beverage transfer between departments in a single hotel, restaurant, or similar enterprise.

Inventory book value   The stores inventory balance, determined from records of transactions affecting inventory. Inventory book value is calculated as follows: opening inventory balance plus purchases (from Receiving Clerk's Daily Report or from invoices), minus issues (from requisitions alone or from requisitions and meat tags).

Inventory differential   The difference between start-of-month and end-of-month dollar values of the bar inventory, used as an adjustment in calculating cost of beverages consumed at the bar.

Inventory turnover   The ratio of cost of food or beverages sold to average inventory of food or beverages for a period.

Inventory turnover method   A method for monitoring the size of a beverage inventory so that judgments can be made about the adequacy of supply.

Invoice   A bill from a vendor for goods or services, often presented as the goods are delivered or the services performed.

Invoice stamp   A rubber stamp used by a receiver to overprint a small form on an invoice for the purpose of recording the date on which goods were received, as well as the signatures of the several individuals verifying the accuracy of data on the invoice.

Jigger   A double-ended, stainless steel measuring device used by bartenders to measure the alcoholic ingredients in drinks.

Job analysis   The process of identifying the nature of a job, as well as the skills, level of education, and other specific qualifications needed to perform the job. It is the first step in preparing a job description.

Job description   A formal definition of a job, which typically includes a summary of the work to be done and a list of specific tasks and duties.

Job specification   A document that outlines the qualifications needed to perform a job. It is an outcome of the job analysis and describes the specific skills, level of education, and experience required for the job.

Job rotation The process of periodically reassigning employees to other jobs.

Labor cost Payroll cost, which includes salaries, wages, and employee benefits.

Labor cost control A process used by managers to direct, regulate, and restrain the actions of people in order to obtain a desired level of employee performance at an appropriate level of cost.

Labor turnover rate The ratio of the number of departing employees to the total number on the staff, expressed as a percentage.

Last-in, first-out method A method for determining the value of a physical inventory that assigns to remaining units the earliest prices paid for units in that category during the period.

Latest purchase price method A method used for determining the value of a physical inventory that assigns the most recent price paid for units in a given category to all units counted in that category.

License state A state in which the government does not sell alcoholic beverages, but licenses those that do.

Lined shot glass A shot glass with a line etched below the brim at a point to which the glass must be filled to measure a given quantity.

Liqueur An alcoholic beverage consisting of spirits that have been sweetened and combined with one or more flavoring agents.

Localized training Training that takes place at the normal work site or at some appropriate facility near the work site.

Market segment A subgroup of potential patrons with similar characteristics. Market segments can be based on such characteristics as age, gender, income level, and occupation.

Meat tag A stock form perforated for division into two parts, used to record in duplicate such information about an item as date of receipt, item, weight, supplier, unit price, total value, and date of issue. One part of the form can be attached to the item described, while the second part can be filed in a remote location as an inventory control device.

Median The value of the middle item in a group.

Menu engineering A technique used to evaluate a menu by assessing sales volume and contribution margin for each item on a given menu and thus to evaluate the individual menu items.

Menu mix percentage As used in menu engineering, the ratio of the number of sales of one menu item to the total number of sales of all menu items, expressed as a percentage.

Menu precost and abstract A form used to calculate standard costs and standard cost percents for both forecasted and actual sales.

Minimum wage   The least gross dollar amount that an hourly employee can legally be paid.

Mixed drink   A drink typically prepared before being poured into the glass or other container from which it is consumed. Mixed drinks are normally stirred, shaken, or blended before being poured for the customer.

Mixed drink differential   An adjustment to the potential sales value of a bottle of liquor, calculated to take into account the varying quantities of liquor used in preparing mixed drinks.

Mixer   A nonalcoholic beverage used both to dilute an alcoholic beverage and to produce a drink of distinctive flavor.

Monitoring   To gather information about employees' work and the results of their work.

Monthly food cost   The cost of food sold for one month.

Non-controllable cost   A cost that management cannot change in the short term. Examples include rent, real estate taxes, and license fees.

Non-perishable foods   Foods that have a comparatively longer useful life than those known as perishables. Because of this longer useful life, nonperishable foods can be ordered less frequently than perishables and can be ordered in comparatively greater quantities.

Off-the-job training   Training that takes place when an employee is not engaged in performing his or her normal job duties.

On-the-job training   Training that takes place while the employee is engaged in performing his or her job.

Opening inventory   The physical inventory at the beginning of a period. It is expressed in terms of units, value, or both of these.

Operating budget   A forecast of sales activity and an estimate of costs that will be incurred in the process of generating those sales.

Operational plan   A statement of the goals and objectives of a business, together with detailed plans for achieving them.

Organization chart   A chart that shows positions and describes reporting relationships within an organization.

Organizational plan   A plan prepared by management to organize an enterprise that identifies the jobs and job titles required for day-to-day operations.

Ounce-control method   A method for monitoring bar operations that compares the number of ounces of alcoholic beverages consumed at the bar with the number of ounces sold as recorded on sales records.

Outsourcing   Arranging to have work done on a contract basis by outside organizations rather than by full-time employees.

Overhead   All costs other than prime costs.

Par stock   Defined in this text as the maximum quantity of an item that should be on hand at any given time. (Other definitions are possible.)

Par stock control   A control technique requiring cooks to sign for and thus accept responsibility for particular numbers of portions of high-cost menu items.

Par stock for bars   The exact number of bottles or other containers that must be on hand at the bar at all times for each item.

Payroll costs   See *labor costs.*

Performance criteria   Written statements describing the minimum level of performance acceptable for a job.

Performance standards   Measures established for making judgments about the quality and quantity of employees' work.

Periodic order method   A method for ordering food or beverages based on fixed order dates and variable order quantities.

Perishable foods   Those foods, typically described as "fresh," that have a comparatively short useful life. Consequently, these must be ordered quite frequently and in relatively small quantities.

Perpetual inventory card   A card or other device used in the perpetual inventory method for recording additions to and issues from inventory, inventory balance, and such other pertinent information as supplier, size, par stock, reorder point, and reorder quantity.

Perpetual inventory method   A method for determining suitable order quantities for nonperishable foods that enables a purchaser to place orders for fixed reorder quantities on varying dates.

Perpetual order method   A method for ordering food or beverages based on variable order dates and fixed order quantities.

Physical inventory   The actual number of units of goods in storage. For food control purposes, there are two physical inventories: directs, which are counted daily for purposes of determining order quantities, and stores, which are counted monthly for purposes of determining values.

Planned cost   An anticipated cost, projected by management, which reflects business plans for the future.

Plowhorse   A term used in menu engineering to describe a menu item for which contribution margin is judged low and sales volume is judged high.

Popularity index   The ratio of the number of portions sold for a given menu item to the total number of portions sold of all menu items.

Portion cost factor   The ratio of the standard cost of a standard portion of a menu item to the dealer price per pound for item as purchased. Portion cost factors are derived from butcher tests or cooking loss tests. When dealers' prices change, one uses portion cost factors to recalculate and update the standard costs of standard portions of menu items.

Portion reconciliation   A comparison of portion sales records and production consumption records to ensure that management is able to account for all portions produced.

Potential sales value   The dollar sales value of a given quantity of alcoholic beverage. It is based on the sales value of the number of drinks in each bottle, assuming that each is sold as a straight drink.

Potential savings   The difference between actual and standard cost. The cost savings that could have been realized if all activities associated with food production and sales had been conducted in strict conformity to the standards and standard procedures established by management.

Pound cost factor   See *cost factor per pound.*

Pourer   A device that replaces an original bottle top and facilitates the pouring of predetermined quantities of the contents.

Pouring brand   An alcoholic beverage served to any customer who does not request a call brand.

Pre-check system   A method for controlling revenue that requires that sales be recorded on checks as drinks are served, that revenues resulting from sales be recorded when customers settle their bills, and that sales records and recorded revenues be reconciled.

Price sensitive   A term used to describe the relative effect of sales price on sales volume. The greater the effect of price on volume, the more price sensitive the product.

Primary ingredient   The principal alcoholic beverage in a drink, the determination of which is necessary for the calculation of mixed drink differentials.

Prime cost   The sum of food cost, beverage cost, and labor cost for a given operating period.

Procedures   Methods used to prepare products or perform jobs.

Production sheet   A form on which one lists the names and quantities of all menu items that are to be prepared for a given date.

Promotion expense   The dollar value of goods and services given away to promote sales in the establishment.

Proof   A measure of the percentage of alcohol in a beverage. In the United States, 1 proof equals .5% alcohol. Thus, 200 proof equals 100.0% alcohol, and 100 proof equals 50.0%.

Proportional share of total sales (PSTS)   The ratio of total dollar sales recorded for an individual item in a given period to the total dollar sales for all items in that period; one element used in the calculation of weighted variable rate and thus of average variable rate.

Purchase journal distribution   That portion of the Receiving Clerk's Daily Report used to separate invoice amounts for delivered items into food direct, food stores, and sundries.

Puzzle A term used in menu engineering to describe a menu item for which contribution margin is judged high and sales volume is judged low.

Quality standards Rules or measures established for making comparisons and judgments about the degree of excellence of raw materials, finished products, or work.

Quantity standards Measures of weight, count, or volume used to make comparisons or judgments.

Receiving Clerk's Daily Report A general term used to identify those forms used in food and beverage operations to record data from invoices for goods received on a given day and, for accounting purposes, to distribute purchases into appropriate categories. Sometimes referred to simply as a *Receiving Report* or *Receiving Sheet*. There are normally separate forms for foods and beverages, each of which may provide varying numbers of columns for separating purchases into categories. Specifics vary from one establishment to another.

Receiving Report (or Sheet) See *Receiving Clerk's Daily Report*.

Recipe detail and cost card A form used to record a standard recipe and to calculate the standard cost of producing the quantity stipulated in the recipe, as well as the standard cost and standard cost percent for one standard portion.

Reorder point The number of units to which an inventory should decrease before an order for additional units is placed.

Reorder quantity The amount of a particular item that will be ordered each time the quantity of that item diminishes to the reorder point.

Reorganization Restructuring the staff of an enterprise to create a different organizational structure.

Requisition A form prepared by a staff member that lists items and quantities the staff member needs in his work area.

Requisition system A formal system that makes provision for recording specific items and quantities needed and issued from inventory.

Revenue control The process used by managers to ensure that all sales result in appropriate dollar income to the enterprise.

Rotation of stock The storing of goods in such a manner that the units received most recently are placed behind those already in storage, resulting in the first units stored being the first units used. This is commonly known as the *first-in, first-out (or FIFO) method of stock rotation*.

Salary A fixed dollar amount paid on a weekly, monthly, or annual basis, regardless of the actual number of hours worked.

Sales Revenue resulting from the exchange of products and services for value.

Sales control The several processes used by managers to optimize numbers of customers, to maximize profits, and to ensure that all sales result in appropriate revenue.

Sales control sheet A form used to record cash and credit sales after guest checks have been settled by customers.

Sales forecast An estimate of future sales-based on sales history and other information deemed relevant by management.

Sales history A record of the number of portions of each menu item sold each time that item has appeared on a menu.

Sales mix The ratio of the number of sales of one menu item to the total number of sales of all menu items. Usually calculated for particular segments of a menu (appetizers, entrees, or desserts, for example).

Sales per seat Total dollar sales for a given time period, divided by the number of seats in the restaurant.

Sales per serving person Total dollar sales attributable to a particular server in a given time period.

Sales price The dollar amount charged for each unit of any given product or service sold.

Seat turnover The number of seats occupied during a given period divided by the number of dining seats in the restaurant; the number of customers (or covers) served in a given period, divided by the number of dining seats available.

Semivariable cost A cost that has both fixed and variable elements, such that one component would not change as sales volume changes, while the other component would.

Service bar A permanent or temporary beverage production and sales facility accessible to servers alone, rather than directly to customers.

Shot glass A small glass used for measuring alcoholic beverages.

Signature book A book used to record the signatures of servers for the numbered guest checks assigned to them.

Signature item A unique food product created for a restaurant to help increase sales volume. A signature item is a differentiated product.

Sparkling wines Those wines containing carbonation, natural or artificial. Asti spumante and sparkling burgundy are examples of sparkling wines.

Special-purpose bar A beverage production and sales facility, established for customers attending a particular function and normally staffed by a bartender.

Spirits Alcoholic beverages produced by the distillation of a fermented liquid.

Standard cost   The cost of goods or services identified, approved, and accepted by management.

Standard cost method   A method for monitoring operations that compares calculated standard product costs with actual product costs to determine whether or not actual costs should be judged excessive.

Standard cost percent   The ratio of standard cost to actual dollar sales for a given period.

Standard deviation method   A method for monitoring bar operations requiring a test period, careful monitoring of operations, and calculation of the difference between actual dollar sales and potential sales value of bottles consumed in the period. This difference, assumed to be attributable to mixed drinks sales, is expressed as a percentage of potential sales for the period and used in succeeding periods to adjust potential sales.

Standard drink cost   The calculated cost of a drink prepared from a standard recipe.

Standard drink recipe   A set of instructions for the preparation of a drink, including ingredients, proportions, and preparation method, intended to be followed each time that drink is prepared.

Standard labor cost   The dollar amount calculated by multiplying the number of standard work hours required to perform a given volume of work by the hourly rate paid those performing the work.

Standard portion cost   The dollar amount that a standard portion should cost, given the standards and standard procedures for its production.

Standard portion size   The specific quantity of any given menu item that is to be served to every customer ordering that item.

Standard procedures   Those procedures that have been established as the correct methods, routines, and techniques for day-to-day operations.

Standard purchase specifications   Carefully written descriptions listing in appropriate detail the specific and distinctive characteristics that best describe an item to be purchased. Standard purchase specifications commonly identify grade, size, weight, degree of freshness, color, and other similar characteristics.

Standard recipe   A recipe that has been designated the correct one to use in a given establishment for the production of a given food or beverage product.

Standard sales price   The established sales price for a given food or beverage product, to be charged each time that product is sold.

Standard staffing requirements   The established number of staff required at various levels of customer count that will result in the desired level of service.

Standard work hours   The number of employee work hours required to perform a given volume of work.

Standing orders   Arrangements made between purveyors and foodservice operators that result in regular delivery of goods without specific orders preceding each delivery.

Standards   Rules or measures established for making comparisons and judgments.

Star   A term used in menu engineering to describe a menu item for which both contribution margin and sales volume are judged high.

Static budget   A budget prepared for one level of business activity.

Steward sales   The dollar value of foods from inventory sold at cost. These are typically sales to employees. Steward sales are cost recoveries and thus serve to decrease food cost in the period during which they occur.

Steward's Market Quotation List   A form often used as a tool by food purchasers for taking daily inventory of perishable foods, determining suitable order quantities, recording market quotations, and selecting vendors.

Stores   Those foods added to inventory when received and charged to cost as issued.

Straight drink   A drink consisting of the appropriate measure of one of the many types of spirits, prepared in the glass or other container from which it is consumed. It may or may not contain a mixer.

Tip   Another term for *gratuity.*

Total available   The sum of opening inventory and purchases for a period. Total available may be expressed in terms of units, values, or both of these.

Total cost   The sum of all unit costs for a given period of time.

Total inventory   The sum of opening inventory and closing inventory, used in calculating average inventory to determine inventory turnover.

Total sales   Total volume of sales revenue for a given period of time expressed in terms of dollars or units.

Total sales per seat   Total dollar sales for a given time period, divided by the number of seats in the establishment.

Training   A process for teaching individuals the skills necessary to perform particular tasks.

Training manual   A manual that provides for standardized training directed towards standardized results. Training manuals take different forms. Some are written guides for trainers; others are aimed at trainees and are designed to give the trainee the information required, even if there is no trainer available to provide instruction.

Training objectives   Objectives that identify the skills, tasks, and behaviors that specific employees will have mastered by the time their training is complete.

Training plan A series of elements or steps that constitute a method for teaching a specific employee the skills required to perform a specific job correctly, in the manner anticipated by management when the standards and standard procedures for the job were developed.

Transfers from bar(s) to kitchen(s) Intraunit transfers of alcoholic beverages previously added to bar inventory. The values of such items are normally recorded and used to adjust food and beverage costs, thus increasing their accuracy.

Transfers from kitchen(s) to bar(s) Intraunit transfers of food previously charged to food cost. The values of such items are commonly determined, recorded, and used to adjust food and beverage costs, thus increasing their accuracy.

Unacceptable costs The unplanned, unwarranted costs that normally develop from spoilage, waste, or pilferage.

Unit cost The cost of one of many like units, such as one portion of a particular menu item (one steak or one martini, for example) or one hour of labor.

Unit sales required to break even The number of average sales required to reach break-even point.

Unplanned costs Any unanticipated costs.

Variable cost A total cost that changes when sales volume changes. Variable costs are linked to business volume, such that total variable cost increases as sales volume increases and decreases as sales volume decreases.

Variable cost personnel Those employees whose numbers and total cost increase or decrease as business volume increases or decreases.

Variable rate The ratio (expressed in decimal form) of variable cost to dollar sales.

Varietal wines Those wines that are named for the varieties of grapes that predominate the wines. Chardonnay is an example.

Void sheet A form used to record information about portions rejected by diners.

Wages Compensation based on an hourly rate of pay. Calculated by multiplying the number of hours worked by the hourly rate.

Weighted average purchase price method A method used for determining the value of a physical inventory that is based on calculating a weighted average value for each unit purchased in a particular category and then applying this value to each of the remaining units in that particular category.

Wine coolers   Blends of wine and fruit juice.

Wines   Alcoholic beverages produced by the fermentation of grapes or various other fruits.

Work schedule   A graphic presentation showing the names of workers and the days and hours they are to work.

Yield   The number of portions produced by a given standard recipe.

Yield factor   The ratio of the weight of part of a product to the weight of that product as purchased. Yield factors are used to make judgments about the values of comparable products and for determining purchase quantities, among other purposes. The term tends to be used interchangeably with *yield percentage.*

Yield percentage   The percentage of a whole purchase unit of meat, poultry, or fish available for portioning after any required in-house processing has been completed. The term tends to be used interchangeably with *yield factor.*

Index

561

Computers (*continued*)
    in programmed instruction,
        496, 504
    requisitions and, 130–131,
        132
    sales control with, 301–302
Conducting business, as reason
    for drinking, 415–416
Containers, for storing food,
    125
Contribution margin (CM), 69–
    70
    in menu engineering
        worksheet, 296–297
    in menu pricing, 278–279
Contribution rate, 65, 66–67
    break-even point and, 67–69
Control, 30. *See also* Beverage
        control; Beverage issuing
        control; Beverage
        production control;
        Beverage purchasing
        control; Beverage
        receiving control;
        Beverage sales control;
        Beverage storing control;
        Food control; Food issuing
        control; Food production
        control; Food purchasing
        control; Food receiving
        control; Food storing
        control; Sales control
    of costs, 31–32
    defined, 31, 310
    instituting, 33–34
    responsibility for, 32–33
    of sales, 32
    techniques of, 34–43
Controllable costs, 10
    in budgets, 43
    in cost/volume/profit
        equation, 62–65
Control process, 47–48
    food control in, 78
    food purchasing and, 80
    for labor cost control, 448–
        449

Control states, liquor laws in,
    319
Control systems, 49–52, 525–
    526
    cost/benefit ratio of, 52–53
    defined, 49
Cooking loss test, 157
    calculating standard portion
        costs with, 153, 164–167
Cooking Loss Test Card, 164–
    166
Cordials, 315
Corrective action, 517–521
    in beverage issuing, storing,
        and receiving control,
        351–352
    in beverage production
        control, 376–377
    in beverage purchasing
        control, 326–327
    for employees, 35, 39
    in food issuing and storing
        control, 135
    in food production control,
        171, 192–198
    in food purchasing control,
        101
    in food receiving control,
        119–120
    in foodservice operations,
        238–239
Cost, 7–12. *See also* Beverage
        costs; Controllable costs;
        Fixed costs; Food costs;
        Labor costs;
        Noncontrollable costs;
        Overhead costs; Standard
        portion costs; Total costs;
        Variable costs
    actual unit, 10
    average unit, 10
    beverage, 9
    calculating menu prices
        from, 278
    controllable, 10
    defined, 7–8
    directly variable, 9

    fixed, 8–9
    food, 9
    guarding against excessive,
        32
    historical, 12
    labor, 9
    monitoring, 23
    in monitoring beverage
        operations, 384–395
    noncontrollable, 10
    overhead, 19
    payroll, 9
    planned, 12
    prime, 11–12
    profit and, 4–7
    relationships to sales of, 60–
        62
    semivariable, 9
    standard, 36
    total, 10–11
    unit, 10–11
    variable, 8, 9
Cost/benefit ratio, 52–53
Cost control. *See also* Control
        process; Control systems;
        Labor cost control
    cost/volume/profit equation
        and, 70–72
    defined, 31–32
Cost factors, in butcher test,
    161–163
Cost of food consumed, 212–
    213
    determining, 214–216
Cost of food issued, 212
    adjustments to, 213–214
Cost of separate issues,
        determining cost of
        employee meals by, 215–
        216
Cost percent methods, for
        monitoring beverage
        operations, 384–393
Cost percents, 17–21. *See also*
        Food cost percent to date
    calculating menu prices
        from, 278